THE INTERNATIONAL LAW OF HUMAN TRAFFICKING

Although human trafficking has a long and ignoble history, it is only recently that trafficking has become a major political issue for States and the international community and the subject of detailed international rules.

This book presents the first-ever comprehensive and in-depth analysis of the international law of human trafficking. Anne T. Gallagher calls on her direct experience working within the United Nations to chart the development of new international laws on this issue. She links these rules to the international law of State responsibility, as well as key norms of international human rights law, transnational criminal law, refugee law, and international criminal law, in the process identifying and explaining the major legal obligations of States with respect to preventing trafficking, protecting and supporting victims, and prosecuting perpetrators. This is a timely and groundbreaking work: a unique and valuable resource for policy makers, advocates, practitioners, and scholars working in this new, controversial, and important field.

Dr. Anne T. Gallagher is recognized as a leading authority on the international legal and policy aspects of human trafficking. She served as a career UN official from 1992 to 2003, including as Adviser on Human Trafficking to the High Commissioner for Human Rights, Mary Robinson, whom she represented in negotiations for the Organized Crime Convention and its Protocols on Trafficking and Migrant Smuggling. Dr. Gallagher oversaw the development of the UN Recommended Principles and Guidelines on Human Rights and Human Trafficking and was founding Chair of the United Nations Inter-Agency Group on Trafficking and Migrant Smuggling. She continues to advise the United Nations on these issues, her most recent assignment being the preparation of a detailed legal commentary on the UN Recommended Principles and Guidelines. Dr. Gallagher has worked directly with criminal justice agencies and legislatures on trafficking in more than forty countries and is currently a technical adviser to the Association of Southeast Asian Nations (ASEAN) and its Member States. A scholar as well as a practitioner, she has taught international law and human rights law at universities and academic institutions in Europe, Asia, and Australia and has published widely on human rights (including women's rights), criminal justice, and trafficking.

The International Law of Human Trafficking

ANNE T. GALLAGHER

CAMBRIDGE UNIVERSITY PRESS
Cambridge, New York, Melbourne, Madrid, Cape Town,
Singapore, São Paulo, Delhi, Mexico City

Cambridge University Press
32 Avenue of the Americas, New York, NY 10013-2473, USA

www.cambridge.org
Information on this title: www.cambridge.org/9781107624559

First published 2010
Reprinted 2011 (twice)
First paperback edition 2012
Reprinted 2012 (twice)

A catalog record for this publication is available from the British Library.

Library of Congress Cataloging in Publication Data

Gallagher, Anne, High Commissioner.
The international law of human trafficking / Anne T. Gallagher.
p. cm.
Includes bibliographical references and index.
ISBN 978-0-521-19107-4 (hardback)
1. Human trafficking. 2. Human trafficking – Prevention – International
cooperation. I. Title.
K5258.G35 2010
345´.025–dc22   2010030167

ISBN 978-0-521-19107-4 Hardback
ISBN 978-1-107-62455-9 Paperback

Mais on ne se bat pas dans l'espoir du succès.

Edmond Rostand, *Cyrano de Bergerac* (1897) (Act V, Scene 6)

[O]ur experience of the revolutionary transformation of national societies has been that the past conditions the future but that it does not finally and inescapably determine it. We have shown that we can think ourselves out of the social jungle.

Philip Allott, *Eunomia: New Order for a New World*
(Oxford, Oxford University Press, 2001) (p. xxxii)

Contents

Preface

This book is not a specialist treatise in the usual sense. More accurately, it represents an attempt to apply the science and tools of international law to a specific, contemporary issue. From this perspective, it is as much about sources of international legal obligation, the formation of international law, the doctrines of responsibility, and theories of compliance as it is about trafficking. The book's focus is essentially a problem-solving one: The international community has identified trafficking as a problem and decided that law will be used to structure and enable at least part of the solution to that problem. By providing a clear and organized explanation of the law as it is, the capacity of those who are in a position to use international law to hold States and others to account is hopefully strengthened.

The book has evolved out of more than a decade of writing and practice. It reflects experiences and insights from my working life as a UN official, as a teacher and scholar of international law, and as a practitioner in the field. From that perspective, more persons than can reasonably be named have contributed, in one way or another, to the final product. I acknowledge in particular Mary Robinson. It was under her leadership as UN High Commissioner for Human Rights that I first began working on trafficking and it was from my time with her that I learned valuable lessons about the politics of international lawmaking. My work in Southeast Asia since 2003 has provided a unique opportunity to test complex theories of legal obligation and State responsibility in the real world. Thanks are due to my stellar ARCPPT/ARTIP team; to ASEAN and its Member States; and to government counterparts in Australia, Brunei Darussalam, Cambodia, Lao PDR, Indonesia, Malaysia, Myanmar, the Philippines, Singapore, Thailand, and Vietnam for allowing me the benefit of this collaboration. The police, prosecutors, and judges with whom I have worked over the past ten years were especially influential in opening my eyes to the central importance of an effective criminal justice response to trafficking for human rights and the rule of law. In this regard, a separate and special thanks is due to my friend and colleague, Paul Holmes.

Janie Chuang has been an intellectual companion on this journey, and I benefited greatly from our constant discussions and her review of parts of the draft manuscript.

Fiona David, Al Moskowitz, Anahred Price, Nina Vallins, Zelie Wood, and Andrea Zakarias also made substantial and much appreciated contributions, as did Cees Flinterman and Theo van Boven, my PhD supervisors at the University of Utrecht during the period 2002–2005. Angela Ha proved to be an exceptional research assistant, and I am grateful for her help in finalizing the manuscript.

Writing is a solitary, if not selfish, occupation, particularly for an independent scholar who insists on maintaining her day job. It is therefore to my family that I owe the greatest debt of gratitude. Thanks to Cees for his critical eye and generous, steadfast support, and to Ruby and Elodie, for providing the perfect reason to hurry and finish up each day.

Anne T. Gallagher
Australia
June 2010

Table of Cases

I. INTERNATIONAL DECISIONS

International Court of Justice

Permanent Court of International Justice

UN Committee against Torture

UN Committee on the Elimination of All Forms of Discrimination against Women

International Criminal Tribunal for Rwanda

Special Court for Sierra Leone

Inter-American Commission on Human Rights

Inter-American Court of Human Rights

International Arbitral Tribunals

Table of Treaties and Other International Instruments

1967

1992

1993

1998

           Organized Crime (2225 UNTS 209)   1, 4, 9, 29, 68–77, 79–83,
                 87–89, 92, 98 n. 310, 125, 140, 163, 260 n. 225, 280, 301, 316,
                 318–319, 323, 350–351, 362, 374–375, 381, 392–393, 395–396,
                 397 n. 118, 401–402, 405–407, 410–413, 416, 443–444,
                 446, 466–467, 472–473, 490, 493

           Art. 1   74 n. 120
           Art. 2(a)   74 n. 124, 123 n. 466
           Art. 2(b)   75 n. 125, 393 n. 95, 400 n. 131
           Art. 2(f)   400 n. 128
           Art. 2(g)   400 n. 128
           Art. 3   443 n. 128
           Art. 3(1)   74 nn. 123–124
           Art. 3(1)(b)   75 n. 125, 393 n. 95, 400 n. 131
           Art. 3(2)   74 n. 123
           Art. 5   75 n. 128, 75 n. 133, 375 n. 25, 407 n. 163
           Art. 6   75 n. 130, 80 n. 181, 407 n. 163, 445 n. 136
           Art. 6(2)(f)   441 n. 118
           Art. 7   445 n. 136
           Art. 8   75 n. 129, 407 n. 163, 443 n. 129
           Art. 8(1)   444 n. 129
           Art. 8(2)   444 n. 129
           Art. 8(3)   444 n. 129
           Art. 9(1)   444 n. 131
           Art. 9(2)   444 n. 132
           Art. 10   80 n. 178, 375 n. 25, 387 n. 74
           Art. 10(4)   393 n. 99
           Art. 11   393 n. 97
           Art. 11(1)   75 n. 132, 80 n. 180, 98 n. 310, 393 n. 96, 444 n. 133
           Art. 11(3)   80 n. 182, 393 n. 97
           Art. 11(4)   393 n. 97
           Art. 11(5)   393 n. 97
           Art. 12   80 n. 183, 401 n. 130, 400 n. 132, 402 n. 133
           Art. 12(7)   72 n. 107
           Art. 13   80 n. 183, 401 n. 130, 402 nn. 133–134
           Art. 13(3)   402 n. 135
           Art. 14   80 n. 183, 401 n. 130, 403 n. 143
           Art. 14(2)   403 n. 143
           Art. 15(1)   72 n. 105, 81 n. 190, 380 n. 44
           Art. 15(2)   81 n. 191
           Art. 15(2)(a)   380 n. 45
           Art. 15(2)(b)   380 n. 46

Table of Common Abbreviations

ACJ	Advisory Council of Jurists (Asia Pacific Forum of National Human Rights Institutions)
APF	Asia Pacific Forum of National Human Rights Institutions
ASEAN	Association of Southeast Asian Nations
AU	African Union
CAHTEH	Ad Hoc Committee on Action against Trafficking in Human Beings (Council of Europe)
CDEG	Steering Committee for Equality between Women and Men (Council of Europe)
CEDAW	Convention on the Elimination of All Forms of Discrimination against Women
CoE	Council of Europe
COMMIT	Coordinated Mekong Ministerial Initiative against Trafficking
CRC	Convention on the Rights of the Child
ECOWAS	Economic Community of West African States
EU	European Union
GRETA	Group of Experts on Action against Trafficking in Human Beings
HCHR	High Commissioner for Human Rights
HRC	Human Rights Committee
ICC	International Criminal Court; also, in Chapter 9: International Coordinating Committee of National Institutions for the Protection and Promotion of Human Rights
ICCPR	International Covenant on Civil and Political Rights
ICESCR	International Covenant on Economic, Social and Cultural Rights
ICJ	International Court of Justice
ICTR	International Criminal Tribunal for Rwanda
ICTY	International Criminal Tribunal for the former Yugoslavia
IGO	International governmental organization
ILC	International Law Commission

ILO	International Labour Organization
IOM	International Organization for Migration
MOU	Memorandum of Understanding
NGO	Nongovernment organization
OAS	Organization of American States
OHCHR	Office of the United Nations High Commissioner for Human Rights
OSCE	Organization for Security and Co-operation in Europe
SAARC	South Asian Association for Regional Cooperation
UN	United Nations
UNHCR	United Nations High Commissioner for Refugees
UNICEF	United Nations Children's Fund
UNIFEM	United Nations Development Fund for Women
UNODC	United Nations Office on Drugs and Crime

THE INTERNATIONAL LAW OF HUMAN TRAFFICKING

Introduction

During 1998 and 1999, I participated in a series of meetings in Vienna convened under the auspices of the United Nations. Their purpose was to hammer out, as quickly as possible, an international agreement on transnational organized crime,[1] as well as a set of supplementary protocols on the specific issues of trafficking,[2] migrant smuggling,[3] and the trade in small arms.[4] My job, as the representative of Mary Robinson, the then-High Commissioner for Human Rights, was to use her voice in persuading States not to dilute or let go of the basic international human rights principles to which they were already committed. We had good reason to be worried. Migrant smuggling had recently been identified as a security threat by the preferred destination countries in Europe, North America, and Australia, and had moved from the margins to the mainstream of international political concern. Human trafficking, an obscure but jealously guarded mandate of the UN's human rights system, had been similarly elevated and, in the process, unceremoniously snatched away from its traditional home.

For those of us from the United Nations' various human rights and humanitarian agencies thrown together in Vienna, the existence of a very real problem was beyond dispute. Despite an impressive, if disparate, array of international legal protections, it was clear to our organizations that forced labor, child labor, debt bondage, forced

---

[1] United Nations Convention against Transnational Organized Crime, 2225 UNTS 209, done Nov. 15, 2000, entered into force Sept. 29, 2003 (Organized Crime Convention).

[2] Protocol to Prevent, Suppress and Punish Trafficking in Persons, Especially Women and Children, supplementing the United Nations Convention against Transnational Organized Crime, done Nov. 15, 2000, GA Res. 55/25, Annex II, UN GAOR, 55th Sess., Supp. No. 49, at 53, UN Doc. A/45/49 (Vol. I) (2001), entered into force Dec. 25, 2003 (Trafficking Protocol).

[3] Protocol against the Smuggling of Migrants by Land, Sea and Air, supplementing the United Nations Convention against Transnational Organized Crime, done Nov. 15, 2000, GA Res. 55/25, Annex III, UN GAOR, 55th Sess., Supp. No. 49, at 62, UN Doc. A/45/49 (Vol. I) (2001), entered into force Jan. 28, 2004.

[4] Protocol against the Illicit Manufacturing of and Trafficking in Firearms, Their Parts and Components and Ammunition, supplementing the United Nations Convention against Transnational Organized Crime GA Res. 255, Nov. 15, 2000, UN Doc. A/RES/55/255 (2001), done May 31, 2001, entered into force July 3, 2005.

marriage, and commercial sexual exploitation of children and adults were flourishing, virtually unchecked in many parts of the world. Globalization, bringing with it the promise of wider markets and greater profits, had created complex new networks and even new forms of exploitation. We all believed that trafficking was an appropriate focus for international law. We also agreed that the existing international legal framework was woefully inadequate, and the chances of the human rights system coming to the rescue were slim. However, it was far from clear that another area of international law, another part of the international system, was up to the challenge. Certainly, among the delegates in Vienna, there seemed to be little understanding or acknowledgment of the role that States play in trafficking or of the moral and legal responsibilities that this involvement entails. I recall, at one of these meetings, a corridor conversation with a very senior member of one of the leading delegations. He was kind but dismissive of our efforts to ensure that human rights were integrated into the final agreements, particularly the one dealing with trafficking. "You have to understand," he said, "this is not like torture. It's not even about human rights. We governments are not the villains here. Traffickers are just criminals. We can't be responsible for what they are doing. In fact, if it wasn't that we needed the cooperation of other countries to catch them, I wouldn't even be here." Those remarks neatly encapsulate many of the issues that lie at the heart of this book.

The end result of the negotiations, at least in respect of the Trafficking Protocol, was better than many had predicted. Following fractious debate, the first international legal definition of trafficking proved to be sufficiently broad to embrace all but a very small range of situations in which women, men, and children are severely exploited for private profit.[5] Importantly, the Protocol's general obligation to criminalize trafficking[6] would, in practice, apply to exploitative practices taking place within as well as across national borders. States also agreed to a limitations clause maintaining the application of existing rights and obligations.[7] It was in relation to specific commitments of protection and support for victims that the Trafficking Protocol disappointed. The flaw, however, was not considered to be a fatal one. International human rights law already provided substantial, if underutilized protections, and subsequent legal developments, particularly at the regional level, were expected to provide ample authority to fill any remaining gaps. As this book demonstrates, that optimism was not misplaced. Over the past decade, the legal and political landscape around this previously marginal issue has been radically transformed. While not quite "high politics," trafficking is now firmly on the international political agenda. It is the subject of a vast array of international legal rules and a plethora of "soft" standards. Previously moribund international legal prohibitions on practices such as slavery, servitude, forced labor, bonded labor, and forced marriage have

---

[5]   Trafficking Protocol, at Art. 3(a).

[6]   Ibid. at Art. 5.

[7]   Ibid. at Art. 14.

been resurrected, reinvigorated, and in some cases reinterpreted as a result of their connection to trafficking. In Africa, Asia, and particularly Europe, regional groupings of States have moved to support or even strengthen the internationally agreed standards.[8] Many States have enacted their own specialist trafficking laws and established new institutions and processes to ensure their effective implementation. Even those States traditionally distrustful of the international legal and political process have had no trouble in joining – or in some cases even leading – this unprecedented international movement.

A Changing Role for Human Rights Law. A full appreciation of the new legal landscape around trafficking requires an understanding of the changing role and position of international human rights law. Until very recently, it would have been difficult, if not impossible, to identify a practitioner working in this area who did not view trafficking solely through the lens of human rights. However, the drafting process for the Trafficking Protocol provided some important and occasionally uncomfortable insights into the place of human rights within a broader international legal and political context. On the positive side, there are not many fields of international law, outside this one, where the gains for the poor and the marginalized are potentially greater than for the rich and the privileged. Making human rights the center of thinking about trafficking stops us from being sidetracked by the slick arguments of those who would prefer it be approached as a straightforward issue of migration, of public order, or of organized crime. It prevents an uncritical acceptance of the strange legal fiction, explored at various points throughout this book, that "trafficking" and "migrant smuggling" are two completely different crimes involving helpless, virtuous victims on the one side, and foolish or greedy adventurers, complicit in their own misfortune, on the other. Perhaps most importantly, a human rights approach

---

[8] See, for example, European Union and African States, "Ouagadougou Action Plan to Combat Trafficking in Human Beings, Especially Women and Children," adopted by the Ministerial Conference on Migration and Development, Nov. 22–23, 2006; "Conclusions and Recommendations of the Meeting of National Authorities on Trafficking in Persons," adopted by the Organization of American States, Docs. OEA/Ser.K/XXXIX and RTP/doc. 16/06 rev. 1, Mar. 17, 2006; European Union, "EU Plan on Best Practices, Standards and Procedures for Combating and Preventing Trafficking in Human Beings," OJ C 2005/C 311/01, Dec. 9, 2005; Memorandum of Understanding on Cooperation against Trafficking in Persons in the Greater Mekong Sub-region, adopted on Oct. 29, 2004 in Yangon (by Cambodia, China, Lao PDR, Myanmar, Thailand, and Vietnam); Organization for Security and Co-operation in Europe (OSCE) Permanent Council, "OSCE Action Plan To Combat Trafficking In Human Beings," OSCE Doc. PC.DEC/557, July 24, 2003; European Union, "Brussels Declaration on Preventing and Combating Trafficking in Human Beings," EU Doc. 14981/02, Nov. 29, 2002; European Union, Council Framework Decision of 19 July 2002 on combating trafficking in human beings (2002/629/JHA), OJ L 203/1, Aug. 1, 2002; Economic Community of West African States, "ECOWAS Initial Plan of Action against Trafficking in Persons (2002–2003)," adopted by the Twenty-Fifth Ordinary Session of Authority of Heads of State and Government, Dec. 20–21, 2001. For a recent overview of regional initiatives against trafficking see "Report submitted by the Special Rapporteur on Trafficking in Persons, Especially Women and Children, Joy Ngozi Ezeilo," UN Doc. A/HRC/14/32, May 4, 2010.

makes clear that trafficking is woven deeply and inextricably into the fabric of an inequitable, unjust, and hypocritical world.

On the negative side, the disadvantages of a traditional, exclusively rights-based response to trafficking are significant. Such disadvantages are connected fundamentally to the inherent political, legal, and structural weaknesses of the international human rights system itself. It cannot be a coincidence that nothing much happened to trafficking in the fifty years it occupied a hallowed, if irrelevant, position on the sidelines of the United Nations' human rights system. During the entire twentieth century, when trafficking and its array of associated practices "belonged" exclusively to the international human rights system, States could not even agree on a definition, much less on specific legal obligations. International oversight of trafficking and related forms of "private" exploitation was almost nonexistent. Despite the presence of relatively straightforward prohibitions in two major treaties, and an impressive selection of related standards in others, trafficking was (and still is) rarely linked to the violation of a specific provision of a specific treaty. All in all, working out the "wrong" of trafficking with reference to international human rights law was a difficult and frustrating task for the human rights lawyer.

I was among those human rights lawyers and activists who, in the late 1990s, decried the removal of trafficking from the sacred chambers of the international human rights system to the area of the United Nations that dealt with drugs and crime. When it became clear that the UN Crime Commission was going to develop a treaty on trafficking, we were, in the best tradition of our profession, righteously outraged. Surely this was the task of human rights? Surely trafficking was too important, too sensitive, to entrust it to an alien UN environment that knew (or, we suspected, cared) little about human rights? A decade later, it is necessary to acknowledge that there is no way the international community would have a definition and an international treaty on trafficking if this issue had stayed within the realms of the human rights system. Even if that troubled system had managed to found its own treaty, such an instrument probably would not have tackled those mundane but critical issues such as criminal jurisdiction, mutual legal assistance, or extradition. No human rights treaty on trafficking or any related issue would have been able to link itself to a parent instrument that set out detailed obligations for tackling corruption, exchanging evidence across national borders, and seizing assets of offenders. No human rights treaty would have received the necessary number of ratifications to permit its entry into force a mere two years after its adoption. Certainly, no human rights treaty would have prompted the raft of international, regional, and national reforms that we have witnessed over the past decade. Perhaps most importantly, no conceivable action of the international human rights system could have focused the same level of global attention and resources on debt bondage, forced labor, sexual servitude, forced marriage, and other exploitative practices that continue to plague all regions and most countries of the world.

Since its adoption, the Trafficking Protocol has served international law very well. It has provided both a framework and an impetus for the generation of a comprehensive range of international, regional, and national norms and standards. These articulate, with much greater clarity than was ever previously possible, the obligations of States in relation to both ending impunity for traffickers and providing support, protection, and justice for those who have been exploited. The level of normative precision secured through this new legal framework and the nature and the intensity of oversight are, for the human rights lawyer, particularly striking. From that perspective, it is not helpful to continue to be aggrieved about the fact that these changes were generated outside the formal human rights system. The international human rights system amply demonstrated over many years that, on its own, it was incapable of taking any serious steps toward eliminating trafficking and other forms of private exploitation. Through the legal instruments developed over the past decade, that system has now been given new and better tools with which to work. The real test of its effectiveness, relevance, and resilience will lie in the way it responds to this challenge.

Accepting the constraints of international human rights law does not require one to renounce the faith. Trafficking goes to the very heart of what human rights law is trying to prevent. From its earliest days to the present, human rights law has loudly proclaimed the fundamental immorality and unlawfulness of one person appropriating the legal personality, labor, or humanity of another. Human rights law has battled the demons of discrimination on the basis of race and sex; it has demanded equal or at least certain key rights for aliens; it has decried and outlawed arbitrary detention, forced labor, debt bondage, forced marriage, and the commercial sexual exploitation of children and women; and it has championed freedom of movement and the right to leave and return to one's own country. There can be no doubt that the spirit of the entire corpus of human rights law rejects, absolutely, the practices and results that are integral to the human trafficking process. As this book will clearly show, human rights law is central to any credible and effective response to trafficking. Human rights law and its enforcement mechanisms are critically important when it comes to ensuring that national responses to trafficking do not violate established rights or circumvent the obligations that States owe to all persons. Ultimately, however, trafficking and its associated harms are multidimensional problems that do not, in the end, belong to one discipline or one branch of law. Combating contemporary exploitation will require a full arsenal of modern, smart weaponry, not just one precious but blunted sword.

The Limits of Knowledge and the Hazards of Objectivity. In trafficking, as in any other area, the attainment of knowledge is an ongoing endeavor. International lawyers working in this field must be part of the journey of discovery and resist the temptation to accept simplistic responses to complex, perhaps intractable problems. An informed understanding of the dynamics of trafficking and an appreciation of the social and political environment within which norms are constructed and implemented are essential when it comes to identifying rules, prioritizing their importance, and applying the law, as carefully and honestly as possible, to specific circumstances. For example, an international legal obligation to address trafficking-related "demand" cannot be effectively applied, or even well described, unless and until the underlying concept is properly understood. This requires an appreciation of the political dimensions of the demand discourse, as well as an insight into the dynamics of the trafficking process itself. An awareness of the gender dimensions of trafficking is a prerequisite for deciding whether a State's response (or nonresponse) to trafficking violates the international legal prohibition of nondiscrimination on the basis of sex. The international legal scholar must be ready to identify limits of current knowledge, for example, on the nature and scope of the problem,[9] and to accept the impact that such limits will impose on the task of identifying and applying legal norms. She or he should also be prepared to venture outside the discipline of international law if this is required to secure an adequate understanding of the problem that international law is seeking to address – or indeed, to assess the potential or actual impact of policy preferences enshrined in law. This is not a matter of diluting or confusing the law through promiscuous alliances. It is an essential aspect of ensuring the relevance and accessibility of legal knowledge.

International legal scholarship around trafficking can only be improved through an awareness of actual or potential biases – and an acknowledgment of the extent to which such biases operate to influence scholarship. The goal is not to produce work that is value-free. Rather it should be to ensure that individual beliefs, preferences, and values are not deliberately used to distort, misrepresent, or otherwise manipulate the description, presentation, or explanation of "the law as it is." This is more difficult than it sounds. On an issue such as trafficking, the temptation to blur the boundaries between moral claims and legal obligations is strong. As noted above, the way in which international law is developed, identified, and applied can

---

[9]   Reliable data on trafficking patterns and numbers is notoriously difficult to secure, a reality that appears lost on many international legal scholars who regularly cite statistics and numbers that are unverified and unverifiable. For an introduction to the "complexities and pitfalls" of measuring trafficking, see E.U. Savona and S. Stefanizzi eds., *Measuring Human Trafficking* (2007). For a withering critique of the oft-cited global figures on trafficking provided by the US Department of State, see US Government Accountability Office, "Human Trafficking: Better Data, Strategy and Reporting Needed to Enhance UN Antitrafficking Efforts Abroad," July 2006, available at http://www.gao.gov/new.items/d06825.pdf (accessed Nov. 22, 2009). See also D.A. Feingold, "Trafficking in Numbers: The Social Construction of Human Trafficking Data," in P. Andreas and K.M. Greenhill eds., *Sex, Drugs and Body Counts: The Politics of Numbers in Global Crime and Conflict* (forthcoming 2010); H.M. Ali, "Data Collection on Victims of Human Trafficking: An Analysis of Various Sources," (2010) 6(1) *Journal of Human Security* 55; K. Kangaspunta, "Measuring the Immeasurable: Can the Severity of Human Trafficking Be Ranked?" (2010) 9 *Criminology & Public Policy* 257; and L.S. Wyler and A. Siskin, "Trafficking in Persons: U.S. Policy and Issues for Congress," Congressional Research Service (2010), available at http://www.fpc.state.gov/documents/organization/139278.pdf (accessed June 9, 2010).

serve to entrench a strategically useful confusion between *lex lata* and *lex ferenda*. Of course, as Rosalyn Higgins has pointed out:

> Reference to "the correct legal view" or "rules" can never avoid the element of choice (though it can seek to disguise it), nor can it provide guidance to the preferable decision. In making this choice, one must inevitably have consideration for the humanitarian, moral and social purpose of the law.[10]

The absence of common agreement over the values and purpose of the law is reflected in a body of scholarly writing that, with a few exceptions, demonstrates an uncanny alignment between policy preference and legal analysis. In other words, scholars are all too frequently succumbing to that understandable temptation to conflate the law as it is with the law as they feel it ought to be. In complex, controversial, and fledgling areas of international law, such as trafficking, it is especially important that *the law make the scholarship*, rather than *the scholarship make the law*.[11] It is on the basis of such considerations that I have conceived my role in writing this book. That role is a modest and essentially technical one: to observe, describe, classify, and explain the law as it currently stands; to separate law from what is not law; to acknowledge rather than ignore or gloss over weaknesses, gaps, and deficiencies; to be objective whenever possible; and to be truthful when the outcome is not optimal or where objectivity is difficult.

The Structure of this Book. Recent legal developments in the field of human trafficking, in particular the expansion of trafficking law outside the traditionally vague domain of human rights, provide a unique opportunity to clarify the relevant obligations, including their scope and substantive content, with a level of exactness that was never previously possible. The task of clarifying obligations is important because, despite more and better laws, there is still abundant evidence of uncertainty and disagreement as to what States must do – or not do – when it comes to human trafficking. Inevitable legal complexities are one explanation but certainly not the only obstacle to clarity. Except where an immediate strategic interest can be met, States are generally reluctant to tie themselves down to obligations that are so specific as to give rise to clear and measurable expectations. Normative imprecision is, in this sense, a tool by which States exercise control over the international political and legislative process. As long as the law remains unclear, they can continue to argue about it. As long as the law remains unclear, they will, almost certainly, not be brought to task for failing to apply it.

---

[10] R. Higgins, *Problems and Process: International Law and How We Use It* (1994), at 5.

[11] See J. d'Aspremont, "Softness in International Law: A Self-Serving Quest for New International Legal Materials," (2008) 19 *European Journal of International Law* 1075, esp. at 1091–3. See also D.J. Bederman, "What's Wrong With International Legal Scholarship?" (2000) 1 *Chicago Journal of International Law* 75.

States are not alone in succumbing to the lure of normative imprecision. For reform-minded advocates, including some international lawyers, the inexactness and ambiguity that has characterized the international legal framework around trafficking has proven irresistible – providing ample and uncritical space within which to articulate and defend certain normative claims, often based on legitimate moral or humanitarian concerns, that may not otherwise have survived rigorous examination. Overly generous interpretations of legal rules, however well intended, are likely just as harmful to the integrity of international law as avoidance of obligation through failure to articulate and specify. There are other reasons for promoting greater normative clarity at the international level. One of the more pressing is the risk that the international legal framework around trafficking will be sidelined or rendered irrelevant through the emergence of a parallel unilateral regime that has adopted its own criteria for measuring State performance.[12]

For those concerned with using legal rules to shape the behavior of States, normative precision in international law is not a luxury but an operational necessity. States must understand exactly what international law requires of them if the international legal system is to have any hope of influencing and attaching consequences to their actions. A clear understanding of relevant rules is also essential for advocacy that purports to draw its authority from international law. This book divides that difficult but necessary process into several steps. The first of these is to identify the "wrong" of trafficking: Which primary international legal rules are implicated, and of these, which are the most relevant and the most important? Under what circumstances will a State actually be held legally responsible for violations of the primary rules and what consequences attach to such responsibility? The second step is to transform commonly vague primary rules, and even more opaque secondary rules, into precise obligations that are capable of measurable implementation. The third and final step is to move beyond the rules and examine the mechanisms and processes that are in place to promote and monitor State behavior with respect to their international legal obligations.

The first task, working out the international legal "wrong" of trafficking, is not as easy as it may first appear. The composite nature of the trafficking phenomenon guarantees that it does not sit comfortably within existing categories and boundaries of international law. Human rights law, for example, does not contain a clear prohibition on trafficking. The question of whether or not such a prohibition exists, or whether it can be inferred, or whether other prohibitions that do exist can be made to fit the trafficking phenomenon, can only be answered (tentatively) with reference to a myriad of sources, instruments, and standards. In addition, international human rights law is no longer the sole (or perhaps even the major) element of the international legal framework around trafficking. International criminal law, international humanitarian law, labor law, migration law, and refugee law are all relevant, to a

---

[12]   See further, discussion of the US reporting and sanctions mechanism in Chapter 9.4.

greater or lesser extent, to the issue of trafficking. Of critical importance is the relatively new field of "transnational criminal law," which includes, alongside treaties on drug trafficking and corruption, the Organized Crime Convention and its previously mentioned Protocol on trafficking in persons. As noted above, these treaties have been supplemented by a number of international and regional instruments, which, with only a few exceptions, add considerably to our understanding of the "wrong" of trafficking. Chapters 1 through 3, addressing, respectively, the international legal definition, the international legal framework, and specific legal issues, together confirm the existence of a strong if not yet fully formed body of relevant primary rules.

As my encounter with the delegate in Vienna demonstrated, States repeatedly deny legal responsibility for trafficking and for the violations of human rights that are integral to the trafficking process. In some cases, refutation of responsibility is based on the argument that the primary wrong (the trafficking) was committed by a private individual or entity and not by the State itself. In other cases, responsibility is not accepted because the State claims to have done everything reasonably possible to avoid the harm. An understanding of the principles of international legal responsibility as they apply in the trafficking context is an essential prerequisite for examining and, if found wanting, rejecting claims of this kind. In all cases, it first becomes a question of working out whether an act or omission can be attributed to the State. In some situations, where the act or omission can be linked directly to State institutions or State officials acting in their official capacity, the question of attribution can be easily settled. It then remains only to demonstrate that the act in question was indeed a breach of an international legal obligation. Taken together, attribution and breach equals responsibility. However, traffickers are people, not States, their institutions, or their representatives. This is a problem because, as the International Law Commission has pointed out: "[a]s a general principle, the conduct of private persons or entities is not attributable to the State under international law."[13] How general is the general rule? Can countries of origin, transit, and destination for trafficked persons absolve themselves of any responsibility to these individuals on the basis that the conduct complained of is not directly attributable to them? Does the content of the primary rule itself (establishing the breach of the international legal obligation) have any bearing on whether or not a State can evade responsibility and its consequences? Chapter 4 engages with the "devilishly difficult"[14] international rules of State responsibility in seeking a response to these and other questions.

The second step in clarifying the international legal framework around trafficking is to identify the specific obligations that flow from the primary and secondary rules.

[13] International Law Commission (ILC), Draft Articles on Responsibility of States for Internationally Wrongful Acts, Report of the International Law Commission on the Work of Its Fifty-third Session, UN GAOR, 56th Sess., Supp. No. 10, at 43, UN Doc. A/56/10 (2001), at Art. 8, para. 1.

[14] D.D. Caron, "The ILC Articles on State Responsibility: The Paradoxical Relationship Between Form and Authority," (2002) 96 *American Journal of International Law* 857, at 872.

As noted above, States must understand what is required of them before it becomes possible for these same requirements to influence their decision making. The more precise and action-oriented the identified obligations are the better. They must be able to answer the basic questions that are asked everywhere and everyday in the context of real situations. For example: Are States required to criminalize trafficking? If so, does international law include specific requirements with regard to criminalization, jurisdiction, and penalties? Does the international legal principle *aut dedere aut judicare* ("extradite or prosecute") apply to trafficking? Are States required, as a matter of international law, to investigate trafficking and, if so, to what standard? Are they required to protect and support all victims? Is there a different standard of protection and support owed to child victims of trafficking? Can victims be prosecuted or detained for status-related offenses? Can States force victims to return home even if this is unsafe? Can they be forced to accept returning victims? Do victims have an enforceable right to remedies? What limits, if any, does international law place on States' response to the crime of trafficking? Must States cooperate with other States and, if so, in what areas and to what extent? Specific legal obligations of States are identified and discussed under the following headings: obligations of protection and support, in Chapter 5; obligations related to repatriation and remedies, in Chapter 6; obligations of an effective criminal justice response, in Chapter 7; and obligations to prevent trafficking and to respond lawfully, in Chapter 8.

The final part of the book, and its final chapter, addresses a difficult but critical question: How can the international legal order around trafficking be made to work? That order includes a range of formal mechanisms established for the specific purpose of overseeing and thereby promoting national implementation of applicable international legal rules. Supplementing (and sometimes supplanting) these mechanisms are less traditional structures and processes including the controversial but highly influential unilateral reporting and sanctions system established by the U.S. government, as well as transnational networks operating within and between national government agencies, intergovernmental organizations, and NGOs. Chapter 9 identifies and explores some of the factors or variables that may help explain and even predict the impact of international legal rules relating to trafficking on the behavior of States. It uses these insights to examine, in turn, the structure, functioning, and potential of the most important compliance mechanisms and processes.

Trafficking was identified as an international legal issue more than a century ago – well before the formation of anything that even vaguely resembled a credible international legal system. Over the past decade, the international community has made clear that trafficking is important enough to be the subject of detailed rules. Ascertaining those rules with certainty is a critical function of the international lawyer. It is, however, only the first one. Until they are applied, laws only exist as abstract concepts and, as such, have little external value. It is therefore also the task of the international lawyer to take those rules, match them with a set of facts, ascertain if they have been broken, identify who is responsible, and determine the consequences of that responsibility. This process is important because international law is ultimately a tool for change: It seeks to positively influence the behavior of States. We use both the primary and the secondary rules to communicate with States and their representatives, to persuade them, to challenge them, to win them over: "If law seeks to condition the choices of those who exercise power, is it not wise to educate power holders in the consequences of their acts, in the responsibility which will attach to their choices?"[15] States are making choices about trafficking every day, choices that could be different and better if they were confronted with clear and unambiguous evidence of their international legal obligations. This book seeks to contribute to a future in which such clarity is both possible and welcomed.

[15] P. Allott, "State Responsibility and the Unmaking of International Law," (1988) 29 *Harvard International Law Journal* 1, at 2.

1

The International Legal Definition

Until December 2000, the term "trafficking" was not defined in international law, despite its incorporation in a number of international legal agreements. The long-standing failure to develop an agreed-upon understanding reflected major differences of opinion concerning the ultimate end result of trafficking, its constitutive acts, and their relative significance, as well as the similarities and differences between trafficking and related issues such as illegal migration and migrant smuggling. It is no coincidence that the various definitions proposed and adopted throughout the twentieth century inevitably mirrored the interests, priorities, and perspectives of their promoters. Only in the late 1990s, when attempts were made to deconstruct understandings about trafficking in order to develop an agreed-upon international definition, were the extent and depth of divisions in both perceptions and priorities revealed.

This chapter commences with an overview of how trafficking was used and evolved as a legal concept throughout the twentieth century. Particular attention will be given to the final decade of that century, when efforts to develop an internationally agreed definition commenced in earnest. It was during this period that many of the most difficult questions were first raised. For example, does "trafficking" cover only the action (recruitment and transport) aspect, or does it also encompass the *outcome* of that action? Can trafficking take place for a range of end purposes, or is it restricted to enforced prostitution and other forms of sexual exploitation? Can men and boys be trafficked as well as women and girls? Must the movement be across an international border, or is it possible for an individual to be trafficked within a country, including her/his own? Can an individual be trafficked with her/his consent? What is the difference between trafficking and illegal migration, and between trafficking and migrant smuggling? The second part of the chapter examines, in detail, the definition contained in the Trafficking Protocol,[1] isolating key

---

[1] Protocol to Prevent, Suppress and Punish Trafficking in Persons, Especially Women and Children, supplementing the United Nations Convention against Transnational Organized Crime, GA Res. 55/25, Annex II, UN GAOR, 55th Sess., Supp. No. 49, at 53, UN Doc. A/45/49 (Vol. I) (2001), done Nov. 15, 2000, entered into force Dec. 25, 2003 (Trafficking Protocol).

elements and identifying, in particular, those aspects of the definition that are controversial, unclear, or otherwise deserving of careful consideration. The third part of the chapter provides a brief summary of post-Protocol developments with respect to the definition. The chapter concludes with a consideration of the scope and limitations of the current international legal definition.

A study of the definition of trafficking is, in many senses, also a study of the history of trafficking in international law. For that reason, the present chapter has important links to the one that follows. A historical analysis of this kind also confirms that discussions around definitions have served as a mask or proxy for infinitely more complicated debates around issues such as prostitution and migration. While a full discourse analysis is beyond the scope of the present work,[2] an examination of the evolution of an international legal definition provides important insights into the ideas, beliefs, and assumptions that have informed and constructed the way in which individuals, States, and the international community have thought about and responded to trafficking.

1.1. HISTORY OF A DEFINITION

Trafficking has a lengthy legal and political history that sets it apart from many contemporary international legal issues. While this fact is noted in much current research, only a few scholars have gone so far as to identify and explore the links between current trafficking discourses and their direct predecessors. As explored in more detail in the following chapter, "trafficking" as it relates to human beings came into international use in the early twentieth century in connection with white slavery: a term that was initially used to refer to forcible or fraudulent recruitment to prostitution. The first Convention against White Slavery, adopted in 1904, sought to suppress the "criminal traffic" of women or girls compulsively procured for "immoral purposes."[3] Six years later, another instrument obliged States to punish:

> Whoever, in order to gratify the passions of another person, has, by fraud, or by means of violence, threats, abuse of authority, or any other method

---

[2] Several scholars, working principally within a feminist and sex-as-work context, have sought to provide such a discourse analysis. See, for example, J. Doezema, *Sex Slaves and Discourse Masters: The Construction of Trafficking* (forthcoming, 2010); J. Sanghera, "Unpacking the Trafficking Discourse," in K. Kempadoo, *Trafficking and Prostitution Reconsidered: New Perspectives on Migration, Sex Work, and Human Rights* 3 (2005); and J. Berman, "(Un)popular Strangers and Crises (Un)Bounded: Discourses of Sex Trafficking, the European Political Community and the Panicked State of the Modern State," (2003) 9 *European Journal of International Relations* 37. For discourse analyses of trafficking from the perspective of migration, see C. Ausserer, "'Control in the Name of Protection': A Critical Analysis of the Discourse of International Human Trafficking as a Form of Forced Migration," (2008) 4 *St Antony's International Review* 96; and C. Dauvergne, *Making People Illegal: What Globalization Means for Migration and Law* (2008), at chapter 5.

[3] International Agreement for the Suppression of the White Slave Traffic, 1 LNTS 83, done May 4, 1904, entered into force July 18, 1905, amended by a Protocol approved by the UN General Assembly on Dec. 3, 1948, 30 UNTS 23.

of compulsion, procured, enticed, or led away a woman or girl over age, for immoral purposes.[4]

References to white slavery were abandoned in 1927 as not reflecting the nature and scope of the problem. Subsequent international agreements concluded under the League of Nations dealt with, *inter alia*, Suppression of the Traffic in Women and Children (1921)[5] and Suppression of the Traffic in Women of Full Age (1933).[6] While none of these treaties defined "traffic" or "trafficking," they were uniformly concerned with the organized and (at least until 1933) coerced movement of women and girls abroad for the purposes of prostitution.[7] Importantly, all of the early agreements were limited to the process of recruitment. The end results of that recruitment, typically the detention of a woman or girl against her will in a brothel, were considered to be outside the scope of international action.[8]

In 1949, the United Nations adopted the Convention for the Suppression of Traffic in Persons and the Exploitation of the Prostitution of Others.[9] The Convention does not define "traffic" or "trafficking," and the absence of any *travaux préparatoires* renders impossible any meaningful analysis of this omission. In principle, elements of a definition could be extracted from the list of prohibited conduct. However, the Convention is extremely broad in this respect, referring in its preamble to "prostitution and the accompanying evil of the traffic in persons for the purposes of prostitution." It requires States Parties to punish:

any person who, to gratify the passions of another:
(1) procures or entices or leads away, for the purposes of prostitution, another person, even with the consent of that person;

---

4   International Convention for the Suppression of the White Slave Traffic, 3 LNTS 278, done May 4, 1910, entered into force Aug. 8, 1912, amended by a Protocol approved by the General Assembly on Dec. 3, 1948, 30 UNTS 23 (1910 White Slavery Convention), at Art. 2.

5   International Convention for the Suppression of Traffic in Women and Children, 9 LNTS 415, done Sept. 30, 1921, entered into force June 15, 1922, amended by a Protocol approved by the General Assembly on Oct. 20, 1947, 53 UNTS 13.

6   International Convention for the Suppression of the Traffic in Women of Full Age, 150 LNTS 431, done Oct. 11, 1933, entered into force Aug. 24, 1934, amended by a Protocol approved by the General Assembly on Oct. 20, 1947, 53 UNTS 13.

7   Under the 1933 Convention, the element of coercion was removed: Procurement was punishable, even if the woman involved had consented.

8   This was made clear in the closing statement of the 1910 White Slavery Convention: "The case of retention, against her will, of a woman or girl in a house of prostitution could not, in spite of its gravity, be included in the present Convention because it is exclusively a question of internal legislation." Cited in M. Wijers and L. Lap-Chew, *Trafficking in Women, Forced Labour and Slavery-Like Practices in Marriage, Domestic Labour and Prostitution* (The Foundation Against Trafficking in Women (STV)/The Global Alliance Against Trafficking in Women (GAATW), 1997) (Wijers and Lap-Chew, *Trafficking in Women, Forced Labour and Slavery-Like Practices in Marriage, Domestic Labour and Prostitution*), at 20.

9   Convention for the Suppression of the Traffic in Persons and of the Exploitation of the Prostitution of Others, 96 UNTS 271, done Dec. 2, 1949, entered into force July 25, 1951 (1949 Trafficking Convention). For an overview of the provisions of this instrument, see Chapter 2 of this volume.

(2) exploits the prostitution of another person, even with the consent of the person.[10]

States Parties are also required to punish those involved in keeping, managing, or financing of brothels,[11] and to refrain from any system of registration or supervision of prostitutes.[12] The Convention thereby attempts to deal with the *process* of trafficking (procurement, etc.) as well as the *result* (exploitation of prostitution). It is unlikely that all acts prohibited under the Convention (process and result) were to be considered "trafficking." It is possible that the first of these – the procurement, enticement, or leading away of a person for purposes of prostitution irrespective of consent (and of the sex of the victim, and of whether an international border is crossed)[13] – captured, in 1949, the contemporary understanding of trafficking. Broad support for this interpretation can be found in the earlier white slavery instruments as well as much of the UN's work on "traffic in persons and exploitation of the prostitution of others" right up to the end of the 1980s.[14]

The specter of innocent women and girls being taken abroad and forced against their will into situations of (usually sexual) exploitation continued to be raised periodically throughout the second half of the twentieth century. This was not,

---

[10] 1949 Trafficking Convention, at Art. 1.

[11] Ibid. at Art. 2.

[12] Ibid. at Art. 6.

[13] The Convention does not appear to have ever been invoked on behalf of men, although its use of gender-neutral language marked a significant shift from the earlier white slavery instruments. Likewise, the absence of any reference to an international element supports an assumption that the provisions of the Convention apply equally to offenses committed solely within the borders of one country.

[14] See, for example, "Inquiry on the Status of Combating of the Traffic in Persons and of the Exploitation of the Prostitution of Others: Report of the Secretary-General," UN Doc. E/CN.4/Sub.2/AC.2/1982/13 (1982). This report explicitly links trafficking and prostitution of women, as do several contemporaneous resolutions of the UN Economic and Social Council. See, for example, UN Economic and Social Council, "Suppression of the Traffic in Persons and of the Exploitation of the Prostitution of Others," UN Doc. E/RES/1982/20, May 4, 1982; UN Economic and Social Council, "Suppression of the Traffic in Persons and of the Exploitation of the Prostitution of Others," UN Doc. E/RES/1983/30, May 26, 1983. In the late 1980s, the Working Group on Contemporary Forms of Slavery (a subsidiary body of the Sub-Commission of the UN Commission on Human Rights) began to pay closer attention to the issues of both prostitution and the cross-border movement of women for exploitative purposes and by 1991, "prevention of traffic in persons and the exploitation of the prostitution of others" was the main agenda item for the Group's annual meeting. Note that an element of confusion was introduced in the 1970s when the UN commenced work on "exploitation of labour through illicit and clandestine trafficking," an area of enquiry that focused on illegal and exploitative movement of migrant workers and only incidentally included the movement of women and girls across national borders for purposes of exploitation. This marked the commencement of an association between migrant smuggling and trafficking that was only disentangled, unsatisfactorily for many, in December 2000 with the conclusion of the Trafficking Protocol closely following that of the Migrant Smuggling Protocol (Protocol against the Smuggling of Migrants by Land, Sea and Air, supplementing the United Nations Convention against Transnational Organized Crime, GA Res. 55/25, Annex III, UN GAOR, 55th Sess., Supp. No. 49, at 62, UN Doc. A/45/49 (Vol. I) (2001), done Nov. 15, 2000, entered into force Jan. 28, 2004). See the further discussion in Chapter 3 of this volume.

however, a widespread concern. Discussions, at least at the international level, were almost exclusively confined to the margins of the relatively low-profile human rights system. It was not until the early 1990s that the issue of trafficking in women and girls began to emerge as a matter of international and national interest and the subject of mainstream academic research. Importantly, the identity of the victims had changed somewhere over the course of the century. They were no longer white and from developed countries, but nonwhite and from relatively poorer countries. Feminists and feminist organizations, predominantly those working for the abolition of prostitution, were instrumental in setting the early parameters of the debate.[15] The advent of HIV/AIDS and fear about transmission of the disease through migration (particularly prostitute migration) played an important, if supplementary, role in reigniting and reorienting interest in the subject.[16] As with the earlier era of the white slave, interest in trafficking coincided with an increase in female migration outside the traditional context of family migration and oriented more toward labor.[17] Several commentators have noted another similarity between the older discourse and its modern equivalent; the new female migration of the early 1990s was, in contrast with male migration, inevitably viewed in negative terms, with little thought given to the possibility of increased autonomy or economic independence: "[w]hereas men [who migrate] tend to be viewed as adventurous, brave and deserving of admiration, for the same behaviour, women are pictured as passive, foolish and naïve, deserving either rescue or punishment."[18]

In the late 1980s and early 1990s, divisions over (and positions on) a definition of trafficking began to emerge in the context of more specific debates relating to prostitution and the inadequacies of the current international legal framework to prevent the sexual exploitation of women.[19] Several major reports released in the early to mid-1990s provided authoritative substance to the claim that cross-border exploitation of women and girls was a serious and worsening problem, particularly in Asia and the newly independent states of Central and Eastern Europe.[20] As this phenomenon

---

[15] See K. Barry, *Female Sexual Slavery* (1979, rev. 1984); UNESCO and the Coalition against Trafficking in Women, *The Penn State Report: Report of an International Meeting of Experts on Sexual Exploitation, Violence and Prostitution*, April 1999, Annex 1 (*Penn State Report*).

[16] As Outshoorn notes, "[p]rostitutes were always seen as sources of contamination, and the authorities were keen to control their activities": J. Outshoorn, "The Political Debates on Prostitution and Trafficking in Women," (2005) 12 *International Studies in Gender, State and Society* 142, at 143.

[17] For one of the earliest acknowledgments and explorations of this shift, see the various articles in M. Morokvasic ed., "Women in Migration" (1984) 18 *International Migration Review*.

[18] M. Wijers, "Keep Your Women Home: European Policies on Trafficking in Women" (unpublished manuscript, 1998), at 12, cited in J. Doezema, "Loose Women or Lost Women? The Re-Emergence of the Myth of 'White Slavery' in Contemporary Discourses of 'Trafficking in Women,'" (2000) 18(1) *Gender Issues* 23, at 40.

[19] See, for example, *Penn State Report*.

[20] Human Rights Watch, *A Modern Form of Slavery – Trafficking of Burmese Women and Girls into Brothels in Thailand* (1993); Human Rights Watch, *Rape for Profit, Trafficking of Nepali Girls and Women to India's Brothels* (1995); International Organization for Migration, *Trafficking and Prostitution: The Growing Exploitation of Migrant Women from Central and Eastern Europe* (1995).

became associated with other global criminal trends, including the facilitated move-ment of migrants across borders for private profit, the discourse began to expand. Literature exploring these issues from the perspectives of migration control and organized crime began to appear around 1997[21] and gained considerable momen-tum over the next few years.[22] It was around this same time that the theoretical and empirical links between trafficking (as presently understood) and broader migration flows, including refugee movements, began to be acknowledged.[23]

The legal and legally focused literature of the 1990s also experienced an evolu-tion: from an incidental consideration of trafficking in the context of other issues – for example, the international legal regulation of prostitution,[24] the prohibition on slavery,[25] or the work of UN human rights mechanisms[26] – toward a more focused consideration of the shortcomings of the international legal framework, including the lack of a clear problem definition.[27] States and intergovernmental organizations took up the issue, and a survey of their attempts to craft a common understanding provides important insights into the origins of the 2000 definition explored further in this chapter – as well as into areas of ongoing controversy and uncertainty.

The UN General Assembly was at the forefront of early definitional struggles. In 1994, in a resolution on trafficking, it referred to:

> the illicit and clandestine movement of persons across national and international borders … with the end goal of forcing women and girl-children into sexually or economically oppressive and exploitative situations for the profit of recruiters,

[21] See, for example, J. Salt and J. Stein, "Migration as a Business: The Case of Trafficking," (1997) 35 *International Migration* 467.

[22] See, for example, International Centre for Migration Policy Development, *The Relationship between Organized Crime and Trafficking in Aliens* (1999); P. Williams ed., *Illegal Immigration and Commercial Sex: The New Slave Trade* (1999) (Williams ed., *Illegal Immigration and Commercial Sex*); A. O'Neill Richard, *International Trafficking in Women to the United States: A Contemporary Manifestation of Slavery and Organized Crime* (2000).

[23] See, generally, various chapters of Williams ed., *Illegal Immigration and Commercial Sex*; J. Morrison and B. Crosland, "The Trafficking and Smuggling of Refugees: The End Game in European Asylum Policy?," UNHCR Evaluation and Policy Analysis Unit (EPAU) Working Paper No. 39 (Apr. 15, 2001).

[24] For example, L. Reanda, "Prostitution as a Human Rights Question," (1991) 13 *Human Rights Quarterly* 202.

[25] For example, N. Lassen, "Slavery and Slave-like Practices: United Nations Standards and Implementation," (1988) 57 *Nordic Journal of International Law* 197.

[26] For example, K. Silferberg, "Suppression of Trafficking in Persons and Exploitation of the Prostitution of Others," (1991) 2 *Finnish Yearbook of International Law* 66.

[27] For example, S. Toepfer and B.S. Wells, "The Worldwide Market for Sex: Review of International and Regional Legal Prohibitions Regarding Trafficking in Women," (1994) 18 *Michigan Journal of Gender and Law* 4; S. Farrior, "The International Law on Trafficking in Women and Children for Prostitution: Making It Live Up to Its Potential," (1997) 10 *Harvard Human Rights Journal* 213; J. Chuang, "Redirecting the Debate over Trafficking in Women: Definitions, Paradigms and Contexts," (1998) 11 *Harvard Human Rights Journal* 65; A. Miller and A. Stewart, "Report from the Roundtable on the Meaning of 'Trafficking in Persons': A Human Rights Perspective," (1998) 20 *Women's Rights Law Reporter* 11.

traffickers, crime syndicates as well as other illegal activities related to trafficking such as forced domestic labour, false marriage, clandestine employment and forced adoption.[28]

The following year, in a report to the General Assembly, the UN Secretary-General took up the spirit of this pronouncement in his examination of the relationship between trafficking and illegal migration:

> Trafficking across international borders is by definition illegal … The question must be asked however, whether trafficking is the same as illegal migration. It would seem that the two are related but different. Migration across frontiers without documentation does not have to be coercive or exploitative. At the same time, persons can be trafficked with their consent. A distinction could be made in terms of the purpose for which borders are crossed and whether movement occurs through the instrumentality of another person. Under this distinction, trafficking of women and girls would be defined in terms of "the end goal of forcing women and girl children into sexually or economically oppressive and exploitative situations" and the fact that it is done "for the profit of recruiters, traffickers and crime syndicates …". [29]

These two efforts to identify the core definitional elements of trafficking are highly significant. Both affirm a link with traditional understandings, for example, that trafficking only affects women and girls. However, they also signal a shift away from certain aspects of the old ideas by, for example, indicating that trafficking can take place for a variety of purposes and need not be limited to sexual exploitation. Notably, only the General Assembly's definition refers to internal trafficking and, while it does not identify coercion as a necessary element of trafficking, this is implied through its reference to "force." It is unclear however, whether "force" refers to the recruitment process alone or whether it also covers the subsequent working and living conditions. The Secretary-General's definition tries to reconcile the reality that trafficked persons may have initially consented to some aspect of their "movement" by focusing on the intention of the trafficker. Under this latter formulation, it is the *process* that defines trafficking, not the end result. In contrast, the General Assembly appears to identify the "illegal activities relating to trafficking," that is, the result of the movement, *as trafficking*. This construction has the potential effect of creating an umbrella definition under which both the process and the result are included. Practices such as forced domestic labor, false marriage, clandestine employment, and forced adoption could therefore be recognized as trafficking provided they are related in some way to the original movement. This was, in many senses, a conceptual breakthrough.

---

[28] UN General Assembly, "Traffic in Women and Girls," UN Doc. A/RES/49/166, Dec. 23, 1994.

[29] UN General Assembly, "Traffic in Women and Girls: Report of the Secretary-General," UN Doc. A/50/369, Aug. 24, 1995, at para. 17.

Confusion surrounding the meaning of trafficking was not limited to the United Nations. The International Organization for Migration (IOM), as the principal intergovernmental organization for migration matters,[30] had begun working in earnest on this issue of "trafficking" in the early 1990s. Progress was complicated from the beginning by a lack of agreement on the features separating "trafficking in migrants" from what IOM characterized as "trafficking in women." In 1994, IOM's definition of trafficking was very similar to the current understanding of migrant smuggling.[31] By 1996, it had determined that the term "trafficking in women" covered "any illicit transporting of migrant women and/or trade in them for economic or other personal gain."[32] As there was no reference to exploitation, this definition would extend to encompass a situation in which a woman paid a third party for her transport and irregular entry into a country other than her own – irrespective of whether or not the arrangement ended at the point of arrival. For IOM in the mid-1990s, therefore, trafficking in women meant exactly what migrant smuggling came to mean in 2000: the organized and illegal movement of persons (in this case, women) for profit. In practice, however, the IOM was researching and attempting to respond to a much more particular phenomenon: the cross-border movement and subsequent exploitation of migrant women (usually in prostitution) against their will and for financial benefit.[33]

The 1990s also saw active engagement on the issue of trafficking on the part of the European intergovernmental organizations. The question of a definition was a major concern during this period, and there was no common view between the

---

[30] Constitution of the International Organization for Migration, 1560 UNTS 440, done Oct. 19, 1953, entered into force Nov. 20, 1954, amended Nov. 14, 1989.

[31] According to a report released by IOM in 1994, international migratory movements were to be considered "trafficking" if the following five conditions were met: (i) money (or another form of payment) changes hands; (ii) a facilitator (trafficker) is involved; (iii) an international border is crossed; (iv) entry is illegal; (v) the movement is voluntary. International Organization for Migration, *International Response to Trafficking in Migrants and the Safeguarding of Migrant Rights* (1994), at 2, cited in International Organization for Migration ed., *Data and Research on Human Trafficking: A Global Survey* (2005) (IOM ed., *Data and Research on Human Trafficking*), at 12.

[32] For example, International Organization for Migration, *Trafficking and Prostitution: The Growing Exploitation of Migrant Women from Central and Eastern Europe* (1995) (IOM, *Central and Eastern Europe*); International Organization for Migration, *Trafficking in Women to Italy for Sexual Exploitation* (1996) (IOM, *Italy*). In this latter report, the IOM sets out examples of various elements of trafficking including "facilitating the illegal movement of women to other countries with or without their consent or knowledge; deceiving migrant women about the purposes of the migration, legal or illegal; physically or sexually abusing migrant women for the purpose of trafficking them; selling women into, or trading in women, for the purpose of employment, marriage, prostitution or other forms of profit-making abuse": at 11. An almost identical list of trafficking "elements" is contained in International Organization for Migration, *Trafficking of Women to the European Union: Characteristics, Trends and Policy Issues*, (1996) (IOM, *European Union*), at 3.

[33] See, for example, IOM, *Central and Eastern Europe*; IOM, *Italy*; IOM, *European Union*; International Organization for Migration, *Trafficking in Women to Austria for Sexual Exploitation* (1996); International Organization for Migration, *Trafficking in Women from the Dominican Republic for Sexual Exploitation* (1996).

different organizations on this point. The Council of Europe in particular initially set itself apart by deciding to focus exclusively on trafficking for sexual exploitation. In 1996, a Plan of Action commissioned by the Council's Steering Committee for Equality Between Women and Men proposed the following definition:

> There is trafficking when a woman is exploited in a country other than her own by another person (natural or legal) for financial gain, the traffic consisting of organising (the stay or) the legal or illegal emigration of a woman, even with her consent, from her country of origin to the country of destination and luring her by whatever means into prostitution or any form of sexual exploitation.[34]

This definition is unclear on whether the concept of trafficking applies to both process and end result. In its subsequent discussions, the Steering Committee did not address this issue but acknowledged that trafficking in human beings takes place for a variety of end purposes and involves men as well as women. It nevertheless justified its narrower definition on the basis that "trafficking ... concerns predominantly women being used for purposes of prostitution and pornography."[35]

This view was largely reflected in a Communication from the European Commission to the Council and the European Parliament, also issued in 1996. The Communication was entitled: "Trafficking in women for purposes of sexual exploitation." Such trafficking was defined as:

> the transport of women from third countries into the European Union (including perhaps subsequent movement between member States) for the purpose of sexual exploitation ... Trafficking for the purpose of sexual exploitation covers women who have suffered intimidation and/or violence through the trafficking. Initial consent may not be relevant as some enter the trafficking chain knowing they will work as prostitutes, but are then deprived of their basic human rights, in conditions which are akin to slavery.[36]

The European Parliament was also attempting to develop its own understanding of trafficking and to encapsulate this understanding into a single definition. In common with other European bodies, its early efforts identified a clear link between trafficking and exploitation of female prostitution.[37] However, by the mid-1990s, the

---

[34] M. Hirsch, "Plan of Action against Traffic in Women and Forced Prostitution," EG (1996) 2, at 11, cited in Wijers and Lap-Chew, *Trafficking in Women, Forced Labour and Slavery-Like Practices in Marriage, Domestic Labour and Prostitution*, at 26.

[35] Steering Committee for Equality between Women and Men, 11th meeting, Doc. CDEG 6 (1996) rev. 10, May 1996, cited in Wijers and Lap-Chew, *Trafficking in Women, Forced Labour and Slavery-Like Practices in Marriage, Domestic Labour and Prostitution*, at 26.

[36] Council of the European Parliament, Commission Communication to the Council and the European Parliament on Trafficking in Women for the Purpose of Sexual Exploitation, COM 1996 567 final, Nov. 20, 1996.

[37] For example, European Parliament Resolution on the exploitation of prostitution and trade in human beings, Resolution A2–52/89 of 14 April 1989, OJ C 120, May 16, 1989, at 352 ff. See also, European Parliament Resolution on trade in women, Resolutions B3–1264, 1283 and 1309/93 of 16 September 1993, OJ C 268, Oct. 4, 1993, at 141 ff.

European Parliament had, in contrast to both the Commission and the Council of Europe, begun to view trafficking as something more than the sexual exploitation of women abroad. In a January 1996 resolution, the Parliament identified coercion and deception as the hallmarks of trafficking in defining this practice as:

> the illegal action of someone who, directly or indirectly, encourages a citizen from a third country to enter or stay in another country in order to exploit that person by using deceit or any other form of coercion or by abusing that person's vulnerable situation or administrative status.[38]

In 1997, the Council of the European Union issued a Joint Action concerning trafficking in human beings and sexual exploitation of children.[39] The definition of trafficking included in the Joint Action was far narrower than that of the European Parliament, with a strong emphasis on the migratory aspects and with sexual exploitation envisaged as the only possible end result. The Joint Action identifies trafficking as:

> any behaviour which facilitates the entry into, transit through, residence in or exit from any territory of a member State for the purposes [of] ... (a) sexually exploiting a person other than a child for gainful purposes where use is made of coercion, in particular violence or threats, or deceit is used, or there is abuse of authority or other pressure which is such that the person has no real and acceptable choice but to submit to the pressure or abuse involved; (b) trafficking in persons other than children for gainful purposes with a view to their sexual exploitation.[40]

That same year, at a Ministerial conference on the subject, EU Member States reverted to the conception of trafficking as a problem only affecting women, albeit reflecting a more nuanced understanding of the way in which traffickers exercise control over their victims. The relevant declaration asserted that:

> trafficking in women relates to any behavior which facilitates the legal or illegal entry into, transit through, residence in or exit from the territory of a country, of women for the purpose of gainful sexual exploitation by means of coercion, in particular violence or threats, or deceit, abuse of authority or other pressure which is such that the person has no real and acceptable choice but to submit to the pressure or abuse involved.[41]

---

[38] European Parliament Resolution on trafficking in human beings, Resolution A4-0326/95 of 18 January 1996, OJ C 032, Feb. 5, 1996.

[39] Joint Action of 24 February 1997 concerning action to combat trafficking in human beings and sexual exploitation of children (97/154/JHA), OJ L 063, Mar. 4, 1997 (Council of Europe 1997 Joint Action on Trafficking).

[40] The Joint Action notes that the term "sexual exploitation" when used in connection with an adult is to be understood as meaning "at least the exploitative use of the adult in prostitution": ibid. at Title I.

[41] EU Ministerial Conference, "Hague Ministerial Declaration on European Guidelines for Effective Measures to Prevent and Combat Trafficking in Women for the Purpose of Sexual Exploitation," Apr. 26, 1997.

Four years later, immediately prior to the adoption of the Trafficking Protocol, the Committee of Ministers of the European Union adopted a Recommendation on Trafficking that included the following definition of trafficking:

> the procurement by one or more natural or legal persons and/or the organisation of the exploitation and/or transport or migration – legal or illegal – of persons, even with their consent, for the purpose of their sexual exploitation, inter alia, by means of coercion, in particular violence or threats, deceit, abuse of authority or a position of vulnerability.[42]

A careful dissection of these various formulations confirms a strong preference on the part of the European States, right up to 2000, to restrict the concept of trafficking to the various processes through which women and children are subject to sexual exploitation outside their country of origin. The European States were generally united on the point that consent of the victim should be rendered meaningless if elements of force, coercion, or abuse of authority were present. There was also some indication of an acknowledgment that the differences between trafficking in adults and children should be reflected in the definition itself.

Definitional struggles were also taking place in other regions. In 1994, the Organization of American States adopted the Inter-American Convention on International Traffic in Minors.[43] The Convention defines traffic in minors as "the abduction, removal or retention, or attempted abduction, removal or retention, of a minor for unlawful purposes or by unlawful means."[44] The term "unlawful purpose" is defined to include prostitution, sexual exploitation, and servitude.[45] "Unlawful means" refers to acts such as kidnapping, fraud, coercion, or payment.[46] Under this definition, it is not necessary to establish an unlawful purpose if the procurement or retention has been achieved through force or by payment. Conversely, the means of procurement or retention are irrelevant if the purpose can be shown to be an unlawful and/or exploitative one. It is relevant to note that this definition strongly resonates with the one finally adopted by the United Nations six years later.

While a number of governments were debating and passing trafficking legislation throughout the 1990s, it was the United States that had the greatest single impact on the evolution of an international consensus on the definition of trafficking. The United States made clear its interest in minimizing differences between an emerging national definition and the one being negotiated in Vienna. Within the United States, trafficking was considered, first and foremost, as a vehicle for the sexual exploitation of

---

[42] Council of Europe, Committee of Ministers, Recommendation No. R (2000) 11 of the Committee of Ministers to member states on action against trafficking in human beings for the purpose of sexual exploitation, adopted on May 19, 2000 (2000 Committee of Ministers Recommendation).

[43] Inter-American Convention on International Traffic in Minors, OAS Doc. OEA/Ser.K/XXI.5, 79 OASTS, done Mar. 18, 1994, entered into force Aug. 15, 1997, reprinted in (1994) 33 ILM 721.

[44] Ibid. at Art. 2(b).

[45] Ibid. at Art. 2(c).

[46] Ibid.

women and children – trafficking of men and trafficking for purposes of labor exploitation were only belatedly acknowledged as aspects of the same phenomenon and, even then, were not given the same priority.[47] The Trafficking Victims Protection Act (TVPA) was signed into law on October 11, 2000,[48] two months before the General Assembly adopted the Trafficking Protocol. While separately identifying a practice of "sex trafficking," the TVPA's operational provisions extend only to "severe forms of trafficking." These are defined as:

(a) sex trafficking in which a commercial sex act is induced by force, fraud, or coercion, or in which the person induced to perform such act has not attained 18 years of age; or

(b) the recruitment, harboring, transportation, provision, or obtaining of a person for labor or services, through the use of force, fraud or coercion for the purpose of subjection to involuntary servitude, peonage, debt bondage, or slavery.[49]

The TVPA definition imposed no gender restriction or requirement for the crossing of an international border. Coercion, force, and fraud were the "means" of trafficking, and "sex trafficking" and exploitative labor, including slavery and debt bondage, were the identified "ends." For "sex trafficking" to occur, the outcome was identified as directly relevant: The individual must have been "induced" to perform a commercial sex act. This is in contrast to trafficking for labor exploitation, in which case it would appear sufficient to establish that the fraudulent, forced, or coercive action was *intended* for one of the stipulated prohibited purposes.

---

[47] See, for example, B. Stolz, "Educating Policymakers and Setting the Criminal Justice Policymaking Agenda: Interest Groups and the 'Victims of Trafficking and Violence Act of 2000,'" (2005) 5 *Criminal Justice* 407, discussing the emphasis by both policymakers and civil society on trafficking for sexual exploitation and of women and children.

[48] Victims of Trafficking and Violence Protection Act of 2000, 22 USC 7101. For a comprehensive summary of the Act and for citations of the major provisions set out below, see S. Feve and C. Finzel, "Trafficking of People," (2001) 38 *Harvard Journal on Legislation* 279, at 283–284.

[49] The key terms of this definition are defined in the Act as follows: "sex trafficking" means the recruitment, harboring, transportation, provision, or obtaining of a person for the purpose of a commercial sex act; "commercial sex act" means any sex act on account of which anything of value is given to or received by any person; "involuntary servitude" includes a condition of servitude induced by means of (a) any scheme, plan, or pattern intended to cause a person to believe that, if the person did not enter into or continue in such condition that person or another person would suffer serious harm or physical restraint; or (b) the abuse or threatened abuse of the legal process; "debt bondage" means the status or condition of a debtor arising from a pledge by the debtor of his or her personal services or of those of a person under his or her control as a security for debt, if the value of those services as reasonably assessed is not applied toward the liquidation of the debt or the length and nature of those services are not respectively limited and defined; "coercion" means (a) threats of serious harm to or physical restraint against any person; (b) any scheme, plan, or pattern intended to cause a person to believe that failure to perform an act would result in serious harm to or physical restraint against any person; or (c) the abuse or threatened abuse of the legal process.

Finally, it is relevant to consider one further definition, proposed by the UN Special Rapporteur on Violence against Women in 2000, shortly before the Trafficking Protocol was adopted:

> Trafficking in persons means the recruitment, transportation, purchase, sale, transfer, harbouring or receipt of persons: (i) by threat or use of violence, abduction, force, fraud, deception or coercion (including the abuse of authority), or debt bondage for the purpose of (ii) placing or holding such person, whether for pay or not, in forced labour or slavery-like practices, in a community other than the one in which such persons lived at the time of the original act described in (i).[50]

This is the broadest and most inclusive of the definitions surveyed above, explicitly acknowledging that trafficking affects men as well as women and takes place for a range of exploitative end purposes. The Special Rapporteur's proposal identifies coercion as a critical element and replaces the widely accepted distinction between internal and cross-border traffic with a focus on the separation of the individual from her or his community. Most significantly, and in contrast to a number of otherwise similar definitions adopted around the same time,[51] the Special Rapporteur attempted to bridge the conceptual gap between process and result by insisting that the "action" aspect of the definition (recruitment, sale, etc.) covers:

> all persons involved in the trafficking chain: those at the beginning of the chain, who provide or sell the trafficked person and those at the end of the chain, who receive or purchase the trafficked person, hold the trafficked person in forced labour and profit from that labour.[52]

She further sought to explain what separated trafficking from other practices with which it is commonly associated:

---

[50] UN Commission on Human Rights, "Report of the Special Rapporteur, Ms. Radhika Coomaraswamy, on violence against women, its causes and consequences, on trafficking in women, women's migration and violence against women," UN Doc. E/CN.4/2000/68, Feb. 29, 2000 (Coomaraswamy, "Report," UN Doc. E/CN.4/2000/68), at para. 13. This definition draws heavily on an earlier one proposed by the Global Alliance Against Trafficking in Women (GAATW). See Global Alliance Against Trafficking in Women, Foundation against Trafficking in Women, International Human Rights Law Group, "Human Rights Standards for the Treatment of Trafficked Persons" (January, 1999).

[51] In June 2000, for example, the Organization for Security and Co-operation in Europe (OSCE) adopted the following working definition of trafficking: "all acts involved in the recruitment, abduction, transport (within or across borders), sale, transfer, harbouring or receipt of persons, by the threat or use of force, deception, coercion (including abuse of authority), or debt bondage, for the purpose of placing or holding such person, whether for pay or not, in involuntary servitude, forced or bonded labour, or in slavery-like conditions, in a community other than the one in which the person lived at the time of the original deception, coercion or debt bondage." OSCE, *Supplementary Human Dimension Meeting on Human Trafficking: Final Report* (2000). Although almost identical to the definition adopted by the Special Rapporteur, the OSCE's draft does not go on to specifically identify the end results of trafficking *as* trafficking.

[52] Coomaraswamy, "Report," UN Doc. E/CN.4/2000/68, para. 14.

it is the combination of the coerced transport and the coerced end practice that makes trafficking a distinct violation from its component parts. Without this linkage, trafficking would be legally indistinguishable from the individual activities of smuggling and forced labour or slavery-like practices.[53]

1.2. THE 2000 DEFINITION OF TRAFFICKING

Given the absence of an agreed-upon definition of trafficking and the divisions outlined earlier in this chapter, it is not surprising that discussions around the definition to be included in the Trafficking Protocol proved to be the most difficult and perhaps the most controversial aspect of the negotiation process. States, intergovernmental organizations, and NGOs were quick to realize the importance of the Protocol with respect to setting the parameters of future action. Many were conscious that other, larger issues loomed. Most particularly, negotiations around the definition of trafficking provided the first chance in more than half a century to revisit the prostitution debate within the context of an international legal drafting process. As the drafting of that instrument is subject to detailed consideration in the following chapter, only those aspects related to the definition of trafficking are discussed further in this chapter. The three elements of that definition are then subject to separate and detailed consideration.

1.2.1. *Key Issues During the Drafting Process*

A preliminary matter that was disposed of relatively quickly concerned the relationship between the various phenomena to be dealt with under the respective Protocols. Initial proposals were for three separate agreements: one on smuggling of migrants by sea; one on smuggling and trafficking of migrants; and one on trafficking of women and children. The developments outlined above had been instrumental in moving States toward accepting the validity and practical utility of a distinction between coerced or fraudulent movement for purposes of exploitation and the much more straightforward facilitation of illegal movement across international borders. As the accepted understanding of trafficking expanded to embrace all children moved into exploitation and all adults moved into exploitation through force, deception, or other means, the definition of migrant smuggling was consequently narrowed to include only those individuals moved across an international border for profit. As a result, there was relatively little debate on what constituted "smuggling of migrants," and States rapidly reached agreement that this practice refers to: "the procurement, in order to obtain, directly or indirectly, a financial or other material benefit, of the illegal entry of a person into a State Party of which the person is not a national or a permanent resident."[54] The reference to "financial or other material

---

[53]   Ibid. at para. 16.
[54]   Migrant Smuggling Protocol, at Art. 3(a).

benefit" identifies the only contentious aspect of the definition. It was included as an additional element, only after lobbying by some States and intergovernmental organizations, in order to ensure that the activities of those who provide support to migrants on humanitarian grounds or on the basis of close family ties do not come within the scope of the Migrant Smuggling Protocol.[55]

Negotiations for a separate instrument on trafficking commenced on the understanding that the final instrument would deal only with trafficking in women and children. However, a proposal to expand the focus to "trafficking in persons" was made at the first session of the drafting group. According to the *travaux préparatoires*, almost every participating country expressed a preference for the Trafficking Protocol to address all persons rather than only women and children, although it was agreed that particular attention should be given to the protection of women and children.[56] It is this formulation that was put to the General Assembly, and the mandate of the drafting group was modified accordingly.[57]

The first substantive stumbling block to agreement was the question of whether noncoerced adult migrant prostitution should be included in the definition of trafficking. One group of States, supported by a coalition of NGOs, argued that any distinction between forced and voluntary prostitution was false and morally unacceptable, and that a coercion requirement in the definition would lend unfounded legitimacy to prostitution.[58] Those opposing this position pointed out that to include noncoerced adult migrant sex work would blur the distinction between trafficking and migrant smuggling.[59] The debate quickly came down to a question of whether

---

[55] United Nations Office on Drugs and Crime, Travaux Préparatoires *of the Negotiations for the Elaboration of the United Nations Convention against Transnational Organized Crime and the Protocols Thereto* (2006) (Travaux Préparatoires *for the Organized Crime Convention and Protocols*), at 469.

[56] Travaux Préparatoires *for the Organized Crime Convention and Protocols*, at 322.

[57] "Progress Report of the Ad Hoc Committee on the Elaboration of a Convention Against Transnational Organized Crime," UN Doc. A/AC.254/30-E/CN.15/2000/4, Mar. 29, 2000, at para. 34.

[58] This position was initially proposed by Argentina and subsequently taken up by the delegation of the Philippines with support from a strong NGO lobby. For a detailed explanation of the NGO rationale, see International Human Rights Network, "Definition of Trafficking: Transnational Crime Convention, Trafficking in Persons Protocol, Informal Submission to the June 2000 Session of the Ad Hoc Committee" (2000) (International Human Rights Network, "Definition of Trafficking Submission").

[59] The United States initially led the move to reject the inclusion of noncoerced sex work into the trafficking definition although its support wavered occasionally, apparently in response to domestic pressures. See, for example, W.J. Bennett and C. Colson, "The Clintons Shrug at Sex Trafficking," *Wall Street Journal*, Jan. 10, 2000, at A-26; H. Rosin and S. Mufson, "Bitter Issues in Crime Treaty Debate: What is Prostitution?" *Washington Post*, Jan. 15, 2000, at A-02. The various nongovernmental organizations advocating a separation between migrant prostitution and coerced sex work organized themselves into a caucus and undertook a comprehensive campaign of lobbying. They were able to draw on supportive statements made by the UN Special Rapporteur on Violence against Women and by various members of an informal coalition of intergovernmental agencies, including the Office of the UN High Commissioner for Human Rights (OHCHR); the UN High Commissioner for Refugees (UNHCR); the United Nations Children's Programme (UNICEF) and the International Organization for Migration (IOM).

the offense of trafficking could occur "irrespective of the consent of the person." On the one side, it was argued that inclusion of the phrase "irrespective of the consent of the person" would ensure traffickers could not escape conviction by using the victim's so-called consent as a defense.[60] Opponents countered that issues of consent should not arise because, according to the noncontested parts of the definition, the trafficking of adults necessarily involves the presence of some kind of consent-nullifying behavior (use of force, abduction, fraud, deception, etc).[61]

A related and hotly debated aspect of the definition concerned the end purposes of trafficking. Reflecting the general direction of international and regional debate surveyed in the previous section, the drafting Committee reached early agreement on the need to move beyond the traditional focus on prostitution and the sex industry in order to ensure the relevance of the Trafficking Protocol to contemporary situations of exploitation including forced labor, debt bondage, and forced marriage. Divisions erupted, however, over whether "use in prostitution" should be included in the definition as a separate end purpose. The battle lines in this debate were identical to those described earlier in the chapter. States and their supporters seeking to maintain the abolitionist thrust of the 1949 Trafficking Convention argued strongly for a specific reference to prostitution. Such a reference would, in their view, confirm international legal opposition to all prostitution while at the same time broadening the scope of the definition and its possible application. Opponents of this position argued that inclusion of "voluntary" prostitution as an end purpose of trafficking would make the definition of trafficking overly broad and lead to a diversion of attention and resources away from the real problem. For example, even minor fraud or deception on the part of an individual recruiting a person into prostitution would amount to trafficking. The question of "consent" was also raised in this context.

After protracted debate, the drafting Committee decided against including the phrase "irrespective of the consent of the person." The final definition now incorporates an unwieldy (and probably unnecessary)[62] provision to the effect that consent

---

[60] International Human Rights Network, "Definition of Trafficking Submission."

[61] For a more detailed explanation of this position, see Human Rights Caucus, "Recommendations and Commentary: Informal Submission to the June 2000 Session of the Ad Hoc Committee" (2000); Human Rights Watch, Women's Rights Division, "Recommendations Regarding the Protocols on Trafficking in Persons and Smuggling of Migrants: Informal Submission to the June 2000 Session of the Ad Hoc Committee," June 5, 2000; and International Human Rights Law Group, "The Proposed Definition of 'Trafficking'", statement to the June 2000 session of the Ad Hoc Committee on the Elaboration of a Convention against Transnational Organized Crime, June 7, 2000. See also J. Doezema, "Who Gets to Choose? Coercion, Consent and the U.N. Trafficking Protocol," (2002) 10 *Gender and Development* 20.

[62] The *travaux préparatoires* note that many delegations were of the view that most of the listed "means" operated to preclude the consent of the victim: Travaux Préparatoires *for the Organized Crime Convention and Protocols*, at 344, note 26. As "means" is an essential element of the definition of adult trafficking, it is difficult to conceive of a situation in which consent would be relevant.

of the victim of trafficking to intended exploitation is to be irrelevant where any of the means (coercion, fraud, abuse of power, etc.) are established.[63] The drafters' clumsy handling of the consent issue has generated considerable confusion. It has been claimed, for example, that the provision "acknowledges the possibility of consent to enslavement."[64] That is, of course, as incorrect for slavery as it is for all other end results of trafficking. The reference to the nonapplicability of consent merely confirms that the means element of trafficking (coercion, deception, abuse of authority, etc.) operates to annul meaningful, informed consent. In other words, "[o]nce it is established that deception, force or other prohibited means were used, consent is irrelevant and cannot be used as a defence."[65] This position reflects a long-standing principle of international human rights law: The intrinsic inalienability of personal freedom renders consent irrelevant to a situation in which that personal freedom is taken away.[66]

A similar compromise was made in respect of the issue of prostitution. The proposal that "use in prostitution" be included as a separate end purpose was rejected in favor of a more narrowly focused reference to "exploitation of the prostitution of others." While the antiprostitution lobby hailed these decisions as victories[67] (and their opponents lamented the outcome as a defeat),[68] it would be incorrect to view the final result as indicative of a majority sentiment on the issue of prostitution. As the debates made clear and subsequent interpretative texts confirmed, States merely agreed to sacrifice their individual views on prostitution to the greater goals of securing an agreed definition and maintaining the integrity of the distinction between

[63] Trafficking Protocol, at Art. 3(b).

[64] J.C. Hathaway, "The Human Rights Quagmire of Human Trafficking," (2008) 49(1) *Virginia Journal of International Law* 1 (Hathaway, "The Human Rights Quagmire of Human Trafficking"), at 11.

[65] UN Office on Drugs and Crime, *Legislative Guides for the Implementation of the United Nations Convention against Transnational Organized Crime and the Protocols Thereto*, UN Sales No. E.05.V.2 (2004) (*Legislative Guide*).

[66] This issue came before the drafters of both the Supplementary Slavery Convention (Supplementary Convention on the Abolition of Slavery, the Slave Trade, and Institutions and Practices Similar to Slavery, 226 UNTS 3, done Sept. 7, 1956, entered into force Apr. 30, 1957) and the ICCPR (International Covenant on Civil and Political Rights, 999 UNTS 171, done Dec. 16, 1966, entered into force Mar. 3, 1976) in the context of proposals to add the qualification "involuntary" to the term "servitude." The proposal was rejected in both instances on the grounds that "[i]t should not be possible for any person to contract himself into bondage": F.G. Jacobs and R.C.A. White, *The European Convention on Human Rights* (1996), at 78, citing "Annotations on the Text of the Draft International Covenants on Human Rights," UN GAOR, 10th Sess., Annexes, Agenda Item 28 pt. II, at 33, UN Doc. A/2929, July 1, 1955 (prepared by the UN Secretary-General). The European Commission on Human Rights has confirmed that "personal liberty is an inalienable right which a person cannot voluntarily abandon": *De Wilde, Ooms & Versyp v. Belgium*, 10 Eur. Ct. H.R. (ser. B) (1969), at 91 (citing *De Wilde, Ooms & Versyp v. Belgium*, (1967) *Yearbook of the European Convention on Human Rights* 420 (Eur. Comm'n on H.R.).

[67] Coalition against Trafficking in Women, "Victory in Vienna" (2000) (unpublished report of the eleventh session of the Ad Hoc Committee on the Elaboration of a Convention against Transnational Organized Crime).

[68] Human Rights Caucus, "U.N. Trafficking Protocol: Lost Opportunity to Protect the Rights of Trafficked Persons" (2000).

trafficking and migrant smuggling. It was agreed, for example, that the *travaux préparatoires* would indicate that the Trafficking Protocol addresses the issue of prostitution only in the context of trafficking, and that these references are without prejudice to how States address this issue in their respective domestic laws.[69]

The final definition contains three separate elements. The first element relates to an *action*: "recruitment, transportation, transfer, harbouring or receipt of persons."[70] The second element relates to the *means* used to secure that action:

> threat or use of force or other forms of coercion, of abduction, of fraud, of deception, of the abuse of power or of a position of vulnerability or of the giving or receiving payments or benefits to achieve the consent of a person having control over another person.[71]

The third element is related to the *purpose* of the action for which the means were used:

> Exploitation shall include, at a minimum, the exploitation of the prostitution of others or other forms of sexual exploitation, forced labour or services, slavery or practices similar to slavery, servitude or the removal of organs.[72]

All three of the listed elements must be present for a situation of "trafficking in persons" to be recognized and for the Trafficking Protocol and Organized Crime Convention to become operational within a given fact-situation. The only exception relates to trafficking in children, in relation to whom the "means" requirement is waived.[73] Accordingly, trafficking will exist in situations where the child has been subject to an act such as recruitment, transportation, or receipt – the purpose of which is the exploitation of that child. Because it is unnecessary to show that force, deception, or any other means were used for trafficking in children, the identification of victims of trafficking *and* the identification of their exploiters can be expected to be easier for child victims as compared to adults.

1.2.2. *The "Action" Element*

The "action" element is one part (and in the case of trafficking in children, the only part) of the *actus reus* of trafficking. This element can be fulfilled by a variety of activities including, but not limited to, the undefined practices of recruitment, transportation, transfer, harboring, or receipt of persons.[74] Such activities may well

---

[69] Travaux Préparatoires *for the Organized Crime Convention and Protocols*, at 374.
[70] Trafficking Protocol, at Art. 3(a).
[71] Ibid.
[72] Ibid.
[73] Ibid. at Art. 3(c).
[74] None of the available interpretative material provides guidance on how these terms should be interpreted or applied. An attempt to do so in a recent EU/UN Study on organ trafficking serves to

be neutral in and of themselves but take on a different character when undertaken in a particular way (means) and/or with an intention to exploit (purpose).

The "action" element is critical in establishing the scope of the Trafficking Protocol's definition. As noted in the previous section, earlier agreements, for example, the 1949 Trafficking Convention, sought to control both the *process* (procurement, enticement, or leading away) and the *result* (exploitation of prostitution). The question to be asked of the Trafficking Protocol definition is whether it deals only with the former or whether it also covers aspects of the result. In this regard, the extension of the range of specified actions to include terms such as *harboring* and *receipt* is critical. As explored below in the context of a more general discussion of the scope of the definition, the references to harboring and receipt operate to bring not just the process (recruitment, transportation, transfer) but also the end situation of trafficking within the definition. In other words, whereas buying or otherwise taking possession of an individual through any of the stipulated means for purposes of exploiting would fall within the definition of trafficking, maintaining an individual in a situation of exploitation through any of the stipulated means would, according to the plain meaning of the text, also amount to trafficking. The breadth of the action element has the effect of bringing, within potential reach of the definition, not just recruiters, brokers, and transporters but also owners and managers, supervisors, and controllers of any place of exploitation such as a brothel, farm, boat, factory, medical facility, or household.

Potentially, this could result in the concept of trafficking being extended to situations of exploitation in which there was no preceding process. Intergenerational

underline the fluidity and potential breadth of these terms: "[r]ecruitment is to be understood in a broad sense, meaning any activity leading from the commitment or engagement of another individual to his or her exploitation. It is not confined to the use of certain means and therefore also includes the use of modern information technologies … *Transportation* is also a general term and does not define any particular means or kinds of transportation. The act of transporting a person from one place to another constitutes this element; as in the cases of trafficking in human beings for sexual or labour exploitation, it is not necessary for the victim to have crossed any borders, nor is it necessary for the victim to be present illegally in a state's territory. The offence therefore includes transnational and national trafficking. The *transfer* of a person includes any kind of handing over or transmission of a person to another person. This is particularly important in certain cultural environments where control over individuals (mostly family members) may be handed over to other people. As the term and the scope of the offence are broad, the explicit or implied offering of a person for transfer is sufficient; the offer does not have to be accepted for the offence of trafficking in human beings to be constituted if the other elements are also present. The *harbouring* of persons means accommodating or housing persons in whatever way, whether during their journey to their final destination or at the place of the exploitation … The *receipt* of persons is not limited to receiving them at the place where the exploitation takes place either, but also means meeting victims at agreed places on their journey to give them further information on where to go or what to do." Council of Europe and United Nations, *Trafficking in Organs, Tissues And Cells and Trafficking in Human Beings for the Purpose of the Removal of Organs* (2009) (CoE/UN Organ Trafficking Study), at 78.

bonded labor is one example of such a situation. A working environment that changes from acceptable to coercively exploitative provides another example of potential trafficking without any preceding process. In both cases, the individuals involved were not trafficked *into* the exploitative situation. However, it could be argued that the situation nevertheless qualifies as trafficking because victims are being "harbored," through one of the stipulated means, for purpose of exploitation. While the text of the definition does appear to support such a conclusion, a close reading of the *travaux préparatoires* provides no evidence to support a contention that this is what the drafters had in mind. Conversely, States appeared to be intent on limiting the potential scope of the concept of trafficking through the development of a complex, three-part test. Expansion of the concept of harboring to include all situations in which individuals are coercively or forcibly exploited (for example, all cases of forced labor) would render redundant that three-part definition.

1.2.3. *The "Means" Element*

The second part of the *actus reus* of trafficking, the means element (force, coercion, abduction, fraud, deception, abuse of power or position of vulnerability, and giving or receiving of payment or benefit to achieve the consent of a person having control over another person) is relevant only to trafficking in adults. This aspect of the definition confirms the position already reflected in the earliest trafficking instruments[75] that individuals can end up in a situation of exploitation through indirect methods such as deception and fraud as well as by brute force. Most components of the "means" element of the definition of trafficking are self-evident, and many are overlapping. The following brief discussion focuses on several of the more interesting or potentially controversial aspects of this element.

Coercion is central to the *idea* of trafficking and to the legal and conceptual separation of trafficking from related phenomena such as migrant smuggling. Coercion is an umbrella term, used previously in the trafficking context to refer to a range of behaviors including violence, threats, and deceit.[76] In the Trafficking Protocol, it is linked with the threat and use of force, signifying a separation between the direct and less direct "means" by which individuals are moved into or maintained in situations of exploitation. Deception and fraud are examples of less direct means and will generally relate to the nature of the promised work or service, and/or the conditions under which an individual is to undertake that work or perform that service. There has been little discussion to date about the requisite seriousness or extent of the

---

[75] See Chapter 1.1 above.

[76] See, for example, European Parliament Resolution on trafficking in human beings, Resolution A4–0326/95 of 18 January 1996, OJ C 032, Feb. 5, 1996 ("deceit or any other form of coercion"); Council of Europe 1997 Joint Action on Trafficking ("coercion, in particular violence or threats, or deceit"); 2000 Committee of Ministers Recommendation ("coercion, in particular violence or threats, deceit, abuse of authority or a position of vulnerability").

coercion, deception, or fraud that could constitute a "means" for the purposes of the definition of trafficking. This absence of clarity provides space for creative interpretations that may go beyond the intention of the drafters. For example, it has been argued, not very convincingly, that "coercion" could move beyond physical and psychological compulsions to include severe economic pressures.[77]

"Abuse of power or of a position of vulnerability" is identified as an additional means through which individuals can be recruited, transported, received, and the like into situations of exploitation. "Abuse of power" has appeared previously in international conventions.[78] No precise definition is provided in the Trafficking Protocol itself, and the *travaux préparatoires* confirm that its exact meaning was disputed during the drafting of this instrument.[79] During discussions on "abuse of authority" (an earlier, alternative formulation), drafters noted that the term "should be understood to include the power that male family members might have over female family members in some legal systems and the power that parents might have over their children."[80]

The concept of abuse of a position of vulnerability is unique to the Trafficking Protocol. The *travaux préparatoires* include an interpretative note to the effect that reference to the abuse of a position of vulnerability "is understood as referring to any situation in which the person involved has no real or acceptable alternative but to submit to the abuse involved."[81] As no further guidance is provided, it is useful to look at subsequent efforts to apply this concept. The Explanatory Report to the European Convention on Action against Trafficking (European Trafficking Convention), which reproduces the Protocol definition, goes much further than the drafters of the Protocol in stating that:

> the vulnerability may be of any kind, whether physical, psychological, emotional, family-related, social or economic. The situation might, for example, involve insecurity or illegality of the victim's immigration status, economic dependence or fragile health. In short, the situation can be any state of hardship in which a human being is impelled to accept being exploited. Persons abusing such a situation flagrantly infringe human rights and violate human dignity and integrity, which no one can validly renounce.[82]

At the international level, recent attempts to develop indicators of abuse of power and position of vulnerability have also focused particularly on the abuse of an individual's

---

[77] See, for example, L.A. Malone, "Economic Hardship as Coercion Under the Protocol on International Trafficking in Persons by Organized Crime Elements," (2001) 25 *Fordham International Law Journal* 54, at 55.

[78] See, for example, the 1910 White Slavery Convention.

[79] Travaux Préparatoires *for the Organized Crime Convention and Protocols*, at 343, note 20.

[80] Ibid.

[81] Ibid. at 347. The wording of the interpretative note appears to have been drawn from the EU Ministerial Conference's "Hague Ministerial Declaration on European Guidelines for Effective Measures to Prevent and Combat Trafficking in Women for the Purpose of Sexual Exploitation," Apr. 26, 1997.

[82] Council of Europe, *Explanatory Report on the Convention on Action against Trafficking in Human Beings*, ETS 197, 16.V.2005 (European Trafficking Convention Explanatory Report) at para. 83.

precarious financial, psychological, and social situation, as well as on linguistic, physical, and social isolation.[83] The UN Office on Drugs and Crime (UNODC) Model Trafficking Law, released in 2009, takes a different approach, suggesting that a focus on the state of mind of the perpetrator, rather than on that of the victim, could be more protective of victims.[84] It proposes a similarly wide range of factors, specifying that abuse of power and of a position of vulnerability could be defined, in national law, as the:

taking advantage of the vulnerable position a person is placed in as a result of …

(i)   Having entered the country illegally or without proper documentation; or
(ii) Pregnancy or any physical or mental disease or disability of the person, including addiction to the use of any substance; or
(iii) Reduced capacity to form judgments by virtue of being a child, illness, infirmity or a physical or mental disability; or
(iv) Promises or giving sums of money or other advantages to those having authority over a person; or
(v)   Being in a precarious situation from the standpoint of social survival; or
(vi) Other relevant factors.[85]

The precise meaning of the term "the giving or receiving of payments or benefits to achieve the consent of a person having control of another person" is similarly opaque. For example, is this aspect of the "means" element limited to situations in which legal control is exercised by one individual over another (for example, a parent over a child), or can it be extended to include de facto control (such as that which may be exercised by an employer over an employee)? How does this means differ from abuse of power or position of vulnerability? The *travaux préparatoires* provide no guidance, and available interpretative documents, including the Legislative Guide and the UNODC Model Law, are equally silent. It can be reasonably presumed that the clause is intended to bring within the definition practices such as payments made to parents in the course of child trafficking. However, as the means element is unnecessary in such cases, this does not provide a complete explanation.

---

[83] See, for example, International Labour Office, "Operational Indicators of Trafficking in Human Beings" (revised ed., September 2009). See also the model law, developed by the United States in 2003, which considers the state of mind of the victim to be relevant: "[a]buse of a position of vulnerability means such abuse that the person believes he or she has no reasonable alternative but to submit to the labor or services demanded of the person, and includes but is not limited to taking advantage of the vulnerabilities resulting from the person having entered the country illegally or without proper documentation, pregnancy or any physical or mental disease or disability of the person, including addiction to the use of any substance, or reduced capacity to form judgments by virtue of being a child." US Department of Justice, Model State Anti-Trafficking Criminal Statute (2003), available at http://www.justice.gov/crt/crim/model_state_law.pdf (accessed Nov. 29, 2009).

[84] United Nations Office on Drugs and Crime, *Model Law on Trafficking in Persons*, UN Sales No. E.09.V.11 (2009) (UNODC Model Law), at 9–10.

[85] Ibid. at 9.

1.2.4. *The "Purpose" Element*

The phrase "for the purpose of" introduces a *mens rea* requirement into the definition: Trafficking will occur if the implicated individual or entity *intended* that the action (which, in the case of trafficking involving adult victims, must be taken through a prohibited means), would lead to one of the specified end results. The UN Office on Drugs and Crime refers to this element in identifying trafficking as a crime of specific or special intent (*dolus specialis*).[86] It defines the *dolus specialis* of trafficking as "the purpose aimed at by the perpetrator when committing the material acts of the offence."[87] Fulfilment of the special intent element does not require the intended aim to actually be achieved. The most important practical result of this is that a situation of trafficking can arise without exploitation taking place.[88] It is sufficient that such exploitation was the intention of the conduct. This element is linked and relates back to the first. The intention to exploit can be held by any of the individuals or entities involved in any of the acts stipulated in the definition: recruitment, transportation, transfer, harboring, or receipt. Accordingly, the requisite intention to exploit could be just as easily held by a final exploiter (brothel owner, factory manager, etc.) as by a recruiter or broker.[89] In fact, such intent should be easier to establish the closer the suspected trafficker is to the situation of exploitation. It may be difficult, for example, to establish the necessary *mens rea* with respect to a recruiter or transporter who may, quite reasonably, deny any knowledge of the final end purpose.

The Trafficking Protocol does not define "exploitation," rather providing an open-ended list that includes, *at a minimum*: "the exploitation of the prostitution

---

[86] United Nations Office for Drugs and Crime, *Anti-Human Trafficking Manual for Criminal Justice Practitioners* (2009), "Module 1: Definition of Trafficking in Persons and Smuggling of Migrants" (*UNODC Anti-Trafficking Practitioners' Manual* (2009), Module 1), at 4. The concept of *dolus specialis* is most frequently raised at the international level in the context of *mens rea* element of the crime against humanity of genocide. See further P. Akhavan, "The Crime of Genocide in the ICTR Jurisprudence," (2005) 3 *Journal of International Criminal Justice* 989.

[87] *UNODC Anti-Trafficking Practitioners' Manual* (2009), Module 1, at 4. UNODC further notes that domestic law could enable *mens rea* to be established on a lesser standard than direct "intent" (such as recklessness, wilful blindness, or criminal negligence): ibid.

[88] *Legislative Guide*, at Trafficking Protocol, at para. 33. The practical implications of this, especially from the perspective of investigation and prosecution of trafficking-related crimes, are considered at various points throughout this study.

[89] This point addresses a common misunderstanding about the third element of the definition that purpose or "intent" is limited only to the initial stage of the trafficking cycle. Under this interpretation, trafficking will only take place when the initial recruitment or movement is motivated by an intention to exploit. If an act that was not initially conceived or executed for exploitative purpose results in exploitation, this would not, according to this erroneous line of analysis, constitute trafficking. See N. Piper, "A Problem by a Different Name: A Review of Research on Trafficking in South East Asia and Oceania," in International Organization for Migration ed., *Data and Research on Human Trafficking: A Global Survey* 203 (2005), at 222: "the definition could be interpreted as being initiation-based – that is, what the intention of the recruiter or broker was at the time when the recruitment or transport was transacted."

of others, or other forms of sexual exploitation, forced labour or services, slavery or practices similar to slavery, servitude, or the removal of organs."[90] In the absence of specific definitions, it may safely be assumed that, in the case of forced labor[91] and slavery,[92] the accepted definitions contained in other international legal instruments (and present, in various forms, in earlier drafts)[93] are applicable. This assumption is supported by the Protocol's own savings clause, which affirms a consistency between that instrument and existing rights, obligations, and responsibilities under international law.[94]

Forced labor is an especially important addition to the list, extending the end purposes of trafficking to include the most seriously exploitative work practices.[95]

---

[90] Trafficking Protocol, at Art. 3(a). The *travaux préparatoires* indicate that the words "at a minimum" were included to ensure that unnamed or new forms of exploitation would not be excluded by implication: Travaux Préparatoires *for the Organized Crime Convention and Protocols*, at 343, note 22 and at 344, note 30.

[91] ILO Convention No. 29 (1930) defines "forced or compulsory labour" as "all work or service which is exacted from any person under the menace of any penalty, and for which the said person has not offered himself voluntarily": Convention Concerning Forced and Compulsory Labour, 39 UNTS 55, ILO No. 29, done June 28, 1930, entered into force May 1, 1932 (Forced Labour Convention), at Art. 2(1). The prohibition contains a subjective element (*involuntariness*) as well as objective requirements, which are met when the State or a private individual orders personal work or service, and a punishment or sanction is threatened if the order is not obeyed. M. Nowak, UN *Covenant on Civil and Political Rights: CCPR Commentary* (2005) (Nowak, *CCPR Commentary*), at 150, and sources cited therein. In relation to the prohibition on forced labor in the European Convention on Human Rights (Convention for the Protection of Human Rights and Fundamental Freedoms, 213 UNTS 222, done Nov. 4, 1950, entered into force Sept. 3, 1953), the European Commission on Human Rights has indicated that the concept of forced or compulsive labor involves two necessary and distinct elements as follows: "that the work or service is performed by the worker against his will and, secondly, that the requirement that the work or service be performed is unjust or oppressive or the work or service itself involves avoidable hardship." *Iverson v. Norway*, (1963) *Yearbook of the European Convention on Human Rights* 278 (Eur. Comm'n on H.R.), at 328.

[92] The 1926 Slavery Convention defines slavery as "the status or condition of a person over whom any or all of the powers attaching to the right of ownership are exercised": Convention to Suppress the Slave Trade and Slavery, 60 LNTS 253, done Sept. 25, 1926, entered into force Mar. 9, 1927, at Art. 1. Note that the UNODC Model Law, at 19, unnecessarily proposes an alternative definition. For a detailed analysis of the definition of slavery and its relationship to trafficking, see Chapter 3 of this volume.

[93] See, for example, "Sixth Revised Draft of the Protocol to Prevent, Suppress and Punish Trafficking in Persons, Especially Women and Children," UN Doc. A/AC.254/4/Add.3/Rev.6, Apr. 4, 2000 ("Sixth Draft of the Trafficking Protocol," UN Doc. A/AC.254/4/Add.3/Rev.6, Apr. 4, 2000), at Art. 2 bis, Option 2.

[94] Trafficking Protocol, at Art. 14.

[95] In a document submitted to the January 2010 session of the Working Group set up to oversee implementation of the Protocol, the Secretariat (UNODC) states that "[t]he notion of exploitation of labour in the definition of trafficking in persons allows for a link to be established between the Trafficking in Persons Protocol and ILO Convention concerning Forced Labour." The document adds, somewhat confusingly, that the inclusion of forced labor or other services in the definition "makes clear that trafficking in persons for the purpose of exploitation is encompassed by the definition of forced or compulsory labor of the Convention. Working Group on Trafficking in Persons, "Analysis of Key Concepts of the Trafficking in Persons Protocol, Background Paper prepared by

The International Labour Office (ILO), which has carriage of the major conventions in this area, has confirmed, in recent years, the breadth of the concept of forced labor, stating that the "threat of penalty" aspect of the definition could involve the loss of rights or privileges (for example, related to immigration status), and that consent is rendered meaningless if a worker has been induced into employment by deceit, false promises, the retention of identity documents, or force.[96] Significantly, the ILO supervisory bodies have also concluded that the worker's right to free choice of employment remains inalienable. Inability to change or leave employment at any time, under threat of a serious penalty, is a strong indication of forced labor.[97]

The inclusion of "practices similar to slavery" is a reference to the 1956 Supplementary Convention on the Abolition of Slavery, the Slave Trade, and Institutions and Practices Similar to Slavery (Supplementary Slavery Convention).[98] It operates to incorporate into the understanding of what constitutes "exploitation" the practices of debt bondage,[99] serfdom,[100] servile forms of marriage,[101] and the

---

the Secretariat," UN Doc. CTOC/COP/WG.4/2010/2, Dec. 9, 2009 (UNODC Key Concepts), at para. 13.

[96] International Labour Office, *Forced Labour: Casebook of Court Decisions* (2009) (*ILO Casebook*), at 12–13.

[97] Ibid.

[98] Supplementary Slavery Convention, at Art. 1.

[99] This is defined as "the status or condition arising from a pledge by a debtor of his personal services or those of a person under his control as security for a debt, if the value of those services as reasonably assessed is not applied towards the liquidation of the debt or the length and nature of those services are not respectively limited and defined": ibid. at Art. 1(a). Unlike forced labor (see at note 162, below), the definition makes no reference to the concept of voluntariness. It would appear, therefore, that international law does not envisage the possibility of an individual being able to consent to debt bondage. Debt bondage is said to be included within the prohibition on servitude contained in the ICCPR: Nowak, *CCPR Commentary*, at 148. This interpretation is supported by the UN human rights treaty bodies' consideration of issues of bonded labor. See, for example, UN Committee on Economic, Social and Cultural Rights, "Concluding Observations: Nepal," UN Doc. E/C.12/NPL/CO/2, Jan. 16, 2008, at para. 18. Bonded labor is identified as one of the "worst forms" of child labor prohibited by the Worst Forms of Child Labour Convention (Convention Concerning the Prohibition and Immediate Action for the Elimination of the Worst Forms of Child Labour, 2133 UNTS 161, ILO No. 182, done June 17, 1999, entered into force Nov. 19, 2000), at Art. 3(a).

[100] This is defined as "the condition or status of a tenant who is by law, custom or agreement bound to live and labour on land belonging to another person and to render some determinate service to such other person, whether for reward or not, and is not free to change his status": Supplementary Slavery Convention, at Art. 1(b).

[101] This is defined as any institution or practice whereby "(i) A woman, without the right to refuse, is promised or given in marriage on payment of a consideration in money or in kind to her parents, guardian, family or any other person or group; or (ii) The husband of a women, his family or his clan, has the right to transfer her to another person for value received or otherwise; or (iii) A woman on the death of her husband is liable to be inherited by another person": Supplementary Slavery Convention, at Art. 1(c). The UNODC Model Trafficking Law, at 16, incorporates this definition. It has been subsequently noted that in relation to domestic trafficking legislation, "[l]egislators may consider updating this definition to include practices in which both women/girls and men/boys can be the subject of forced or servile marriages. This may cover trafficking for marriage and certain forms of 'mail order bride' practices." UNODC Key Concepts, at para. 19.

sale of children for exploitation,[102] as well as, potentially, the forced or compulsory recruitment of children into armed conflict.[103] These are all common forms of exploitation associated with trafficking, and their indirect inclusion significantly expands the scope of the third element of the definition.[104]

Victims of "practices similar to slavery" are identified in international law as "persons of servile status."[105] As explored further in Chapter 3, the concept of servitude remains undefined in international law, although it is generally considered to refer to forms of exploitation that are less severe than slavery.[106] Some delegations objected to the inclusion of servitude in the list of exploitative purposes because of the lack of clarity as to the meaning of the term and the duplication with "slavery and practices similar to slavery."[107] A draft definition, negotiated within the Ad Hoc Committee, provided that, in the context of trafficking, servitude was to mean:

> the condition of a person who is unlawfully compelled or coerced by another to render any service to the same person or to others and who has no reasonable alternative but to perform the service, and shall include domestic service and debt bondage.[108]

The definition survived up to October 2000 but was inexplicably omitted from the final text. A rather awkward alternative, apparently based on an interpretation of the prohibition of servitude set out in the Universal Declaration of Human Rights and the ICCPR, is proposed by the UNODC Model Law.[109]

---

[102] This is defined as "any institution or practice whereby a child or young person under the age of 18 years, is delivered by either or both if his natural parents or by his guardian to another person, whether for reward or not, with a view to the exploitation of the child or young person or of his labour": Supplementary Slavery Convention, at Art. 1(d). See further the discussion on illegal adoption at notes 125 to 129 and the accompanying text. Note that the prohibition applies only to the sale of children into exploitation. The UNODC Model Law, at 17, and UNODC Key Concepts Paper, at para. 23, erroneously state that the Supplementary Slavery Convention "specifically prohibits the exploitation of children and adolescents."

[103] The Worst Forms of Child Labour Convention identifies the worst forms of child labor as including "all forms of slavery or practices similar to slavery such as ... forced or compulsory labour, including forced or compulsory recruitment of children for use in armed conflict": at Art. 3. See also UNODC Model Law, at 29.

[104] Note that the UNODC Handbook for Parliamentarians mistakenly identifies practices associated with slavery and the slave trade (and thereby prohibited by the Supplementary Slavery Convention), such as transportation and branding of slaves, as "practices similar to slavery": United Nations Office on Drugs and Crime, *Trafficking in Persons, Handbook for Parliamentarians* (2009), at 18.

[105] Supplementary Slavery Convention, at Art. 7(b).

[106] See Chapter 3.3 below.

[107] Travaux Préparatoires *for the Organized Crime Convention and Protocols*, at 344, note 29.

[108] "Seventh Revised Draft of the Protocol to Prevent, Suppress and Punish Trafficking in Persons, Especially Women and Children," UN Doc. A/AC.254/4/Add.3/Rev.7, July 19, 2000 ("Seventh Draft of the Trafficking Protocol," UN Doc. A/AC.254/4/Add.3/Rev.7, July 19, 2000), at Art. 2 bis(c).

[109] The UNODC Model Law, at 18, proposes that servitude: "shall mean the labour conditions and/or the obligation to work or to render services from which the person in question cannot escape and which he or she cannot change."

The *travaux préparatoires* confirm that two terms included in the purpose element, "exploitation of the prostitution of others" and "other forms of exploitation", were deliberately left undefined, thereby ensuring that the Protocol was "without prejudice to how States parties address prostitution in their respective domestic laws."[110] The first term is not unknown to international law as it echoes the 1949 Trafficking Convention as well as the CEDAW Convention, which requires States Parties to "suppress all forms of trafficking in women and exploitation of the prostitution of women."[111] During the negotiations, the Chairperson of the drafting group affirmed the accepted meaning of "exploitation of prostitution," noting that "exploitation" as used in connection with prostitution distinguished individuals who might derive benefit from their own prostitution and those who derived some benefit from the prostitution of others.[112] The UNODC Model Law on Trafficking notes that the term *exploitation of prostitution of others* could be defined in any number of ways, proposing that it refer to "the unlawful obtaining of financial or other material benefit from the prostitution of another person."[113]

The concept of "sexual exploitation" is more problematic, in particular when applied to adults. In international law, sexual exploitation is most commonly used to refer to the exploitative use of children in prostitution and related practices.[114] However, even within this narrow area, there is little common agreement on its precise definition. At one stage in the negotiation process, the rolling text contained a definition of "sexual exploitation."[115] It was subsequently decided that there was no need to define the term.[116] The potential impact of the drafting committee's failure to provide authoritative guidance on the substantive content of this term should not be underestimated. A broad interpretation could, when accompanied by an expansive interpretation of the means element (for example, "abuse of authority or position of vulnerability"), potentially place a range of practices – including, but not limited to, adult prostitution and the production, possession, or use of pornography – within

[110] Travaux Préparatoires *for the Organized Crime Convention and Protocols*, at 347.
[111] Convention on the Elimination of All Forms of Discrimination Against Women, 1249 UNTS 13, done Dec. 13, 1979, entered into force Sept. 3, 1981, at Art. 6. For further discussion, see Chapter 2 of this volume.
[112] Travaux Préparatoires *for the Organized Crime Convention and Protocols*, at 344, note 27.
[113] UNODC Model Law, at 13. The UNODC Model Law clarifies that "[t]he term 'unlawful' was added to indicate that this has to be unlawful in accordance with the national laws on prostitution," at 14.
[114] Convention on the Rights of the Child, 1577 UNTS 3, done Nov. 20, 1989, entered into force Sept. 2, 1990, at Art. 34; Optional Protocol to the Child Convention on the Sale of Children, Child Prostitution and Child Pornography, GA Res. 54/263, Annex I, 54 UN GAOR Supp. (No. 49), 7, UN Doc. A/54/49, Vol. III (2000), done May 25, 2000, entered into force Jan. 18, 2002, at Art. 3. See further, Chapter 2.1.4 below.
[115] "'Sexual exploitation' shall mean: (i) of an adult [forced] prostitution, sexual servitude or participation in the production of pornographic materials for which the person does not offer himself or herself with free and informed consent; (ii) Of a child, prostitution, sexual servitude or use of a child in pornography": "Sixth Draft of the Trafficking Protocol," UN Doc. A/AC.254/4/Add.3/Rev.6, Apr. 4, 2000, at Art. 2(bis), Option 1.
[116] Travaux Préparatoires *for the Organized Crime Convention and Protocols*, at 342, note 14.

the scope of the definition of trafficking. Such an interpretation would go against the intention of the drafters: There was clear consensus within the drafting group that the Trafficking Protocol definition was not to extend to prostitution or pornography per se.[117] Since the Protocol was concluded, several different definitions of "sexual exploitation" have emerged, confirming that many of the earlier controversies documented above are alive and well.[118]

A proposal to include organ removal as an end purpose of trafficking was made very late in the negotiations[119] and survived, despite objections that the Trafficking Protocol was dealing with trafficking in persons, not organs.[120] At the time of the Protocol's drafting, the addition of "removal of organs" into the list of "purposes" was generally viewed to have been an unnecessary accommodation by the Ad Hoc Working Group.[121] However, since the definition was adopted, the nature of the organ trade, including its links with trafficking, has become more apparent and

---

[117] See discussion of pornography as trafficking below at note 163 and accompanying text.

[118] For example, the Global Alliance Against Trafficking in Women (a key member of the Human Rights Caucus that lobbied actively during the development of the Trafficking Protocol) has proposed that if States must clarify what is meant by "sexual exploitation," they define it as follows: "the participation by a person in prostitution, sexual servitude, or the production of pornographic materials as a result of being subjected to a threat, deception, coercion, abduction, force, abuse of authority, debt bondage or fraud. Even in the absence of any of these factors, where the person participating in prostitution, sexual servitude or the production of pornographic materials under the age of 18 [sic], sexual exploitation shall be deemed to exist." Global Alliance Against Trafficking in Women, *Human Rights and Trafficking in Persons: A Handbook* (2000), at 26. As part of its zero-tolerance policy toward sexual exploitation in its field operations, the United Nations has defined the concept very broadly, referring to "any actual or attempted abuse of a position of vulnerability, differential power, or trust, for sexual purposes, including but not limited to, profiting monetarily, socially or politically from the sexual exploitation of another": "Secretary-General's Bulletin: Special Measures for Protection from Sexual Exploitation and Sexual Abuse," UN Doc. ST/SGB/2003/13, Oct. 9, 2003. The UN's Office of Internal Oversight Services, responsible for investigating misconduct, has stated that "engaging in sex with prostitutes" is an example of sexual exploitation: UN Office of Internal Oversight Services, "Frequently Asked Questions" (2008), available at http://huwu.org/Depts/oios/pages/id_faq.html (accessed Nov. 29, 2009). In its model law (building blocks) approach for countries that need to reform their legal framework around trafficking, the United States has proposed that the term "sexual exploitation" be defined as: "[e]ngaging in any other form of commercial sexual exploitation, including but not limited to pimping, pandering, procuring, profiting from prostitution, maintaining a brothel, child pornography." US Department of Justice, Model State Anti-Trafficking Criminal Statute (2003), available at http://www.justice.gov/crt/crim/model_state_law.pdf (accessed Nov. 29, 2009). The UNODC Model Law on Trafficking proposes that sexual exploitation be defined as "the obtaining of financial or other benefits through the involvement of another person in prostitution, sexual servitude or other kinds of sexual services, including pornographic acts or the production of pornographic materials." UNODC Model Law, at 19.

[119] "Seventh Draft of the Trafficking Protocol," UN Doc. A/AC.254/4/Add.3/Rev.7, July 19, 2000, at note 22.

[120] Ibid. at note 12. See also Travaux Préparatoires *for the Organized Crime Convention and Protocols*, at 344, note 28.

[121] This is illustrated by the European Union's deletion of organ removal from the definition of trafficking contained in its Council Framework Decision of 19 July 2002 on combating trafficking in human beings (2002/629/JHA), OJ L 203/1, Aug. 1, 2002 (2002 European Framework Decision on Trafficking).

better understood.[122] For example, there is now general consensus on the point that trafficking in persons for purposes of organ removal is technically and legally distinct from "trafficking" in organs, cells, and tissues.[123] The official documentation provides no additional guidance on this aspect of the definition beyond an interpretative note to the effect that the removal of a child's organs for legitimate medical or therapeutic reasons cannot form an element of trafficking if the parent or guardian has validly consented.[124]

The question of whether abusive, illegal, unethical, or otherwise undesirable adoption practices fall within the international definition of trafficking has been periodically raised since the definition was finalized, without satisfactory resolution. While adoption is not included in list of exploitative purposes, the open-ended nature of the list means that the omission is not conclusive. The *travaux préparatoires* contain a curious interpretative note to the effect that *illegal adoption* will fall within the scope of the Trafficking Protocol (that is, will be considered an exploitative purpose under the third element of the definition) where it amounts to "a practice similar to slavery" under the 1956 Supplementary Slavery Convention.[125] As explored further

---

[122] See, for example, N. Scheper-Hughes, "Illegal Organ Trade: Global Justice and the Traffic in Human Organs," in R.W.G. Gruessner and E. Benedetti eds., *Living Donor Organ Transplantation* 106 (2008); UN Office of Drugs and Crime, "Human Trafficking for the Removal of Organs and Body Parts," workshop background paper for Vienna Forum to Fight Human Trafficking, Feb. 13–15, 2008, available at http://www.unodc.org/documents/human-trafficking/Marika-Misc/BP011HumanTraffickingfortheRemovalofOrgans.pdf (accessed Nov. 30, 2009); and CoE/UN Organ Trafficking Study. Note also that in the proposed successor instrument to the 2002 European Framework Decision on Trafficking, organ removal is proposed to be included in the revised understanding of exploitation for the purposes of trafficking: Commission of the European Communities, Proposal for a Framework Decision on preventing and combating trafficking in human beings, and protecting victims, repealing Framework Decision 2002/629/JHA, COM(2009) 136 final, Mar. 25, 2009, at preambular para. 4 and Art. 1(3); European Commission, Proposal for a Directive of the European Parliament and of the Council on preventing and combating trafficking in human beings, and protecting victims, repealing Framework Decision 2002/629/JHA, COM(2010) 95 final, Mar. 29, 2010, at Art. 2(3).

[123] "Some trafficking in OTC [organs, tissues and cells] may originate in trafficking in human beings and will therefore fall within the scope of [the specialist trafficking treaties]. But trafficking in OTC is much broader in scope than trafficking in human beings for the purpose of organ removal ... trafficking in organs, tissues and cells differs from trafficking in human beings for organ removal in one of the constituent elements of the crime – the object of the criminal offence. In the former case, the object of the crime is the organs, tissues and cells, while in the latter case it is the trafficked person." CoE/UN Organ Trafficking Study, at 93. Note that there is not yet an agreed definition of "trafficking" in organs, tissues and cells: ibid, at 96–97.

[124] Travaux Préparatoires *for the Organized Crime Convention and Protocols*, at 347. The CoE/UN Organ Trafficking Study, at 80–81, notes that this also sets the limit for legitimate consent of parents or guardians: "if they consent to removal of organs other than for legitimate medical or therapeutic reasons, the offence of trafficking in human beings is committed. Regarding the question of what legitimate medical or therapeutic reasons are, reference must ... be made to recognised medical and ethical standards."

[125] Ibid. at 347. Note that the reference to "illegal" adoption creates a further complication as it is unclear whether legality is to be judged with reference to international law, the laws of the country of adoption, or the laws of the country of placement.

in Chapter 3, "practices similar to slavery" are defined in that instrument to include debt bondage and forced marriage, as well as:

> any institution or practice whereby a child or young person under the age of 18 years, is delivered by either or both of his natural parents, or by his guardian, to another person, whether for reward or not, *with a view to the exploitation of the child or young person or of his labour.*[126]

This provision is obscure in several important respects. It does not define exploitation and is unclear on the point of whether the intent to exploit must be held by the parent/guardian, the receiver, or both.

Leaving aside these limitations, the reference to the 1956 Supplementary Slavery Convention creates a circular and therefore unhelpful line of reasoning. As one commentator has noted, "children are subject to a practice similar to slavery if they are exploited, and they are exploited if they are subject to a practice similar to slavery."[127] The reference does however appear to support a view that adoption per se is not exploitative – only illegal adoption intended to result in the exploitation of the child (for example, through forced labor or sexual exploitation) will fall within the third element of the trafficking definition. Such a result would mean that the organized recruitment, transportation, receipt, and the like of children for purposes of illegal but nonexploitative adoption would not be trafficking – irrespective of the manner in which the child was procured, the scale of the operation, or any other factor.

This interpretation, based on the plain meaning of the text, is not universally accepted. Many States, as well as the leading international organizations involved in this issue, see a clear link between the commodification of children in the international adoption market and more typical end purposes of trafficking. The stealing, buying, and selling of children for adoption is even more readily identified with practices commonly associated with trafficking. Unfortunately, the legal aspects of that link have not been explored in any great depth. For example, the custodian of the Trafficking Protocol, the UN Office on Drugs and Crime, has held, without further explanation, that "illicit adoption practices … can be prosecuted under the umbrella of trafficking crimes."[128] Several commentators have grappled with the relationship between trafficking and international adoption, with only limited success.[129]

---

[126] Supplementary Slavery Convention, at Art. 1(d) (emphasis added).

[127] D.M. Smolin, "Intercountry Adoption as Child Trafficking," (2004) 39 *Valparaiso University Law Review* 281 (Smolin, "Intercountry Adoption as Child Trafficking"), at 296.

[128] *UNODC Anti-Trafficking Practitioners' Manual* (2009), Module 1, at 7.

[129] Dillon, for example, has proposed that trafficking for adoption involves bringing into the adoption process children who would not otherwise have been placed for adoption by their families of origin. This practice, she argues, should be considered distinct from profiteering: "a term that indicates officials and others taking portions of adoption fees in the course of what is otherwise a legal, normal adoption process involving finding families for children who would have been in the system even in the absence of the fees being paid." Dillon does not engage with the Protocol's definition of trafficking. S. Dillon, "Making Legal Regimes for Intercountry Adoption Reflect Human Rights

It remains to be seen whether (and if so, how) the intuitive connection between trafficking and unethical adoption practices, particularly those involving denial of the rights of birth parents and profiteering, will be reconciled with a definition that prioritizes an *intent to harm* and thereby, perhaps accidentally, excludes such practices.[130]

1.3. POST-2000 DEVELOPMENTS

The adoption of the Trafficking Protocol at the end of 2000 was widely considered to be the final word in the long-standing impasse over an international legal definition of trafficking. In many respects, this is indeed the case. The Protocol's understanding of trafficking has been adopted, explicitly or implicitly, by all relevant UN organs and agencies, as well as by other intergovernmental organizations working on this issue.[131] Belying the extent and depth of divisions revealed during the negotiation process, the core elements of that definition have been equally embraced by nongovernmental organizations working on trafficking and related issues.[132] Since 2000, the majority of States have enacted comprehensive antitrafficking laws that generally reflect the internationally agreed definition.[133]

Principles: Transforming the United Nations Convention on the Rights of the Child with the Hague Convention on Intercountry Adoption," (2003) 21 *Boston University International Law Journal* 179, at 188. See also K.M. Wittner, "Curbing Child Trafficking in Intercountry Adoptions: Will International Treaties and Adoption Moratoriums Accomplish the Job In Cambodia?" (2003) 12 *Pacific Rim Law and Policy Journal* 595; Smolin, "Intercountry Adoption as Child Trafficking" and D.M. Smolin, "Child Laundering: How the Intercountry Adoption System Legitimizes and Incentivizes the Practices of Buying, Trafficking, Kidnapping, and Stealing Children," (2006) 52 *Wayne Law Review* 113.

[130] See the further discussion of the concept of "sale of children" in Chapter 2.1.4.

[131] It is difficult to locate any exceptions to this trend. Among the numerous and varied examples of explicit adoption of the new definition, see, for example: UN Economic and Social Council, Office of the United Nations High Commissioner for Human Rights, *Recommended Principles and Guidelines on Human Rights and Human Trafficking*, UN Doc E/2002/68/Add.1, May 20, 2002 (*UN Trafficking Principles and Guidelines*); United Nations Children's Fund, *Guidelines for the Protection of Child Victims of Trafficking* (September 2006); UN Committee against Torture, "Concluding Observations: Poland," UN Doc. CAT/C/POL/CO/4, July 25, 2007, at para. 18; UN Committee on the Elimination of Discrimination against Women, "Concluding Observations: Singapore," UN Doc. CEDAW/C/SGP/CO/3, Aug. 10, 2007, at para. 22; *ILO Casebook*, at 15–16.

[132] Once again, exceptions to this trend are rare. A review of reports and statements issued since the adoption of the Trafficking Protocol by both generalist NGOs (such as Amnesty International and Human Rights Watch) and specialist antitrafficking NGOs (such as the Global Alliance Against Trafficking in Women [GAATW] and the Coalition Against Trafficking in Women [CATW]) reveals uniform acceptance of the international definition.

[133] United Nations Office on Drugs and Crime, *Global Report on Trafficking in Persons* (2009). The report reveals that by 2008, 80 percent (125 countries) of the 155 countries surveyed had specific antitrafficking legislation: at 22. Sixty-three percent (98 countries) of all surveyed countries had criminalized trafficking for at least forced labor and sexual exploitation, irrespective of both age and gender: ibid. A time analysis of relevant data shows that 45 percent of the surveyed countries had adopted an offense of trafficking in persons for the first time only after the Trafficking Protocol

Since the adoption of the Trafficking Protocol, several regional treaties and treaty-like instruments on trafficking have been developed, in particular: the 2002 South Asian Association for Regional Cooperation Convention on Preventing and Combating Trafficking in Women and Children for Prostitution (SAARC Convention);[134] the 2002 Council of the European Union Framework Decision on Trafficking Human Beings (2002 European Framework Decision on Trafficking);[135] and the 2005 European Convention on Action against Trafficking (European Trafficking Convention).[136] Of these instruments, only the European Trafficking Convention faithfully reflects the Trafficking Protocol's definition. The SAARC Convention, considered in more detail in the following chapter, explicitly aims to prevent the use of women and children in international prostitution networks, and this goal clearly influenced the SAARC States' choice of a definition. The Convention defines trafficking as: "the moving, selling or buying of women or children for prostitution[137] within and outside a country for monetary or other considerations with or without the consent of the person subject to trafficking."[138] The "person subject to trafficking" refers to: "women and children victimised or forced into prostitution by the traffickers by deception, threat, coercion, kidnapping, sale, fraudulent marriage, child marriage or any other unlawful means."[139] While the SAARC Convention identifies the same three elements (action, means, and purpose) as the Protocol, the substantive content of each element is significantly different, with the SAARC definition being much narrower than that of the Protocol on all three points. For example, the action element consists simply of the moving, selling, or buying of women and children.[140] Failure to include transfer and receipt could operate to exclude from the definition the actions of those involved in holding individuals in situations of exploitation. A similar narrowing of the potential scope of the Convention occurs through a constrained understanding of means element, which does not include abuse of power or position of vulnerability, or the giving or receiving of payments or benefits to achieve the consent of a person having control over another.[141] The

entered into force in December 2003, and that most of the countries with long-standing antitrafficking provisions had amended their criminal codes to more closely reflect the broader concept of trafficking set out in the Trafficking Protocol since 2003: ibid. at 22, 24–25.

[134] South Asian Association for Regional Cooperation, Convention on Preventing and Combating Trafficking in Women and Children for Prostitution, done Jan. 5, 2002, entered into force Dec. 1, 2005 (SAARC Convention).

[135] Council Framework Decision of 19 July 2002 on combating trafficking in human beings (2002/629/JHA), OJ L 203/1, Aug. 1, 2002 (2002 European Framework Decision on Trafficking).

[136] Council of Europe Convention on Action against Trafficking in Human Beings and its Explanatory Report, ETS 197, 16.V.2005, done May 16, 2005, entered into force Feb. 1, 2008 (European Trafficking Convention).

[137] The Convention defines "prostitution" as "the sexual exploitation or abuse of persons for commercial purposes." SAARC Convention, at Art. I(2).

[138] Ibid. at Art. I(3).

[139] Ibid. at Art. I(5).

[140] Ibid. at Art. I(3).

[141] Ibid. at Art. I(5).

most significant limitation however, is imposed through the purpose element of the definition, which refers only to prostitution.

Initial drafts of the EU's 2002 Framework Decision on Trafficking in Persons revealed distinct differences between the proposed definition and the one that eventually emerged out of the Trafficking Protocol negotiations.[142] There was no separate definition of trafficking in children and the draft separated trafficking into labor exploitation and sexual exploitation, an approach that the UN High Commissioner for Human Rights suggested was:

> unnecessarily complicating and somewhat artificial … imprecise and … beyond current understandings of trafficking while at the same time potentially excluding certain end-practices which cannot readily be identified as either labour or sexual exploitation.[143]

Following similarly strong encouragement from external commentators, the EU position moved slowly toward the definition finally agreed upon in Vienna.[144] Timing was important in narrowing differences in understanding. The one-year gap

---

[142] Article 2 of the draft definition required that Member States: "shall take the necessary measures to ensure that the recruitment, transportation or transfer of a person, including harbouring and subsequent reception and the exchange of control over him or her is punishable, where the fundamental rights of that person have been and continue to be suppressed for the purpose of exploiting him or her in the production of goods or provision of services in infringement of labour standards governing working conditions, salaries and health and safety, and: (a) use is made of coercion, force or threats, including abduction, or (b) use is made of deceit or fraud, or (c) there is a misuse of authority, influence or pressure, or (d) there is another form of abuse." Article 3 of the draft definition required Member States to: "take the necessary measures to ensure that the recruitment, transportation or transfer of a person, including harbouring and subsequent reception and the exchange of control over him or her is punishable, where the purpose is to exploit him or her in prostitution or in pornographic performances or in production of pornographic material, and: (a) use is made of coercion, force or threats, including abduction, or (b) use is made of deceit or fraud, or (c) there is a misuse of authority, influence or pressure, or (d) there is another form of abuse." Commission of the European Communities, Combating trafficking in human beings and combating the sexual exploitation of children and child pornography, Proposal for a Council Framework Decision on combating trafficking in human beings, Brussels, Jan. 22, 2001, COM(2000) 854 final /2.

[143] Note by the United Nations High Commissioner for Human Rights on the Proposed EU Council Framework Decision on Combating Trafficking in Human Beings (Brussels (COM) 2000 854 final/2), 2000 to the European Commission and the Swedish President of the European Union, Mar. 21, 2001, at para. 4.

[144] The initial proposal for a Council Framework Decision required member States to "ensure that the recruitment, transportation or transfer of a person, including harbouring and subsequent reception and the exchange of control over him or her is punishable, where the fundamental rights of that person have been and continue to be suppressed for the purpose of exploiting him or her in the production of goods or provision of services in infringement of labour standards governing working conditions, salaries and health and safety, and: (a) use is made of coercion, force or threats, including abduction; or (b) use is made of deceit or fraud, or (c) there is a misuse of authority, influence or pressure, or (d) there is another form of abuse." The purpose of exploiting a person "in prostitution or in pornographic performances or in production of pornographic materials" was dealt with in a separate article. Council of the European Union, Proposal for a Council Framework Decision on Combating Trafficking in Human Beings, OJ C 62 E/24, Feb. 27, 2001.

between adoption of the Protocol and the finalization of the Framework Decision provided the opportunity for a well-organized lobbying effort, aimed at ensuring maximum consistency between the two instruments, to gain momentum.[145] In its final form, the 2002 Framework Decision does not contain a definition of trafficking as such. Rather, the first article, entitled "Offences concerning trafficking in human beings for the purposes of labour exploitation or sexual exploitation," requires Member States and Candidate Countries to take measures to ensure certain acts are punishable.[146]

In terms of substance, the 2002 Framework Decision definition is almost entirely consistent with the Trafficking Protocol's definition. Both instruments identify trafficking as a problem affecting "persons," not just women and children, and both envisage trafficking as taking place for a wide range of end purposes, not just sexual exploitation, presumably putting an end to long-standing differences on this point within the various European organizations. The issue of consent is dealt with in an identical fashion in both instruments, and a separation is made between trafficking in children and trafficking in adults in connection with the means used to effect both initial and subsequent "action." Notable differences between the Trafficking Protocol and the Framework Decision's conception of trafficking can only be discerned in relation to the "purpose" element. These include the latter's maintenance of an apparently legally inconsequential distinction between trafficking for exploitative labor and trafficking for sexual exploitation, and the omission of removal of organs as a possible end purpose of trafficking. It is relevant to note that the proposal for a new Framework Decision to replace the 2002 instrument identified these discrepancies as unhelpful to the broader goal of coordinating national responses to trafficking.[147]

---

[145] For an account of this process, which involved the United Nations as well as a well organized NGO coalition, see A.T. Gallagher, "Recent Legal Developments in the Field of Human Trafficking: A Critical Review of the 2005 European Convention and Related Instruments," (2006) 8 *European Journal of Migration and Law* 163.

[146] Article 1 of the 2002 European Framework Decision on Trafficking requires States Parties to punish "the recruitment, transportation, transfer, harbouring, subsequent reception of a person, including exchange or transfer of control over that person, where: (a) use is made of coercion, force or threat, including abduction, or (b) use is made of deceit or fraud, or (c) there is an abuse of authority or of a position of vulnerability, which is such that the person has no real or acceptable alternative but to submit to the abuse involved, or (d) payments or benefits are given or received to achieve the consent of a person having control, over another person," where that act was performed either "for the purpose of exploitation of that person's labour or services, including at least forced or compulsory labour or services, slavery or practices similar to slavery or servitude," or "for the purpose of the exploitation of prostitution of others or other forms of sexual exploitation, including in pornography." The remainder of Article 1 then proceeds to clarify: "(2) The consent of a victim of trafficking in human beings to the exploitation, intended or actual, shall be irrelevant where any of the means set forth in paragraph 1 have been used. (3) Where the conduct referred to in paragraph 1 involves a child, it shall be a punishable trafficking offence even if none of the means set forth in paragraph 1 have been used."

[147] "Accompanying Document to the proposal for a Council Framework Decision in preventing and combating trafficking in human beings, and protecting victims, repealing Framework Decision 2002/629/JHA – Impact Assessment," Mar. 25, 2009, SEC (2009) 358, at 30.

The draft text, released in 2009 and discussed in detail in Chapter 2, incorporated the Trafficking Protocol and European Trafficking Convention definitions verbatim, "in order to enhance the process of approximation of legislation," only supplementing the list of open-ended examples of exploitation with "exploitation of activities associated with begging or of unlawful activities."[148] At the time of writing, this 2009 draft was no longer active due to disagreements over other aspects of the draft, and the 2002 Framework Decision remains in force. However, the part of the 2009 proposal for a new Framework Decision that proposes a definition of trafficking consistent with that of the Trafficking Protocol is currently being reconsidered for adoption in a recently tabled Proposal for a Directive on trafficking.[149]

By 2002, it had become possible to discern a distinct, if fragile, international consensus on the critical elements of trafficking, those elements being the ones contained in the Trafficking Protocol definition and reiterated in the 2002 European Framework Decision on Trafficking. The adoption of a different definition by the SAARC countries did not upset this situation, and by the time the European Trafficking Convention was adopted in 2005, that consensus had strengthened further. It was therefore no surprise that the Council of Europe reversed its previous position on trafficking being restricted to women and girls for the purposes of prostitution. The European Trafficking Convention incorporates precisely the Trafficking Protocol's definition of trafficking. It also goes one step further by defining a "victim" of trafficking, considered by the drafters to be an important means of ensuring that the provisions of the Convention, especially those related to protection, were applied correctly.[150] The recent proposal of the European Union to change the definition of trafficking set out in its 2002 Framework Decision to that contained in the Trafficking Protocol and European Trafficking Convention provides further compelling evidence of the impact and reach of the 2000 definition.[151]

---

[148] Commission of the European Communities, Proposal for a Framework Decision on preventing and combating trafficking in human beings, and protecting victims, repealing Framework Decision 2002/629/JHA, COM(2009) 136 final, Mar. 25, 2009, at Art. 1 and preambular para. 4. See further discussion of the Framework Decision in Chapter 2.

[149] A new proposal for a Directive on trafficking was tabled in March 2010. The new proposal "is, to its content, essentially identical to the previous Proposal for a Framework Decision": European Commission, Proposal for a Directive of the European Parliament and of the Council on preventing and combating trafficking in human beings, and protecting victims, repealing Framework Decision 2002/629/JHA, COM(2010) 95 final, Mar. 29, 2010 (EC Directive 2010 Proposal), at 6. This proposal also includes, verbatim, the definition of trafficking under the Trafficking Protocol: ibid. at Art. 2(1).

[150] European Trafficking Convention Explanatory Report, at 99. A victim of trafficking is anyone who is subject to trafficking as it is defined in the Convention. European Trafficking Convention, at Art. 2.

[151] Commission of the European Communities, Proposal for a Framework Decision on preventing and combating trafficking in human beings, and protecting victims, repealing Framework Decision 2002/629/JHA, COM(2009) 136 final, Mar. 25, 2009, at Art. 1 and preambular para. 4. As noted above, although this proposal is no longer active at the time of publication, that part that proposes a revised

1.4. THE SCOPE AND LIMITS OF THE DEFINITION

In terms of the questions set out in the introduction to this section, the following responses can now be given. First, the concept of trafficking in international law does not just refer to the *process* by which an individual is moved into a situation of exploitation: It extends to include the maintenance of that person in a situation of exploitation. Accordingly, it is not just the recruiter, broker, or transporter who can be identified as a trafficker, but also the individual or entity involved in initiating or sustaining the exploitation. Second, trafficking can take place for a range of end purposes including, but not limited to, sexual exploitation and can involve as victims men and boys as well as women and girls. Third, it is legally possible for trafficking to take place within a single country, including the victim's own. Fourth, the "means" of trafficking in adults – an inherent part of the trafficking definition – will operate to nullify consent. As such means are not required to be established in relation to trafficking in children, consensual trafficking of either adults or children is a legal impossibility.

The evolution of consensus on what constitutes trafficking does not necessarily mark the end of definitional controversies. A major point of critique has been the apparent narrowness of the current international legal understanding. For example, it has been argued that the three-element definition means that States are under no obligation to do anything about the actual exploitation that is the end purpose of trafficking.[152] It has also been argued that the definition is constrained further by the requirement that, in the case of adult victims, the "action" intended to lead to exploitation must have been made possible through the use of a specified means such as coercion, deception, or the abuse of authority.[153]

To what extent do these two features of the definition – exploitation as an element rather than as a separate offense, and an additional requirement of "means" – operate to limit the scope or impact of the definition and thereby the legal obligations to which it is attached? The short answer is, in its practical application, not at all. Although the legal instruments that incorporate the new definition do not specifically require State Parties to address the exploitative practices that are the end purpose of trafficking, and while they do require, at least for adults, that the relevant action is secured through a specific means, it is difficult to identify a contemporary form of private exploitation that would not fall within the generous parameters of the definition. Because the definition encompasses both the bringing of a person into exploitation and the maintenance of that person in a situation of exploitation, it is equally difficult to identify an exploiter who would escape its reach. For example, as noted above, it is possible to argue very convincingly that even in the absence of a preceding process, trafficking is present in traditional debt bondage systems

definition was broadly accepted and has been proposed for adoption in a subsequent draft instrument: EC Directive 2010 Proposal, at Art. 2(1).

[152] Hathaway, "The Human Rights Quagmire of Human Trafficking," at 10.

[153] Ibid. at 11.

of South Asia where individuals are harbored or received and often also transported and transferred (act) through coercion (means) in order to exploit their labor
through debt bondage (purpose).[154] Certainly, trafficking is present in chattel slavery
in Africa where individuals are bought, sold, transported, harbored, and received
(act) through force and coercion (means) into situations of slavery (purpose). The
sale of children into prostitution by their parents also falls within the international
legal definition: Children are recruited, transported, transferred, harbored, and
received (act) in order to sexually exploit them (purpose).[155] Trafficking is also present in the Australian sex industry in the form of Thai and Korean women held
in debt bondage;[156] in the Russian construction sector where thousands of workers
from Tajikistan and Kyrgyzstan are abused and deceived;[157] on fishing boats off the
gulf of Thailand where Burmese and Cambodian men are isolated and exploited
for long periods of time without being paid the wages they were led to expect;[158] in
the brothels of Bali and the private homes of Jakarta to which Indonesian girls and
young women have been sent or lured with promises of a better life;[159] on the cocoa
farms of Côte d'Ivoire, made profitable through the almost zero-cost labor of child
workers from Mali;[160] on the beaches of Thailand where children are procured for
sexual exploitation by foreign "tourists,"[161] and in the private household of North
America where Guatemalan maids sleep on the floor and are not allowed outside.[162]

---

[154] See further discussion of the relationship between forced/bonded labor and trafficking below at note
162 and the accompanying text.

[155] Note that as this situation specifically concerns children, the requirement of "means" is
waived: Trafficking Protocol, at Art. 3(c).

[156] See, for example, *R v. Tang*, (2008) 249 ALR 200 (Aus. HC, Aug. 28, 2008); and F. David, *Trafficking
of Women for Sexual Purposes*, Australian Institute of Criminology Research and Public Policy
Series No. 95 (2008), available at http://www.aic.gov.au/documents/1/C/E/{1CE51DE9–5346–4565-
A86B-778F895BF9E1}rpp95.pdf (accessed Nov. 30, 2009).

[157] See, for example, Human Rights Watch, *"Are You Happy to Cheat Us?" Exploitation of Migrant
Construction Workers in Russia* (2009).

[158] See, for example, United Nations Inter-Agency Project on Human Trafficking, "Exploitation of
Cambodian Men at Sea: Facts about the Trafficking of Cambodian Men onto Thai Fishing Boats"
(2009), available at http://www.no-trafficking.org/reports_docs/siren/siren_cb3.pdf (accessed Nov. 30,
2009).

[159] See, generally, Human Rights Watch, *Workers in the Shadows: Abuse and Exploitation of Child
Domestic Workers in Indonesia* (2009); A. Hamim, "Provincial Assessments: Riau Islands," in
K.L. Sugiarti, J. Davis and A. Dasgupta eds., *When They Were Sold: Trafficking of Women and Girls
in 15 Provinces of Indonesia* 79 (2006); R. Surtees, "Commercial Sex Work," in R. Rosenburg ed.,
Trafficking of Women and Children in Indonesia 63 (2005).

[160] See C. Off, *Bitter Chocolate: Investigating the Dark Side of the World's Most Seductive Sweet* (2006),
at 121–22, 143; see also G.B. Nkamleu and A. Kielland, "Modeling Farmers' Decisions on Child
Labor and Schooling in the Cocoa Sector: A Multinomial Logit Analysis in Côte d'Ivoire," (2006)
35 *Agricultural Economics* 319.

[161] See, for example, H. Montgomery, *Modern Babylon? Prostituting Children in Thailand* (2001);
Human Rights Watch, Asia Watch and Women's Rights Project divisions, *A Modern Form of
Slavery: Trafficking of Burmese Women and Girls into Brothels in Thailand* (1993).

[162] See, for example, *United States v. Tecum*, 48 Fed. Appx. 739 (US CA11, Aug. 28, 2002) (finding Jose
Tecum guilty of violating several federal laws when he kidnapped a young Guatemalan woman

Even child sex tourism, not specifically referred to in the Trafficking Protocol or any of the other specialist trafficking treaties – and often identified separately from trafficking in laws and policies – appears to satisfy the "act" and "purpose" elements of the international legal definition: In such situations, children are recruited, transported, and so on for the purpose of sexual exploitation. As the "act" element includes receipt, the definition extends beyond those involved in moving the child into the situation of exploitation to potentially include the individual exploiter (the child sex tourist).

Ironically, it is not the narrowness of its scope but the potential breadth of the definition that will most likely nurture future debate. It could be argued, for example, that a unified definition, eminently defensible with reference to the plain meaning of the text of the definition, obscures important differences between trafficking and exploitation as well as between different exploitative practices. The understandable (and perhaps inescapable) absence of a standard measure of what constitutes "exploitation" is a major cause of definitional fluidities. For example, in the case of children, how unpleasant or exploitative does an employment situation have to be before it is possible to say that a child was recruited or moved or harbored "for purposes of exploitation"? Uncertainties around the limits of the "means" element of the definition are another potential source of confusion. For example, what degree of deception or coercion is required to satisfy the "means" element of the definition? Is it really possible to interpret the concept of "coercion" to include economic pressures?

There is general agreement that not all undesirable practices involving the exploitation of individuals could or should be identified as trafficking. Most activists and scholars appear to accept the validity of some kind of a "seriousness" threshold. Beyond this, the lines remain blurred. Disagreements on whether sale of children for purposes of adoption should be considered trafficking provide a case in point, while also serving to confirm that lack of clarity may be as much about politics and strategy as it is about law. Ongoing debates about the relationship between trafficking and forced labor furnish another example. The ILO, for example, continues to use the well-established legal concept of "forced labor," rather than trafficking, as its overarching conceptual framework around work-related exploitation. By emphasizing the movement aspect of the "action" element, the ILO has sought to distinguish trafficking from what it considers to be the broader category of forced labor.[163] While

by threats of violence and inveiglement from her family home in remote Guatemala, smuggled her across the US-Mexico border, transported her to and harbored her in his home in Florida, and forced her to perform domestic and agricultural work and to submit to his sexual demands); and the Brief for the Appellee in that case at 2–3, available at http://www.usdoj.gov/crt/briefs/tecum.pdf (accessed Nov. 30, 2009).

[163] "Trafficking is a process that very often ends in forced labour – be it forced commercial sexual exploitation or different forms of economic exploitation. *Forced labour* is defined in the ILO Forced Labour Convention (No. 29) that dates back to 1930. The term covers all work or service

the capacity of the international legal definition to swallow up other prohibited practices may well be a legitimate cause of concern, it is not at all clear that the ILO
position on this point is supported by the legal analysis of the definition presented
above.

Overly broad interpretations of the definition of trafficking, designed to take
advantage of the political and legal momentum around this issue for purposes
of advancing a particular policy agenda, are a related worry. While many would
accept that trafficking is fundamentally different to its identified end purposes,
that view is no longer a consensus one. Maladroit attempts to identify pornography
as "trafficking" are one manifestation of a potentially troubling expansionist trend.[164]

that any woman, man or child is coerced to do under the threat of a penalty, and for which they
have not offered themselves voluntarily. In common usage today, the term *slavery* is often used
to connote forced labour or 'slavery-like' conditions. *Slavery* was first defined by the League of
Nations in 1926 as a situation where rights of ownership are exercised by one person over another;
and subsequently, in 1956, a UN instrument addressed slavery-like practices, including debt bondage, serfdom and related practices. There are many ways in which a person can be coerced into
undertaking work against their free will. Those most commonly associated with the forced labour
resulting from human trafficking include the confiscation of personal identity documents, the
threat of denunciation of irregular migrants to the authorities in the host country, deception of
a trafficked person about the type of work he or she will eventually undertake, and withholding
of wages over prolonged periods. Threats of – or actual – physical or sexual violence against the
victim, or his or her family members, are also used to keep victims in work against their will. Debt
bondage, often associated with more 'traditional' forms of forced labour, is among the most prevalent means now used to keep trafficked victims in situations of forced labour. Debts incurred by the
victim during the trafficking process – for transportation, forged documents, smuggling through
borders and so on – as well as at the destination (for food, lodging, securing a 'job') accumulate to
such a proportion that the victim will never be able to pay them off through the meagre income
earned, effectively bonding them to work for the trafficker or employer for an indeterminate period
of time. *Forced labour* is closely linked to human *trafficking*, but is not identical to it. While most
victims of trafficking end up in forced labour, not all victims of forced labour are in this situation as a result of trafficking. For example, people who are coerced to work in their place of origin have not been considered in the ILO's own estimates of forced labour as trafficking victims.
A distinction must also be drawn between those people who are under some form of economic
compulsion to accept sub-standard working conditions because they simply have no alternative
(exploitation or abuse of vulnerability, but not necessarily forced labour) and those against whom
actual coercion is exercised by a third party to force them to undertake a job against their will
(forced labour)": International Labour Organization, "Fighting Human Trafficking: The Forced
Labour Dimensions," background paper prepared for the Vienna Forum on Human Trafficking,
Vienna, Feb. 13–15, 2008, available from: http://www.oit.org/sapfl/Events/ILOevents/lang–en/
WCMS_090236/index.htm (accessed Feb. 5, 2010). See also, International Labour Office, *The Cost
of Coercion* (2009), especially at 28–35.

[164] Catherine Mackinnon has argued that: "[p]ornography is clearly covered as sex trafficking [sic]
under this [Trafficking Protocol] definition. For pornography, women and children are received,
transported, provided and obtained for sex acts on account of which, typically, money is given to pornography pimps and received by lesser pimps. Then, each time the pornography is exchanged, the
trafficking continues as the women and children in it are transported and provided for sex, sold and
bought again. Doing all these things for the purpose of exploiting the prostitution of others – which
prostitution intrinsically does – makes it trafficking in persons." C.A. Mackinnon, "Pornography
as Trafficking," (2004) 26 *Michigan Journal of International Law* 993, at 1004. Leaving aside its

The attention and resources that are being directed toward fighting trafficking provide some explanation for what are undoubtedly well-intentioned efforts to expand the definition. To make pornography "trafficking," for example, radically expands the range and force of available legal weapons as well as, in many cases, the political and financial capital available to support its elimination. To characterize all cases of forced labor as trafficking has a similar effect, also operating to considerably expand the pool of potential victims and perpetrators. However well-intentioned, attempts to stretch the concept of trafficking beyond the clear intention of the drafters and, at least in relation to the pornography example provided above, beyond the plain meaning of the text should be resisted. As has happened with the concept of slavery,[165] expansionist interpretations weaken the force of the underlying legal prohibition. They also operate to undermine broader goals related to international cooperation and the standardization of concepts that require shared understanding of the nature of the problem to be addressed.

Another important area of ongoing controversy and concern is the relationship between the international legal concepts of trafficking and migrant smuggling. There is certainly substance to the claim that the distinction between trafficking and migrant smuggling is an oversimplification of a much more complicated reality, and critics have rightly highlighted the essential artificiality of a legal distinction between two such closely related phenomena.[166] A careful analysis of both definitions reveals significant potential for overlap, in particular between trafficking on

---

clumsiness, this effort to equate pornography with trafficking misrepresents the definition in several important respects. Certainly there are situations in which the various acts involved in the *production* (although not the dissemination or consumption) of pornography could amount to trafficking. In the case of child pornography, for example, the definition would be satisfied by showing that the child was recruited, transported, transferred, harbored, or received for the purpose of using that child in pornography. In the case of adults, however, the additional requirement of means operates to restrict application of the definition to only those situations in which the recruitment, transport, receipt etc. was made possible through deception, force, coercion, abuse of authority etc. The argument that sale and resale of images amounts to retrafficking is equally difficult to sustain. Equating pornography with prostitution does not strengthen Mackinnon's argument, as the drafters of the Trafficking Protocol were explicit on the point that the definition did *not* operate to regulate or even pronounce on prostitution: Travaux Préparatoires *for the Organized Crime Convention and Protocols*, at 347.

[165] For further discussion, see Chapter 3.3 below.

[166] See, for example, C. Brolan, "An Analysis of the Human Smuggling Trade and the Protocol Against the Smuggling of Migrants by Land, Air and Sea (2000) from a Refugee Protection Perspective," (2002) 14 *International Journal of Refugee Law* 561, at 596; M.V. McCreight, "Smuggling of Migrants, Trafficking in Human Beings and Irregular Migration on a Comparative Perspective," (2006) 12 *European Law Journal* 106; B.S. Buckland, "Human Trafficking & Smuggling: Crossover & Overlap", in C. Friesendorf ed., *Strategies Against Human Trafficking: The Role of the Security Sector* 132 (2009) (Buckland, "Human Trafficking & Smuggling") (arguing that "smuggled and trafficked people fall along a continuum of abuse – quite clearly distinguishable at the extremes but increasingly hard to tell apart at the centre": at 163; and International Council on Human Rights

the one hand and aggravated smuggling (involving, e.g., "inhuman or degrading treatment, including for exploitation")[167] on the other.

While acknowledging potential problems, it is also important to accept that no legal definition of trafficking, no matter how carefully crafted, can ever be expected to respond fully to the shades and complexities of the real world. The distinction that has been created in international law between trafficking in persons on the one hand and smuggling of migrants on the other is a clear example of such a limitation. It is nevertheless understandable and defensible. Unless States were prepared to invent exploitation where it did not necessarily exist – or deny it where it did – they had little option but to separate formally the (inherently exploitative) practice of trafficking from the (only incidentally exploitative) practice of migrant smuggling. As a result, States were required to disregard the reality that both trafficking and migrant smuggling are *processes* that are often interrelated and almost always involve shifts, flows, overlaps, and transitions.[168] An individual can be smuggled one day and trafficked the next. A single "shipment" could well include persons destined for exploitation (victims of trafficking) and persons who are merely being moved from one country to the next in exchange for a fee (smuggled migrants). In many cases, not even the individuals involved will, at the movement stage, be able to classify their precise situation with certainty. The risks of incorrect identification – in particular, the risk of trafficked persons being misidentified as smuggled or illegal migrants, and especially the risk to the human rights of all victims of exploitation – was recognized during the drafting of both international definitions[169] and continues to occupy States[170] and

Policy, *Irregular Migration, Migrant Smuggling and Human Rights: Towards Coherence* (2010), at 71–85 ("the ambiguous reality of migratory movement is somewhat obscured by the pretence in the Protocols that clean distinctions can be made between people who are forced to move and people who choose to move voluntarily": at 78).

[167] Migrant Smuggling Protocol, at Art. 6(3)(b). The Migrant Smuggling Protocol does not define exploitation. Presumably the concept of exploitation as set out in the Trafficking Protocol and discussed in detail above would be applicable.

[168] Many commentators have also explored this argument. See, for example, UN High Commissioner for Refugees, *Guidelines on International Protection: The application of Article 1(A)(2) of the 1951 Convention and/or 1967 Protocol relating to the Status of Refugees to victims of trafficking and persons at risk of being trafficked*, UN Doc. HCR/GIP/06/07 (Apr. 7, 2006); L. Kelly, "'You Can Find Anything You Want': A Critical Reflection on Research on Trafficking in Persons within and into Europe," (2005) 43 *International Migration* 235, at 238; see also Global Commission on International Migration, *Migration in an Interconnected World: New Directions for Action* (2005), esp. at 34.

[169] See, for example, "Note by the Office of the United Nations High Commissioner for Human Rights, the Office of the United Nations High Commissioner for Refugees, the United Nations Children's Fund and the International Organization for Migration on the Draft Protocols Concerning Migrant Smuggling and Trafficking in Persons," UN Doc. A/AC.254/27, Feb. 8, 2000 and UN Doc. A.AC.254/27/Corr.1, Feb. 22, 2000; J. Bhabha and C. Alfirev, "The Identification and Referral of Trafficked Persons to Procedures for Determining International Protection Needs" (United Nations High Commissioner for Refugees, 2009).

[170] The European Trafficking Convention, for example, requires State Parties to ensure that trained and qualified individuals are involved in identifying victims, including children. It further requires

intergovernmental agencies,[171] as well as individuals and nongovernmental organizations working to promote rights-based responses to trafficking.[172]

Constant interrogation of the differences and similarities between trafficking and migrant smuggling is an important means of exploring the definitional uncertainties outlined above. Such interrogation should also serve to establish, over time, whether the qualitative distinctions outlined above are valid or, conversely, whether trafficking and smuggling are "mere points on a poorly defined continuum."[173] Much will depend on how the definitions are applied in practice. If uniform and consistent application of the two concepts proves difficult or impossible, this will inevitably compromise the legitimacy of the distinction as well as of the underlying norms.[174]

In the euphoria of securing an internationally agreed-upon definition, many legal and practical matters remain to be fully considered. States, international organizations, and civil society are only now coming to terms with both the scope and the limitations of the new understanding of trafficking, and it is likely to be some time before the issues raised in this chapter are fully resolved. In the meantime, other questions and controversies will surely arise. International forums, including the supervisory mechanism established under the Organized Crime Convention as well as the various human rights bodies (explored in detail in Chapter 9), will have an important role to play in fleshing out the substantive content of the definition. It should also be recalled that as trafficking is now a criminal offense in most countries of the world, the application of this new definition to real situations involving real people will likely yield additional important insights.

---

different authorities to collaborate with each other and with relevant support organizations to ensure victims can be identified in a procedure that duly takes account of the special situation of both women and children. European Trafficking Convention, at Art. 10. The commentary to this provision notes that failure to identify quickly and accurately victims of trafficking renders any rights granted to such persons "purely theoretical and illusory": European Trafficking Convention Explanatory Report, at para. 131.

[171] See, for example, UN Office on Drugs and Crime, *Toolkit to Combat Trafficking in Persons* (2008), at 251–302; International Organization for Migration, *Identification and Protection Schemes for Victims of Trafficking in Persons in Europe: Tools and Best Practices* (2005); see also the UN *Trafficking Principles and Guidelines*.

[172] See, for example, Global Alliance Against Trafficking in Women, *Collateral Damage: The Impact of Anti-Trafficking Measures on Human Rights Around the World* (2007).

[173] Buckland, "Human Trafficking & Smuggling," at 149.

[174] For a useful illustration of such difficulties, see E. Gjerdingen, "Suffocation inside a Cold Storage Truck and Other Problems with Trafficking as 'Exploitation' and Smuggling as 'Choice' along the Thai-Burmese Border," (2009) 26 *Arizona Journal of International & Comparative Law* 699.

2

The International Legal Framework

Modern, positivist approaches to international law accept the central place of consent in both the formation and continuing acceptance of international legal rules. In other words, States are bound by international laws because they choose to be. Consent to be bound is most clearly and unambiguously adduced from the purposeful decision of a State to enter into a treaty. However, other "traditional" sources of law,[1] custom and general principles, are similarly dependent on the State making some kind of tangible commitment that serves to express its will. While non-State actors play an important role in shaping international law, the task of identifying the source and nature of specific legal obligations is best served by a conservative position that accepts that international law is made, or recognized or accepted through the will of States, and that "nothing becomes law for the international system from any other source."[2]

This chapter confines itself to a survey and analysis of international legal rules that generally pass this test. Its primary focus is the web of international treaties that have developed over the past century to address trafficking and related forms of exploitation and whose coverage of the topic is, today, remarkably comprehensive. The chapter also provides a brief analysis of customary law as it relates to trafficking and of secondary and subsidiary sources of international law, including general principles and judicial decisions. It concludes with an analysis of the rather elusive concept of "soft" law as it relates to trafficking, with a view to determining the nature of the contribution that this "category" of materials makes to the international legal framework around trafficking.

2.1. A BRIEF HISTORY OF TRAFFICKING IN INTERNATIONAL HUMAN RIGHTS TREATY LAW

Unlike many contemporary human rights issues, trafficking has an extended and somewhat complex legal history, aspects of which have already been touched upon

---

[1] The generally recognized "sources" of international law are set out in Article 38(1) of the Statute of the International Court of Justice, 961 UNTS 183, done June 26, 1945, entered into force Oct. 24, 1945 (ICJ Statute).

[2] L. Henkin, *International Law, Politics and Values* (1995) (Henkin, *International Law*), at 27.

in the definitional survey contained in the previous chapter. The following, more detailed overview considers the evolution of trafficking as a legal issue. It alludes to, without fully exploring, the various narratives that have shaped or otherwise reflect normative developments in this area.

2.1.1. *Trafficking and White Slavery*

The legal aspects of the relationship between trafficking and the international prohibition on slavery are subject to separate and detailed consideration in the following chapter. For present purposes, it is sufficient to note that the raft of international agreements on slavery, which were concluded in the latter part of the nineteenth century and the first decades of the twentieth century, did not purport and were never considered to cover the practices that are now associated with trafficking, including sexual exploitation, forced labor, debt bondage, and child labor. However, the international movement to abolish the transatlantic slave trade provided the framework within which another battle – this time for the virtue of white women – would be waged.[3] The concept of "white slavery" was originally developed by activists intent on abolishing systems of regulated prostitution in Europe. It served to distinguish "female sexual slavery" from the enslavement of Africans, while at the same time serving to draw a moral comparison between the two different types of exploitation.[4] In its original form, the term referred to migrant prostitution.[5] By the second half of the nineteenth century, the concept of "white slavery" was associated with recruitment to prostitution by force or fraud.[6] The sensationalized image of young and innocent white women being coerced into prostitution in foreign lands was at least partially responsible for the internationalization of the abolitionist movement and

---

[3]   E.A. Nadelmann, "Global Prohibition Regimes: The Evolution of Norms in International Society," (1990) 44 *International Organisation* 479 (Nadelmann, "Global Prohibition Regimes"), at 514–515. On the early international movement to abolish prostitution and "white slavery," see F.K. Grittner, *White Slavery: Myth, Ideology and American Law* (1990) (Grittner, *White Slavery*); J. Walkowitz, *Prostitution and Victorian Society: Women, Class and the State* (1980) (Walkowitz, *Prostitution and Victorian Society*) and M.A. Irwin, "'White Slavery' as Metaphor: Anatomy of a Moral Panic," (1996) 5 *Ex-Post Facto: the History Journal* 1 (Irwin, "'White Slavery' as Metaphor"). See also J. Doezema, *Sex Slaves and Discourse Masters: The Construction of Trafficking* (forthcoming, 2010) (Doezema, *Sex Slaves*).

[4]   Irwin, "'White Slavery' as Metaphor," at 5. Irwin notes that in comparing the taking of black slaves for labor with the enslavement of white women for sexual purposes, commentators generally placed a higher value on the suffering of the women, "whose purer natures made sexual contact particularly abhorrent": ibid.

[5]   Nadelmann, "Global Prohibition Regimes," at 514. Josephine Butler, a prominent reformist of the late nineteenth century, argued that regulation of prostitution crated a permanent "slave class of women" and was "nothing else than … the protection of the white-slave trade, in a word, the organisation of female slavery." J.E. Butler, *Personal Reminisces of a Great Crusade* (1911). See further, S.A., Limoncelli, "Paths to the Abolition of Regulated Prostitution in Europe, 1875–1950: International Voluntary Associations, Local Social Movements and State," (2006) 21 *International Sociology* 31.

[6]   Nadelmann, "Global Prohibition Regimes," at 514.

the resulting emphasis on trafficking of women for purposes of sexual exploitation.[7] A focus on the international dimension also provided anti-prostitution crusaders with "the essential transnational hook needed to pursue the abolition of licensed prostitution"[8] – itself associated with "disfavored racial minorities."[9]

The white slavery campaign has been described as an early and classic example of a "moral panic."[10] It created and sustained a powerful cultural myth,[11] one that survived intact despite the discrepancy between the claimed size of the phenomenon and the number of documented cases.[12] The essence of that myth lay in the idea of male exploitation of innocence, a notion that provided the foundation for the subsequent, idealized victim: a young girl, kidnapped or tricked into leaving her family, finds herself locked up in a foreign brothel servicing numerous faceless men against her will. A 1921 League of Nations report neatly encapsulates the international perception of the problem of white slavery, decrying the fact that:

> women, for the most part underage, were engaged for lucrative posts and then, always in complete ignorance of the abominable lot which awaited them, were transported to foreign countries and finally flung penniless into houses of debauchery.[13]

Significantly, the early focus on prostitution did not prevent attempts to broaden the scope of the campaign against white slavery to include exploitation of women's labor in all sectors. However, through international agreements set out further in

---

[7] See generally Nadelmann, "Global Prohibition Regimes"; Irwin, "'White Slavery' as Metaphor" and Doezema, *Sex Slaves.*

[8] Nadelmann, "Global Prohibition Regimes," at 515.

[9] Ibid. Irwin adds another dimension to the connection between race and white slave trader: "[b]y forwarding frighteningly plausible tales of continental predators scouring train terminals and country villages for English virgins, Britons were invoking race as a morally acceptable explanation for the rising tide of prostitution at home." Irwin, "'White Slavery' as Metaphor," at 11.

[10] See, for example, Irwin, "'White Slavery' as Metaphor." Generally, on the concept of "moral panic," see S. Cohen, *Folk Devils and Moral Panics: The Creation of the Mods and Rockers* (2002).

[11] Doezema adopts Grittner's conception of a myth: "[a]s an uncritically accepted collective belief, a myth can help explain the world and justify social institutions and actions … When it is repeated in similar form from generation to generation, a myth discloses a moral content, carrying its own meaning, secreting its own values. The power of myth lies in the totality of explanation. Rough edges of experience can be rounded off. Looked at structurally, a cultural myth is a discourse, 'a set of narrative formulas that acquire, through specifiable historical action, a significant ideological charge'." Grittner, *White Slavery,* cited in Doezema, *Sex Slaves,* at 4–5. Note that Doezema does not equate myth with falsehood, proposing that analysis of "political myths" such as white slavery and trafficking can proceed without analysis of its status as "true" or "false": ibid. at 22.

[12] Historians and sociologists generally agree that the actual number of cases of "white slavery," particularly those involving exploitation across national borders, were very few and certainly much less than was claimed by activists. See, generally, Grittner, *White Slavery* and M. Connelly, *The Response to Prostitution in the Progressive Era* (1980).

[13] Cited as League of Nations 1921, in S. Jeffries, *The Idea of Prostitution* (1997), at 11. See also the opening speech of the President, League of Nations, Records of the International Conference on Traffic in Women and Children, June 1921, available at: http://www.archive.org/stream/convention-internooleagrich/conventioninternooleagrich_djvu.txt (accessed Feb. 5, 2010).

this chapter, the emphasis narrowed, first to prostitution and then exclusively to cross-border prostitution.[14] During this period, no international effort was made to regulate sexual exploitation and prostitution taking place within national borders – it being understood that such matters were properly the subject of domestic regulation. As Jones-Pauly notes:

> It was as if exploitation of women and prostitutes at home lay only within the jurisdiction of the sovereign State, subject to its own sense of morality and immorality. But the export of immorality across borders had to be stopped.[15]

Between 1904 and 1933, four different international conventions dealing with the (white slave) traffic in women and girls were concluded.[16] The earliest agreement in this series, concluded in 1904, covered only situations in which women were forced or deceived into prostitution or "debauchery" in foreign countries. The focus was on the social obligations of the State – particularly as these related to the welfare of victims. The 1904 Convention also emphasized the centralization of information as a means of facilitating cross-border cooperation. The second agreement, concluded in 1910, extended its scope to situations of enticement and procurement not necessarily involving force, and within as well as across national boundaries. It shifted the emphasis away from social concerns and more toward the criminalization of procurement and related acts, as well as the prosecution and punishment of offenders. The 1910 Convention also introduced a distinction that has survived to the present day – between young victims (in relation to whom the "means" by which they were procured were irrelevant) and adult victims (in relation to whom some evidence of compulsion was required).

The third and fourth agreements in this series were concluded under the auspices of the League of Nations, which itself was mandated to supervise the execution of agreements with regard to the traffic in women and children.[17] The 1921 Agreement

[14] C.C. Jones-Pauly, *Report on Anti-Trafficking Laws in Six Countries (Austria, Belgium, Czech Republic, Federal Republic of Germany, Italy, Poland) and Compliance with the International Conventions against Trafficking* (1999) (Jones-Pauly, *Report on Anti-Trafficking Laws*), at 162.

[15] Ibid.

[16] International Agreement for the Suppression of the White Slave Traffic, 1 LNTS 83, done May 4, 1904, entered into force July 18, 1905. There were thirteen signatories, all of which were European States. International Convention for the Suppression of the White Slave Traffic, 3 LNTS 278, done May 4, 1910, entered into force Aug. 8, 1912. There were thirteen signatories, all European States except for Brazil. (Both amended by a protocol approved by the General Assembly on May 4, 1949, 30 UNTS 23.) International Convention for the Suppression of Traffic in Women and Children, 9 LNTS 415, done Sept. 30, 1921, entered into force June 15, 1922. There were thirty-three signatories from Europe, North America, Asia, and Oceania. International Convention for the Suppression of the Traffic in Women of Full Age, 150 LNTS 431, done Oct. 11, 1933, entered into force Aug. 24, 1934. There were twenty-six signatories from Europe, Oceania, Asia, the Americas, and Africa. (Both instruments were amended by a Protocol approved by the General Assembly on Nov. 12, 1947, 53 UNTS 13.)

[17] Covenant of the League of Nations, 225 CTW 195, done June 28, 1919, entered into force Jan. 10, 1920, at Art XXIII. The same article called on Member States of the League to "ensure fair and humane conditions of labour for men, women, and children, both in their own countries and in all countries to which their commercial and industrial relations extend."

avoided any references to "white slavery" and applied a new notion of "immoral trafficking" to individuals of both sexes under the age of twenty-one, as well as women over twenty-one years if they had been constrained or deceived. The 1921 Convention continued the earlier emphasis on emigration and immigration controls, as well as on the prosecution of all those involved in the trafficking process.

The final trafficking-related Convention of this period, concluded in 1933, expanded the end results of trafficking to include all sexual and immoral purposes, not just prostitution. The notion of consent was eliminated, which meant that, at least in relation to cross-border cases, force or coercion was no longer a constitutive element of trafficking for either adults or children. The offense of trafficking under this instrument thus involved the procuring, enticing, or leading away of any women of any age across an international border for immoral purposes. The cross-border element was removed with respect to the offenses of procurement, enticement, or leading away, thereby subjecting certain domestic activities, particularly in the country of origin, to the Convention's provisions. Like each of its predecessors, the 1933 Convention required States Parties to protect victims and to exchange information with each other.

The major themes identified by Jones-Pauly in her overview of the interwar, pre-1949 debates on trafficking strongly echo aspects of the contemporary trafficking discourse. An emphasis on rehabilitation of the victim through education and vocational training emerged,[18] as did the realization that banning of foreign prostitutes could be conveniently passed off as a measure to reduce trafficking supply.[19] Almost no attention was given to the demand side of the prostitution/trafficking equation, with the result that international political and legislative attention was overwhelmingly focused on countries of origin.[20] While the League of Nations strongly advocated the supported repatriation of victims over deportation, States of destination pushed for a system of compulsory return.[21] It is also relevant to note that while all four instruments encouraged the criminalization of recruitment of women for prostitution abroad, they carefully preserved the authority of those States that had chosen to regulate internal prostitution.

2.1.2. *The 1949 Trafficking Convention*

In 1949, the various white slavery/trafficking agreements were consolidated into one instrument: the Convention for the Suppression of the Traffic in Persons and of the Exploitation of the Prostitution of Others.[22] The 1949 Convention, which, as

---

[18]   Jones-Pauly, *Report on Anti-Trafficking Laws*, at 167.

[19]   Ibid.

[20]   Ibid. at 168.

[21]   Ibid. at 168–169.

[22]   Convention for the Suppression of the Traffic in Persons and of the Exploitation of the Prostitution of Others, 96 UNTS 271, done Dec. 2, 1949, entered into force July 25, 1951 (1949 Trafficking Convention). For an overview of the legislative history of the Convention, see UNESCO and

of May 2010, had eighty-one States Parties,[23] is limited to trafficking for prostitution and ostensibly applies to both women and men. It aims to prohibit and control the (undefined) practices of trafficking, procurement,[24] and exploitation, whether internal or cross-border, and irrespective of the victim's age or consent. It declares both trafficking and prostitution to be "incompatible with the dignity and worth of the human being" and a danger to "the welfare of the individual, the family and the community."[25] By extending its scope beyond the "movement" issue to identify prostitution and forced prostitution as matters for international regulation, the Convention set itself apart from the earlier legislative measures outlined earlier in the chapter, with their deference to matters traditionally seen as within a State's domestic jurisdiction.

States Parties to the Convention are required to punish:

> Any person who, to gratify the passions of another: (1) procures or entices or leads away, for the purposes of prostitution, another person, even with the consent of that person; (2) exploits the prostitution of another person, even with the consent of the person.[26]

States Parties are also required to punish those involved in the keeping, managing, or financing of brothels[27] and to refrain from any system of registration or supervision of prostitutes.[28] Despite its avowed abolitionist stance, the Convention does not, in fact, prohibit prostitution nor demand its criminalization, instead requiring States Parties only to take social and economic measures aimed at preventing prostitution.[29] This somewhat contradictory position was no doubt an attempt to forge consensus between those countries that outlawed prostitution and those that tolerated it under certain conditions, thereby ensuring the widest possible ratification. Framers of the Convention were also aware that outright criminalization or

---

the Coalition against Trafficking in Women, *The Penn State Report: Report of an International Meeting of Experts on Sexual Exploitation, Violence and Prostitution*, April 1999, Annex 1 (*Penn State Report*).

[23] Information in accordance with the UN Treaty Collection: http://treaties.un.org/pages/showDetails.aspx?objid=080000028002d016 (accessed May 27, 2010). Note that there appear to be some historical inconsistencies in the ratification information.

[24] Note that contrary to the 1933 Convention, procurement is prohibited only if it is for purposes of prostitution, not for the more general "immoral purposes."

[25] 1949 Trafficking Convention, at Preamble.

[26] Ibid. at Art. 1.

[27] Ibid. at Art. 2.

[28] Ibid. at Art. 6: "[e]ach Party … agrees to take all the necessary measures to repeal or abolish existing law, regulation or administrative provision by virtue of which persons who engage in or suspected of being engaged in prostitution are subject either to special registration or to the possession of a special document or to any exceptional requirements for supervision or notification."

[29] Ibid. at Art. 16: "[t]he Parties … agree to take or to encourage, through their public and private educational, health, social, economic and other related services, measures for the prevention of prostitution and for the rehabilitation and social adjustment of the victims of prostitution and of the offences referred to in the present Convention."

prohibition would drive the practice underground, and that such laws would likely be applied selectively only against the prostitutes.[30]

Cross-border cooperation is seen to be an important tool in the fight against immigrant prostitution/trafficking, and the Convention contains a number of substantive and procedural provisions on this issue.[31] It envisages extradition of offenders, as well as the prosecution and punishment of nationals for offenses committed abroad.[32] Detailed guidance is also provided on the internal coordination and centralization of antitrafficking efforts.[33] Protection and rehabilitation are central themes. Foreign victims of trafficking are to have the same rights as nationals with respect to their being party to proceedings against traffickers[34] – presumably including equality of access to compensation for crimes. Victims of prostitution are to be identified, and reasons and circumstances behind their situation are to be established prior to their repatriation.[35] Victims of both prostitution and trafficking are to be provided with social services for prevention of prostitution, as well as for "rehabilitation and social adjustment."[36] States Parties are also obliged to maintain and care for destitute trafficking victims prior to their repatriation.[37] Repatriation (for alien prostitutes, as well as for trafficked persons) is envisaged if so desired by the alien prostitute or trafficked person, or if their "expulsion is ordered in conformity with the law."[38] The Convention sets out a

---

[30] United Nations Department of International Economic and Social Affairs, "Activities for the Advancement of Women: Equality, Development and Peace," UN Doc. ST/ESA/174, (1985), 11, cited in J. Chuang, "Redirecting the Debate over Trafficking in Women: Definitions, Paradigms and Contexts," (1998) 11 *Harvard Human Rights Journal* 65, at 77.

[31] 1949 Trafficking Convention, at Arts. 13, 14, 15, and 18. Article 13 establishes/facilitates direct communications between "judicial authorities" as well as between Ministers of Justice in signatory countries. Article 13 attempts to ease the burden of passing requests/communications through ordinary diplomatic channels, thereby increasing the efficacy of cooperation. Article 14 establishes a standing body to coordinate/track investigations into offenses under the Convention. It also assists cross-border cooperation by promoting regular contact between each domestic body as well as establishing a standing body of knowledge about previous offenders/cases. Article 15 provides for the transfer of information about offenders between the bodies established under Article 14. It covers the particulars of an offense, attempts to commit an offense, investigations into an offense, the movements of persons, and biodata of offenders/suspected offenders. It is possible the effectiveness of this Article may be circumscribed by its first clause: i.e. "to the extent permitted by domestic law and to the extent which the authorities … judge desirable." Its success also depends upon each State having formed a working (and thorough) central body.

[32] Ibid. at Arts. 8 and 9.

[33] Ibid. at Art. 14.

[34] Ibid. at Art. 5.

[35] 1949 Trafficking Convention, Article 18 authorizes officials to take declarations from "alien" prostitutes to establish their identity/civil status/reasons for leaving their country of origin, with the view to eventual repatriation. This information is to be communicated to officials from the State of origin. While this article may assist in cross-border cooperation, it may also endanger/frighten victims of trafficking who do not want officials in their home country to know of their whereabouts. It is unclear whether this information is to be included in the database/body of knowledge set out in Article 4.

[36] Ibid. at Art. 16.

[37] Ibid. at Art. 19(1).

[38] Ibid. at Art. 19(2). As most trafficked persons can be presumed to be in an irregular migration situation, this clause would allow States to deport victims.

range of measures to be taken by States Parties to prevent trafficking and prostitution, including provision of public information warning of the dangers of trafficking;[39] supervision of employment agencies;[40] railway stations, airports, and other public places;[41] and regulation of immigration and emigration.[42]

The Convention attracted and has retained a measure of political support from some States and sectors of civil society. However, it has also come under considerable and wide-ranging attack. Many human rights activists and States that operate systems of legalized, licensed, or otherwise regulated prostitution have criticized this instrument for not focusing sufficiently or solely on the more serious, coercive forms of sexual exploitation and for failing to distinguish between consensual and forced prostitution.[43] It has also been noted that the Convention does not cover contemporary forms of sexual exploitation[44] and provides no protection against the coerced or fraudulent movement of individuals into sectors other than prostitution.[45] The trenchant critique offered in 2000 by the UN Special Rapporteur on Violence against Women is representative of this position:

> The 1949 Convention has proved ineffective in protecting the rights of trafficked women and combating trafficking. The Convention does not take a human rights approach. It does not regard women as independent actors endowed with rights and reason; rather, the Convention views them as vulnerable beings in need of protection from the "evils of prostitution". As such, the 1949 Convention does very little to protect women from and provide remedies for the human rights violations committed in the course of trafficking, thereby

---

[39] Ibid. at Art. 17(2).

[40] Ibid. at Art. 20.

[41] Ibid. at Art. 17(3).

[42] Ibid. at Art. 17(1).

[43] L. Chew, *Programme Consultation Meeting on the Protection of Domestic Workers Against the Threat of Forced Labour and Trafficking* (Anti-Slavery International, 2003), at 25, 35; UN Commission on Human Rights, "Report of the Special Rapporteur, Ms. Radhika Coomaraswamy, on violence against women, its causes and consequences, on trafficking in women, women's migration and violence against women," UN Doc. E/CN.4/2000/68, Feb. 29, 2000 (Coomaraswamy, "Report," UN Doc. E/CN.4/2000/68), at para. 22; P. Saunders, "Working on the Inside: Migration, Sex Work and Trafficking in Persons," (2000) 11(2) *Legal Link* 44; A. Derks, "From White Slaves to Trafficking Survivors: Notes on the Trafficking Debate," paper presented at the Conference on Migration and Development, May 4–5, 2000; J. Bindman and J. Doezema, "Redefining Prostitution as Sex Work on the International Agenda," (Anti-Slavery International, 1997), at Section 2; N.V. Demleitner, "Forced Prostitution: Naming an International Offence," (1994) 18 *Fordham International Law Journal* 163, at 174 ("[w]hile the title of the ... Convention speaks of the 'exploitation of prostitution,' the text tends to refer solely to prostitution. This created a certain degree of ideological confusion, since the [1949] Convention's focus remained ambiguous as to whether all kinds of prostitution or only forced prostitution were at issue").

[44] L. Reanda, "Prostitution as a Human Rights Question," (1991) 13 *Human Rights Quarterly* 202, at 210.

[45] K. Knaus, A. Kartusch and G. Reiter, "Combat of Trafficking in Women for the Purpose of Forced Prostitution" (Institute for Human Rights, 2000) (Knaus, Kartusch and Reiter, "Combat of Trafficking"), at 16.

increasing trafficked women's marginalization and vulnerability to human rights violations.[46]

Even those who support the Convention's abolitionist perspective have, on occasion, held it responsible for helping legitimize sexual exploitation by obscuring the manner in which prostitution violates women's rights and by ignoring the role of prostitution in the overall subordination of women in society.[47] All commentators appear to agree with the UN's own assessment that the enforcement mechanism under the Convention (annual reports to the UN Secretary-General to be published periodically)[48] is extremely weak.[49]

Despite these trenchant criticisms, the Convention survived as the only specialist treaty on trafficking for more than half a century, and thereby as the primary source of reference and authority on this matter. For example, the Beijing Platform for Action that emerged from the 1995 World Conference on Women contains detailed and specific references to the Convention, including calls for review and strengthening of its implementation.[50] Interest in the Convention was revived in the last years of the twentieth century as a result of efforts to develop another international legal instrument on trafficking (discussed further in this chapter).

It is important to consider the possibility that the 1949 Convention will, in time, become obsolete. In terms of international treaty law, this situation is generally referred to as *desuetude*. A treaty falls into *desuetude* when its nonapplication over a period of time indicates an intention by the parties to let it lapse.[51] The consent of the parties to abandon a treaty is to be implied from their conduct in relation to that

---

[46] Coomaraswamy, "Report," UN Doc. E/CN.4/2000/68, at para. 22.

[47] Statement of the Representative of UNESCO to the 1991 session of the Working Group on Contemporary Forms of Slavery, in UN Doc. E/CN.4/Sub.2/1991/41, 1991, at 38. See also *Penn State Report*, at 8–11.

[48] Since 1974, States Parties have been required to submit these reports to the Sub-Commission on Prevention of Discrimination and Protection of Minorities (now the Sub-Commission on the Protection and Promotion of Human Rights): ECOSOC Decision 16 (LVI), UN Doc. E/5514, May 17, 1974. These reports have generally been received by the now-defunct Working Group on Contemporary Forms of Slavery, which was not empowered to take any action on them. The mandate of the Special Rapporteur on Contemporary Forms of Slavery, established in 2007 to replace the Working Group, does not refer to the 1949 Convention: UN Human Rights Council, "Special Rapporteur on contemporary forms of slavery," UN Doc. A/HRC/Res/6/14, Sept. 28, 2007.

[49] In 1996, the Secretary-General proposed that the reporting problems under the 1949 Trafficking Convention be at least partially addressed by States, including information on measures taken to address trafficking in their reports to the Committee on the Elimination of Discrimination against Women: "Traffic in Women and Girls: Report of the Secretary-General," UN Doc. A/51/309, Aug. 27, 1996, at para. 42.

[50] "Beijing Declaration and Platform for Action," Fourth World Conference on Women, UN Doc. A/CONF.177/20 and UN Doc. A/CONF.177/20/Add.1, Sept. 15, 1995 (Beijing Declaration and Platform for Action), at para 122.

[51] See, generally, N. Kontou, *The Termination and Review of Treaties in the Light of New Customary International Law* (1994), at 25–27.

treaty.[52] In the present case, it would be necessary to identify a range of actions and inactions that, taken together, demonstrate the collective disregard of States Parties for the provisions of the 1949 Convention. From that perspective, the signals are mixed. Certainly the adoption of a new, not wholly consistent treaty on the same subject matter is highly relevant. The absence of any apparent link between the 1949 Convention and recent legal developments is also significant,[53] as is the failure of the United Nations to provide for continuity of monitoring functions following the abolition of the Convention's de facto guardian, the Working Group on Contemporary Forms of Slavery.[54] These indications that the 1949 Convention has been eclipsed, if not fully obliterated, by its successor treaty must be weighed against the fact that it managed to attract seven new States Parties during the period 2002–8. Ultimately, it is the nature of the treaty itself that is likely to render problematic any charge of termination through *desuetude*. The absence of any significant reporting or oversight mechanism will make the task of implying consent (or absence of consent) through behavior particularly difficult.

There is also the question of compatibility between the 1949 Convention and subsequent instruments, in particular the Trafficking Protocol[55] and the European Trafficking Convention.[56] International legal rules regarding application of successive treaties relating to the same subject matter are laid down in the Vienna Convention on the Law of Treaties as follows:[57]

- When all the parties to the earlier treaty [1949 Convention] are parties also to the later treaty [in this case, the Trafficking Protocol and/or the European Trafficking Convention], but the earlier treaty is not terminated or suspended in accordance with the relevant international legal rules, the earlier treaty applies only to the extent that its provisions are compatible with those of the later treaty.

---

[52] Ibid. at 25–26, citing the International Law Commission and the International Court of Justice in the *Nuclear Tests Cases* (Australia v. France) Request for Interim Measures, 1973 and Merits, 1974.

[53] For example, the European Convention on Trafficking does not refer to the 1949 Convention despite its preamble "contain[ing] an enumeration of the most important international legal instruments which deal directly with trafficking": Council of Europe, *Explanatory Report on the Convention on Action against Trafficking in Human Beings*, ETS 197, 16.V.2005 (European Trafficking Convention Explanatory Report), at para. 49.

[54] See note 48 above.

[55] Protocol to Prevent, Suppress and Punish Trafficking in Persons, Especially Women and Children, supplementing the United Nations Convention against Transnational Organized Crime, done Nov. 15, 2000, GA Res. 55/25, Annex II, UN GAOR, 55th Sess., Supp. No. 49, at 53, UN Doc. A/45/49 (Vol. I) (2001), entered into force Dec. 25, 2003 (Trafficking Protocol).

[56] Council of Europe Convention on Action against Trafficking in Human Beings and its Explanatory Report, ETS 197, 16.V.2005, done May 16, 2005, entered into force Feb. 1, 2008 (European Trafficking Convention).

[57] Vienna Convention on the Law of Treaties, 1155 UNTS 331, done May 23, 1969, entered into force Jan. 27, 1980 (VCLT), at Art. 30. For a detailed examination of this provision, see M.E. Villiger, *Commentary on the 1969 Vienna Convention on the Law of Treaties* (2009), at 395–412 (chapter entitled "Application of Successive Treaties Relating to the Same Subject-Matter").

- When the parties to the later treaty do not include all the parties to the earlier one: (i) as between States Parties to both treaties, the same rule applies as above; (ii) as between a State Party to both the earlier and later treaties and a State Party to only one of the treaties, the treaty to which both States are parties governs their mutual rights and obligations.

The likelihood of a genuine conflict erupting over the 1949 Convention is remote. Despite its important place in ongoing political battles over prostitution, the Convention currently occupies a marginal position within the international legal framework around trafficking. As its successors consolidate their position, this situation is unlikely to change in its favor.

2.1.3. *The CEDAW Convention*

The 1949 Convention maintained its status as the last official word on trafficking in international law for thirty years. In 1979, the General Assembly of the United Nations adopted the Convention on the Elimination of All Forms of Discrimination Against Women (CEDAW), which obliges States Parties to take all appropriate legislative and other measures to "suppress all forms of traffic in women and exploitation of the prostitution of women."[58] The vagueness of this provision ("appropriate measures") makes it difficult to ascertain the precise nature of States Parties' obligations under this instrument. An additional difficulty is presented by the Convention failing to define "all forms of traffic in women" or "exploitation of the prostitution of women." The full *travaux préparatoires* to the Convention are unavailable, and existing information on its drafting history does not shed additional light on these points.[59]

The CEDAW Convention marks a departure from the earlier treaties on white slavery and trafficking, including the 1949 Convention, in several important respects. The focus on *exploitation* of prostitution can be read as a tacit rejection of the explicit abolitionist stance of the preceding instruments, including the 1949 Convention. This interpretation has been confirmed, albeit somewhat unevenly, through the work of the Committee established to oversee the implementation of the Convention (CEDAW Committee).[60] The CEDAW Convention also treads a new path by requiring States Parties to address not just the phenomena of trafficking

---

[58] Convention on the Elimination of All Forms of Discrimination Against Women, 1249 UNTS 13, done Dec. 13, 1979, entered into force Sept. 3, 1981 (CEDAW), at Art. 6.

[59] Parts of the *travaux préparatoires* were mislaid within the UN and have not been recovered. The most substantive, publicly available collection is L.A. Rehof, *Guide to the* Travaux Préparatoires *of the Convention on the Elimination of All Forms of Discrimination against Women* (1993).

[60] See J. Chuang, "CEDAW Article 6," in C. Chinkin, M. Freeman and B. Rudolf, eds., *Commentary to the Convention on the Elimination of All Forms of Discrimination against Women* (forthcoming 2010) (Chuang, "Article 6").

and exploitation of prostitution, but also the underlying causes.[61] In the matter of scope, it has been argued that the reference to *all forms of traffic* expands the prohibition contained in the 1949 Trafficking Convention to cover trafficking for other typical end purposes, such as forced labor or forced marriage as well as forced prostitution.[62] That interpretation has been confirmed by the work of the CEDAW Committee.[63] These and related issues are considered in more detail in the context of the following chapter's analysis of trafficking as a form of gender-based violence and discrimination against women.

2.1.4. *The Convention on the Rights of the Child and its Optional Protocol*

The Convention on the Rights of the Child (CRC),[64] adopted by the General Assembly in 1989, is the only contemporary international human rights treaty apart from the CEDAW Convention to refer explicitly to trafficking. As noted at various points throughout this study, the CRC provides a comprehensive framework for the protection of the rights and dignity of children as well as of their empowerment. As such, it should be considered, in its entirety, as a tool for understanding and responding to the trafficking and related exploitation of children.[65] Article 35 of that instrument requires States Parties to "take all appropriate national, bilateral and multilateral measures to prevent the abduction of, the sale of or traffic in children[66] for any purpose or in any form."[67] Under Article 34, children are to

---

[61] J. Connors, A. Byrnes and C. Beyani, *Assessing the Status of Women: A Guide to Reporting under the Convention on the Elimination of All Forms of Discrimination Against Women* (International Women's Rights Action Watch (IRWAW) USA and the Commonwealth Secretariat, 1996, 2nd edition), at 19.

[62] Knaus, Kartusch and Reiter, "Combat of Trafficking," at 17.

[63] Chuang, "Article 6."

[64] Convention on the Rights of the Child, 1577 UNTS 3, done Nov. 20, 1989, entered into force Sept. 2, 1990 (CRC).

[65] A UNICEF-sponsored report on children and prostitution has noted the importance of looking beyond those articles of the CRC that directly address the practice under consideration. The report notes that one of the major strengths of the CRC is its ability to be used as a framework for understanding and measuring child trafficking and related commercial sexual exploitation of children in the broadest possible context. Basic articles relating to definition of the child, children's identity, and dignity are critical in this regard as these are the aspects that are violated when trafficking-related exploitation takes place and "indeed the reasons why all 'protection' articles are necessary": J. Ennew, K. Gopal, J. Heeran, and H. Montgomery, *Children and Prostitution: How Can We Measure the Commercial Sexual Exploitation of Children? Literature Review and Annotated Bibliography*, (UNICEF, 2nd edition, 1996), at Part 2, 1. Other important provisions of the CRC from this perspective include those relating to nondiscrimination, consent, power, maturity, the best interests of the child, service provision, education, family support, community, and health care. See further the remainder of the UNICEF-sponsored report on the use of the Convention as a holistic tool for understanding and responding to sexual exploitation of children.

[66] The Convention defines "child" as any individual under the age of 18 unless majority is attained at an earlier age under domestic laws: CRC, at Art. 1.

[67] Ibid. at Art. 35. The terms "abduction," "sale" and "trafficking" are not defined in the Convention.

be protected from all forms of economic exploitation,[68] sexual exploitation, and sexual abuse.[69]

The CRC also requires States Parties to take all appropriate national, bilateral, and multilateral measures to prevent the inducement or coercion of a child to engage in any unlawful sexual activity; the exploitative use of children in prostitution or other unlawful sexual practices; the exploitative use of children in pornographic performances and materials;[70] and the illicit transfer and nonreturn of children abroad.[71] The CRC also requires States Parties to:

> take all appropriate measures to promote physical and psychological recovery and social integration of a child victim of ... any form of ... exploitation ... in an environment which fosters the health, self-respect and dignity of the child.[72]

Other relevant provisions include the obligation on States Parties to ensure that a child is not separated from his or her guardians against his or her will, except where such separation is determined to be in the best interests of the child;[73] and the right of a child residing in a different State from her or his parents to leave any country, including his or her own, and to enter his or her own country.[74]

The Committee on the Rights of the Child, established under the CRC to monitor its implementation, has regularly raised and pronounced on trafficking-related issues in its concluding observations on States Parties' reports, and have found trafficking and child prostitution to directly implicate both Articles 34 and 35 of the CRC.[75] While the emphasis has been firmly on trafficking for sexual exploitation, the Committee has also (and increasingly) recognized the phenomenon of trafficking for economic exploitation, including forced and bonded labor, and trafficking for adoption.[76]

---

[68] Ibid. at Art. 32.

[69] Ibid. at Art. 34.

[70] Ibid. at Arts. 19 and 34.

[71] Ibid. at Art. 11.

[72] Ibid. at Art. 39.

[73] Ibid. at Art. 9.

[74] Ibid. at Art. 10(2).

[75] Specific references to the work of the Committee in this area are provided throughout this book in the context of discussion on particular rights and obligations. See especially the references in Chapter 5.5.

[76] See, for example, UN Committee on the Rights of the Child, "Concluding Observations: Democratic Republic of the Congo," UN Doc. CRC/C/COD/CO/2, Feb. 10, 2009, at paras. 82–83 (sexual and economic exploitation); "Concluding Observations: Moldova," UN Doc. CRC/C/MDA/CO/3, Jan. 30, 2009, at para. 68 (sexual and economic exploitation); "Concluding Observations: Chile," UN Doc. CRC/C/OPSC/CHL/CO/1, Feb. 18, 2008, at para. 23 (forced labor); "Concluding Observations: Sweden," UN Doc. CRC/C/OPAC/SWE/CO/1, June 8, 2007, at para. 6 (war service and forced labor); "Concluding Observations: Kenya," UN Doc. CRC/C/KEN/CO/2, Feb. 2, 2007, at para. 40 (adoption); "Concluding Observations: Malaysia," UN Doc. CRC/C/MYS/CO/1, Feb. 2, 2007, at para. 95 (sexual exploitation, forced labor, and adoption).

Despite some opposition, including from the CRC Committee itself,[77] an Optional Protocol to the CRC, purporting to extend the scope and reach of the Convention's provisions in relation to sale of children, child prostitution, and child pornography, was concluded through the United Nations Commission on Human Rights in 2000.[78] The CRC Protocol entered into force in early 2002 and, as of June 2010, had 137 States Parties. It goes beyond the CRC in several important respects, in particular, by adopting an explicitly criminal justice approach to the issue and detailing obligations accordingly. In that sense, the CRC Protocol has much in common with the criminal justice instruments discussed in the following section. States Parties are, for example, required to prohibit, criminalize, and appropriately punish the relevant acts;[79] to establish appropriate jurisdiction over offenses; and to extradite offenders.[80] Other provisions deal with mutual legal assistance[81] and confiscation of proceeds.[82] The Protocol details the rights of child victims and witnesses in the criminal justice process and the protections to be afforded them.[83] It also sets out specific obligations with regard to prevention[84] and international cooperation.[85]

For present purposes, it is important to establish the relevance of the CRC Protocol for the issue of trafficking. The CRC Protocol does not deal specifically with this issue, referring to trafficking only in its preamble. It does, however, provide a definition of "sale of children" that is sufficiently broad to encompass most situations in which children are trafficked.[86] The link is confirmed by the practice of the CRC Committee, which reveals a marked tendency to associate sale of children with trafficking.[87] The Committee has, however, been careful to maintain a

---

[77] The Committee argued that the CRC already provided an appropriate framework for dealing with these issues, and that efforts would be better concentrated on the implementation of the existing instruments rather than on developing a new treaty: U. Cedrangolo, "The Optional Protocol to the Convention on the Rights of the Child on the Sale of Children, Child Prostitution and Child Pornography and the Jurisprudence of the Committee on the Rights of the Child" (UNICEF: Innocenti Research Paper, April 2009) (Cedrangolo, "The Optional Protocol"), at 7.

[78] Optional Protocol to the Child Convention on the Sale of Children, Child Prostitution and Child Pornography, GA Res. 54/263, Annex I, 54 UN GAOR Supp. (No. 49), 7, UN Doc. A/54/49, Vol. III (2000), done May 25, 2000, entered into force Jan. 18, 2002 (CRC Optional Protocol).

[79] Ibid. at Arts. 1, 3.

[80] Ibid. at Arts. 4–5. Note that Article 4(3) includes a requirement of *aut dedere aut judicare* (extradite or prosecute).

[81] Ibid. at Art. 6.

[82] Ibid. at Art. 7.

[83] Ibid. at Arts. 8, 9(4).

[84] Ibid. at Art. 9.

[85] Ibid. at Art. 10.

[86] The CRC Optional Protocol at Article 2 defines sale of children as "any act or transaction whereby a child is transferred by any person or group of persons to another for remuneration or any other consideration."

[87] See, for example, UN Committee on the Rights of the Child, "General Comment No. 6: Treatment of Unaccompanied and Separated Children Outside Their Country of Origin," UN Doc. CRC/GC/2005/6, June 3, 2005, at para. 2, where conversely the sale of children by parents is listed as an example of trafficking. See also the linkage of sale and trafficking of children in: UN Committee

distinction between the two concepts, noting, for example, that some cases of sale of children may not involve the element of exploitation that is essential to the definition of trafficking.[88] On this point, Cedrangolo concludes that while sale of children and trafficking will coincide when the sale is made for any consideration and involving an exploitative purpose, not all cases of trafficking involving children constitute acts of sale of children.[89]

2.2. TRAFFICKING IN TRANSNATIONAL CRIMINAL LAW

As noted in the introduction, the 1990s marked an important shift in the international legal framework around trafficking as the issue began to be considered from perspectives other than human rights. Of particular significance was the link established between trafficking and the newly identified international threats of "migrant smuggling" and transnational organized crime. These changes led eventually to the development of a new treaty that has been acknowledged by States to be "the principal legally binding global instrument to combat trafficking in persons."[90] The present section considers that treaty, the Trafficking Protocol, as well as its parent instrument, the UN Convention against Transnational Organized Crime, in detail. It also analyzes the origins and principal features of the Migrant Smuggling Protocol, recognizing the "substantial overlap in the conduct involved in the two offences."[91]

Proposals for an international treaty on transnational organized crime were first tabled at the World Ministerial Conference on Organized Transnational Crime in Naples, Italy, in November 1994.[92] While not received enthusiastically by all

---

on the Rights of the Child, "Concluding Observations: Sierra Leone," UN Doc. CRC/C/SLE/CO/2, June 6, 2008, at para. 75; UN Committee on the Rights of the Child, "Concluding Observations: Kuwait," UN Doc. CRC/C/OPSC/KWT/CO/1, Feb. 1, 2008, at para. 17; UN Committee on the Rights of the Child, "Concluding Observations: Sudan," UN Doc. CRC/C/OPSC/SDN/CO/1, June 8. 2007, at para. 39; UN Committee on the Rights of the Child, "Concluding Observations: Malaysia," UN Doc. CRC/C/MYS/CO/1, Feb. 2, 2007, at para. 95; UN Committee on the Rights of the Child, "Concluding Observations: Syrian Arab Republic," UN Doc. CRC/C/OPSC/SYR/CO/1, Oct. 31, 2006, at para. 28; UN Committee on the Rights of the Child, "Concluding Observations: China," UN Doc. CRC/C/OPSC/CHN/CO/1, Nov. 24, 2005, at para. 19.

[88] Cedrangolo, "The Optional Protocol", at 4.

[89] Ibid. Cedrangolo cautions, however, that trafficking may enter the purview of the Protocol by other means, for example, through its link with child prostitution and child pornography: ibid. at 10.

[90] Conference of Parties to the United Nations Convention on Transnational Organized Crime, Decision 4/4, "Trafficking in Human Beings," reproduced in Conference of Parties to the United Nations Convention on Transnational Organized Crime, "Report of the Conference of Parties to the United Nations Convention on Transnational Organized Crime on its fourth session, held in Vienna from 8 to 17 October 2008," UN Doc. CTOC/COP/2008/19, Dec. 1, 2008, at para. (d).

[91] UN Office on Drugs and Crime, *Legislative Guides for the Implementation of the United Nations Convention against Transnational Organized Crime and the Protocols Thereto*, UN Sales No. E.05.V.2 (2004) (*Legislative Guide*), at 340.

[92] On the history of United Nations engagement on this issue and on developments leading up to the establishment of the Ad Hoc Committee, see United Nations Office on Drugs and Crime,

States, the proposal was generally supported, and in late 1997, the United Nations General Assembly established an intergovernmental group of experts to prepare a preliminary draft.[93] Following receipt of the report of the group of experts,[94] the General Assembly decided to establish an open-ended, intergovernmental Ad Hoc Committee

> for the purpose of elaborating a comprehensive international convention against transnational crime and of discussing the elaboration, as appropriate, of international instruments addressing trafficking in women and children ... and illegal trafficking in, and transporting of migrants, including by sea.[95]

In October 2000, after only eleven sessions, the Ad Hoc Committee concluded its work.[96] The drafting process for both the Convention and its Protocols was highly participatory,[97] belying uninformed suggestions made subsequently that western States, nursing specific agendas, were able to intimidate or trick their less sophisticated rivals into accepting a set of agreements they did not particularly want.[98]

Travaux Préparatoires of the Negotiations for the Elaboration of the United Nations Convention against Transnational Organized Crime and the Protocols Thereto (2006) (Travaux Préparatoires *for the Organized Crime Convention and Protocols*), at ix–xxvi. For a more informal analysis of this period, see D. Vlassis, "The UN Convention Against Transnational Organized Crime," in M.R. Berdal and M. Serrano eds., *Transnational Organized Crime and International Security: Business as Usual?* 83 (2002) (Vlassis, "The UN Convention Against Transnational Organized Crime"), at 85; and D. Vlassis, *The Global Situation of Transnational Organized Crime, the Decision of the International Community to Develop an International Convention and the Negotiation Process,* in UN Asia and Far East Institute for the Prevention of Crime and the Treatment of Offenders, Annual Report and Resource Materials Series No. 59 (Vlassis, UNAFEI), at 475, 492. See also D. McClean, *Transnational Organized Crime: A Commentary on the UN Convention and its Protocols* (2007) (McClean, *Transnational Organized Crime*), esp. at 2–7.

93 UN General Assembly, "Follow-up to the Naples Political Declaration and Global Action Plan against Organized Transnational Crime," UN Doc. A/RES/52/85, Dec. 12, 1997.

94 *Report of the Meeting of the Inter-Sessional Open-Ended Intergovernmental Group of Experts on the Elaboration of a Preliminary Draft of a Possible Comprehensive International Convention against Organised Transnational Crime,* UN Doc. E/CN.15/1998/5 (Warsaw, Feb. 2–6, 1998). Note that the idea of additional protocols was first discussed in this forum. On the question of whether specific offenses should be included in the draft convention, the group concluded that that the negotiating process would be simplified if such offenses were dealt with separately: ibid. at para. 10(b).

95 UN General Assembly, "Transnational Organized Crime," UN Doc. A/RES/53/111, Jan. 20, 1999.

96 For observations on the drafting process, see McClean, *Transnational Organized Crime*, at 11–15; Vlassis, "The UN Convention Against Transnational Organized Crime"; and Vlassis, UNAFEI.

97 Over 100 States were actively involved in the negotiation process: McClean, *Transnational Organized Crime*, at 12.

98 This claim was made by J.C. Hathaway, "The Human Rights Quagmire of Human Trafficking," (2008) 49(1) *Virginia Journal of International Law* 1, and refuted by the present author in her response published in the same journal, A.T. Gallagher, "Human Rights and Human Trafficking: Quagmire or Firm Ground? A Response to James Hathaway," (2009) 49(4) *Virginia Journal of International Law* 789 (Gallagher, "Human Rights and Human Trafficking: Quagmire or Firm Ground?"). Note that according to the Secretary of the drafting group, the Western group did not particularly want a convention on transnational organized crime. "The vast majority of developing countries favored the idea of a new convention. Dealing with transnational crime in a global forum such as the UN

The centerpiece of the new regime is the United Nations Convention against Transnational Organized Crime (Organized Crime Convention)[99]. The Organized Crime Convention is supplemented by three additional treaties (Protocols), dealing respectively with Smuggling of Migrants;[100] Trafficking in Persons, Especially Women and Children; and Trafficking in Firearms.[101] The first three of these instruments were adopted by the General Assembly in November 2000[102] and opened for signature at a high-level intergovernmental conference convened in Palermo, Italy, in December 2000. The Convention entered into force on September 29, 2003 and the Trafficking Protocol on December 25, 2003. As of June 2010, the Convention had attracted 155 States Parties and the Trafficking Protocol 137 States Parties. The Migrant Smuggling Protocol, with 123 States Parties as of June 2010, entered into force on January 28, 2004.

The significance of these developments should not be underestimated. The Vienna Process, as it came to be known, represented the first serious attempt by the international community to invoke international law as a weapon against transnational organized crime. Perhaps even more notable was the selection of trafficking and migrant smuggling as the subjects of additional agreements. Both issues were, at

offered developing countries relative parity with their Western counterparts because the UN tended to prefer consensus decisionmaking ... Smaller countries lack the resources and negotiating power to influence the content of bilateral agreements in criminal matters. Developing states thus threw their support behind a new convention." Vlassis, "The UN Convention against Transnational Organized Crime," at 83, 85. Vlassis refers to the first meeting of what was to become the highly influential and inclusive "Friends of the Chair" in 1998: "[t]his meeting marked the formation of a core group of delegates, experts in their fields ... The core group was highly participatory, in the sense that it included representatives from virtually all regions and all systems of the world." Ibid. at 90. Berdal and Serrano also reject any simplistic assessment of power relations and influence within the drafting group: "[t]he energy and urgency that characterized the process was not limited to the contribution of dominant powers, but was also the result of 'entrepreneurial middle-power action' by States as diverse as Italy, Colombia, Poland and Argentina. The distinct interests of these countries was reflected not only in the three additional protocols to the UN Convention, but also in the emphasis placed upon the need to financially assist developing countries in order to bolster their capacity to prevent and combat transnational organized crime." M.R. Berdal and M. Serrano, "Introduction" in M.R. Berdal and M. Serrano eds., *Transnational Organized Crime and International Security: Business as Usual?* 1 (2002), at 4.

[99] United Nations Convention Against Transnational Organized Crime, 2225 UNTS 209, done Nov. 15, 2000, entered into force Sept. 29, 2003 (Organized Crime Convention).

[100] Protocol against the Smuggling of Migrants by Land, Sea and Air, supplementing the United Nations Convention against Transnational Organized Crime, done Nov. 15, 2000, GA Res. 55/25, Annex III, UN GAOR, 55th Sess., Supp. No. 49, at 62, UN Doc. A/45/49 (Vol. I) (2001), entered into force Jan. 28, 2004 (Migrant Smuggling Protocol).

[101] Protocol against the Illicit Manufacturing of and Trafficking in Firearms, Their Parts and Components and Ammunition, supplementing the United Nations Convention against Transnational Organized Crime GA Res. 255, Nov. 15, 2000, UN Doc. A/RES/55/255 (2001), done May 31, 2001, entered into force July 3, 2005 (Firearms Protocol).

[102] UN General Assembly, *Report of the Ad Hoc Committee on the Elaboration of a Convention against Transnational Organized Crime on the work of its first to eleventh sessions*, UN Doc. A/55/383, Nov. 2, 2000; "United Nations Convention against Transnational Organized Crime," UN Doc. A/RES/55/25, Jan. 8, 2001.

the time of drafting, high on the international political agenda. While human rights concerns may have provided some impetus (or cover) for collective action, it was clearly the sovereignty/security issues surrounding trafficking and migrant smuggling, as well as the perceived link with organized criminal groups operating across national borders, that provided the true driving force behind such efforts.[103]

Before considering the substantive provisions of the Convention and its Protocols, it is relevant to briefly touch on several aspects of the drafting process that were both unusual and influential. First, the level of civil society participation, particularly in the trafficking negotiations, was unprecedented. Unlike its human rights counterpart, the crime prevention and criminal justice system of the United Nations is not of great interest to the international NGO community. The annual sessions of the UN Crime Commission are almost devoid of NGO input, and the deliberations of the Commission are very rarely exposed to civil society scrutiny. In the context of protocol negotiations, government delegations and the Secretariat were forced to deal with a swelling group of vocal and increasingly well-organized NGOs. While many of the organizations represented in Vienna had little international lobbying experience, the great number of submissions and interventions made by them suggest that this was not an obstacle to action. As a group, the NGOs focused almost exclusively on the Trafficking Protocol, and only passing attention was paid to the issue of migrant smuggling. Of particular interest to NGOs was the issue of prostitution and the way in which it was to be dealt with through the definition of trafficking.[104]

Another very unusual aspect of the negotiations was the sustained involvement of an informal group of intergovernmental agencies and instrumentalities – the UN High Commissioner for Human Rights, the United Nations Children's Fund, the International Organization for Migration, the UN High Commissioner for Refugees, and, on one occasion, the UN Special Rapporteur on Violence Against Women. The aim of the this coalition ("the Inter-Agency Group") was to ensure that both Protocols represented a net advance for the human rights of women, children, asylum-seekers, refugees, and migrants. The High Commissioner for Human Rights was particularly active, submitting, as an official document, a detailed examination of both Protocols, making a number of oral interventions, and coordinating a joint intervention on behalf of the concerned international agencies.

While it is difficult to gauge the effect of these actions with any certainty, a close analysis of the negotiations supports a conclusion that the sustained and active IGO/NGO involvement had a strong educative effect on members of the drafting group. A number of delegations freely admitted their lack of legal expertise on

---

[103] See generally Gallagher, "Human Rights and Human Trafficking: Quagmire or Firm Ground?" at 833–841.

[104] See further, A.T. Gallagher, "Human Rights and the New UN Protocols on Trafficking and Migrant Smuggling: A Preliminary Analysis," (2001) 23 *Human Rights Quarterly* 975, at 1002.

the trafficking issue and their unfamiliarity with the trafficking phenomenon. Both intergovernmental agencies and NGOs, through their submissions and informal lobbying efforts, went at least some way toward filling this gap, and their efforts certainly contributed to the rapid pace of negotiations. In addition, sustained pressure from these quarters clearly influenced the decision of States to include/adopt: (1) a coercion-based definition of trafficking that recognizes a number of end purposes in addition to sexual exploitation; (2) specific references to international law including human rights law, refugee law, and humanitarian law (both Protocols); (3) an anti-discrimination clause (both Protocols); and (4) the protection of rights as a principal objective (both Protocols).

Levels of Obligation. The Convention and its Protocols create varying levels of legal obligation. Some provisions are mandatory;[105] some require either consideration or positive effort;[106] and others are entirely optional.[107] While no longer an unusual feature of modern international treaty law,[108] the existence of "soft obligations" presents certain interpretation challenges that are addressed in Chapter 2.4.3, as well as in the following chapters, in the specific context in which they arise.

Interpretative Materials. A legal analysis of the Convention and its Protocols is facilitated by the existence of several kinds of interpretative material. The official records (*travaux préparatoires*) of the negotiation process for all three instruments were released in 2006[109] and, in accordance with the Vienna Convention on the Law of Treaties, have been used in the present volume as a secondary source in interpreting the text.[110] Two years earlier, the United Nations Office for Drugs and Crime issued a Legislative Guide to the Convention and its Protocols. While not intended to be authoritative or otherwise deliver a definitive legal interpretation

---

[105] For example, "[e]ach State Party shall adopt such measures as may be necessary to establish its jurisdiction over the offences established in accordance with articles 5, 6, 8, and 23 of this Convention": Organized Crime Convention, at Art. 15(1).

[106] For example, "[e]ach State Party shall endeavour to provide for the physical safety of victims of trafficking while they are within its territory": Trafficking Protocol, at Art. 6(5).

[107] For example, "States Parties may consider the possibility of requiring that an offender demonstrate the lawful origin of alleged proceeds of crime or other property liable to confiscation, to the extent that such a requirement is consistent with the principles of their domestic law and with the nature of the judicial and other proceedings": Organized Crime Convention, at Art. 12(7).

[108] See, for example, Convention on Access to Information, Public Participation in Decision-Making and Access to Justice in Environmental Matters, 2161 UNTS 447, done June 25, 1998, entered into force Oct. 30, 2001; Framework Convention on Climate Change, 1771 UNTS 107, done May 9, 1992, entered into force Mar. 21, 1994; Convention Concerning the Protection of the World Cultural and Natural Heritage, 1037 UNTS 151, done Nov. 16. 1972, entered into force Dec. 17, 1975. See also J. d'Aspremont, "Softness in International Law: A Self-Serving Quest for New Legal Materials," (2008) 19 *European Journal of International Law* 1075 (d'Aspremont, "Softness in International Law").

[109] Travaux Préparatoires *for the Organized Crime Convention and Protocols.*

[110] VCLT, at Arts. 31–32.

of these instruments,[111] the Guide is nevertheless a useful source of additional insight, particularly with regard to legislative implementation obligations.[112] Finally, in an apparent effort to facilitate negotiations, the drafters of the Convention and Protocols issued more than one hundred "Interpretative Notes." These notes, which form part of the *travaux préparatoires*, cover phrases, paragraphs, and whole articles and, by showing the reasoning behind a particular approach, can promote uniform interpretation of the text.[113]

The Relationship between the Convention and its Protocols. The general rules governing the relationship between the Convention and its Protocols are set out in the Convention itself, with additional guidance provided by particular provisions of the Protocols. When read together, it is possible to identify four basic principles. First, as the Protocols were not intended to become stand-alone treaties, States must ratify the Convention before ratifying any of its Protocols.[114] A State Party to the Convention is not bound by a Protocol unless it also becomes party to that Protocol.[115] Second, the Convention and its Protocols must be interpreted together, taking into account their stated purposes.[116] Third, the provisions of the Convention apply, *mutatis mutandis*, to the Protocols.[117] This means that in applying the Convention to the Protocols, modifications of interpretation or application should be made only

---

[111] *Legislative Guide*, at xv–xvi.

[112] Note that additional guidance has subsequently been provided by the United Nations in the form of draft model laws relating to both the Trafficking and Migrant Smuggling Protocols: United Nations Office on Drugs and Crime, *Model Law on Trafficking in Persons*, UN Sales No. E.09.V.11 (2009) (UNODC Model Law); United Nations Office on Drugs and Crime, *Model Law against Smuggling in Migrants* (forthcoming, 2010).

[113] McClean, *Transnational Organized Crime*, at 13. However, McClean also observes that this approach is not without its problems. Interpretative Notes were used by the Ad Hoc Committee as a device to speed up negotiations by placating minority views, thereby distorting the real weight of that view. McClean also points out that in some cases, the relevant Interpretative Note is not fully consistent with the text, thereby creating uncertainty in interpretation: ibid. The Interpretative Notes are contained in UN General Assembly, Ad Hoc Committee on the Elaboration of a Convention Against Transnational Organized Crime, "Report of the Ad Hoc Committee on the Elaboration of a Convention Against Transnational Organized Crime on the Work of its First to Eleventh Sessions, Addendum: Interpretative Notes for the Official Records (*Travaux Préparatoires*) of the Negotiation of the United Nations Convention Against Transnational Organized Crime and the Protocols Thereto," UN Doc. A/55/383/Add.1, Nov. 3, 2000. All Interpretative Notes are also included in the Travaux Préparatoires *for the Organized Crime Convention and Protocols*. For ease of reference, throughout this study, references to Interpretative Notes have been given as references to the part of the *Travaux Préparatoires* in which they appear.

[114] Organized Crime Convention, at Art. 37(2). See also *Legislative Guide*, at 253. As the *Legislative Guide* points out, this provision ensures that in a case arising under one of the Protocols to which the States concerned are parties, all of the general provisions of the Convention (for example, relating to mutual legal assistance and protection of victims) will also be available and applicable.

[115] Organized Crime Convention, at Art. 37(3).

[116] Ibid. at Art. 37(4); Trafficking Protocol, at Art. 1(1). See further, *Legislative Guide*, at 253–255.

[117] Trafficking Protocol, at Art. 1(2).

when and to the extent that they are necessary.[118] Fourth, offenses established by the Protocols are to be regarded as offenses established by the Convention. As a result, the Convention's general provisions, for example on matters such as victim protection, law enforcement cooperation, mutual legal assistance, and extradition are available and applicable to States in their implementation of the more specific and detailed provisions of the Protocols.[119]

2.2.1. *The Organized Crime Convention*

The Organized Crime Convention is essentially an instrument of international cooperation, its stated purpose being to promote interstate cooperation in order to combat transnational organized crime more effectively.[120] In this respect, its goal is to enlarge the number of States taking effective measures against transnational crime and to forge and strengthen cross-border links.[121] More specifically, the Convention seeks to eliminate "safe havens" where organized criminal activities or the concealment of evidence or profits can take place by promoting the adoption of basic minimum measures.[122]

There are three prerequisites for application of the Convention to a particular situation. First, the relevant offense must have some kind of transnational aspect.[123] Second, it must involve an organized criminal group.[124] Third, it must constitute

---

[118] *Legislative Guide*, at 254. The Interpretive Note on Article 1 of the Trafficking Protocol states that: "[t]his paragraph was adopted on the understanding that the words 'mutatis mutandis' meant 'with such modifications as circumstances require' or 'with the necessary modifications'. Provisions of the United Nations Convention Against Transnational Organized Crime that are applied to the Protocol under this article would consequently be modified or interpreted so as to have the same essential meaning or effect in the Protocol as in the Convention": Travaux Préparatoires *for the Organized Crime Convention and Protocols*, at 330.

[119] Trafficking Protocol, at Art. 1(3). See also *Legislative Guide*, at 254.

[120] Organized Crime Convention, at Art. 1. Note there is no preamble. McClean refers to the General Assembly resolution adopting the Convention ("United Nations Convention against Transnational Organized Crime," UN Doc. A/RES/55/25, Jan. 8, 2001) for additional insight into its purpose. McClean, *Transnational Organized Crime*, at 35–36.

[121] *Legislative Guide*, at xvii–xviii.

[122] United Nations Office for Drug Control and Crime Prevention, "Summary of the United Nations Convention Against Transnational Organized Crime and Protocols Thereto," December 2000.

[123] Organized Crime Convention, at Art. 3(1). The Convention defines a transnational offense as one which is committed in more than one State; or committed in one State but substantially planned, directed, or controlled in another State; or committed in one State but involving an organized criminal group operating in more than one State: or committed in one State but having substantial effects on another State: ibid. at Art. 3(2).

[124] Ibid. at Art. 3(1). An organized criminal group is defined as "a structured group of three or more persons existing for a period of time and acting in concert with the aim of committing one or more serious crimes or offences ... in order to obtain, directly or indirectly, a financial or other material benefit": ibid. at Art. 2(a). An Interpretative Note confirms that "financial or other benefit" is to be understood broadly to include, for example, personal or sexual gratification: Travaux Préparatoires *for the Organized Crime Convention and Protocols*, at 17. See also ibid. at 12, 14–15. On the function and status of the Interpretative Notes to the Organized Crime Convention and its Protocols, see McClean, *Transnational Organized Crime*, at 13.

a "serious crime."[125] As all three elements are defined very broadly, States are able to use this instrument to address a wide range of contemporary criminal activity including trafficking and related exploitation as well as migrant smuggling.[126] This is especially important in view of the fact that States may become party to the Convention without having to ratify any or all of the Protocols.[127]

The core obligation of the Convention is that of criminalization. States Parties are required to criminalize a range of offenses, whether committed by individuals or corporate entities, including: participation in an organized criminal group;[128] public sector corruption;[129] laundering of the proceeds of crime;[130] and obstruction of justice.[131] These offenses are also to be made subject to sanctions that take into account the gravity of the offense.[132] Critically, the obligation of criminalization stands independently of the transnational nature or the involvement of an organized criminal group.[133] In other words, these are not to be considered elements of the offense for criminalization purposes.[134]

A lack of communication and cooperation between national law enforcement authorities has been identified as one of the principal obstacles to effective action against transnational organized crime, including both trafficking and migrant smuggling. The Convention sets out a range of measures to be adopted by States Parties to enhance effective law enforcement in this area through, *inter alia*, improving information flows and enhancing coordination between relevant bodies.[135]

---

[125] Organized Crime Convention, at Art. 3(1)(b). "Serious crime" refers to conduct constituting a criminal offense punishable by a maximum deprivation of liberty of at least four years or a more serious penalty: ibid. at Art. 2(b). This definition is based on the results of a study of legislation in UN Member States contained in General Assembly, Ad Hoc Committee on the Elaboration of a Convention Against Transnational Organized Crime, "Analytical Study on Serious Crime," UN Docs. A/AC.254/22, Nov. 30, 1999; A/AC.254/22/Add.1, Dec. 13, 1999; A/AC.254/22/Corr.1, Dec. 16, 1999.

[126] For a trenchant critique of the breadth of these new international legal definitions, see V. Mitsilegas, "From National to Global, From Empirical to Legal: The Ambivalent Concept of Transnational Organized Crime," in M.E. Beare ed., *Critical Reflections on Transnational Organized Crime, Money Laundering and Corruption* (2005). See also the introduction by M.E. Beare in the same volume.

[127] Organized Crime Convention, at Art. 37(3).

[128] Ibid. at Art. 5.

[129] Ibid. at Art. 8. Corruption is not directly defined. Instead, States Parties are required to criminalize a range of conduct when committed intentionally, specifically "the promise, offering or giving to a public official, directly or indirectly, of an undue advantage, for the official himself or herself or another person or entity, in order that the official act or refrain from acting in the exercise of his or her duties" and "[t]he solicitation or acceptance by a public official, directly or indirectly, of an undue advantage for the official himself or herself or another person or entity, in order that the official act or refrain from acting in the exercise of his or her duties": ibid.

[130] Ibid. at Art. 6. "Proceeds of crime" is defined in Article 2(e).

[131] Ibid. at Art. 23.

[132] Ibid. at Art. 11(1).

[133] Ibid. at Art. 34(1). This provision does not apply to the extent that the Convention itself (at Art. 5) would require the involvement of an organized criminal group: ibid.

[134] Travaux Préparatoires *for the Organized Crime Convention and Protocols,* at 285.

[135] Organized Crime Convention, at Art. 26.

The practical application of these provisions is likely to be enhanced by the inclusion of a detailed legal framework on mutual legal assistance in investigations, prosecutions, and judicial proceedings in relation to applicable offenses.[136] The relevant provisions constitute, in effect, a mini-treaty that can be used by States as the legal basis of a request for mutual legal assistance for a range of purposes including the taking of evidence, effecting service of judicial documents, execution of searches, identification of the proceeds of crime, and production of information and documentation. States Parties are also encouraged to establish joint investigative bodies;[137] come to formal agreement on the use of special investigative techniques;[138] consider the transfer of criminal proceedings[139] and sentenced persons;[140] and facilitate extradition procedures for applicable offenses.[141] National law enforcement structures are also to be strengthened through education and training of relevant officials in order to prevent, detect, and control transnational organized crime.[142] States Parties are also to endeavor to take certain legal and financial steps to prevent transnational organized crime.[143] The reality that developing countries will require economic and technical assistance to fully implement the Convention's provisions is acknowledged in a detailed article that sets out a range of international cooperation measures including the establishment of a dedicated UN funding mechanism.[144]

The Convention contains several important provisions on victims of transnational organized crime. States Parties are to take appropriate measures within their means to provide assistance and protection to victims, particularly in cases of threat of retaliation or intimidation.[145] Appropriate procedures to provide access to compensation and restitution are to be established[146] and, subject to their domestic laws, States Parties are to enable the views and concerns of victims to be presented and considered during criminal proceedings against offenders.[147] Appropriate measures are also to be taken to protect witnesses (including victims who are witnesses) from potential retaliation or intimidation.[148] The only other provision touching upon victims relates to the requirement that States Parties participate, as appropriate, in international projects to prevent transnational organized crime, "for example, by

---

[136] Ibid. at Art. 18.
[137] Ibid. at Art. 19.
[138] Ibid. at Art. 20.
[139] Ibid. at Art. 21.
[140] Ibid. at Art. 17.
[141] Ibid. at Art. 16.
[142] Ibid. at Art. 29.
[143] Ibid. at Art. 31.
[144] Ibid. at Art. 30.
[145] Ibid. at Art. 25(1).
[146] Ibid. at Art. 25(2).
[147] Ibid. at Art. 25(3).
[148] Ibid. at Art. 24.

alleviating the circumstances that render socially marginalized groups vulnerable to the action of transnational organized crime."[149]

The Convention establishes a Conference of the Parties to promote and review its implementation as well as to improve more generally the capacity of States Parties to combat transnational organized crime.[150] The Conference of Parties is envisaged to have a special role in facilitating several of the cooperative measures envisaged under the Convention, including: the provision of technical assistance; information exchange; and cooperation with international and non-governmental organizations.[151] It is also responsible for periodic examination of the implementation of the Convention as well as making recommendations to improve the Convention and its implementation[152] and for setting up any additional review mechanisms that may be required.[153] The nature and functioning of the Convention's implementation machinery (which extends to its Protocols) is subject to detailed consideration in Chapter 9.

2.2.2. *The Trafficking Protocol*

The origins of the Trafficking Protocol can be traced back to Argentina's interest in the issue of trafficking in minors and its dissatisfaction with the slow progress on negotiating an additional protocol to the CRC to address child prostitution and child pornography.[154] Argentina was also concerned that a purely human rights perspective to this issue would be insufficient and accordingly lobbied strongly for trafficking to be dealt with as part of the broader international attack on transnational organized crime.[155] Argentina's proposal for a new convention against trafficking in minors was discussed at the 1997 session of the UN Commission on Crime Prevention and Criminal Justice.[156] Its timing was fortuitous. Powerful European institutions had recently decided to take the issue of trafficking seriously and were in the midst of developing detailed policies and responses.[157] The United States had also become active, with its President preparing to issue a detailed memorandum on measures to be taken by its own government to combat violence against women and trafficking

---

[149] Ibid. at Art. 31(7).

[150] Ibid. at Art. 32(1).

[151] Ibid. at Art. 32(3)(a)-(c).

[152] Ibid. at Art. 32(3)(d)-(e).

[153] Ibid. at Art. 32(4). Vlassis observes that this latter provision was an indirect reference to the system of "peer review": Vlassis, "The UN Convention Against Transnational Organized Crime," at 92.

[154] Vlassis, UNAFEI, at 492.

[155] Ibid.

[156] UN Commission on Human Rights, "Measures to Prevent Trafficking in Children, Report of the Secretary-General," UN Doc. E/CN.15/1997/12, Feb. 28, 1997.

[157] On the early European response, see "Trafficking in Women and Girls: Note prepared by the Office of the High Commissioner for Human Rights and the ECE Secretariat," UN Doc. E/ECE/RW.2/2000/3, Dec. 1, 1999, esp. at 29–35.

in women and girls.[158] A general awareness was also developing among an influential group of States of the need for a holistic approach where the crime control aspects of trafficking were addressed along with traditional human rights concerns.[159]

Argentina's original proposals related only to the trafficking of women and children. At the first session of the Ad Hoc Committee, the United States produced an initial draft that referred to "trafficking in persons."[160] Those supporting the latter approach argued that limiting the proposed instrument to women and children was unnecessarily restrictive – particularly if the end purposes of trafficking were expanded beyond sexual exploitation. According to the *travaux préparatoires*, almost all countries expressed their preference for the Protocol to address all persons rather than only women and children, although it was agreed that particular attention should be given to the protection of women and children.[161] Following a recommendation of the Ad Hoc Committee, the UN General Assembly modified the Committee's mandate so as to enable the scope of the proposed Protocol to be expanded to cover trafficking in persons, especially women and children.[162]

As the substantive obligations of the Protocol are subject to a detailed and contextual analysis in Part Three of this book (Chapters 5–9), the following is restricted to a brief identification and analysis of the Protocol's major features, including an insight into issues and controversies that arose during the drafting process.

Overview of the Protocol. The Protocol's definition of trafficking has been considered in detail the previous chapter, necessitating only a brief summary at this point. Under Article 2, trafficking comprises three separate elements: an action (recruitment, transportation, transfer, harboring, or receipt of persons); a means (threat or use of force or other forms of coercion, abduction, fraud, deception, abuse of power, or abuse of a position of vulnerability, or the giving or receiving of payments or benefits to achieve the consent of a person having control over another person); and a purpose (exploitation).[163] Exploitation is defined to include, at a minimum, exploitation of prostitution, other forms of sexual exploitation, forced labor or services, slavery or practices similar to slavery, servitude, or the removal of organs.[164] The definition includes a provision to the effect that the consent of a victim to the intended

---

[158] President W.J. Clinton, "Memorandum on Steps to Combat Violence Against Women and Trafficking in Women and Girls," prepared for the Secretary of State, the Attorney General, the Administrator of the Agency for International Development, the Director of the United States Information Agency, Mar. 11, 1998, reprinted in (1998) 3(4) *Trends in Organized Crime* 20.

[159] See generally, Vlassis, UNAFEI.

[160] "Draft Protocol to Combat International Trafficking in Women and Children, Supplementary to the United Nations Convention against Transnational Organized Crime: Proposal/Submitted by the United States of America," UN Doc. A/AC/254/4/Add.3, Nov. 25, 1998.

[161] Travaux Préparatoires *for the Organized Crime Convention and Protocols*, at 322.

[162] "Progress Report of the Ad Hoc Committee on the Elaboration of a Convention Against Transnational Organized Crime," UN Doc. A/AC.254/30-E/CN.15/2000/4, Mar. 29, 2000, at para. 34.

[163] Trafficking Protocol, at Art. 3.

[164] Ibid.

exploitation is irrelevant where any of the means set out above have been used.[165] In other words, "[o]nce it is established that deception, force or other prohibited means were used, consent is irrelevant and cannot be used as a defence."[166]

The stated purpose of the Trafficking Protocol is threefold: first, to prevent and combat trafficking in persons, paying particular attention to the protection of women and children; second, to protect and assist victims of trafficking; and third, to promote and facilitate cooperation among States Parties to this end.[167] The structure of the Protocol generally follows this three-part approach. In terms of its scope of application, it is relevant to note that some commentators have misunderstood the Protocol as requiring States Parties to take action against trafficking only in respect to situations with a transnational element or involving an organized criminal group.[168] This interpretation does hold up with respect to the interstate *cooperation* obligations of the Trafficking Protocol, but it fails to capture accurately the nature of State Party obligations under the instrument as a whole. The provisions of both the Convention and the Protocol operate to require that the offense of trafficking be established in the domestic law of every State Party, independently of its transnational nature or the involvement of an organized criminal group.[169]

Criminalization, Investigation, and Punishment of Trafficking.[170] The obligation to criminalize trafficking when committed intentionally is contained in Article 5 and, as noted in Chapter 7, is a central and mandatory provision of that instrument.[171] Article 5 also obliges States Parties to criminalize attempting to commit such an offense;[172] participating as an accomplice in such an offense;[173] organizing

---

[165] Ibid. at Art. 3(b).

[166] *Legislative Guide*, at 270. See further the discussion of this issue in Chapter 1.

[167] Trafficking Protocol, at Art. 2.

[168] Hathaway, for example, asserts incorrectly that "slavery or other forms of exploitation that occur entirely within the borders of one country without the involvement of outside parties are beyond the scope of the Trafficking Protocol": J.C. Hathaway, *The Rights of Refugees under International Law* (2005), at 11.

[169] Organized Crime Convention, at Art. 34(2); see also Conference of the Parties to the UN Convention against Transnational Organized Crime, "Criminalization Within the Scope of the United Nations Convention Against Transnational Organized Crime and the Protocols Thereto," UN Doc. CTOC/COP/2008/4, Sept. 9, 2008, at para. 2 ("the offences need to be criminalized in domestic law independently of the transnational nature or the involvement of an organized criminal group"); *Legislative Guide*, at 276 ("transnationality is not required as an element of domestic offences") and also at 18–19, 275–276, 341; *Travaux Préparatoires for the Organized Crime Convention and Protocols*, at 285. On the matter of involvement of an organized criminal group, see also, for example, *Legislative Guide*, at 276 ("the involvement of an organized criminal group must not be required as a proof in a domestic prosecution").

[170] See further Chapter 7, below.

[171] *Legislative Guide*, at 269–270.

[172] "[S]ubject to the basic concepts" of the legal system of the State: Trafficking Protocol, at Art. 5(2)(a). The *Legislative Guide* at 271–272 notes that this caveat was introduced to accommodate legal systems which do not recognise the criminal concept of "attempt."

[173] Trafficking Protocol, at Art. 5(2)(b).

or directing others to commit such an offense;[174] and obstruction of justice when carried out with respect to offenses established by the Protocol.[175] Importantly, the obligation extends only to "trafficking" as defined in that instrument and not to "related conduct."[176] In other words, it is the combination of constituent elements making up the crime of trafficking that are to be criminalized, not the elements themselves.[177] The obligation extends to both natural and legal persons, although the liability for legal persons does not need to be "criminal."[178]

Interestingly, the requirement that States Parties impose appropriate penalties for trafficking, accepted without question throughout the negotiation process, was quietly omitted from the final text of the Protocol.[179] Absent a specific provision on the subject, the relevant provisions of the Organized Crime Convention apply. In accordance with their obligations under that instrument, States Parties are required to ensure that sanctions adopted within domestic law take into account and be proportionate to the gravity of the offenses.[180] The *mutatis mutandis* requirement also means that there are further mandatory provisions of the Convention that create obligations on States Parties to take certain measures with respect to offenses established under the Protocol. These include obligations to:

- Criminalize the laundering of the proceeds of trafficking[181]
- Take appropriate measures to ensure that conditions of release for defendants do not jeopardize the ability to secure their presence at subsequent criminal proceedings[182]
- Establish a long statute of limitations period for trafficking offenses
- Provide, to the greatest extent possible, for the tracing, freezing, and confiscating of the proceeds of trafficking in both domestic cases and in aid of other State Parties[183]
- Provide other States Parties with mutual legal assistance in investigation, prosecution, and judicial proceedings for trafficking offenses[184]

---

[174] Ibid. at Art. 5(2)(c).

[175] Organized Crime Convention, at Art. 23.

[176] *Legislative Guide*, at 267–269. The Legislative Guide notes that this limitation is unique to the Trafficking Protocol. Both the Firearms Protocol and the Migrant Smuggling Protocol require criminalization of certain specified "related conduct."

[177] *Legislative Guide*, at 268–269. See Chapter 6 for a detailed discussion of whether international law supports an obligation to criminalize component acts and related offenses.

[178] Organized Crime Convention, at Art. 10; *Legislative Guide*, at 270.

[179] The obligation to "impose penalties that take into account the grave nature of those offences" appeared in all drafts. While noting the decision to omit this reference, the *travaux préparatoires* do not explain it: Travaux Préparatoires *for the Organized Crime Convention and Protocols*, at 363. It can be assumed that as such a provision was already included in the Convention (see the *Travaux Préparatoires*), its repetition in the Protocol was considered to be unnecessary.

[180] Organized Crime Convention, at Art. 11(1).

[181] Ibid. at Art. 6.

[182] Ibid. at Art. 11(3).

[183] Ibid. at Arts. 12–14.

[184] Ibid. at Art. 18.

- Criminalize obstruction of justice[185]
- Protect victims and witnesses from potential retaliation or intimidation[186]
- Take appropriate measures to encourage those involved in trafficking to cooperate with or assist national authorities[187]
- Provide for channels of communication and police-to-police cooperation in relation to the investigation of trafficking offenses.[188]

Establishment of Jurisdiction.[189] The obligations of States Parties with regard to establishment of criminal jurisdiction over trafficking offenses and extradition of offenders are also set out in the Organized Crime Convention and not in the Trafficking Protocol itself. The Convention requires States Parties to establish jurisdiction to investigate, prosecute, and punish all relevant offenses committed within their territorial jurisdiction, including their marine vessels and aircraft.[190] The Convention encourages, but does not require, States Parties to establish jurisdiction in other circumstances, for example, when nationals of a State are either victims or perpetrators of relevant offenses.[191] States Parties must treat offenses established under the Protocol as extraditable offenses under their relevant treaties and laws. Where extradition has been refused on the grounds of nationality, the State is required to submit the offenses to competent authorities for prosecution.[192] In other words, if domestic legislation prohibits extradition of a State's nationals, then that State Party is required to establish jurisdiction over trafficking-related offenses committed by its nationals anywhere in the world.[193] In summary, and in addition to the general requirement to prosecute for offenses committed within the territory, States Parties to the Convention and Trafficking Protocol are therefore required to prosecute for offenses of their nationals committed abroad *and/or* to make trafficking an extraditable offense.

Victim Protection and Support.[194] Part Two of the Trafficking Protocol, dealing with protection of the trafficked person, contains several important protective provisions. However, to the general disappointment of many commentators,[195]

---

[185] Ibid. at Art. 23.
[186] Ibid. at Arts. 24–25.
[187] Ibid. at Art. 26. For examples of measures that could be taken to this end, see the *Legislative Guide*, at 275.
[188] Organized Crime Convention, at Art. 27.
[189] See further, Chapter 7.1.2.
[190] Organized Crime Convention, at Art. 15(1).
[191] Ibid. at Art. 15(2).
[192] Ibid. at Art. 16.
[193] Ibid. at Art. 16(10).
[194] See further, Chapters 5 and 6.2.
[195] Coomaraswamy, "Report," UN Doc. E/CN.4/2000/68, at para. 7; S. Scarpa, *Trafficking in Human Beings: Modern Slavery* (2008), at 63–65; T. Obokata, *Trafficking of Human Beings from a Human*

there is very little in the way of "hard" or detailed obligation. States Parties are required to:

- Protect the privacy and identity of trafficking victims in appropriate cases and to the extent possible under domestic law, including by making legal proceedings confidential to the extent that this is also possible under domestic law[196]
- Ensure that in appropriate cases, victims receive information on relevant court and administrative proceedings as well as assistance to enable their views to be presented and considered during criminal proceedings[197]
- Endeavor to provide for the physical safety of trafficking victims within their territory[198]
- Ensure that domestic law provides victims with the possibility of obtaining compensation.[199]

In relation to the issue of compensation, it is relevant to note that a draft provision on the seizure, confiscation, and disposal of gains from trafficking was deleted following agreement that the corresponding article of the Convention would apply *mutatis mutandis*.[200] However, the essence of the provision was lost in this move, and

Rights Perspective: Towards a Holistic Approach (2006) (Obokata, *Trafficking of Human Beings from a Human Rights Perspective*), at 164.

[196] Trafficking Protocol, at Art. 6(1). The *Legislative Guide*, at 283, notes that this may include courts being given authority to shield identities or otherwise protect the privacy of victims in appropriate cases. Reference should also be made to Article 24(2)(b) of the Organized Crime Convention, which provides for witnesses to be able to give evidence in safety.

[197] Trafficking Protocol, at Art. 6(2). Note that this is one of the few mandatory victim assistance provisions and should already have been implemented through legislation as required under Article 25(3) of the Organized Crime Convention. The *Legislative Guide*, at 284, notes a number of ways in which this provision could be given practical effect, including through provision of a right to submit a post-conviction, pre-sentencing victim impact statement.

[198] Trafficking Protocol, at Art. 6(5). Note that this is a minimum standard which, in certain cases (such as in relation to witnesses), would be supplemented by additional requirements contained in Articles 24 and 25 of the Organized Crime Convention. See further, *Legislative Guide*, at 285.

[199] Trafficking Protocol, at Art. 6(6). Note that the provision does not specify types of compensation. The *Legislative Guide*, at 60, identifies a range of options including provisions allowing victims to sue offenders for civil damages, provisions allowing criminal courts to award criminal damages or compensation, and provisions establishing special funds or schemes for the benefit of victims of trafficking.

[200] The original provision, from the first session of the Ad Hoc Working Group, stipulated that "States Parties shall take all necessary and appropriate measures to allow the seizure and confiscation of gains obtained by the criminal organization from the offences described in article 3 of this Protocol. The proceeds from such seizure and confiscation shall be allocated towards defraying the costs of providing due assistance to the victim, where deemed appropriate by States Parties and as agreed by them, in conformity with individual guarantees enshrined in domestic legislation." Travaux Préparatoires *for the Organized Crime Convention and Protocols*, at 443. In explaining the deletion, the *travaux préparatoires* note at 444: "[i]t was agreed that the seizure and forfeiture scheme in … the draft convention should apply, mutatis mutandis, to the Protocol and that these draft provisions covered most of the same content. It was decided not to retain text calling for use of seized proceeds to defray the cost of assistance to victims because this was not consistent with compromises reached in negotiating the scheme in the draft convention and because of the practical and legal implementation problems in many States."

States Parties will now *not* be required to use the proceeds from seizure and confiscation to fund assistance and compensation for victims of trafficking.[201]

In terms of victim assistance and support, the relevant provision requires States Parties to: "consider adopting legislative or other appropriate measures to provide for the physical, psychological and social recovery of victims of trafficking."[202] Special reference is made to the provision of housing, counseling, and information in a language the victim understands; medical, psychological, and material assistance; and employment, education, and training opportunities.[203] According the Legislative Guide, the expected high cost of such measures, and the fact that their provision would be required of all States in which victims are found, precluded them from being made obligatory.[204]

As the more detailed analysis set out in Chapter 5.3.4 confirms, a State will not be breaching either the letter or the spirit of the Convention if it decides to provide no material, medical, or other assistance whatsoever to any victim of trafficking within its territory. States also retain an implied right under the Convention to link the provision of such assistance to victims' willingness to cooperate with criminal justice agencies. The conditional and qualified nature of the victim assistance and protection provisions did not escape criticism. In a joint submission, the Inter-Agency Group pointed out that the discretionary nature of the protection provisions was unnecessarily restrictive.[205] Similar criticisms were leveled by the Special Rapporteur on Violence against Women and by the International Labour Organization.[206]

---

[201] The original provision stipulated that "States Parties shall take all necessary and appropriate measures to allow the seizure and confiscation of gains obtained by the criminal organisations from the offences covered by this Protocol. The proceeds from such seizure and confiscation shall be used to defray the costs of providing due assistance to the victim, where deemed appropriate by States Parties and as agreed by them, in conformity with individual guarantees enshrined in their domestic legislation." "Sixth Draft of the Protocol to Prevent, Suppress and Punish Trafficking in Persons, Especially Women and Children," UN Doc. A/AC.254/4/Add.3/Rev.6, Apr. 4, 2000, at Art. 5 bis.

[202] Trafficking Protocol, at Art. 6(3). The type of assistance set forth in this paragraph is applicable to both the receiving State and the State of origin of the victims of trafficking in persons, but only as regards victims who are in their respective territory. Paragraph 3 is applicable to the receiving State until the victim of trafficking in persons has returned to his or her State of origin, after which paragraph 3 will apply to the State of origin. The relevant Interpretative Note stipulates that "[t]he type of assistance set forth in this paragraph is applicable to both the receiving State and the State of origin but only as regards victims who are in their respective territory": Travaux Préparatoires *for the Organized Crime Convention and Protocols*, at 373.

[203] Trafficking Protocol, at Art. 6(3).

[204] *Legislative Guide*, at 288.

[205] "Note by the Office of the United Nations High Commissioner for Human Rights, the Office of the United Nations High Commissioner for Refugees, the United Nations Children's Fund and the International Organization for Migration on the Draft Protocols Concerning Migrant Smuggling and Trafficking in Persons," UN Doc. A/AC.254/27, Feb. 8, 2000 and UN Doc. A.AC.254/27/Corr.1, Feb. 22, 2000 (Inter-Agency Submission), at 7.

[206] For a useful summary of these interventions, see the Travaux Préparatoires *for the Organized Crime Convention and Protocols*, at 368.

Special Protections for Trafficked Children.[207] Despite the genesis of the Trafficking Protocol in this issue, the matter of child trafficking did not especially occupy delegations during the negotiations. Early in the negotiations, the UN High Commissioner for Human Rights urged the Ad Hoc Committee to include special provisions to prevent trafficking in children and to protect child victims.[208] These calls were echoed in a separate submission by the Special Rapporteur on the Sale of Children, Child Prostitution and Child Pornography.[209] In February 2000, the Inter-Agency Group, alarmed at the lack of any progress on this issue, made the following strong recommendation:

> The Protocol should include an explicit acknowledgment of the fact that children have special rights under international law and, in particular in the light of the Convention on the Rights of the Child that child victims of trafficking have special needs that must be recognised and met by States Parties; that States are obliged to take measures to prevent trafficking of children; and that in dealing with child victims of trafficking, the best interests of the child (including the specific right to physical and psychological recovery and social integration) are to be at all times paramount. Also important is clear recognition of the need to fight the impunity of those responsible for the trafficking, while at the same time ensuring that the child is not criminalised in any way. In that context it should be noted that the overwhelming majority of States are already under such legal obligations through their ratification of the Convention on the Rights of the Child. Existing international law would also appear to require States to ensure, *inter alia*, that assistance and protection of child victims of trafficking is not made discretionary or otherwise dependent on the decision of national authorities. In accordance with article 2 of the Convention, child victims of trafficking are entitled to the same protection as nationals of the receiving State in all matters including those related to protection of their privacy and physical and moral integrity.[210]

While the final version of the Protocol falls far short of this standard, it does contain several provisions aimed at ensuring relatively greater protection for trafficked children.[211] The most significant of these relates to the definition of trafficking in children – specifically, the omission of a means element.[212] In applying the Protocol's protection and assistance provisions, States Parties are required to take into account the special needs of child victims including appropriate housing, education, and

---

[207] See further, Chapter 5.5.

[208] "Informal Note by the United Nations High Commissioner for Human Rights," UN Doc. A/AC.254/16, June 1, 1999 (HCHR Submission), at 13–14.

[209] The Special Rapporteur proposed, *inter alia*, that the preamble should contain a paragraph recognizing the vulnerability of children as distinct and separate from circumstances attendant upon the vulnerability of women, as well as reference to the CRC: Travaux Préparatoires *for the Organized Crime Convention and Protocols*, at 324.

[210] Inter-Agency Submission, at 6.

[211] The Protocol defines children as persons under the age of eighteen: Trafficking Protocol, at Art. 3(d).

[212] See Chapter 1.2.3.

care.[213] The Legislative Guide has expanded on these provisions by providing examples of the kinds of steps that States could take to protect and assist child victims of trafficking.[214] These are considered further in Chapter 5.5, in the context of a discussion on the substantive content of the obligation to protect and support trafficked children.

Legal Status and Repatriation.[215] The status of the victim in the receiving State was a critical issue in the negotiations. While NGOs and the Inter-Agency Group argued strongly for the inclusion of some kind of right of trafficked persons to remain in the receiving country, at least temporarily, this option was never seriously under consideration. According to the *travaux préparatoires*, "[m]ost delegations were concerned that the Protocol might inadvertently become a means of illicit migration if States Parties were obliged to adopt legislation permitting victims to remain in the countries to which they were trafficked."[216] States recognized, however, that in some cases there would be a legitimate need for victims to remain in their country of destination, for example: "for humanitarian purposes and to protect them from being victimized again by traffickers."[217] The final text provides that the State Party is to consider adopting legislative or other measures permitting victims of trafficking to remain in their territories temporarily or permanently in appropriate cases,[218] with appropriate consideration being given to humanitarian and compassionate factors.[219]

---

[213] Trafficking Protocol, at Art. 6(4). The provision requires consideration of "age, gender and special needs of victims of trafficking in persons, in particular the special needs of children." McClean points out that at one stage, this provision was limited to the special needs of children, and that the widening of its scope of application to include considerations of both gender and special needs may have weakened its force: McClean, *Transnational Organized Crime*, at 340.

[214] The *Legislative Guide* makes specific reference to the CRC and the principle of the best interests of the child enshrined therein. The Guide encourages States to ensure that even those whose age is uncertain are treated in accordance with the CRC until age is verified. It also sets out a list of possible measures that could be taken by States in order to assist and support victims of trafficking, including appointment of a guardian to protect the child's interests; ensuring no direct contact between the child and the suspected offender; providing shelter for children which guards against revictimization; ensuring that those dealing with child victims are properly trained to understand their needs and rights; and considering the best interests of the child in relation to decisions about her or his repatriation. *Legislative Guide*, at 289–290.

[215] See further, Chapters 5.4 and 6.1.

[216] Travaux Préparatoires *for the Organized Crime Convention and Protocols*, at 380.

[217] "Seventh Draft of the Protocol to Prevent, Suppress and Punish Trafficking in Persons, Especially Women and Children," UN Doc. A/AC.254/4/Add.3/Rev.7, July 7, 2000, at footnote 27.

[218] Trafficking Protocol, at Art. 7(1). The *travaux préparatoires* confirm that delegations were in agreement that "it was not the intention of the paragraph to confer the right to remain, but that the decision whether or not to grant temporary or permanent residence was always at the discretion of the State party." Travaux Préparatoires *for the Organized Crime Convention and Protocols*, at 380.

[219] Trafficking Protocol, at Art. 7(2). The *travaux préparatoires* note that many delegations supported the view that the words "compassionate factors" referred to personal circumstances such as family situation, age, common-law marital relationship, and other factors that should be considered on an

The related issue of repatriation, dealt with in a separate article, was also very sensitive. The Ad Hoc Committee proved somewhat receptive to the view of the UN High Commissioner for Human Rights that "safe and, as far as possible, voluntary return must be at the core of any credible protection strategy for trafficked persons."[220] However, it did reject another proposal put forward by the Inter-Agency Group that identification of a person as a trafficked person be sufficient to ensure that immediate expulsion that goes against the will of the victim does not occur, and that the protection and assistance provisions of the Protocol become immediately applicable.[221] There was general agreement that repatriation was a burden to be shared between States of origin and States of destination[222] and, importantly, that the Protocol's repatriation provisions were to be understood as being without prejudice to existing obligations under customary international law regarding the return of migrants.[223]

The final article on repatriation provides that States Parties of origin are to facilitate and accept, without undue or unreasonable delay, the return of their trafficked nationals and those who have a right of permanent residence within their territories.[224] In returning a trafficking victim to another State Party, States Parties of destination are required to ensure that such return takes place with due regard both for the safety of the trafficked person and the status of any legal proceedings relating to the fact of that person being a victim of trafficking.[225] While such return "shall preferably be voluntary,"[226] these words are to be understood as not placing any obligation on the returning State Party.[227] In order to facilitate repatriation, States Parties are required to communicate with each other in verifying nationalities as well as travel and identity documents.[228] The relevant article also contains several savings

---

individual and case-by-case basis. "Humanitarian factors" were applicable to all persons, being the rights established in the human rights instruments. Travaux Préparatoires *for the Organized Crime Convention and Protocols*, at 380. McClean questions whether this is correct, pointing out that if human rights are applicable to all, "it is strange to find they are to be given merely 'appropriate consideration' in this context": McClean, *Transnational Organized Crime*, at 343.

[220] HCHR Submission, at 20. An early draft of the relevant provision stated that return of victims "shall be with due regard for the safety of that person, as well as the status of any legal proceedings related to the fact that the person is a victim of trafficking [and, as far as possible, voluntary]." The majority of delegations subsequently agreed to delete the bracketed text. See further Travaux Préparatoires *for the Organized Crime Convention and Protocols*, at 387.

[221] Inter-Agency Submission, at 9.

[222] Travaux Préparatoires *for the Organized Crime Convention and Protocols*, at 383–389.

[223] Ibid. at 389.

[224] Trafficking Protocol, at Art. 8(1). See further, Travaux Préparatoires *for the Organized Crime Convention and Protocols*, at 386, 397.

[225] Trafficking Protocol, at Art. 8(2).

[226] Ibid.

[227] Travaux Préparatoires *for the Organized Crime Convention and Protocols*, at 388. On the issue of repatriation in the absence of consent, the Ad Hoc Committee agreed, during negotiations, that "bilateral and multilateral agreements should be encouraged": ibid. at 384.

[228] Trafficking Protocol, at Arts. 8(3)–8(4).

clauses, preserving the rights that may be afforded victims under domestic law, as well as any other bilateral or multilateral agreements that govern the issue of return of victims of trafficking.[229]

Prevention and Cooperation.[230] Article 31 of the Organized Crime Convention contains a comprehensive list of measures to be taken by States to prevent, *inter alia*, trafficking in persons.[231] Prevention provisions in the Trafficking Protocol itself operate to supplement those measures. These provisions are, for the most part, couched in qualified terms, making it difficult to isolate specific obligations.[232] States Parties are required to establish policies, programs, and other measures aimed at preventing trafficking and protecting trafficked persons from revictimization.[233] They are further required to endeavor to undertake additional measures, including information campaigns and social and economic initiatives, to prevent trafficking.[234] These measures should include cooperation with NGOs, relevant organizations, and other elements of civil society.[235] States Parties are also required to adopt legislative or other measures "to discourage the demand that fosters all forms of exploitation of persons, especially women and children, that leads to trafficking."[236]

Despite its attention being drawn to the issue,[237] the Ad Hoc Committee did not directly address the problem of national antitrafficking measures being used for discriminatory purposes or with discriminatory results. This gap is, however, at least partly ameliorated by a provision that the application and interpretation of measures pursuant to the Protocol: "shall be consistent with internationally recognized principles of non-discrimination."[238] Discussions on the need to avoid conflict with existing principles of international law also produced a broad savings clause to the effect that nothing in the Protocol is to affect the rights, obligations, and responsibilities of States under international law, including international humanitarian law,

---

[229] Ibid. at Arts. 8(5)–8(6). See also Travaux Préparatoires *for the Organized Crime Convention and Protocols*, at 389.

[230] See further, Chapters 7.5 and 8.

[231] Organized Crime Convention, at Art. 31(7).

[232] Article 9 of the Trafficking Protocol uses terms such as "shall establish," "shall endeavour to undertake," "shall take measures," and "shall adopt measures." The *Legislative Guide*, at 297, confirms that all of the measures referred to in Article 9 are mandatory but only in the sense that "some action on each point must be taken." Apart from confirming that the substantive content of the relevant Article expanded considerably over time (due, at least in part, to interventions from United Nations agencies and entities), the *travaux préparatoires* do not shed additional light on this aspect: Travaux Préparatoires *for the Organized Crime Convention and Protocols*, at 391–395.

[233] Trafficking Protocol, at Art. 9(1).

[234] Ibid. at Art. 9(2).

[235] Ibid. at Art. 9(3).

[236] Ibid. at Art. 9(5).

[237] HCHR Submission, at 25; Inter-Agency Submission, at 13.

[238] Trafficking Protocol, at Art. 14(2).

international human rights law, and, in particular, refugee law and the principle of *non-refoulement*.[239]

More specific obligations of prevention are set out in relation to law enforcement and border controls, supplementing the extensive ones set out in the Organized Crime Convention itself.[240] In the area of law enforcement, States Parties accept a general obligation to cooperate through information exchange aimed at identifying perpetrators or victims of trafficking, as well as methods and means employed by traffickers.[241] States Parties are also to provide or strengthen training for law enforcement, immigration, and other relevant personnel aimed at preventing trafficking as well as prosecuting traffickers and protecting the rights of victims.[242] Training is to include a focus on methods to protect the rights of victims.[243] It should take into account the need to consider human rights, children, and gender-sensitive issues, and to encourage cooperation with NGOs as well as other relevant organizations and elements of civil society.[244]

Border controls, sanctions on commercial carriers, and measures relating to travel or identity documents are all seen as an important means of making it more difficult for traffickers to operate. During the drafting process, the Inter-Agency Group recommended that emphasis in relation to border control should be on measures to assist border authorities in identifying and protecting victims, as well as intercepting traffickers.[245] The final text requires States Parties to strengthen border controls as necessary to detect and prevent trafficking;[246] to take legislative or other appropriate measures to prevent commercial transport being used in the trafficking process; and to penalize such involvement.[247] States Parties are also to take steps to ensure the

---

[239] Ibid. at Art. 14(1). The Interpretative Notes further clarify that "[t]he protocol does not cover the status of refugees," and that "[t]his protocol is without prejudice to the existing rights, obligations or responsibilities of States Parties under other international instruments, such as those referred to in this paragraph. Rights, obligations and responsibilities under another instrument are determined by the terms of that instrument and whether the State concerned is a party to it, not by this protocol. Therefore, any State that becomes a party to this protocol but is not a party to another international instrument referred to in the protocol would not become subject to any right, obligation or responsibility under that instrument": Travaux Préparatoires *for the Organized Crime Convention and Protocols*, at 421.

[240] In particular, Arts. 27–29 of the Organized Crime Convention.

[241] Trafficking Protocol, at Art. 10(1).

[242] Ibid. at Art. 10(2).

[243] Ibid.

[244] Ibid.

[245] Inter-Agency Submission, at para. 10. See also Travaux Préparatoires *for the Organized Crime Convention and Protocols*, at 407.

[246] Trafficking Protocol, at Art. 11(1).

[247] Ibid. at Arts. 11(2)–11(4). An Interpretative Note confirms that "[v]ictims of trafficking in persons may enter a State legally only to face subsequent exploitation, whereas in cases of smuggling of migrants, illegal means of entry are more generally used. This may make it more difficult for common carriers to apply preventive measures in trafficking cases than in smuggling cases and legislative or other measures taken in accordance with this paragraph should take this into account": Travaux Préparatoires *for the Organized Crime Convention and Protocols*, at 409. States are reminded, also

integrity of travel documents issued on their behalf and to prevent their fraudulent use.[248] Following concerns expressed by delegations and the Inter-Agency Group, several draft provisions were modified in order to ensure that measures taken under this Part did not prejudice the free movement of persons or compromise other internationally recognised human rights, including the right of asylum.[249]

Improved cooperation between countries on the issue of trafficking is the *raison d'être* of the Protocol,[250] and the obligation of cooperation is accordingly integrated into a range of provisions, including those related to the sharing of information[251] and the repatriation of victims.[252] Cross-border cooperation is also envisaged with respect to the strengthening of border controls and general law enforcement against trafficking.[253] These specific provisions are supplemented by the Convention, which, as noted above, constructs a detailed model of mutual legal and other assistance to facilitate cooperation between States in the prevention and suppression of transnational organized crime. The Protocol also makes brief reference to the need for improved cooperation *within* countries: specifically, between criminal justice and victim support agencies in matters related to the prevention of trafficking and the provision of assistance to victims.[254]

2.2.3. *The Migrant Smuggling Protocol*

The origins of the Migrant Smuggling Protocol can be traced back to the 1990s, when several European states, backed by Australia and the United States, began pushing for greater international legal cooperation against the organized movement of migrants for profit.[255] Their advocacy found a receptive audience. Almost all of the preferred destination countries in Europe, North America, and elsewhere had experienced a significant increase in the number of "unauthorized arrivals."[256]

---

through an Interpretative Note, of their discretion not to hold carriers liable in cases where they have transported undocumented refugees: ibid. at 80 and 521.

[248] Trafficking Protocol, at Art. 12. For examples of the kinds of measures that could be taken to this end, see the *Legislative Guide*, at 298–299.

[249] HCHR Submission, at 8; Inter-Agency Submission, at 11. On the issue of smuggling/trafficking of asylum-seekers and refugees, see Chapter 3.5, below.

[250] Trafficking Protocol, at Preamble.

[251] Ibid. at Art. 10.

[252] Ibid. at Art. 8.

[253] Ibid. at Arts. 11–13.

[254] Ibid. at Arts. 6(3) and 9(3). The *Legislative Guide*, at 313, provides examples of cooperation between governmental agencies working on trafficking and NGOs. It also notes the need to ensure that victim support agencies manage to retain their distance from the State in order to preserve their value as an independent refuge and source of support for victims.

[255] McClean, *Transnational Organized Crime*, at 21–24; Vlassis, UNAFEI.

[256] See generally F. David, "Human Smuggling and Trafficking: An Overview of the Responses at the Federal Level" (Australian Institute of Criminology Research and Public Policy, 2000) (David, "Human Smuggling and Trafficking"); A. Schloenhardt, "Migrant Smuggling: Illegal Migration and Organised Crime in Australia and the Asia Pacific Region" (2003) (Schloenhardt, "Migrant

There was growing evidence that criminal groups who were organized and sophisticated enough to exploit legislative, policy, and law enforcement weaknesses were facilitating much of this movement.[257] Deficiencies in international law were seen as particularly acute and detrimental; there was no definition of smuggling, no domestic obligation to criminalize smuggling, and no obligation to extradite or prosecute perpetrators,[258] resulting in a "legal lacuna under international law [that] is increasingly perceived as an obstacle to the effort of the international community to cope, in an efficient manner, with the phenomenon of smuggling of illegal migrants for criminal purposes."[259] The major receiving countries were quick to understand that the default position – a purely national approach to sanctioning those who facilitated such migration, supplemented by *ad hoc* and largely ineffective international cooperation – played directly into the hands of smugglers and traffickers.[260]

In 1997, the Government of Austria formally proposed the development of a new legal instrument to deal with the smuggling of migrants.[261] The Italian Government had, in the meantime, approached the International Maritime Organization (IMO) with a proposal for the issuance of directives regarding "trafficking" of migrants by sea.[262] The IMO was not interested, and Italy subsequently decided to join forces with Austria in pushing for the development of a legal instrument against migrant smuggling within the context of the Crime Commission's work against transnational organized crime.[263] This goal was secured in late 1998 when the Ad Hoc Committee established to develop a convention on transnational organized crime was also mandated to discuss the elaboration of an international instrument on "illegal trafficking in, and transportation of migrants, including by sea."[264]

Overview of the Migrant Smuggling Protocol. The stated purpose of the Migrant Smuggling Protocol is to prevent and combat migrant smuggling, to promote international cooperation to that end, and to protect the rights of smuggled migrants.[265] "Smuggling of migrants" is defined as "the procurement, in order to obtain, directly

---

Smuggling"); S. Zhang and K. Chin, "Characteristics of Chinese Human Smugglers: A Cross-National Study" (October, 2002) (Zhang and Chin, "Chinese Human Smugglers").

[257] David, "Human Smuggling and Trafficking"; Schloenhardt, "Migrant Smuggling"; Zhang and Chin, "Chinese Human Smugglers."

[258] "Letter from the Austrian Permanent Representative to the United Nations to the United Nations Secretary-General dated 16 September, 1997 accompanying the Draft International Convention against the Smuggling of Illegal Migrants," UN Doc. A/52/357, Sept. 17, 1997 (transmitting a draft of the proposed convention), cited in McClean, *Transnational Organized Crime,* at 21–22.

[259] McClean, *Transnational Organized Crime,* at 22.

[260] See generally Vlassis, UNAFEI.

[261] "Letter from the Austrian Permanent Representative to the United Nations to the United Nations Secretary-General dated 16 September, 1997 accompanying the Draft International Convention against the Smuggling of Illegal Migrants," UN Doc. A/52/357, Sept. 17, 1997.

[262] Vlassis, UNAFEI, at 493.

[263] Ibid.

[264] UN General Assembly, "Transnational Organized Crime," UN Doc. A/RES/53/111, Jan. 20, 1999.

[265] Migrant Smuggling Protocol, at Art. 2.

or indirectly, a financial or other material benefit, of the illegal entry of a person into a State Party of which the person is not a national or a permanent resident."[266] The reference to "financial or other material benefit" was included as an element of the definition in order to ensure that the activities of those who provide support to migrants on humanitarian grounds or on the basis of close family ties do not come within the scope of the Protocol.[267] The focus is on those who procure or otherwise facilitate the smuggling of migrants. The Protocol does not address mere illegal entry and takes a neutral position on whether those who migrate illegally should be the subject of any offenses.[268]

The structure of this instrument is similar to the Trafficking Protocol. Its direct application is limited to situations of international migrant smuggling involving an organized criminal group (which, owing to the breadth of that concept, operates to bring within the operation of the Protocol almost every conceivable situation of migrant smuggling).[269] States Parties are required to criminalize the smuggling of migrants as well as related offenses including the production, provision, and possession of fraudulent travel or identity documents.[270] In criminalizing migrant smuggling, States Parties are required to ensure that offenses involving dangerous or degrading circumstances are subject to at least the risk of harsher penalties.[271]

Reflecting the impetus behind its development, the Migrant Smuggling Protocol includes a detailed section on preventing and suppressing the smuggling of migrants by sea through, *inter alia*, empowering States to take appropriate action against ships that are or that may be engaged in the smuggling of migrants.[272] The involvement of commercial carriers in smuggling of migrants is addressed by way of a requirement that States Parties adopt appropriate legal and administrative measures to ensure the vigilance of commercial carriers and their liability in the event of complicity or negligence.[273]

The Migrant Smuggling Protocol requires the adoption of general measures to prevent migrant smuggling with a particular focus on prevention through improved law enforcement. As with the Trafficking Protocol, great emphasis is given to the strengthening of border controls. States Parties are required to strengthen

---

[266] Ibid. at Art. 3(a).

[267] Travaux Préparatoires *for the Organized Crime Convention and Protocols*, at 469.

[268] Migrant Smuggling Protocol, at Art. 5. See also, *Legislative Guide*, at Part Three, 340, 347. But see Article 6(4) of the Protocol, which provides that nothing in the Protocol limits the existing rights of States Parties to take action against those whose conduct constitutes an offense under national law.

[269] Migrant Smuggling Protocol, at Art. 4.

[270] Ibid. at Art. 6. In accordance with Article 34(2) of the Convention, these corequisites (of transnationality and involvement of an organized criminal group) do not apply to the obligation of criminalization except, as noted by the *Legislative Guide*, where the language of the criminalization requirement specifically incorporates one of these elements. *Legislative Guide*, at 333–334.

[271] Migrant Smuggling Protocol, at Art. 6(3). See further, *Legislative Guide*, at 346–347.

[272] Migrant Smuggling Protocol, at Arts. 7–9. Importantly, when taking such action, States Parties are to ensure the safety and humane treatment of the persons on board: ibid. at Art. 9(1)(a).

[273] Ibid. at Arts. 11(2)–11(4).

border controls to the extent possible and necessary to prevent and detect migrant smuggling.[274] They are also encouraged to establish and maintain direct channels of communication between each other as a way of intensifying cooperation among border control agencies.[275] States Parties are to take steps to ensure the integrity of travel documents issued on their behalf and to cooperate in preventing their fraudulent use.[276] Specialized training aimed at preventing, combating, and eradicating migrant smuggling is to be provided or strengthened for immigration and other officials. Little attention is given to the root causes of migrant smuggling.[277] A key preventative element is seen to be the dissemination of negative information aimed at discouraging potential migrants.[278]

In contrast to the Trafficking Protocol, States Parties to the Migrant Smuggling Protocol are not required to consider the possibility of permitting victims to remain in their territories temporarily or permanently. Smuggled migrants also fare worse when it comes to repatriation. States Parties of origin are to facilitate and accept, without delay, the return of their smuggled nationals and those who have a right of permanent abode within their territories[279] once the nationality or right of permanent residence of the returnee is verified.[280] There is no requirement for either the State of origin or the State of destination to take account of the safety of smuggled migrants in the repatriation process.[281] This is despite the fact that the involvement of organized crime (itself a prerequisite for application of the Convention) is likely to pose a serious risk to returnees. Smuggled migrants are also not entitled to any of the special protections that States Parties may choose to afford trafficked persons in relation to their personal safety and physical and psychological well-being. No entitlements are envisaged with respect to legal proceedings or remedies against smugglers. The Ad Hoc Committee did not take up suggestions that the Protocol include special protective measures for smuggled children.[282]

---

[274] Ibid. at Art. 11(1).

[275] Ibid. at Art. 11(6).

[276] Ibid. at Arts. 12–13.

[277] Root causes are referred to briefly in the Protocol's preamble as well as in Article 15(3) in relation to development programs and cooperation aimed at combating "the root socio-economic causes of the smuggling of migrants, such as poverty and underdevelopment."

[278] Ibid. at Art. 15(1).

[279] Ibid. at Art. 18(1).

[280] Travaux Préparatoires *for the Organized Crime Convention and Protocols*, at 552.

[281] Article 18(5) does require returning States Parties to "carry out the return in an orderly manner and with due regard for the safety and dignity of the person." It is evident from the *travaux préparatoires* that this reference to safety and dignity refers only to the process of return and not to the eventual fate of the individual concerned. See Travaux Préparatoires *for the Organized Crime Convention and Protocols*, at 547–552.

[282] Inter-Agency Submission, at 19. The only reference to children is in Article 16(4) of the Protocol, which provides that the limited protection and assistance measures specified in that article are to take into account the special needs of women and children.

Human Rights, Asylum-seekers, and Refugees. The potential impact of the Migrant Smuggling Protocol on individual human rights, including the rights of asylum-seekers and refugees, was a point of discussion during negotiations. However, the issue did not gain the level of traction secured with respect to the Trafficking Protocol. With only a few exceptions, most participating States appeared reluctant to support the inclusion of strong human rights protections in the draft Protocol.[283] It should nevertheless be noted that a public record of strong and persistent intervention on the part of the involved international agencies confirms their awareness of potential risks, especially to the rights of asylum-seekers, posed by the new Protocol.[284] A major submission delivered by the Inter-Agency Group in February 2000 provides a useful summary of principal concerns, in particular with respect to the issue of asylum:[285]

> The Office [OHCHR], [UNHCR], UNICEF and IOM welcome the explicit references [in the draft text] to obligations of States Parties under the 1951 Convention relating to the Status of Refugees and the Protocol relating to the Status of Refugees of 1967 as safeguards aimed at ensuring that the adoption of the Migrant Protocol does not jeopardize the obligations of States Parties to the 1951 Convention or impinge on the ability of asylum seekers to secure protection from persecution.
>
> The Office [OHCHR], [UNHCR], UNICEF and IOM urge that the above-mentioned safeguards be maintained and, where appropriate, further strengthened … In this context, it is essential to acknowledge that increasing numbers of asylum seekers, including those with genuine claims to refugee status, are being transported by means covered in the draft Migrant Protocol. The principle of *non-refoulement*, which is the core of international refugee protection, and which is recognized as a norm of customary international law, must be explicitly preserved in the Migrant Protocol. The Office [OHCHR], [UNHCR], UNICEF and IOM strongly advocate the inclusion of a provision to the effect that illegality of entrance into a State will not adversely affect a person's claim for asylum. Further, in order to make such a provision effective, signatories should be required to ensure that smuggled migrants are given full opportunity (including through the provision of adequate information) to make a claim for asylum or to present any other justification for remaining in the country, and that such claims be considered on a case-by-case basis. Such a provision could be inserted as a safeguard clause or, if more appropriate, added to the [proposed] savings clause.[286]

---

[283] See notes 288 and 294 for this chapter.

[284] See, for example, Inter-Agency Submission; HCHR Submission.

[285] Inter-Agency Submission, at paras. 16–18. Note that the UNHCR was originally omitted from the list of agencies preparing this submission. This was amended in the corrigendum.

[286] The point about illegality of entry not affecting a person's claim for asylum was also made in a joint NGO submission to the same session of the working group. "NGO Joint Submissions on the Protocol against the Smuggling of Migrants by Land, Air and Sea and Protocol to Prevent, Suppress and Punish Trafficking in Persons, Especially Women and Children" (2000), available at www.december18.net/web/general/page.php?pageID=161&menuID=36&lang=EN (accessed Sept. 30, 2009).

In the same submission, the Inter-Agency Group also pointed out the conceptual confusion between "smuggled migrants" and "trafficked persons" as embodied in the border protection provisions in the draft Trafficking Protocol:

> The current draft provisions on border controls [in Article 8 of the Trafficking Protocol] appear somewhat at odds with the stated purposes of the Trafficking Protocol, and call into question the distinction between trafficked persons and smuggled migrants. The [OHCHR], [UNHCR], UNICEF and IOM agree with the comments made by several delegations at the sixth session of the Ad Hoc Committee that such provisions could operate to restrain the liberty of movement of the persons who are subject to protection under the Protocol. Given that the majority of trafficked persons are women and girls, the imposition of such restrictions would be, prima facie, discriminatory. It is clear that the strengthening of border controls is an important aspect of preventing trafficking. However, emphasis should be placed, in Article 8, on measures to assist border authorities in identifying and protecting victims as well as intercepting traffickers.
>
> In addition, while States have a legitimate interest in strengthening border controls in order to detect and prevent trafficking, the [OHCHR], [UNHCR], UNICEF and IOM are concerned that these measures do not limit the rights of individuals to seek and enjoy in other countries asylum from persecution as provided for under the Convention relating to the Status of Refugees. In particular, provisions of the draft Protocol should not undermine the fundamental principle of *non-refoulement*.[287]

In its final version, the Migrant Smuggling Protocol does indeed require States to criminalize smuggling and related conduct, to strengthen their borders against smugglers, and to cooperate in preventing and combating smuggling. However, the Protocol also includes a number of provisions aimed at protecting the basic rights of smuggled migrants and preventing the worst forms of exploitation that often accompany the smuggling process.[288] When criminalizing smuggling and related offenses, States Parties are required to establish, as aggravating circumstances, situations that

---

[287] Inter-Agency Submission, at paras. 10–11. Note that the UNHCR was originally left off the list of agencies preparing this submission. This was amended in the corrigendum.

[288] The Secretariat reported that at the seventh session of the Ad Hoc Committee, the Group of Latin American and Caribbean States "were of the view that it was important to develop a legal instrument that would effectively target smugglers while protecting the rights of migrants. Therefore the protocol must take into account the relevant United Nations instruments on protection of migrants in connection with correcting social and economic imbalances ... it [is] important for the Migrants Protocol not to penalise migration ... or to convey an ambiguous message to the international community that would stimulate xenophobia, intolerance and racism. The negotiation process should take into account the causes of migration and the reasons for the increasing vulnerability of migrants": "Progress Report of the Ad Hoc Committee on the Elaboration of a Convention Against Transnational Organized Crime," UN Doc. A/AC.254/30-E/CN.15/2000/4, Mar. 29, 2000, at para. 18. See also, HCHR Submission, at 4–8 and the Inter-Agency Submission, at 15–22. Protection of the rights of smuggled migrants was finally included as one of the purposes of the Protocol: Migrant Smuggling Protocol, at Art. 2.

endanger the lives or safety of migrants or entail inhuman or degrading treatment, including exploitation.[289] Importantly, migrants themselves are not to become liable to criminal prosecution under the Protocol for the fact of having being smuggled.[290] States Parties are also required to take all appropriate measures, consistent with their obligations under international law, to preserve and protect the rights of smuggled migrants, including: the right to life; the right not to be subject to torture or other cruel, inhuman, or degrading treatment or punishment; and the right to consular access.[291] They are further required to afford migrants protection against smuggling-related violence and appropriate assistance if their lives and safety are endangered through the smuggling process.[292]

The Migrant Smuggling Protocol contains a savings clause, identical to that contained in Article 14 of the Trafficking Protocol.[293] The savings clause was hard won,[294] and its significance should not be underestimated. While a collision of norms could still occur (for example, between the obligation to act against smuggling of migrants and the obligation to ensure the rights of refugees and asylum-seekers), the correct outcome has been clearly articulated: A State that acts against the letter or spirit of international law, including international refugee law, in implementing its obligations under the Migrant Smuggling Protocol is in violation of one of its central provisions.

2.3. REGIONAL LEGAL AGREEMENTS

The renewed interest in trafficking that provided the impetus for the development of an international treaty also prompted the elaboration of similar regional agreements. This section considers the evolution and substantive content of the trafficking-specific legal instruments developed at the regional level over the past decade.

---

[289] Migrant Smuggling Protocol, at Art. 6(3).

[290] Ibid.

[291] Ibid. at Arts. 16(1), (5).

[292] Ibid. at Arts. 16(2)–16(4).

[293] "Nothing in this Protocol shall affect the other rights, obligations and responsibilities of States and individuals under international law, including international humanitarian law and international human rights law and, in particular, where applicable, the 1951 Convention and the 1967 Protocol relating to the Status of Refugees and the principle of non-refoulement as contained therein": ibid. at Art. 19(1).

[294] As late as March 2000, the draft of the Migrant Smuggling Protocol did not contain a savings clause, despite States agreeing on the inclusion of such a clause in the Trafficking Protocol. In its joint submission to the Ad Hoc Committee on the Elaboration of a Convention against Transnational Organized Crime, the Inter-Agency Group "recommended that a savings clause such as that contained in the Trafficking Protocol be inserted, with reference being made to the rights, obligations and responsibilities of States and individuals under international law, including applicable international humanitarian law and international human rights law and, in particular, the 1951 Convention and the 1967 Protocol relating to the Status of Refugees": Inter-Agency Submission, at para. 17. The proposal received support from many States and was finally taken up at the end of the drafting session.

2.3.1. *European Union Instruments*

The European Union (EU) became actively involved in the issue of trafficking from the mid-1990s, releasing, in 1997, a detailed Joint Action on the subject[295] and confirming, several years later, trafficking in persons as a priority for the EU in relation to cooperation for combating and preventing crime.[296] Article 5 of the 2000 EU Charter of Fundamental Rights, which came into effect in November 2009, prohibits trafficking in human beings.[297] During the period 2002–4, the Council of the European Union adopted two legal instruments on this issue: the 2002 Framework Decision on Combating Trafficking in Human Beings[298] (to replace the 1997 Joint Action); and a Joint Action on short-term residency permits for victims of trafficking.[299] In 2009, following an implementation review of the Framework Decision, the Council released a proposal for the repeal of that instrument and adoption of a new Framework Agreement.

2.3.1.1. EU Framework Decision on Combating Trafficking (2002)[300]

On June 12, 2002, eighteen months after it was first proposed by the European Commission, the Council of the European Union adopted a Framework Decision

---

[295] Joint Action of 24 February 1997 concerning action to combat trafficking in human beings and sexual exploitation of children (97/154/JHA), OJ L 063/2, Mar. 4, 1997 (Joint Action on Trafficking).

[296] Treaty on European Union, OJ C 191/1, done Feb. 7, 1992, entered into force Nov. 1, 1993, at Title VI, Art. 29.

[297] Charter of Fundamental Rights of the European Union, OJ C 364/1, Dec. 18, 2000, done Dec. 7, 2000, entered into force Dec. 1, 2009 with the Lisbon Treaty (Treaty of Lisbon amending the Treaty on European Union and the Treaty establishing the European Community, OJ C 306/1, done Dec. 13, 2007, entered into force Dec. 1, 2009). The Charter was proclaimed in December 2000 and had been incorporated in 2004 as Part Two of the now-defunct Treaty establishing a Constitution for Europe, OJ C 310, Dec. 16, 2004, done Oct. 29, 2004 (rejected by French and Dutch voters in 2005). With the entry into force of that treaty's successor, the Lisbon Treaty, the Charter became binding on all EU Member States except those who had opted out by that point. The European Union is required to act and legislate consistently with the Charter as are Member States when implementing EU law. Article 5 provides that "[n]o one shall be held in slavery or servitude. No one shall be required to perform forced or compulsory labour. Trafficking in human beings is prohibited."

[298] Council Framework Decision of 19 July 2002 on combating trafficking in human beings (2002/629/JHA), OJ L 203/1, Aug. 1, 2002 (2002 Framework Decision on Trafficking).

[299] Council Directive 2004/81/EC of 29 April 2004 on the residence permit issued to third-country nationals who are victims of trafficking in human beings or who have been the subject of an action to facilitate illegal immigration, who decide to cooperate with the competent authorities, OJ L 261/19, Aug. 6, 2004 (EU Council Directive on the residence permit).

[300] While not considered a "treaty" in the usual sense, the adoption of the Framework Decision imposed specific obligations on Member States of the European Union, as well as Candidate Countries, to ensure that their laws and practices conform to its substantive provisions. They could, in effect, be viewed as obligations of result. See Treaty on European Union, OJ C 325/5, Dec. 24, 2002, done Feb. 7, 1992, entered into force Nov. 1, 1993, at Art. 34(2)(b). Adopted as instruments of the third pillar, which was in place until December 1, 2009, Framework Decisions entered into

on Combating Trafficking in Human Beings.[301] The Framework Decision was a response to a generally perceived need to address the serious criminal offense of trafficking at the EU level.[302] It built on a range of initiatives and developments, in particular the Council's 1997 Joint Action on trafficking and child sexual exploitation, which had sought, with only very limited success,[303] to promote common action in the areas of definitions, jurisdiction, criminal procedure, assistance to victims, and police/judicial cooperation.[304] All EU Member States were required to have transposed the provisions of the Framework Decision into domestic legislation by July 31, 2004.[305]

The link between the 2002 Framework Decision and the Trafficking Protocol was, from the outset, a strong one. The original proposal envisaged an instrument that would go well beyond the Protocol: extending its minimum standards and, in the words of the Commission, "providing more far-reaching definitions and sanctions."[306] It was not expected that there would be any competition between the two instruments.[307] The European Union had already ratified the Protocol, and the Framework Decision was expected to improve implementation of the international treaty.[308] As noted in Chapter 1, initial differences in the definition of trafficking

force quickly without the requirement of formal ratification. They generally set out a restricted period for implementation. Member States are required to notify both the Council and the Commission on measures taken to implement a Framework Decision. Such implementation is to be evaluated in an implementation report from the Commission that is later assessed by the Council. While the Commission has no legal ability to enforce implementation of a Framework Decision, the European Court of Justice is entitled to interpret Framework Decisions via preliminary rulings and, by 2009, 16 Member States had accepted the authority of the European Court in this regard: "Accompanying Document to the proposal for a Council Framework Decision in preventing and combating trafficking in human beings, and protecting victims, repealing Framework Decision 2002/629/JHA, Impact Assessment," Mar. 25, 2009, SEC (2009) 358 at 30 (Framework Decision Impact Assessment).

[301] 2002 Framework Decision on Trafficking.

[302] Ibid. at preambular para. 7: "It is necessary that the serious criminal offence of trafficking in human beings be addressed not only through individual action by each Member State but by a comprehensive approach … this Framework Decision confines itself to the minimum required in order to achieve those objectives at European level."

[303] C. Rijken, *Trafficking in Persons: Prosecution from a European Perspective* (2003), at 123.

[304] Joint Action on Trafficking. Through the Joint Action, EU Member States agreed to review existing laws and practices with a view to improving judicial cooperation and ensuring appropriate penalties (including confiscation of the proceeds of trafficking). Member States were also to ensure protection for witnesses and assistance for victims and their families. The Joint Action made extensive provision for strengthening cooperation between Member States in all relevant areas including judicial processes and information exchange. Note that the legal status and effect of Joint Actions is subject to some dispute. See Obokata, *Trafficking of Human Beings from a Human Rights Perspective*, at 97–98, and also at chapter 3 of that book on other important antecedents.

[305] 2002 Framework Decision on Trafficking, at Art. 10(1).

[306] "EU Urges Higher Priority on Trafficking in Women and Children," Europa Press Release IP/01/325, Mar. 7, 2001.

[307] Ibid.

[308] Ibid.

were smoothed out over time and the final version reflected the one set out in the Protocol in relation to all but a few, relatively minor elements.[309]

The Framework Decision retained and, in some respects, significantly expanded the Trafficking Protocol's criminal justice focus.[310] EU countries are required to criminalize and penalize a full range of trafficking-related offenses whether committed by natural or legal persons.[311] The inclusion of precise rules on penalties, as well as their broad application to legal persons, represents a general strengthening of the relevant provisions of the Protocol. For example, in addition to establishing a standard of "effective, proportionate and dissuasive" criminal penalties,[312] the Framework Decision introduced the concept of aggravated offenses in relation to which the stipulated minimum penalties are to apply.[313] The jurisdiction clause is broader than that of the Protocol, although Member States retain a right to opt out of its more innovative aspects.[314] In another departure from the Protocol, Member States are required to ensure that, at least in relation to offenses committed in their territory, the investigation and prosecution of trafficking cases do not rely on victim complaints.[315] The stipulation that investigations and prosecutions can proceed *ex officio* is clearly intended to address one aspect of victim intimidation that particularly compromises an effective criminal justice response to trafficking. The final text weakens the victim protection provisions that appeared in early drafts, and the only two substantive provisions on this aspect both concern children. Children are to be

---

[309] These differences relate to the element of "purpose." Unlike the Protocol, the list set out in the Framework Decision appears to be an exhaustive one. It adds "compulsory labour" and "pornography" and omits "removal of organs": 2002 Framework Decision on Trafficking, at Art. 1.

[310] Note, however, that most commentators and the European Union itself have failed to appreciate the relationship between the Protocol and the Convention, which operates to bring the comprehensive criminal justice provisions of the latter into the former (see notes 112-115 and accompanying text above). See, for example, H. Askola, *Legal Responses to Trafficking in Women for Sexual Exploitation in the European Union* (2007) (Askola, *Legal Responses to Trafficking in Women*), at 125; and Framework Decision Impact Assessment. For example, while the Protocol itself does not contain any specific provision on sanctions, the Convention operates to require States to ensure that the relevant offenses are made subject to sanctions that take into account the gravity of the offense: Organized Crime Convention, at Art. 11(1).

[311] 2002 Framework Decision on Trafficking, at Arts. 1–5.

[312] Ibid. at Art. 3(1).

[313] Ibid. at Art. 3(2). Note that this provision appears to respond to a proposal made by the UN High Commissioner for Human Rights in "Note by the United Nations High Commissioner for Human Rights on the Proposed EU Council Framework Decision on Combating Trafficking in Human Beings (Brussels (COM) 2000 854 final/2)," April, 2001, at para. 7. As noted above, the concept of aggravated offenses was subsequently incorporated into the European Trafficking Convention.

[314] 2002 Framework Decision on Trafficking, at Art. 6. States can choose whether or not to establish jurisdiction over situations in which: (1) the offender is a national and the offense is committed abroad; and (2) the offense is committed abroad for the benefit of a legal person established in the Member State: ibid. at Art. 6(2). Note, however, that in respect of the first situation, reserving Member States would still be bound by the rule of "extradite or prosecute": ibid. at Art. 6(3). Note also that there is no provision for jurisdiction in relation to offenses committed abroad against a national of a Member State.

[315] Ibid. at Art. 7(1).

considered "particularly vulnerable victims" in relation to European Union rules on the standing of victims in criminal proceedings.[316] Member States are required to take measures to ensure that child victims and their families receive appropriate assistance.[317]

The greatest criticisms of the 2002 Framework Decision on Trafficking can be made in respect of what was left out. As noted above, provisions with respect to victims are both weak and narrow. There is no real acknowledgement of the need to protect the rights and interests of trafficked children. There are no provisions at all on victim repatriation, prevention of trafficking, or remedies. Critically, the 2002 Framework Decision does not contain an antidiscrimination clause or any kind of savings clause that would operate to affirm and protect rights already established under international law, including refugee law and human rights.[318] For many, both within and outside the EU, the initiative of a Framework Decision provided the perfect opportunity for the EU to demonstrate its oft-stated commitment to protecting the rights of trafficked persons and their families, as well as to addressing the root causes behind the movement and the demand which feeds it. Despite great encouragement from a diverse range of agencies and organizations including the European Parliament itself,[319] the EU decided not to take up this challenge, arguing that certain issues were outside its competence and promising that some of the more obvious weaknesses would be taken up at a later date.[320] The end result is an instrument that, on the positive side, has proved to be influential in ensuring maximum uniformity between Member States with respect to their criminal law approaches to trafficking.[321] However, in terms of victims' rights and the prevention of trafficking, the 2002 Framework Decision offers very little and in fact can be seen to represent a substantial retreat from previous commitments of the EU, for example, those contained in the 1997 Joint Action on Trafficking repealed as a result of the 2002 Framework Decision.[322] That these weaknesses have recently been officially acknowledged and acted upon (see Chapter 2.3.1.3), is a welcome development.

---

[316] Ibid. at Art. 7(2).

[317] Ibid. at Art. 7(3).

[318] These points are addressed in the HCHR Submission and further explored in a subsequent, joint submission, from the High Commissioner for Human Rights and the High Commissioner for Refugees, "Observations by the United Nations High Commissioner for Human Rights and the United Nations High Commissioner for Refugees on the proposal for an EU Council Framework Decision on Combating Trafficking in Human Beings," June 27, 2001. See also the European Parliament submission in the following note.

[319] European Parliament, Committee on Citizens' Freedoms and Rights, Justice and Home Affairs, "Report on the proposal for a Council framework decision on combating trafficking in human beings (COM(2000) 854 – C5–0042/2001 – 2001/0024(CNS))," A5–0183/2001, May 30, 2001.

[320] Askola, *Legal Responses to Trafficking in Women*, at 126.

[321] "Report from the Commission to the Council and the European Parliament based on Article 10 of the Council Framework Decision of 19 July 2002 on combating trafficking in human beings," COM(2006) 187 final, May 2, 2006 (2002 Framework Decision Implementation Report).

[322] In accordance with Article 9 of the 2002 Framework Decision on Trafficking.

2.3.1.2. EU Council Directive on Short-term Residency Permits

As noted above, the retreat on victims' rights through the 2002 Framework Decision was made possible, at least in part, by vague but frequent promises from the EU that such matters would be dealt with in a subsequent instrument concerning the question of short-term stays or residency for victims of trafficking.[323] Unfortunately, the EU Council Directive 2004/81/EC on the residence permit issued to third-country nationals who are victims of trafficking in human beings or who have been the subject of an action to facilitate illegal immigration, who decide to cooperate with authorities, which entered into force almost two years later,[324] did not fulfill these promises. The Directive seeks to prevent migrant smuggling and trafficking by providing victims of such practices with incentives to come forward and cooperate with authorities in the detection and prosecution of smugglers and traffickers. It was prompted by a growing realization within the European countries of the inherent obstacles in obtaining and sustaining the cooperation of individuals who fear for their safety and wellbeing and who have little to gain in complaining to the police or otherwise assisting in investigations.[325]

The Directive adopts a "minimum-standard" version of the national regimes that had already been established in a number of European countries to enable victims of trafficking to cooperate with law enforcement authorities by providing assistance and temporary residence permits.[326] It applies to third-country victims of trafficking and may also apply to victims of illegal migration if Member States wish to

---

[323] Such assurances were given informally to the Office of the United Nations High Commissioner for Human Rights and the United Nations High Commissioner for Refugees as well as to various NGO groups lobbying the EU for greater victim protection in the 2002 Framework Decision (personal information); see also an undated briefing paper released by Anti-Slavery International and ECPAT (UK), "Briefing on a proposal for: European Union Council Directive (COM (2000) 71 Final), On the Short-term Residence Permit Issued to Victims of Action to Facilitate Illegal Immigration or Trafficking in Human Beings Who Co-operate with the Competent Authorities" (ASI-ECPAT Briefing Paper), which noted that "[p]rotection mechanisms for victims of trafficking were omitted from the [2002 Framework Decision on Trafficking], despite recommendation for their inclusion by the European Parliament, the United Nations High Commissioner for Human Rights and numerous non-governmental organisations (NGOs). Indeed, during discussion of the Framework Decision it was implied that protection measures would be dealt with in the current directive."

[324] EU Council Directive on the residence permit. All EU States, with the exception of Denmark and the UK, who have both negotiated an opting-out clause, were required to bring their national law in line with the directive before August 6, 2006.

[325] This dilemma, and its obvious solution, had already been acknowledged by the EU itself on a number of different occasions: see European Parliament Resolution on the exploitation of prostitution and trade in human beings, Resolution A2–52/89 of 14 April 1989, OJ C 120, May 16, 1989, at 352 ff; European Parliament Resolution on trade in women, Resolutions B3–1264, 1283 and 1309/93 of 16 September 1993, OJ C 268, Oct. 4, 1993, 141 ff, points 2 and 10; and Report on trafficking in human beings, European Parliament Resolution on trafficking in human beings, Resolution A4–0326/95 of 18 January 1996, OJ C 032, Feb. 5, 1996, 88 ff, point 25.

[326] Belgium (1994); Italy (1998); the Netherlands (2000); Spain (2000); France (2002); and Greece (2002).

extend its application in this way.[327] Victims are to be informed, at the discretion of national authorities, of the possibility of being granted temporary residence permits in exchange for cooperation with police or judicial authorities.[328] Victims are to be granted a period of grace (a "reflection period," the duration of which is to be fixed by Member States) allowing them to escape the influence of traffickers so they can make an informed decision as to whether to cooperate with criminal justice agencies in the investigation and prosecution of these persons. During that period, identified victims will not be expelled and will be entitled to emergency medical and psychological care and material assistance.[329] In order to secure optimum cooperation from victims, Member States are also to provide them with free legal aid, translation, and interpretation services.[330] The reflection period can be terminated on grounds of public policy and national security.[331] It can also be terminated if the victim actively, voluntarily, and on her or his own initiative renews contact with the trafficker.[332] A temporary residence permit may be issued during or following expiration of the "reflection period" on the basis of various requirements, each decided by authorities of the receiving State.[333]

The explanatory memorandum accompanying the initial proposal explicitly stated that it is not concerned with either victim protection or witness protection, and that such protection is neither its aim nor its legal basis. Clearly, the overwhelming concern of the Commission was to ensure that the proposed visa regime was not open to opportunistic abuse or to otherwise aggravating the problem of illegal

---

[327] EU Council Directive on the residence permit, at Art. 3. The initial proposal covered both victims of trafficking and victims of illegally facilitated migration. It was noted, at the time, that "the concept of 'victim of action to facilitate illegal immigration' has a very specific meaning, in that it does not cover all those who seek assistance in illegal immigration, only those who might be reasonably regarded as victims ... who have suffered harm, for example having their lives endangered or physical injury." European Council Proposal for a Council Directive on the short-term residence permit issued to victims of action to facilitate illegal immigration or trafficking in human beings who cooperate with the competent authorities, COM(2002) 71 final – 2002/0043 (CNS), Feb. 11, 2002, at para. 2.1. The proposal includes both the draft Directive and a detailed Explanatory Memorandum (Explanatory Memorandum on the short-term residence permit). This clarification was subsequently dropped in favor of granting States full discretion to decide whether or not to grant residence permits to victims of illegal migration.

[328] EU Council Directive on the residence permit, at Art. 5. There appears no obligation on Member States to inform *all* victims of trafficking of the possibility of obtaining a temporary residence permit, and Member States further retain the right to decide whether NGOs can also have a role to play providing such information: ibid.

[329] Ibid. at Art. 7.

[330] Ibid. See also the Explanatory Memorandum on the short-term residence permit on this point.

[331] EU Council Directive on the residence permit, at Art. 6.

[332] Ibid. As noted by Raffaelli, this type of requirement is typically imposed on criminal informants who decide to cooperate with criminal justice authorities. Its purpose in this context is unclear. See R. Raffaelli, "The European Approach to the Protection of Trafficking Victims: The Council of Europe Convention, the EU Directive and the Italian Experience," (2009) 10 *German Law Journal* 205.

[333] Ibid. at Art. 8.

migration into the European Union.[334] From that perspective, the highly restrictive approach adopted by the Directive is entirely understandable. However, the trade-off is most likely to be felt by victims of trafficking: those who, for one reason or another, are unable or not required to give testimony or otherwise cooperate in investigations; and those who have cooperated, benefited from the regime, and are then repatriated against their will. For the former category, likely to include the most vulnerable, including the deeply traumatized, the absence of substantive victim protection provisions in the 2002 Framework Decision on Trafficking ultimately means, at least under the EU regime, little or no entitlement to basic assistance and support and inevitable deportation. For beneficiaries of the new visa regime, important protection concerns will remain. As some have pointed out,[335] safety risks are not necessarily ameliorated by criminal proceedings, and trafficked persons who have cooperated in a prosecution are much more likely than others to compromise the safety of themselves and their families. The failure of the proposal to prohibit or at least warn against return in cases where the victim is likely to be subjected to serous human rights violations is another serious omission.

Other objections to the Directive are more fundamental, questioning, for example, a logic so focused on restrictions, it can only see a solution in "carving out limited exceptions to generally ungenerous rules."[336] In June 2009, the Group of Experts on Trafficking in Human Beings, established by the European Commission in 2007,[337] issued a detailed opinion on a possible revision to the Directive.[338] The opinion criticized the current text for "insufficiently address[ing] the legitimate needs and rights of victims to support and assistance," in particular the tying of such assistance and support to victim cooperation in criminal proceedings.[339] It proposed, *inter alia*, that a new Directive should focus exclusively on victims of trafficking; that its scope should be broadened to cover all victims, not just those from outside

---

[334] This was confirmed at the September 2002 European Conference on Trafficking by the outcome document, which noted that "[t]he implementation of such a residence permit must be carefully monitored and evaluated to prevent the incidence of 'procedure shopping' whereby the capacity to accommodate and support genuine trafficked victims is eroded by the claims of fraudulent victims." "Recommendations, Standards and Best Practices Brussels," in "Declaration on Preventing and Combating Trafficking in Human Beings," Annex, adopted by the European Conference on Preventing and Combating Trafficking in Human Beings – Global Challenge for the 21st Century, Brussels, Sept. 18–20, 2002, at 11.

[335] ASI-ECPAT Briefing Paper.

[336] Askola, *Legal Responses to Trafficking in Women*, at 94. See also M.-H. Chou, "The European Union and the Fight against Human Trafficking: Comprehensive or Contradicting?" (2008) 4 *St Antony's International Review* 76, esp. at 76–82.

[337] European Commission Decision of 17 October 2007 setting up the Group of Experts on Trafficking in Human Beings (2007/675/EC), OJ L 277/29, Oct. 20, 2007.

[338] Opinion No. 4/2009 of the Group of Experts on Trafficking in Human Beings on a possible revision of Council Directive 2004/81/EC of 29 April 2004 on the residence permit issued to third-country nationals who are victims of trafficking in human beings or who have been the subject of an action to facilitate illegal immigration, who cooperate with the competent authorities, June 16, 2009.

[339] Ibid. at 2.

the European Union; that the granting of the reflection period be automatic, its purpose broadened, and its duration extended; that the conditions under which residence permits can be granted be expanded; and that international protection obligations be incorporated.[340]

2.3.1.3. Proposal for a Replacement to the 2002 Framework Decision (2009–2010)

Evaluation and monitoring of the European Union's response to trafficking over the period 2006–8 confirmed that there were a number of significant problems, most particularly that "the number of criminal proceedings and victims assisted were not high enough compared to the estimated scale and the gravity of the crime."[341] In March 2009, the Commission adopted and submitted to the Council of the European Union two proposals – one for a new Framework Decision on trafficking,[342] the other for a Framework Decision on combating sexual abuse and sexual exploitation of children – each aimed at strengthening the provisions of its predecessor instrument.[343] The structure of the two proposals was very similar, and many provisions, for example those relating to penalties and jurisdiction, were virtually identical. As explored further below, both Framework Decisions were also linked by a provision that recognized an overlap in scope of application between them. It should be noted that neither of the proposed Framework Decisions was adopted before the entry into force of the Treaty of Lisbon on December 1, 2009. Under the new decision-making processes put in place by the Treaty of Lisbon, the drafts of the proposed Framework Decisions were inactivated. However, those parts of the proposed Framework Decisions that are relevant to the following discussion have received general support and have been resubmitted in substance for continued negotiation. A new proposal for a Directive on trafficking was tabled on March 29, 2010, and it "is, to its content, essentially identical to the previous Proposal for a Framework Decision."[344] Although the following discussion

---

[340] Ibid. at 3–5.

[341] "Proposal for a Framework Decision on preventing and combating trafficking in human beings, and protecting victims, repealing Framework Decision 2002/629/JHA," Europa Press Release MEMO/01/131, Mar. 23, 2009. See also, 2002 Framework Decision Implementation Report, and Commission of the European Communities, Evaluation and monitoring of the implementation of the EU Plan on best practices, standards and procedures for combating and preventing trafficking in persons, COM (2008) 657 final, Oct. 17, 2008.

[342] Commission of the European Communities, Proposal for a Framework Decision on preventing and combating trafficking in human beings, and protecting victims, repealing Framework Decision 2002/629/JHA, COM(2009) 136 final, Mar. 25, 2009 (Framework Decision 2009 Proposal), at 4.

[343] Commission of the European Communities, Proposal for a Framework Decision on combating the sexual abuse, sexual exploitation of children and child pornography, repealing Framework Decision 2004/68/JHA, COM(2009) 135 final, Mar. 25, 2009.

[344] European Commission, Proposal for a Directive of the European Parliament and of the Council on preventing and combating trafficking in human beings, and protecting victims, repealing Framework Decision 2002/629/JHA, COM(2010) 95 final, Mar. 29, 2010 (EC Directive 2010 Proposal), at 6. See also "Proposal for a Directive on preventing and combating trafficking in human

focuses on the now-lapsed proposed Framework Decision on Trafficking, its analysis is equally applicable to the successor proposal. Any changes made to that text through the subsequent draft are noted.

The process for elaborating the new Framework Decision on Trafficking was significantly more open than had been the case for its predecessor, comprising a series of wide-ranging consultative meetings involving Member States, technical experts, and NGOs including representatives of victim support groups.[345] Those consultations, together with the Commission's own research, confirmed that criminals were generally not being brought to justice; that victims were not receiving adequate assistance, protection, or compensation; that there were insufficient measures in place to prevent trafficking; and that the situation itself was being poorly monitored, leading to lack of knowledge and coordination.[346] The Impact Assessment accompanying the proposed new Framework Decision identified a range of options, eventually favoring the most expansive one: new legislation on prosecution, victim support, prevention, and monitoring, accompanied by a series of nonlegislative options (such as training, preventative measures in countries of origin and destination, and victim support schemes) that would support the effective implementation of the Framework Decision.[347]

The proposed Framework Decision declared trafficking to be a serious crime and "a gross violation of human rights" and identified as its objectives more rigorous prevention and prosecution, and protection of victims' rights.[348] The substantive provisions of the proposal are considered below.

Criminal Law and Prosecutions. In order to enhance approximation of legislation, the proposed Framework Decision provided a definition of trafficking that was identical to the one set out in the Trafficking Protocol, except that it extended the open-ended list of practices that are to be included as "exploitation" to "exploitation of activities associated with begging or of unlawful activities."[349] The purpose of this

---

beings and protecting victims, repealing Framework Decision 2002/629/JHA," MEMO/10/108, Mar. 29, 2010. The new proposed Directive was tabled as the present volume was being finalized for publication; this volume's discussion of recent EU policy focuses on the lapsed Framework Decision 2009 Proposal but remains equally relevant to the "essentially identical" (at 6) successor EC Directive 2010 Proposal.

[345] Framework Decision 2009 Proposal, at 4.
[346] Framework Decision Impact Assessment, at 11–14.
[347] Ibid.
[348] Framework Decision 2009 Proposal, at preambular paras. 1, 3.
[349] Ibid. at Art. 1 and preambular para. 4. It appears that the reference to trafficking for the purpose of exploitation in unlawful activities is meant to refer to, for example, trafficking for drug trafficking. Note however that the lack of clarity around both "begging" and "other unlawful activities" was raised as a concern by the Council in its consideration of the draft: Council of the European Union, "Note of the Presidency: Proposal for a Council Framework Decision on combating the sexual abuse, sexual exploitation of children and child-pornography, repealing Framework Decision 2004/68/JHA – State of play; Proposal for a Council Framework Decision on preventing and combating trafficking in human beings, and protecting victims, repealing Framework Decision 2002/629/

expansion was to "make easier the task of interpreters and national legislators."[350] The revised text affirmed the need for penalties to be "effective, dissuasive and proportionate to the gravity of the crime," as well as to contribute to more effective investigation and prosecution and international cooperation.[351] To that end, it set precise maximum penalties for all trafficking-related offenses while retaining the concept introduced in the 2002 Framework Decision of aggravated offenses with penalties adapted to the seriousness of the offense.[352]

The jurisdictional reach of the proposed Framework Decision was significantly expanded in comparison with its 2002 predecessor, in an effort to address the extreme mobility of criminal groups within the EU area.[353] Member States would now be required to exercise jurisdiction over trafficking-related offenses that had any connection with that State, whether through the place of offense or the nationality or habitual residence of either perpetrator or victim.[354] In relation to offenses committed outside the territory, Member States would further be required to ensure that application of the principle of double criminality was not applied to thwart the establishment of jurisdiction,[355] and further, that establishment of such jurisdiction would not depend on the complaint of the victim in the State where the offense occurred or on a positive action of that State with regard to the offense.[356] In cases where jurisdiction could be established in two or more States, Member States were required to cooperate in identifying the most suitable location for prosecution with view to centralizing proceedings, and a role was envisaged for Eurojust in settling such matters.[357]

JHA – State of play," Doc. 9892/09, May 18, 2009 (Council Review, May 2009), at 7. This concern notwithstanding, the successor proposal to the Framework Decision 2009 Proposal contains an identical provision: EC Directive 2010 Proposal, at Art. 2(3).

[350] Framework Decision Impact Assessment, at 24.

[351] Framework Decision 2009 Proposal, at preambular para. 5.

[352] Ibid. at Art. 5. Note that the concept of aggravated offenses has been expanded beyond the 2002 Framework Decision on Trafficking to include offenses committed against children. Note further that under the proposed Framework Decision, legal persons are also subject to criminal liability (at Art. 4) and sanctions (at Art. 5). The penalty provisions attracted some criticism during the review of the proposed Framework Decision in the Council. Concerns were expressed, for example, over the severity of the penalties, the lack of differentiation in the level of penalties according to the types and gravity of the offenses, and the structure of the corresponding Articles that did not appear to specify the basic elements of crime on one hand and aggravating circumstances on the other: Council Review, May 2009, at 4.

[353] Framework Decision Impact Assessment, at 25.

[354] A Member State is required to take necessary measures to establish jurisdiction when the offense is committed in its territory; where the offender is a national or having habitual residence in its territory; where the victim is a national or having habitual residence in its territory; and where the offense is committed for the benefit of a legal person established in its territory: Framework Decision 2009 Proposal, at Art. 8(1).

[355] Ibid. at Art. 8(2).

[356] Ibid. at Art. 8(3).

[357] Ibid. at Art. 8(4). Factors to be taken into account in making this determination were provided. Note, however, that the provision on coordination of prosecutions has been superseded by a subsequent

The requirement in the 2002 Framework Decision that investigation and prosecution of trafficking cases not be dependent on victim complaints was retained in the new instrument, with the addition that criminal proceedings might continue even if the victim withdraws his or her complaint.[358] Initiation of proceedings should also be possible after child victims of trafficking reach the age of majority.[359] Member States were further required to ensure that investigators and prosecutors be trained and that the full range of investigative tools be made available to them.[360]

Victim Protection and Support. It was in relation to victim protection and support that the new Framework Decision most radically departed from its predecessor. Member States were required to establish "appropriate measures aimed at early identification and support to victims."[361] Background documents confirmed that such mechanisms were to be for the benefit of *all* victims of trafficking, including persons in relation to whom there are "indications" they have been trafficked,[362] irrespective of whether or not they

Framework Decision of 30 November 2009 on prevention and settlement of conflicts of jurisdiction, OJ L 328/42, Dec. 15, 2009, although this Framework Decision does not contain binding rules on how possible conflicts of jurisdiction are to be resolved. That Framework Decision on conflicts of jurisdiction is noted at preambular paragraph 2 of the new EC Directive 2010 Proposal, the successor to the lapsed Framework Decision 2009 Proposal. The EC Directive 2010 Proposal does not otherwise address the coordination of prosecutions.

[358] Framework Decision 2009 Proposal, at Art. 7(1).

[359] Ibid. at Art. 7(2).

[360] Ibid. at Arts. 7(3)–7(4). This provision was prompted by a concern that trafficking investigations were being carried at an inappropriately low level, and that Member States required encouragement to ensure that such investigations were tackled as serious and organized crimes, by specially trained law enforcement officials who had at their disposal appropriate investigative tools and techniques: Framework Decision Impact Assessment, at 26.

[361] Framework Decision 2009 Proposal, at Art. 10(3); see similarly the EC Directive 2010 Proposal, at Art. 10(4). Note that under the third pillar, the proposed Framework Decision could only provide for an obligation to establish such victim support schemes and would not be able to stipulate quality standards or any other matter relating to their establishment and functioning. The Impact Assessment document notes that these matters "would be the object of a separate non binding document": Framework Decision Impact Assessment, at 27. Note further that provisions dealing with assistance are intended to apply to victims who do not fall within the scope of application of the EU Council Directive on the residence permit, thereby addressing the protection gap that currently exists with respect to EU nationals: ibid.

[362] Framework Decision 2009 Proposal, at Art. 10(2). Note that there was no explicit provision to the effect that a victim who appears to be a child is to be presumed to be a child (and thereby entitled to additional measures of protection and support) until otherwise established, though the Framework Decision 2009 Proposal did cross-reference, at Article 11, a presumption of age provision in another proposed (and now-lapsed) Framework Decision: Commission of the European Communities, Proposal for a Council Framework Decision on combating the sexual abuse, sexual exploitation of children and child pornography, repealing Framework Decision 2004/68/JHA, COM(2009) 135 final, Mar. 25, 2009, at Art. 14(1). The absence of an explicit presumption of age provision is rectified in the successor EC Directive 2010 Proposal, which provides that "where the age of a person subject to trafficking in human beings is uncertain and there are reasons to believe that the person is a child, the person is presumed to be a child in order to receive immediate access to assistance, support and protection": at Art. 12(2).

cooperate with criminal justice agencies.[363] However, the effect of this provision was lessened somewhat by all other measures, including specific provisions relating to protection and support, being framed within the context of criminal proceedings[364] with only children being entitled to expansive protections solely on the basis of their status as victims.[365] For example, victims were to receive assistance and support to "enable them to recover and escape from the influence of perpetrators" and to "enable their rights and interests to be presented and considered in criminal proceedings."[366]

Victims of trafficking (including persons in relation to whom there are "indications" that they have been trafficked)[367] would be entitled to a wide range of assistance measures. Significantly, however, these measures were all framed within the context of criminal proceedings. The most extensive victim support provisions related to measures aimed at avoiding secondary victimization of vulnerable persons (all children and adult victims assessed as such) in criminal proceedings.[368] Member States were, for example, required to provide all such victims with access to free legal counseling and legal representation, as well as to protection based on risk assessment and special measures in the legal process itself, such as identity protection and alternatives to direct testimony.[369] It should be noted, however, that the newly proposed Directive on trafficking, the successor to the lapsed draft Framework Decision, includes a new clause clarifying these seeming inconsistencies firmly in favor of nonconditionality: "Member States shall take the necessary measures to ensure that assistance and support for a victim are not made conditional on the victim's willingness to act as a witness."[370]

The draft Framework Decision addressed the issue of status offenses: the problem of victims being detained, prosecuted, or punished for minor offenses that are typically associated with the victimization process, such as violation of immigration laws and involvement in unlawful activities such as prostitution. A general but "soft"

---

[363] Framework Decision Impact Assessment, at 27.

[364] See further, discussion of the protection and support provisions of the draft Framework Decision in Chapter 5.

[365] This entitlement was secured, indirectly, through Article 11, which links the proposed Framework Decision on trafficking to provisions of the proposed Framework Decision on child sexual exploitation that require, for example, measures to ensure protection and assistance of all child victims independently of their involvement in criminal proceedings; presumption of minor age; and appointment of a guardian/representative:ibid. at Art. 9. It was unclear whether Article 11 would operate in situations where the exploitation of the child did not relate to sexual abuse, sexual exploitation, or child pornography.

[366] Ibid. at Art. 10(4). Note that these aspects have been deleted from the equivalent Article 10 of the revised EC Directive 2010 Proposal.

[367] Framework Decision 2009 Proposal, at Art. 10(2).

[368] The provisions on victims' rights in criminal proceedings supplemented those set out in the European Union Council Framework Decision of 15 March 2001 on the standing of victims in criminal proceedings, OJ L 82/1, Mar. 22, 2001, which is expected to be revised in the near future. For a comprehensive discussion of that Framework Decision, see Project Victims in Europe, *Implementation of the EU Framework Decision on the standing of victims in the criminal proceedings in the Member States of the European Union* (2009).

[369] Framework Decision 2009 Proposal, at Art. 9.

[370] EC Directive 2010 Proposal, at Art. 10(3).

decriminalization provision required Member States to provide for the *possibility* of not prosecuting or imposing penalties on victims for their involvement in unlawful activities that are a direct consequence of their having been trafficked.[371]

Prevention of Trafficking. The draft Framework Decision contained several important prevention provisions. In an effort to promote rapid and accurate victim identification as well as the provision of immediate support to the most vulnerable, Member States were required to "promote" regular training for officials likely to come into contact with victims and potential victims of trafficking.[372] They were also required to "seek to" discourage the demand that fosters "all forms of exploitation" (presumably related to trafficking).[373] Finally, and most controversially, Member States were required to "consider taking measures" to establish as a criminal offense the use of services of a victim of trafficking with the knowledge that the individual is a victim of a trafficking-related offense.[374] The successor Proposal for a Directive on trafficking includes a further provision requiring Member States to take measures to raise awareness and reduce the risk of people, especially children, becoming trafficking victims, "such as information and awareness raising campaigns, research and education programmes, where appropriate in cooperation with civil society organisations."[375]

Implementation and Monitoring. The thin and inconclusive report submitted in 2006 by the Council to the Commission on implementation of the 2002 Framework Decision served to confirm the weaknesses of the implementation arrangements for that instrument.[376] The proposed Framework Decision nevertheless adopted a similar approach: Member States were given a two-year period in which to take the necessary

---

[371] Framework Decision 2009 Proposal, at Art. 6. The reference is to nonprosecution or nonpenalization for involvement in unlawful activities "as a direct consequence of having been subjected to any of the illicit means," for example, force, coercion, or abuse of authority. It is unclear whether this wording (as opposed to a general reference to involvement in unlawful activities as a direct consequence of having been trafficked) narrows the range of potential situations in which victims of trafficking could benefit from this provision. The wording also introduces potential confusion with respect to status offenses involving children, as the element of "means" is not part of the definition of trafficking in children. Note that this provision attracted some criticism during scrutiny of the draft proposal in the Council, with some delegations expressing the view that introduction of a nonpunishment clause entailed certain risks: Council Review, May 2009, at 4. It should be noted that as the present volume was going to press, the latest draft of the EC Directive 2010 Proposal obtained by the author (dated June 28, 2010) contained a much stronger nonprosecution and nonpenalization clause in the form "Member States shall not prosecute or impose penalties on victims" for involvement in such offenses. If it does survive, this provision will be the most emphatic affirmation of the principle that victims of trafficking should not be prosecuted or penalized for status-related offenses.

[372] Framework Decision 2009 Proposal, at Art. 12(1).

[373] Ibid. at Art. 12(2).

[374] Ibid. at Art. 12(1). Further on the discussions on this point, see Framework Decision Impact Assessment, at 29.

[375] EC Directive 2010 Proposal, at Art. 15(2).

[376] 2002 Framework Decision Implementation Report. A significant portion of the report is occupied with describing the failure of Member States to meet agreed reporting deadlines.

measures required of them and to report on the relevant parts of their national law to the Council. The Council would analyze implementation on the basis of individual State reports and prepare a consolidated report to the Commission.[377] However, an important additional measure was provided through a requirement that Member States establish National Rapporteurs or similar mechanisms with the task of (at least) monitoring the implementation of measures envisaged in the Framework Decision.[378] Background documents confirmed that the drafters envisaged such monitoring mechanisms eventually joining together in a regional network that would facilitate the exchange of information between Member States as well as harmonization of both methodology and practice.[379] The implementation provisions of the new Proposal for a Directive on trafficking are substantially the same, except for the additional provisions that State reports would include a "correlation table" comparing national laws with the provisions of the Directive[380] and that the Commission would prepare a consolidated report not only in the first four years but also every three years thereafter.[381]

Next Steps. The reaction to the proposed new Framework Decision had generally been positive, although, as noted throughout the analysis presented above, several of its more innovative elements attracted some criticism, particularly from Member States. The proposed requirement of National Rapporteurs was especially contentious. In addition, some concern was expressed that the new instrument may not have been necessary, particularly in light of the 2005 European Trafficking Convention.[382] As noted above, the Treaty of Lisbon entered into force before the adoption of the proposed Framework Decision, and in doing so abolished the

[377] Framework Decision 2009 Proposal, at Art. 16.

[378] Ibid. at Art. 13. The Impact Assessment noted that this measure is crucial as "better knowledge of the situation of trafficking is the necessary starting point for the establishment of effective anti-trafficking policy." The Assessment identified a range of tasks and functions of such monitoring measures while noting that such details would not be covered by the Framework Decision: Framework Decision Impact Assessment, at 29. Note that under the successor EC Directive 2010 Proposal, the tasks of the National Rapporteur are amended from "monitoring of the implementation of measures envisaged in this Framework Decision" (Framework Decision 2009 Proposal, at Art. 13) to "the carrying out of assessments on trafficking in human beings trends, the measuring of results of anti-trafficking actions and reporting to the relevant national authorities" (EC Directive 2010 Proposal, at Art. 16).

[379] Framework Decision Impact Assessment, at 29. Note that as this volume was going to press, the EU was also taking steps to establish a new EU Anti-Trafficking Coordinator under a revised version of the proposed EC Directive.

[380] EC Directive 2010 Proposal, at Art. 18(1).

[381] Ibid. at 19(1).

[382] Council of Europe Convention on Action against Trafficking in Human Beings and its Explanatory Report, ETS 197, 16.V.2005, done May 16, 2005, entered into force Feb. 1, 2008 (European Trafficking Convention). The European Scrutiny Committee of the UK Parliament, for example, queried whether full implementation of the 2002 Framework Decision and the Council of Europe Convention "[m]ight … be a more effective means to counter trafficking in human beings and help victims than creating new legislative requirements": UK House of Commons, European Scrutiny Committee, Twentieth Report: Documents considered by the Committee on 3 June 2009, at para. 11.8, available at http://www.publications.parliament.uk/pa/cm200809/cmselect/cmeuleg/19-xviii/1913.htm (accessed Oct. 13, 2009).

decision-making system used to produce Framework Decisions. This notwithstanding, there appeared to remain considerable interest in resubmitting the substance of the proposed Framework Decision for further negotiation under the reformed EU processes, and indeed an "essentially identical" proposal for a new Directive on trafficking was tabled on March 29, 2010.[383]

2.3.2. *The Council of Europe Convention against Trafficking*

The Council of Europe's work on trafficking can be traced back to the early 1990s when the issue was still one of marginal relevance for international organizations and national governments.[384] The first high-level political statement on trafficking came at a summit held in Strasbourg in 1997. The Final Declaration from this event refers specifically to violence against women and makes a direct link between exploitation of women and threats to security and democracy in Europe.[385] Since 1997, much Council of Europe activity in this area has been directed toward encouraging and supporting comprehensive national and subregional responses to trafficking that identify and assign responsibility to key players including legislators, criminal justice officials, consular officials, educators, and the media.[386] Increasingly, the attention of the Council focused on countries of origin and transit in south and southeastern Europe, with particular attention to legislative reform.[387] By involving these countries, the Council was able to make and foster important connections with the major destination points in western Europe.

The Council of Europe's somewhat unfocused approach to the issue of trafficking took a turn in the first years of the twenty-first century with the development of two instruments by the Committee of Ministers. The first instrument, adopted in 2000, related to trafficking for sexual exploitation.[388] The second instrument,

---

[383] European Commission, Proposal for a Directive of the European Parliament and of the Council on preventing and combating trafficking in human beings, and protecting victims, repealing Framework Decision 2002/629/JHA, COM(2010) 95 final, Mar. 29, 2010, at 6. See also "Proposal for a Directive on preventing and combating trafficking in human beings and protecting victims, repealing Framework Decision 2002/629/JHA," MEMO/10/108, Mar. 29, 2010.

[384] In 1991, the Council of Europe adopted Recommendation No. R (91) 11 on sexual exploitation, pornography, and prostitution of and trafficking in children and young adults. That same year, the Committee of Ministers Committee for Equality between Women and Men (CDEG) organized a seminar on the subject, already identifying trafficking as a violation of human rights and already delimiting the scope of action and concern to women and children. Following the seminar, CDEG set up a Group of Experts on Traffic in Women that identified for the Council the key elements of an action plan including recommendations regarding both criminal justice action against trafficking and measures to protect and support victims.

[385] Council of Europe, "Final Declaration and Action Plan," adopted Oct. 11, 1997 by the Second Summit of Heads of State and Government, Strasbourg, CM(97)169, at preambular para. 7.

[386] See European Trafficking Convention Explanatory Report, at paras. 12–22.

[387] Ibid.

[388] Council of Europe, Committee of Ministers, Recommendation No. R (2000) 11 of the Committee of Ministers to member states on action against trafficking in human beings for the purpose of sexual exploitation, adopted on May 19, 2000.

adopted the following year, outlined measures to protect children against sexual exploitation, including through trafficking.[389] Together, these instruments proposed a comprehensive strategy to deal with trafficking throughout and beyond Europe, focusing on harmonization of definitions, research, criminal justice measures, assistance to victims, and international cooperation. The proposal for a convention on trafficking first emerged in 2002 through a recommendation of the Parliamentary Assembly.[390] At that stage, it appeared likely the future convention would reflect the Council's perception of the problem to be addressed as limited to trafficking of women for sexual exploitation.[391]

That same year, the Parliamentary Assembly developed a much more specific recommendation on the subject of a future convention, which referred specifically to the need to ensure that this instrument "will bring added value to other international instruments."[392] The Recommendation provided explicit instructions on what the Assembly considered to be important provisions, focusing heavily on criminalization, harmonization of penalties, and introduction of the "extradite or prosecute" rule to improve prosecutions.[393] Several additional recommendations, issued during 2003 and 2004, reaffirmed the need for a European treaty against trafficking.[394] These developments took place during a period of heightened activity in the Council's Steering Committee for Equality between Women and Men (CDEG). The CDEG commissioned a study on a possible convention, which confirmed the desirability of developing a legally binding instrument "geared towards

[389] Council of Europe, Committee of Ministers, Recommendation No. R (2001) 16 of the Committee of Ministers to member states on the protection of children against sexual exploitation, adopted on Oct. 31, 2001.

[390] Council of Europe, Parliamentary Assembly, Recommendation 1545 (2002) on a campaign against trafficking in women, adopted on Jan. 21, 2002.

[391] This issue was raised at a meeting organized by the United Nations High Commissioner for Human Rights and the Council of Europe during the 2002 session of the UN Commission on Human Rights. Mary Robinson, the then-High Commissioner for Human Rights, urged the Council of Europe to further the consensus developed through the Trafficking Protocol by adopting the same definitions: Office of the High Commissioner for Human Rights, Council of Europe, "Panel Discussion on Combating Trafficking in Human Beings: A European Convention," Palais des Nations, Apr. 9, 2002, Address by the United Nations High Commissioner for Human Rights (copy on file with the author) (HCHR: CoE Statement).

[392] Council of Europe, Parliamentary Assembly, Recommendation 1610 (2003) on migration connected with trafficking in women and prostitution, adopted June 25, 2003.

[393] In particular, Recommendation 1610 (2003), cited in the previous note, at section 3(ii) calls for the Council to ensure the following provisions: "(a) introducing the offence of trafficking in the criminal law of Council of Europe member states; (b) harmonising the penalties applicable to trafficking; (c) ensuring the effective establishment of jurisdiction over traffickers or alleged traffickers, particularly by facilitating extradition and the application of the principle *aut dedere aut iudicare* in all cases concerning trafficking."

[394] Council of Europe, Parliamentary Assembly, Recommendation 1611 (2003) on trafficking in organs in Europe, adopted on June 25, 2003; Council of Europe, Parliamentary Assembly, Recommendation 1663 (2004) on domestic slavery: servitude, au pairs and mail order brides, adopted on June 22, 2004.

the protection of victim's rights and the respect of human rights, and aiming at a proper balance between matters concerning human rights and prosecution."[395] In its explanation accompanying the European Trafficking Convention, the Committee of Ministers explains, in detail, the benefits of a regional instrument in an area already covered by an international treaty. These include the possibility of more precisely defined and even stricter standards. The Explanatory Report notes that the treaty:

> does not aim at competing with other instruments adopted at a global or regional level but at improving the protection afforded by them and developing the standards contained therein, in particular in relation to the protection of the human rights of the victims of trafficking.[396]

The legislative process began in April 2003 with the formal establishment, by the Committee of Ministers, of an Ad Hoc Committee on Action against Trafficking in Human Beings (CAHTEH), specifically tasked with preparing a European convention on trafficking. CAHTEH commenced actual drafting in September 2003 and its work was finalized in a little over a year. The finalized text was transmitted through the Committee of Ministers to the Parliamentary Assembly for its opinion in late 2004. The Assembly's opinion was delivered in January 2005 and considered by CAHTEH at its final meeting the following month.[397] A tense period followed in which the draft Convention, along with several others, was left in limbo while EU States pushed for a "disconnection" clause that would permit them to apply existing and future EC or EU rules rather than those set out in the CoE treaties. NGOs and others rightly pointed out that such a clause risked dilution of the human rights protections contained in the draft.[398] The EU bloc eventually withdrew this request, and the Council of Europe Convention on Action against Trafficking in Human Beings[399] was formally adopted by the Council of Ministers at its 925th meeting, on May 3 and 4, 2005.

The Drafting Process. In comparison to the drafting process for the Trafficking Protocol, development of the Council of Europe Convention was a relatively private affair, with significantly greater internal control.[400] The meetings of the CAHTEH

---

[395] European Trafficking Convention Explanatory Report, at para. 29. See also Council of Europe Steering Committee for Equality between Women and Men (CEDG), *Feasibility Study for a Convention of the Council of Europe on Trafficking in Human Beings*, Doc. DG-11 (2002), at 5.

[396] European Trafficking Convention Explanatory Report, at para. 30.

[397] Ibid. paras. 33–35.

[398] See Amnesty International, Public Statement, "European institutions must cooperate to ensure the highest standards of human rights protection," AI Index IOR 30/008/2005 (2005).

[399] Council of Europe Convention on Action against Trafficking in Human Beings and its Explanatory Report, ETS 197, 16.V.2005, done May 16, 2005, entered into force Feb. 1, 2008 (European Trafficking Convention).

[400] See further, A.T. Gallagher, "Recent Legal Developments in the Field of Human Trafficking: A Critical Review of the 2005 European Convention and Related Instruments," (2006) 8 *European Journal of Migration and Law* 163.

were closed to those without observer status, and attempts by some international NGOs to gain access failed. Reports of CAHTEH's meetings were restricted and, in the early stages, even the drafts of the Convention were not publicly available. This only changed after concerted pressure from NGOs, including Amnesty International and Anti-Slavery International. While the CAHTEH accepted (and took some account of) external submissions and even permitted some NGO representatives to address later meetings, it held no public hearings.[401] The inability of outsiders to follow negotiations certainly made it much harder to ascertain motivations once the drafting process was completed. The following analysis of the Convention utilizes personal observations, public documentation,[402] and submissions made to the drafting committee by NGOs and others.[403]

Scope and Purpose. The timing of the European Trafficking Convention, coming so soon after the adoption of the first contemporary international treaty on

---

[401] A request for such a hearing was formally made in a letter to the Chair of the Ad Hoc Committee on Action against Trafficking in Human Beings (CAHTEH) from both Anti-Slavery International and Amnesty International on Mar. 30, 2003 (copy on file with author).

[402] Ad Hoc Committee on Action against Trafficking in Human Beings (CAHTEH), "Revised Draft: European Convention against Trafficking in Human Beings," Strasbourg, Oct. 28, 2004; Ad Hoc Committee on Action against Trafficking in Human Beings (CAHTEH), "Revised Draft: European Convention against Trafficking in Human Beings," Strasbourg, July 5, 2004; Ad Hoc Committee on Action against Trafficking in Human Beings (CAHTEH), "Revised Draft: European Convention against Trafficking in Human Beings," Strasbourg, Feb. 12, 2004 (Preliminary Draft, Feb. 12, 2004); Ad Hoc Committee on Action against Trafficking in Human Beings (CAHTEH), "Preliminary Draft: European Convention against Trafficking in Human Beings," Strasbourg, Oct. 29, 2003.

[403] The NGO campaign on the draft Convention was informally coordinated by Amnesty International (AI) and Anti-Slavery International (ASI). Major joint position papers included: Amnesty International and Anti-Slavery International, "Council of Europe: Recommendations to Strengthen the December 2004 Draft of the European Convention on Action against Trafficking in Human Beings," AI Index IOR 61/001/2005, Jan. 1, 2005 (AI/ASI January 2005 Submission); Amnesty International and Anti-Slavery International, "Council of Europe: Recommendations to Strengthen the October 2004 Draft of the European Convention on Action against Trafficking in Human Beings," AI Index IOR 61/024/2004, Nov. 12, 2004 (AI/ASI November 2004 Submission); Amnesty International and Anti-Slavery International, "Council of Europe: Enhancing the Protection of the Rights of Trafficked Persons: Amnesty International and Anti-Slavery International's recommendations to strengthen provisions of the July 2004 draft of the European Convention on Action against Trafficking in Human Beings," AI Index IOR 61/016/2004, Aug. 31, 2004 (AI/ASI August 2004 Submission); Amnesty International and Anti-Slavery International, "Memorandum on the Draft European Convention on Action against Trafficking in Human Beings: Protection of the Rights of Trafficked Persons," AI Index IOR 61/011/2004, May 2004 (AI/ASI May 2004 Submission). Other NGO submissions more or less followed the main points being advocated by AI and ASI. See, for example, European Women Lawyers Association (EWLA), "Resolution on Trafficking in Human Beings regarding the future European Convention on Action against Trafficking in Human Beings," adopted by the EWLA General Assembly, Mar. 18, 2005 (EWLA Resolution); and "Joint NGO Statement on the draft European Convention on Trafficking in Human Beings," signed by 179 national and international NGOs (text reproduced with list of signatories in AI/ASI January 2005 Submission) (Joint NGO Statement).

trafficking, inevitably impacted on its scope and purpose. As noted above, the Convention positions itself as a supplement to the Trafficking Protocol: a means of adding value to a regime that is implicitly recognized as an international minimum standard.[404] In short, the European Trafficking Convention is defined, at least in part, by what the UN Trafficking Protocol *is not*.

The perception of the European Trafficking Convention being different to the Trafficking Protocol – because of the latter's emphasis on crime prevention aspects of trafficking and the former's emphasis on human rights and victim protection – is reinforced in the Convention's preamble, which specifically refers to the need to improve the protections afforded under the Protocol and to develop the standards which it establishes.[405] In a specific provision setting out the relationship between the two instruments, it is further noted that the Convention "is intended to enhance the protection afforded by [the Protocol] and develop the standards contained therein."[406]

The stated purposes of the Convention are: to prevent and combat trafficking; to protect the human rights of victims; to ensure effective investigation and prosecution; and to promote international cooperation.[407] Reflecting the terms of reference of the drafting committee (which required it to take gender equality into account), special reference is made to the importance of guaranteeing gender equality in relation to both prevention and protection.[408] In terms of its scope, Article 2 of the Convention confirms the demise of the Council of Europe's long-standing attachment to trafficking of women for purposes of sexual exploitation. The Convention applies to *all* forms of trafficking and to trafficking in women, men, and children. In addition, and in a clear attempt to widen the scope of the Trafficking Protocol, the Convention applies to trafficking committed within as well as between countries and whether or not related to organized crime.[409] The Convention's status as a human rights instrument is further established by its explicit recognition, in the

---

[404] "The added value provided by the ... Convention lies firstly in the affirmation that trafficking in human beings is a violation of human rights and violates human dignity and integrity, and that greater protection is therefore needed for all of its victims. Secondly, the Convention's scope takes in all forms of trafficking (national, transnational, linked or not to organised crime ...) in particular with a view to victim protection measures and international cooperation. Thirdly, the Convention sets up monitoring machinery to ensure that parties implement its provisions effectively. Lastly, the Convention mainstreams gender equality in its provisions": European Trafficking Convention Explanatory Report, at para. 36; see also para. 51, which contains a detailed list of the various ways in which the Convention adds value to the pre-existing international legal framework.

[405] European Trafficking Convention, at Preamble.

[406] Ibid. at Art. 39.

[407] Ibid. at Art. 1(1).

[408] Ibid. For a full explanation of the meaning of gender quality in relation to the work of the Council of Europe in general and the Convention in particular, see European Trafficking Convention Explanatory Report, at paras. 54–55.

[409] European Trafficking Convention, at Art. 2. See also the European Trafficking Convention Explanatory Report, at paras. 60–61.

preamble, of trafficking as a violation of human rights as well as an offense to the dignity and integrity of the human being.[410]

The Definition of Trafficking. As noted in the previous chapter, the timing of the European Trafficking Convention proved to be decisive in terms of the definition of trafficking. Following the adoption of the Trafficking Protocol, it became increasingly unlikely that the Council of Europe's understanding of trafficking as relating only to the sexual exploitation of women and girls could be sustained. The final definition mirrors exactly the corresponding provision of the Trafficking Protocol.[411] The Explanatory Report accompanying the Convention gives a number of important insights into several aspects of the definition that can also shed light on the corresponding provisions of the Protocol. These include:

- That trafficking can occur even where a border was crossed legally and presence on national territory is lawful.[412]
- That abuse of a position of vulnerability (one of the "means" by which the action element is secured) encompasses "any state of hardship in which a human being is impelled to accept being exploited," including "abusing the economic insecurity or poverty of an adult hoping to better their own and their family's lot."[413]
- That there is no need for exploitation to have occurred for trafficking to take place.[414]
- That while the Convention does not refer to illegal adoptions, such practices would fall within its scope if they amounted a "practice similar to slavery."[415]
- That the fact an individual is willing to engage in prostitution does not mean that she or he has consented to exploitation.[416]

The Convention also defines a "victim" of trafficking, something that is not done in the Trafficking Protocol. This was considered to be an important means of ensuring that the provisions of the Convention, especially those related to protection, were applied correctly.[417]

---

[410] An alternative wording, which would have seen the Convention recognizing trafficking as seriously undermining the enjoyment of human rights (rather than being a violation of rights in and of itself) was eventually rejected by the drafters. It is likely that NGO pressure on this point (see, for example, AI/ASI November 2004 Submission, at 3–4) was influential in securing adoption of the stronger option.

[411] See notes 163 to 166 above and the accompanying text.

[412] European Trafficking Convention Explanatory Report, at para. 80.

[413] Ibid. at para. 83.

[414] Ibid. at para. 87.

[415] This term is as defined in the Supplementary Convention on the Abolition of Slavery, the Slave Trade, and Institutions and Practices Similar to Slavery, 226 UNTS 2, done Sept. 7, 1956, entered into force Apr. 30, 1957: European Trafficking Convention Explanatory Report. at para. 94.

[416] Ibid. at para. 97.

[417] Ibid. at para. 99. A victim of trafficking is anyone who is subject to trafficking as it is defined in the Convention: European Trafficking Convention, at Art. 2.

Protection and Assistance for Trafficked Persons.[418] Even before drafting formally commenced, the UN High Commissioner for Human Rights expressed the view that protection and support for victims of trafficking was too important to be made optional, and that the relevant provisions of the Trafficking Protocol should be incorporated into the proposed European Convention as basic obligations.[419] This call was later taken up by NGOs seeking to ensure that the weaknesses of the Protocol in this area could be remedied for at least one significant group of States. That ambitious goal may not have been entirely secured but, in terms of legal obligations to victims of trafficking, the European Trafficking Convention is much more generous, considerably broader, and more strongly worded than its international equivalent. The victory was not, however, an easy one. While the drafters were, from the outset, determined to ensure that the Convention distinguished itself in terms of its commitment to victims, there was little agreement on how this could best be done.

Perhaps the most important of all victim protection provisions is the one relating to identification. In a landmark development for the international legal framework related to trafficking, the Convention explicitly acknowledges that correct identification of victims is essential to the provision of protection and assistance, and that failure to correctly identify a victim will likely lead to a denial of that person's rights as well as problems in the prosecution process.[420] States Parties are therefore required to ensure the necessary legal framework is in place as well as the availability of competent personnel for the identification process. They are also required to cooperate with each other and internally with victim support agencies in this process.[421]

States Parties to the European Trafficking Convention are required to provide basic assistance to all victims of trafficking – even if only provisionally identified as such[422] – within their territory.[423] These provisions cannot be reserved only for those agreeing to act as witnesses[424] or otherwise agreeing to cooperate in investigations or criminal proceedings.[425] They should aim to assist victims in their physical, psychological, and social recovery. The elements of such assistance include: standards of living capable of ensuring their subsistence, including appropriate and secure accommodation; psychological and material assistance; access to emergency

---

[418] See further, Chapter 5.

[419] HCHR: CoE Statement.

[420] European Trafficking Convention Explanatory Report, at para. 127.

[421] European Trafficking Convention, at Arts. 10(1)–10(2).

[422] Ibid. at Art. 10(2).

[423] Ibid. at Art. 12. The Explanatory Report emphasizes that the protection obligations do not fall on "each party" but only on that Party in whose territory the victim is physically located: European Trafficking Convention Explanatory Report, at para. 148.

[424] European Trafficking Convention, at Arts. 10(1), 12(6).

[425] European Trafficking Convention Explanatory Report, at para. 168. Note that this provision could not be relied on by a victim in refusing to act as a witness when she or he is legally required to do so: ibid. at para. 170.

medical treatment; translation and interpretation services; and counseling, information, and assistance including in relation to the legal process.[426] For victims lawfully within the territory of a State Party (legal migrants, victims who have been granted a reflection period or residency permit, and victims who have returned home), additional obligations are placed on the State with regard to the provision of full medical and other assistance as well as access to the labor market, vocational training, and education.[427] All protection and support measures are to be provided on a nondiscriminatory,[428] consensual, and informed basis.[429]

Protection of victims from further harm is an important theme of the Convention, and "States Parties are required to take due account of the victim's safety and protection needs."[430] The European Trafficking Convention recognizes that protection needs are likely to increase when victims cooperate with criminal justice authorities. A detailed provision sets out the specific measures that must be implemented to provide "effective and appropriate protection" to victims and others (including families, witnesses, and victim support agencies) from potential retaliation and intimidation, in particular during and after the investigation and prosecution process.[431] The Explanatory Report (but crucially, not the Convention itself) recognizes the potentially intrusive and damaging effect of protection in noting that such measures must not be taken without the consent of the subject.[432]

Finally, the Convention explicitly recognizes the importance of avoiding criminalization of victims of trafficking. States Parties are required, in accordance with the basic principles of their legal systems, to "provide for the possibility of not imposing penalties on victims for their involvement in unlawful activities, to the extent that they have been compelled to do so."[433] The provision is weakened by the limited scope of application. For example, States Parties do not appear to be required to consider nonpunishment for involvement in offenses through deception or abuse of authority rather than coercion. As the provision only covers punishment, States Parties also remain technically free to detain and prosecute trafficked

---

[426] European Trafficking Convention, at Art. 12(1).

[427] Ibid. at Arts. 12(3)–12(4). The Explanatory Report notes that this latter provision does not grant an actual right of access to the labor market, vocational training, and education. European Trafficking Convention Explanatory Report, at para. 166. The withholding of certain assistance provisions for those not lawfully within the territory of the State was strongly criticized by NGOs. See, for example, AI/ASI November 2004 Submission, at 9–10.

[428] European Trafficking Convention, at Art. 3.

[429] Ibid. at Art. 12(7).

[430] Ibid. at Art. 12(2). Note that this provision will also apply to victims who have only been provisionally identified as such: ibid. at Art. 10(2).

[431] Ibid. at Art. 28.

[432] European Trafficking Convention Explanatory Report, at para. 289. Note, however, that informed consent is required in relation to the provision of general assistance and protection measures: European Trafficking Convention, at Art. 12(7).

[433] European Trafficking Convention, at Art. 26. See also the European Trafficking Convention Explanatory Report, at paras. 272–274.

victims for compelled involvement in unlawful activities. The soft nature of the underlying obligation (States Parties only needing to provide for the *possibility* of nonprosecution for status-related offenses) further weakens its force and likely impact. While serious, these shortcomings do not detract from the significance of the provision. As in all other parts of the world, trafficked persons who end up in Europe have regularly been detained and then either prosecuted or deported, usually for offenses related to their immigration status or their involvement in the sex industry. Until this point, no international or regional legal agreement had acknowledged this reality.

Special Measures for Children.[434] As noted above, the Trafficking Protocol was considered a major disappointment in relation to recognition and protection of the rights of children. It is therefore not surprising that both intergovernmental and non-governmental organizations turned to the Council of Europe to extend the rather miserly protections provided in the international treaty.[435] In comparison with the Protocol, the European Trafficking Convention is indeed extremely detailed when it comes to the protection of child victims of trafficking, despite the fact that NGO requests to make protection of the rights of child victims a specific purpose of the Convention were not successful.[436]

In addition to the protection and assistance measures available to all victims, the European Trafficking Convention provides further measures for children, including the following:

- A victim of trafficking is presumed to be a child where his or her age is uncertain and there are reasons to believe that s/he is a child.
- Such presumed victims of trafficking are to be accorded special measures of protection pending verification of age (Article 10(3)).
- A representative shall be appointed for unaccompanied child (and presumed child) victims of trafficking to act in the best interests of that child (Article 10(4)(a)).
- States Parties are required to take the necessary steps to establish the child's identity and nationality (Article 10(4)(b)).
- States Parties are required to make every effort to locate the child's family when this is in her/his best interests (Article 10(4)(c)).
- Child victims are to have access to education (Article 12(1)(f)).
- The right to privacy of child victims is subject to special protection (Article 11(2)).

---

[434] See further, Chapter 5.5.

[435] The UN High Commissioner for Human Rights, for example, urged that the Convention "acknowledge that the problem of child trafficking is a distinct one requiring special attention. The best interests of child victims must be considered paramount at all times. Children should be provided with appropriate assistance and protection. Full account should be taken of their special vulnerabilities, rights and needs": HCHR: CoE Statement.

[436] See, for example, AI/ASI November 2004 Submission, at 5–6.

- Child victims are to be given special protection measures during a trafficking investigation taking into account their best interests (Article 28(3)).
- Child victims are not to be repatriated if there is an indication, following a risk and security assessment, that such return would not be in their best interests (Article 16(7)).
- States Parties are required to take specific measures to reduce children's vulnerability to trafficking.[437]
- States Parties are required to ensure that in the provision of accommodation, education, and appropriate health care to child victims of trafficking, due account is taken of their special needs and rights (Article 12(7)).
- Considerations of the best interests of the child victim shall govern the issuing and renewal of residence permits by States Parties (Article 14(2)).

Legal Status, Repatriation, and Remedies.[438] The legal status of victims of trafficking in countries of destination was one of the major points of contention during the drafting process. Countries of the European Union were already at the forefront of developing genuine incentives for victims to cooperate with national criminal justice authorities in the investigation and prosecution of trafficking cases. However, many European States remained concerned that provision of special treatment to trafficked persons in this way would seriously compromise national migration regimes. Recognizing the danger of a retreat from previously agreed positions, the major lobbying groups, including both Amnesty International and Anti-Slavery International, developed detailed arguments and proposals around this issue and fought hard to have them considered.[439]

While the Convention did not go as far as many observers would have liked, its provisions on legal status and repatriation represent a vast improvement on what is available to victims under the Trafficking Protocol or indeed under the EU's Directive on this issue. In brief, victims or presumed victims are to be granted a thirty-day period of grace (a "recovery and reflection period"), during which time they will be given support and assistance and permitted to decide whether or not to cooperate with the competent authorities.[440] Victims cannot be repatriated against

---

[437] "... notably by creating a protective environment for them": European Trafficking Convention, at Art. 5(5).

[438] See further, Chapters 5.4 and 6.

[439] See, for example, Joint NGO Statement, at 15; AI/ASI January 2005 Submission, at 2, 8–12; AI/ASI November 2004 Submission, at 13–15; AI/ASI August 2004 Submission; and AI/ASI May 2004 Submission, at 4. The main lobbying point was for inclusion of a provision providing for a minimum three-month recovery and reflection period for all victims and provisionally identified victims, during which time they would be given all necessary assistance aimed at enabling their recovery and ability to make an informed decision on whether or not to cooperate with investigations and/or prosecutions.

[440] European Trafficking Convention, at Art. 13. Both Amnesty International and Anti-Slavery International were calling for a minimum ninety-day reflection period. See, for example, AI/ASI January 2005 Submission, at 10–11; AI/ASI November 2004 Submission, at 13–15.

their will during this period.[441] Once this thirty-day period is up, States Parties are to issue a renewable residence permit to victims if, in the State Party's opinion, an extended stay is necessary owing to the victim's personal situation *or* for the purposes of their cooperation in an investigation or prosecution.[442] This provision has the practical effect of ensuring that States Parties retain the right to grant residence permits only to those victims cooperating with the authorities. There is no obligation to even consider the granting of residence permits to victims to pursue remedies or for the possibility of family reunification during the period of legal residence. Victims have no right, under the Convention, to appeal negative decisions regarding residency applications or provision of further assistance.[443]

For those who wish to return or who do not qualify for the residence permit, the European Trafficking Convention sets out a number of provisions aimed at protecting the rights and dignity of trafficked persons in the repatriation process. Perhaps most important is the obligation on countries of destination to conduct return "with due regard for the rights, safety and dignity" of the victim and for the status of any related legal proceedings, and to ensure that such return "shall preferably be voluntary."[444] Countries of origin have two specific obligations with regard to repatriation. First, they are to facilitate and accept the return of a trafficked national or resident, also "with due regard for the rights, safety and dignity" of that person and without undue delay.[445] Second, they are to cooperate in return, including through verification of victim nationality or residence and issuing of necessary travel documents.[446] All States Parties have an obligation to provide victims being repatriated with information,[447] to promote their reintegration, and to work to avoid their revictimization.[448] The practical effect of these provisions is that victims of trafficking can indeed be returned against their will. The fact that no risk assessment is required in such cases (except for children) means that States are ultimately not accepting legal or moral responsibility for the safety and security of returned victims.

---

[441] European Trafficking Convention, at Art. 13.

[442] Ibid. at Art. 14. Note that this final provision is weaker than that proposed in the preliminary draft, which would have seen victims being eligible for such residency visas if they had suffered serious abuse or harm; if they or their families were in danger; *or* if they were assisting the authorities in their investigation: Preliminary Draft, Feb. 12, 2004.

[443] The lack of any appeal procedure was identified as a major flaw in the draft by NGOs. See, for example, AI/ASI January 2005 Submission, at 14; AI/ASI November 2004 Submission, at 20; and EWLA Resolution, at 14(vi).

[444] European Trafficking Convention, at Art. 16(2) (regarding the "preferably voluntary" provision). The language on this point echoes a call from the UN High Commissioner for Human Rights when she called for safe and, as far as possible, voluntary return with legal alternatives to repatriation being offered where it is reasonable to conclude that such repatriation would pose a serious risk to the safety of victims and/or that of their families: HCHR: CoE Statement.

[445] European Trafficking Convention, at Art. 16(1).

[446] Ibid. at Arts. 16(3)–16(4).

[447] Ibid. at Art. 16(6).

[448] Ibid. at Art. 16(5).

The issue of adequate and appropriate remedies for victims of trafficking was critical for those urging a rights-based and victim-centered Convention.[449] In its final form, the European Trafficking Convention takes a comprehensive, if imperfect, approach to the issue of victim compensation and legal redress.[450] It requires, first of all, that victims are provided with appropriate information including procedures they can use to obtain compensation,[451] as "people cannot claim their rights if they do not know about them."[452] Victims are also to be given access to legal assistance.[453] The Convention specifically provides that victims have a right to monetary compensation from traffickers in respect of both material injury and suffering.[454] Finally, and in recognition of the fact that, in practice, the State will rarely be able to force traffickers to compensate victims fully, the Convention requires States Parties to take steps to guarantee compensation of victims. Examples given in the Convention include establishment of a special fund or initiatives aimed at social assistance or reintegration of victims.[455] The possibility of State compensation schemes being funded by the seized proceeds of trafficking is also noted.[456]

Criminalization, Investigation, and Prosecution.[457] While the European Trafficking Convention pays more attention to the rights and needs of victims than its international equivalent, this is not done at the expense of the criminal justice and immigration aspects of trafficking. In this context, it is important to acknowledge that despite their generosity, the victim protection provisions are clearly geared

---

[449] In early 2002, well before the formal drafting process had commenced, the High Commissioner for Human Rights stated that the Convention should guarantee to trafficked persons the right of access to adequate and appropriate remedies: HCHR: CoE Statement. See also AI/ASI January 2005 Submission, at 13; AI/ASI November 2004 Submission, at 16–18; Joint NGO Statement, at 19.

[450] One significant weakness is the lack of any provision enabling States Parties to permit a victim to stay in the country to pursue compensation or other claims. In addition, the Convention does not provide for the possibility of other forms of reparation beyond compensation.

[451] European Trafficking Convention, at Art. 15(1). This provision could, however, have been considerably strengthened if it were attached to the minimum assistance standards set out in Article 12, which require States Parties to provide assistance to victims to enable their rights and those of interested parties to be presented and considered only in relation to criminal proceedings against traffickers.

[452] European Trafficking Convention Explanatory Report, at para. 192. The Explanatory Report also notes that provision of information on the possibility of obtaining a residency permit will be very important for victims who are illegally in the country, as it would be very difficult for a victim to obtain compensation if she is unable to remain in the country.

[453] European Trafficking Convention, at Art. 15(2). On the extent of required assistance and the much-litigated question of whether it includes a right to free legal aid, see the European Trafficking Convention Explanatory Report, at para. 196.

[454] European Trafficking Convention, at Art. 15(3). See also the European Trafficking Convention Explanatory Report, at paras. 197–198.

[455] European Trafficking Convention, at Art. 15(4).

[456] Ibid. The final provision on use of seized assets is weaker than in the preliminary draft, which called for States to ensure that such assets be used, as a first priority, to pay compensation claims or fund victim support activities: Preliminary Draft, Feb. 12, 2004, at Art. 11(2).

[457] See further, Chapter 7.

toward making sure that criminal justice authorities are given the best possible chance to secure prosecutions and convictions through the cooperation of victims. It is extremely unlikely that provisions such as the recovery and reflection period, and even those related to immediate support and assistance, could have been possible without this understanding of their dual purpose.

The criminal law aspects of trafficking are dealt with in chapters IV and V of the European Trafficking Convention. The purpose is clearly to ensure approximation of legislation and the improvements to regional law enforcement that this can be expected to deliver. Shared definitions, similar laws, and common approaches promote information exchange and cooperation, as well as strengthen the comparability of data.[458] The criminalization provisions of the Convention are almost identical to those contained in the Trafficking Protocol, with some important extensions. States Parties are required to criminalize trafficking as well as certain acts committed for the purpose of enabling trafficking such as document fraud.[459] They are also required to criminalize attempting, aiding, and abetting.[460] There is provision for legal persons to be held liable for a criminal offense established under the Convention.[461] The compulsory jurisdiction of States Parties is extremely wide, covering territoriality, nationality, or passive personality. In other words, a State Party *must* establish jurisdiction over an offense when committed in its territory, by one of its nationals, or *against* one of its nationals.[462] States are required to either prosecute or extradite.[463] Overall, the jurisdictional elements of the Convention are extremely broad and, with one exception, can be expected to cover all cases involving victims or perpetrators who are present in the territory of, or citizens of, States Parties.[464]

---

[458] European Trafficking Convention Explanatory Report, at para. 216.

[459] European Trafficking Convention, at Arts. 18, 20.

[460] Ibid. at Art. 21.

[461] Ibid. at Art. 18. Corporate liability is limited to situations in which the offense was committed for the benefit of the legal person by a natural person in a leading position acting under its authority and/or where lack of supervision and control by a natural person made possible the commission of an offense. This provision echoes a broader trend toward recognition of corporate liability in criminal law.

[462] Ibid. at Art. 31. Note that jurisdiction under the territoriality principle is also to apply when the offense was committed on board a ship flying a State Party's flag or on aircraft registered under its laws: ibid. Note further that the jurisdictional scope of the Convention is potentially compromised by States being entitled to enter reservations to the jurisdiction grounds relating to both the nationality of the victim and of the perpetrator: ibid.

[463] No reservation can be made against this aspect of the jurisdictional requirement: ibid.

[464] The sole exception relates to the fact that the Convention provides for no specific jurisdiction over persons involved in trafficking while carrying out functions as part of an international military or peacekeeping or related force. Under Article 31, States would only acquire the necessary jurisdiction to prosecute one of their nationals if the offense (trafficking) is punishable under the criminal law where it was committed. Given that European forces are invariably operating in countries with underdeveloped legal frameworks and dysfunctional criminal justice systems, it can be expected that States would *not* be required to exercise jurisdiction in such cases. See further, AI/ASI January 2005 Submission, at 16–17; AI/ASI November 2004 Submission, 26–27; and Joint NGO Statement, at 23.

The European Trafficking Convention is much more explicit than the Trafficking Protocol when it comes to penalties. The offenses established under the Convention are all to be punishable by "effective, proportionate and dissuasive" sanctions – to include deprivation of liberty giving rise to extradition.[465] In determining penalties, a number of situations are to be considered "aggravating circumstances." These include instances where the offense was committed against a child; by a public official; where it endangered the life of the victim; or where it was committed within the framework of a criminal organization.[466] The penalties provision of the European Trafficking Convention also includes an obligation on States to ensure an ability to confiscate the instrumentalities and proceeds of trafficking and to close establishments used for trafficking.[467]

One original provision in chapter IV of the Convention relates to recognition of previous convictions in foreign courts. Generally, in Europe and elsewhere, only convictions by a court in the country where a case is being heard can count toward a harsher penalty. The drafters of the European Trafficking Convention acknowledged that this rule is now out of step with modern criminal practices, especially in the area of transnational organized crime. In recognition of the difficulties in setting clear standards on international recidivism, the Convention does not place a positive obligation on judicial bodies to seek out such information and to include it in their deliberations.[468] Rather, States Parties are required to "provide for the possibility" of taking sentences handed down in the court of another State Party into account when determining penalties.[469]

Through one of its most innovative provisions, the European Trafficking Convention requires States Parties to consider criminalization of those *using the services* of a victim of trafficking.[470] This provision could be used to prosecute owners of establishments using trafficked persons in cases where it is difficult or impossible to prove the required action and means for trafficking. It could also be used to prosecute someone who knowingly uses the services of a trafficker to procure a sexual service or even an organ.[471] The uniqueness of this provision can only be fully appreciated with reference to the long and complicated legal history around trafficking, which has never even considered the *possibility* of attaching criminal responsibility to the brothel owners, pimps, and clients of trafficked women and

---

[465] European Trafficking Convention, at Art. 23.

[466] Ibid. at Art. 24. Note that while "criminal organisation" is not defined in the Convention, the accompanying Explanatory Report makes specific reference to the definition contained in Article 2(a) of the Organized Crime Convention: European Trafficking Convention Explanatory Report, at para. 264.

[467] Ibid. at para. 264.

[468] Ibid. at para. 270.

[469] European Trafficking Convention, at Art. 25.

[470] Ibid. at Art. 19.

[471] These examples are drawn from the European Trafficking Convention Explanatory Report, at para. 232.

children – or indeed the wholesale buyers of products made in factories and sweat-shops taking advantage of prices that could only be possible through the use of exploited labor. As explored further in Chapter 8, implementation of this provision will undoubtedly prove difficult in practice. A successful prosecution will require establishing both action (use of services) and knowledge (of the fact the services were only made available through trafficking). The educative effect of this provision was clearly uppermost in the minds of the drafters and, on balance, is likely to outweigh these evidentiary concerns.

Most law enforcement agencies anywhere in the world will only initiate an investigation into trafficking following a complaint from the victim. The problems associated with this approach are numerous. Victims are rarely willing to make complaints against traffickers. Some are intimidated into silence; others are worried about possible repercussions for themselves and their families. Most victims of trafficking, once they have escaped, just want to go home or get a decent job. The European Trafficking Convention requires States Parties to ensure that investigations or prosecutions can be initiated *ex officio*, in other words, that they are not dependent on victim complaints if the offense has been committed in its territory in whole or in part.[472] Victims must also be able to make complaints from outside the country where the offense was committed, for example, after they return home. The State Party to which such a complaint is made must transmit the complaint to the State Party in which the offense was committed for the latter State's action.[473]

As explored further in Chapters 4 and 7, the way in which a State's criminal justice response is organized is one measure of whether or not it is meeting the traditional due diligence test with regard to the obligation to investigate and prosecute trafficking. Europe is home to some of the first and still the best law enforcement units specializing in human trafficking.[474] It is therefore no surprise that the Convention carves out a role for specialization at both the individual and organizational levels. States Parties are required to adopt the necessary measures to ensure that specialists are independent and have the necessary training and resources to do their job properly. Coordination of the criminal justice response is another key theme, as is the need for comprehensive, rights-based training across key agencies.

Preventing Trafficking.[475] The European Trafficking Convention's specific purpose is to *prevent* and *combat* trafficking. Prevention, in this context, refers to

---

[472] European Trafficking Convention, at Art. 27(1).

[473] Ibid. at Art. 27(2). Note that this provision was modelled on Article 11(2) of the European Union Council Framework Decision of 15 March 2001 on the standing of victims in criminal proceedings, OJ L 82/1, Mar. 22, 2001. Note further that the obligation is only to forward the complaint to the competent authority; the State of residence is not obliged to commence an investigation or otherwise institute proceedings: European Convention Explanatory Report, at para. 278.

[474] See A.T. Gallagher and P. Holmes, "Developing an Effective Criminal Justice Response to Human Trafficking: Lessons from the Front Line," (2008) 18 *International Criminal Justice Review* 318.

[475] See further, Chapter 8.

positive measures to stop future acts of trafficking from occurring. Most trafficking prevention measures focus on two areas: decreasing vulnerability of potential victims and increasing the risks to traffickers of apprehension and prosecution. In this sense, many of the measures set out in the Convention aimed at combating trafficking (such as strengthening the criminal justice response and border controls, imposing criminal liability on end users, etc.) can also be expected to have a preventative effect.

In terms of specific preventative strategies, the Convention's approach is fairly orthodox. The general obligations are so broad as to be almost meaningless in terms of monitoring compliance and measuring impact. First, States are required to coordinate, internally, their preventative strategies.[476] Second, they are required to either establish or strengthen effective policies and programs to prevent trafficking.[477] Such policies and programs are to promote a human rights-based approach as well as use gender mainstreaming and child-sensitive approaches.[478] States Parties are also required to take appropriate measures to ensure that migration can take place legally[479] and specific measures to reduce the vulnerability of children to trafficking through creation of "a protective environment."[480]

International Cooperation.[481] As with the Trafficking Protocol, international cooperation is the *raison d'être* of the European Trafficking Convention. Provisions related to international cooperation are therefore integrated into a range of broader obligations regarding investigation and prosecution, prevention, and protection of victims. In relation to the first category, it is relevant to note that the Convention does not establish a complex system of mutual legal assistance applicable to trafficking such as was set up within the Organized Crime Convention and the Trafficking Protocol. Sensibly, the drafting committee instead noted the existence of a comprehensive and relatively effective web of bilateral and multilateral agreements already in existence between States Parties.[482] They therefore confined themselves to highlighting key areas for cooperation and articulating certain basic principles.

The general obligation is for States Parties to cooperate with each other, to the widest extent possible, for the purposes of preventing and combating trafficking, protecting and supporting victims, and investigating and prosecuting offenses. This general obligation is, of course, supplementary to specific ones that relate, for example, to: (1) provision of information on risks to victims and the results of any

---

[476] European Trafficking Convention, at Art. 5(1).
[477] Ibid. at Art. 5(2).
[478] Ibid. at Art. 5(3).
[479] Ibid. at Art. 5(4).
[480] Ibid. at Art. 5(5).
[481] See further, Chapter 7.5.
[482] European Trafficking Convention Explanatory Report, at paras. 335–337. A sample list of relevant mutual legal assistance, extradition, and related matters is set out at paras. 343–345, ibid.

follow-up in respect of such persons;[483] and (2) provision of information necessary to enable application of the entitlements of victims to a recovery and reflection period, residency, or safe repatriation.[484] There is no obligation on States Parties to cooperate with civil society, although the frequent references to NGOs and victim support agencies are indicative of a view, on the part of the drafters, that the Convention's objectives can best be achieved through the development of cooperative relationships with these groups.[485]

Evaluating the European Trafficking Convention. According to the Secretary-General of the Council of Europe, the European Trafficking Convention is one of the most important achievements of the Council of Europe during its sixty years of existence, and the most important human rights treaty of the last ten years.[486] If its political significance is beyond question, it remains to consider the technical quality of this instrument. Such an evaluation depends, to a great extent, on one's point of reference. In comparison to the Trafficking Protocol, the Convention represents a significant improvement in recognition of the rights of victims and of the connection between protection of those rights and improved criminal justice responses to trafficking. When measured against higher standards, for example, those set out in the 2002 UN Trafficking Principles and Guidelines,[487] certain aspects of the Convention fall short. Nevertheless, it comes closer than any other international legal instrument in reflecting both the letter and spirit of that ambitious ideal.

In evaluating the strength and potential of the Convention, particularly from the perspective of human rights, it is essential to recognize just how far and how quickly international standards have shifted upwards. Those lobbying at the Trafficking Protocol negotiations did not even bother to seriously advocate for a mandatory recovery and reflection period or for an independent monitoring body. As demonstrated in Chapter 3 of this book, new standards, first articulated in the European

---

[483] European Trafficking Convention, at Arts. 32, 34(1).

[484] Ibid. at Arts. 16, 34(3).

[485] For example, references to the role of NGOs and civil society in relation to: preventing trafficking (Art. 5(6)); repatriation and return (Art. 16(6)); assistance and support during criminal proceedings (Art. 27(3)); and being protected against retaliation and intimidation (Art. 28(4)). On a general level, States Parties to the Convention are required to *encourage* State authorities and public officials to cooperate with NGOs and other relevant organizations "in establishing strategic partnerships with the aim of achieving the purpose of [the] Convention": ibid. at Art. 35. The Explanatory Report to the Convention observes that such partnerships can be achieved through regular dialogue as well as the establishment of more formal mechanisms such as memoranda of understanding between governmental authorities and national NGOs working with victims: European Trafficking Convention Explanatory Report, at para. 353.

[486] GRETA Report, February 2009, at para. 2.

[487] UN Economic and Social Council, UN High Commissioner for Human Rights, *Recommended Principles and Guidelines on Human Rights and Human Trafficking*, UN Doc E/2002/68/Add.1, May 20, 2002 (UN Trafficking Principles and Guidelines). See further Chapter 2.4.3, below. Note that the Explanatory Report accompanying the European Trafficking Convention draws heavily on language used in the UN Trafficking Principles and Guidelines.

Trafficking Convention, have now become widely accepted. Perhaps even more importantly, the European Trafficking Convention embodies a revolutionary way of thinking about trafficking and victims of trafficking. It explicitly recognizes trafficking as a violation of human rights. It requires States to provide minimum standards of assistance and protection to all victims of trafficking, irrespective of their willingness to cooperate with criminal justice authorities. No victim or presumed victim can be automatically deported. Cooperating victims and witnesses are entitled to extra help and extra protection as befits their increased need. Child victims of trafficking are also given special help in accordance with the "best interests" principle. The strengths of the Convention extend beyond its victim protection provisions. States are required to criminalize trafficking and to exercise their jurisdiction in a manner that almost guarantees no safe havens for traffickers within Europe. The Convention recognizes the concept of "aggravated offences" and in so doing acknowledges the special dangers associated with violent trafficking, organized trafficking, trafficking in children, and trafficking with official complicity. In a world-first, the Convention requires States to criminalize those knowingly using the services of victims of trafficking, thereby sending an important message that the end beneficiaries of trafficking are also complicit in the exploitation of victims.

The Convention's imperfections confirm that, within the realities of current migration regimes, there is a natural limit to what States will grant victims of trafficking. It is a common and not altogether unreasonable fear of countries of destination that too much recognition of and support to victims of trafficking will strain resources and capacities and will create a flood of both valid and fraudulent claims – all requiring expensive and time-consuming investigation. These fears are reflected in the careful wording of the various assistance and protection clauses. Ultimately, it is likely to be only those who can give something back to the State – a prosecution – who will be substantially supported and allowed to stay. Despite the inclusion of a non-penalty clause, there is still nothing to stop States from treating victims of trafficking as criminals and from arresting and prosecuting them for violations of labor and migration laws.

Chapter 9.2.2 analyzes the compliance machinery established by the Convention and considers, from this perspective, its broader impact on the behavior of States.

2.3.3. *The SAARC Convention*

The first-ever regional treaty on trafficking was developed within the framework of the South Asian Association for Regional Cooperation (SAARC), an intergovernmental organization bringing together the hugely divergent States of South Asia: India, Pakistan, Bangladesh, Sri Lanka, Nepal, the Maldives, Bhutan, and, most recently, Afghanistan. SAARC Member States have a combined population of close to 1.5 billion, giving this relatively weak and ineffective body the largest "membership" of any regional organization in the world.

SAARC Foreign Ministers formally took up the issue of trafficking (in women and children) in late 1996.[488] At the Ninth SAARC Summit, held in the Maldives the following year, participants adopted a resolution on trafficking in women and children that called for the elaboration of a regional convention.[489] The government of Bangladesh took responsibility for elaborating the first draft, with the government of India producing a second version. The draft Convention was formally considered by the SAARC heads of State or government at the Tenth SAARC Summit, held in Colombo in July 1998. After some delays due to regional political tensions involving India and Pakistan, the SAARC Convention on Preventing and Combating Trafficking in Women and Children for Prostitution was finally adopted at the Eleventh SAARC Summit, held in Nepal in January 2002,[490] the eight Member States expressing their collective resolve "to treat the trafficking in women and children for commercial sexual exploitation as a criminal offence of a serious nature."[491]

The drafting process for the SAARC Convention was not a transparent one. While some regional NGOs made submissions,[492] the lack of any formal avenue for communication and dialogue clearly affected the level and quality of civil society engagement, as well as the impact of any contributions that did get through. At the international level, both the United Nations High Commissioner for Human Rights and the Special Rapporteur on Violence against Women provided formal submissions on the second draft.[493] However, as detailed further below, these contributions did not appear to exercise any noticeable influence on the process or its outcome. The SAARC Secretariat informally advised those who did make submissions that the Convention would be adopted as drafted, on the understanding that it would be subject to review within the next few years. That review has not taken place.

---

[488] For additional details on the drafting history of the Convention, see International Movement Against All Forms of Discrimination and Racism, *Final Report: South Asian Dialogue on Trafficking in Women and Children, Towards the Adoption of a SAARC Convention*, Feb. 11–12, 1999, Colombo, Sri Lanka (IMADR SAARC Report).

[489] Declaration of the Ninth Summit of the Heads of State or Government of the Member Countries of the South Asian Association for Regional Cooperation, issued on May 14, 1997, in Male, Maldives.

[490] South Asian Association for Regional Cooperation, Convention on Preventing and Combating Trafficking in Women and Children for Prostitution, done Jan. 5, 2002, entered into force Dec. 1, 2005 (SAARC Convention).

[491] Declaration of the Eleventh Summit of the Heads of State or Government of the Member Countries of the South Asian Association for Regional Cooperation, issued on Jan. 6, 2002, in Kathmandu, Nepal, at para. 22 (SAARC Kathmandu Declaration).

[492] See, for example, IMADR SAARC Report; "Letter from the Participants of the SAARC People's Forum to the Honourable Heads of the State and Government of the SAARC Countries: Proposed amendments to the SAARC Convention on Preventing and Combating Trafficking in Women and Children for Prostitution," July 27, 1998 (copy on file with the author).

[493] "Letter from the United Nations High Commissioner for Human Rights to the Heads of State and Government of SAARC Member Countries," July 5, 1999 (copy on file with the author); Special Rapporteur on Violence against Women, Its Causes and Consequences, "Position Paper on the draft SAARC Convention on Preventing and Combating Trafficking in Women and Children for Prostitution," Aug. 27, 1999 (copy on file with the author).

Overview of the SAARC Convention. The stated purpose of the SAARC Convention is to promote regional cooperation to effectively deal with the prevention, interdiction, and suppression of trafficking and the repatriation and rehabilitation of victims. The Convention also seeks to prevent the use of women and children in international prostitution networks, especially within SAARC Member States.[494] The Convention defines trafficking as "the moving, selling or buying of women or children for prostitution[495] within and outside a country for monetary or other considerations with or without the consent of the person subject to trafficking."[496] The person subject to trafficking refers to "women and children victimised or forced into prostitution by the traffickers by deception, threat, coercion, kidnapping, sale, fraudulent marriage, child marriage or any other unlawful means."[497] As noted in Chapter 1, this definition varies in several critical respects from that set out in the Trafficking Protocol. It does not cover trafficking in men, nor does it cover trafficking for debt bondage, exploitative labor, or other nonsexual forms of exploitation.

States Parties are required to make trafficking and involvement in trafficking criminal offenses to which appropriate penalties apply.[498] These offenses are also to be regarded as extraditable offenses in any existing extradition treaty and, in addition, to the extent possible under national law.[499] Where extradition is not possible, States Parties are to ensure that offending nationals are prosecuted and punished by their own court.[500] The Convention sets out a range of "aggravating circumstances" that can be taken into account during the judicial consideration of trafficking offenses, including involvement in an organized criminal group or international organized criminal activities, the use of arms or violence, and the victimization of or trafficking in children.[501] Abuse of public authority to commit trafficking offenses is also to be considered an aggravating circumstance.[502]

The SAARC Convention contains detailed provisions on mutual legal assistance, designed to ensure improved cooperation in relation to investigations, inquiries, trials, and other proceedings.[503] Such assistance is to include regular information exchange aimed at identifying trafficking patterns and routes, as well as possible bilateral mechanisms.[504] At the national level, States Parties are required to provide the resources, training, and assistance necessary for the investigation and

---

[494] SAARC Convention, at Art. II.
[495] The Convention defines "prostitution" as "the sexual exploitation or abuse of persons for commercial purposes": ibid. at Art. I(2).
[496] Ibid. at Art. I(3).
[497] Ibid. at Art. I(5).
[498] Ibid. at Art. III.
[499] Ibid. at Art. VII.
[500] Ibid.
[501] Ibid. at Art. III.
[502] Ibid.
[503] Ibid. at Art. VI.
[504] Ibid. at Arts. VIII(4)–VIII(5).

prosecution of trafficking offenses.[505] Law enforcement officials and the judiciary are to be sensitized to the issue of trafficking, including the factors that encourage such trafficking.[506] The Convention includes an optional provision relating to the supervision of employment agencies to prevent trafficking under the guise of employment.[507]

In terms of protection and assistance to victims, key provisions for countries of destination are framed within the context of repatriation. States Parties are required to provide assistance (including legal advice and health care) to trafficking victims pending their repatriation.[508] States Parties (presumably countries of origin) are also to establish protective homes or shelters for the rehabilitation of trafficked persons.[509] The Convention encourages States Parties to seek the involvement of "recognised non-governmental organisations" in the establishment of such homes or shelters, as well as more generally in prevention, intervention, and rehabilitation.[510] The Convention requires States Parties to promote awareness of the problem of trafficking and its underlying causes, "including the projection of negative images of women," as well as to endeavor to focus preventative and developmental efforts on source areas for trafficking.[511]

The SAARC Convention requires the establishment of a regional taskforce, consisting of officials of the Member States, to facilitate implementation of the Convention as well as to undertake periodic reviews. The taskforce will also make recommendations regarding the establishment of a voluntary fund for the rehabilitation and reintegration of victims of trafficking.[512]

Substantive Issues and Concerns. One of the principal objections expressed to SAARC about the Convention in its draft form was its narrow scope of application: specifically, that the definition dealt with only one aspect of the trafficking problem. While such a narrow view of trafficking may have been common while the Convention was being drafted in the late 1990s, it was clearly outdated by the time of its adoption in 2002. Another aspect that troubled human rights groups and the United Nations was the Convention's identical treatment of women and children. No allowance is made for the relatively greater agency of women, nor indeed for the particular situation and needs of trafficked children[513] beyond a passing, preambular

---

[505] Ibid. at Art. VIII(1).
[506] Ibid. at Art. VIII(2).
[507] Ibid. at Art. VIII(6).
[508] Ibid. at Arts. IX(1)–IX(2).
[509] Ibid. at Art. IX(3).
[510] Ibid. at Arts. IX(4)–IX(5).
[511] Ibid. at Art. VIII(8).
[512] SAARC Kathmandu Declaration, at para. 23.
[513] The only concession in this respect is the identification of trafficking in children as an aggravating circumstance, which courts can take into account as part of the factual circumstances which make the commission of such offenses particularly grave: SAARC Convention, at Art. IV(1)(e).

reference to the Convention on the Rights of the Child.[514] The Convention also assumes automatic repatriation of all trafficked persons to the country of origin and does not even acknowledge a possibility that legal alternatives to repatriation be made available in cases where it is reasonable to conclude that such return would pose a serious risk that person's safety or the safety of their families.

The Convention includes a number of important assistance and protection provisions, several of which go beyond their strictly optional equivalents contained in the UN Trafficking Protocol. For example, as noted above, States Parties are required to provide legal advice and health care to victims of trafficking pending their repatriation, as well as suitable provision for their care and maintenance.[515] Rehabilitation of trafficked persons in protective homes or shelters is also envisaged with States Parties being required to make "suitable provisions" for granting legal advice, counseling, job training, and health care facilities.[516] During the drafting stage, objections were made to the use of the term "rehabilitation," with its inference that victims of trafficking are social misfits who need to be re-educated before being permitted to rejoin mainstream society. However, the reference to NGO involvement in rehabilitation[517] was seen as potentially ameliorating the danger of such an approach being adopted.

An Uncertain Future. The SAARC Convention was not immediately ratified by any eligible State and only entered into force in late 2005. To date, there is little evidence that the Convention has exerted any influence over antitrafficking law, policy, or practice at either the regional or national levels. Two bodies mandated by the Convention – a regional taskforce responsible for implementation of its provisions and a regional voluntary fund for the rehabilitation and reintegration of victims of trafficking – are yet to be established. While a regional consultation on the Convention was organized shortly after its entry into force, the promised review has not yet taken place. Over time, references to the Convention in SAARC documentation have become markedly less frequent and less specific.[518]

---

[514] Ibid. at Preambular para. 3.

[515] Ibid. at Art. IX(2).

[516] Ibid. at Art. IX(3).

[517] Ibid. at Art. IX(5).

[518] For example, the Declaration of the Fifteenth Summit of the Heads of State or Government of the Member Countries of the South Asian Association for Regional Cooperation, Aug. 2–3, 2008, in Colombo, Sri Lanka, does not refer to trafficking or to the Convention. The most recent, substantive reference appears to be contained in the SAARC Social Charter, done at the Twelfth Summit of the Heads of State or Government of the Member Countries of the South Asian Association for Regional Cooperation, Jan. 4, 2004, in Islamabad, Pakistan. Under Article 5 of that instrument, "States Parties re-affirm their commitment to effectively implement the SAARC Convention on Combating the Trafficking of Women and Children for Prostitution and to combat and suppress all forms of traffic in women and exploitation of women, including through the cooperation of appropriate sections of the civil society." Subsequent public references to the Convention (for example in a communiqué issued by SAARC ministers responsible for matters related to children in July 2009) have been cursory and non-specific.

It is conceivable that the SAARC Convention will, at some point in the future, become obsolete and thereby terminate through *desuetude*. The argument for *desuetude*, based on inferred consent, could possibly be made more strongly for this instrument than for the 1949 Trafficking Convention.[519] The majority of SAARC Member States are now party to the UN Trafficking Protocol and thereby to a treaty that is inconsistent with the SAARC Convention in a number of important respects. Failure of States Parties to the SAARC Convention to take steps to establish mandated mechanisms is another indication of collective disregard that may contribute to its eventual termination through *desuetude*.

2.4. NONTREATY ASPECTS OF THE INTERNATIONAL LEGAL FRAMEWORK

The international law of trafficking is essentially treaty-based, and most of the obligations identified in this book find their basis and authority in multilateral legal agreements. However, other sources of international legal rules (or avenues through which such rules can be identified) are also relevant, and these are considered briefly further in this chapter.

2.4.1. *Customary Law,* Jus Cogens, *and Trafficking*

International customary law is defined as "evidence of a general practice accepted as law."[520] Such law is not written, although it may subsequently be "codified" into treaties. International legal doctrine asserts that a rule is customary if (1) it reflects general and uniform State practice, and (2) that practice is accompanied by a subjective sense of legal obligation (*opinio juris*).[521] It is not necessary that all countries recognize a rule of customary international law for the norm to exist and to bind them. All that is required is a general consensus that the rule in question is in fact an obligation and a sufficient level of conforming State practice, particularly from specially affected States.[522] In principle, custom and treaty law are equal in value.

---

[519] See notes 51 to 53 to this chapter and the accompanying text.

[520] ICJ Statute, at Art. 38(1)(b).

[521] "Not only must the acts concerned be a settled practice, but they must also be such, or be carried out in such a way, as to be evidence of a belief that this practice is rendered obligatory by the existence of a rule requiring it. ... The States concerned must feel that they are conforming to what amounts to a legal obligation." *North Sea Continental Shelf Cases (Federal Republic of Germany v. Denmark; Federal Republic of Germany v. Netherlands)*, [1969] ICJ Rep 3, at 44. See also I. Brownlie, *Principles of Public International Law* (2008), at 7–10.

[522] While the nature and quality of State practice needed remains controversial, the ICJ has indicated that it need not be uniform. In the *Nicaragua Case*, the Court held that "[i]n order to deduce the existence of customary rules, the Court deems it sufficient that the conduct of States should in general be consistent with such a rule; and that instances of State conduct inconsistent with a given rule should generally have been treated as breaches of that rule, not as indications of the recognition of a new rule." *Military and Paramilitary Activities in and against Nicaragua*

In the case of a conflict, a treaty rule (as *lex specialis*) would generally override the *lex generalis* of custom.[523]

While the legal definition of custom is well settled, its ephemeral nature has caused considerable difficulties in application. These difficulties are both conceptual (how does custom begin? Where does a sense of legal obligation come from before practice hardens into custom? How can States follow a rule from a sense of legal obligation without already having the required *opinio juris*? How should one distinguish between what States *believe* and what they say or do?) and operational (how much and what sort of practice is required to establish the first part of the custom test? How consistent should that practice be? What kind of evidence is required to establish *opinio juris*? What contribution do international organizations, international courts, and tribunals make to the development of customary international law?),[524] and have generally proved resistant to satisfactory resolution. In relation to the more practical concerns, Henkin observes that such questions have also never been definitively settled "because every 'piece' of customary law is different; develops in different circumstances, at a different rate of growth."[525]

Problems in the identification and application of custom have been exacerbated by the distinction commonly made between *traditional custom*, which is evolutionary, heavily reliant on State practice, and best established through inductive reasoning; and what has been termed *modern custom*, which emphasizes *opinio juris* over State practice (or even collapses the two), is identified through a deductive process of reasoning that commences with a general statement of rules, and uses the multitude of sources commonly identified as "soft law," such that it can develop relatively quickly.[526] This opening up of the concept of customary international law

---

(*Nicaragua v. United States*), [1986] ICJ Rep 14, at para. 186. Note also the well-established rule that States objecting to a norm of international customary law when it is being formed are not bound by it (the rule of the "persistent objector"): "in principle, a State that indicates its dissent from a practice while the law is still in the process of development is not bound by that rule even after it matures": American Law Institute, *Restatement (Third) of the Foreign Relations Law of the United States* (Philadelphia: ALI, 1990), 102. See also *Anglo-Norwegian Fisheries (United Kingdom v. Norway)* [1951] ICJ Rep 116, at 131.

[523] International Law Commission, *Fragmentation of International Law: Difficulties Arising from the Diversification and Expansion of International Law*, UN Doc. A/CN.4/L.682 (Apr. 13, 2006), at Part C. But see also Part D (*lex posterior*), *ibid*.

[524] Henkin, *International Law*, at 29–31. See also A. D'Amato, *The Concept of Custom in International Law* (1971). For a discussion of the growing influence of international jurisprudence on customary international law, see R.B. Baker, "Customary International Law in the 21st Century: Old Challenges and New Debates," (2010) 21 *European Journal of International Law* 173. (Baker, "Customary International Law in the 21st Century").

[525] Henkin, *International Law*, at 30.

[526] This separation (identified as two aspects of the same source of law rather than as opposing concepts) is carefully described and analyzed within the framework of a broader consideration of the theory of custom in A.E. Roberts, "Traditional and Modern Approaches to Customary International Law: A Reconciliation," (2001) 95 *American Journal of International Law* 757 (Roberts, "Traditional and Modern Approaches").

has likely been a necessary aspect of the system's adaptation to a more complex operating environment.

However, some of the dangers discussed below with reference to soft law apply here, particularly the danger of a separation between *what is said to be law* and what States have bound themselves to through explicit or implicit consent.[527] In keeping with its generally conservative approach to identification of obligations, the present study largely restricts its consideration of customary norms to those already widely accepted to have met the required evidentiary threshold.[528] In relation to the question of whether certain contemporary rules or norms not falling within that category may have moved toward or attained the status of customary law, the analysis is cautious, weighed in favor of traditional evidentiary sources of both custom and *opinio juris* including treaties, national legislation, and decisions of international and regional courts. Provisions of multilateral treaties that have secured wide ratification, been effectively implemented through legislation and other positive measures, and also been applied by nonparties (especially when out of a sense of obligation) are identified as particularly strong evidence (and contributors to the development) of customary norms.[529]

Despite the great codification project of the last century, the growing importance of treaties, and a range of objections to its legitimacy, integrity, and relevance,[530] custom continues to be recognized as an essential, independent source of international legal obligation. In the present context, customary international law is important for several reasons. First, not all States are party to all relevant instruments. The characterization of a rule as part of customary international law elevates that rule (and any resulting obligation) to one of universal applicability. For example, the prohibitions on torture and discrimination are widely considered to be norms of customary international law operating to constrain all States, not just those party to the relevant international and regional conventions. This book includes a consideration of how such prohibitions relate to trafficking. Its conclusions in that regard would therefore apply to all States. Another example is provided by the Vienna Convention on the

---

[527] See further, J. Kelly, "The Twilight of Customary International Law," (2000) 40 *Virginia Journal of International Law* 449.

[528] Of course, that threshold is itself highly contested. The International Court of Justice in the *Nicaragua* case, for example, appeared to reverse the traditional test by emphasizing *opinio juris* (evidenced through United Nations resolutions) over State practice. See *Military and Paramilitary Activities in and Against Nicaragua (Nicaragua v. United States)*, [1986] ICJ Rep 14, as cited in Roberts, "Traditional and Modern Approaches," at 758–759.

[529] Note that even in such cases, treaties are themselves only a source of evidence of custom and/or opinio juris. As noted by the ICJ in the Continental Shelf case: "[i]t is of course axiomatic that the material of customary international law is to be looked for primarily in the actual practice and *opinio juris* of States, even though multilateral conventions may have an important role to play in recording and defining rules deriving from custom, or indeed in developing them": *Continental Shelf (Libyan Arab Jamahiriya v. Malta)*, [1985] ICJ Rep 13, para. 27.

[530] See further Roberts, "Traditional and Modern Approaches," esp. at 759–761.

Law of Treaties, which largely codifies customary rules relating to the formation and interpretation of treaties. These customary rules operate to bind all States, not just those party to that Convention.[531]

In this area as in all others, customary international law can also play an important role in shedding light on the actual content of codified rules. For example, it has been frequently argued that the international prohibition on slavery, as codified in various human rights treaties, has been subsequently expanded (by *opinio juris* as well as State practice) to include contemporary manifestations of slavery, such as trafficking. Such a conclusion, if proved, would significantly strengthen the legal basis of a general prohibition against trafficking.[532] Custom is also an important constitutive element of the so-called "secondary rules" of international law – those rules that concern the circumstances under which a State is to be held responsible for a particular violation of international law – and the consequences of a finding of responsibility. It is therefore of particular relevance to the discussion of State responsibility as it relates to trafficking in Chapter 4.

International law also recognizes the existence of rules of *jus cogens*. A *jus cogens* rule is an established rule designated to be a "peremptory norm of general international law," one that is:

> accepted and recognized by the international community of States as a whole as a norm from which no derogation is permitted and which can be modified only by a subsequent norm of general international law having the same character.[533]

There is no definitive list of such peremptory norms, although there is strong evidence available to support the inclusion of rules outlawing aggression, as well as prohibitions on racial discrimination, apartheid, and genocide.[534] The prohibition on slavery and the slave trade, considered in detail in the following chapter, is also generally accepted to be a peremptory norm of international law.[535] While *jus cogens*

---

[531] See, for example, *Maritime Delimitation and Territorial Questions (Qatar v. Bahrain)*, [1995] ICJ Rep 6, at 18 (interpretation); *Fisheries Jurisdiction (United Kingdom v. Iceland)*, [1974] ICJ Rep 3, at para. 36 (change of circumstances); *Legal Consequences for States of the Continued Presence of South Africa in Namibia (South West Africa) Notwithstanding Security Council Resolution 276 (1970) (Advisory Opinion)*, [1971] ICJ Rep 16, at para. 94 (material breach); *Gabcikovo-Nagymaros Project (Hungary v. Slovakia)*, [1997] ICJ Rep 7, at para. 99 (termination and suspension). As the International Law Commission has stated, "a codifying convention purporting to state existing rules of customary law may come to be regarded as the generally accepted formulation of the customary rules in question even by States not parties to the convention": *Draft Articles on the Law of Treaties with Commentaries*, adopted by the International Law Commission at its 18th session, 1966, in *Yearbook of the International Law Commission*, 1966, vol. 11, UN Doc. A/6309/Rev.1, at 231.

[532] See generally Chapter 3.3 below.

[533] VCLT, at Art. 53.

[534] International Law Commission, *Fragmentation of International Law: Difficulties Arising from the Diversification and Expansion of International Law*, UN Doc. A/CN.4/L.682, Apr. 13, 2006, at para. 374; International Law Commission, *Commentaries to the Draft Articles on Responsibility of States for Internationally Wrongful Acts*, UN Doc. A/56/10 (2001), Supp. No 10, at Art. 15, para. 2.

[535] See Chapter 3.3 below.

norms are clearly customary in nature, their legitimacy derives less from the consent of individual States evidenced through practice accompanied by *opinio juris* than from what Henkin has termed "authentic systemic consensus"[536] implicating the international system as a whole.

Certain basic norms, arising either through custom or treaties, are considered to be universal in character and thereby in *effect*. Such norms are owed to all States and give all States a legal interest in their protection. The right of all States to take action to protect an obligation *erga omnes* subsists irrespective of whether the State itself has suffered direct harm.[537] While all norms of *jus cogens* will inevitably give rise to *erga omnes* obligations,[538] not all such obligations will necessarily meet the test of *jus cogens*.[539]

2.4.2. *Secondary and Subsidiary Sources of International Law*

Traditional statements of the sources of international law include general principles of law as a category that is secondary to both treaties and custom. This term is commonly understood to refer to principles that are consistent across the major legal systems of the world or, even further, "a proposition of law so fundamental that it will be found in virtually every legal system."[540] The nature of a "general principle of law" is that it could be applied by a State in a dispute with another State or by an international court or tribunal that is adjudicating such a dispute or otherwise pronouncing on a particular point of law, even if it is not part of a treaty or has not entered into international law as custom.[541] General principles are in accordance with the consensual view of international law because they cover matters in relation to which States have already consented to be bound at the national level.

---

[536] Henkin, *International Law*, at 39.

[537] The basis for this right was recognized by the International Court of Justice in *Barcelona Traction, Light and Power Company Limited (Belgium v. Spain)*, [1970] ICJ Rep 3, at 32.

[538] In *Barcelona Traction*, ibid., the Court stated at 32 that "[s]uch obligations derive, for example, in contemporary international law, from the outlawing of acts of aggression, and of genocide, as also from the principles and rules concerning the basic rights of the human person, including protection from slavery and racial discrimination."

[539] See generally, M. Beyers, "Conceptualizing the Relationship Between Jus Cogens and Erga Omnes Rules," (1997) 66 *Nordic Journal of International Law* 211. See also M. Ragazzi, *The Concept of International Obligations Erga Omnes* (2000), esp. at chapter 10. Ragazzi considers direct comparisons to be a category mistake as the concept of *jus cogens*, in his view, refers to *rules*, while the concept of *erga omnes* refers to *obligations*: at 193.

[540] M. Janis, *An Introduction to International Law* (2003) (Janis, *An Introduction to International Law*), at 56.

[541] See B. Cheng, *General Principles of Law as Applied by International Courts and Tribunals* (1987) (Cheng, *General Principles*), esp. at chapter 1, "Introduction". See also M.C. Bassiouni, "A Functional Approach to General Principles of International Law," (1990) 11 *Michigan Journal of International Law* 786.

General principles have been used most often in situations where there is perceived to be a gap in the law that is not readily filled by available treaties and customary law. Those invoked by international courts are usually of a procedural and administrative kind: part of the science or structure of "the law" and thereby part of international law because it is a system of law.[542] Examples include the principle of *res judicata* (once a matter has been definitely decided by a court, it cannot be decided again), good faith, judicial impartiality, and proportionality. General principles of law can also exist at the regional, rather than universal, level. For example, the right to remain silent when charged with a crime may well be a general principle of law in Europe and the Americas, as most countries in both regions recognize it in their legal system. However, it is unclear whether it would constitute a general principle of law internationally, because many countries in other parts of the world do not specifically recognize it. General principles of law are occasionally relevant to the issue of trafficking and are therefore referred to at several points in this book.

The traditional doctrine also identifies two subsidiary "sources" of international law: the writings of "the most highly qualified publicists" and decisions of international courts and tribunals.[543] In relation to the former, it is now generally recognized that such writings cannot create law and are at best of evidential weight.[544] A positivist understanding of the role of consent in international lawmaking is inimical to the idea that an individual or a group of individuals can have a determinative effect on shaping legal obligations. It could further be argued that in relation to an issue as divisive and sensitive as trafficking, strong or unreflective reliance on scholars is potentially dangerous. The warning, given by Judge Huber in the *Spanish Zones of Morocco Claims Case*,[545] that writers are "frequently politically inspired"[546] is, as noted in the introduction to this book, just as relevant today as it may have been in 1925. The following chapter's discussion of international legal scholarship around trafficking as slavery provides just one example of the kind of campaigning scholarship that should not be relied upon when ascertaining the state of the law in this area.[547] The work of the International Law Commission in relation to State responsibility, cited extensively in Chapter 4, provides a much more positive example of writings that have clearly contributed, whether directly or by presenting evidence of custom, to the development of law in this area.

---

[542] Janis, *An Introduction to International Law*, at 41 and Henkin, *International Law*, at 32–33.

[543] ICJ Statute, at Art. 38(1).

[544] M. Dixon, *Textbook on International Law* (2007) (Dixon, *Textbook on International Law*), at 47. Elias is even stronger on the point, identifying such writings as "little more than points of reference or examples in illustration of legal arguments": T.O. Elias, *The International Court of Justice and Some Contemporary Problems* (1983), at 14.

[545] (1925) 2 RIAA 615.

[546] Cited in Dixon, *Textbook on International Law*, at 47.

[547] See further the discussion on slavery in Chapter 3.3.

The decisions of courts and tribunals are becoming increasingly significant as a source of law (or perhaps as a source of *evidence of law*)[548] as a greater number of such bodies are established to deal with an ever-widening range of issues – from international criminal law (for example, the International Criminal Court and the ad hoc and hybrid tribunals that preceded or have followed it), to law of the sea (for example, the International Tribunal for the Law of the Sea), to matters related to international trade (for example, the World Trade Organization and its Appellate Body), to regional and human rights courts (for example, the European Court of Human Rights). The capacity of a particular court or tribunal to generate international law through its jurisprudence will depend on a range of factors including the rules under which it operates, its jurisdiction, and its composition. In most cases, such bodies will have a less direct role, their proceedings and judgments providing insight or confirmation into the state of a particular customary rule,[549] the existence of a general principle of law,[550] or the substantive content of a particular treaty-based norm.[551] A useful example of the latter is provided by the series of cases cited in Chapter 3 in relation to the evolution of the 1926 treaty-based definition of slavery.

Note that national courts will often make use of international law, and their decisions can be helpful in the task of determining the substantive content of particular rules. Such bodies can also be a source of State practice and thereby contribute to the making or identification of customary norms.[552] However, their determinations do not, of themselves, constitute a source of international law or of binding international legal authority. Decisions of national courts are not generally referred to in this book.

2.4.3. The "Soft" Law of Trafficking

Soft law is less a term of art than "a moderately useful shorthand"[553] employed to describe a dizzying range of norms and instruments that have in common only the

---

[548] This is the position taken by Henkin, on the basis that judges only purport to apply law that has already come into existence through one of the primary sources. Henkin, *International Law*, at 27. For a contrasting view, see Dixon, *Textbook on International Law*, at 42–46. For a more contemporary analysis of the role of international jurisprudence on the development of customary international law, see Baker, "Customary International Law in the 21st Century."

[549] Dixon notes that the contribution of courts (particularly major international courts such as the International Court of Justice) to customary law can be substantial, "bring[ing] the process of crystallization of customary law to a swift conclusion" or "accelerat[ing] the creation of customary law and by confirming trends in state practice and by 'discovering' the necessary opinio juris": Dixon, *Textbook on International Law*, at 45. While judicial decisions are also considered a "subsidiary source," since, at least "[i]n theory, they do not make law but are declaratory of pre-existing law," this classification belies somewhat the often highly influential nature of judicial decisions from well respected international and national tribunals: ibid. at 42–46.

[550] See further, Cheng, *General Principles*.

[551] But see Baker, "Customary International Law in the 21st Century."

[552] M. Akehurst, "Custom as a Source of International Law," (1975) 47 *British Yearbook of International Law* 1.

[553] I. Brownlie, "To What Extent are the Traditional Categories of Lex Lata and Lex Ferenda Still Viable?" in A. Cassese and J.H. Weiler eds., *Change and Stability in International Law-Making* 62 (1988), at 66.

inability to be identified simply as "law." In current parlance, it is used to describe two related phenomena of international law. It can refer to principles contained in treaties that do not prescribe precise rights or obligations or otherwise provide "precise directives as to which behaviors its authors are committed to."[554] In this case, it is the *content* of the treaty itself that, through lack of solid legal content, can be described as "soft." An example is provided by a treaty that requires States Parties to "endeavor" to implement certain measures or to secure certain results. The term "soft law" is also used to refer to nontreaty instruments that, despite often employing the "hard" language of obligation, do not, of themselves, bind States. In this case, it is the *instrument* that can be described as soft. Resolutions of IGOs are a commonly cited example of soft law instruments. D'Aspremont locates the widespread acceptance of soft law as rooted in an appreciation of its flexibility that appears well suited to addressing "the growing complexity of contemporary international relations ... and the multi-dimensional problems of the modern world."[555]

Soft law, of the *negotium* and *instrumentum* varieties, is a significant aspect of the international legal framework around trafficking. In relation to the first category, many of the treaty-based rules examined in this study have been formulated as "soft" obligations. For example, as previously noted, States Parties to the Trafficking Protocol are variously required to "consider" certain measures, to "endeavour" to undertake or provide other measures, and to take action "in appropriate cases" or "to the extent possible." Some of these already vague provisions are qualified still further through reference to measures being taken in accordance with the domestic law of the State Party. The European Trafficking Convention also contains obligations that may be considered soft. States Parties are variously required to "promote" a human rights approach, to "aim to promote" gender equality, to "consider adopting" certain measures, and to "take other measures" where appropriate and under conditions provided for by their internal law. While the precise legal content of such provisions is arguable (for example, the requirement to "endeavor to provide for the physical safety of victims"[556] has been identified as placing on States an obligation to do *something*),[557] the absence of an unambiguous right or obligation is marked.

Determining the weight of soft, treaty-based norms is, at least in the area of trafficking, a fairly straightforward process. Perhaps the most important point to make is that the majority of such provisions are not completely devoid of legal substance, and it will generally be possible to objectively ascertain the scope of required behavior.

---

[554] d'Aspremont, "Softness in International Law," at 1084.
[555] Ibid. at 1076. See further, K. Raustiala and A.-M. Slaughter, "International Law, International Relations and Compliance," in W. Carlnaes, T. Risse and B.A. Simmons eds., *The Handbook of International Relations* 538 (2002) (Raustiala and Slaughter, "International Law, International Relations and Compliance"), at 551–552.
[556] Trafficking Protocol, at Art. 6(5).
[557] According to the Legislative Guide to the Protocol, the consequence of this provision is that "each State party is obliged to actually take at least some steps that amount to an 'endeavour' to protect safety." *Legislative Guide*, at 285.

In the case of the major instruments cited previously, as well as the Organized Crime Convention, such determination can be made with reference to an extensive and growing body of interpretative material that includes *travaux préparatoires*,[558] legislative guides,[559] and commentaries.[560] The basic rules of treaty interpretation, as set out in the Vienna Convention on the Law of Treaties,[561] are an additional and important source of guidance for this kind of soft law.

Particularly over the past decade, trafficking has generated a considerable body of soft law of the instrumentalist kind, some of which has been clearly normative in intent and much of which has been of the "promotional inspiration" variety.[562] One of the most prominent examples of the former category is the 2002 United Nations Principles and Guidelines on Human Rights and Human Trafficking (UN Trafficking Principles and Guidelines).[563] This instrument is the product of an internal process involving United Nations officials and a small group of experts. No State had a direct input into its drafting and while it is regularly referred to by the Human Rights Council, it has never been submitted to States for their consideration or approval. More recently, the United Nations Children's Fund released a set of Guidelines for the Protection of Child Victims of Trafficking (UNICEF Guidelines)[564] that was developed in a similar way. The United Nations High Commissioner for Refugees has also produced its own guidelines on the application of international refugee law to those who have been or are at risk of being trafficked.[565] Within the United Nations itself, the General Assembly and the Human Rights Council have been issuing resolutions on trafficking and related matters for many years.[566] At the regional and subregional levels, soft law instruments on trafficking abound. They

---

[558] For example, Travaux Préparatoires *for the Organized Crime Convention and Protocols.*

[559] For example, *Legislative Guide.*

[560] For example, European Trafficking Convention Explanatory Report.

[561] VCLT, at Arts. 31–32.

[562] This distinction is drawn from an American Society of International Law study on soft law, the results of which were published as D. Shelton ed., *Commitment and Compliance: The Role of Non-Binding Norms in the International Legal Process* (2003).

[563] UN Economic and Social Council, UN High Commissioner for Human Rights, *Recommended Principles and Guidelines on Human Rights and Human Trafficking*, UN Doc E/2002/68/Add.1, May 20, 2002 (UN Trafficking Principles and Guidelines). For information on the development of the UN Trafficking Principles and Guidelines and on how they have been used as a normative tool, see the introductory chapter to Office of the UN High Commissioner for Human Rights, *Commentary to the United Nations Recommended Principles and Guidelines on Human Rights and Human Trafficking* (forthcoming, 2010).

[564] United Nations Children's Fund, *Guidelines for the Protection of Child Victims of Trafficking* (September 2006).

[565] UN High Commissioner for Refugees, *Guidelines on International Protection: The application of Article 1(A)(2) of the 1951 Convention and/or 1967 Protocol relating to the Status of Refugees to victims of trafficking and persons at risk of being trafficked*, UN Doc. HCR/GIP/06/07 (Apr. 7, 2006).

[566] For example, in 2009, the General Assembly adopted a resolution on "Improving the Coordination of Efforts against Trafficking in Persons," UN Doc. A/RES/63/194, Jan. 23, 2009, and the Human Rights Council adopted "Trafficking in Persons, Especially Women and Children," UN Doc. A/HRC/11/L.6, June 17, 2009.

include declarations and resolutions of IGOs,[567] intergovernmental "action plans,"[568] professional standards developed by or through intergovernmental bodies,[569] memoranda of understanding between groups of countries,[570] and a growing web of bilateral agreements that focus particularly on standards relating to the repatriation and treatment of victims.[571] The "soft law" around trafficking also includes instruments of broader scope and application. For example, international normative standards on the administration of criminal justice are highly pertinent to a consideration of the legal framework around detention of trafficked persons, including children.[572] Nontreaty standards on treatment of victims of crime,[573] victims of gross

[567] For example, "Conclusions and Recommendations of the Meeting of National Authorities on Trafficking in Persons," adopted by the Organization of American States, Docs. OEA/Ser.K/XXXIX and RTP/doc. 16/06 rev. 1, Mar. 17, 2006; "ASEAN Declaration against Trafficking in Persons Particularly Women and Children," adopted by the Association of Southeast Asian Nations, Nov. 29, 2004; "Brussels Declaration on Preventing and Combating Trafficking in Human Beings" adopted by the European Conference on Preventing and Combating Trafficking in Human Beings, Sept. 20, 2002; and "Declaration A/DC12/12/01 on the Fight Against Trafficking in Persons," adopted by the Economic Community of West African States, Dec. 21, 2001.

[568] For example, the "Ouagadougou Action Plan to Combat Trafficking in Human Beings, Especially Women and Children" adopted by the Ministerial Conference on Migration and Development of the European Union and African States, Nov. 23, 2006; European Union, "EU Plan on Best Practices, Standards and Procedures for Combating and Preventing Trafficking in Human Beings," OJ 2005/C 311/1, Dec. 9, 2005; Organization for Security and Cooperation, "Action Plan to Combat Trafficking in Human Beings," OSCE Doc. PC.DEC/557, July 24, 2003; "ECOWAS Initial Plan of Action Against Trafficking in Persons (2002–2003)" annexed to the "Declaration A/DC12/12/01 on the Fight Against Trafficking in Persons," adopted by the Economic Community of West African States, Dec. 21, 2001.

[569] For example, Association of Southeast Asian Nations (ASEAN), *Criminal Justice Responses to Trafficking in Persons – ASEAN Practitioner Guidelines* (Jakarta, 2007); C. Zimmermann and C. Watts (World Health Organization), WHO *Ethical and Safety Recommendations for Interviewing Trafficked Women* (2003).

[570] For example, Memorandum of Understanding on Cooperation against Trafficking in Persons in the Greater Mekong Sub-region, adopted on Oct. 29, 2004 in Yangon (Cambodia, China, Lao PDR, Myanmar, Thailand, and Vietnam). See also "ASEAN Declaration against Trafficking in Persons Particularly Women and Children," adopted by the Association of Southeast Asian Nations, Nov. 29, 2004.

[571] For example, Agreement between the Government of Greece and the Government of Albania on the Protection and Assistance of Children Victims of Trafficking, Feb. 27, 2006; Memorandum of Understanding for the Protection of Women and Children who are Victims of Human Trafficking and Smuggling on the Border between Mexico and Guatemala, adopted on Apr. 23, 2004; Accord de Cooperation entre le Gouvernement de la République du Sénégal et le Gouvernement de la République du Mali en Matière de Lutte contre la Traite et le Traffic Transfrontaliers des Enfants, adopted on July 22, 2004 in Dakar; Memorandum of Understanding between the Royal Government of the Kingdom of Cambodia and the Royal Government of the Kingdom of Thailand on Bilateral Cooperation for Eliminating Trafficking in Children and Women and Assisting Victims of Trafficking, adopted on May 31, 2003 in Siem Reap.

[572] UN General Assembly, "United Nations Rules for the Protection of Juveniles Deprived of Their Liberty," UN Doc. A/RES/45/113, Dec. 14, 1990. For example, UN General Assembly, "Body of Principles for the Protection of All Persons under Any Form of Detention or Imprisonment," UN Doc. A/RES/43/173, Annex, Dec. 9, 1988.

[573] UN General Assembly, "Declaration of Basic Principles for Victims of Crime and Abuse of Power," UN Doc. A/RES/40/34, Nov. 29, 1985.

human rights violations,[574] and child victim-witnesses[575] address many issues that are of direct relevance to the rights of victims of trafficking and the obligations of States toward those persons.

The question of what weight to give such soft law instruments in determining the existence and substantive content of a claimed right or obligation is a complicated one. Of primary concern, particularly to those of a more conservative and positivist-leaning bent, is the danger that actions or instruments never meant by States to create binding obligations are somehow construed in that way, to the general detriment of international law's legitimacy and impact. One commentator has charged that international legal scholars intent on finding "new legal materials" to expand their own fields of study have led the way in creating for soft law a power and influence that goes well beyond what is deserved.[576] In the field of trafficking, a related danger is presented by the less-than-careful "scholar-activists," in particular those who have arrived at a particular policy position that is not well supported by "hard" international law and who then turn to soft law in order to bolster that "legal" position. The campaign to bring trafficking within the international legal prohibition on slavery, recounted in the following chapter, is an instructive example. Efforts to identify prostitution and pornography as trafficking, referred to in the previous chapter, have been similarly manipulative of international legal materials.

Misuse or incorrect application of sources does not provide adequate justification for their outright rejection. It would be incorrect to state that the multitude of soft law instruments cited above are collectively irrelevant to determining the nature and substantive content of individual rights and State obligations in relation to trafficking. There can be no doubt that in the present case, at least some soft law agreements "are not just failed treaties but can be a superior institutional choice"[577] with measurable legal effects. The most important of these instruments may directly contribute to the formation and recognition of customary law. They can, for example, provide examples or instances of both State practice and *opinio juris*. Soft law instruments in this field may also contribute to clarifying the nature and scope of a "soft" or even a hard legal norm. For example, the rather vague, treaty-based obligation to take measures to prevent trafficking in persons has been rendered more precise through a range of nontreaty instruments that specify, in considerable detail, the minimum steps that are required of a serious effort to prevent

---

574 UN General Assembly, "Basic Principles and Guidelines on the Right to a Remedy and Reparation for Victims of Gross Violations of International Human Rights Law and Serious Violations of International Humanitarian Law," UN Doc. A/RES/60/147, Dec. 16, 2005.

575 UN Economic and Social Council, "Guidelines on Justice in Matters involving Child Victims and Witnesses of Crime," adopted by ECOSOC Res. 2005/20, July 22, 2005.

576 d'Aspremont, "Softness in International Law."

577 Raustiala and Slaughter, "International Law, International Relations and Compliance," at 552.

trafficking.[578] The vague treaty-based obligation to protect victims referred to above has been similarly clarified.[579] In other cases, soft law instruments do not appear to have had this effect, underlining the importance of considering each right or obligation (or proposed right or obligation) and its associated authorities individually.

[578] See Chapter 8.
[579] See Chapter 5.

3

Specific Legal Issues

This chapter seeks to further explore and explain the international legal framework around trafficking by identifying a series of legal issues of special relevance to current debates and practice and subjecting each to detailed analysis. The issues selected are not exhaustive, and many others are raised at various points throughout this book.

3.1. TRAFFICKED PERSONS AS NONCITIZENS

The position of noncitizens or "non-nationals"[1] (including stateless persons) under international law is of particular relevance to an assessment of the rights of trafficked persons and the duties owed to them by States. Except in cases of internal trafficking, the most serious violations committed against a trafficked person will almost invariably take place outside the victim's country of residence or citizenship. This is not to deny the reality of substantive violations occurring during the recruitment and initial transportation phases. However, the purpose of that recruitment and transport is exploitation; it is for this reason that the country of destination is an especially dangerous one for trafficked persons and their rights. It is also the place where these rights often can be most effectively protected. Trafficked persons outside their usual country of residence may fall into a particular category of noncitizen (such as refugee, asylum-seeker, or migrant worker). This categorization, like the status of being a trafficked person, may operate to alter the nature of the rights to

---

[1] The terms "alien," "non-national," and "noncitizen" have been used interchangeably although "noncitizen" now appears to be the preferred term within the international human rights system. The United Nations has defined a noncitizen as "any individual who is not a national of a State in which he or she is present": UN General Assembly, "Declaration on the Human Rights of Individuals who are not Nationals of the Countries in Which They Live," UN Doc. A/RES/40/144, Dec. 13, 1985 ("Declaration on Human Rights of Non-Nationals"), at Art. 1. The term "noncitizen" also applies to stateless persons, that is, individuals who have never formally acquired citizenship of the country in which they were born or who have somehow lost their citizenship without gaining another: D. Weissbrodt, "The Protection of Non-Citizens in International Human Rights Law," in R. Cholewinski, R. Perruchoud and E. MacDonald eds., *International Migration Law: Developing Paradigms and Key Challenges* 221 (2007), at 222.

which they are entitled and the obligations owed to them. The following general discussion is applicable to all noncitizens but should be read in light of the information provided elsewhere in this chapter on the various supplemental regimes that operate in respect of certain categories of noncitizens, including stateless persons.

The rights of noncitizens have their roots in traditional international law of State responsibility, which recognized that certain duties (either "equal treatment" or an "international minimum standard") were owed by a host State to aliens or non-nationals within its territory.[2] In other words, States were obliged under customary international law not to mistreat foreign nationals present in their territory. A State would be held legally responsible for injury to aliens resulting from acts that were contrary to international law,[3] irrespective of how it treated its own citizens.[4] However, as the individual lacked formal legal status, it was to the State of origin that such rights accrued,[5] and the decision of whether to extend diplomatic protection was one for that State to make. The question of the standard of treatment to be afforded foreign nationals has always been controversial, with some States arguing for "international minimum standards" and others for a standard that accords to the treatment, by the host State, of its own citizens.[6]

3.1.1. *Human Rights Protections for Noncitizens*

While not totally supplanting the traditional law of State responsibility for injury to aliens,[7] the development of international human rights law introduced norms

---

[2] On the general subject of State responsibility for injury to aliens with particular reference to human rights, see M.M. McDougal, H.D. Lasswell, and L. Chen, "The Protection of Aliens from Discrimination and World Public Order: Responsibility of States Conjoined with Human Rights," (1976) 70 *American Journal of International Law* 432 (McDougal, et al., "The Protection of Aliens"); R. Cholewinski, *Migrant Workers in International Human Rights Law* (1997) (Cholewinski, *Migrant Workers*), at 40–47. See also the introductory section to Chapter 4.

[3] The usual citation for this principle is *Mavrommatis Palestine Concessions* (*Greece v. Great Britain*), [1924] PCIJ Rep, Series A, No. 2.

[4] "[A] State is entitled to treat both its own nationals and stateless persons at discretion and … the manner in which it treats them is not a matter with which International Law, as a rule, concerns itself": L. Oppenheim, *International Law: A Treatise* (1955) (Oppenheim, *International Law*), at 640.

[5] Cholewinski, *Migrant Workers*, at 45. See also M. Dixon, *Textbook on International Law* (2007), at 255–258.

[6] B. Opeskin, *The Influence of International Law on the International Movement of Persons*, United Nations Development Programme, Human Development Research Paper 2009/18 (2009), at 12–13.

[7] D.J. Harris, *Cases and Materials on International Law* (1991), at 499–500: "[t]hat the law of State responsibility for aliens is not made redundant by the emergence of international human rights law follows from the uncertainty as to the rules on the enforcement of customary human rights law and the less than perfect remedies and universal acceptance of human rights treaties. For the time being at least, the possibility of diplomatic protection by one's national State is a valuable alternative and supplement to such guarantees and procedures under international human rights law as may exist," cited in Cholewinski, *Migrant Workers*, at 47. Cholewinski, ibid., also draws attention to the view of McDougal, et al., "The Protection of Aliens," at 464–465, that "[t]he traditional channels of protection through a state, together with the newly developed procedures under the contemporary human rights program of claims by individuals, would appear to achieve a cumulative beneficial impact, each reinforcing each other, in defense and fulfilment of the human rights of the individual."

that regulated the way in which the State was to treat all persons, by virtue of their common humanity, with the added advantage of such rights being vested in the individual and not the State. Accordingly, the question of whether a trafficked person outside his or her own country benefits from the protection of international human rights law can, in principle, be answered in the affirmative. International law generally accepts that treaties apply to all individuals within a State's jurisdiction.[8] By extension, human rights law will apply to everyone within a State's territory or jurisdiction, regardless of nationality or citizenship and how they came to be within the territory. Many human rights instruments either explicitly or implicitly confirm this position. For example, the Universal Declaration of Human Rights (UDHR), adopted in 1948, speaks of that instrument being "a common standard of achievement for all peoples and all nations."[9] It refers to "equal and inalienable rights of all members of the human family"[10] and confirms that *everyone* is entitled to all enumerated rights and freedoms "without distinction of any kind, such as race, colour, sex, language, religion, political or other opinion, national or social origin, property, birth or other status."[11]

Despite the generous sweep of the UDHR, and notwithstanding repeated affirmations of the universality of human rights,[12] the scope and extent of human rights protection for aliens or noncitizens remains controversial, uneven, and, in some cases, uncertain. Certainly, State practice appears to support a different level of treatment of noncitizens with respect to many aspects of public and private life. In addition, and despite the use of inclusive terminology, most of the major international human rights treaties contain numerous provisions excluding non-nationals or otherwise permitting differential treatment. Aliens unlawfully within the territory of a State

---

[8] See *Treatment of Polish Nationals in the Danzig Territory (Advisory Opinion)* [1932] PCIJ Rep, Series A/B, No. 44 (identifying a difference between a State's right to control admission of foreigners versus the right of individuals found within the State); Vienna Convention on the Law of Treaties, 1155 UNTS 331, done May 23, 1969, entered into force Jan. 27, 1980 (VCLT), at Art. 29 (inferring that treaties apply to all individuals within the jurisdiction of the State Party: "Territorial scope of treaties: Unless a different intention appears from the treaty or is otherwise established, a treaty is binding upon each party in respect of its entire territory"). For a provocative extension of the concept of "jurisdiction" in relation to human rights treaties, see H. King, "The Extraterritorial Rights Obligations of States," (2009) 9 *Human Rights Law Review* 521.

[9] Universal Declaration of Human Rights, adopted by UNGA Res. 217A (III), UN Doc. A/810 at 71, Dec. 10, 1948 (UDHR), at Preamble.

[10] Ibid.

[11] Ibid at. Art. 2(1). Note the list of prohibited grounds excludes nationality. For an interpretation of this exclusion in the context of the identical nondiscrimination clause set out in the International Covenant on Civil and Political Rights, 999 UNTS 171, done Dec. 16, 1996, entered into force Mar. 3, 1976 (ICCPR), see note 13 to this chapter.

[12] See, for example, the "Vienna Declaration and Programme of Action," UN Doc. A/CONF.157/23, July 12, 1993, at Art. 1: "The World Conference on Human Rights reaffirms the solemn commitment of all States to fulfil their obligations to promote universal respect for and observance and protection of all human rights and fundamental freedoms for all in accordance with the Charter of the United Nations, other instruments relating to human rights and international law. The universal nature of these rights and freedoms is beyond question."

are often subject to even greater restrictions. In deciding whether such restrictions or distinctions are lawful, it is important to consider the precise terms of the treaty in question – including the scope of its nondiscrimination clause. The following paragraphs briefly consider this issue in relation to the human rights treaties that are of most relevance to trafficked persons. The subsection concludes with a general finding on the applicability of international human rights law to noncitizens.

Application of the International Covenant on Civil and Political Rights (ICCPR) is specifically extended to:

> all individuals within [the] territory [of the State Party] and subject to its juris-
> diction ... without distinction of any kind such as race, colour, sex, language,
> religion, political or other opinion, national or social origin, property, birth or
> other status.[13]

The ICCPR also guarantees to "all persons" equality before the law and equal protection of the law without discrimination.[14] The Human Rights Committee has affirmed that:

> The rights set forth in the Covenant apply to everyone, irrespective of reciprocity,
> and irrespective of his or her nationality or statelessness. Thus, the general rule is
> that each one of the rights of the Covenant must be guaranteed without discrimi-
> nation between citizens and aliens.[15]

---

[13] ICCPR, at Art. 2(1). Note that as with the UDHR, the list of prohibited grounds does not include nationality. The significance of this omission is generally played down, with one influential commentator arguing, unconvincingly, that "the list clearly is intended to be illustrative and not comprehensive" and, further, that nationality would anyway "appear to fall into the category of 'distinction of any kind'": R.B. Lillich, *The Human Rights of Aliens in Contemporary International Law* (1984), at 43, cited in Office of the United Nations High Commissioner for Human Rights, *The Rights of Non-Citizens* (2006) (OHCHR, *Non-Citizens*), at 36.

[14] ICCPR, at Art. 26.

[15] UN Human Rights Committee, "General Comment No. 15: The Position of Aliens under the Covenant" (1986), UN Doc. HRI/GEN.1/Rev.7, May 12, 2004, at 140 (HRC General Comment No. 15), at para. 2. See also UN Human Rights Committee, "General Comment No. 31: The Nature of the General Legal Obligation Imposed on States Parties to the Covenant" (2004), UN Doc. HRI/GEN.1/Rev.7, May 12, 2004, at 192, at para. 10. The UN Special Rapporteur on the Rights of Non-Citizens noted that ICCPR General Comment No. 15 very much reflects the substance of the UN General Assembly, "Declaration on the Human Rights of Individuals who are not Nationals of the Countries in Which They Live," UN Doc. A/RES/40/144, Dec. 13, 1985; "Prevention of Discrimination and Protection of Indigenous Peoples and Minorities: The Rights of Non-Citizens: Preliminary Report of the Special Rapporteur, Mr. David Weissbrodt, submitted in accordance with Sub-Commission decision 2000/103," UN Doc. E/CN.4/Sub.2/2001/20, June 6, 2001, at para. 103. For an overview of the development of this Declaration as well as an examination of its contents, see Cholewinski, *Migrant Workers*, at 72–75. In the present context it is relevant to note that the Declaration specifically provides that nothing in it "shall be interpreted as legitimising any alien's illegal entry into and presence in a State, nor shall any provision be interpreted as restricting the right of any State to promulgate law and regulations concerning the entry of aliens and the terms and conditions of their stay or to establish differences between nationals and aliens. However, such laws and regulations shall not be incompatible with the international legal obligations of that State, including those in the field of human rights": at Art. 2(1).

The Human Rights Committee has further specified that:

> Aliens ... have an inherent right to life, protected by law, and may not be arbitrarily deprived of life. They may not be subjected to torture or to cruel, inhumane or degrading treatment or punishment; nor may they be held in slavery or servitude. Aliens have the full right of liberty and security of the person. If lawfully deprived of their liberty, they shall be treated with humanity and with respect for the inherent dignity of their person. Aliens may not be imprisoned for failure to fulfil a contractual obligation. They have the right to liberty of movement and free choice of residence; they shall be free to leave the country. Aliens shall be equal before the courts and tribunals, and shall be entitled to a fair and public hearing by a competent, independent and impartial tribunal established by law in the determination of any criminal charge or of rights and obligations in a suit at law. Aliens shall not be subject to retrospective penal legislation and are entitled to recognition before the law. They may not be subjected to arbitrary or unlawful interference with their privacy, family, home or correspondence. They have the right to freedom of thought, conscience and religion and the right to hold opinions and to express them. Aliens receive the benefit of the right of peaceful assembly and of freedom of association. They may marry when at marriageable age. Their children are entitled to those measures of protection required by their status as minors. In those cases where aliens constitute a minority within the meaning of Article 27, they shall not be denied the right, in community with other members of their group, to enjoy their own culture, to profess and practice their own religion and to use their own language. Aliens are entitled to equal protection by the law. There shall be no discrimination between aliens and citizens in the application of these rights. These rights of aliens may be qualified only by such limitations as may be lawfully imposed under the Covenant.[16]

In terms of lawful qualifications, reference should be made to Article 4(1) of the ICCPR, which permits derogations from certain nonfundamental rights in times of public emergency that threaten the life of the nation, provided that such measures are strictly required by the exigencies of the situation and do not amount to discrimination "solely on the ground of race, colour, sex, language, religion or social origin."[17] It is relevant to note that nationality and even national origin are excluded from this list of prohibited grounds. According to the *travaux préparatoires*, this omission reflected a general understanding that States will often find it necessary to discriminate against aliens in times of national emergency.[18] In addition, and as

---

[16] HRC General Comment No. 15, at para. 7.

[17] Among the rights in the ICCPR that may be subject to such restrictions are freedom of association (Article 22), freedom of movement (Article 12), freedom of expression (Article 19), and peaceful assembly (Article 21).

[18] M. Nowak, *UN Covenant on Civil and Political Rights: CCPR Commentary* (2005) (Nowak, *CCPR Commentary*), at 99–100. Note that the word "solely" has been interpreted as confirming that emergency measures affecting a particular population group are permissible, "as long as they do not intentionally target these population groups": ibid.

explored further in Chapter 5 in the context of a consideration of the lawfulness of detention of trafficked persons, the ICCPR restricts application of the right to free-dom of movement[19] and safeguards against arbitrary expulsion[20] to persons *lawfully* within the territory of the State Party.[21] Within these restrictions, the Human Rights Committee has generally upheld the principle of equality of rights between citizens and noncitizens. Its work nevertheless reflects an assumption that differentiation based on citizenship can sometimes be reasonable and therefore not a breach of the Covenant's guarantee of equality and equal treatment.[22] However, the jurispru-dence on this point is limited, with the result that the parameters of reasonableness have not yet been clearly defined.[23]

The International Covenant on Economic, Social and Cultural Rights (ICESCR) includes a nondiscrimination clause that is identical to that found in the ICCPR.[24] As with the ICCPR's clause, commentators are divided on the question of whether this provision would admit further grounds of discrimination such as nationality or alienage.[25] In two important respects, the ICESCR is weaker on noncitizen rights

---

[19] ICCPR, at Art. 12(1).

[20] Ibid. at Art. 13.

[21] Note also that the right to participate in public affairs, to vote and hold office, and to have access to public service under Article 25 is restricted to "every citizen."

[22] For a detailed analysis of this aspect of the work of the Human Rights Committee, see J.C. Hathaway, *The Rights of Refugees under International Law* (2005) (Hathaway, *The Rights of Refugees*), at 131–147.

[23] Writing in 2005, Hathaway concludes that "[t]he present moment can thus be most accurately described as one of legal uncertainty on this point: until and unless the jurisprudence of the Human Rights Committee assesses the propriety of categorical differentiation based on citizenship across a broader range of issues, it will be difficult to know which forms of exclusion are likely to be found valid and which are in breach of Art. 26": ibid. at 133. Hathaway is generally critical of the Committee's analysis of equality and nondiscrimination as these principles apply to non-nationals, describing it as formalistic and superficial, failing to grapple with a genuinely effects-based approach, and granting too wide a margin of appreciation to States: ibid. at 133–137, 150–151.

[24] "The States Parties to the present Covenant undertake to guarantee that the rights enunciated in the present Covenant will be exercised without discrimination of any kind as to race, colour, sex, language, religion, political or other opinion, national or social origin, property, birth or other sta-tus": International Covenant on Economic, Social and Cultural Rights, 993 UNTS 3, done Dec. 16, 1966, entered into force Jan. 3, 1976 (ICESCR), at Art. 2(2).

[25] See, for example, Cholewinski, *Migrant Workers*, at 57–58. The Committee on Economic, Social and Cultural Rights has said, in relation to the prohibition against discrimination, that it "[e]ncom-passes all internationally prohibited grounds of discrimination": UN Committee on Economic, Social and Cultural Rights, "General Comment No. 13: The Right to Education (Art.13)," UN Doc. E/C.12/1999/10, Dec. 8, 1999, at para. 31. In a subsequent general comment on the right to health, the Committee also held that the Covenant proscribed "any discrimination on the grounds of race, colour, sex, language, religion, political or other opinion, national or social origin, property, birth, physical or mental disability, health status (including HIV/AIDS), sexual orientation and civil, polit-ical, social or other status which has the intention or effect of nullifying or impairing the equal enjoyment or exercise of the right to health": UN Committee on Economic, Social and Cultural Rights, "General Comment No. 14: The Right to the Highest Attainable Standard of Health," UN Doc. E/C.12/2000/4, Aug. 11, 2000, at para. 18. On the basis of the General Comment, the Special Rapporteur on the Rights of Non-Citizens has asserted that States Parties cannot discriminate

than the ICCPR. First, there is no specific extension of applicability of Convention rights to all individuals within the territory or under the jurisdiction of the State Party. Second, developing countries are explicitly permitted to determine the extent to which they will guarantee the *economic* rights set forth in the Covenant to non-nationals.[26]

The Committee on Economic, Social and Cultural Rights (ICESCR Committee) has generally taken the view that the Convention applies to all persons under the jurisdiction of the State Party, regardless of citizenship and status. This approach has been widely supported[27] and is strengthened by the fact that, apart from a general limitations clause,[28] specific restrictions on the rights of aliens are limited to those discussed above. The language of certain Articles further reinforces this interpretation. In relation to the right to education, for example, the relevant Article refers to the right of "everyone."[29] The ICESCR Committee has also indicated that the principle of nondiscrimination in relation to access to educational institutions "extends to all persons of school age residing in the territory of the State Party including non-nationals and irrespective of their legal status."[30] Another example of particular relevance to the present context is Article 6, establishing the right of "everyone" to "gain his living by work which he freely chooses or accepts."[31] The Special Rapporteur on the rights of noncitizens has interpreted the Committee's General Comments on the right to health and the right to adequate housing as supportive of extending both

against non-nationals with respect to the right to health if that discrimination intentionally or effectively nullifies or impairs their enjoyment to exercise of that right: "Prevention of Discrimination and Protection of Indigenous Peoples and Minorities: The Rights of Non-Citizens: Preliminary Report of the Special Rapporteur, Mr. David Weissbrodt, submitted in accordance with Sub-Commission decision 2000/103," UN Doc. E/CN.4/Sub.2/2001/20, June 6, 2001, at para. 60. Note that the Limburg Principles, developed by a group of experts and advocates in 1987 to clarify the nature of State obligations under the ICESCR and to guide its effective implementation, assert that the grounds of discrimination mentioned in Article 2(2) are not exhaustive: "Limburg Principles on the Implementation of the International Covenant on Economic, Social and Cultural Rights," UN Doc. E/CN.4/1987/17, Annex, Jan. 8, 1987 (Limburg Principles), at para. 36.

[26] "Developing countries, with due regard to human rights and their national economy, may determine to what extent they would guarantee the rights recognized in the present Covenant to non-nationals": ICESCR, at Art. 2(3). It can be argued that this provision implies an obligation on *developed* States Parties to guarantee provision of the relevant rights to non-nationals and on *all States* to guarantee provision of all noneconomic rights. Further on controversies and ambiguities surrounding this provision, see Cholewinski, *Migrant Workers*, at 58–60.

[27] See, for example, Limburg Principles, at para. 42: "[a]s a general rule the Covenant applies equally to nationals and non-nationals."

[28] ICESCR, at Art. 4, provides that: "[t]he States Parties to the present Covenant recognise that, in the enjoyment of those rights provided by the State in conformity with the present Covenant, the State may subject such rights only to such limitations as are determined by law only in so far as this may be compatible with the nature of these rights and solely for the purpose of promoting the general welfare in a democratic society."

[29] Ibid. at Art. 13.

[30] UN Committee on Economic, Social and Cultural Rights, "General Comment No. 13: The Right to Education," UN Doc. E/C.12/1999/10, Dec. 8, 1999, at para. 34.

[31] ICCPR, at Art. 6.

rights to non-nationals.[32] These expansive interpretations receive confirmation in the ICESCR Committee's most recent General Comment No. 20, which states:

> The ground of nationality should not bar access to Covenant rights, e.g. all children within a State, including those with an undocumented status, have a right to receive education and access to adequate food and affordable health care. The Covenant rights apply to everyone including non-nationals, such as refugees, asylum-seekers, stateless persons, migrant workers and victims of international trafficking, regardless of legal status and documentation.[33]

However, this position is weakened somewhat by an accompanying footnote, which indicates that the statement is not to prejudice the application of Article 2(3) of ICESCR: "Developing countries, with due regard to human rights and their national economy, may determine to what extent they would guarantee the economic rights recognized in the present Covenant to non-nationals."[34]

While repeatedly affirming in its General Comments the principle of equality, the ICESCR Committee has in practice demonstrated what one commentator identifies as a "flexible" approach in tailoring its views of State Party obligations depending on the legal status of the individual.[35] Judging from the practice of the ICESCR Committee in its Concluding Observations, it appears that those lawfully within the territory of the State Party (including stateless persons, refugees, and asylum-seekers) are, for the most part, entitled to enjoy Covenant rights on an equal basis with citizens and to a relatively greater extent than individuals illegally present.[36] This de facto categorical differentiation may operate to exclude from the protection of the ICESCR, individuals, including trafficked persons, who have not entered the destination country lawfully and who are not able to make or sustain a claim for asylum. It remains to be seen whether this disadvantageous distinction based on legal status will continue following the ICESCR Committee's recent General Comment No. 20.

---

[32] "Prevention of Discrimination and Protection of Indigenous Peoples and Minorities: The Rights of Non-Citizens: Preliminary Report of the Special Rapporteur, Mr. David Weissbrodt, submitted in accordance with Sub-Commission decision 2000/103," UN Doc. E/CN.4/Sub.2/2001/20, June 6, 2001, at 60–61. But see Cholewinski, *Migrant Workers*, at 61, arguing that the Committee's various pronouncements on the right to housing do not necessarily support a conclusion that this right applies to non-nationals.

[33] UN Committee on Economic, Social and Cultural Rights, "General Comment No. 20: Non-Discrimination in Economic, Social and Cultural Rights," UN Doc. E/C.12/GC/20, July 2, 2009, at para. 30 (footnotes omitted).

[34] Ibid. at note 22.

[35] M.M. Sepúlveda, *The Nature of the Obligations under the International Covenant on Economic, Social and Cultural Rights* (2003), at 262.

[36] For a detailed and balanced consideration of the practice of the Committee with respect to the issue of non-citizens, see ibid. at 262–277. For a less nuanced view of the Committee's work in this area (which concludes by finding that "a compelling argument can be made that all non-nationals possess ICESCR rights"), see J.A. Dent, *Research Paper on the Social and Economic Rights of Non-Nationals in Europe* (European Council on Refugees and Exiles, 1998) (Dent, *Research Paper on the Social and Economic Rights of Non-Nationals in Europe*), at 3–4.

The Convention on the Elimination of All Forms of Racial Discrimination (CERD) contains the most unambiguous statement of differentiation between citizens and noncitizens. CERD qualifies its broad definition of racial discrimination[37] by declaring, in Article 1(2), that: "[t]his Convention shall not apply to distinctions, exclusions, restrictions or preferences made by a State Party to this Convention between citizens and non-citizens."[38] In practice, the provision has been interpreted as "providing for the possibility of differentiating between citizens and non-citizens."[39] In its detailed General Comment on this issue, the relevant treaty body (the Race Discrimination Committee) confirmed its much earlier stance that Article 1(2):

> must be construed so as to avoid undermining the basic prohibition of discrimination. Hence, it should not be interpreted to detract, in any way, from the rights and freedoms recognized and enunciated in particular in the Universal Declaration of Human Rights, the International Covenant on Civil and Political Rights and the International Covenant on Economic, Social and Cultural Rights.[40]

While recognizing limited exceptions, it affirms that "human rights are, in principle, to be enjoyed by all persons" and that "States parties are under an obligation to guarantee equality between citizens and non-citizens in the enjoyment of these rights to the extent recognized under international law."[41]

The Race Discrimination Committee has provided a clear test for determining whether a particular measure that differentiates between persons on the basis of citizenship or immigration status cannot be justified as a special measure under Article 1(4):

> Under the Convention, differential treatment based on citizenship or immigration status will constitute discrimination if the criteria for such differentiation, judged in the light of the objectives and purposes of the Convention, are not applied pursuant to a legitimate aim, and are not proportional to the achievement of this aim.[42]

---

[37] "The term 'racial discrimination' shall mean any distinction, exclusion, restriction or preference based on race, colour, descent, or national or ethnic origin which has the purpose of effect of nullifying or impairing the recognition, enjoyment or exercise, on an equal footing, of human rights and fundamental freedoms in the political, economic, social, cultural or any other field of public life": Convention on the Elimination of All Forms of Racial Discrimination, 660 UNTS 195, done Dec. 21, 1965, entered into force Jan. 4, 1969 (CERD), at Art. 1(1).

[38] Ibid. at Art. 1(2). Note that Article 1(3) provides that: "[n]othing in this Convention may be interpreted as affecting in any way the legal provisions of States Parties concerning nationality, citizenship or naturalization, provided that such provisions do not discriminate against any particular nationality."

[39] UN Committee on the Elimination of Racial Discrimination, "General Recommendation No. 30: Discrimination against Non-Citizens," UN Doc. CERD/C/64/Misc.11/rev.3, Mar. 12, 2004 (CERD General Recommendation No. 30), at para. 1.

[40] Ibid. at para. 2. See also UN Committee on the Elimination of Racial Discrimination, "General Recommendation 1 on States Parties' Obligations," UN Doc. A/8718 at 37, Feb. 25, 1972.

[41] CERD General Recommendation No. 30, at para. 3.

[42] Ibid.

In its own deliberations, the Race Discrimination Committee has examined and pronounced on a wide range of situations involving discriminatory treatment of non-nationals, including migrant domestic workers as well as persons who have been trafficked.[43] Since its adoption of a General Comment on the subject in 2004, in which States Parties were directed to report on discrimination against non-nationals,[44] the Race Discrimination Committee has routinely addressed this issue in its consideration of States Parties' reports.[45]

At the heart of the Convention on the Elimination of Discrimination Against Women (CEDAW)[46] is a broad prohibition on sex-based discrimination, the implications of which are considered at various points throughout this study. With respect to the application of this prohibition to non-nationals, the Convention is silent: While it does not specifically extend its application to all women within the territory or under the jurisdiction of a State Party, it also does not contain a CERD-type exclusionary clause. The CEDAW Committee has not directly addressed the issue through, for example, an explicit affirmation that non-nationals should receive the benefit of the rights guaranteed under CEDAW without discrimination. However, the CEDAW Committee does appear to base its own work on an assumption of broad applicability. It has, for example, repeatedly examined and expressed its concern for the situation of trafficked women (vis-à-vis countries of destination) and other noncitizens such as female migrant domestic workers, smuggled migrants, unaccompanied or undocumented female children, asylum-seekers, and refugees, both in Concluding Observations and in a General Recommendation specifically on women migrant workers.[47] The CEDAW Committee has also affirmed that States Parties should

---

43 For a detailed but now dated overview of the Committee's consideration of the rights of non-nationals, see Cholewinski, *Migrant Workers*, at 62–64. See also the various reports of the Special Rapporteur on the Rights of Non-Citizens ("The Rights of Non-Citizens: Progress Report of the Special Rapporteur, Mr David Weissbrodt," UN Doc. E/CN.4/Sub.2/2002/25, June 5, 2002; "The Rights of Non-Citizens: Final Report of the Special Rapporteur, Mr David Weissbrodt," UN Doc. E/CN.4/Sub.2/2003/23, May 26, 2003; "The Rights of Non-Citizens: Preliminary Report of the Special Rapporteur, Mr David Weissbrodt," UN Doc. E/CN.4/Sub.2/2001/20, June 6, 2001) and OHCHR, *Non-Citizens*, esp. at 29–32.

44 CERD General Recommendation No. 30, at para. 5.

45 See, for example, UN Committee on the Elimination of Racial Discrimination: "Concluding Observations: United Arab Emirates," UN Doc. CERD/C/UAE/CO/17, Aug. 31, 2009; "Concluding Observations: Russian Federation," UN Doc. CERD/C/RUS/CO/19, Aug. 20 2008; "Concluding Observations: United States of America," UN Doc. CERD/C/USA/CO/6, Mar. 5, 2008; "Concluding Observations: Norway," UN Doc. CERD/C/NOR/CO/18, Oct. 19, 2006.

46 Convention on the Elimination of All Forms of Discrimination Against Women, 1249 UNTS 13, done Dec. 18, 1979, entered into force Sept. 3, 1981 (CEDAW).

47 See, for example, UN Committee on the Elimination of Discrimination against Women: "Concluding Observations: Germany," UN Doc. CEDAW/C/DEU/CO/2, Nov. 14, 2009, at para. 34 (refugees and asylum-seekers); "Concluding Observations: Bahrain," UN Doc. CEDAW/C/BHR/CO/2, Nov. 14, 2008, at paras. 30 (children of non-citizen parents) and 35 (migrant domestic workers); "Concluding Observations: Ecuador," UN Doc. CEDAW/C/ECU/CO/7, Nov. 7, 2008, at para. 26 (migrants, refugees, and asylum-seekers); "Concluding Observations: Belize," UN Doc. CEDAW/C/BLZ/CO/4, Aug. 10, 2007, at para. 33 (undocumented girl children); "Concluding Observations: Singapore,"

ensure that foreign women are aware of their rights and have access to effective remedies when those rights are breached.[48] The need for an explicit statement from the CEDAW Committee on the applicability of its provisions to noncitizens has recently been recognized in the context of a possible General Comment on Article 2.[49]

Of all the core human rights instruments, the Convention on the Rights of the Child (CRC) provides [the most clarity on the point of its application to non-nationals. All provisions of the CRC apply to all children within the jurisdiction of the State Party, without discrimination of any kind.[50] All trafficked children within the jurisdiction of a State Party would therefore be entitled to the full protection of that instrument, irrespective of any other factor. The Committee on the Rights of the Child (CRC Committee), established to oversee implementation of this

---

UN Doc. CEDAW/C/SGP/CO/3, Aug. 10, 2007, at paras. 21 (trafficked women and girls) and 23–24 (migrant domestic workers); "Concluding Observations: Greece," UN Doc. CEDAW/C/GRC/CO/6, Feb. 2, 2007, at paras. 31–32 (children of immigrant women); "Concluding Observations: Poland," UN Doc. CEDAW/C/POL/CO/6, Feb. 2, 2007, at para. 28 (refugees, asylum-seekers, and migrants); "Concluding Observations: China," UN Doc. CEDAW/C/CHN/CO/6, Aug. 25, 2006, at paras. 33 (refugees and asylum-seekers, and noting the precarious status and vulnerability of North Korean women to abuse, trafficking, forced marriage, and virtual slavery) and 41 (migrant domestic workers); "Concluding Observations: The Former Yugoslav Republic of Macedonia," UN Doc. CEDAW/C/MKD/CO/3, Feb. 3, 2006, at para. 29 (refugees and asylum-seekers); "Concluding Observations: Malawi," UN Doc. CEDAW/C/MWI/CO/5, Feb. 3, 2006, at paras. 35–36 (trafficking and smuggling of refugee women from neighboring countries). See also UN Committee on the Elimination of Discrimination against Women, "General Recommendation No. 26: Women Migrant Workers," UN Doc. CEDAW/C/2009/WP.1/R, Dec. 5, 2008 (CEDAW General Recommendation No. 26), at para. 4: "The Committee ... emphasizes that all categories of women migrants fall within the scope of the obligations of States parties to the Convention and must be protected against all forms of discrimination by the Convention." The Committee noted that "this general recommendation will not address the circumstances relating to trafficking ... however ... many elements of the present general recommendation are also relevant in situations where women migrants have been victims of trafficking": ibid. at note 4.

48 See, for example, UN Committee on the Elimination of Discrimination against Women, "Concluding Comments: Germany", UN Doc A/53/38 at 29, Aug. 17, 2000, at para. 318, cited in A. Byrnes, M. Herminia Graterol and R. Chartres, "State Obligation and the Convention on the Elimination of All Forms of Discrimination Against Women," UNSW Law Research Paper No. 2007-48 (July 19, 2007) (Byrnes et al, "State Obligation and CEDAW"), at 56. See also CEDAW General Recommendation No. 26, at paras. 24(b)(i), 26(c) and 26(l).

49 See Byrnes et al, "State Obligation and CEDAW," Annex 2, proposing at para. 5 that a General Comment on Article 2 include the following: "[t]he obligations of the State party under the Convention apply both to its citizens and to non-citizens in its territory or under its jurisdiction. Aliens should in general receive the benefit of the rights guaranteed by the Convention without discrimination, although there are a number of rights in the sphere of political life that may be limited in the case of non-citizens, provided that there is no discrimination between male and female non-citizens in these areas," and at para. 30 that "[a policy of eliminating discrimination against women] should identify women within the jurisdiction of the State party (including non-citizens) as the rights-bearers."

50 States Parties are required to "[r]espect and ensure the rights set forth in the present Convention to each child within their jurisdiction without discrimination of any kind, irrespective of the child's or his or her parent's or legal guardian's race, colour, sex, language, religion, political or other opinion, national, ethnic or social origin, property, disability, birth or other status": Convention on the Rights of the Child, 1577 UNTS 3, done Nov. 20, 1989, entered into force Sept. 2, 1990 (CRC), at Art 2(1).

instrument, has specifically stated that domestic implementation must ensure that the rights contained in the Convention protect all children, including noncitizens.[51] The CRC Committee routinely deals with issues affecting noncitizens including refugees and asylum-seekers, stateless persons, child migrant workers, and victims of trafficking.[52] The CRC Committee has also, through the mechanism of its General Comments, addressed the matter of unaccompanied children, identifying specific obligations towards this category of noncitizen vis-à-vis the destination State.[53]

The level of variation found within the international human rights instruments with respect to non-nationals is reflected in the regional human rights instruments. The African Charter on Human and Peoples' Rights is perhaps the most inclusive, with almost every substantive right applying to "every individual" or "every human being"; a broad nondiscrimination clause also referring to "every individual";[54] and an open-ended list of grounds of prohibited discrimination.[55] The Charter's specific reference to "every citizen" in relation to the right to participate in government and public service[56] lends weight to the view that its other provisions apply to all persons without distinction as to nationality or alienage. This position has been confirmed by the African Commission on Human and Peoples' Rights with respect to several

---

[51] "[T]he enjoyment of rights stipulated in the Convention is not limited to children who are citizens of a State party and must therefore, if not explicitly stated otherwise in the Convention, also be available to all children – including asylum-seeking, refugee and migrant children – irrespective of their nationality, immigration status or statelessness": UN Committee on the Rights of the Child, "General Comment No. 6: Treatment of Unaccompanied and Separated Children Outside Their Country of Origin," UN Doc. CRC/GC/2005/6, Sept. 1, 2005 (CRC General Comment No. 6), at para. 12.

[52] See, for example, UN Committee on the Rights of the Child: "Concluding Observations: Chad," UN Doc. CRC/C/TCD/CO/2, Feb. 12, 2009, at paras. 40 (children of refugees and nomads), 71 (protection of refugee children from recruitment into military service), 73–74 (refugee children, including unaccompanied and separated children) and 77–78 (protection of refugee children from child labor); "Concluding Observations: Georgia," UN Doc. CRC/C/GEO/CO/3, June 23, 2008, at para. 59 (asylum-seeking and refugee children, including unaccompanied and separated children); "Concluding Observations: Jordan," UN Doc. CRC/C/JOR/CO/3, Sept. 29, 2007, at para. 80 (asylum-seeking and refugee children, particularly unaccompanied children); "Concluding Observations: Costa Rica," UN Doc. CRC/C/OPSC/CRI/CO/1, May 2, 2007, at para. 20 (migrant, smuggled, and trafficked children); "Concluding Observations: Latvia," UN Doc. CRC/C/LVA/CO/2, June 28, 2006, at para. 17 (identifying noncitizen, stateless, refugee, and minority group children as requiring special attention); "Concluding Observations: Mexico," UN Doc. CRC/C/MEX/CO/3, June 8, 2006, at paras. 60–61 (unaccompanied migrant and refugee children); "Concluding Observations: Qatar," UN Doc. OPSC/QAT/CO/1, June 2, 2006, paras. 31–37 (trafficking in children and exploitation of children as camel jockeys).

[53] CRC General Comment No. 6.

[54] "Every individual shall be entitled to the enjoyment of the rights and freedoms recognised and guaranteed in the present Charter without distinction of any kind such as race, ethnic group, colour, sex, language, religion, political or any other opinion, national and social origin, fortune, birth or any other status": African Charter on Human And Peoples' Rights, 1520 UNTS 217, done June 27, 1981, entered into force Oct. 21, 1986 (African Charter), at Art. 2.

[55] Ibid.

[56] Ibid. at Art. 13.

key Articles of the Charter.[57] The African Charter on the Rights and Welfare of the Child refers to "every child" being entitled to the enjoyment of the rights and freedoms recognized and guaranteed in that instrument.[58]

The American Convention on Human Rights guarantees almost every right contained in that instrument to "all persons subject to [the State Parties'] jurisdiction"[59] and confirms that "[f]or the purposes of this Convention, 'person' means every human being."[60] However, the Convention's nondiscrimination clause does not appear to leave room for the inclusion of non-traditional grounds such as national origin or alienage.[61]

The European Human Rights Convention contains a broad, open-ended nondiscrimination clause,[62] and States Parties are required to "[s]ecure to everyone within their jurisdiction the rights and freedoms defined in [the Convention]."[63] The exclusion of "aliens" from the protection of the nondiscrimination clause with respect to one area[64] supports a contention that the remaining provisions of the Convention apply to all persons, not just nationals. The European Court of Human Rights has affirmed, on a number of occasions, the application of certain of the Convention's provisions to noncitizens – including those who are also not citizens of other Member States.[65]

---

[57] See "The Rights of Non-Citizens: Progress Report of the Special Rapporteur, Mr David Weissbrodt: Addendum 2: Examples of Practices," UN Doc. E/CN.4/Sub.2/2002/25/Add.2, June 5, 2002, at 2–22.

[58] African Charter on the Rights and Welfare of the Child, OAU Doc. CAB/LEG/2.49/49, done July 1990, entered into force Nov. 29, 1999 (African Children's Charter), at Art. 6(3).

[59] American Convention on Human Rights, 1144 UNTS 123, done Nov. 22, 1969, entered into force July 18, 1978 (American Convention on Human Rights), at Art. 1. Article 22 of the Convention, dealing with freedom of movement and residence, applies only to "every person lawfully in the territory of a State Party." Article 23 guarantees the right to participation in government to "every citizen."

[60] Ibid. at Art. 1(2). The inclusive nature of the American Convention is reinforced by the following paragraph of the preamble: "[r]ecognizing that the essential rights of man are not derived from one's being a national of a certain State but are based upon attributes of the human personality, and that they therefore justify international protection in the form of a Convention reinforcing or complementing the protection provided by the domestic law of the American States."

[61] "The States Parties to this Convention undertake to respect the rights and freedoms recognized herein and to ensure to all persons subject to their jurisdiction the free and full exercise of those rights and freedoms, without any discrimination for reasons of race, color, sex, language, religion, political or other opinion, national or social origin, economic status, birth or any other social condition": ibid. at Art. 1. The term "social condition" is the only novel ground and its parameters are yet to be explored.

[62] "The enjoyment to the rights and freedoms set forth in this Convention shall be secured without discrimination on any ground such as sex, race, colour, language, religion, political or other opinion, national or social origin, association with a national minority, property, birth or other status": Convention for the Protection of Human Rights and Fundamental Freedoms, 213 UNTS 221, done Nov. 4, 1950, entered into force Sept. 3, 1953 (European Human Rights Convention), at Art. 14.

[63] Ibid. at Art. 1.

[64] Ibid. at Art. 16, relating to the political activities of aliens.

[65] See *Conka v. Belgium*, (2002) 34 EHRR 54 (ECHR, Feb. 5, 2002); *Mehemi v. France*, (2000) 30 EHRR 739 (ECHR, Sept. 26, 1997), at 750–751, 753; *Beldjoudi v. France*, (1992) 14 EHRR 801 (ECHR, Feb. 26, 1992), at 830–831, 833–834; *Moustaquim v. Belgium*, (1991) 13 EHRR 802

By way of conclusion, it is possible to point to a general consensus on the applicability of core human rights to noncitizens. These rights include (but may not be limited to) the right to life, liberty, and security of person; liberty of movement including the right to return to one's own country; protection from *non-refoulement*; protection from arbitrary expulsion; freedom of thought, conscience, and religion; the right to privacy; the right to recognition and equal protection before the law; the right not to be discriminated against on the basis of race, sex, language, religion, or other prohibited ground; and the right to health, education, and housing.[66] As noted in the introduction to this subsection, certain categories of noncitizens, such as stateless persons, migrant workers, asylum-seekers, refugees, and children, will be entitled to additional status-related protection.[67] In short, it is clear that the fundamental rights likely to be of most relevance to the trafficked person cannot be denied to them solely on the basis of their status as aliens or noncitizens.

In terms of deciding whether a category distinction between citizens and non-citizens is lawful, international human rights treaty bodies and regional courts tend to base such decisions on considerations of reasonableness and proportionality.[68] This appears to accord with customary international law, under which substantive distinctions in treatment between nationals and non-nationals require a legitimate aim, objective justification, and reasonable proportionality between the distinction

(ECHR, Jan. 18, 1991), at 813–815; see also "The Rights of Non-Citizens: Final Report of the Special Rapporteur, Mr David Weissbrodt, Addendum: Regional Activities," UN Doc. E/CN.4/Sub.2/2003/23/Add.2, May 26, 2003, at paras. 2–13; "The Rights of Non-Citizens: Progress Report of the Special Rapporteur, Mr David Weissbrodt, Addendum," UN Doc. E/CN.4/Sub.2/2002/25/Add.2, June 3, 2002, at paras. 23–57; "The Rights of Non-Citizens: Preliminary Report of the Special Rapporteur, Mr David Weissbrodt, Addendum," UN Doc. E/CN.4/Sub.2/2001/20/Add.1, June 6, 2001, at paras. 126–128.

[66] This list is drawn from the various reports of the Special Rapporteur on the Rights of Non-Citizens ("The Rights of Non-Citizens: Final Report of the Special Rapporteur, Mr David Weissbrodt," UN Doc. E/CN.4/Sub.2/2003/23, May 26, 2003; "The Rights of Non-Citizens: Progress Report of the Special Rapporteur, Mr David Weissbrodt," UN Doc. E/CN.4/Sub.2/2002/25, June 5, 2002; "The Rights of Non-Citizens: Preliminary Report of the Special Rapporteur, Mr David Weissbrodt," UN Doc. E/CN.4/Sub.2/2001/20, June 6, 2001) and from a distillation of the findings of those reports published in OHCHR, *Non-Citizens*, esp. at 15–26.

[67] See further OHCHR, *Non-Citizens*, at 28–34.

[68] For example, the UN Human Rights Committee has stated that "[a] differentiation which is compatible with the provisions of the Covenant and is based on reasonable grounds does not amount to prohibited discrimination within the meaning of article 26": *Simunek et al v. Czech Republic*, UNHRC Comm. No. 516/1992, UN Doc. CCPR/C/54/D/516/1992, July 19, 1995, at para. 11.5. See also *Juridical Conditions and Rights of Undocumented Migrants*, Advisory Opinion OC=18/03, Inter-American Court of Human Rights (ser. A) No. 18, Sept. 17, 2003 (*Undocumented Migrants*), at para. 119: "States may not discriminate or tolerate discriminatory situations that prejudice migrants. However, the State may grant a distinct treatment to documented migrants with respect to undocumented migrants, or between migrants and nationals, provided that this differential treatment is reasonable, objective, proportionate and does not harm human rights. For example, distinctions may be made between migrants and nationals regarding ownership of some political rights."

and its aims.[69] A summary of the generally accepted approach, advanced in 1983, is still applicable today:

> Distinctions are reasonable if they pursue a legitimate aim and have an objective justification, and a reasonable relationship of proportionality exists between the aim sought to be realized and the means employed. These criteria will usually be satisfied if the particular measures can reasonably be interpreted as being in the public interest as a whole and do not arbitrarily single out individuals or groups for invidious treatment.[70]

While acknowledging the protections available to noncitizens, it is important not to overstate their legal strength and political worth. States have studiously avoided locking themselves into a binding statement of rights of noncitizens, and many continue to resist efforts aimed at formalizing obligations owed to this category of persons. Progress in articulating and defending the rights of noncitizens has been incremental and continues to be hampered by the terms of some of the major treaties that permit differentiation under certain circumstances.

3.1.2. *A Note on Trafficking and Statelessness*

Another important category of noncitizen is the stateless person, defined in international law as anyone who is "not considered a national by any State under the operation of its law."[71] There are important links between statelessness and trafficking. Statelessness increases vulnerability to trafficking, and stateless people who are trafficked face unique difficulties, for example in relation to establishing their identity and accessing protection and support. Measures such as compulsory birth registration are especially important in reducing the vulnerability of stateless persons, particularly children, to trafficking and related exploitation. Trafficking can sometimes result in

---

[69] Goodwin-Gill, for example, cites Judge Tanaka's dissenting judgment in the *South West Africa Cases* as support for the claim that the reasons for a distinction must first be relevant and the measures subsequently adopted must be both reasonable and proportional: "[i]f individuals differ from one another … their needs will be different, and accordingly, the content of the law may not be identical. Hence is derived the relativity of law to individual circumstances … A different treatment comes into question only when and to the extent that it corresponds to the nature of the difference … The issue is whether the difference exists … Different treatment must not be given arbitrarily; it requires reasonableness, or must be in conformity with justice." *South West Africa Cases (Second Phase) (Ethiopia v. South Africa; Liberia v. South Africa)*, [1966] ICJ Rep 6, at 305, 313, cited in G.S. Goodwin-Gill, "Forced Migration and Human Rights," paper presented at the Expert Meeting on International Legal Norms and Migration, May 23–25, 2002. See also McDougal, et al., "The Protection of Aliens," at 469: while "it is seldom seriously asserted that States cannot differentiate between nationals and aliens," such differentiation must "bear reasonable relations to the differences in their obligations and loyalties."

[70] Dent, *Research Paper on the Social and Economic Rights of Non-Nationals in Europe*, at 9, citing W. McKean, *Equality and Discrimination under International Law* (1983), at 287.

[71] Convention Relating to the Status of Stateless Persons, 360 UNTS 117, done Sept. 28, 1954, entered into force June 6, 1960 (Status of Stateless Persons Convention), at Art. 1(1).

statelessness; for example, women who are trafficked abroad for marriage or other purposes may (often because of nationality laws that discriminate on the basis of sex) lose their nationality and/or that of their children in the process.[72] More common is a situation of de facto statelessness imposed on foreign victims of trafficking who, without formal papers, languish in detention centers and shelters for long periods of time.[73]

The rights and obligations identified above apply, as minimum standards, to stateless persons. Such persons may also, under certain circumstances and in relation to certain rights, be entitled to additional or special rights.[74] The specialist framework around this issue is established through two treaties, the Convention Relating to the Status of Stateless Persons (1954) and the Convention on the Reduction of Statelessness (1961),[75] and is reinforced by the major international and regional human rights treaties.[76] International law prohibits States from depriving an individual of his or her nationality if this would result in statelessness.[77] States are also generally required to avoid actions that would result in statelessness.[78] This latter obligation extends to situations where statelessness may arise through omission or neglect.[79] In the present context, this obligation would be violated when destination countries fail to undertake timely and effective identity checks in respect of victims of trafficking who are unable to prove their nationality though the usual means. Failure by countries of origin to cooperate in such processes would be similarly violative of the obligation to avoid actions that result in statelessness.[80]

3.2. TRAFFICKED PERSONS AS MIGRANTS AND MIGRANT WORKERS

Migrants and migrant workers are non-nationals of the country in which they find themselves, and their position under international law is linked to, and has

---

[72] See further, United States Department of State, "Trafficking in Persons Report" (2009), at 31; Vital Voices, "Stateless and Vulnerable to Human Trafficking in Thailand" (2007). For a review of issues of displacement and statelessness from a gender perspective, see UN Committee on the Elimination of Discrimination against Women, "Summary of background paper entitled 'Displacement, Statelessness and Questions of Gender Equality and the Convention on the Elimination of All Forms of Discrimination against Women,'" UN Doc. CEDAW/C/2009/II/WP.3, July 1, 2009.

[73] See further the discussion on detention of victims of trafficking in Chapter 5.2.3.

[74] For a detailed consideration of these status-based rights, see D. Weissbrodt and C. Collins, "The Human Rights of Stateless Persons," (2006) 28 *Human Rights Quarterly* 245.

[75] Convention on the Reduction of Statelessness, 989 UNTS 175, done Aug. 30, 1961, entered into force Dec. 13, 1975 (Reduction of Statelessness Convention).

[76] For example, Article 7 of CRC and Article 24 of the ICCPR effectively require the State to grant citizenship to children born in their territories who would otherwise be rendered stateless.

[77] Reduction of Statelessness Convention, at Art. 8(1).

[78] See generally, Reduction of Statelessness Convention.

[79] UN High Commissioner for Refugees, *Guidelines on International Protection: The application of Article 1(A)(2) of the 1951 Convention and/or 1967 Protocol relating to the Status of Refugees to victims of trafficking and persons at risk of being trafficked*, UN Doc. HCR/GIP/06/07, Apr. 7, 2006 (UNHCR Trafficking Guidelines), at para. 41.

[80] Ibid. at paras. 42–43, confirming this interpretation.

traditionally been determined by their status as aliens and noncitizens. The reluctance of States to tie themselves down to specific legal obligations in relation to noncitizens, explored in the previous section, has been carried through to migrants and migrant workers. This is despite repeated affirmations of the special vulnerabilities faced by migrants and the particular nature of the violations to which they are subject.[81] The increasingly important place that migrant workers occupy in a globalized and highly competitive economy has not yet operated to lessen the gulf between the rhetoric and reality of protection.[82]

The key question for the present section is a straightforward one: Does international law offer separate or additional protection to migrants or migrant workers that may, under certain circumstances, be applicable to individuals who have been trafficked? This question is first addressed by way of a consideration of legal issues relating to emigration and immigration, specifically the right to enter, leave, and return. The section then analyzes the international legal framework around migrant workers, with special attention to the 1990 Migrant Workers Convention[83] and relevant ILO instruments.

3.2.1. *Right to Leave and Return*

The sovereign power of a State to control the entry of non-nationals into its territory is well established in international law. States have been extremely careful, in relation to both standard setting and institution building, to preserve this power from any significant erosion.[84] A corollary to this power is, of course, the absence of a right

---

[81] See, for example: "Vienna Declaration and Programme of Action," UN Doc. A/CONF.157/23, July 12, 1993, at chapter III, Programme of Action, at Part I, para. 24 and Part II, paras. 33–35; World Conference against Racism, Racial Discrimination, Xenophobia and Related Intolerance, "Durban Declaration," UN Doc. A/CONF.189/12, Sept. 8, 2001, at paras. 16, 38, 48–51 and Programme of Action, at paras. 24–33; UN General Assembly, "Protection of Migrants," UN Doc. A/RES/63/184, Mar. 17, 2009; UN General Assembly, "International Migration and Development," UN Doc. A/RES/63/225, Mar. 10, 2009; UN Human Rights Council, "Human Rights of Migrants: Migration and Human Rights of the Child," UN Doc. A/HRC/RES/12/6, Oct. 1, 2009; UN Human Rights Council, "The Human Rights of Migrants in Detention Centres," UN Doc. A/HRC/RES/11/9, June 18, 2009; "Declaration on Human Rights of Non-Nationals."

[82] See the final report of the Global Commission on International Migration: "there is an urgent need to fill the gap that currently exists between the principles found in the legal and normative framework affecting international migrants and the way in which legislation, policies and practices are interpreted and applied at the national level." Global Commission on International Migration, *Migration in an Interconnected World: New Directions for Action* (2005), at 58.

[83] International Convention on the Protection of the Rights of All Migrant Workers and Members of their Families, UN Doc. A/RES/45/158, done Dec. 18, 1990, entered into force July 1, 2003 (Migrant Workers Convention).

[84] See, for example, the Constitution of the International Organization for Migration, which specifically recognizes that "control of standards of admission and the number of immigrants to be admitted are matters within the domestic jurisdiction of States": Constitution of the International Organization for Migration, 1560 UNTS 440, done Oct. 19, 1953, entered into force Nov. 20, 1954, amended Nov. 14, 1989, at Art. 1(3).

of individuals to enter or reside in the territory of other States. Aside from certain exceptions of limited applicability, international law does not recognize the existence of a right to enter or reside in a country other than one's own.[85] In the context of a discussion on trafficking, the typical exceptions (such as family reunification under the obligation of respect for family life) would be of potential but uncommon application. Other exceptions to the general absence of a right to enter and reside in a country other than one's own can arise in relation to refugee and asylum claims. These matters are considered further in Chapter 6 in the context of a general discussion on legal obligations regarding the repatriation of individuals who have been trafficked.

Can a State lawfully prevent a citizen from leaving his or her own country? More particularly, is a State allowed (or even required) to prevent departure by irregular or unauthorized means, and can such departure be subject to prosecution or other sanction? These are not theoretical questions but ones with routine practical significance for many individuals. A number of countries have reacted to the growth in exploitative migration practices such as trafficking and migrant smuggling by imposing a range of restrictions on departure. States wishing to control entry on noncitizens into their territories will often encourage and even facilitate the imposition of such restrictions on departure by countries of origin. The typical emigration restriction will apply to certain categories of persons wishing to move abroad for purposes of employment. Restrictions associated with countertrafficking efforts generally prevent women within a certain age group from emigrating to specified destinations or for specified occupations.[86] Such practices reflect and are strengthened by a long established trend of relatively higher intervention by States in the emigration of women, as compared to men.[87] Extralegal methods (such as

[85]　For example, the UN Human Rights Committee has held that the ICCPR "[d]oes not recognise the right of aliens to enter or reside in the territory of a State Party. ... However, in certain circumstances an alien may enjoy the protection of the Covenant even in relation to entry or residence, for example, when considerations of non-discrimination, prohibition of inhumane treatment and respect for family life arise": HRC General Comment No. 15, at para. 5.

[86]　Regarding emigration restrictions on young women from Myanmar, see Physicians for Human Rights, *No Status: Migration, Trafficking and Exploitation of Women in Thailand: Health and HIV/AIDS Risks for Burmese and Hill Tribe Women and Girls* (2004), at 21, available at http://physicians-forhumanrights.org/library/documents/reports/report-2004-july-nostatus.pdf (accessed Nov. 18, 2009); regarding emigration restrictions on young and unaccompanied women from Nepal, see E. Pearson, "Preventing What?" in *Prevention of Trafficking: Alliance News*, Issue 21 (July 2004), 15. On trafficking-related emigration restrictions in both Nepal and Romania, see UN Commission on Human Rights, "Report of the Special Rapporteur, Ms. Radhika Coomaraswamy, on violence against women, its causes and consequences, on trafficking in women, women's migration and violence against women," UN Doc. E/CN.4/2000/68, Feb. 29, 2000 (Coomaraswamy, "Report," UN Doc. E/CN.4/2000/68), at paras. 47–48. For a comprehensive detailing of emigration restrictions on female migration in place throughout Asia circa 2000, see N. Oishi, *Women in Motion: Globalization, State Policies and Labor Migration in Asia* (2005) (Oishi, *Women in Motion*).

[87]　For example, in the early 1920s, Great Britain imposed emigration restrictions on sixteen-year-old girls, prohibiting their leaving the country for employment without approval from a magistrate

the seizure of passports of women working in prostitution in order to prevent their emigration altogether) have been recorded.[88] Returning migrants have also been sanctioned for their unauthorized departure.[89]

The right to leave is a core component of the international right to freedom of movement. The UDHR states clearly that "[e]veryone has the right to leave his country."[90] Freedom to leave any country, including one's own, is also protected by the ICCPR,[91] CERD,[92] the Migrant Workers Convention,[93] and all major regional human rights treaties.[94] In its implementation, the right to leave has always been limited by practical realities relating to, for example, the individual's status as a minor or as a convicted criminal. The relevant instruments accommodate this reality by envisaging the possibility of lawful derogation in certain prescribed circumstances. The ICCPR, for example, does not permit restrictions on the right to leave "except those which are provided by law, are necessary to protect national security, public order (ordre public), public health or morals or the rights and freedoms of others, and are consistent with other rights."[95] Accordingly, the lawfulness of any restriction on the right to leave is to be measured with reference to whether it is: (1) provided by law; (2) necessary on the basis of one or more stipulated grounds; and (3) consistent with other rights including, for example, the prohibition on discrimination.

As Hannum has noted, the right to leave is formulated in absolute terms, indicating that the appropriate point of departure is the widest possible scope of the freedom to move out of any country including one's own.[96] That interpretation has been confirmed by the UN Human Rights Committee, the only international body to have examined this right in any detail. In its General Comment No. 27 on freedom of movement, adopted in 1999, the Committee confirmed the right to leave as

---

who was also to approve the conditions of supervision: LN Doc. A.9(1).1922.IV, July 4, 1922, cited in C.C. Jones-Pauly, *Report on Anti-Trafficking Laws in Six Countries (Austria, Belgium, Czech Republic, Federal Republic of Germany, Italy, Poland) and Compliance with the International Conventions against Trafficking* (1999), at 163. See also Oishi, *Women in Motion*, at 59–61. Note that some countries continue to restrict the unaccompanied or unapproved international travel of their female citizens in situations unrelated to migration for work.

[88] See, for example, Coomaraswamy, "Report," UN Doc. E/CN.4/2000/68, at para. 48.

[89] For example, in Lao PDR. See A.T. Gallagher, "A Shadow Report on Human Trafficking in Lao PDR: The US Approach vs. International Law," (2006) 15 *Asian and Pacific Migration Journal* 525.

[90] UDHR, at Art. 13(2). See also Art. 29, which sets out applicable restrictions on this and other rights.

[91] ICCPR, at Art. 12(2).

[92] CERD, at Art. 5(d)(ii).

[93] Migrant Workers Convention, at Art. 8(1).

[94] Protocol No. 4 to the Convention of 4 November 1950 for the Protection of Human Rights and Fundamental Freedoms, 1496 UNTS 263, done Sept. 16, 1963, entered into force May 2, 1968 (European Convention, Protocol No. 4), at Art. 2(2); American Convention on Human Rights, at Art. 22(2); African Charter, at Art. 12(2).

[95] ICCPR, at Art. 12(3). For generally equivalent provisions, see European Convention, Protocol No. 4, at Art. 2(3); American Convention on Human Rights, at Art. 22(3); African Charter, at Art. 12(2).

[96] H. Hannum, *The Right to Leave and Return in International Law and Practice* (1987) (Hannum, *The Right to Leave and Return*), at 19.

essentially a right to travel.[97] From this perspective, an action such as the withholding or withdrawal of a vital travel document such as a passport without permissible justification would operate to violate the right to leave.[98] More broadly, General Comment No. 27 requires that any restrictions on the right to leave not impair the essence of the right.[99] Such restrictions must be proportionate, appropriate under the circumstances, and the "least intrusive instrument amongst those which might achieve the desired result."[100] Application of restrictions must, "in any individual case, be based on clear legal grounds and meet the test of necessity and the requirements of proportionality."[101]

Harvey and Barnidge have addressed the link between obligations on States to address smuggling and trafficking and the right to leave. Referencing the legal regime established under the Organized Crime Convention and its Protocols, they conclude that:

> restrictions on the movement of the smuggled [or trafficked] person will have to be justified within the terms of [ICCPR] article 12(3). The state must demonstrate that these restrictions meet the tests of legality and necessity, are consistent with the other provisions of the ICCPR, and come under one of the listed grounds. A state must be in a position to argue that any direct or indirect restrictions are for the purpose of tackling the pressing problem of smuggling and trafficking.[102]

It is apparent that at least some of the common practices used by States to restrict the departure of their citizens in the name of addressing trafficking and smuggling will fail to meet the test mandated by the Human Rights Committee. Such practices would include restrictions on the issuing of passports and the requirement of special exit visas.[103] Even if a State is able to argue that its emigration restrictions

---

[97] UN Human Rights Committee, "General Comment No. 27: Freedom of Movement," UN Doc. CCPR/C/21/Rev.1/Add.9, Nov. 2, 1999 (HRC General Comment No. 27), at para. 9.

[98] See, for example, *Loubna El Ghar v. Socialist People's Libyan Arab Jamahiriya*, UNHRC Comm. No. 1107/2002, UN Doc. CCPR/C/82/D/1107/2002, decided Mar. 29, 2004.

[99] HRC General Comment No. 27, at para. 13: "the relation between right and restriction, between norm and exception, must not be reversed."

[100] Ibid. at para. 14.

[101] Ibid. at para. 16.

[102] C. Harvey and R.P. Barnidge, Jr., "Human Rights, Free Movement and the Right to Leave in International Law," (2007) 19 *International Journal of Refugee Law* 1 (Harvey and Barnidge, "Human Rights, Free Movement and the Right to Leave in International Law"), at 14.

[103] For an overview of the jurisprudence of the UN Human Rights Committee on the issues of passports and exit visas, see generally: Hannum, *The Right to Leave and Return*; Harvey and Barnidge, "Human Rights, Free Movement and the Right to Leave in International Law." The UN Human Rights Committee has provided a list of practices and rules that will operate to obstruct the right to leave: "lack of access for applicants to the competent authorities and lack of information regarding requirements; the requirement to apply for special forms through which the proper application documents for the issuance of a passport can be obtained; the need for supportive statements from employers or family members; exact description of the travel route; issuance of passports only on payment of high fees substantially exceeding the cost of the service rendered by the administration; unreasonable delays in the issuance of travel documents; restrictions on family members travelling

are based on a need to preserve public order or public morals though preventing trafficking and that the measures taken are both necessary and in proportion to their stated aim, that same State must also be able to show that its restriction is nondiscriminatory in both intention and effect. Practices that are directed toward or that disproportionately affect one group such as women will not meet this standard. In addition, as restrictions must be provided by law, extralegal measures such as passport confiscation by law enforcement officials would also be contrary to the right to leave. The penalizing of returning migrants for unauthorized departure in circumstances where the original restriction cannot be justified is another example of a practice unlikely to meet the test set out above.

The question of whether migrants can be sanctioned for using fraudulent travel documents is slightly more complicated. Harvey and Barnidge cite the provision of the Migrant Smuggling Protocol excluding smuggled migrants from criminal liability for the fact of their having been smuggled[104] to support their contention that "states cannot legitimately prosecute migrants when they leave their own states with documents that they know to be fraudulent assuming that the facts and circumstances would position the migrants to be otherwise prosecuted."[105] This analysis fails to capture the nature of the Migrant Smuggling Protocol, which is specifically directed towards suppressing the activities of organized criminal groups. Drafters of the Protocol were careful to preserve the right of States to take measures against individuals whose conduct constitutes an offense under national law.[106] In other words, while the procuring and use of false travel documentation may not make an individual liable to criminal prosecution *under the Protocol itself,* States would remain free to apply their own criminal laws to such a situation.

---

together; requirement of a repatriation deposit or a return ticket; requirement of an invitation from the State of destination or from people living there; harassment of applicants, for example by physical intimidation, arrest, loss of employment or expulsion of their children from school or university; refusal to issue a passport because the applicant is said to harm the good name of the country." HRC General Comment No. 27, at para. 17.

[104] Harvey and Barnidge, "Human Rights, Free Movement and the Right to Leave in International Law." The cited provision is Article 5 of the Protocol against the Smuggling of Migrants by Land, Sea and Air, supplementing the United Nations Convention against Transnational Organized Crime, GA Res. 55/25, Annex III, UN GAOR, 55th Sess., Supp. No. 49, at 62, UN Doc. A/45/49 (Vol. I) (2001), done Nov. 15, 2000, entered into force Jan. 28, 2004 (Migrant Smuggling Protocol). Note that the Interpretative Notes to the Migrant Smuggling Protocol indeed make clear that its provisions on possession of fraudulent documentation do not apply to a migrant who is in possession of fraudulent documents to enable his or her own smuggling: United Nations Office on Drugs and Crime, Travaux Préparatoires *of the Negotiations for the Elaboration of the United Nations Convention against Transnational Organized Crime and the Protocols Thereto* (2006) (Travaux Préparatoires *for the Organized Crime Convention and Protocols*), at 489. On the function and status of the Interpretative Notes to the Organized Crime Convention and its Protocols, see D. McClean, *Transnational Organized Crime: A Commentary on the UN Convention and its Protocols* (2007), at 13.

[105] Harvey and Barnidge, "Human Rights, Free Movement and the Right to Leave in International Law," at 16.

[106] Migrant Smuggling Protocol, at Art. 6(4).

The international legal rules governing repatriation of victims of trafficking are considered in detail in Chapter 6. At this point, therefore, it is only necessary to provide a brief overview of the corollary of the right to leave: the right to return. International law has traditionally recognized an obligation on a State to accept return of its nationals when demanded by another State on whose territory they are found.[107] Both this obligation and the rights to which it gives rise resided in the States concerned and not in the individual. It was only with the UDHR that the international community expressly acknowledged that "[e]veryone has the right to ... return to his country."[108] The ICCPR confirms that "[n]o-one shall be arbitrarily deprived of the right to enter his own country."[109] The right to return to one's own country is also protected by CERD,[110] the Migrant Workers Convention,[111] and all major regional human rights treaties.[112] Other closely related (and sometimes overlapping) internationally recognized rules, such as the prohibition on exile[113] and on the expulsion of nationals,[114] provide further support for the right of all persons to return to their country. Academic discussion on the scope and substantive content of the right of return has tended to focus on particular situations involving entire populations, such as the Palestinians in relation to Israel and the Greek population of Turkish-occupied Cyprus.[115] As yet, there has been little analysis of how this right may operate in respect of individuals whose presence in a country other than their own has been facilitated through practices such as trafficking and smuggling.

3.2.2. *Trafficked Persons as Migrant Workers*

Until recently, the connection between trafficking and migration for work was rarely made.[116] This may have been one result of a widespread reluctance on the part of States and others to identify common purposes of trafficking (such as child labor and enforced prostitution) as "work." Another contributing factor is likely to be the

---

[107] Oppenheim, *International Law*, at 645–646.

[108] UDHR, at Art. 13(2).

[109] ICCPR, at Art. 12(4).

[110] CERD, at Art. 5(d)(ii).

[111] Migrant Workers Convention, at Art. 8(2).

[112] European Convention, Protocol No. 4, at Art. 3(2); American Convention on Human Rights, at Art. 22(5); African Charter, at Art. 12(2).

[113] See, for example, UDHR, at Art. 9: "[n]o one shall be subjected to arbitrary arrest, detention or exile."

[114] See further, J.M. Henckaerts, *Mass Expulsion in Modern Law and Practice* (1998), esp. at 78–82.

[115] See, for example, Y. Zilbershatz, "International Law and the Palestinian Right of Return to the State of Israel," in E. Benvenisti, C. Gans and S. Hanafi eds., *Israel and the Palestinian Refugees* 191 (2007); J. M. Bracka, "Past the Point of No Return? The Palestinian Right of Return in International Human Rights Law," (2005) 6 *Melbourne Journal of International Law* 272.

[116] For example, the only book-length study of human rights and migrant workers (Cholewinski, *Migrant Workers*) contains no reference to trafficking or to typical end results of trafficking, such as enforced prostitution.

relative invisibility of the typical forms of exploitation with which trafficking is commonly associated, which exist firmly within the private sector (domestic servitude, coerced marriage, etc.) and are consequently largely impervious to external regulation. A result of the disconnection between trafficking and migration for work is that the rights of trafficked persons *as workers* – migrant or otherwise – have rarely been articulated or pursued. The following paragraphs provide an overview and analysis of the relevant international legal standards with a view to determining the extent to which they may offer different and/or additional protection to trafficked persons.

ILO Instruments to Protect Migrant Workers. The International Labour Organization (ILO), a Specialized Agency of the United Nations, was the first intergovernmental body to take up the rights of migrant workers.[117] As the only UN agency with a constitutional mandate to protect this group, its role continues to be central. The eight "core" ILO Conventions,[118] dealing with issues that include social security, the right to organize, forced labor, and child labor, are all relevant, in one way or another, to the rights of migrant workers.[119] In addition, the ILO has developed two conventions specifically protecting the rights and interests of migrant workers. The first of these, adopted in 1949, is the Migration for Employment Convention (Revised),[120] which covers individuals who migrate from one country to another

---

[117] On the history of ILO involvement with migrant workers, see N. Valticos, *International Labour Law*, (1979), at chapter 14.

[118] Convention Concerning Forced and Compulsory Labour, 39 UNTS 55, ILO No. 29, done June 28, 1930, entered into force May 1, 1932; Convention Concerning Freedom of Association and Protection of the Right to Organise, 68 UNTS 17, ILO No. 87, done July 9, 1948, entered into force July 4, 1950; Convention Concerning Right to Organise and Collective Bargaining, 96 UNTS 257, ILO No. 98, done July 1, 1949, entered into force July 18, 1951; Convention Concerning Equal Remuneration for Men and Women Workers for Work of Equal Value, 165 UNTS 303, ILO No. 100, done June 19, 1951, entered into force May 23, 1953; Convention Concerning the Abolition of Forced Labour, 320 UNTS 291, ILO No. 105, done June 25, 1957, entered into force Jan. 17, 1959; Convention Concerning Discrimination in Respect of Employment and Occupation, 362 UNTS 31, ILO No. 111, done June 25, 1958, entered into force June 15, 1960; Convention Concerning Minimum Age for Admission to Employment, 1015 UNTS 298, ILO No. 138, done June 26, 1973, entered into force June 19, 1976; Convention Concerning the Prohibition and Immediate Action for the Elimination of the Worst Forms of Child Labour, 2133 UNTS 161, ILO No. 182, done June 17, 1999, entered into force Nov. 19, 2000 (Worst Forms of Child Labour Convention).

[119] The ILO is clear on the point that "[a]ll international labour standards apply to migrant workers, unless otherwise stated," and that "migrant workers should benefit from the principles and rights in the 1998 ILO Declaration on Fundamental Principles and Rights at Work and its Follow-up, which are reflected in the eight fundamental ILO Conventions and the relevant United Nations human rights Conventions": International Labour Organization, International Migration Programme, *ILO Multilateral Framework on Labour Migration: Non-Binding Principles and Guidelines for a Rights-Based Approach to Labour Migration* (2006), at 15–16.

[120] Convention Concerning Migration for Employment (Revised), 20 UNTS 79, ILO No. 97, done July 1, 1949, entered into force Jan. 22, 1952 (ILO Migration for Employment Convention). The Convention is accompanied by "Recommendation No. 86 concerning Migration for Employment (Revised 1949)," adopted July 1, 1949, reproduced in 1 *International Labour Conventions and Recommendations* 508.

with a view to working for an employer (that is, not in a self-employed capacity). The Convention requires States Parties, *inter alia*, to maintain or facilitate a reasonable and free service in order to assist migrant workers and to provide them with correct information; to take all appropriate steps against misleading propaganda concerning immigration and emigration; and to ensure legal equality in matters of work (opportunity and treatment) between documented migrants and nationals. The Convention does not specifically address the question of undocumented or illegal migrants apart from requiring States to impose "appropriate penalties" on those promoting clandestine or illegal migration.[121]

In 1975, the ILO adopted Convention No. 143 Concerning Migrations in Abusive Conditions and the Promotion of Equality of Opportunity and Treatment of Migrant Workers.[122] The Convention obliges States Parties to respect the basic human rights of *all* migrant workers[123] irrespective of their legal status in the country of employment.[124] However, as with the 1949 Migration for Employment Convention, this obligation does not extend to the right to equal opportunity and treatment on the same level as nationals.[125] The first part of the Convention is devoted in its entirety to suppression of migration in abusive conditions.[126] States Parties are required to establish the situation of migrant workers within their own territory and whether the conditions under which they are living and working contravene relevant laws and regulations,[127] and to take necessary and appropriate measures within their jurisdictions or in cooperation with other States to combat clandestine migration and the illegal employment of migrants.[128] Measures are to be taken to ensure that persons responsible for "manpower trafficking" are prosecuted.[129] Provision must also be made for civil or criminal sanctions for organizing migration with a view

---

[121] ILO Migration for Employment Convention, at Annex I, Art. 8; Annex II, Art. 13.

[122] Convention Concerning Migrations in Abusive Conditions and the Promotion of Equality of Opportunity and Treatment of Migrant Workers, 1120 UNTS 324, ILO No. 143, done June 24, 1975, entered into force Dec. 9, 1978 (ILO Convention No. 143).

[123] Ibid. at Art. 1.

[124] Cholewinski, *Migrant Workers*, at 103, citing International Labour Conference, "Report of the Committee of Experts on the Application of Conventions and Recommendations," 66th session, 1980, reproduced in International Labour Office, *General Survey of the Reports Relating to Conventions Nos. 97 and 143 and Recommendations Nos. 86 and 151 concerning Migrant Workers* (1980) at 69, 257. The term "basic human rights" is not defined, and the breadth of application of this provision continues to remain uncertain. Cholewinski cites an ILO Committee of Experts in support of the contention that the reference to basic rights is, in fact, extremely limited and should be taken to refer to the most fundamental of rights including the right to life, the prohibition on torture, and the right to a fair trial: ibid. at 133.

[125] In both Conventions, the right to equal opportunity and treatment with nationals is extended only to migrants "lawfully" within the territory of the country of employment: ILO Migration for Employment Convention, at Art. 6; ILO Convention No. 143, at Part II.

[126] ILO Convention No. 143, at Part I.

[127] Ibid at Art. 2.

[128] Ibid at Art. 3.

[129] Ibid at Art. 5.

to abusive employment as well as for illegal employment and trafficking of migrant workers.[130]

While the 1975 ILO Convention No. 143 is notable as the first international legal instrument to address the issue of illegal or irregular migration from a rights perspective, it has failed to attract widespread support, not just from migrant-receiving States[131] but also from migrant-sending States who have traditionally been skeptical of the capacity of the ILO to improve the lot of migrant workers.[132] Apart from these two instruments, ILO mechanisms have, on occasion, pronounced on certain rights of direct relevance to migrant workers, including those in an irregular situation.[133]

The Migrant Workers Convention. The question of migrant workers' rights and the issue of exploitation of some migrants "in conditions akin to slavery and forced labour"[134] entered the UN's human rights agenda in the early 1970s.[135] A 1975 report of the Sub-Commission on Prevention of Discrimination and Protection of Minorities (a subsidiary body of the Commission on Human Rights) identified significant gaps in international legal protection for migrant workers, particularly those in an irregular situation, and recommended the development of a new standard.[136] Countries of

---

[130] Ibid. at Art. 6(1).

[131] To date, only twenty-three States have ratified the Convention: International Labour Organization, ILO Convention No. 143 Ratification Information, available at http://www.ilo.org/ilolex/cgi-lex/ratifce.pl?C143 (accessed Feb. 7, 2010).

[132] This scepticism in revealed in the speed with which key migrant-sending countries, including Morocco and Mexico, pushed for a new Convention outside the ILO before "[t]he ink on ILO Convention No. 143 had hardly dried": R. Bohning, "The ILO and the New UN Convention on Migrant Workers: The Past and the Future," (1991) 25 *International Migration Review* 698 (Bohning, "The ILO and the New UN Convention on Migrant Workers"), at 699. See the discussion of the Migrant Workers Convention further in this chapter.

[133] For example, the ILO Committee on Freedom of Association has upheld the equal application of the right to freedom of association to all workers, including those who are unauthorized: *Case No. 2227 (United States): Report in which the Committee Requests to Be Kept Informed of Developments*, Complaints against the Government of the United States presented by the American Federation of Labor and the Congress of Industrial Organizations (AFL-CIO) and the Confederation of Mexican Workers (CTM), in *332nd Report of the Committee on Freedom of Association*, ILO Doc. GB.288/7 (Part II), 288th Session, November 2003, cited in B. Lyon, "The Unsigned United Nations Migrant Worker Rights Convention: An Overlooked Opportunity to Change the Brown Collar Migration Paradigm," (2010) 42 *New York Journal of International Law and Politics* (forthcoming) (Lyon, "The Unsigned United Nations Migrant Worker Rights Convention").

[134] UN Economic and Social Council Resolution 1706 (LIII), July 28, 1972, at Preamble.

[135] Prior to that time, the UN generally adhered to a competencies agreement it had reached with the ILO in 1947, which stipulated that the ILO would be concerned with migrants as workers and the UN with their status as aliens. See further, M. Hasenau, "ILO Standards on Migrant Workers: The Fundamentals of the UN Convention and their Genesis," (1991) 25 *International Migration Review* 693.

[136] UN Economic and Social Council, "Exploitation of Labour Through Illicit and Clandestine Trafficking," UN Doc. E/CN.4/Sub.2/1986/6 (1986). See also Commission on Human Rights, Sub-Commission on Prevention of Discrimination and Protection of Minorities, "Exploitation of Labour through Illicit and Clandestine Trafficking, Note by the Secretary-General and Study by Ms. H. Embarek Warzazi," UN Doc. E/CN.4/Sub.2/L.629, July 4, 1975.

origin for migrant workers, led by Mexico and Morocco, were aware that the work of the ILO on this issue was not widely supported by countries of employment.[137] The UN's human rights system was seen to offer greater flexibility as well as the comfort of a more traditional (State-centered) decision-making structure.[138] Following up on a recommendation of the Economic and Social Council,[139] a number of General Assembly resolutions on the subject,[140] reports of the Secretary-General,[141] and a recommendation of the 1978 World Conference against Racism,[142] the General Assembly established in 1980 a working group to elaborate an international convention for protection of migrant workers and their families.[143]

The International Convention on the Protection of the Rights of All Migrant Workers and Members of their Families was adopted by the General Assembly in 1990 after a decade of complex negotiation and significant compromise between what one of the principal drafters has characterized as the "visionaries" and the "conservatives."[144] The Convention is intended to expand upon rather than to replace or modify existing rights.[145] It adopts an inclusive definition of "migrant worker"[146] and applies to all migrant workers and their families without distinction of any

---

[137] Bohning, "The ILO and the New UN Convention on Migrant Workers".

[138] Ibid. at 700–702.

[139] UN Economic and Social Council Resolution 2083 (LXII), May 13, 1977. The resolution noted that while there were a number of conventions and recommendations established at the international level to protect migrant workers, there were areas where migrant workers were not protected and where a UN instrument (as opposed to a new ILO instrument) would have wider applicability.

[140] UN General Assembly, "Measures to Improve the Situation and Ensure the Human Rights and Dignity of All Migrant Workers," UN Doc. A/RES/32/120, Dec. 16, 1977; UN General Assembly, "Measures to Improve the Situation and Ensure the Human Rights and Dignity of All Migrant Workers," UN Doc. A/RES/33/163, Dec. 20, 1978.

[141] For example, see UN Economic and Social Council, "Welfare of Migrant Workers and Their Families: Principles Concerning Migrant Workers and Their Families Already Embodied in International Instruments Adopted by the United Nations Organisation, Report of the Secretary-General," UN Doc. E/CN.5/564, Dec. 11, 1978; and UN Economic and Social Council, "Welfare of Migrant Workers and Their Families: Progress Report of the Secretary-General," UN Doc. E/CN.5/568, Dec. 22, 1978.

[142] The Programme of Action that emerged from the Conference recommended that "States consider the possibility of adopting an international convention on the protection of all migrant workers": UN Economic and Social Council, "Report of the World Conference to Combat Racism and Racial Discrimination, 14–25 August, 1978," UN Doc. A/CONF.92/40 (1979), at para. 13(x).

[143] UN General Assembly, "Measures to Improve the Situation and Ensure the Human Rights and Dignity of All Migrant Workers," UN Doc. A/RES/34/172, Dec. 17, 1979. For an overview of opposition to this decision as well as an insight into why developing countries wished to use the UN human rights system rather than the ILO to advance the rights of migrant workers, see Bohning, "The ILO and the New UN Convention on Migrant Workers," at 700–702.

[144] J. Lonnroth, "The International Convention on the Rights of all Migrant Workers and Members of their Families in the Context of International Migration Policies: An Analysis of Ten Years of Negotiation," (1991) 24 *International Migration Review* 721 (Lonnroth, "Migrant Workers Convention: An Analysis of Ten Years of Negotiation").

[145] Migrant Workers Convention, at Preamble.

[146] Ibid. at Art. 2: "[t]he term 'migrant worker' refers to a person who is to be engaged, is engaged or has been engaged in a remunerated activity in a State of which he or she is not a national."

kind.[147] It recognizes that migrant workers and members of their families, being non-nationals residing in States of employment or in transit, are vulnerable to exploitation and abuse.[148] The Convention explicitly extends fundamental human rights to all migrant workers and their families, both documented and undocumented. It reiterates the prohibition on torture[149] and stipulates that migrant workers must not be held in slavery or servitude and that forced labor must not be demanded of them.[150] States Parties must effectively protect all migrant workers "[a]gainst violence, physical injury, threats and intimidation."[151] Importantly, such protection must be provided irrespective of whether such violence or the like has been perpetrated "by public officials or by private individuals, groups or institutions."[152] States Parties must also provide for sanctions against persons or groups who use violence against migrant workers, employ them in irregular circumstances, threaten them, or intimidate them.[153] All migrant workers are granted the right of equal treatment with nationals in relation to conditions of employment and work, trade union rights, social security rights, the right to emergency health care, the right to education (of migrant children), and the right to culture.[154] All migrant workers, including those in an irregular situation, are protected against unfair or arbitrary expulsion.[155] The Convention replicates the structure of ILO Convention No. 143 by creating a set of additional rights that are applicable only to documented migrant workers and their families. These additional rights include equality of treatment with nationals of States of employment in a number of legal, political, economic, social, and cultural areas.[156]

The Migrant Workers Convention was developed well before trafficking emerged as a matter of international concern – or indeed as a mainstream human rights issue. While clearly seeking to contribute toward preventing and eliminating the exploitation of all migrants, including an end to their illegal or clandestine movements and

---

The Convention also defines the following terms in Article 2: "frontier worker," "seasonal worker," "seafarer," "worker on an offshore installation," "itinerant worker," "project-tied worker," "specified-employment worker," and "self-employed worker."

[147] Ibid. at Art. 1.

[148] Ibid. at Preamble.

[149] Ibid. at Art. 10.

[150] Ibid. at Art. 11.

[151] Ibid. at Art. 16(2).

[152] Ibid. This provision has potentially important consequences with respect to invoking the responsibility of States for failure to protect trafficked persons from harm caused by traffickers and their accomplices. See further, Chapter 5.

[153] Migrant Workers Convention, at Art. 68(1)(c).

[154] The Migrant Workers Convention includes rights relating to remuneration, work, and employment conditions (Art. 25); trade union rights (Art. 26(1)); right to social security (Art. 27); right to emergency medical care (Art. 28); right of access to education for migrant children (Art. 30); and respect for cultural identity (Art. 31(1)).

[155] Ibid. at Art. 22. Expulsion would generally not be considered arbitrary if the individual had violated the laws of the host country with respect to his or her entry or stay, or through involvement in criminal activities.

[156] Ibid. at Part IV, Arts. 36–56.

to irregular or undocumented situations,[157] its sole reference to trafficking is brief and preambular.[158] The place of the Convention within the international human rights framework around trafficking is therefore not immediately clear. On the one hand, it could be argued that the "remunerated activity" requirement of the definition of migrant worker was not intended to cover typical trafficking end-situations such as enforced prostitution, forced marriage, and begging.[159] It could also be argued that to identify such practices as "work" may obscure their fundamentally exploitative character and alter the direction of the debate regarding the need for their elimination. On the other hand, it would be counterintuitive (and perhaps counterproductive) to ignore the link between trafficking and migration for work. While not all migrant workers have been trafficked, many trafficked persons are migrant workers in the very real sense that they have left their homes in search of gainful employment in another country. To deny that such a person is a migrant worker, and therefore to exclude him or her from any added value provided by the Convention, would appear to go against the Convention's inclusive approach; its recognition of the vulnerability of migrant workers, especially those who are undocumented or otherwise "irregular";[160] and its avowed goal of ensuring the fundamental rights of *all* migrants.[161] It is nevertheless important to note this goal of inclusiveness is compromised in the Convention itself – a potential precedent for excluding "problematic" categories of potential beneficiaries.[162]

---

[157] Ibid. at Art. 68. Commentators have argued that the Convention's attempts to achieve a compromise between protecting the rights of undocumented migrants and preventing irregular migration are flawed because of the essentially irreconcilable nature of these two principles: Cholewinski, *Migrant Workers*, at 188.

[158] "[A]ppropriate action should be encouraged in order to prevent and eliminate clandestine movements and trafficking in migrant workers": Migrant Workers Convention, at Preamble. The reference has been criticized as an example of the Convention's tendency toward "over-inclusiveness." Nafziger and Bartel, for example, argue that "a separate instrument to address the problem of trafficking in undocumented aliens, that is, workers in an irregular situation, is preferable to the incorporation of anti-trafficking provisions in a more general human rights instrument, so as to stigmatize those aliens." They add, somewhat confusingly, "[t]he lot of undocumented workers is bad enough without enlisting a new corpus of human rights law, in effect, against them." J. Nafziger and B.C. Bartel, "The Migrant Workers Convention: Its Place in Human Rights Law," (1991) 25 *International Migration Review* 771 (Nafziger and Bartel, "The Migrant Workers Convention"), at 788.

[159] According to Cholewinski, the term "remunerated activity" in the definition of migrant worker was understood by the drafters as meaning "gainful employment" and not referring to an activity regarded by State laws as contrary to the rules of *ordre public*: Cholewinski, *Migrant Workers*, at 151.

[160] Migrant Workers Convention, at Preamble.

[161] Ibid.

[162] Ibid. Note that Article 3 specifically excludes certain categories of persons from the protection of the Convention including both refugees and stateless persons. These two groups were apparently excluded on the basis that that they are protected under other international instruments and therefore possess a specific international status: Cholewinski, *Migrant Workers*, at 153, citing deliberations of the drafting group. It could be argued that with the recent development of a specific and comprehensive international instrument covering the situation of trafficked persons, this group is also excluded on the basis of being in a position to benefit from an alternative regime of protection.

The Migrant Workers Convention entered into force thirteen years after its adoption, on July 1, 2003, and, as of June 2010, had forty-two States Parties.[163] Its drafting history reveals little political support from the wealthy developed destination countries,[164] which, despite participating in the negotiation process, made abundantly clear their objection to "the fact that migrant workers in an irregular situation should become subjects of an international convention"[165] and their view that such a convention "accord[s] them too many rights, and that ... included within the scope of the ... Convention [are] categories of persons [who are] not truly migrant workers."[166] The pattern of ratifications and accessions to date (a strong preponderance of migrant-sending countries and none of the major countries of employment) indicates that the polarization of views that marked the Convention's development has persisted.[167] Despite a global campaign[168] and apparent support from regional political bodies,[169] the current situation is not expected to change dramatically in

---

[163] "International Convention on the Protection of the Rights of All Migrant Workers and Members of their Families" in *Multilateral Treaties Deposited with the Secretary-General*, at chapter IV, no. 13, available at http://treaties.un.org/Pages/ViewDetails.aspx?src=TREATY&mtdsg_no=IV-13-&chapter=4&lang=en (accessed Feb. 7, 2010). Lyon notes that the slow rate of ratifications was a surprise because many States, from both sides of the migrant worker debate, had been involved in the complex negotiations: Lyon, "The Unsigned United Nations Migrant Worker Rights Convention," at 7 (manuscript reference of forthcoming publication).

[164] For a comprehensive review and analysis of the Convention's drafting history, see Lonnroth, "Migrant Workers Convention: An Analysis of Ten Years of Negotiation" and Cholewinski, *Migrant Workers*, at chapter 4.

[165] Cholewinski, *Migrant Workers*, at 203, note 285, quoting a statement of the representative of Germany to the drafting group.

[166] Ibid.

[167] See further A. Pécoud and P. de Guchteneire, "Migration, Human Rights and the United Nations: An Investigation into the Low Ratification Record of the UN Migrant Workers Convention" (Global Comm'n on Int'l Migration, Global Migration Perspectives No. 3, 2004) (analyzing the results of research conducted by UN Educational, Scientific and Cultural Organization into obstacles to the ratification of the Migrant Workers Convention), available at http://www.iom.int/jahia/webdav/site/myjahiasite/shared/shared/mainsite/policy_and_research/gcim/gmp/gmp3.pdf (accessed Nov. 19, 2009); S. Vucetic, "Democracies and Human Rights: Why is There No Place for Migrant Workers?" (2007) 11 *International Journal of Human Rights* 403 (exploring the causes of the poor ratification record of the Migrant Workers Convention in OECD countries). See also, generally, R. Cholewinski, P. de Guchteneire and A. Pécoud eds., *Migration and Human Rights: The United Nations Convention on Migrant Workers' Rights* (2009). For a consideration of obstacles to ratification/accession and effective implementation of the Migrant Workers Convention in particular regions and countries, see the chapters in that volume by N. Piper (Asia); V. Piché, E. Depatie-Pelletier and D. Epale (Canada); G. Diaz and G. Kuhner (Mexico); J. Crush, V. Williams and P. Nicholson (South Africa); B. Ryan (United Kingdom); H. Oger (France); F. Hillmann and A. Klekowski Von Koppenfels (Germany); K. Touzenis (Italy); and E. Macdonald and R. Cholewinski (European Union).

[168] The *Global Campaign for Ratification of the Convention on Rights of Migrants* involves both intergovernmental organizations (ILO and Office of the United Nations High Commissioner for Human Rights) and NGOs. See further http://www.migrantsrights.org/campaign.htm.

[169] Lyon reports that the European Parliament, the European Economic and Social Committee, and the Organization of American States have all favorably reported on the Migrant Worker Convention and called on Member States to ratify it: Lyon, "The Unsigned United Nations Migrant Worker Rights Convention," at 8 (manuscript reference of forthcoming publication).

the foreseeable future. Accordingly, the Convention is unlikely to become a major source of obligation for many States, including those that are primary destinations for trafficked persons.

Even leaving aside the critical issue of political support, the Convention itself is plagued by weaknesses, duplications, and inconsistencies that seriously compromise its ability to provide a comprehensive framework for the international legal protection of migrant workers and their rights.[170] It is "a child of its time"[171] and "deeply rooted in the migratory problems and policies of the 1960s and 1970s,"[172] calling into question its relevance and usefulness in an ever-changing and increasingly complex environment. The Convention's ambivalent view toward irregular migration is, when seen through a contemporary lens, especially troubling.[173]

An additional problem from the present perspective is that apart from a few minor concessions on language,[174] the Convention lacks any meaningful gender

---

[170] Cholewinski provides the most concise analysis of the Convention's shortcomings, including specific problems with the exercise of Convention rights (particularly for irregular migrants), omissions with respect to certain rights, and technical obstacles to ratification: Cholewinski, *Migrant Workers*, at 190–192, 201–204. See also Nafziger and Bartel, "The Migrant Workers Convention." On the issue of the relationship between the Convention and the ILO's protection regime for migrant workers including potential conflicts, see M. Hasenau, "Setting Norms in the United Nations System: The Draft International Convention on the Rights of All Migrant Workers and Members of their Families in Relation to ILO Standards on Migrant Workers," (1990) 28 *International Migration Review* 133 and Bohning, "The ILO and the New UN Convention on Migrant Workers," at 702–708.

[171] Lonnroth, "Migrant Workers Convention: An Analysis of Ten Years of Negotiation" at 714.

[172] Ibid. at 716.

[173] While excluding irregular migrants from the scope of certain important rights, the Convention's protection of this group is greater and more explicit than any other human rights instrument. At the same time, it affirms, in a number of places, the sovereign right of States to decide who should be admitted into or excluded from its territory. States Parties are permitted to pursue the immigration controls they see fit (Article 79) and to undertake measures to end clandestine migration and the presence and employment of irregular migrants (Articles 68 and 69). Article 34 of the Convention states that: "Nothing in the present part of the Convention shall have the effect of relieving migrant workers and the members of their families from either the obligation to comply with the laws and regulations of any State of transit and State of employment or the obligation to respect the cultural identity of the inhabitants of such States." Bosniak argues that the ultimate result of the tensions inherent in these conflicting provisions is "a hybrid instrument, at once a ringing declaration of individual rights and a staunch manifesto in support of state territorial sovereignty": L. Bosniak, "Human Rights, State Sovereignty and Protection of Undocumented Migrants under the International Migrant Workers Convention," (1991) 25 *International Migration Review* 737 (Bosniak, "Human Rights, State Sovereignty and Protection of Undocumented Migrants under the International Migrant Workers Convention"), at 742. Hammer sees the Convention as "exemplify[ing] the jurisdictional struggle between State sovereignty and its control over immigration versus the obligation on the State to protect the human rights of all individuals found within a State's territory": L.M. Hammer, "Migrant Workers in Israel: Towards Proposing a Framework of Enforceable Customary International Human Rights," (1999) 17 *Netherlands Quarterly of Human Rights* 5.

[174] For example, the definition of migrant worker contained in Article 2 refers to "he or she." Hune notes that the adoption of gender-neutral language was not automatic but in fact generated some discussion amongst States: S. Hune, "Migrant Women in the Context of the International Convention on the Rights of all Migrant Workers and Members of their Families," (1991) 25 *International Migration Review* 809 (Hune, "Migrant Women in the Context of the Migrant Workers Convention").

perspective. It ignores the reality that work of male and female migrants can be very different, and that the principle of equality of treatment with nationals will not generally be sufficient to ensure that migrant women are protected from inequality in wages as well as occupational segregation.[175] Certain protected rights, such as those related to social security and trade union involvement, are clearly inapplicable to those working in unprotected, unregulated sectors such as entertainment and domestic service, the majority of whom are likely to be women. Critically in the present context, the Convention contains no reference to the special vulnerabilities of women migrant workers or to the gendered nature of abuses to which they are subject.[176] The omission appears to be deliberate. While certainly not as high-profile as they became, practices such as trafficking for enforced prostitution and the abuse of female migrant domestic workers were well-known and acknowledged at the time of the Convention's drafting.[177] In her analysis of the Convention, Hune notes that certain provisions of the Convention, including those dealing with protection against torture (Article 10), protection against slavery and servitude (Article 11), and protection by the State against violence, physical injury, threats, and intimidation (Article 16(2)), should be interpreted to address "the exceptional vulnerability of women in the areas of sexual exploitation, physical abuse and forced prostitution and illicit trafficking."[178] Overall, however, she concludes that the Convention:

> does not adopt specific language that addresses the situation of women who are recruited without their knowledge for the purposes of prostitution, and sexual entertainment and who are subject to sexual abuses such as rape and other forms of violence and harassment as part of their work conditions. If the above articles are gendered, that is, interpreted from the experiences of men, then women

[175] Ibid. at 812. Generally on these issues, see the various contributors to N. Piper ed., *New Perspectives on Gender and Migration: Livelihood, Rights and Entitlements* (2007).

[176] See further ibid. at 811–812.

[177] The special vulnerabilities of female migrant workers was recognized at the World Conference of the International Women's Year, held in Mexico in 1975, and reflected in the resulting Plan of Action: *Report of the World Conference on the International Women's Year, Mexico City, June 19 to July 2, 1975*, UN Sales No. E.76.IV.1, at 88. Five years later, at Copenhagen, the plight of migrant women workers was identified as one of a number of "[p]riority areas requiring special attention": Hune, "Migrant Women in the Context of the Migrant Workers Convention," at 803. In 1995, the mid-point in negotiations over the new migrant workers instrument, States meeting in Nairobi highlighted the prevalence of sex tourism, violence against women, forced prostitution, and the international transport, exchange, and sale of women and committed themselves to taking measures against such activities: Hune, "Migrant Women in the Context of the Migrant Workers Convention." Note also that problems and practices specific to women migrant workers were highlighted in the report of the Special Rapporteur that provided the initial impetus for the Convention's development: UN Commission on Human Rights, Sub-Commission on Prevention of Discrimination and Protection of Minorities, "Exploitation of Labour through Illicit and Clandestine Trafficking, Note by the Secretary-General and Study by Ms. H. Embarek Warzazi," UN Doc. E/CN.4/Sub.2/L.629, July 4, 1975.

[178] Hune, "Migrant Women in the Context of the Migrant Workers Convention," at 817.

migrant workers remain at risk. In other words, the universality of men does not necessarily incorporate a women's perspective.[179]

More recent scholarship has echoed the concern that the Convention's failure to provide any form of explicit protection to women migrant workers against gender-related harms is a major weakness.[180] There is some indication that the Committee on Migrant Workers (the monitoring mechanism established under the Convention) intends to redress this weakness through its own work processes.[181] Whether this is possible remains to be seen.

By way of a summary, the Migrant Workers Convention can best be viewed as a potential source of rights and obligations that echoes and, to some extent, builds upon those to which the broader group of noncitizens are entitled. The Convention also provides an additional source of authority for the proposition, still resisted by many States, that irregular migrants are owed certain rights by the country in which they find themselves. The extent to which the Migrant Workers Convention operates to substantially alter the balance between migrant workers on the one hand and noncitizens on the other will depend a great deal on its future acceptance as a common standard for all countries. Some commentators have persuasively argued that rather than focusing exclusively on ratification efforts for the Convention, efforts should be directed toward ensuring that the more widely ratified human rights treaties are interpreted so as to extend protection to migrant workers.[182] These treaties can also be used to challenge the capacity (and growing propensity) of States to prosecute, punish, and deport migrants for immigration-related offenses, which

---

[179] Ibid.

[180] M. Satterthwaite, "Crossing Borders, Claiming Rights: Using Human Rights Law to Empower Women Migrant Workers," (2005) 8 *Yale Human Rights and Development Law Journal* 1 (Satterthwaite, "Crossing Borders, Claiming Rights").

[181] The Migrant Workers Committee has expressly requested that periodic reports from States Parties include information on "[s]pecific procedures that have been put in place in order to deal with mixed migratory flows, in particular to establish the special protection needs of … victims of trafficking" (at para. 5(g)) and "[p]rocedures assisting victims of trafficking, especially women and children" (at para. 5(k)): UN Committee on the Protection of the Rights of All Migrant Workers and Members of Their Families, "Guidelines for the Periodic Reports to be Submitted by States Parties under Article 73 of the Convention," UN Doc. CMW/C/2008/1, May 22, 2008. It has engaged with trafficking in various concluding observations, for example: "Concluding Observations: El Salvador," UN Doc. CMW/C/SLV/CO/1, Feb. 4, 2009, at paras. 6–7, 47–48; "Concluding Observations: Bolivia," UN Doc. CMW/C/BOL/CO/1, May 2, 2008, at paras. 9, 41–42; "Concluding Observations: Egypt," UN Doc. CMW/C/EGY/CO/1, May 25, 2007, at paras. 50–51; "Concluding Observations: Mali," UN Doc. CMW/C/MLI/CO/1, May 31, 2006, at paras. 22–23. Further on the work of the Committee, see C. Edelenbos, "Committee on Migrant Workers and Implementation of the ICRMW," in R. Cholewinski, P. de Guchteneire and A. Pécoud eds., *Migration and Human Rights: The United Nations Convention on Migrant Workers' Rights* 100 (2009).

[182] Satterthwaite, "Crossing Borders, Claiming Rights," at 2–4. See also J.S. Hainsfurther, "A Rights-Based Approach: The Utilization of CEDAW to Protect the Human Rights of Migrant Workers," (2009) 24 *American University International Law Review* 843 and I. Slinckx, "Migrants' Rights in UN Human Rights Conventions," in R. Cholewinski, P. de Guchteneire and A. Pécoud eds., *Migration and Human Rights: The United Nations Convention on Migrant Workers' Rights* 122 (2009).

inevitably works to limit migrants' ability to exercise the rights they have, in theory, secured.[183] For victims and potential victims of trafficking, the Migrant Workers Convention may, in the end, be more a tool of advocacy than a source of substantive rights additional to those already secured through the more widely accepted international human rights treaties.

While the past decade has produced abundant policy and even "soft law" on the rights of both documented and irregular migrant workers,[184] there have been few significant legal developments beyond the entry into force of the Migrant Workers Convention. One important exception is an advisory opinion, issued by the Inter-American Court of Human Rights in 2003, on the *Legal Status and Rights of Undocumented Migrants*.[185] The request for the Advisory Opinion came from Mexico, which expressed concern that:

> [The unauthorized workers'] vulnerability makes them an easy target for violations of their human rights, based, above all, on criteria of discrimination and, consequently, places them in a situation of inequality before the law as regards the effective enjoyment and exercise of these rights.[186]

In its opinion, the Court affirmed that "States may not discriminate or tolerate discriminatory situations that prejudice migrants"[187] and that:

> The regular situation of a person in a State is not a prerequisite for that State to respect and ensure the principle of equality and non-discrimination, because ... this principle is of a fundamental nature and all States must guarantee it to their citizens and to all aliens who are in their territory. This does not mean that they cannot take any action against migrants who do not comply with national laws. However, it is important that, when taking the corresponding measures, States should respect human rights and ensure their exercise and enjoyment to all persons who are in their territory, without any discrimination owing to their regular or irregular residence, or their nationality, race, gender or any other reason.[188]

---

[183] Bosniak, "Human Rights, State Sovereignty and Protection of Undocumented Migrants under the International Migrant Workers Convention," at 759.

[184] See for example, "ASEAN Declaration on the Protection and Promotion of the Rights of Migrant Workers," adopted by the Association of Southeast Asian Nations, Jan. 13, 2007; International Labour Organization, International Migration Programme, *ILO Multilateral Framework on Labour Migration: Non-Binding Principles and Guidelines for a Rights-Based Approach to Labour Migration* (2006); Council of Europe, "Parliamentary Assembly Recommendation 1755 (2006) on Human Rights of Irregular Migrants and Reply Adopted by the Committee of Ministers," CM/AS(2006) Rec1755 final, Dec. 15, 2006; Organization of American States General Assembly, "The Human Rights of All Migrant Workers and Their Families," Doc. OR OEA/Sen./AG/Res. 1898 (XXXII-O/02), June 4, 2002.

[185] *Undocumented Migrants.*

[186] Ibid. at para. 2.

[187] Ibid. at para. 119.

[188] Ibid. at para. 118.

In applying the principles of equality and nondiscrimination, the Court held that States may treat documented migrants differently to undocumented migrants, and citizens differently to noncitizens, but only to the extent that such differential treatment is "reasonable, objective, proportionate and does not harm human rights."[189] While permissible distinctions may be made, for example between migrants and nationals regarding ownership of some political rights and in relation to employment rights,[190] "the migratory status of a person can never be a justification for depriving him of the enjoyment and exercise of his human rights, including those related to employment."[191] The Court pointed out that the State and individuals in a State need not offer employment to undocumented migrants. However, "if undocumented workers are engaged, they immediately become possessors of the labor rights corresponding to workers and may not be discriminated against because of their irregular situation."[192]

3.3. TRAFFICKING AND SLAVERY

The link between trafficking and traditional chattel slavery is immediately obvious. Both practices involve the organized movement of individuals, generally across national borders, for exploitative purposes. Both are primarily conducted outside the public realm by private entities for private profit. Both seek to secure control over individuals by minimizing or even eliminating personal autonomy. Neither system can be sustained without massive and systematic violations of human rights. References to slavery in the new international legal framework around trafficking, and vice versa to trafficking in contemporary rules on slavery, have reinforced this connection.[193]

As a matter of international law, the link between trafficking and slavery is not well understood. The notion of trafficking as "slavery" or as "a modern form of slavery" is widespread in both academic and general public discourse.[194] More significantly,

---

[189] Ibid. at para. 119.
[190] Ibid.
[191] Ibid. at para. 134.
[192] Ibid. at para. 133.
[193] For example, the reference to slavery in the definition of trafficking: Protocol to Prevent, Suppress and Punish Trafficking in Persons, Especially Women and Children, supplementing the United Nations Convention against Transnational Organized Crime, done Nov. 15, 2000, GA Res. 55/25, Annex II, UN GAOR, 55th Sess., Supp. No. 49, at 53, UN Doc. A/45/49 (Vol. I) (2001), entered into force Dec. 25, 2003 (Trafficking Protocol) at Art. 2; and the reference to trafficking in the definition of enslavement in the Rome Statute of the International Criminal Court, 2187 UNTS 90, done July 17, 1998, entered into force July 1, 2002 (ICC Statute), at Art. 7(2)(c).
[194] See examples cited in A.T. Gallagher, "Using International Human Rights Law to Better Protect Victims of Trafficking: The Prohibitions on Slavery, Servitude, Forced Labour and Debt Bondage," in L. Sadat and M.P. Scharf eds., *The Theory and Practice of International Criminal Law: Essays in Honour of M. Cherif Bassiouni* 397 (2008) (Gallagher, "Using International Human Rights Law to Better Protect Victims of Trafficking"), at 413–415.

from a legal perspective, the concept of slavery has been interpreted or applied in a manner that seeks or claims to extend its reach to situations that are generally associated with trafficking, including debt bondage, forced labor, and enforced prostitution.[195] The rationale behind such an approach is not difficult to understand or appreciate. The slavery label carries a political and emotional weight (particularly in the United States) that can add considerably to the persuasive force of an argument. However, to identify a practice such as trafficking as slavery (or slavery as including practices associated with trafficking) does more than raise the emotional ante. It also brings a very special kind of legal pressure to bear; as shown further in this chapter, the prohibition on slavery is recognized as a rule of customary international law.[196] It is also regularly identified as a legal obligation *erga omnes*[197] and as a part of *jus cogens* – a peremptory norm of international law.[198]

The present section will consider the definition of slavery and the substantive content of the international legal prohibition with which it is associated – with the

---

[195] The leading public advocate for an expanded vision of "slavery" is sociologist and activist Kevin Bales. His major works include: K. Bales, *The Slave Next Door: Human Trafficking and Slavery in America Today* (2009); K. Bales, *Understanding Global Slavery: A Reader* (2005); K. Bales, *Ending Slavery: How We Free Today's Slaves* (2007); and K. Bales, *Disposable People: New Slavery In The Global Economy* (1999; revised edition, 2004). Despite being based on shaky legal grounds, Bales' expansionist vision of slavery as encompassing the full range of contemporary forms of exploitation has been adopted, unquestioningly, by a number of legal scholars writing in this area. See, for example, J.C. Hathaway, "The Human Rights Quagmire of Human Trafficking," (2008) 49 *Virginia Journal of International Law* 1 (Hathaway, "The Human Rights Quagmire of Human Trafficking"); Y. Rassam, "International Law and Contemporary Forms of Slavery: An Economic and Social Rights-Based Approach," (2005) 23 *Penn State International Law Review* 809 (Rassam, "International Law and Contemporary Forms of Slavery"), at 811; and J. Quirk, "Unfinished Business: A Comparative Survey of Historical and Contemporary Slavery" (UNESCO, 2008).

[196] *Prosecutor v. Kunarac, Kovac and Vukovic*, Case IT-96–23-T and IT-96–23/1-T, ICTY Trial Chamber, Feb. 22, 2001 (*Kunarac Judgment*), at para. 520. For an overview of this customary prohibition and its development, see M.C. Bassiouni, "Enslavement as an International Crime," (1991) 23 *New York University Journal of International Law and Politics* 445 (Bassiouni, "Enslavement as an International Crime").

[197] A legal obligation *erga omnes* is considered to be universal in character giving any State a legal interest in its protection and a capacity to bring suit against another State in the International Court of Justice. This legal right is vindicated irrespective of whether the State has suffered direct harm. The basis for this right was recognized by the International Court of Justice in *Barcelona Traction, Light and Power Company Limited (Belgium v. Spain)*, [1970] ICJ Rep 3 (*Barcelona Traction*), at paras. 33–34.

[198] The international law principle of *jus cogens* is a "peremptory norm of general international law," and is "a norm accepted and recognized by the international community as a whole as a norm from which no derogation is permitted and which can be modified only by a subsequent norm of general international law having the same character": VCLT, at Art. 53. In *Barcelona Traction*, at para. 34, the International Court of Justice stated, in regard to obligations *erga omnes*: "[s]uch obligations derive, for example, in contemporary international law, from the outlawing of acts of aggression, and of genocide, as also from the principles and rules concerning the basic rights of the human person, including protection from slavery and racial discrimination." Further on the status of the prohibition on slavery as an obligation *erga omnes* and as a *jus cogens* norm, see Bassiouni, "Enslavement as an International Crime."

express purpose of determining the nature of its relationship with trafficking and the extent of any overlap between the two concepts. The key question is whether it is possible to sustain an argument that trafficking is a form of slavery and therefore subject to the same strict legal prohibition as exists in respect of slavery and the slave trade.

3.3.1. *The Definition and Indicia of Slavery*

Freedom from chattel slavery was one of the first rights to be recognized under public international law, with prohibitions on slavery and the trading in slaves being a central feature of more than seventy-five multilateral and bilateral conventions from the early nineteenth century onward.[199] It was not until 1926, however, with the adoption of the League of Nations Slavery Convention,[200] that an international legal definition of slavery was formally articulated. Article 1 of that instrument defines slavery as "the status or condition of a person over whom any or all of the powers attaching to the right of ownership are exercised."[201] The same instrument also called upon States to bring about "progressively and as soon as possible, the complete abolition of slavery *in all its forms*."[202] Unfortunately, the "powers attaching to the right of ownership" and the "forms" of slavery that were to be progressively abolished were not specified. It is these ambiguous provisions that have been used by activists and scholars to propose or justify an expanded definition of slavery beyond the strict confines of the 1926 definition.[203] However, this expansionist interpretation, given wide

[199] See, for example, the Definitive Treaties of Peace of Paris (Peace Treaties of Paris), 63 CTS 171, May 30, 1814 and 65 CTS 251, Nov. 20, 1815; the Declaration and Final Act of the Congress of Vienna, 64 CTS 453, June 9, 1815; Congress of Verona, "Declaration Respecting the Abolition of the Slave Trade" (Declaration of Verona), Nov. 28, 1822; bilateral treaties between Great Britain and France abolishing the slave trade (1831, 1833 and 1845), the Treaty of London for the Suppression of the African Slave Trade. 92 CTS 437, Dec. 20, 1841; Treaty between the United States of America and the United Kingdom of Great Britain for the Suppression of the African Slave Trade (Treaty of Washington), 12 Stat 1225, TS No. 126, Apr. 7, 1862; and the General Act of the Berlin Conference regarding Africa, 10 Martens NRG, 2nd ser. 409, Feb. 26, 1885, which affirmed at Article 9 that "trading in slaves is forbidden in conformity with the principles of international law." See also, the General Act of the Brussels Conference, 173 CTS 293, July 2, 1890; and the Convention of St. Germain-en-Laye, 226 CTS 186, Sept. 10, 1919. For a detailed examination of relevant international and State practice during the eighteenth and nineteenth century, see J.H.W. Verzijl, *International Law in Historical Perspective* (1976), at 238–260; Bassiouni, "Enslavement as an International Crime." On the special courts that were set up under several of these bilateral agreements, see J.S. Martinez, "Anti-Slavery Courts and the Dawn of International Human Rights Law," (2007) 117 *Yale Law Journal* 550.

[200] Convention to Suppress the Slave Trade and Slavery, 60 LNTS 253, done Sept. 25, 1926, entered into force Mar. 9, 1927 (Slavery Convention).

[201] Ibid. at Art. 1.

[202] Ibid. at Art. 2 (emphasis added).

[203] See, for example, J. Quirk, "The Anti-Slavery Project: Linking the Historical and Contemporary," (2006) 28 *Human Rights Quarterly* 565, at 568; K. Bales and P.T. Robbins, "No One Shall Be Held in Slavery or Servitude: A Critical Analysis of International Slavery Agreements and Concepts of Slavery," (2001) 2 *Human Rights Review* 18 (Bales and Robbins, "No One Shall Be Held in Slavery or Servitude"), at 21–33.

currency through a series of UN reports,[204] has now been rejected. A meticulous
analysis of the relevant *travaux préparatoires* undertaken by Allain reveals this broad
interpretation of the Slavery Convention is an incorrect interpretation of the provision as well as a misreading of the intention of the drafters.[205] Allain's analysis confirms that the phrase "slavery in all its forms" was not intended and does not operate
to expand the definition beyond those practices involving the demonstrable exercise
of powers attached to the right of ownership.[206] Efforts to expand the notion of slavery, even to include the closely related concept of servitude, were explicitly rejected
by States who were generally united in their efforts to ensure that the scope of the
prohibition was strictly limited.[207] This did not mean that institutions and practices
such as debt bondage or sale of children were automatically excluded. What it did
mean, however, was that such institutions and practices, irrespective of their des-
ignations, would be considered "slavery" within the terms of the Convention *only
if* they involved the exercise of "any or all of the powers attaching to the right of
ownership."[208]

---

[204] These reports were prepared for the Sub-Commission on Promotion and Protection of Human
Rights (previously the Sub-Commission on Prevention of Discrimination and Protection of
Minorities) by D. Weissbrodt and Anti-Slavery International. The authors of the report use a document of the Drafting Committee for the Slavery Convention in addition to an earlier report
of the Temporary Slavery Committee (the report which prepared the ground for drafting of the
Convention) to argue that the terms "any or all of the powers of ownership" as well as "aboli-
tion of slavery in all its forms" indicate that the Convention covers a broad range of practices.
See UN Sub-Commission on Promotion and Protection of Human Rights, "Contemporary Forms
of Slavery: Updated Review of the Implementation of and Follow-Up to the Conventions on Slavery
Working Paper Prepared by Mr. David Weissbrodt and Anti-Slavery International," UN Doc. E/
CN.4/Sub.2/2000/3, May 26, 2000; UN Sub-Commission on Promotion and Protection of Human
Rights, "Consolidation and Review of the Conventions on Slavery: Executive Summary of the
Working Paper Prepared by David Weissbrodt and Anti-Slavery International," UN Doc. E/CN.4/
Sub.2/AC.2/1999/6, June 3, 1999; UN Sub-Commission on Promotion and Protection of Human
Rights, "Consolidation and Review of the Conventions on Slavery: Working Paper Prepared by David
Weissbrodt and Anti-Slavery International," UN Doc. E/CN.4/Sub.2/AC.2/1999/1, May 25, 1999.

[205] J. Allain, *The Slavery Conventions: The Travaux Préparatoires of the 1926 League of Nations
Convention and the 1956 United Nations Convention* (2008) (Allain, *The Slavery Conventions*).

[206] Ibid. esp. at 50–79. Allain considers the efforts of Weissbrodt and Anti-Slavery International to
expand the definition of slavery to include debt bondage, trafficking, and other forms of exploitation in J. Allain, "A Legal Consideration of 'Slavery' in Light of the *Travaux Préparatoires* of the
1926 Convention," paper presented at the conference "Twenty-First Century Slavery: Issues and
Responses" in Hull (UK), Nov. 23, 2006 (Allain, "A Legal Consideration of 'Slavery' in Light of the
Travaux Préparatoires of the 1926 Convention"), available at http://www.lawvideolibrary.com/docs/
Definition%20of%20Slavery.pdf (accessed Nov. 17, 2009).

[207] See Allain, *The Slavery Conventions*, at 69–79.

[208] This interpretation is supported by the reports of the drafting Committee as well as by the 1936
Advisory Committee of Experts on Slavery established to review the Convention with a view to
determining whether amendments or a supplementary instrument were necessary. See Allain, "A
Legal Consideration of 'Slavery' in Light of the *Travaux Préparatoires* of the 1926 Convention," at 7–9;
Allain, *The Slavery Conventions*, at 207–218. In relation to "debt slavery," the Advisory Committee
noted that: "[i]t is right, perhaps, that one should realise quite clearly that the [practice] – whatever
form it may take in different countries – is not 'slavery' within the definition set forth in Article 1 of

A decision of the United Nations in the 1950s to elaborate a new legal instrument that would, *inter alia*, address itself to certain institutions and practices resembling slavery lends additional support to the narrow interpretation of the 1926 definition set out above. In other words, if the international legal definition of slavery adopted in 1926 had indeed included related institutions and practices, there would have been no need to develop a new instrument. The 1956 Supplementary Convention on the Abolition of Slavery, the Slave Trade and Institutions and Practices Similar to Slavery[209] did not, as one leading commentator asserts, "give more detail" to the prohibition of slavery set out in the 1926 Convention.[210] The central feature of this latter instrument is its extended application to the institutions and practices held to be *similar to slavery*, specifically debt bondage, serfdom, servile forms of marriage, and exploitation of children.[211] States Parties are required to abolish these institutions or practices "where they still exist and *whether or not* they are covered by the [1926 Convention's] definition of slavery."[212] In addition to retaining the 1926 definition of slavery, the Supplementary Slavery Convention introduces a new concept: "a person of servile status."[213] This concept was intended to differentiate a victim of slavery (a "slave") from a victim of one of the institutions or practices referred to as "slave-like" (a "person of servile status").[214]

International human rights law reflects the 1956 Supplementary Slavery Convention's division between slavery and servitude or "slave-like practices." Both

the 1926 Convention, unless any or all the powers attaching to the right of ownership are exercised by the master": League of Nations, *Slavery: Report of the Advisory Committee of Experts, Third (Extraordinary) Meeting of the Advisory Committee*, LN Doc. C.189(I).M.145.1936.VI, Apr. 13–14, 1936, at 24–25.

209 Supplementary Convention on the Abolition of Slavery, the Slave Trade, and Institutions and Practices Similar to Slavery, 226 UNTS 3, done Apr. 1, 1957, entered into force Apr. 30, 1957 (Supplementary Slavery Convention), at Art. 1.

210 Hathaway, "The Human Rights Quagmire of Human Trafficking," at 9. Other scholars have made similar claims, including Rassam, "International Law and Contemporary Forms of Slavery," at 829. Rassam asserts that the Supplementary Slavery Convention expanded the earlier definition of slavery to include institutions and practices similar to slavery, such as debt bondage, servile forms of marriage, serfdom, and the exploitation of child labor.

211 The phrase "practices similar to slavery" occurs in the title as well as in the preamble of the Supplementary Slavery Convention. For an insight into its development during the drafting process, see Allain, *The Slavery Conventions*, at 219–247.

212 Supplementary Slavery Convention, at Art. 1 (emphasis added).

213 "'A person of servile status' means a person in the condition or status resulting from any of the institutions or practices mentioned in article I of this Convention": ibid. at Art. 7(b).

214 Ibid. at Art. 7(b). Allain has noted that the opportunity presented by the Convention to explicitly define and prohibit "servitude" was considered and rejected. Drafters of the Convention instead favored a more restrictive approach that required States only to take all practicable measures to bring about "progressively and as soon as possible the complete abolition or abandonment" of the four servitudes specified in that Convention: J. Allain, "On the Curious Disappearance of Human Servitude from General International Law," (2009) 11 *Journal of the History of International Law* 25 (Allain, "On the Curious Disappearance of Human Servitude from General International Law"), at 25.

the UDHR and the ICCPR prohibit slavery and the slave trade and further stipulate that no person shall be held in *servitude* – a term that, although not defined by either instrument, is related normatively to the pre-human rights era concept of "servile status."[215] As such, it is generally seen to be separate from[216] and broader than slavery, referring to "all conceivable forms of domination and degradation of human beings by human beings."[217] Another interpretation separates the two concepts according to relative severity:

> Slavery indicates that the person concerned is wholly in the legal ownership of another person, while servitude concerns less far-reaching forms of restraint and refers, for instance, to the total of the labour conditions and/or the obligations to work or to render services from which the person in question cannot escape and which he cannot change.[218]

While the relationship between the two concepts is not fully settled, most agree that the distinction between slavery and servitude is both distinct and qualitative: "[s]ervitude should be understood as human exploitation falling short of slavery."[219] The *travaux préparatoires* to the ICCPR reveal general acceptance of the concept of slavery as implying destruction of an individual's juridical personality.[220] Drafters

---

[215] UDHR, at Art. 4 ("[n]o one shall be held in slavery or servitude; slavery and the slave trade shall be prohibited in all their forms"); ICCPR, at Arts. 8(1) and 8(2) ("[n]o one shall be held in slavery; slavery and the slave-trade in all their forms shall be prohibited": at Art. 8(1); "[n]o one shall be held in servitude": at Art. 8(2)).

[216] Drafters of the ICCPR changed the formulation of the UDHR by separating "slavery" and "servitude" on the grounds that they were two different concepts and should therefore be dealt with in separate paragraphs: M.J. Bossuyt, *Guide to the* Travaux Préparatoires *of the International Covenant on Civil and Political Rights* (1987) (Bossuyt, *Guide to the* Travaux Préparatoires *of the ICCPR*), at 164. See also Allain, "On the Curious Disappearance of Human Servitude from General International Law."

[217] Manfred Nowak, in his Commentary on the ICCPR, cites the relevant *travaux préparatoires* to the ICCPR to support his argument that "servitude" covers practices similar to slavery involving economic exploitation such as debt bondage, servile forms of marriage, and all forms of trafficking in women and children: Nowak, *CCPR Commentary*, at 199–201. See also Bossuyt, *Guide to the* Travaux Préparatoires *of the ICCPR*, at 167. That interpretation can be justified at least for debt bondage, servile forms of marriage, and trafficking in children by reference to the Supplementary Slavery Convention, which defines a person of "servile status" as being a victim of such practices.

[218] P. van Dijk and G.J.H. van Hoof, *Theory and Practice of the European Convention on Human Rights* (1990), at 242 (discussing Article 4 of the European Convention on Human Rights). The European Commission on Human Rights has endorsed this interpretation by stating that "in addition to the obligation to provide another with certain services, the concept of servitude includes the obligation on the part of the 'serf' to live on another's property and the impossibility of changing his condition": *Van Droogenbroeck v. Belgium*, (1982) 4 EHRR 443 (Eur Comm'n on HR, June 24, 1980). See also the discussion at notes 245 to 248 and accompanying text on the 2005 judgment of the European Court in *Siliadan v. France*, (2006) 43 EHRR 16 (ECHR, July 26, 2005).

[219] Allain, "On the Curious Disappearance of Human Servitude from General International Law."

[220] Bossuyt, *Guide to the* Travaux Préparatoires *of the ICCPR*, at 167.

were also explicit on the point that the reference to the slave trade in Article 8 was *not* meant to encompass trafficking in women.[221]

What then is the substantive content of the international legal prohibition on slavery? Do the powers attached to the right of ownership include, as some have asserted, factors such as loss of free will, the appropriation of labor power, and the use or threat of violence?[222] Is the related definitional reference of one legal commentator to "any form of dealing with human beings leading to the forced exploitation of their labour"[223] justifiable, or does it bring his definition within the lesser realm of "practices similar to slavery"? While the *travaux préparatoires* to the 1926 Convention are not particularly helpful on this point, historical evidence, including those aspects of the *travaux préparatoires* to the ICCPR cited earlier, generally supports an interpretation that is consonant with the ordinary meaning of the terms found in the 1926 definition and, to this extent, incompatible with the expansionist definitions that have recently gained currency.

Additional insight is provided by a 1953 report to the Economic and Social Council in which the UN Secretary-General referred to the "reasonable assumption" that the drafters had in mind the Roman law notion of *dominica potestas*: the absolute authority of the master over the slave.[224] Significantly, the report also notes that the definition departs from the traditional Roman law concept of slavery by extending the prohibition to slavery *de facto* (condition) as well as slavery *de jure* (status). In other words, the existence of slavery does not depend on the existence of a legal right of ownership. Slavery can occur even where there is no legal right of ownership over the victim if the attributes that would normally be attached to the right of legal ownership are exercisable and exercised. The report identified six characteristics of

---

[221] During the drafting process, a suggestion was made to substitute "trade in human beings" for "slave trade" in order that this provision would cover traffic in women as well. The suggestion was rejected on the grounds that the clause should be only dealing with the slave trade as such: UN Doc. E/CN.4/SR.199, at paras. 101 (France), 102 (Great Britain) and 103 (France), UN Doc. E/CN.4/SR.93, at 3–4, both cited in Bossuyt, *Guide to the* Travaux Préparatoires *of the ICCPR*, at 165.

[222] Bales and Robbins, "No One Shall Be Held in Slavery or Servitude," at 32.

[223] Hathaway, "The Human Rights Quagmire of Human Trafficking," at 9.

[224] "This authority was of an absolute nature, comparable to the rights of ownership, which included the right to acquire, to use or to dispose of a thing or of an animal or of its fruits or its off-spring": UN Economic and Social Council, "Slavery, the Slave Trade and Other Forms of Servitude: Report of the Secretary-General," UN Doc. E/2357, Jan. 27, 1953 (ECOSOC 1953 Slavery Report), at 40. See Gallagher, "Using International Human Rights Law to Better Protect Victims of Trafficking," at 411. Even though such powers may be constrained by law, those most commonly associated with slavery have usually included the right to buy, possess, and sell the slave, as well as to compel and gain from the slave's labor: J. Allain, "The Definition of 'Slavery' in General International Law and the Crime of Enslavement within the Rome Statute," speech given at the Guest Lecture Series of the Office of the Prosecutor, International Criminal Court, Apr. 26, 2007 (Allain, "The Definition of 'Slavery' in General International Law and the Crime of Enslavement within the Rome Statute"), at 11, available at http://www.icc-cpi.int/NR/rdonlyres/069658BB-FDBD-4EDD-8414–543ECB1FA9DC/0/ICCOTP20070426Allain_en.pdf (accessed Nov. 22, 2009).

the various "powers attaching to the right of ownership," the exercise of which give rise to a situation of slavery:

(1) The individual may be made an object of purchase.
(2) The master may use the individual, in particular his or her capacity to work, in an absolute manner.
(3) The products of the individual's labor become the property of the master without any compensation commensurate to the value of the labor.
(4) The ownership of the individual can be transferred to another person.
(5) The status/condition of the individual is permanent in the sense that it cannot be terminated at the will of the individual.
(6) The status/condition is inherited/inheritable.[225]

Despite the obvious attractions of such a clear exposition, it would be unwise to allow a single, relatively ancient Secretariat report to secure its place as the final word on the substantive content of the international prohibition on slavery.[226] Although supplementary interpretative guidance remains scarce, that which is available deserves close scrutiny.

In this regard, recent developments in international criminal law are, with the important caveat of contextual and legal difference,[227] particularly relevant. The Rome Statute of the International Criminal Court identifies *enslavement* as a crime against humanity when committed as part of a widespread or systematic attack directed against any civilian population, with knowledge of the attack.[228] The statute's definition of enslavement is identical to that provided in the 1926 Convention – with the curious addition of a clause that specifically includes within that definition

---

[225] ECOSOC 1953 Slavery Report, at 48.

[226] Note, for example, that in relation to international criminal law, what is relevant is the state of customary international law at the time the crimes were committed. See, for example, *Kunarac Judgment*, at para. 515: "[w]hat falls to be determined here is what constitutes 'enslavement' as a crime against humanity; in particular, the customary international law content of this offence at the time relevant to the Indictment."

[227] The prohibition of slavery in general international law is based in international human rights law and directed to States: Violation of that prohibition will invoke the international legal responsibility of the offending State. By contrast, the prohibition on *enslavement*, as set out in international criminal law, was developed in the context of war and carries individual criminal responsibility. The meaning of "enslavement" is not necessarily the same as slavery. As explored previously and considered further at Chapter 3.6.2, evidence for a more expansive reading of the range of practices to be included in the definition is currently greater for the international crime of enslavement than for the human rights violation of slavery. Allain argues that this reflects fundamental differences between international criminal law and general international law/human rights law, because the latter regimes have made clear normative distinctions between various types and degrees of exploitation (servitude) "while international criminal law seeks to subsume all within the grander definition of 'enslavement'": J. Allain, "Mobilization of International Law to Address Trafficking and Slavery," paper presented at the 11th Joint Stanford-University of California Law and Colonialism in Africa Symposium, Mar. 19–21, 2009, available at http://lawvideolibrary.com/docs/mobilization.pdf (accessed Nov. 22, 2009).

[228] ICC Statute, at Art. 7(1)(c).

the exercise of powers attaching to the right of ownership "in the course of trafficking in persons, in particular women and children."[229] The (technically nonbinding)[230] elements of the crime of enslavement are identified as including the exercise, by the perpetrator, of:

> any or all of the powers attaching to the right of ownership over one or more persons, such as by purchasing, selling, lending or bartering such a person or persons, or by imposing on them a similar deprivation of liberty.[231]

A footnote explains that such deprivation of liberty "may in some circumstances, include exacting forced labour or otherwise reducing a person to a servile status as defined in the [1956 Supplementary Slavery Convention]."[232] It is also understood that the conduct described in this element includes "trafficking in persons, in particular women and children."[233] The elements of the crime of enslavement reveal that, although the ICC Statute continues the firm attachment to attributes of ownership enshrined in the 1926 definition, it also admits a cautious expansion of the concept by acknowledging that certain practices not intrinsic to slavery could, under certain circumstances, *become* slavery.

In the case of *Prosecutor v. Kunarac* before the International Criminal Tribunal for the Former Yugoslavia, where the charges were of "enslavement as a crime against humanity," the Trial Chamber extensively reviewed the international legal definition of slavery in customary international law. The Chamber confirmed the core 1926 definition applies to enslavement in customary international law,[234] defining the *actus reus* of enslavement as "the exercise of any or all of the powers attaching to the right of ownership over a person."[235] In a judgment that explicitly recognized

---

[229] Ibid. at Art. 7(2)(c). See further the discussion on this point in the context of trafficking in international humanitarian law at Chapter 3.6.

[230] The ICC Statute at Article 9 specifies that the "Elements of Crimes *shall* assist the Court in the interpretation and application of [the law]" (emphasis added). Article 9(3) further provides that "[t]he elements of crimes and amendments thereto shall be consistent with this Statute." For the *travaux préparatoires* of the Elements of Crimes see K. Dorman, *Elements of War Crimes under the Rome Statute of the International Criminal Court, Sources and Commentary* (2003), esp. at 8. For a critical analysis of the elements of crimes and the development of international criminal law under the Rome Statute, see generally D. Hunt, "The International Criminal Court: High Hopes, Creative Ambiguity, and an Unfortunate Mistrust in Judges," (2004) 2 *Journal of International Criminal Justice* 56.

[231] Preparatory Commission for the International Criminal Court, "Report of the Preparatory Commission for the International Criminal Court, Addendum, Part II: Finalized Draft Text of the Elements of Crimes," UN Doc. PCNICC/2000/1/Add.2, Nov. 2, 2000 (ICC Elements of Crimes).

[232] Ibid. at note 11.

[233] Ibid.

[234] *Kunarac Judgment*, at para. 539: "[e]nslavement as a crime against humanity in customary international law consists of the exercise of any or all of the powers attaching to the right of ownership over a person." The *Krnojelac* Trial Judgment also upheld the customary international law basis of the prohibition against slavery: *Prosecutor v. Krnojelac*, Case IT-97-25-T, ICTY Trial Chamber, Mar. 15, 2002 (*Krnojelac Trial Judgement*), at para. 353 and the authorities cited therein.

[235] *Kunarac Judgment*, at para. 540. See also the *Krnojelac Trial Judgment*, at para. 350.

the evolution of this definition in international law, the Trial Chamber identified
that factors to be taken into account in properly identifying whether enslavement
was committed include:

> control of someone's movement, control of physical environment, psychological
> control, measures taken to prevent or deter escape, threat of force or coercion,
> duration, assertion of exclusivity, subjection to cruel treatment and abuse, control
> of sexuality and forced labour.[236]

The Trial Chamber curbed the potential breadth of this list with several caveats. It
noted, for example, that in certain situations, the presence of multiple factors may
be required to reach a determination that someone has been enslaved; no single
factor or combination of factors is decisive or necessary in determining whether or
not enslavement exists. For example, "[d]etaining or keeping someone in captivity,
without more, would, depending on the circumstances of a case, usually not constitute enslavement."[237] Importantly, the judgment specifically noted that although
the buying, selling, trading, or inheriting of a person or his or her labors or services
could be a relevant factor, the "mere ability" to engage in such actions was insufficient to constitute enslavement.[238]

On appeal, the Appeals Chamber accepted the Trial Chamber's definition of
enslavement as an accurate reflection of customary international law.[239] In so doing,
it endorsed the Trial Chamber's thesis that:

> the traditional concept of slavery, as defined in the 1926 Slavery Convention and
> often referred to as "chattel slavery" has evolved to encompass various contempo-
> rary forms of slavery *which are also based on the exercise of any or all of the powers
> attaching to the right of ownership.*[240]

The Appeals Chamber noted, however, that the distinction between chattel slavery and more contemporary forms was a matter of degree and not of substance: "in
all cases, as a result of the exercise of any or all of the powers attaching to the
right of ownership, there is some destruction of the juridical personality."[241] The
Appeals Chamber accepted, as a nonexhaustive list and subject to the caveats set
out above, the factors of enslavement identified by the Trial Chamber.[242] In considering the issue of consent, the Appeals Chamber conceded that, while consent may

---

[236] *Kunarac Judgment*, at paras. 542–543.

[237] Ibid. at para. 543.

[238] Ibid.

[239] *Prosecutor v. Kunarac, Kovac and Vukovic*, Case IT-96-23-T and IT-96-23/1-T, ICTY Appeals
Chamber, June 12, 2002 (*Kunarac Appeal*), at para. 124.

[240] Ibid. at para. 117 (emphasis added).

[241] Ibid.

[242] Ibid. at para. 119. The Appeals Chamber notes that "the question whether a particular phenomenon
is a form of enslavement will depend on the operation of the factors or indicia of enslavement identified by the Trial Chamber."

be relevant from an evidential point of view,[243] there is no requirement that lack of consent be proven as an element of the crime as it is "often rendered impossible or irrelevant by a series of influences such as detention, captivity or psychological oppression."[244]

Unfortunately, the only other recent international jurisprudence available on the "powers attaching to the rights of ownership" demonstrates that the concept of slavery, and the substantive content of the legal prohibition, remains controversial, even within the strict realms of international law. In *Siliadin v. France*, the European Court of Human Rights was called upon to consider whether a situation of domestic exploitation involving a child constituted slavery.[245] (While the case was not prosecuted on the basis of trafficking, the agreed facts would have supported such a charge.) In a unanimous decision, the Court held that being deprived of personal autonomy, even in the most brutal way, is not, of itself, sufficient to constitute slavery.[246] In referring briefly to the possibility that the applicant was a slave within the meaning of Article 1 of the 1926 Slavery Convention, the Court held:

> Although the applicant was, in the instant case, clearly deprived of her personal autonomy, the evidence does not suggest that she was held in slavery in the proper sense, in other words that Mr and Mrs B exercised a genuine right of legal ownership over her, thus reducing her to the status of an "object."[247]

The reasoning of the Court on this point has been criticized as involving a misinterpretation of the 1926 definition: the Court reading that definition as linked to traditional chattel slavery and thereby requiring a "genuine right of legal ownership."[248]

---

[243] Ibid. at para. 120.

[244] Ibid. at para. 113. See also *Kunarac Judgment*, at para. 542.

[245] *Siliadan v. France*, (2006) 43 EHRR 16 (ECHR, July 26, 2005) (*Siliadin v. France*). This case concerned Article 4 of the European Convention on Human Rights. Article 4 prohibits – without defining the terms – slavery, servitude, and forced labor. A domestic worker complained that French criminal law did not afford her sufficient and effective protection against "servitude" or at least "forced or compulsory" labor.

[246] The Court held that the applicant had been held in "servitude" within the meaning of Article 4 of the European Convention on Human Rights and that she had also been subject to forced labor. For a detailed analysis of the case including of the Court's finding that the State had breached its positive obligation to provide specific and effective protection against violations of the Convention, see H. Cullen, "*Siliadin v. France*: Positive Obligations under Article 4 of the European Convention on Human Rights," (2006) 6 *Human Rights Law Review* 585.

[247] *Siliadin v. France*, at 33.

[248] Ibid. In his brief but dismissive analysis of this case, Allain notes the potential for a schism between international criminal law and human rights law on this point. Unlike the situation in international criminal law, human rights law generally links the prohibition on slavery with both servitude and forced labor, thereby creating an implied hierarchy of severity. The existence of "lesser" alternatives to slavery, in particular servitude, provides a possibility, perhaps confirmed by *Siliadin v. France*, for the threshold for slavery to be elevated beyond what has been recognized in judgments such as *Kunarac*. See Allain, "The Definition of 'Slavery' in General International Law and the Crime of Enslavement within the Rome Statute," at 18. Allain refines this argument in his critical analysis of a recent judgment of the ECOWAS Community Court of Justice, *Koraou v. Republic*

A more recent contribution to the "trafficking as slavery" question is provided by the European Court of Human Rights in *Rantsev v. Cyprus and Russia*.[249] In this case, the Court was required to consider whether the response of Cyprus and Russia to a suspected case of trafficking resulting in death violated the obligations of those States under Article 4 of the European Human Rights Convention (prohibiting slavery and servitude as well as forced or compulsory labor).[250] The Court considered its own jurisprudence in *Siliadin* as well as that of the ICTY in *Kunarac* (and a few less persuasive authorities)[251] in deciding that:

> trafficking in human beings, by its very nature and aim of exploitation, is based on the exercise of powers attaching to the right of ownership. It treats human beings as commodities to be bought and sold and put to forced labour, often for little or no payment, usually in the sex industry but also elsewhere. It implies close surveillance of the activities of victims, whose movements are often circumscribed. It involves the use of violence and threats against victims, who live and work under poor conditions. It is described … as the modern form of the old worldwide slave trade.[252]

---

of Niger, Judgment No. ECW/CCJ/JUD/06/08, ECOWAS Community Court of Justice, Oct. 27, 2008: J. Allain, "Slavery – positive obligations – nonapplicability of the rule of exhaustion of domestic remedies (*Koraou v. Republic of Niger*)," (2009) 103 *American Journal of International Law* 311. See also Gleeson CJ in *R v. Tang*, (2008) 249 ALR 200 (Aus. HC, Aug. 28, 2008), at para. 31, stating that "it is to be noted that the Court [in *Siliadin v. France*] did not refer to the definition's reference to condition in the alternative to status, or to powers as well as rights, or to the words 'any or all'."

[249] *Rantsev v. Cyprus and Russia*, Dec. No. 25965/04 (not yet reported) (ECHR, Jan, 7, 2010) (*Rantsev v. Cyprus and Russia*), at para 282.

[250] The applicant, a Russian national, brought a complaint against the Republic of Cyprus and Russia in relation to the death of his daughter, Oxana Rantseva, who traveled (and was almost certainly trafficked) to Cyprus to work in a cabaret under an "artiste" visa scheme. (The Court noted a report by the Cypriot Ombudsman that "the word 'artiste' in Cyprus has become synonymous with 'prostitute'": ibid. at para. 83.) After several weeks, Rantseva informed her employer she wished to return to Russia. Her employer took her to the local police station claiming she was illegally residing in Cyprus. The police advised that Rantseva had a valid working visa and asked the manager to bring her back to the police station the next morning for further questioning. The manager took her to an apartment where she was detained. Rantseva was found dead the following morning. An inquest into the death held that Rantseva died in "strange circumstances" while attempting to escape but that there was no evidence to suggest any criminal liability. Her body was returned to Russia, and, upon the applicant's request, a separate autopsy was conducted that concluded that the circumstances surrounding the death were unestablished. Russian authorities requested the Cypriot government to conduct further investigations. In October 2006, the Cypriot Ministry of Justice confirmed that further investigations would not be undertaken stating that inquest into Rantseva's death had been completed in 2001 and that the verdict was final. The applicant alleged violations of the European Human Rights Convention arising from: (1) the failure of the Cypriot authorities to investigate his daughter's death and to protect her while she was living in Cyprus; and (2) the failure of the Russian authorities to investigate the alleged trafficking and subsequent death and to protect her.

[251] For example, the Cypriot Ombudsman's statement that sexual exploitation and trafficking in that country took place "under a regime of modern slavery": *Rantsev v. Cyprus and Russia*, at para. 282.

[252] Ibid (internal references omitted).

The Court avoided pronouncing specifically on whether trafficking is slavery:

> There can be no doubt that trafficking threatens the human dignity and fundamental freedoms of its victims and cannot be considered compatible with a democratic society and the values expounded in the Convention. In view of its obligation to interpret the Convention in light of present-day conditions, the Court considers it unnecessary to identify whether the treatment about which the applicant complains constitutes "slavery", "servitude" or "forced and compulsory labour". Instead, the Court concludes that trafficking itself, within the meaning of Article 3(a) of the [Trafficking] Protocol and Article 4(a) of the [European Trafficking] Convention, falls within the scope of Article 4 of the Convention.[253]

The *Rantsev* judgment is a significant one, not least because of its contribution to clarifying the substantive content of certain key obligations considered at various points throughout this book.[254] The Court's finding that trafficking falls within the parameters of Article 4 is also an important and timely contribution. It could nevertheless have been more explicit and direct. Even taking into account the extensive consideration of "trafficking as slavery," it remains unclear *why* trafficking falls within the parameters of Article 4.

3.3.2. *Trafficking as Slavery?*

To what extent have other legal developments, more particularly in the field of trafficking, impacted on the question of its relationship with slavery? The definition set out in the Trafficking Protocol and explored in detail in Chapter 1 refers to movement, through various means, for the purposes of exploitation (including, at a minimum, the exploitation of the prostitution of others, or other forms of sexual exploitation, forced labor or services, *slavery or practices similar to slavery*, servitude, or the removal of organs).[255] Several observations are warranted here. First, it could be argued that conceptually, the definition does not seem to leave room for the possibility that trafficking itself is a form of slavery: Slavery is identified as one of several end purposes for which a person may be trafficked. Second, the kind of exploitation traditionally linked to trafficking, such as sexual exploitation and forced labor, is separately identified from slavery and slave-like practices, thereby inferring that they are distinct from each other. On balance, however, the reference to slavery and slave-like practices in an instrument that deals solely and specifically with trafficking would appear to be sufficient to override these potential caveats. At the very least, it could be convincingly argued that the inclusion of slavery and slave-like practices in the definition of trafficking is strong evidence of a substantive link between the two concepts.

---

[253] Ibid. at para. 282.

[254] In particular, the obligation of an effective criminal justice response and obligations of prevention. See further, Chapters 7 and 8.

[255] Trafficking Protocol, at Art. 3 (emphasis added).

The 1999 ILO Convention on the Worst Forms of Child Labour provides further evidence of such a link. That instrument calls for "immediate and effective measures to secure the prohibition and elimination of the worst forms of child labour as a matter of urgency,"[256] including *"all forms of slavery or practices similar to slavery such as the sale and trafficking of children,* debt bondage and servitude and forced or compulsory labour."[257] It is possible to interpret this provision as a recognition that at least one of the listed practices is in fact slavery, rather than the less legally significant "similar to slavery." The European Trafficking Convention provides a further legislative link to trafficking. The Convention's preamble specifically recognizes that "trafficking can lead to slavery."[258] Also significant is the 2000 Charter of Fundamental Rights of the European Union.[259] Article 5 of the Charter, entitled "Prohibition on Slavery," includes a specific prohibition on trafficking in human beings.[260]

These and other indications recounted earlier are not definitive on the question of trafficking as slavery. They nevertheless serve to confirm that the substantive content of the international legal prohibition on slavery – in relation to both the customary norm and its treaty-based equivalent – is both less settled and less expansive than many have assumed. Certainly there is strong evidence that the legal understanding of what constitutes slavery has evolved to *potentially* include contemporary forms of exploitation such as debt bondage and trafficking. The core element of the 1926 definition, however, remains intact. A situation of trafficking, debt bondage, bonded labor, or forced labor will be identifiable as slavery only if it has involved, as required by the 1926 Convention, "the exercise of any or all of the powers attached to the right of ownership." All cases of slavery are likely to be also capable of being characterized as trafficking. Conversely, and despite indications that legal conceptions of slavery have expanded to embrace practices that go beyond chattel slavery, it is difficult to sustain an absolute claim that trafficking, in all its modern manifestations, is included in the customary and *jus cogens* norm prohibiting slavery and the slave trade. Egregious cases of trafficking, involving the clear exercise of powers attached to the right of ownership as identified earlier in this chapter, would provide the

---

[256] Worst Forms of Child Labour Convention, at Art. 1.

[257] Ibid. at Art. 3(a) (emphasis added).

[258] Council of Europe Convention on Action against Trafficking in Human Beings and its Explanatory Report, ETS 197, 16.V.2005, done May 16, 2005, entered into force Feb. 1, 2008, at Preamble.

[259] The European Charter of Fundamental Rights is not a treaty but was "solemnly proclaimed" by the European Commission, the European Parliament, and the Council of the European Union in December 2000: OJ C 364/1, Dec. 18, 2000, done Dec. 7, 2000. Most but not all of its provisions reflect the principles and rules contained in the European Convention on Human Rights. The Charter gained binding legal force with the entry into force of the Treaty of Lisbon: Treaty of Lisbon amending the Treaty on European Union and the Treaty establishing the European Community, OJ C 306/1, done Dec. 13, 2007, entered into force Dec. 1, 2009.

[260] "No-one shall be held in slavery or servitude. No one shall be required to perform forced or compulsory labour. Trafficking in Human Beings is prohibited." Ibid. at Art. 5.

strongest base for arguing the existence of slavery and the consequential application of the slavery norm.

In summary, it is clear that international law on this point is in a state of flux, and that changes to the customary law prohibition on slavery are currently underway. While the full extent and effect of those changes remains to be seen, the developments outlined above point to a gradual but definite evolution of the legal definition of slavery that reflects a more contemporary and nuanced understanding of the elements of ownership.

3.4. TRAFFICKING AS A FORM OF DISCRIMINATION AND VIOLENCE AGAINST WOMEN

It has been argued that trafficking constitutes a violation of international law because it is contrary to the international prohibition on sex-based discrimination. A refinement of this position identifies trafficking as a form of violence against women and therefore a violation of the norm prohibiting inequality and discrimination on the basis of sex.[261] These various claims are analyzed further in this chapter with particular but not exclusive reference to the provisions of the CEDAW and the work of its Committee. The CEDAW Convention defines sex-based discrimination as:

> any distinction, exclusion or restriction made on the basis of sex which has the effect or purpose of impairing or nullifying the recognition, enjoyment or exercise by women, irrespective of their marital status, on a basis of equality of men and women, of human rights and fundamental freedoms in the political, economic, social, cultural, civil or any other field.[262]

States Parties to CEDAW are obliged to condemn such discrimination in all its forms and to pursue, by all appropriate means and without delay, a policy of eliminating discrimination against women.[263] The prohibition on sex-based discrimination is related to and reinforces the duty of equal application of the law.[264] It is generally agreed that this prohibition requires States Parties to take action to prevent private as well as public acts of discrimination.[265]

---

[261] Charter of the United Nations, 1 UNTS 16, done June 26, 1945, entered into force Oct. 24, 1945, at Preamble, and Art. 1(3); ICCPR, at Arts. 2, 3, 26; ICESCR, at Arts. 2, 3, 7; African Charter, at Arts. 2, 18(3); American Convention on Human Rights, at Art. 1; European Convention on Human Rights, at Art. 14.

[262] CEDAW, at Art. 1.

[263] Ibid. at Art. 2.

[264] Article 26 of the ICCPR, for example, provides that "[a]ll persons are equal before the law and are entitled without any discrimination to the equal protection of the law. In this respect, the law shall prohibit any discrimination and shall guarantee to all persons equal and effective protection against discrimination on any ground such as ... sex."

[265] See UN Committee on the Elimination of Discrimination against Women, "General Recommendation No. 19: Violence Against Women," UN Doc. A/47/38, Jan. 29, 1992 (CEDAW General Recommendation No. 19), at para. 9; UN General Assembly, "Declaration on the Elimination

Violence against women is not directly addressed in the CEDAW Convention or in any of the major international or regional human rights instruments.[266] However, attitudes are changing, and the issue is now a fixture on the mainstream human rights agenda. Two UN instruments are significant: General Recommendation No. 19 on violence against women issued by the CEDAW Committee,[267] and the Declaration on Violence against Women adopted by the General Assembly in 1993.[268] Also relevant, both in a regional context and in terms of its overall influence on the direction and content of the debate on violence against women, is the 1994 Inter-American Convention on Violence against Women.[269] Each of these instruments is considered briefly further in the chapter.

General Recommendation No. 19 brings the issue of violence against women within CEDAW by stipulating that the definition of discrimination contained in Article 1 includes "gender-based violence," that is, violence that is directed against a woman because she is a woman or that affects women disproportionately.[270] Gender-based violence is identified as "a form of discrimination that seriously inhibits women's ability to enjoy rights and freedoms on a basis of equality with men."[271] According to the CEDAW Committee, gender-based violence includes "acts that inflict physical, mental or sexual harm or suffering, threats of such acts, coercion and other deprivations of liberty."[272] That the Recommendation establishes a clear link between gender-based violence and the international legal prohibition on discrimination has been widely accepted.[273]

---

of Violence against Women," UN Doc. A/48/49, Dec. 20, 1993 ("Declaration on Violence against Women"), at Art. 4(c); "Preliminary Report submitted by the Special Rapporteur on violence against women, its causes and consequences, Ms. Radhika Coomaraswamy," UN Doc. E/CN.4/1995/42, Nov. 22, 1994, at para. 72. See also T. Meron, *Human Rights Law-Making in the United Nations* (1986), at 60 and Byrnes et al, "State Obligation and CEDAW" at 30–33 (citing Articles 1 and 2(e) and General Recommendations 19 and 25 on temporary special measures).

[266] This omission and the reasons behind it have been the subject of extensive analysis. For a useful overview, see "Preliminary Report submitted by the Special Rapporteur on violence against women, its causes and consequences, Ms. Radhika Coomaraswamy," UN Doc. E/CN.4/1995/42, Nov. 22, 1994.

[267] CEDAW General Recommendation No. 19.

[268] "Declaration on Violence against Women."

[269] American Convention on the Prevention, Punishment, and Eradication of Violence against Women, 1438 UNTS 63, done June 9, 1994, entered into force Mar. 5, 1995 (Inter-American Convention on Violence against Women).

[270] CEDAW General Recommendation No. 19, at paras. 1, 6 and 7. "Gender based violence, which impairs or nullifies the enjoyment by women of human rights and fundamental freedom under general international law or under human rights conventions, is discrimination within the meaning of article 1of the Convention": ibid. at para. 7.

[271] Ibid. at para. 1.

[272] Ibid. at para. 6.

[273] See, for example, the 2006 report of the Secretary-General on violence against women that affirms that CEDAW General Recommendation No. 19 "decisively established the link: it asserted unequivocally that violence against women constitutes a form of gender-based discrimination and that discrimination is a major cause of such violence. This analysis added the issue of violence against women to the terms of the Convention and the international legal norm of non-discrimination

General Recommendation No. 19 confirms that trafficking is a form of violence against women incompatible with the equal enjoyment of rights by women and with respect for their rights and dignity, putting women at special risk of violence and abuse.[274] In relation to Article 6 of CEDAW (requiring States to take all appropriate measures, including legislation, to suppress all forms of traffic in women and exploitation of prostitution of women),[275] General Recommendation No. 19 also notes that poverty and unemployment increase opportunities for trafficking in women and may force many women, including young girls, into prostitution; that prostitutes are especially vulnerable to violence because their status, which may be unlawful, tends to marginalize them; that prostitutes need the equal protection of laws against rape and other forms of violence; that in addition to established forms of trafficking, there are new forms of sexual and/or gendered exploitation, such as sex tourism, the recruitment of domestic labor from developing countries to work in developed countries, and organized marriages between women from developing countries and foreign nationals. These practices are incompatible with the equal enjoyment of rights by women and with respect for their rights and dignity. They put women at special risk of violence and abuse. It also observes that wars, armed conflicts, and the occupation of territories often lead to increased prostitution, trafficking in women, and sexual assault on women, which require specific protective and punitive measures.[276]

As General Recommendation No. 19 makes clear, gender-based violence "impairs or nullifies the enjoyment by women of human rights and fundamental freedoms under general international law or under human rights conventions." Importantly, the General Recommendation points out that discrimination prohibited under CEDAW is not restricted to action by or on behalf of governments[277] and requires States to "take appropriate and effective measures to overcome all forms of gender-based violence, *whether by private or public act.*"[278] This point has been reaffirmed by the CEDAW Committee on many separate occasions, including in its consideration of communications under the CEDAW Optional Protocol.[279]

---

on the basis of sex, and thus directly into the language, institutions and processes of human rights": "In-depth Study on All Forms of Violence against Women: Report of the Secretary General," UN Doc. A/61/122/Add.1, July 6, 2006 (UN Secretary-General's Violence against Women Report), at para. 31.

[274] Ibid. at para. 14.

[275] Further on this Article, see Chapter 2.1.3.

[276] UN Secretary-General's Violence against Women Report, at paras. 13–16.

[277] Ibid. at para. 9.

[278] Ibid. at para. 24(a) (emphasis added).

[279] Optional Protocol to the Convention on the Elimination of All Forms of Discrimination against Women, 2131 UNTS 83, done Oct. 6, 1999, entered into force Dec. 22, 2000. See, for example, *AT v. Hungary,* CEDAW Comm. No. 2/2003, UN Doc. CEDAW/C/32/D/2/2003, decided Jan. 26, 2005, at para. 9.2; and *Fatma Yildirim (deceased) v. Austria,* CEDAW Comm. No. 6/2005, UN Doc. CEDAW/C/39/D/6/2005, decided Oct. 1, 2007, at para. 12.1.1.

The Declaration on Violence against Women, adopted by consensus in the United Nations General Assembly, adopts a slightly different definition, identifying violence against women as:

> any act of gender-based violence that results in, or is likely to result in physical, sexual or psychological harm or suffering to women, including threats of such actions, coercion or arbitrary deprivation of liberty, whether occurring in public or in private.[280]

This definition and the provisions of the Declaration apply to all forms of gender-based violence within the family and the general community[281] as well as violence "perpetrated or condoned by the State wherever it occurs."[282] States are to "exercise due diligence to prevent, investigate and … punish acts of violence against women *whether these are perpetrated by the State or private persons.*"[283] As a resolution of the UN General Assembly, the Declaration does not have automatic force of law and does not carry the important interpretative weight of the General Recommendation. However, its potential capacity to contribute to the development of a customary international norm on the issue of violence against women (including the question of State responsibility for acts of violence perpetrated by private individuals or entities) should not be discounted,[284] particularly in light of its adoption by consensus.

The Inter-American Convention on Violence against Women is currently the only international legal agreement specifically addressing the issue of violence against women.[285] Its purpose is to prevent, punish, and eradicate all forms of violence against women, defined as "any act or conduct, based on gender, which causes death or physical, sexual or psychological harm or suffering to women whether in the *public or private sphere.*"[286] The Convention specifically recognizes trafficking (undefined) as community-based violence against women[287] (as opposed to domestic violence or violence perpetrated or condoned by the State or its agents), thereby acknowledging that the harm of trafficking generally originates in the private sphere. Under the Convention, States Parties are required to: (1) refrain from engaging in any act or

---

[280] Declaration on Violence Against Women, at Art. 1.

[281] Ibid. at Art. 2.

[282] Ibid.

[283] Ibid. at Art. 4(c) (emphasis added).

[284] *Military and Paramilitary Activities in and against Nicaragua (Nicaragua v. United States of America), Jurisdiction*, [1984] ICJ Rep 392 (identifying General Assembly resolutions adopted by consensus as important sources of *opinio juris*). See further the discussion on customary international law in Chapter 2.

[285] At the time of writing, preparations were underway to achieve a European convention on violence against women. See Council of Europe, Ad Hoc Committee on Preventing and Combating Violence against Women and Domestic Violence, "Interim Report," CAHVIO (2009) 4 FIN, May 27, 2009.

[286] Inter-American Convention on Violence against Women, at Art. 1 (emphasis added).

[287] Ibid. at Art. 2.

practice of violence against women; (2) ensure that their authorities or agents act in conformity with this obligation; (3) exercise due diligence in preventing, investigating, and imposing penalties for violence against women; and (4) establish fair and effective legal procedures for women who have been subjected to violence.[288] States Parties are also required to "take special account of the vulnerability of women to violence by reason of among others, their race or ethnic background or their status as migrants, refugees or displaced persons."[289] The Convention provides for a range of potentially effective enforcement mechanisms including reporting and a complaints procedure open to both individuals and groups.[290] The authority of the Inter-American Court of Human Rights to integrate this Convention into its interpretation of the American Convention on Human Rights was established in 2006.[291]

At the international political level, two outcome documents of major world conferences, the Vienna Declaration[292] and the Beijing Platform for Action,[293] identify trafficking as a form of gender-based violence, as does a key report on the subject released by the UN Secretary-General in 2006 entitled "In-depth Study on All Forms of Violence against Women."[294] Of all the human rights bodies, the CEDAW Committee has been most explicit in identifying trafficking as a form of gender-based violence and therefore as unlawful discrimination.[295] The work of other treaty

---

[288] Ibid. at Art. 7.

[289] Ibid. at Art. 9.

[290] Ibid. at Arts. 10, 12.

[291] *Miguel Castro-Castro Prison v. Peru*, Inter-Am Ct. H.R. (ser. C) No. 160, Nov. 25, 2006 (*Miguel Castro-Castro Prison v. Peru*), at paras. 276, 377–379, 408 (García Ramírez J., individual opinion, at paras. 2–32), cited in *Gonzalez, Herrara, Monreal and Ramos Monarrez v. The United Mexican States*, Cases 12.496, 12.497 and 12.498, Expert testimony of Professor Rhonda Copelon, proffered by the Inter-American Commission on Human Rights, Santiago, Chile, Apr. 28, 2009, revised June 12, 2009 (Copelon Expert Testimony), at para. 5, available at http://ccrjustice.org/files/Rhonda%20Copelon%20declaration.doc (accessed Nov. 19, 2009).

[292] "Vienna Declaration and Programme of Action," UN Doc. A/CONF.157/23, July 12, 1993, at Art. 18.

[293] "Beijing Declaration and Platform for Action," Fourth World Conference on Women, UN Doc. A/CONF.177/20 and UN Doc. A/CONF.177/20/Add.1, Sept. 15, 1995, at chapter IV, Strategic Objective D.3., para. 131.

[294] UN Secretary-General's Violence against Women Report, at paras. 135–138; UN High Commissioner for Human Rights, "Women 2000: The Future of Human Rights," speech given at Columbia University, June 4, 2000, available at http://www.unhchr.ch/huricane/huricane.nsf/0/74EE87E151FF942E802568F600495B90?opendocument (accessed Nov. 19, 2009).

[295] CEDAW General Recommendation No. 19; see also, for example, the following concluding observations of the UN Committee on the Elimination of Discrimination against Women: "Concluding Observations: Guatemala," UN Doc. CEDAW/C/GUA/CO/7, Feb. 12, 2009, at para. 24; "Concluding Observations: El Salvador," UN Doc. CEDAW/C/SLV/CO/7, Nov. 7, 2008, at para. 26; "Concluding Observations: Kazakhstan," UN Doc. CEDAW/C/KAZ/CO/2, Feb. 2, 2007, paras. 17–18; "Concluding Observations: Bosnia and Herzegovina," UN Doc. CEDAW/C/BIH/CO/3, June 2, 2006, at para. 28.

bodies[296] and international agencies[297] has provided additional authority on this point.

In considering whether trafficking can be identified as a form of gender-based violence and thereby a manifestation of discrimination against women, it is important to acknowledge that not all violence against women is gender-based. Deciding whether a particular act of violence is gender-based (and therefore a form of sex-based discrimination) will involve consideration of the two prongs of the definition: first, whether women are targeted *qua* women (involving considerations of the characteristics of the target, the nature of the violence, its purpose, and the general context);[298] and second, whether women are disproportionately affected. In relation to the latter, it is clear that the appropriate measure is qualitative as well as quantitative: Violence directed equally toward women and men can still be characterized as gender-based if it has a disproportionate effect on women.[299] Using this framework of analysis, it is not difficult to identify trafficking involving women and girls as a form of gender-based violence. Discrimination against women has been widely identified as a root cause of trafficking and as a factor aggravating existing vulnerabilities. Certain forms of trafficking including trafficking for sexual exploitation, trafficking for forced marriage, and trafficking for domestic servitude are both directed toward and impact disproportionately upon women and girls. Victims of trafficking also suffer gender-specific forms of harm including sexual assault, forced abortion,

---

[296] For example, the UN Committee against Torture recently addressed trafficking in its concluding observations of a State Party report under the heading "Violence against women and children, including trafficking": "Concluding Observations: Russian Federation," UN Doc. CAT/C/RUS/CO/4, Feb. 6, 2007, at para. 11; "Concluding Observations: Ukraine," UN Doc. CAT/C/UKR/CO/5, Aug. 3, 2007, at para. 14. See also UN Committee on Economic, Social and Cultural Rights, "General Comment No. 16: The Equal Right of Men and Women to the Enjoyment of Economic, Social and Cultural Rights," UN Doc E/C.12/2005/4, Aug. 11, 2005, at para. 27: "[g]ender-based violence is a form of discrimination that inhibits the ability to enjoy rights and freedoms, including economic, social and cultural rights, on a basis of equality."

[297] "[Trafficking] of women and children for purposes of forced prostitution or sexual exploitation is a form of gender-related violence, which may constitute persecution," within the legal definition of "refugee". UNHCR Trafficking Guidelines, at para. 19, citing UNHCR, *Guidelines on International Protection: Gender-Related Persecution within the Context of Article 1A(2) of the 1951 Convention and/or its 1967 Protocol relating to the Status of Refugees*, UN Doc. HCR/GIP/02/01, May 7, 2002 (UNHCR Gender Guidelines), at para. 18.

[298] Copelon Expert Testimony, at para. 15. Copelon explains further: "[t]he gendered character of violence against women may be indicated by various characteristics of the violence, such as if sexualized violence is involved; if the methods used involve more direct application of physical violence (strangulation, beating or cutting etc); if the aspects relating to the condition or disposal of the body indicate the targeting of the woman qua woman; if the treatment is part of a pattern indicating gender violence; if communications by the perpetrator or those who claim credit indicates the targeting of women (what is said or written); if the timing of the attack indicates gender animus, etc." Ibid. at note 20.

[299] Ibid. at paras. 16–17, citing *Miguel Castro-Castro Prison v. Peru*, in which the Inter-American Court of Human Rights recognized that in certain circumstances, female detainees experience the presence of male guards differently from male detainees.

and sexually transmitted diseases.[300] State responses to trafficking can also involve gender-based violence such as the assault of women and girls in detention or other official custody.[301]

The consequences of identifying trafficking as a form of gender-based violence and thereby as a violation of human rights are considered at various points throughout this study, including in relation to State responsibility as well as in the context of specific obligations identified in Chapters 5 to 9.

3.5. TRAFFICKING AND ASYLUM

International law as it relates to refugees seeks to provide some measure of legal protection for persons forced to flee their countries of origin because of persecution for reasons of race, religion, nationality, membership of a particular social group, or political opinion.[302] Victims of trafficking who are also refugees are entitled to the full range of rights and protections that their status as trafficked persons and as refugees provides.[303] There are two main questions that arise in respect of trafficking and international refugee law. The first relates to whether trafficked persons are entitled to seek and receive asylum. A more complex question is whether trafficking can itself form the basis of a claim for refugee status. These issues are considered in detail below. The section concludes with a brief note on trafficking and the rules that apply to internal displacement. The core refugee law principle of

[300] Further on trafficking as a form of gender-based violence, see Coomaraswamy, "Report," UN Doc. E/CN.4/2000/68; S. Dariam, "Uses of CEDAW in Addressing Trafficking in Women" (International Women's Rights Action Watch, 2003); A.T. Gallagher, "Trafficking and the Human Rights of Women: Using the CEDAW Convention and Committee to Strengthen National and International Responses to Trafficking in Women and Girls," background paper for the UN Economic and Social Commission for Asia and the Pacific, Expert Group Meeting on the Promotion and Implementation of CEDAW, Trafficking in Women and Violence against Women, Oct. 3–5, 2005; S. Warnath, "Examining the Intersections between Trafficking in Persons and Domestic Violence" (USAID and Creative Associates, 2007); La Strada International, *Violation of Women's Rights: A Cause and Consequence of Trafficking in Women* (La Strada, 2008); and J. Chuang, "CEDAW Article 6," in C. Chinkin, M. Freeman and B. Rudolf eds., *Commentary to the Convention on the Elimination of All Forms of Discrimination against Women* (forthcoming 2010).

[301] See, for example, United States Department of State, "Trafficking in Persons Report" (2009), at 96 (Cambodia), 127 (Egypt), 144 (Greece), 236 (Papua New Guinea), and 277–278 (Tajikistan).

[302] The Refugee Convention, as amended by the Refugee Protocol, defines a refugee as anyone who, "[o]wing to a well-founded fear of being persecuted for reasons of race, religion, nationality, membership of a particular social group or political opinion, is outside the country of his nationality and is unable, or owing to such fear, is unwilling to avail himself of the protection of that country; or who, not having a nationality and being outside the country of his former habitual residence as a result of such events, is unable, or, owing to such fear, is unwilling to return to it": Convention Relating to the Status of Refugees, 189 UNTS 137, July 28, 1951, entered into force Apr. 22, 1954 (Refugee Convention), at Art. 1A(2), as amended by the Protocol Relating to the Status of Refugees, 606 UNTS 267, done Jan. 31, 1967, entered into force Oct. 4, 1967.

[303] For a comprehensive analysis of the human rights of refugees, see Hathaway, *The Rights of Refugees*.

non-refoulement is considered separately in Chapter 6.1.3 in the specific context of State responses to trafficking.

3.5.1. *Trafficking and the Right to Seek and Receive Asylum*

Everyone has the right to seek asylum from persecution.[304] The right to receive asylum is not absolute but predicated on a particular claim meeting the international standards set out in the Refugee Convention. In the case of trafficked persons, questions may arise with regard to the applicant's means of entry. However, international law is clear on the point that asylum claims are to be considered on their substantive merits and not on the basis of the applicant's means of entry.[305] In other words, an individual cannot be denied refugee status – or, most importantly, the opportunity to make a claim for such status – solely because that person was trafficked or otherwise illegally transported into the country of destination. This rule has important practical significance. Many States impose penalties for unlawful entry, use of fraudulent travel documents, and so on, and it has been noted that such penalties increasingly consist of denial of rights in the context of refugee determination procedures.[306]

The possibility that some victims or potential victims of trafficking may be entitled to international refugee protection is explicitly recognized in Article 14 of the Trafficking Protocol and Article 40 of the European Trafficking Convention. The Explanatory Report to the latter instrument confirms that:

> The fact of being a victim of trafficking in human beings cannot preclude the right to seek and enjoy asylum and Parties shall ensure that victims of trafficking have access to appropriate and fair asylum procedures.[307]

That some victims or potential victims of trafficking may fall within the international legal definition of refugee is also implicit in the savings clause of the Trafficking Protocol, which makes specific reference to rights, obligations, and responsibilities arising under international refugee law.[308] The United Nations High Commissioner for Refugees has gone further, calling upon States to ensure that their asylum systems are open to receiving claims from individual victims of

---

[304] UDHR, at Art. 14.

[305] See Refugee Convention, at Art. 31; see also G.S. Goodwin-Gill, "Article 31 of the 1951 Convention Relating to the Status of Refugees: Non-Penalization, Detention, and Protection," in E. Feller, V. Türk and F. Nicholson eds., *Refugee Protection in International Law: UNHCR's Global Consultations on International Protection* 183 (2003), at 185, 187; and Hathaway, *The Rights of Refugees*, at 406–412.

[306] Hathaway, *The Rights of Refugees*, at 408.

[307] Council of Europe, *Explanatory Report on the Convention on Action against Trafficking in Human Beings*, ETS 197, 16.V.2005, at para. 377.

[308] Trafficking Protocol, at Art. 14. Note that the Migrant Smuggling Protocol contains an identical savings clause, at Art. 19. See also the Trafficking Protocol, at Art. 7, which requires States Parties to "consider adopting legislative or other appropriate measures that permit victims of trafficking in persons to remain in its territory, temporarily or permanently, in appropriate cases."

trafficking.[309] The effect of these various provisions is to confirm that all persons, including both smuggled migrants and trafficked persons, are entitled to – and should be given – full opportunity (including through the provision of adequate information) to make a claim for asylum or to present any other justification for remaining in the country of destination.

3.5.2. *Trafficking as the Basis of a Claim for Refugee Status*

The question of whether trafficking or fear of trafficking could itself ever constitute a valid basis for asylum is more complex. In order to be recognized as a refugee, the individual concerned must be found to have a "well-founded fear of persecu-tion" that is linked to one or more Convention grounds.[310] In 2006, the United Nations High Commissioner for Refugees (UNHCR) issued a set of Guidelines on International Protection on the application of refugee law to victims of traffick-ing and persons at risk of being trafficked (UNHCR Trafficking Guidelines).[311] The Guidelines acknowledge that not all victims or potential victims of trafficking fall within the scope of the refugee definition, and that being a victim of trafficking does not, per se, represent a valid ground for claiming refugee status.[312] However, as previously confirmed by the UNHCR:

> in some cases, trafficked persons may qualify for international refugee protection if the acts inflicted by the perpetrators would amount to persecution for one of the reasons contained in the 1951 Convention definition, in the absence of effective national protection.[313]

---

[309] United Nations High Commissioner for Refugees, "Agenda for Protection," UN Doc. A/AC96/965/Add.1, June 26, 2002, at Goal 2, Objective 2. See also UN Economic and Social Council, Office of the United Nations High Commissioner for Human Rights, *Recommended Principles and Guidelines on Human Rights and Human Trafficking*, UN Doc E/2002/68/Add.1, May 20, 2002 (UN Trafficking Principles and Guidelines) (recommending States take appropriate measures to consider asylum applications by trafficked persons).

[310] See further, *Reasons for Persecution*, from page 203 below.

[311] UNHCR Trafficking Guidelines. The UNHCR Trafficking Guidelines form part of a series issued by UNHCR ("Guidelines on International Protection") to provide interpretative legal guidance on Article 1 of the Refugee Convention for governments, legal practitioners, decision makers, and the judiciary as well as for UNHCR staff carrying out refugee status determination in the field: ibid. They are intended to be read in conjunction with other guidelines relating to gender-related per-secution and membership of a social group (cited further in the chapter) and complement the UNHCR's *Handbook on Procedures and Criteria for Determining Refugee Status under the 1951 Convention and the 1967 Protocol Relating to the Status of Refugees*, 1979, UN Doc. HCR/IP/4/Eng/REV.1 (1979, reissued Jan. 2002) (UNHCR Handbook): ibid. For a useful overview of the UNHCR Trafficking Guidelines, see R. Piotrowicz, "The UNHCR's Guidelines on Human Trafficking," (2008) 20 *International Journal of Refugee Law* 242.

[312] UNHCR Trafficking Guidelines, at para. 6.

[313] "Refugee Protection and Migration Control: Perspectives from UNHCR and IOM," Global Consultations on International Protection, 2nd Meeting, UN Doc. EC/GC/01/11, May 31, 2001, at para. 32.

The various elements of the international legal requirements for international refugee protection are considered below.

A Well-founded Fear of Persecution. A claim for international protection by a victim or potential victim of trafficking can arise in different circumstances. The victim could, for example, have been trafficked abroad, have escaped his or her exploiters, and be seeking the protection of the State of destination. A victim could have been trafficked internally, have escaped, and have fled abroad in search of international protection. A potential victim may have fled abroad to escape the threat of trafficking.[314] To be considered a refugee under any of these scenarios, the individual must, as noted above, be found to have a well-founded fear of persecution based on one or more of the Convention grounds. While the Refugee Convention does not define persecution, there is some authority for an interpretation that emphasizes systematic and severe violations of human rights that are themselves indicative of a failure of State protection.[315]

What amounts to a well-founded fear of persecution that would validate a claim to asylum will depend on the facts of each individual case[316] with the following points being considered relevant in the context of trafficking:

- Forms of exploitation inherent in the trafficking experience (such as abduction, incarceration, rape, sexual enslavement, enforced prostitution, forced labor, and physical beatings) constitute serious violations of human rights that will generally amount to persecution.[317]
- Individuals who have been trafficked may experience fear of persecution that is particular to the experience of being trafficked. They may, for example, face reprisals and retrafficking as well as ostracism, discrimination, or punishment should they be returned. Reprisals from traffickers (directed at the individual and/or the family of that person) could amount to persecution depending on the seriousness of the acts feared. Retrafficking would usually amount to persecution. Severe ostracism, discrimination, or punishment may amount to persecution particularly if aggravated by trafficking-related trauma or if linked to an increased risk of retrafficking.[318]
- The impact of previous persecution may, under certain circumstances, be severe enough to render return to the country of origin intolerable.[319]

---

[314] Each of these different scenarios is identified in the UNHCR Trafficking Guidelines, at para. 13.

[315] J.C. Hathaway, *The Law of Refugee Status* (1991), at 104–105. For extensive discussion of subsequent authority accepting this position, see M.M. Foster, *International Refugee Law and Socio-Economic Rights: Refuge from Deprivation* (2007), at 246. For contrary approaches, see ibid. at 243–247.

[316] UNHCR Trafficking Guidelines, at para. 14.

[317] Ibid. at para. 15.

[318] Ibid. at paras. 17–18.

[319] Ibid. at 16.

The following additional points are relevant when the situation involves women or children who have been trafficked or who are at risk of trafficking:

- Trafficking of women and girls for purposes of enforced prostitution or sexual exploitation is a form of gender-related violence that may amount to persecution within the legal definition of "refugee."[320]
- Trafficked women and children can be particularly susceptible to severe reprisals, retrafficking, ostracism, and discrimination.[321]

Agents of Persecution. As discussed further in Chapter 4, both State agents and non-State actors can be involved or otherwise complicit in trafficking. Persecution in the context of international refugee law is normally related to action by national authorities, with the State being identified as the agent of persecution. However, it is now widely accepted that the nature of persecution does not require it to emanate from the State or be imputable to the State.[322] Accordingly, it is technically possible for non-State entities, such as traffickers and their accomplices, to inflict harm sufficient to warrant international protection under the refugee regime. Persecution by non-State actors does not need to be at the hands of traffickers and could, for example, take the form of social ostracism by communities and individuals.[323] The UNHCR Trafficking Guidelines confirm that the persecutory acts relevant to the definition of "refugee" can indeed be perpetrated by individuals if they are "knowingly tolerated by the authorities or if they refuse, or prove unable to offer effective protection."[324] Seen from this perspective, the critical factor is not the origin of the persecution but rather the ability and willingness of the concerned State to protect the victim or potential victim upon return.[325]

State Protection International refugee law provides an alternative to State protection when such protection is unavailable or otherwise inaccessible to the individual in need. A decision as to whether or not the State meets the required standard is

---

[320] Ibid. at para.19, citing the UNHCR Gender Guidelines, at para. 18.

[321] UN High Commissioner for Refugees, *Guidelines on International Protection: "Membership of a Particular Social Group" within the context of Article 1A (2) of the 1951 Convention and/or its 1967 Protocol Relating to the Status of Refugees*, UN Doc. HCR/GIP/02/02, May 7, 2002 (UNHCR Social Group Guidelines), at para. 18.

[322] UNHCR Handbook, at para. 65.

[323] UNHCR Trafficking Guidelines, at para. 18. See also the case analysis in K. Saito, "International Protection for Trafficked Persons and Those Who Fear Being Trafficked," UNHCR Research Paper No. 149 (2007), available at http://www.unhcr.org/research/RESEARCH/476652742.pdf (accessed Nov. 19, 2009) (Saito, "International Protection for Trafficked Persons and Those Who Fear Being Trafficked"), at 17, confirming that refugee determination procedures have variously found brothel owners, organized crime syndicates, and parents to be "agents of persecution" in determination proceedings involving individuals who had been trafficked, in the absence of effective State protection.

[324] UNHCR Handbook, at para. 65, cited in UNHCR Trafficking Guidelines, at para. 21.

[325] UNHCR Trafficking Guidelines, at para. 21.

therefore an essential aspect of the refugee determination procedure. Proper application of this test requires consideration of both ability and willingness to protect, both of which must be based in objective fact. Symbolic gestures or those that do not deliver real protection will, of themselves, be insufficient.

In the present context, the question of whether the State is considered able and willing to protect victims can be expected to depend on a range of factors – most importantly, whether mechanisms are in place to prevent and combat trafficking, and whether such mechanisms are being effectively implemented.[326] The UNHCR Trafficking Guidelines are clear on the point that:

> Where a State fails to take such reasonable steps as are within its competence to prevent trafficking and provide effective protection and assistance to victims, the fear of persecution of the individual is likely to be well founded.[327]

Until recently, it would have been difficult to accurately identify the "reasonable steps" required to meet this standard. However, developments in international law and policy recounted in the present study serve to confirm a growing commonality of understanding on what is required to deal effectively with trafficking. The rights and obligations set out under the Trafficking Protocol, as well as those derived from international human rights law, provide especially important guidance in assessing the adequacy of protection and assistance.[328] In all cases, assessment of capacity and willingness to protect should look beyond formal measures such as the passing of an antitrafficking law or the development of a national action plan to deal with trafficking. It would be necessary to consider whether the identified source of protection is effective or being effectively implemented, *and* whether the individuals concerned are, in fact, able to access the protections provided. Absent indications of effectiveness and access, "the state may be deemed unable to extend protection to the victim, or potential victim, of trafficking."[329] The evidentiary problems associated with making such a determination in the context of antitrafficking responses are, as detailed further below, considerable.

Trafficked persons or those who fear being trafficked may be unable or unwilling to seek the protection of the State because of a fear that this will make their situation worse. Where States are complicit in or tolerate trafficking, such fears may be particularly well-founded. The UNHCR Trafficking Guidelines do not address the question of whether applicants for asylum must seek State protection in order to demonstrate that it has failed. It appears that where the risks are real, failure to seek State protection would not compromise an application for asylum. However, the burden of proof will be on the applicant to demonstrate that no meaningful, accessible, and effective remedies were available in or from the country of origin.[330]

---

[326] Ibid.
[327] Ibid. at para. 23.
[328] Ibid.
[329] Ibid.
[330] Saito, "International Protection for Trafficked Persons and Those Who Fear Being Trafficked," at 19.

The Place of Persecution. As noted above, the legal concept of "refugee" requires an individual to be outside her or his country of origin and, owing to a well-founded fear of persecution, be unable or unwilling to avail him- or herself of the protection of that country.[331] International refugee law is clear on the point that the individual does not need to have left the country *because* of a well-founded fear of persecution.[332] Such a fear could arise (and, in cross-border trafficking cases, will typically arise) *after* that person has left the country. It must, however, relate to the applicant's country of nationality or habitual residence. An individual who has been internally trafficked, or who fears such trafficking and escapes to another country in search of international protection would generally be able to establish the required link "between the fear of persecution, the motivation for flight, and the unwillingness to return."[333]

Even where the harm experienced by a victim of trafficking occurs outside the country of origin, this does not preclude the existence of a well-founded fear of persecution in that person's own country.[334] A determination on this point would require consideration of the full circumstances under which the victim had been trafficked, including the existence of a threat of harm to the victim in their country of origin.

Reasons for Persecution. To qualify for refugee status, there must be a causal link between an individual's "well-founded fear of persecution" and one or more of the *grounds* specified in the definition contained in the Refugee Convention: "race, religion, nationality, membership of a particular social group or political opinion."[335] The general rules relating to this causal link will apply to trafficking cases. For example, it is sufficient that the "ground" is a relevant factor contributing to the persecution; it does not need to be the sole or even dominant cause.[336] In addition, attribution or imputation of a Convention ground by the persecutor to the individual will be sufficient to establish the necessary causal link.[337] That link works both ways. In cases where there is a risk of persecution by a non-State actor for reasons related to one or more Convention grounds, the causal link is established irrespective of whether the inability or unwillingness of the State to protect is based on one of the grounds.[338] Even where the persecution is unrelated to any of the accepted grounds, a causal link will still be established if the inability/failure of the State to protect is based on one of the grounds.[339] Despite general agreement on these points,

---

[331] Refugee Convention, at Art. 1A(2).
[332] UNHCR Trafficking Guidelines, at para. 25, citing UNHCR Handbook, at para. 94.
[333] UNHCR Trafficking Guidelines, at para. 26.
[334] Ibid. at para. 27.
[335] Refugee Convention, at Art. 1A(2).
[336] UNHCR Trafficking Guidelines, at para. 29.
[337] Ibid.
[338] Ibid. at para. 30.
[339] Ibid.

other aspects of the "causal link" element of the refugee definition (for example, the nature and degree of connection required, and whether the intention of the persecutor is relevant) remain unsettled.

The UNHCR Trafficking Guidelines acknowledge that the motivation of trafficking is almost always economic and unrelated to other considerations such as race. However, the Guidelines point out that this reality accommodates a possibility of certain Convention-related grounds being used in the targeting and selection of victims of trafficking. For example, members of a particular race or ethnic group may be especially vulnerable to trafficking as a result of conflict or even because of specific market demands.[340] In the same way, religious affiliation or ethnicity could be a factor in the targeting or profiling of victims. Even in situations where they are not specifically targeted in this way, members of such groups may also be less effectively protected by authorities in the country of origin.[341]

While a particular trafficking situation may involve more than one "ground,"[342] experience to date has confirmed that such cases most often invoke "membership of a particular social group" as the factor linked to a well-founded fear of persecution. In order to sustain a determination that a victim or potential victim of trafficking qualifies for refugee status on this basis, it is necessary to show that members of this group share common, innate, and unchangeable characteristics (other than being persecuted) and are generally recognized as a group.[343] Not all members of the social group need to be at risk of persecution: It is sufficient to show that the claimant's well-founded fear of persecution is based on his or her membership of that group.[344] Women, men, and children (as well as subsets of these groups, such as unaccompanied children) may constitute a particular social group for the purposes of refugee status determination.[345] The fact of belonging to one of these groups might be one of the factors contributing to an individual's fear of being subject to persecution, such as sexual exploitation, through trafficking.[346] Former victims of trafficking might also be considered as constituting a social group for whom past trafficking experience would constitute a defining element, and in relation to whom future persecution, involving reprisals, punishment, and ostracism, could form an additional defining element.[347] The link between trafficking and membership of "a particular

---

[340] Ibid. at paras. 32, 34.

[341] Ibid. at para. 32.

[342] According to the UNHCR Trafficking Guidelines, "although a successful claim need only establish a causal link with one ground, a full analysis of trafficking cases may frequently reveal a number of interlinked, cumulative grounds": at para. 33.

[343] Ibid. at para. 37. See also UNHCR Social Group Guidelines, at para. 11.

[344] UNHCR Trafficking Guidelines, at para. 37; UNHCR Social Group Guidelines, at para. 17.

[345] UNHCR Trafficking Guidelines, para. 38.

[346] Ibid.

[347] Ibid. at para. 39. Note, however, that particular social groups cannot be defined solely by the persecution that members of that group suffer or by a common fear of being persecuted: UNHCR Social Group Guidelines, at para. 14. Accordingly, it is the past trafficking experience that would constitute

social group" continues to be explored at the national level in the context of specific refugee status determination procedures.[348]

3.5.3. *Conclusion on Trafficking as a Basis for Asylum*

In conclusion, it can be said that while not all victims or potential victims of trafficking fall within the scope of the refugee definition, and being a victim of trafficking does not represent a valid ground for claiming refugee status per se, refugees can be trafficked and, conversely, trafficked persons can qualify for international refugee protection. In the latter case, a positive determination will require that the individual has a well-founded fear of persecution based on one of the reasons contained in the Refugee Convention definition, and that the country of origin is unwilling or unable to provide effective protection.

Acceptance of the possibility that trafficking can form the basis for a valid asylum claim has paved the way for reinterpretations of core aspects of the much-contested refugee definition. The link between trafficking and membership of "a particular social group" is particularly relevant and is the subject of a growing body of national case law. A recent UK case granting two trafficking victims asylum provides a useful insight into the evolution of views on the question of membership of a social group and the broader issue of risk of persecution:

> The Albanian Government and authorities are taking steps to protect trafficked women who return but such steps are not always effective ... Trafficked women from Albania may well be members of a particular social group on that account alone. Whether they are at risk of persecution on account of such membership and whether they will be able to access sufficiency of protection from the authorities will depend upon their individual circumstances including but not limited to the following: 1) The social status and economic standing of the trafficked woman's family. 2) The level of education of the trafficked woman or her family. 3) The trafficked woman's state of health, particularly her mental health. 4) The presence of an illegitimate child. 5) The area of origin of the trafficked woman's family. 6) The trafficked woman's age.[349]

---

one of the elements defining the group, "rather than the future persecution now feared in the form of ostracism, punishment, reprisals, or re-trafficking": UNHCR Trafficking Guidelines, at para. 39.

[348] For a comprehensive analysis of recent trafficking-related asylum applications and relevant case law in four major destination countries (Australia, Canada, the United Kingdom, and the United States), see Saito, "International Protection for Trafficked Persons and Those Who Fear Being Trafficked." For a detailed and nuanced analysis of how the various aspects of international refugee law (most particularly the definition of "refugee") have been applied in Australia in the trafficking context, see A. Dorevitch and M. Foster, "Obstacles on the Road to Protection: Assessing the Treatment of Sex-Trafficking Victims under Australia's Migration and Refugee Law," (2008) 9 *Melbourne Journal of International Law* 1 (Dorevitch and Foster, "Obstacles on the Road to Protection").

[349] *AM and BM (Trafficked women) Albania CG* [2010] UKUT 80 (IAC) (UK Upper Tribunal (Immigration and Asylum Chamber), Mar. 18, 2010), at introductory paras. (e)–(f).

Both national and international refugee determination proceedings have also considered a range of related issues, including trafficking as persecution, trafficking as a form of gender-based persecution, retrafficking and reprisals against victims and their families as persecution, trafficking-related trauma, discrimination and ostracism as persecution, traffickers as agents of persecution, and the question of State protection against trafficking.[350] Asylum is, in short, an essential measure to protect those targeted by trafficking and, as one commentator has pointed out, may, in fact, be "the only option available in countries where there is no other means of protection."[351]

While acknowledging the very real progress that has been made in linking trafficking with international refugee law, it is important not to underestimate the challenges to developing a reliable and consistent practice in this area. The lack of verifiable information on trafficking[352] renders extremely difficult the making of an accurate assessment as to the nature of the risk faced by an individual asylum-seeker. Refugee determination procedures have been found to be using incomplete, unverified, and sometimes unreliable information to decide critical questions such as whether there is a risk of reprisals or retrafficking and whether effective State protection is available.[353] In addition, the capacity of an individual to exercise a right to seek and receive asylum from persecution depends on that person's knowledge of the existence of such a right and its applicability to his or her situation. States are adept at avoiding their responsibilities through both omission (for example, failing to require relevant officials to inform trafficked persons of their right to seek asylum or failing to provide access to the specialist legal advice that may be required[354]) and commission (for example, actively

---

[350] Saito, "International Protection for Trafficked Persons and Those Who Fear Being Trafficked." See also J. Monheim, "Human Trafficking and the Effectiveness of Asylum Policies," Saarland University Center for the Study of Law and Economics (CSLE) Discussion Paper No. 2008–01 (2008); and Dorevitch and Foster, "Obstacles on the Road to Protection." See also *AM and BM (Trafficked women) Albania CG* [2010] UKUT 80 (IAC) (UK Upper Tribunal (Immigration and Asylum Chamber), Mar. 18, 2010) for a useful illustration of how these issues have been treated.

[351] Saito, "International Protection for Trafficked Persons and Those Who Fear Being Trafficked," at 27.

[352] See further, the Introduction to this book.

[353] Saito, "International Protection for Trafficked Persons and Those Who Fear Being Trafficked," at 14–15, 18–19 (citing UK reliance on out-of-date and/or incomplete country assessments and US State Department reports), and Dorevitch and Foster, "Obstacles on the Road to Protection" (citing Australian reliance on US Department of State reports). Further on problems with the methodology used by the U.S. Department of State in the compilation of its country reports on trafficking, see U.S. Government Accountability Office, "Human Trafficking: Better Data, Strategy and Reporting Needed to Enhance UN Antitrafficking Efforts Abroad," July 2006, available at http://www.gao.gov/new.items/d06825.pdf (accessed Nov. 22, 2009); and the discussion at Chapter 9.4.

[354] The UNHCR Trafficking Guidelines note the importance of providing proper legal counseling if trafficked persons are to lodge an asylum claim effectively. A UK study has also confirmed the importance of specialist legal advice in ensuring that valid asylum claims are determined correctly. See S. Richards, M. Steel and D. Singer, "Hope Betrayed: An Analysis of Women Victims of Trafficking and Their Claims for Asylum" (POPPY Project, Feb. 2006).

screening out potential applicants from refugee determination).[355] Obstacles to rapid and accurate victim identification of trafficked persons, explored in detail in Chapter 5, further undermine effective procedures for determining international protection needs of individuals who have been trafficked.[356] While agencies such as UNHCR and the UN High Commissioner for Human Rights have recognized the importance of *access*,[357] this aspect is yet to be formally integrated into the international legal framework in any meaningful way.

This issue must also be considered within the broader context of the challenges facing international refugee law in the twenty-first century. Those challenges have been widely acknowledged,[358] and few disagree that the body of law set up to deal with post–World War II refugee flows is straining under the burden of providing an adequate framework of protection for the growing number of people who are forced to leave their countries because of poverty, environmental degradation, conflict, persecution, or a lack of opportunity for a decent life.[359] States that are in a position to assist migrants have come up with an ingenious array of obstacles and deterrents to minimize the impact of their already highly circumscribed international legal obligations.[360] Refugees and their advocates have been equally enterprising in their attempts to both locate and create flexibility within current legal constraints, in particular by seeking expansion of the substantive criteria for refugee status[361] and through increased reliance on complementary or "subsidiary" protection against *non-refoulement* for individuals who do not meet the criteria for asylum.[362] Ultimately, the advances recounted earlier are as constrained as international refugee law itself. They are but minor expansions to a "strictly limited safety valve" that

---

[355] See, for example, Dorevitch and Foster, "Obstacles on the Road to Protection," at 15–16.

[356] See J. Bhabha and C. Alfirev, "The Identification and Referral of Trafficked Persons to Procedures for Determining International Protection Needs" (United Nations High Commissioner for Refugees, 2009).

[357] UNHCR Trafficking Guidelines, at para. 45; UN Trafficking Principles and Guidelines, at Guideline 2, para. 7.

[358] See, for example, Hathaway, *The Rights of Refugees*; see also M.J. Gibney, *The Ethics and Politics of Asylum: Liberal Democracy and the Response to Refugees* (2004).

[359] The current situation has been characterized by one commentator as "a battle between the strategies of states and counter-strategies of asylum seekers ... in the market place of protection": R. Byrne, "Changing Paradigms in Refugee Law," in R. Cholewinski, R. Perruchoud and E. MacDonald eds., *International Migration Law: Developing Paradigms and Key Challenges* 163 (2007) (Byrne, "Changing Paradigms in Refugee Law"), at 163.

[360] These efforts have included the introduction of a range of procedural barriers, including visa requirements, carrier sanctions, detention, the deflection of asylum claims through the concept of "safe third countries," and resistance to efforts to reinterpret the core definitions of the relevant international agreements. See generally E. Feller, V. Türk and F. Nicholson eds., *Refugee Protection in International Law: UNHCR's Global Consultations on International Protection* (2003).

[361] This has occurred through, for example, the recognition of persecution perpetrated by non-State actors and a broader interpretation of the term "membership of a particular social group" described by Byrne as "the most ambiguous of the five grounds of persecution": Byrne, "Changing Paradigms in Refugee Law," at 165.

[362] See further, discussion of the obligation of *non-refoulement* in Chapter 6.1.3.

will likely only permit a small fraction of individuals moved into exploitation across national borders to secure the protection they need.[363]

3.5.4. *A Note on Trafficking and Internal Displacement*

Trafficking within the borders of one country shares many common features with internal displacement, and it has been argued that individuals who have been internally trafficked should be considered as internally displaced persons (IDPs).[364] The UN Commission on Human Rights' Guiding Principles on Internal Displacement[365] define IDPs as "persons or groups of persons who have been forced or obliged to flee or leave their homes or places of habitual residence ... and who have not crossed an ... international boundary."[366] The Handbook for applying the Guiding Principles confirms that:

> the distinctive feature of internal displacement is coerced or involuntary movement that takes place within national borders. The reasons for flight may vary and include armed conflict, situations of generalized violence, violations of human rights, and natural or human-made disasters.[367]

The elements of coercion and involuntary movement certainly fall within the definition of trafficking,[368] and it is widely accepted that conflict, disaster, and violation of human rights all contribute to increasing the vulnerability of individuals and groups to trafficking and related exploitation.[369] The trafficking of individuals from camps established for the internally displaced is just one manifestation of this link.

---

[363] J. Bhabha, "Internationalist Gatekeepers? The Tension Between Asylum Advocacy and Human Rights," (2002) 15 *Harvard Human Rights Journal* 155, at 161.

[364] S. Martin, "Internal Trafficking," (2006) 25 *Forced Migration Review* 12, at 12.

[365] UN Commission on Human Rights, "Guiding Principles on Internal Displacement," UN Doc. E/CN.4/1998/53/Add.2 (Annex), Feb. 11, 1998 ("Guiding Principles on Internal Displacement"). The Guiding Principles, which "are based upon existing international humanitarian law and human rights instruments," were developed to "serve as an international standard to guide governments as well as international humanitarian and development agencies in providing assistance and protection to IDPs." Statement by the Under-Secretary-General for Humanitarian Affairs, Sergio Vieria de Mello in W. Kälin, *The Annotations to the Guiding Principles on Internal Displacement* (2000) (Kälin, *The Annotations to the Guiding Principles on Internal Displacement*).

[366] Kälin, *The Annotations to the Guiding Principles on Internal Displacement*, at "Introduction."

[367] Brookings Project on Internal Displacement and the UN Office for the Coordination of Humanitarian Affairs, "Handbook for Applying the Guiding Principles on Internal Displacement" (2000) (IDP Handbook), at 5.

[368] It is less clear that internal trafficking involving less direct "means" such as deception would meet the definition of IDP provided above. See further, discussion of the "means" element of the definition of trafficking in Chapter 1.

[369] See further, Chapter 3.6 on the link between conflict and trafficking. See also note 45 to this chapter for a sample of concluding observations by the UN Committee on the Elimination of Discrimination against Women discussing the vulnerability of refugees and asylum-seekers. Note that the gender dimension of this aspect of trafficking has also been acknowledged: see, for example, "In-Depth Study on All Forms of Violence against Women: Report of the Secretary-General," UN Doc. A/61/122/Add.1, July 6, 2006, esp. at 44–46, 67–68.

The Guiding Principles on Internal Displacement identify the rights and guarantees relevant to the protection of persons who have become internally displaced. They are grounded in and consistent with international human rights law. Guiding Principle 1 provides that IDPs enjoy, "in full equality, the same rights and freedoms" as other persons in the country and shall not be discriminated against in the enjoyment of their rights because of their status as displaced persons. The Guiding Principles set out a detailed range of measures that are required to protect, support, and assist those who have been internally displaced including through trafficking. Of particular importance are principles relating to longer-term solutions to displacement, including return, resettlement, and local integration.[370] Note that the special needs of certain categories of IDPs (including unaccompanied minors, mothers, female heads of household, and women and girls) are explicitly recognized in the Guiding Principles on Internal Displacement and elsewhere.[371]

3.6. TRAFFICKING IN INTERNATIONAL HUMANITARIAN LAW AND INTERNATIONAL CRIMINAL LAW

There can be little doubt that many of the worst practices associated with armed conflict would today fall within the agreed international legal definition of trafficking. Under most circumstances, the forcible recruitment of child soldiers, the enlistment of civilians into situations of forced or highly exploitative labor, and the organized prostitution of women would all meet the three elements of action, means, and purpose explored in detail in Chapter 1. Still, trafficking and (with a few exceptions) the gender-based harms with which it is associated have never been explicitly prohibited or even regulated by international humanitarian law. The humanitarian law conventions contain no reference to trafficking, and even contemporary analyses of relevant custom are similarly silent.[372] A consideration of trafficking in international humanitarian law (IHL) and international criminal law (addressing individual criminal

---

[370] Further on the "Guiding Principles on Internal Displacement" see the IDP Handbook and W. Kälin, "The Guiding Principles on Internal Displacement as International Minimum Standard and Protection Tool," (2005) 24 *Refugee Survey Quarterly* 27.

[371] See, for example, Principle 4 (nondiscrimination; protection and assistance to take account of special needs of certain IDPs including unaccompanied minors, mothers, and female heads of household); Principles 7 and 18 (involvement of affected women in planning and decision making about their relocation as well as the distribution of supplies); Principle 11 (protection against gender-based violence); Principle 19 (special attention to the health needs of IDP women); and Principle 23 (involvement of IDP women and girls in education programs). The Beijing Platform for Action, at para. 58(I) calls on governments to "ensure that internally displaced women have full access to economic opportunities and that the qualifications and skills of refugee women are recognized": "Beijing Declaration and Platform for Action," Fourth World Conference on Women, UN Doc. A/CONF.177/20 and UN Doc. A/CONF.177/20/Add.1, Sept. 15, 1995.

[372] See, for example, J.-M. Henckaerts and L. Doswald-Beck, *Customary International Humanitarian Law* (ICRC, 2005) (Henckaerts and Doswald-Beck, *Customary International Humanitarian Law*) (references to trafficking only in the context of the ICC definition of enslavement).

responsibility for the most serious of all crimes often, but not always, associated with situations of armed conflict) must therefore proceed indirectly via an examination of related prohibitions including those that cover practices such as enslavement and sexual violence. The following brief overview focuses first on rape and other forms of sexual violence in international humanitarian law as well as in the law and practice of the ad hoc tribunals and the International Criminal Court. It then addresses the question of whether (and if so, under what circumstances) trafficking can be considered a war crime and a crime against humanity.

3.6.1. *Sexual Violence and Other International Crimes Related to Trafficking*

Rape has been prohibited under the customary laws of war for centuries,[373] despite being commonly observed in the breach and rarely prosecuted as a war crime.[374] International humanitarian law, through the Geneva Conventions, prohibits, in situations of armed conflict, "outrages upon personal dignity, in particular inhumane and degrading treatment or punishment, enforced prostitution and any form of indecent assault,"[375] including rape.[376] Women and children are required to be protected against rape, enforced prostitution, and any other form of indecent assault.[377] Other laws of war aimed at protecting civilians can also be invoked against sexual violence.[378]

The use of sexual violence as a method of warfare, and even as a tool of genocide, emerged as a matter of international concern during the 1990s as a steady drip of dispatches from Europe and Africa confirmed the prevalence and seriousness of this phenomenon in contemporary conflict.[379] International commitment to addressing

---

[373] See T. Meron, "Rape as a Crime Under International Humanitarian Law," (1993) 87 *American Journal of International Law* 424. For an analysis of the relevant State practice and *opinio juris* supporting a finding that prohibitions on rape, enforced prostitution, and other forms of severe sexual violence during situations of armed conflict are part of customary international law and thereby binding on all States, see Henckaerts and Doswald-Beck, *Customary International Humanitarian Law*, at 324–326.

[374] See generally, R. Copelon, "Surfacing Gender: Re-Engraving Crimes against Women in International Humanitarian Law," (1994) 5 *Hasting Women's Law Journal* 243.

[375] Protocol Additional to the Geneva Conventions of 12 August 1949, and Relating to the Protection of Victims of International Armed Conflicts, 1125 UNTS 3, done June 8, 1977, entered into force Dec. 7, 1978 (Additional Protocol I), at Art. 75. See similarly Protocol Additional to the Geneva Conventions of 12 August 1949, and Relating to the Protection of Victims of Non-International Armed Conflicts, 1125 UNTS 609, done June 8, 1977, entered into force Dec. 7, 1978 (Additional Protocol II), at Art. 4; Geneva Convention Relative to the Protection of Civilian Persons in Time of War, 75 UNTS 287, done Aug. 12, 1949, entered into force Oct. 21, 1950 (Fourth Geneva Convention), at Art. 3(2).

[376] Additional Protocol I, at Art. 76; Additional Protocol II, at Art. 4; Fourth Geneva Convention, at Art. 27.

[377] Fourth Geneva Convention, at Art. 27; Additional Protocol I, at Arts. 76–77.

[378] For example, the grave breach of the Fourth Geneva Convention of "wilfully causing great suffering or serious injury to body or health" at Art. 147.

[379] See, for example, Human Rights Watch, "Shattered Lives: Sexual Violence During the Rwandan Genocide and Its Aftermath" (1996); "Interim Report of the Commission of Experts Established

individual criminal responsibility for sexual violence in war became increasingly well-organized and gained considerable momentum during this period.[380] The structure and functioning of the three ad hoc international criminal tribunals established during the period 1993–2000 reflect this fundamental shift in thinking about the nature and limits of war.[381] The Statutes of the Special Court for Sierra Leone and the International Criminal Tribunal for Rwanda (ICTR) both identify rape, enforced prostitution, and any form of indecent assault as war crimes.[382] Rape is further identified as a crime against humanity under the Statutes of the International Criminal Tribunals for both Rwanda and the Former Yugoslavia (ICTY).[383] These ad hoc tribunals have made significant doctrinal advances in relation to the international legal prohibitions that are potentially implicated in or associated with trafficking. They have, for example, prosecuted individuals for sexual violence, and several defendants have been convicted of the crime against humanity of rape,[384] defined for the first time in 1998 by the ICTR.[385] Sexual violence has been recognized as an act

Pursuant to Security Council Resolution 780," UN Doc. S/25274, Feb. 10, 1993, at paras. 58–60, 66(c).

[380] See K.D. Askin, "Prosecuting Wartime Rape and Other Gender-Related Crimes under International Law: Extraordinary Advances, Enduring Obstacles," (2003) 21 *Berkeley Journal of International Law* 288; and R. Copelon, "Gender Crimes as War Crimes: Integrating Crimes against Women into International Criminal Law," (2000) 46 *McGill Law Journal* 217.

[381] For a comprehensive analysis of the law and practice of the ad hoc tribunals, see W. Schabas, *The UN International Criminal Tribunals: The Former Yugoslavia, Rwanda and Sierra Leone* (2006).

[382] Statute of the Special Court for Sierra Leone, 2178 UNTS 138, Jan 16, 2002, at Art. 3(e) (when committed as part of a widespread or systematic attack against any civilian population); Statute of the International Criminal Tribunal for Rwanda, UN Doc. S/RES/955, Nov. 8, 1994 (ICTR Statute), at Art. 4(e) (when committed as part of a widespread or systematic attack against any civilian population on national, political, ethnic, racial, or religious grounds).

[383] ICTR Statute, at Art. 3(g) (when committed as part of a widespread or systematic attack against any civilian population on national, political, ethnic, racial, or religious grounds); Statute of the International Criminal Tribunal for the Former Yugoslavia, UN Doc. S/RES/827, May 25, 1993, and amended by UN Doc. S/RES/1166, May 13, 1998, at Art. 5(g) (when committed in armed conflict and directed against any civilian population).

[384] For a comprehensive overview of these cases, see J. Mertus, "The Prosecution of Rape Under International Law: Justice that is Long Overdue," (2002) 35 *Vanderbilt Journal of Transnational Law* 1269. For background information on several of the major indictments see K.D. Askin, "Sexual Violence in Decisions and Indictments of the Yugoslav and Rwandan Tribunals: Current Status," (1999) 93 *American Journal of International Law* 97. For a more recent and detailed analysis, see A.-M. de Brouwer, *Supranational Criminal Prosecution of Sexual Violence: The ICC and the Practice of the ICTY and ICTR* (2005).

[385] "[A] physical invasion of a sexual nature, committed on a person under circumstances which are coercive": *Prosecutor v. Akayesu*, Case No. ICTR-96-4-T, ICTR Trial Chamber, Sept. 2, 1998 (*Akayesu*), at para. 598. Note that this definition does not require evidence of non-consent, which may be assumed from the existence of generally coercive circumstances such as armed conflict. For a discussion on post-*Akayesu* developments in both the ICTY and ICTR with regard to the definition of rape, see F. de Londras, "Prosecuting Sexual Violence in the Ad Hoc International Criminal Tribunals for Rwanda and the Former Yugoslavia," in M. Fineman ed., *Transcending the Boundaries of Law* (2010, *forthcoming*) (de Londras, "Prosecuting Sexual Violence in the Ad Hoc International Criminal Tribunals"), at 5–6. See also the discussion in Chapter 1 of this volume on coercion and consent in the context of the international legal definition of trafficking.

of genocide as well as a form of torture, enslavement, persecution, and inhumane act and as the *actus reus* for these and other crimes.[386] As detailed in the discussion on slavery above, the ICTY has also identified sexual and related violence as constituting the crime against humanity of enslavement.[387] While highly significant, these developments are seen by many to represent only a partial victory in the struggle for recognition of sexual violence during conflict. The under-prosecution of sexual violence by the ad hoc tribunals has been identified as particularly problematic.[388]

The International Criminal Court (ICC), established in 2002, has jurisdiction over genocide, war crimes, crimes against humanity, and the crime of aggression (which is yet to be defined).[389] The jurisdiction of the ICC is limited to situations where national systems fail to investigate or prosecute, or where they are "unable" or "unwilling" to do so genuinely.[390] The Statute provides for individual criminal responsibility for persons who commit, attempt to commit, order, solicit, induce, aid, abet, assist, or intentionally contribute to the commission of a crime within the ICC's jurisdiction.[391] This covers all persons without distinction, including on the basis of official capacity such as head of State, member of Government, or elected representative.[392] Importantly, the ICC Statute also provides for the responsibility of military commanders and other superior authorities for crimes committed by subordinates under their control.[393]

The ICC Statute is even more explicit than those of the ad hoc international criminal tribunals with respect to sexual violence and other offences typically associated with trafficking. It provides that war crimes committed in situations of international armed conflict include "[c]ommitting rape, sexual slavery, enforced prostitution, forced pregnancy … enforced sterilisation, or any other form of sexual violence also constituting a grave breach of the Geneva Conventions."[394] War crimes in situations

---

[386] See, for example, *Akayesu* (acts of sexual violence can form the *actus reus* for the crime of genocide).

[387] See discussion of the *Kunarac Judgment* at note 236 to this chapter and accompanying text. Note that a similar fact situation would likely give rise to a prosecution for "sexual slavery" under the statute of the ICC. This option was not open to the ICTY.

[388] See, for example, de Londras, "Prosecuting Sexual Violence in the Ad Hoc International Criminal Tribunals."

[389] ICC Statute, at Art. 5(1).

[390] Ibid. at Art. 17. "Inability" is determined by considering "whether, due to a total or substantial collapse or unavailability of its national judicial system, the State is unable to obtain the accused or the necessary evidence and testimony or otherwise unable to carry out its proceedings": ibid. at Art. 17(3). In determining "unwillingness", the Court will consider whether one or more of the following exist as applicable: "(a) The proceedings were or are being undertaken or the national decision was made for the purpose of shielding the person concerned from criminal responsibility … ; (b) There has been an unjustified delay in the proceedings … inconsistent with an intent to bring the person concerned to justice; (c) The proceedings were not or are not being conducted independently or impartially": ibid. at Art. 17(2).

[391] Ibid. at Art. 25.

[392] Ibid. at Art. 27.

[393] Ibid. at Art. 28.

[394] Ibid. at Art. 8(2)(b)(xxii).

of noninternational armed conflict likewise include "[c]omitting rape, sexual slavery, enforced prostitution, forced pregnancy … enforced sterilisation, and any other form of sexual violence also constituting a serious violation of article 3 common to the four Geneva Conventions."[395]

The ICC Statute further provides that the constituent acts of "crimes against humanity" (which must, by jurisdictional necessity, be committed as part of a widespread or systematic attack directed against any civilian population, with knowledge of the attack)[396] include "[r]ape, sexual slavery, enforced prostitution, forced pregnancy, enforced sterilisation or any other forms of sexual violence of comparable gravity."[397] Enslavement is also listed as a constituent act of crimes against humanity. As discussed previously and considered further in this chapter, the Statute provides that "enslavement" means "the exercise of any or all of the powers attaching to the right of ownership over a person and includes the exercise of such power in the course of trafficking in persons, in particular women and children."[398] Additional acts identified as war crimes and/or crimes against humanity that are of potential relevance to a situation of trafficking include deportation or forcible transfer,[399] "committing outrages upon personal dignity, in particular humiliating and degrading treatment,"[400] and "other inhumane acts of a similar character intentionally causing great suffering, or serious injury to body or to mental or physical health."[401]

The inclusion of "sexual slavery" as distinct and separate from enslavement in the ICC Statute is a significant recognition of both the links and the differences between the two concepts. One important difference relates to the scope of application. Sexual slavery is identified as both a war crime and a crime against humanity. Enslavement is only identified as a crime against humanity. Secondary legislation identifies the "Elements of Crime" attaching to sexual slavery as a war crime and

---

[395] Ibid. at Art. 8(2)(e)(vi). Note the elements of crime for the war crimes of enslavement, sexual slavery, and enforced prostitution are identical to those set out for the equivalent crimes against humanity: ICC Elements of Crimes, at 10, 13.

[396] ICC Statute, at Art. 7(1). Note there is no requirement of a nexus to armed conflict. For a detailed consideration of the three constitutive elements of "crime against humanity" (widespread and systematic attack; directed against any civilian population; with knowledge of the attack), see D. Robinson, "Defining 'Crimes against Humanity' at the Rome Conference," (1999) 93 *American Journal of International Law* 43; and S. Chesterman, "Altogether Different Order: Defining the Elements of Crimes against Humanity," (2000) 10 *Duke Journal of Comparative and International Law* 307.

[397] ICC Statute, at Art. 7(1)(g).

[398] Ibid. at Art. 7(2)(c). Note that "trafficking in persons" is not defined in the ICC Statute.

[399] Ibid. at Art. 7(1)(d) (crime against humanity of "[d]eportation or forcible transfer of population" and Art. 8(2)(a)(vii) (war crime of "[u]nlawful deportation or transfer or unlawful confinement"). For an argument that trafficking can fall within the crime against humanity of "forcible transfer of population," see T. Obokata, *Trafficking of Human Beings from a Human Rights Perspective* (2006) (Obokata, *Trafficking of Human Beings from a Human Rights Perspective*) at 135–136.

[400] ICC Statute, at Art. 8(2)(b)(xxi) (war crime in situations of international armed conflict); and Art. 8(c)(ii) (war crime in situations of noninternational armed conflict).

[401] Ibid. at Art. 7(1)(k) (crime against humanity).

crime against humanity to include enslavement as defined above (incorporating the reference to trafficking) *and* "caus[ing] such person or persons to engage in one or more acts of a sexual nature.'[402] Acts of enslavement that include a sexual element will, accordingly, be capable of being characterized as both enslavement and sexual slavery.

The elements of the war crime and crime against humanity of enforced prostitution confirm that the distinction between enforced prostitution and sexual slavery is a matter both of degree (the former not requiring the exercise of any or all of the powers attaching to the rights of ownership) and of substance (the former requiring a measure of force, coercion, or abuse of authority and conducted with the expectation of advantage or reward).[403] Enforced prostitution could clearly rise to sexual slavery should the elements of both crimes be satisfied. The ICC Statute also criminalizes persecution, including gender-based persecution, if committed in connection with any inhumane act enumerated in the Statute or any crime within the jurisdiction of the Court.[404]

3.6.2. *Trafficking as a Crime Against Humanity*

The above overview confirms that a number of practices associated with trafficking, including various forms of sexual violence such as enforced prostitution, can, subject to certain specific conditions, be identified as both war crimes and crimes against humanity, attracting individual criminal responsibility. However, the question of whether (and if so, under what circumstances) trafficking *qua* trafficking can be characterized as a crime against humanity is much more complex. The implications of such a characterization are significant. If trafficking is identified as a crime against humanity, then it is considered to be a "most serious crime of concern to the international community as a whole,'[405] and all States are under an obligation to prevent and repress its commission as well as to prosecute those responsible.[406] So characterized, trafficking *qua* trafficking would also fall under the jurisdiction of the ICC, even if committed in peace time, provided the relevant acts can be

---

[402] ICC Elements of Crimes, at Art. 7(1)(g), para. 2.

[403] Ibid. at Art. 7(1)(g), para. 3 ("Caus[ing] one or more persons to engage in one or more acts of a sexual nature by force, or by threat of force or coercion, such as that caused by fear of violence, duress, detention, psychological oppression or abuse of power, against such person or persons or another person, or by taking advantage of a coercive environment or such person's or persons' incapacity to give genuine consent; [and t]he perpetrator or another person obtained or expected to obtain pecuniary or other advantage in exchange for or in connection with the acts of a sexual nature").

[404] Ibid. at Art. 7(1)(h). Article 7(2)(g) of the ICC Statute defines persecution as: "the intentional and severe deprivation of fundamental rights contrary to international law by reason of the identity of the group or collectivity."

[405] Ibid. at Art. 5.

[406] F. Pocar, "Human Trafficking: A Crime against Humanity" in E.U. Savona and S. Stefanizzi eds., *Measuring Human Trafficking: Complexities and Pitfalls* 5 (2007) (Pocar, "Human Trafficking: A Crime against Humanity"), at 10.

characterized as "part of a widespread and systematic attack directed against any civilian population, with knowledge of the attack."[407] Such a result would significantly strengthen the international legal framework around trafficking, particularly in relation to the obligation of States to criminalize and prosecute trafficking. It is therefore unsurprising that a flexible interpretation of the concept of "crimes against humanity," explicitly aimed at supporting the inclusion of trafficking, has gained currency.[408]

As noted previously, the only direct reference to trafficking in the ICC Statute is in the definition attached to the war crime and crime against humanity of enslavement. The Statute defines enslavement as "the exercise of any or all powers attaching to the right of ownership over a person and includes the exercise of such power in the course of trafficking in persons, in particular women and children."[409] This is a faithful reproduction of the classic 1926 Slavery Convention definition of slavery, modified only by the reference to trafficking. The elements of the crime of enslavement are confirmed to include the exercise by the perpetrator of "any or all of the powers attaching to the right of ownership over one or more persons."[410] The ways in which such power can be exercised are identified as including "purchasing, selling, lending or bartering such a person or persons, or by imposing on them a similar deprivation of liberty."[411] A note attached to the elements of the crime of enslavement confirms that "the conduct described in this element includes trafficking in persons, in particular women and children."[412] Trafficking in persons is not defined in the ICC Statute or the ICC Elements of Crime.

The reference to trafficking in persons in the definition of the crime against humanity of enslavement has attracted very little comment or analysis but appears to have caused considerable confusion. Bales and Robbins assert that the ICC definition has served to return the definition of slavery to its original 1926 Slavery Convention version, "with the addition of the practice of trafficking."[413] The assumption that the ICC Statute "includes trafficking as a crime against humanity,"[414] or alternatively, that it "established a new definition of enslavement which includes

---

[407] ICC Statute, at Art. 7(1). This means a course of conduct involving the multiple commission of serious violations of fundamental human rights, pursuant to or in furtherance of a State or organizational policy to commit such attack.

[408] See, for example, Obokata, *Trafficking of Human Beings from a Human Rights Perspective*, at 136–139 and Pocar, "Human Trafficking: A Crime against Humanity."

[409] ICC Statute, at Art 7(2)(c).

[410] Ibid. at Art. 7(1)(c).

[411] ICC Elements of Crimes.

[412] Ibid. at note 11.

[413] Bales and Robbins, "No One Shall Be Held in Slavery or Servitude," at 26.

[414] M. Mattar, "The International Criminal Court (ICC) Becomes a Reality: When Will the Court Prosecute the First Trafficking in Persons Case?" (Protection Project, 2002) (Mattar, "The ICC Becomes a Reality"), at para. 2.

trafficking in persons,"[415] is widespread. While there are slight differences between them, each of these interpretations accepts that trafficking itself has somehow become a form of slavery that can then be subsumed into the crime against humanity of enslavement (or even prosecuted as a separate crime).[416] Allain is one of very few commentators to resist this egregiously expansive reading of the ICC Statute. He rightly concludes that "the definition of enslavement (not slavery) found in the Rome Statute does not add trafficking as an additional type of slavery."[417] However, he then claims that the opposite interpretation is true: "the Statute acknowledges that slavery is but one possible component part of the definition of trafficking".[418] That is not correct. The Statute does not concern itself at all with the definition of trafficking. Rather, it foresees that the (undefined) act of trafficking in persons can be a *vehicle* for the exercise of a power attaching to the right of ownership of the kind required to constitute enslavement.

Under this more conservative reading, an act of trafficking would first be required to satisfy the core requirement of the definition of enslavement – "the exercise of any or all of the powers attached to the right of ownership" – *before* it could be potentially identified as enslavement undertaken *in the course of trafficking in persons* that can be characterized as a crime against humanity. The relevant Elements of Crime provide an open-ended list of examples of the powers attached to the right of ownership. These include actions normally associated with the assertion of ownership, such as buying, selling, and lending, but also the imposition of a similar level of deprivation of liberty. A somewhat ambiguous explanatory note attached to this latter term confirms that deprivation of liberty "may in some circumstances, include exacting forced labour or otherwise reducing a person to a servile status as defined in the [1956 Supplementary Slavery Convention]."[419] The reference to the 1956 Convention operates to bring debt bondage, serfdom, forced marriage, and child exploitation[420] into the group of practices that could, potentially, be identified as "deprivations of liberty" of sufficient severity to constitute a power attaching to the right of ownership. Trafficking in persons could, according to the Elements of Crimes, be included in the same way.[421]

That practices associated with trafficking are now a recognized part of international humanitarian law and criminal law is indisputable. The place of trafficking *qua* trafficking is less certain and will likely depend on future ICC jurisprudence.

---

[415] B. Bedont, "Gender Specific Provisions in the Statute of the International Criminal Court," in F. Lattanzi and W.A. Schabas eds., *Essays on the Rome Statute of the International Criminal Court: Volume 1* 183 (1999), at 199.

[416] "[T]he International Criminal Court may prosecute cases of trafficking in persons": Mattar, "The ICC Becomes a Reality," at para. 7.

[417] Allain, *The Slavery Conventions*, at 231.

[418] Ibid.

[419] Ibid. at note 11.

[420] These are the four "servitudes" proscribed by the Supplementary Slavery Convention.

[421] ICC Elements of Crime.

The work of the ad hoc criminal tribunals will undoubtedly be highly influential. One ICTY case cited previously, *Kunarac*, can be expected to be of lasting importance. The significance of this judgment for the present discussion lies in its acceptance of an evolution of the concept of enslavement, away from highly prescribed notions of property and ownership and toward a more nuanced understanding, reflected in the definition of trafficking, of the many and varied ways in which individuals can and do exercise complete and effective control over others.[422]

---

[422] See discussion of the *Kunarac Judgment* and *Appeal* at notes 234 to 244 above and the accompanying text.

4

State Responsibility for Trafficking

In every system of law, responsibility as a legal institution plays a leading part because it both organizes and reveals the level of integration of this system, as well as the prevailing conceptions inside it regarding the nature of rights and of obligations, the consequences of their infringement and, perhaps more deeply, the ethical and social foundations of the whole. The establishment of a certain type of responsibility requires contemplation of the relationship it defines between the subjects of law, their acts and the community to which they belong.[1]

The allocation of responsibility for violations of international law is critical to that system's effectiveness and credibility. The central claim of this study is that international law requires States (and, under certain circumstances, other entities) to be held answerable for their acts and omissions that cause or otherwise contribute to trafficking. The scant attention paid to State responsibility in the legal literature on trafficking[2] suggests that this aspect of law is of marginal, perhaps only historical importance. This is both a legal and strategic mistake. Certainly, formal recourse to doctrines of State responsibility through international courts and tribunals is relatively uncommon. Such recourse is expensive, time-consuming, and often not seen to be in the long-term interests of even those States directly affected by a breach of legal obligation. It is to be expected that the development of treaty regimes establishing supervisory mechanisms and compliance procedures will further lessen the perceived need for formal invocation of responsibility. However, the practical value of State responsibility rules extends far beyond their capacity to enable a technical legal determination as to whether or not one State has a legitimate and enforceable international claim against another that is subject to binding international adjudication. Rules of State responsibility help determine the existence of a breach of

---

[1]   P.-M. Dupuy, "The International Law of State Responsibility: Revolution or Evolution?" (1989) 11 *Michigan Journal of International Law* 105, at 126.

[2]   For example, none of the recent legal monographs on the subject – S. Scarpa, *Trafficking in Human Beings: Modern Slavery* (2008); H. Askola, *Legal Responses to Trafficking in Women for Sexual Exploitation in the European Union* (2007); C. Rijken, *Trafficking in Persons: Prosecution from a European Perspective* (2003); T. Obokata, *Trafficking of Human Beings from a Human Rights Perspective* (2006) – index any references to State responsibility.

obligation. They can, therefore, be used and applied in any setting in which such a determination is useful. This extends their utility beyond international courts and tribunals to include forums where States may make less formal claims of violations of international law, for example, intergovernmental commissions and human rights treaty bodies. Responsibility claims can also be "domesticated" and brought before national courts.[3] A finding of responsibility can, in short, be used in many ways, by different mechanisms and different parties, to enforce, encourage, and facilitate compliance with international law.[4]

As noted in the Introduction to this volume, States consistently deny responsibility for trafficking. In some cases, the refutation of responsibility is justified with reference to the primary wrong (trafficking) being committed by a criminal or groups of criminals and not by the State itself. In other cases, responsibility is not acknowledged because the State claims to have done everything reasonably possible to avoid the harm. An understanding of the principles of international legal responsibility as they apply in the trafficking context is an essential prerequisite for examining and, if justified, rejecting claims of this kind, as well as defining, with precision, the nature of a State's obligations in a particular situation. This chapter seeks to explore the doctrine of State responsibility with a view to determining whether and, if so, under what circumstances, to what extent, and with what effect States can be held legally responsible for trafficking. The chapter commences with a short overview of the rules of State responsibility and their origin before examining the two specific requirements of responsibility: attribution and breach of obligation. Issues around State responsibility for trafficking-related harm originating in the conduct of private persons or entities are subject to separate and detailed discussion. The chapter then addresses the consequences of a finding of responsibility, rules relating to invocation of responsibility, and countermeasures. The question of legal responsibility of non-State actors, international organizations, individuals, and private entities is subject to brief consideration prior to a summary of the key principles of State responsibility relevant to trafficking.

4.1. A GENERAL THEORY OF INTERNATIONAL RESPONSIBILITY

It is a basic principal of international law that every internationally wrongful act entails the responsibility of the State, giving rise to an obligation of reparation. The terms "international responsibility" and "State responsibility" "cover[] the relations which arise under international law from the internationally wrongful act of a State."[5] Classical doctrines that traditionally governed this area of law, which traditionally

---

[3]   J. Crawford and S. Olleson, "The Nature and Forms of International Responsibility," in M.D. Evans ed., *International Law* 451 (2006) (Crawford and Olleson, "The Nature and Forms of International Responsibility"), at 456.

[4]   Further on compliance, see Chapter 9.

[5]   International Law Commission (ILC), *Draft Articles on Responsibility of States for Internationally Wrongful Acts, Report of the International Law Commission on the Work of Its Fifty-third Session*, UN

restricted the issue to State responsibility vis-à-vis aliens,[6] were nevertheless based on this same premise:

> The origin of responsibility lay in the commission by a state of an internationally wrongful act. The damage produced by such an act … gave rise to the existence of an injured state. This latter, the right of which had been harmed, was able to seek reparation from the responsible state through, the means appropriate to the nature of the damage suffered. The main, if not the only consequence of the wrongful act was to burden the responsible state with the subsidiary obligation of making reparation for the tortious results of its wrongdoing.[7]

While the scope of State responsibility eventually expanded beyond the treatment of aliens to cover the whole corpus of international law, the essence of the basic doctrine has remained remarkably unchanged. Put simply, the breach of an international obligation is a predicate to responsibility. The "secondary rules" of State responsibility operate to require the State to make reparations for a failure to comply with an international legal obligation.

The question of State responsibility for violation of international rules has been considered by international courts and tribunals on numerous occasions and has generated substantial State practice. Formal codification efforts began under the auspices of the League of Nations and the topic was taken up by the International Law Commission (ILC) at its first session in 1949 following a referral from the General Assembly. The ILC's initial work focused, as the League's had done, on the specific issue of responsibility for injury to aliens and their property. By 1963, the focus had expanded to encompass rules of general application concerning State responsibility applicable to all substantive areas of international law.[8] That expansion took place on the basis of a methodological separation between the primary and secondary rules of international law. The ILC was clear on the point that its focus would not be on the "primary rules" that define the content of legal obligation,[9] but rather on the "secondary rules" that determine by whom an obligation has been violated and the consequences of that violation.[10] This distinction is an important one in the present

---

GAOR, 56th Sess., Supp. No. 10, at 43, UN Doc. A/56/10 (2001) (referred to in this chapter as "ILC Draft Articles" or "ILC Commentary"), at Art. 1, para. 5.

[6] See generally, R. Jennings and A. Watts, *Oppenheim's International Law* (9th ed., 1992), at Chapter 4; and R. Lillich ed., *International Law of State Responsibility for Injury to Aliens* (1983).

[7] P.-M. Dupuy, "Reviewing the Difficulties of Codification: On Ago's Classification of Obligation of Means and Obligation of Result in Relation to State Responsibility," (1999) 10 *European Journal of International Law* 371, at 372.

[8] J. Crawford, *The International Law Commission's Articles on State Responsibility: Introduction, Text and Commentaries* (2002) (Crawford, *The ILC's Articles on State Responsibility*), at 2. See also R. Rosenstock, "The ILC and State Responsibility," (2002) 96 *American Journal of International Law* 792, at 792–793.

[9] For example, the content of obligations under the "primary law" of a particular treaty regime.

[10] Crawford, *The ILC's Articles on State Responsibility*, at 2. As ILC Rapporteur Ago remarked: "it is one thing to define a rule and the content of the obligation it imposes, and another to determine

context, as will be seen in the following discussion, in particular as it relates to State responsibility for the actions of private individuals.

The ILC's work on State responsibility was only completed in 2001, with the finalization of a set of principles ("Articles") for consideration by the UN and its Member States.[11] It is not yet clear whether this process will result in a multilateral treaty,[12] although the impact of the ILC's work has already been felt and is expected to be considerable.[13] As the major statement on the international law of State responsibility, the Articles on State Responsibility (along with the accompanying Commentaries by the ILC) provide a useful, if not wholly authoritative, framework for the questions to be addressed in this part. It is therefore important to note, at the outset, certain key features of the text. With respect to their scope, the Articles establish general principles of State responsibility applicable to all areas of international law and "to the whole field of international obligations of States, whether the obligation is owed to one or several States, to an individual or group, or to the international community as a whole."[14] They are limited to State responsibility and do not pronounce on important questions concerning the responsibility of individuals, of international organizations, and of States for the acts of international organizations.[15] The Articles do not apply where and to the extent that the issues they cover are governed by

whether that obligation has been violated and what should be the consequences of the violation." R. Ago, "Second Report on State Responsibility," UN Doc. A/8010/Rev.1, reprinted in [1970] 2 *Yearbook of the International Law*, UN Doc. A/CN.4/SER.A/1970/Add.1, 271, at 306, para. 66(c).

[11]   The official text of the draft Articles and Commentaries appear in the 2001 report of the International Law Commission (ILC), *Draft Articles on Responsibility of States for Internationally Wrongful Acts, Report of the International Law Commission on the Work of Its Fifty-third Session*, UN GAOR, 56th Sess., Supp. No. 10, at 43, UN Doc. A/56/10 (2001) (referred to in this chapter as "ILC Draft Articles" or "ILC Commentary"). The notes and references in this chapter are to the Articles and Commentary as set out in Crawford, *The ILC's Articles on State Responsibility*.

[12]   The complete text of the Articles was adopted by the ILC at its fifty-third session in 2001 and subsequently referred to the General Assembly for its consideration. In its recommendation to the General Assembly, the ILC proposed a two-stage approach for taking its work forward: some form of endorsement or taking note of the Articles, followed by the possible conversion of the Articles into a multilateral convention at a later stage. See Provisional Summary Record of the 2675th Meeting, UN Doc. A/CN.4/SR.2675, May 11, 2001, at 18–19. On issues around possible adoption of a convention on State responsibility, see J. Crawford and S. Olleson, "The Continuing Debate on a UN Convention on State Responsibility," (2005) 54 *International and Comparative Law Quarterly* 959.

[13]   D.D. Caron, "The ILC Articles on State Responsibility: The Paradoxical Relationship between Form and Authority," (2002) 96 *American Journal of International Law* 857 (Caron, "The ILC Articles on State Responsibility: The Paradoxical Relationship between Form and Authority"). The ILC's principles have also been applied, in particular, by human rights courts and treaty bodies. See R. McCorquodale, "Impact on State Responsibility," in M.T. Kamminga and M. Scheinin eds., *The Impact of Human Rights on General International Law* 235 (2009) (McCorquodale, "Impact on State Responsibility"), at 236.

[14]   ILC Commentary, at Introduction, para. 5.

[15]   "[S]pecial considerations apply to the responsibility of other international legal persons and these are not covered in the articles": ibid. at Art. 1, para. 7. Note that Article 57 confirms that the Articles are without prejudice to the question of responsibility under international law of an organization or of any State for the conduct of an international organization. See further, Chapter 4.6.

special rules of international law (*lex specialis*).[16] With respect to their legal force, it should be noted that the authority of the ILC's work as a source of law is not universally accepted.[17] Many of the Articles have a long and generally uncontroversial history and appear to be an authoritative codification of relevant customary law doctrine. However, other parts of the text are new and as such are better considered as examples of progressive development that are yet to receive the level of international consensus required for their acceptance as customary norms.[18]

4.2. STATE RESPONSIBILITY FOR VIOLATIONS OF INTERNATIONAL LAW ASSOCIATED WITH TRAFFICKING

The core principle of State responsibility, firmly established in international law,[19] is that "[e]very internationally wrongful act of a State entails the international responsibility of that State."[20] The characterization of an act as internationally wrongful is governed by international law.[21] It is well settled that an act of a State which breaches an international obligation will be internationally wrongful even if it does not contravene the State's own internal law, and the ILC Articles reflect this position.[22]

---

[16] ILC Draft Articles, at Art. 55.

[17] Caron points out at 867 that the ILC text and commentaries are not, of themselves, a source of law but rather "evidence of a source of law": Caron, "The ILC Articles on State Responsibility: The Paradoxical Relationship between Form and Authority." He expresses particular concern that the dynamics of decision-making in arbitral tribunals (tending toward uncritical deference to such texts) and the treaty-like structure of the Articles themselves ("false concreteness and false consensus") will contribute to their being "inappropriately and essentially accorded the authority of a formal source of law": ibid. at 861, 868.

[18] The precise status of the ILC Articles has not been clarified. Prior to their finalization, the draft texts were used on occasion by the International Court of Justice – pointing, perhaps, to an acceptance of its central provisions as declaratory of customary international law. See, for example, *Gabcikovo-Nagymaros Project (Hungary v. Slovakia)*, [1997] ICJ Rep 7, at paras. 47, 50–54 (especially), 79 and 83. Commenting on the status of the (at that point, still draft) texts, Meron argued that the work of the ILC in this area "constitutes a stage in the U.N. work of codification and progressive development of international law and as such it may demonstrate practice of States and international organisations": T. Meron, *Human Rights and Humanitarian Norms as Customary Law* (1989) (Meron, *Human Rights and Humanitarian Norms as Customary Law*), at 137. However, as noted above, this view is not universally shared, and the decision not to submit the drafts to the scrutiny of a law-making conference has been particularly criticized. See, for example, Caron, "The ILC Articles on State Responsibility: The Paradoxical Relationship between Form and Authority," at 858.

[19] The ILC Commentary on Article 1 (at paras. 2–3) notes that along with leading commentators and international arbitral tribunals, the International Court of Justice has repeatedly confirmed and applied this basic principle including in *Corfu Channel (UK v. Albania)*, [1949] ICJ Rep 4, at 23; *Reparation for Injuries Suffered in the Service of the United Nations (Advisory Opinion)*, [1949] ICJ Rep 174 (*Reparation for Injuries Case*), at 184; and *Military and Paramilitary Activities in and against Nicaragua (Nicaragua v. United States), Merits*, [1986] ICJ Rep 14 (*Nicaragua Case, Merits*), at paras. 283, 292.

[20] ILC Draft Articles, at Art. 1. Note that an internationally wrongful act of a State can consist of one or more acts or omissions, or a combination of both: ILC Commentary, at Art. 1, para. 1.

[21] ILC Draft Articles, at Art. 3.

[22] Ibid. See also the ILC Commentary to Article 3, which provides a succinct overview of the instances in which this principle has been affirmed and upheld by international courts and tribunals, including

Similarly, the consequences of a finding of responsibility (discussed further in this chapter) are also located within international law. Internal law is therefore irrelevant with regard to the obligations of cessation and reparation.[23]

There are two elements to determining whether an internationally wrongful act has occurred: first, whether the act (or omission)[24] is attributable to the State under international law;[25] and second, whether the act or omission constitutes a breach of an international obligation of the State[26] in force at the relevant time. It is these two components of State responsibility that are considered in detail below.

4.2.1. *Requirement of Attribution*

As noted above, a determination of whether or not the State is responsible for a particular act or omission will depend, in the first instance, on whether the relevant acts or omissions can be regarded as acts or omissions of that State, that is, whether they are attributable[27] to the State. International law generally recognizes as attributable only the conduct of the organs of government or of others who have acted under the direction, instigation, or control of those organs and thereby as agents of the State.[28] While determining attribution may initially appear to be a straightforward process, the reality is, in fact, quite different. The primary obstacle lies in the fact that "the State" is, in the present context, an abstraction. Despite their position as full legal entities under international law, "States can only act by and through their agents and representatives."[29] In determining the responsibility of the State, it is therefore

the International Court of Justice in the *Reparation for Injuries Case*, at 180, and *Elettronica Sicula S.p.A (ELSI)*, [1989] ICJ Rep 15. Note also the Vienna Convention on the Law of Treaties: "[a] party may not invoke the provisions of its internal law as justification for its failure to perform a treaty." Vienna Convention on the Law of Treaties, 1155 UNTS 331, done May 23, 1969, entered into force Jan. 27, 1980 (VCLT), at Art. 27.

[23] ILC Draft Articles, at Art. 32 and the accompanying Commentary at paras. 1–3.

[24] International law, as confirmed by ILC Article 2 and accompanying Commentary (at para. 4), is clear on the point that international legal responsibility for breach of an obligation can be engaged through both an act *and* an omission attributable to the State. The traditional authority on this point is the judgment of the International Court of Justice in the *Corfu Channel Case*, where the Court held that Albania knew or should have known about the illegal act of another State. Its failure to act meant that the conduct of that other State was therefore imputable to Albania: *Corfu Channel Case*, at 23.

[25] ILC Draft Articles, at Art. 2(a).

[26] Ibid. at Art. 2(b).

[27] The terms "attributable" and "imputable" are often used interchangeably to refer to "the operation of attaching a given act or omission to a State": ILC Commentary, at Art. 2, para. 12. During its lengthy consideration of this issue, the ILC also used both terms while eventually deciding in favor of "attribution" as it "avoids any suggestion that the legal process of connecting conduct to the State is a fiction, or that the conduct in question is 'really' that of someone else": ibid.

[28] Ibid. at Chapter II, para. 2.

[29] *German Settlers in Poland (Advisory Opinion)*, [1923] PCIJ Rep, Series B, No. 6, at 22, cited in ILC Commentary, at Art. 2, para. 5.

the acts and omissions of individuals that must be examined. When is an individual acting in his or her private capacity and when is she or he acting for or on behalf of the State? This is a central conundrum of the State responsibility issue and one that is addressed in considerable detail by the ILC in Chapter II of its Articles.

Attribution can generally be established without difficulty when the conduct in question is clearly that of an organ of the State. The ILC formulates its principle on this point as follows:

> The conduct of any State organ acting in that capacity shall be considered an act of that State under international law, whether the organ exercises legislative, executive, judicial or other functions, whatever position it holds in the organisation of the State, and whatever its character as an organ of the central government or of a territorial unit of the State.[30]

That the conduct of any organ of the State will be regarded as an act of that State is a well-established rule of international law and one affirmed by the International Court of Justice (ICJ) to be "of a customary character."[31] Article 4 has been framed very broadly and clearly indicates that any entity or authority exercising public powers in the State is considered an organ of that State for the purposes of attributing responsibility.[32] In addition, Article 4 supports the contention that no distinction is to be made between the acts of "superior" and "subordinate" officials[33] (provided, of course, that both are acting in their official capacity), a refinement of the general principle of attribution that has been strengthened considerably by recent decisions of international criminal tribunals.[34] Attribution is not compromised even in the

---

[30] ILC Draft Articles, at Art. 4.

[31] *Difference Relating to Immunity from Legal Process of a Special Rapporteur of the Commission on Human Rights (Advisory Opinion)*, [1999] ICJ Rep 87, at para. 62, cited in ILC Commentary, at Art. 4, para. 6.

[32] Note paragraph 2 of ILC Draft Article 4: "[a]n organ includes any person or entity which has that status in accordance with the internal laws of the State." The ILC Commentary notes that the use of the word "includes" denies the State any opportunity of avoiding responsibility for the conduct of a body which is, in reality, an organ of that State by denying it that status under its own law: ILC Commentary, at Art. 4, para. 11.

[33] Ibid. at Art. 4, para. 7.

[34] See, for example, *Prosecutor v. Bemba*, Case ICC-01/05–01/08, ICC Pre-Trial Chamber II, June 15, 2009 (command responsibility, preferring the standard enunciated by the ICTY Trial Chamber in *Blaskic*); *Prosecutor v. Brima et al.*, Case SCSL-04–16-T, SCSL Trial Chamber, June 20, 2007; *Prosecutor v. Naletilic and Martinovic*, Case IT-98–24-A, ICTY Appeals Chamber, May 3, 2006 (command responsibility and failure to prevent or punish); *Prosecutor v. Hadzihasanovic*, Case IT-01–47-T, ICTY Trial Chamber, Mar. 15, 2006 (command responsibility and failure to punish); *Prosecutor v. Halilovic*, Case IT-01–48-T, ICTY Trial Chamber, Nov. 16, 2005 (command responsibility as imposing criminal liability for a superior's "failure to act when under a duty to do so," at para. 38); *Prosecutor v. Kajelijeli*, Case ICTR-98–44A-A, ICTR Appeals Chamber, May 23, 2005 (command responsibility and the superior-subordinate relationship); *Prosecutor v. Ntagerura et al.*, Case ICTR-99–46-T, ICTR Trial Chamber, Feb. 25, 2004; *Prosecutor v. Baglishema*, Case ICTR-95–1A-A, ICTR Appeals Chamber, July 3, 2002 (command responsibility and the superior-

case of gross incompetence on the part of the offending State organ and even if the conduct has been disowned by other organs of the State.[35]

Some State organs almost invariably act only in their public capacity. In other words, they do not have a private capacity in the same way that other State entities may. A determination of responsibility involving such a State entity is not likely to be overly complicated. An executive act prohibiting all women from emigrating in search of work or a judicial decision upholding the use of torture in the administration of justice would both be readily identified as an act of the State. The State will, of course, be responsible for its legislative and other omissions as well as its acts. A legal and administrative system that failed to provide trafficked persons with reasonable access to remedies would, for example, directly implicate the State concerned. Subject to a finding that the act or omission itself constituted a breach of an international obligation of that State (such as the prohibition on sex-based discrimination, the right to freedom of movement, the prohibition on torture, or the right of access to remedies), then the international responsibility of the State would be directly engaged in relation to both these situations.

In other cases, it will not be readily apparent whether a person who is part of a State organ acts within the capacity of that organ and thereby on behalf of the State. In making such a determination, the ILC Commentary clearly indicates that the central question will be whether the individual concerned is acting in an apparently official capacity or under color of authority.[36] Importantly, "it is irrelevant for this purpose that the person concerned may have had ulterior or improper motives or may be abusing public power."[37] That the act in question was unauthorized, or *ultra vires*, is also irrelevant in determining whether or not it is to be characterized as an act of the State.[38] These are both important principles

subordinate relationship); *Prosecutor v. Krnojelac*, Case IT-97–25-T, ICTY Trial Chamber, Mar. 15, 2002 (superior authority); *Prosecutor v. Kvocka et al.*, Case IT-98–30/1, ICTY Trial Chamber, Nov. 2, 2001 (superior authority); *Prosecutor v. Kordic and Cerkez*, Case IT-95–14–2, ICTY Trial Chamber, Feb. 21, 2001 (command responsibility); *Prosecutor v. Delalic et al.*, Case IT-96–21-A, ICTY Appeals Chamber, Feb. 20, 2001 (command responsibility); *Prosecutor v. Blaskic*, Case IT-95–14-T, ICTY Trial Chamber, Mar. 3, 2000 (command responsibility); *Prosecutor v. Aleksovski*, Case IT-95–14/1-T, ICTY Trial Chamber, June 25, 1999 (authority – *de jure* or *de facto* – of the defendant); *Prosecutor v. Kayishema and Ruzindana*, Case ICTR-95–1-T, ICTR Trial Chamber, May 21, 1999 (command responsibility and *mens rea*); *Prosecutor v. Delalic et al.*, Case IT-96–21-T, ICTY Trial Chamber, Nov. 16, 1998 (command responsibility); *Prosecutor v. Erdemovic*, Case IT-96–22-T, ICTY Trial Chamber, May 31, 1996. See also J. Dungel, "Command Responsibility in International Criminal Tribunals," paper presented at the National Consultative Summit on Extrajudicial Killings and Enforced Disappearances: Searching for Solutions, July 16–17, 2007, available at http://sc.judiciary. gov.ph/publications/summit/Summit%20Papers/Dungel%20-%20Command%20Responsibility%20 in%20ICT.pdf (accessed Nov. 29, 2009).

[35]   ILC Commentary, at Art. 7, para. 2.

[36]   Ibid. at Art. 4, para. 13.

[37]   Ibid.

[38]   Ibid. See also ILC Draft Articles, at Art. 7. Note that this Article provision applies both to organs of the State and to "a person or entity empowered to exercise elements of the governmental authority": ibid.

in the present context. States will often defend themselves against allegations of public sector involvement in trafficking by pointing out that such involvement is contrary to national law and policy. Under the rules of attribution, a national prohibition against trafficking is insufficient for the State to avoid its international legal responsibility. Two cases mentioned in the ILC's Commentary serve to confirm the rule that "conduct carried out by persons cloaked by governmental authority"[39] is attributable to the State. In the *Caire* case, a French national was killed by two Mexican officials who had tried to rob him. The Commission held:

> That the two officers, even if they are deemed to have acted outside their competence … and even if their superiors countermanded an order, have involved the responsibility of the State, since they acted under the cover of their status as officers and used means placed at their disposal on account of that status.[40]

In the *Velásquez Rodríguez Case*, the Inter-American Court of Human Rights stated that a determination as to whether a breach of the American Convention on Human Rights had occurred did not depend on whether or not provisions of internal law had been contravened or authority exceeded:

> Under international law, a State is responsible for the acts of its agents undertaken in their official capacity and for their omissions, even when those agents act outside the sphere of their authority or violate internal law.[41]

The task then becomes one of distinguishing, not between authorized and unauthorized conduct, but between "official" conduct and "private" conduct. Some situations will be relatively straightforward. In many parts of the world, border authorities are complicit in trafficking, turning a blind eye to suspicious movements in return for money or other rewards. Such practices are invariably contrary to internal law, and the individuals involved are thereby exceeding their lawful authority. However, it is their official position that enables the conduct. The attribution of this conduct to the State and a consequential finding of responsibility against that State should therefore not be particularly difficult.

Complications arise when the acts or omissions in question appear to be those of private individuals who also happen to be agents of the State. What is the situation, for example, in respect of an individual law enforcement official who maintains a commercial interest in a brothel that uses the services of trafficked persons? The ILC notes that attribution will not extend to conduct that is "so removed from the

---

[39] *Petrolane Inc. v. Islamic Republic of Iran,* (1991) 27 Iran-USCTR 92 (Iran-US Claims Tribunal), cited in ILC Commentary, at Art. 7, para. 7.

[40] *Caire (France v. Mexico),* (1929) 5 UNRIAA 516 (French-Mexican Claims Commission), at 531, cited in ILC Commentary, at Art. 7, para. 5.

[41] *Velásquez Rodríguez v. Honduras,* Inter-Am Ct. H.R. (ser. C) No. 4, July 29, 1988 (*Velásquez Rodríguez*), at para. 170, cited in ILC Commentary, at Art. 7, para. 6.

scope of … official functions that it should be assimilated to that of private individuals, not attributable to the state.'[42] It suggests, somewhat inconclusively, that:

> The problem of drawing the line between unauthorized but still "official" conduct, on the one hand, and "private" conduct on the other, may be avoided if the conduct complained of is systematic or recurrent, such that the State knew or should have known of it and should have taken steps to prevent it.[43]

In all cases, a distinction will need to be made between unauthorized conduct that is nevertheless undertaken with apparent authority and unauthorized conduct that is purely private. Apparent authority could be inferred in the above example by showing that it is the official position of a particular individual that gives him or her the knowledge and protection to operate and maintain an unlawful business of this kind. In other words, the conduct was only possible because of the individual's official position and use of apparent authority. While such a finding would appear to point to a presumption in favor of such conduct being attributable to the State, more evidence may be required to satisfy the standard set by the ILC – for example, the use of official vehicles to transport trafficked persons, the use of police intelligence to avoid raids, or the use of law enforcement colleagues to provide "protection."[44]

Increasingly, individuals and entities that are not "organs" of the State are nevertheless empowered to exercise elements of governmental authority. Private security firms, for example, are often contracted by States to exercise public powers of detention and even border control. Commercial carriers are routinely empowered to exercise certain immigration control functions. The "privatization" of governmental functions should not allow States to avoid responsibility. The ILC Draft Articles are clear on the point that the conduct of persons or entities so empowered will be attributable to the State provided that the person or entity is acting in that capacity in the particular instance.[45] If the actions of a private entity attributable to the State breaches international obligations, then the State's international responsibility will be engaged. The denial, by a commercial carrier, of a trafficked person's right to seek asylum provides one example. The government-authorized or government-tolerated detention of trafficked persons in a private shelter provides another.

---

[42] ILC Commentary, at Art. 7, para. 7.

[43] Ibid. at Art. 7, para. 8.

[44] On this point, see the discussion in Chapter 3.1. Note also Lawson's observation that "the police official does not perform an act of his State if, when off duty and out of personal motives, he kills his wife and her lover; nor would his conduct be attributed to the State if he used the gun supplied to him by the State for the performance of his official duties": R. Lawson, "Out of Control: State Responsibility and Human Rights: Will the ILC's Definition of the 'Act of State' Meet the Challenges of the 21st Century?" in M. Castermans-Holleman, R. van Hoof, and J. Smith eds., *The Role of the Nation-State in the 21st Century: Human Rights, International Organisations and Foreign Policy: Essays in Honour of Peter Baehr* 91 (1998) (Lawson, "Out of Control: State Responsibility and Human Rights"), at 97.

[45] ILC Draft Articles, at Art. 5.

Is it possible for conduct outside the official structure of the State by individuals or groups not specifically empowered to exercise State functions to nevertheless be attributable to that State? The ILC Draft Articles envisage this possibility if the person or group of persons "is in fact acting on the instructions of, or under the direction and control of, that State in carrying out the conduct."[46] A typical example would involve private persons being recruited by the State to perform auxiliary law enforcement or military activities outside the formal State structure.[47] This head of responsibility could be relevant in times of conflict when individuals who are not *de jure* officials engage in trafficking, sexual slavery, and other forms of unlawful exploitation under circumstances that suggest they may, in fact, be acting under the *instructions, direction,* or *control* of their State. Only one of these three elements is required and must relate to the conduct in question.[48] Judicial consideration of this issue has focused particularly on the level of direction or control required to establish attribution. In considering whether the violative conduct of the *contras* in Nicaragua was attributable to the United States, the ICJ held that the dependency of the *contras* on the U.S. was insufficient. It was necessary to prove that the U.S., in fact, exercised "effective control" to the point that it was apparent the *contras* were acting on its behalf.[49] The Appeals Chamber of the International Criminal Tribunal for the Former Yugoslavia (ICTY) (in considering the question of attribution in the context of individual criminal responsibility rather than State responsibility) rejected the "effective control" test on the basis that it was contrary to the very logic of State responsibility and inconsistent with State and judicial practice. It concluded that the degree of control required for attribution varied according to the factual circumstances, and that "overall control" was the preferred test.[50] The ICJ subsequently rejected the ICTY standard, affirming, in its *Bosnian Genocide* judgment, the stricter "complete" and "effective" control tests first articulated in *Nicaragua.*[51] In rejecting the ICTY test of overall control, the ICJ expressed concern that such a test would have the effect of "broadening state responsibility well beyond the principles governing the law of state responsibility."[52]

---

[46] Ibid. at Art. 8.

[47] Ibid.

[48] ILC Commentary, at Art. 8, para. 7.

[49] *Nicaragua Case, Merits,* at 62, 64–65, cited in ILC Commentary, at Art. 8, para. 4.

[50] *Prosecutor v. Tadic,* Case IT-94–1-A, ICTY Appeals Chamber, July 15, 1999, at para. 117, cited in ILC Commentary, at Art. 8, para. 5. Note that this lower threshold of control required for attribution appeared to be accepted by the European Court of Human Rights, which subsequently decided that the question was whether the entity in question was operating "under the effective authority or at least under the decisive influence" of the State: *Ilaşcu and Others v. Moldova and Russia,* (2005) 40 EHRR 46 (ECHR, July 8, 2004), at para. 392.

[51] *Application of the Convention on the Prevention and Punishment of the Crime of Genocide (Bosnia and Herzegovina v. Serbia and Montenegro),* (2007) ICJ Gen. List No. 91, decided Feb. 26, 2007 (*Bosnian Genocide Case*). Generally on the judgment as it related to the issue of State responsibility, see M. Milanovic, "State Responsibility for Genocide: A Follow-Up," (2007) 18 *European Journal of International Law* 669 (Milanovic, "State Responsibility for Genocide: A Follow-Up").

[52] *Bosnian Genocide Case,* at para. 404. Note the ICJ rejected the application of the ICTY's test on several other grounds. See further Milanovic, "State Responsibility for Genocide: A Follow-Up."

The *Bosnian Genocide* judgment was widely criticized as setting too high a threshold for attribution of responsibility. Critics focused on the unreasonableness of the result[53] as well as apparent deficiencies in the Court's interpretation and application of the relevant law, including of the ICTY judgment.[54] Others affirmed the judgment as a reasonable application of the current customary norm.[55] Certainly, in relation to both practice and doctrine, this aspect of State responsibility appears to be in flux, as those responsible for the interpretation and application of international law are confronted with new situations and new challenges that strain traditional doctrines of attribution. There is some evidence that, at least in relation to State practice, the threshold is being lowered as States find the traditional "effective control" or even "overall control" tests "insufficient to address the threats posed by global criminals and the states that harbor them."[56] In potentially uncomfortable partnership are human rights advocates arguing for the recognition of an exceptional (lower) test of control under international human rights law in relation to potentially problematic non-State entities such as private military contractors.[57]

The ILC Draft Articles envisage several additional bases for attribution: when the conduct is of an insurrectional or other movement that becomes the new government of a State or succeeds in establishing a new State;[58] when elements of governmental authority are exercised in the absence of such authority and in circumstances such as to call for the exercise of those elements of authority;[59] and when the State acknowledges and adopts otherwise nonattributable conduct as the State's own.[60] These additional bases of attribution serve to confirm both the nature and the limits of the general rules. In relation to the conduct of private persons or entities, attribution relies on the existence of a special circumstance linking apparently private behavior to the State itself. In other words, in order to establish attribution for the conduct of non-State entities, it is necessary to show the existence of a link between that entity and the State. The link establishing attribution can manifest itself in the public nature of the act. It can also rely upon a range of other factors including control, authorization, approval,

---

[53] See, for example, Gibney ("if extraterritorial state responsibility could not be established in this particular case, it is difficult to imagine under what circumstances it could ever be established"): M. Gibney, "Genocide and State Responsibility," (2007) 7 *Human Rights Law Review* 760, at 771, cited in McCorquodale, "Impact on State Responsibility," at 244.

[54] See A. Cassese, "The *Nicaragua* and *Tadic* Tests Revisited in Light of the ICJ Judgment on Genocide in Bosnia," (2007) 18 *European Journal of International Law* 649.

[55] Milanovic, "State Responsibility for Genocide: A Follow-Up."

[56] A.-M. Slaughter and W. Burke-White, "An International Constitutional Moment," (2002) 43 *Harvard International Law Journal* 1, at 20, cited in D. Jinks, "State Responsibility for the Acts of Private Armed Groups," (2003) 4 *Chicago Journal of International Law* 83, at 90.

[57] See, for example, McCorquodale, "Impact on State Responsibility," esp. at 245–246. McCorquodale cites the ICJ judgment in *Armed Activities in the Territory of the Congo (Democratic Republic of Congo v. Uganda)*, (2005) ICJ Gen. List 116, decided Dec. 19, 2005, as indicative of a different and lower threshold of control in relation to international human rights law: ibid.

[58] ILC Draft Articles, at Art. 10.

[59] Ibid. at Art. 9

[60] Ibid. at Art. 11.

awareness, or support. Outside of these situations, and absent specific undertakings or guarantees, the State will not be responsible for the conduct of private persons or entities. The identified situations are therefore not exceptions but additional refinements of the long-standing rule of international law attributing responsibility to the State for the conduct of its organs and representatives. In the words of Vattel:

> if the nation, or its ruler, approve and ratify the act of the citizen, it takes upon itself the act, and may then be regarded by the injured party as the real author of the affront of which the citizen was perhaps only the instrument.[61]

While these general rules set out a framework for attributing conduct, they do not provide a full response to the question of whether and, if so, under what circumstances the State can be held responsible when it is not the immediate agent of harm. This issue is dealt with more fully and with specific reference to the trafficking phenomenon in Chapter 4.3.

4.2.2. *Requirement of a Breach of Obligation*

As noted above, the second mandatory condition for an internationally wrongful act of a State is that the conduct attributable to the State constitutes a breach of an international obligation of that State. The ILC has emphasized the importance of distinguishing between the question of attribution and the characterization of conduct as internationally wrongful: "To show that conduct is attributable to the State says nothing, as such, about the legality or otherwise of that conduct."[62] Conduct attributable to a State that does not constitute a breach of an international obligation of that State will not be characterized as an internationally wrongful act and will not thereby engage its responsibility. In the same way, a breach of an international obligation owed by that State that cannot be attributed to the State will not be considered an act of that State and will therefore also fail to engage that State's responsibility under international law.

It is therefore only when both of these two elements – conduct attributable to the State and conduct constituting a breach of that State's obligation – have been proven that the standard for establishing international legal responsibility of the State will have been satisfied. The only possible way for a State to escape a finding of responsibility when these two elements are present with respect to a specific situation is for it to successfully claim the existence of "special circumstances precluding wrongfulness."[63] Such a claim may operate to preclude responsibility

---

[61] E. de Vattel, *The Law of Nations: Book III* (reprinted 1974), at 136, cited in G. Townsend, "State Responsibility for Acts of De-Facto Agents," (1997) 14 *Arizona Journal of International and Comparative Law* 635, at 636.

[62] ILC Commentary, at Part One, Chapter II, para. 4.

[63] The law of State responsibility recognizes that certain circumstances will operate to preclude an otherwise liable State from responsibility for its unlawful acts or omissions. The ILC Draft Articles

for the period during which the special circumstance exists, while not affect-ing the underlying obligation.[64] A relevant example could involve a State citing the special circumstance of necessity to justify otherwise unlawful restrictions on the freedom of movement of non-nationals or even on emigration restrictions directed against its own nationals.[65] In the context of international human rights law, these "special circumstances precluding wrongfulness" under the secondary rules of State responsibility are paralleled at the primary level by provisions in a number of international human rights treaties permitting derogation from certain rights under strict circumstances of public emergency threatening the life of the nation.[66]

How should one determine whether a particular act or omission constitutes a breach of an international obligation of the State concerned? It is at this point that reference must be made to the underlying primary rule as "there is no such thing as a breach of an international obligation in the abstract."[67] Under ILC Draft Article 12, "there is a breach of an international obligation by a State when an act of that State is not in conformity with what is required of it by that obligation, regardless of its ori-gin or character."[68] Accordingly, absent special considerations relating, for example, to circumstances precluding wrongfulness, the question of whether and when there has been a breach of an obligation will depend on "the precise terms of the obliga-tion, its interpretation and application, taking into account its object and purpose and the facts of the case."[69] In other words, the exact nature of the obligations (and

identify six such circumstances as being presently recognized under general international law: con-sent (Article 20), self-defense (Article 21), countermeasures (Article 22), *force majeure* (Article 23), distress (Article 24), and necessity (Article 25).

[64] Circumstances precluding wrongfulness do not annul or otherwise terminate the obligation in ques-tion. Rather, they provide a justification for nonperformance of an obligation, a justification that continues for as long as the applicable circumstance continues: ILC Commentary, at Part One, Chapter V, paras. 2–3. The duty to comply with the obligation in question will revive once the cir-cumstance precluding wrongfulness ceases to exist. Importantly, none of these circumstances will operate to preclude the wrongfulness of a State with respect to a peremptory norm of international law: ILC Draft Articles, at Art. 26. The work of the ILC on this particular aspect of State responsi-bility has attracted some controversy and criticism. See, for example, P. Allott, "State Responsibility and the Unmaking of International Law," (1988) 29 *Harvard International Law Journal* 1 (Allott, "State Responsibility and the Unmaking of International Law").

[65] The special circumstance precluding wrongfulness of necessity is recognized in Article 25 of the ILC Draft Articles.

[66] International Covenant on Civil and Political Rights, 999 UNTS 171, done Dec. 16, 1966, entered into force Mar. 3, 1976 (ICCPR), at Art. 4; Convention for the Protection of Human Rights and Fundamental Freedoms, 213 UNTS 222, done Nov. 4, 1950, entered into force Sept. 3, 1953 (European Human Rights Convention), at Art. 15; American Convention on Human Rights, 1144 UNTS 123, done Nov. 22, 1969, entered into force July 18, 1978 (American Convention on Human Rights), at Art. 27. See also UN Human Rights Committee, "General Comment No. 29: States of Emergency," UN Doc. CCPR/C/21/Rev.1/Add.11, Aug. 31, 2001.

[67] ILC Commentary, at Part One, Chapter III, para. 2.

[68] ILC Draft Articles, at Art. 12.

[69] ILC Commentary, at Art. 12, para. 1.

therefore the nature of any possible breach) can only be ascertained with reference to the primary rule, which could reside in a treaty, in customary international law, or in any other accepted source of international legal obligation – or indeed, in a combination of sources.

As the ILC has indicated, the possible range of conduct proscribed (or prescribed) by an international obligation is extremely wide. Transnational criminal law, for example, may require the State to pass new legislation or to modify or repeal existing legislation. It may require the State to cooperate with another State in specified areas or to provide specified services. International human rights law may require the State to refrain from certain actions and from intruding into certain spheres. Many human rights treaties go beyond a negative obligation of noninterference in requiring States Parties to take positive steps – to "respect and ensure";[70] toward "realization";[71] to "secure";[72] to "prohibit and bring to an end";[73] and to "pursue, by all appropriate means."[74] The general formulation requires States Parties to secure rights for everyone within their own territory or subject to their jurisdiction.[75] Additionally, States have repeatedly been held responsible, under the major international and regional human rights treaties, for acts and omissions that produce effects outside their territory.[76] As explored further in this chapter, these and other provisions may operate to impose on States Parties certain obligations with respect to the conduct of non-State actors, even in cases where the conduct of the non-State actor is not attributable to the State. In relation to these cases – and indeed every other case – "it is by comparing the conduct in fact engaged in by the State with the conduct legally prescribed by the international obligation that one can determine whether or not there is a breach of that obligation."[77]

It is well settled that an act of a State does not constitute a breach of an international obligation unless the State is bound by the obligation at the time the act in question occurs.[78] It follows that conduct that amounted to a breach at the time of

---

[70] ICCPR, at Art. 2; American Convention on Human Rights, at Art. 1(1).

[71] ICCPR, at Art. 1(3); American Convention on Human Rights, at Art. 26; Convention on the Elimination of All Forms of Discrimination against Women, 1249 UNTS 13, done Dec. 13, 1979, entered into force Sept. 3, 1981 (CEDAW), at Art. 2(a).

[72] European Human Rights Convention, at Art. 1.

[73] International Convention on the Elimination of All Forms of Racial Discrimination, 660 UNTS 195, done Dec. 21, 1965, entered into force Jan. 4, 1969 (CERD), at Art. 2(1).

[74] CEDAW, at Art. 2(f).

[75] See further the discussion on the rights of noncitizens at Chapter 3 of this volume.

[76] For a detailed consideration of this issue from the differing perspectives of the major international and regional human rights treaties, see F. Coomans and M.T. Kamminga eds., *Extraterritorial Application of Human Rights Treaties* (2004).

[77] ILC Commentary, at Art. 12, para. 2.

[78] ILC Draft Articles, at Art. 13. The ILC Commentary on Article 13 (at para. 1) notes that this provision reflects the general principle of intertemporal law as stated in the *Island of Palmas* case: "A juridical fact must be appreciated in the light of the law contemporary with it, and not of the law in force at the time when a dispute in regard to it arises or falls to be settled" ((1949) 2UNRIAA 829, at

its occurrence but which, had it occurred at some time in the future, would not be considered a breach because of a subsequent change in the applicable law, would also engage the responsibility of the relevant State. The principle of no retrospective assumption of responsibility is particularly important in relation to a "new" area of international legal regulation such as trafficking. The obligation to criminalize trafficking, for example, explored in detail in Chapter 7, is relatively recent. A State would not be held responsible for failing to criminalize trafficking unless and until that obligation came into existence for that State (through, for example, ratification by that State of the Trafficking Protocol[79] and its subsequent entry into force). However, if the prohibition on trafficking were considered to be part of the general peremptory norm prohibiting slavery and the slave trade,[80] then it could be argued that all States have been obliged to eliminate trafficking for as long as this interpretation of the prohibition on slavery has existed. These examples serve to underlie the importance of establishing, with as much precision as possible, the substantive content of the primary rule.

In terms of identifying when a wrongful act begins or ends, the rules are also clear. A breach by way of an act that is noncontinuing in nature is deemed to have taken place at the time the relevant act takes place, irrespective of whether and for how long the effects of that act are felt.[81] A single act of torture, even if it has ongoing negative effects for the victim, would fall into this category of noncontinuing breach. In contrast, a breach by way of an act that has a continuing character extends for as long as the nonconforming act continues.[82] For example, the right to freedom of movement and the right to leave one's country as well as the prohibition on sex-based discrimination are all potentially violated through the passing of legislation preventing women from leaving the country in search of work.[83] The breach in question begins with the passing of that act and continues for as long as it remains in force. In the case of an obligation to prevent the occurrence of a given event (for

---

845). The Commentary provides a relevant example on this point: In the mid-nineteenth century, a mixed arbitration tribunal was called upon to decide whether British action to seize American vessels engaged in the slave trade and to free slaves belonging to American nationals was unlawful. Certain of these acts were held to have taken place at a time when the slave trade was considered lawful. Accordingly, the British authorities were held to have breached the international legal obligation to protect and respect the property of foreign nationals. It was only the later incidents that were held to have occurred at a time when the slave trade had been "prohibited by all civilised nations." The responsibility of Great Britain was therefore not engaged by the later incidents. ILC Commentary, at Art. 13, para. 2.

[79] Protocol to Prevent, Suppress and Punish Trafficking in Persons, Especially Women and Children, supplementing the United Nations Convention against Transnational Organized Crime, done Nov. 15, 2000, GA Res. 55/25, Annex II, UN GAOR, 55th Sess., Supp. No. 49, at 53, UN Doc. A/45/49 (Vol. I) (2001), entered into force Dec. 25, 2003 (Trafficking Protocol).

[80] See further, Chapter 3.3.

[81] ILC Draft Articles, at Art. 14(1).

[82] Ibid. at Art. 14(2).

[83] See further, Chapter 5.2.3.

example, the obligation on States to prevent violence against trafficked women), the State is generally in breach for however long it remains not in conformity with that obligation.[84]

Many of the core international obligations relevant to trafficking, such as the prohibition on discrimination and obligations of prevention, are composite in nature and likely to be breached by a composite act, involving "some aggregate of conduct and not individual acts as such."[85] Under these circumstances, the actual breach will occur at the time when the particular act or omission occurs that, when taken together with other acts or omissions, is sufficient to constitute the wrongful act.[86] In such cases, the rules of State responsibility serve to identify the "breach" as having commenced from the first of the acts or omissions in the series of acts constituting the wrongful conduct.[87] In the trafficking context, these rules would apply if "trafficking" was recognized as internationally wrongful, and the corresponding "prohibition against trafficking" thereby recognized as a separate source of international legal obligation for States. While the single acts and omissions making up the aggregate wrong of trafficking (for example, failure to protect victims, failure to investigate and prosecute perpetrators, failure to provide access to remedies) would be individually wrongful of themselves in accordance with other obligations, the aggregate wrong of trafficking would be separately identifiable and actionable. For the purposes of State responsibility, the breach occurs at the "threshold" point at which the contents of the obligation (the prohibition on trafficking) are satisfied with reference to the conduct of the State. Once this threshold is crossed, the time of commission extends, in the words of the ILC: "over the whole period during which any of the acts were committed."[88]

Unlike traditional doctrines, the modern laws of State responsibility do not identify damage as an essential aspect of an internationally wrongful act, giving rise to State responsibility. In other words, it is the violation of the obligation and not the resulting damage that constitutes the inherent legal injury and therefore entails responsibility.[89] In a similar vein, the question of "fault," generally understood as an intention to harm, will be irrelevant to a determination of responsibility for an internationally wrongful act, absent a specific requirement of such an element in the primary obligation.[90] As explored further below, this is the case even with respect

---

[84] ILC Draft Articles, at Art. 14(3).
[85] ILC Commentary, at Art. 15, para. 2.
[86] ILC Draft Articles, at Art. 15(1).
[87] Ibid. at Art. 15(2)
[88] ILC Commentary, at Art. 15, para. 3.
[89] Ibid. at Art. 2, para. 9. See further, T. Meron, *The Humanization of International Law* (2006), at 252–253.
[90] ILC Commentary, at Art. 2, para. 10. For an analysis of the ILC's position on "fault," see A. Gattini, "Smoking/No Smoking: Some Remarks on the Current Place of Fault in the ILC Draft Articles on State Responsibility," (1999) 10 *European Journal of International Law* 397. See also J. Crawford, "Revising the Draft Articles on State Responsibility," (1999) 10 *European Journal of International Law* 438 (Crawford, "Revising the Draft Articles on State Responsibility"), esp. at 4.

to the question of State responsibility for private acts, where the absence of fault on the part of State organs or officials is not, of itself, sufficient to avoid a finding of responsibility.

4.3. STATE RESPONSIBILITY FOR TRAFFICKING-RELATED BREACH OF OBLIGATIONS ORIGINATING IN THE CONDUCT OF PRIVATE PERSONS OR ENTITIES

The previous section outlined the basic principles of attribution applicable to State responsibility as these are generally recognized in international law and as they have been codified by the ILC. In the context of trafficking, it was shown that acts of trafficking or acts related to trafficking committed by a State that are in breach of its international legal obligations entail the international responsibility of that State. The notion of "act of State" will be extended, in certain situations, to cover acts committed by non-State entities that are under the control of the State or that are adopted or otherwise made its own by the State. However, "[a]s a general rule the conduct of private persons or entities is not attributable to the State under international law."[91] In other words, absent the existence of carefully defined special circumstances outlined above, private action will be considered as such and will not implicate the responsibility of the State.

4.3.1. *Implications of the General Rule of Nonattribution of Private Conduct*

In the majority of trafficking situations, direct State involvement is either not present or unable to be conclusively established. Two typical examples that may apply to any of a number of countries serve to illustrate this point. The trafficking of persons between Country A and Country B is controlled and conducted by individual entrepreneurs and loosely organized criminal groups. While facilitated by systemic, low-level public sector corruption, cases of direct official involvement in trafficking are relatively rare in either country, and both have taken at least some preliminary steps to outlaw trafficking and to cooperate in its eradication. The trafficking of women from Country X and Country Y is firmly in the hands of highly organized and sophisticated international criminals. The Governments of Country X and Country Y do not control these criminal syndicates. They have not condoned or otherwise taken steps to adopt the conduct of these groups as their own. As in the previous example, individual officials in both States have undoubtedly facilitated this trade through their inaction, inertia, and occasional active involvement. However, the

---

[91] ILC Commentary, at Art. 8, para. 1. See also the Commentary to Article 11, at para. 2: "The general principle, drawn from state practice and international judicial decisions, is that the conduct of a person or group of persons not acting on behalf of the State is not considered as an act of the State under international law. This conclusion holds irrespective of the circumstances in which the private person acts and of the interests affected by the person's conduct."

harm of trafficking, in terms of both the process and the end result, is very much a direct consequence of actions taken by private entities.

How do these realities square with the general principle of nonattribution for acts of private persons? Can countries of origin, transit, and destination for trafficked persons absolve themselves of any responsibility to these individuals – and to the international community as a whole – on the basis that the conduct complained of is not directly attributable to them? If this were indeed the case, international rules on State responsibility would appear to offer very little scope for securing the accountability of States for trafficking taking place within their territories or involving their nationals. This would, in fact, render almost totally ineffective the complex web of international norms that have evolved to protect trafficked and other vulnerable persons from exploitation and abuse. In other words, by holding the State responsible only for the harm that that State directly causes by its actions (or by the actions of another that it explicitly adopts), the international legal order would be failing in its greater purpose of securing accountability and justice. Most importantly, it would also be failing to recognize the actual and potential capacity of States to structure their internal order (including through regulation and control of private conduct) in a way that can either facilitate or obstruct trafficking and related forms of exploitation.

Such a result would appear to be contrary to the object and purpose of much international law, not least international human rights law and transnational criminal law, the two major areas of focus for the present study. More generally, it would serve to remove from the sphere of international law an ever-increasing range of conduct that has a direct impact on the enjoyment by individuals of their rights and freedoms. The issue of State responsibility for the acts of private persons has become an immensely important one in recent years, as the near-exclusive power of the State is eroded in favor of private individuals and entities including business corporations, criminal organizations, rebel groups, and terrorists. These entities clearly have the capacity to engage in acts that compromise not just human rights but also laws relating to organized crime, the conduct of warfare, maintenance of international peace and security, trade, and environmental protection. It is therefore important to consider in more detail the circumstances under which States will be held responsible for such acts and their consequences.

Importantly, this is not a separate discussion invoking new or previously unexplored rules. Rather, it is a more careful consideration of the two conditions of responsibility explored in the previous section and summarized above: existence of a breach of obligation and attribution of that breach to the State.

4.3.2. *Moving Beyond the General Rule: State Responsibility to Prevent, Protect, and Respond*

While not departing from the general principle of nonattribution of private conduct, the ILC has acknowledged that the rules governing attribution have a cumulative effect, "such that a State may be responsible for the effects of the conduct of private parties, if it failed to take necessary measures to prevent those effects."[92] This concession reflects a discernible movement toward a more nuanced conception of State responsibility. Particularly in the area of human rights, there is growing acceptance that the State will be responsible, not only if it abrogates human rights in the traditional sense (sometimes referred to as *direct responsibility* arising out of *vertical application* of legal obligations), but also if it fails to adequately protect those within its jurisdiction from the actions of others that result in a violation of rights (sometimes referred to as *indirect responsibility* arising out of *horizontal application* of legal obligations).[93] In other words, the State can incur international responsibility for a private act in the case of an action or omission of the State's own organs "where [these organs] are guilty of not having done everything within their power to prevent the injurious act of the private individual or to punish it suitably if it has occurred despite everything."[94] Therefore, in the present context, the fact that the State was not the cause of the initial harm (trafficking) may not, of itself, be sufficient to absolve the State from responsibility for that harm and the consequences flowing from it.

This expanded view of State responsibility is not in conflict with the ILC position because of the latter's deference to the primary rules. In other words, the secondary rules of State responsibility only envisage the *possibility* of State responsibility for private harm. Whether or not such responsibility exists in a particular case will invariably be a matter for the applicable primary rules. An example is provided by the *Bosnian Genocide Case*. The actual commission of genocide was ultimately not attributable to Serbia under the standard of attribution adopted by the ICJ. However, the Court found that Serbia was nevertheless responsible for breaching its specific

---

[92] ILC Commentary, at Part One, Chapter II, para. 4. An example drawn from the *Tehran Hostages Case* is used to illustrate this point: The seizing of the American embassy in Tehran by private individuals did not immediately engage the international legal responsibility of the State of Iran. It was only after the Government failed to assert control over the situation that the conduct of the private individuals became attributable to the State itself. It was therefore Iran's failure "to take appropriate steps" to protect the Embassy that "by itself, constituted a clear and serious violation": *United States Diplomatic and Consular Staff in Tehran (United States v. Iran)*, [1980] ICJ Rep 3 *(Tehran Hostages Case)*, at para. 67. The Court noted that the Iranian authorities were aware of their obligations to protect consular and diplomatic staff and premises and that they had the means at their disposal but "completely failed to comply": ibid. at para. 68.

[93] The seminal text in relation to indirect/horizontal application of international human rights law remains A. Clapham, *Human Rights in the Private Sphere* (1996). For a more recent exploration of these same themes, including a considered analysis of the major objections to an expansion of international human rights law to include non-State actors, see A. Clapham, *Human Rights Obligations of Non-State Actors* (2006).

[94] Lawson, "Out of Control: State Responsibility and Human Rights," at 96. This position echoes the one taken by Jiménez de Arechaga, writing in 1978: "The basis of State responsibility for acts of private individuals is not complicity with the perpetrator but solely failure of the State to perform its international duty of preventing the unlawful act or, failing that, to arrest the offender and bring him to justice." E. Jiménez de Arechaga, "International Responsibility," in M. Sorensen ed., *Manual of Public International Law* 531 (1976) (Jiménez de Arechaga, "International Responsibility"), at 560.

treaty obligation to *prevent* genocide.[95] International human rights law provides many similar examples of "positive obligations" whereby the State is required to do more than merely abstain from committing violations. These are commonly identified as obligations to *protect*, to *respect*, to *fulfill*, and, more recently, to *promote*.[96] This three- or four-level typology of a State's obligations under international human rights law is now widely accepted,[97] although it is important to acknowledge that its application will differ depending on the nature and substantive content of the particular right or obligation under consideration. Generally, however, failure on the part of the State to protect (including from private interference), respect, or fulfill its human rights obligations – owed to every person within its jurisdiction – is something that is directly attributable to the State and therefore sufficient to trigger its international legal responsibility. In this connection, it is relevant to note that many of the most important human rights, including the right to life, the prohibition on torture and cruel and inhuman treatment, the prohibition on discrimination, the right to education, and the right to privacy, can only be properly implemented by imposing duties on private individuals.

Regional human rights courts in particular have been instrumental in confirming that a State may be held responsible *for its own acts* if it has encouraged individuals to engage in acts contrary to human rights;[98] if it has failed to "secure" specified rights and freedoms in its domestic law;[99] or if it has failed to take "reasonable and

---

[95]   *Bosnian Genocide Case*. See also A. Gattini, "Breach of the Obligation to Prevent and Reparation Thereof in the ICJ's Genocide Judgment," (2007) 19 *European Journal of International Law* 695.

[96]   See, for example, ICCPR, at Art. 6(1) ("[e]very human being has the inherent right to life. This right shall be *protected* by law"); European Human Rights Convention, at Art. 1 ("[t]he High Contracting Parties shall *secure* to everyone in their jurisdiction the rights and obligations defined in Section I"); American Convention on Human Rights, at Art. 1 ("[t]he States Parties to this Convention undertake to *respect* the rights and freedoms recognized herein and to *ensure* to all persons subject to their jurisdiction the free and full exercise of those rights and freedoms"); African Charter on Human And Peoples Rights, 1520 UNTS 217, done June 27, 1981, entered into force Oct. 21, 1986 (African Charter), at Art. 18(3) ("[t]he State shall *ensure* the elimination of every discrimination against women and also ensure the protection of the rights of the woman and the child"); Convention on the Rights of Persons with Disabilities, UN Doc. A/61/611, done Dec. 13, 2006, entered into force May 3, 2008, at Art 1. ("[t]he purpose of the present Convention is to *promote*, *protect* and *ensure* the full and equal enjoyment of all human rights and fundamental freedoms by all persons with disabilities, and to *promote* respect for their inherent dignity") (all emphases added).

[97]   See A. Eide, "Economic, Social and Cultural Rights as Human Rights," in A. Eide, C. Krause and A. Rosas eds., *Economic, Social, and Cultural Rights: A Textbook* 21 (1995). For an application of the methodology see *Social and Economic Rights Action Center and Center for Economic and Social Rights v. Nigeria*, Case No. ACPHR/COMM/A044/1 (African Commission on Human and Peoples' Rights, May 27, 2002) (*SERAC and CESR v. Nigeria*).

[98]   *Lopez Ostra v. Spain*, (1995) 20 EHRR 277 (ECHR, Dec. 9, 1994).

[99]   *X and Y v. the Netherlands*, (1986) 8 EHRR 235 (ECHR, Mar. 26, 1985) (*X and Y v. the Netherlands*); see also *Costello-Roberts v. United Kingdom*, (1995) 19 EHRR 112 (ECHR, Mar. 25, 1993), regarding the potential responsibility of the State for acts perpetrated in a private school, because the duty on the State to provide an education system could not be delegated. See also *Airey v. Ireland*, (1979) 2 EHRR 305 (ECHR, Oct. 9, 1979), a decision subsequently cited by the Court in *X and Y v. the*

appropriate measures" of protection.[100] Highlights of the relevant case law are provided immediately below.

X and Y v. the Netherlands, a decision of the European Court of Human Rights, is especially instructive in the present context. As a result of a gap in Dutch criminal procedure, a sixteen-year-old mentally disabled rape victim was unable to initiate criminal proceedings. The act of rape itself, which had been committed by a private individual, was not attributable (or attributed) to the Netherlands. However, the Court found that the girl was offered insufficient protection under Dutch law. Two aspects of the ruling are particularly relevant. First, the Court noted that the right in question (the right to private life protected under Article 8 of the European Convention on Human Rights) not only protects the individual against arbitrary interference from the State, but also includes a positive obligation on the State to take measures "designed to secure respect for private life, even in the sphere of the relations of individuals between themselves."[101] Further, the authorities had "a degree of responsibility resulting from the deficiency in the legislation which gave rise to the violation of Article 8."[102] The Court reasoned that the European Human Rights Convention entailed positive as well as negative obligations on the part of the State. The gap in Dutch law was an omission by the State, which was, in essence, a failure of protection, resulting in the violation of an established right.[103]

Does this ruling require domestic law to oblige private individuals to act in accordance with the provisions of human rights treaties to which a particular State is party? If this is indeed the case, then the failure of domestic legislation to require individuals to so act could provide the basis for a claim of responsibility for breach of an international obligation. Some writers have asserted that *X and Y v. the Netherlands* supports the position that "the State is held responsible for a private violation, due to its failure to legislate or take other preventive action."[104] Others argue that this interpretation is too broad, and that case law, particularly of the European Court, indicates that a finding of State responsibility under such circumstances requires the establishment of a direct link between the quality of the law and the treatment of the complainant.[105] Even under a conservative reading of *X and Y v. the Netherlands*, a legal system that prevents a trafficked person from initiating criminal proceedings (for example, because of his or her status as an alien or because of a legislative

---

Netherlands, which held that the right to private life guaranteed under Article 8 of the European Human Rights Convention required the State to ensure *access* to that right.

[100] See *Platform "Ärtze Für das Leben" v. Austria*, (1991) 13 EHRR 204 (ECHR, June 21, 1988).

[101] *X and Y v. the Netherlands*, at para. 23.

[102] Ibid. at para. 40.

[103] Ibid. at paras. 11–12.

[104] Clapham, *Human Rights in the Private Sphere*, at 183. This reasoning was described as "erroneous" by Lawson, who adds: "[i]t should be emphasised that the act of rape itself, which had been committed by a private individual, was not attributed to the Netherlands." Lawson, "Out of Control: State Responsibility and Human Rights," at 106.

[105] Lawson, "Out of Control: State Responsibility and Human Rights," at 107.

requirement of immediate deportation) would likely be found to have given rise to the violation of certain established rights and thereby to invoke the responsibility of the State. On the other hand, the absence of a law prohibiting trafficking would not automatically give rise to a finding of responsibility unless it could be found that this legislative gap was directly connected to the violation of an established right.

Ultimately it is the primary rule, and not secondary rules of State responsibility, that will be decisive in ascertaining the nature and scope of the obligation to secure specified rights and freedoms in domestic law. In the 1981 *Young, James and Webster Case (Closed Shop Case)*, the plaintiffs were dismissed by a private company for failing to join a trade union. In considering whether responsibility for the dismissal could be attributed to the respondent State, the European Court of Human Rights noted that Article 1 of the European Human Rights Convention requires States Parties to "secure to everyone under [its] jurisdiction the rights and freedoms defined in … [the] Convention." It concluded:

> if a violation of one of those rights and freedoms is the result of non-observance of that obligation in the enactment of domestic legislation, the responsibility of that State for the violation is engaged. Although the proximate cause of the events giving rise to this case was [a private agreement between private parties] it was the domestic law in force at the relevant time that made lawful the treatment of which the applicant complained. The responsibility of the respondent State for any resultant breach of the Convention is thus engaged on this basis.[106]

Therefore, while the applicants' dismissal was not, as such, attributable to the State, the legislation that paved the way for that dismissal was indeed attributable, and it was on this basis that the claim for responsibility could be made.

Can a State be held responsible under international law for omissions such as failure to prosecute trafficking or failure to regulate and control entities such as employment agencies that engage in trafficking? From the perspective of the law of State responsibility, there is certainly no obstacle to such a finding, provided the relevant primary rule supports the existence of an obligation to that effect.[107] International tribunals have previously recognized State inaction in the face of certain private conduct (that is, failure to protect) as evidence of complicity and therefore as invoking that State's responsibility.[108] A failure on the part of the State

---

[106] *Young, James and Webster v. United Kingdom*, (1981) 4 EHRR 38 (ECHR, Aug. 13, 1981), at para. 49.

[107] See, for example, *Rantsev v. Cyprus and Russia* in which the European Court of Human Rights held that Article 4 of the European Human Rights Convention required Member States to "put in place adequate measures regulating businesses often used as a cover for human trafficking": *Rantsev v. Cyprus and Russia*, Dec. No. 25965/04 (not yet reported) (ECHR, Jan, 7, 2010) (*Rantsev v. Cyprus and Russia*), at para. 285.

[108] *Zafiro Case (Great Britain v. United States)*, (1925) 6 UNRIAA 160 (concerning liability for injuries inflicted by the civilian crew of a naval ship under circumstances in which State officials had not adopted effective measures to prevent), cited in R.J. Cook, "State Responsibility for Violations of

to prosecute private wrongs has also, on a number of occasions, led to findings of responsibility.[109]

The above analysis has been borne out by a recent European Court of Human Rights decision, its first to engage directly with trafficking-related wrongs as such. In *Rantsev v. Cyprus and Russia*, a Russian national and probable victim of trafficking had died in Cyprus after falling from the apartment of her employer's associate. While her death itself and her likely exploitation as a "cabaret artiste" were not attributed to Cyprus or Russia, both States were held to have violated related human rights obligations, for example, through failure to regulate employment and through inaction in the face of private conduct. These violations included the failure to carry out an effective investigation into the death (including securing the relevant evidence from overseas as well as domestically, and investigating whether there had been any trafficking-related corruption);[110] the maintenance of a regime of artiste visas that did not afford protection against trafficking;[111] and failure to investigate trafficking.[112]

4.3.3. *Identifying Violations Giving Rise to Responsibility: The Due Diligence Standard*

What measure is to be used in judging whether or not a State has taken adequate steps to meet its obligations – for example, to protect established rights from private interference and to respond to such interferences when they have occurred? Once again, this is not a test for the secondary rules of State responsibility. Whether or not a breach has occurred must be determined with reference to the primary rule. As discussed further below, a primary rule requiring States to "respect," "ensure," or "secure" human rights will impose a different standard with regard to protection from private interference than one requiring the State to refrain from certain conduct.

Despite differences in the nature of the primary obligations, the standard most commonly cited in the human rights context is that of "due diligence." Under this standard, a State is obliged to exercise a measure of care in preventing and responding to the acts of private entities that interfere with established rights. Failure to prevent an anticipated abuse or violation by a private individual or entity will therefore invoke the responsibility of the State. In the same vein, legal responsibility will arise when the State fails to remedy abuses or violations of international law – not

---

Women's Human Rights," (1994) 7 *Harvard Human Rights Journal* 125 (Cook, "State Responsibility for Violations of Women's Human Rights"), at 145.

[109] *Janes Case (United States v. Mexico)*, (1926) 4 UNRIAA 82, at 87 (concerning liability for failure to prosecute), cited in Cook, "State Responsibility for Violations of Women's Human Rights," at 145. See also *Velásquez Rodríguez*.

[110] *Rantsev v. Cyprus and Russia*, at paras. 238–242.

[111] Ibid. at para. 293.

[112] Ibid. at para. 309.

only because access to remedies is of itself an established right,[113] but also because the failure of the State to provide remedies in cases involving non-State interference with rights is a breach of the standard of due diligence. In other words, the State could have made the situation better for the victim but failed to do so.

The "due diligence" standard has a long history in the law of State responsibility for injury to aliens[114] and is a central doctrine of a number of areas of international law, including international environmental law.[115] It entered international human rights law through a landmark decision of the Inter-American Court of Human Rights in 1988. In the *Velásquez Rodríguez Case*,[116] the Court found that the disappearance of the complainant had been carried out by State officials. However, more importantly for the present discussion, the Court further held that "even had that fact not been proven," the State would have been liable for its lack of due diligence in preventing or punishing the violative conduct of putatively private actors.[117] The Court confirmed that responsibility is incurred when:

> a violation of … rights … has occurred with the support or the acquiescence of the government, [or when] the State has allowed the act to take place without taking measures to prevent it or to punish those responsible.[118]

As noted above, attribution is not enough: There must also be breach of an obligation. In this case, liability derived from a breach by the State of the rule contained in Article 1 of the American Convention on Human Rights requiring States Parties to *"respect"* the rights guaranteed by the Convention and to *"ensure"* their full and free exercise to all persons.[119] In a judgment with implications for the international and regional human rights treaties that also impose on States an obligation to "protect" or "ensure" human rights for persons within their territories or under their jurisdictions, the Court held that States are required: "to organize the governmental apparatus and, in general, all the structures through which public power is exercised, so that they are capable of juridically ensuring the free and full enjoyment of human rights."[120]

---

[113] See further, Chapter 6.

[114] M. Shaw, *International Law* (2003) (Shaw, *International Law*), at 721–724; D. Shelton, "Private Violations, Public Wrongs and the Responsibilities of States," (1989) 23 *Fordham International Law Journal* 13 (Shelton, "Private Violations, Public Wrongs"), at 21–23.

[115] On the development and application of the doctrine of due diligence in international environmental law, see P. Birnie, A. Boyle and C. Redgwell, *International Law and the Environment* (2009), at chapter 3, section 4(2).

[116] Note that the most relevant aspects of the *Velásquez Rodríguez* judgment for the present study are also reflected in another case that was considered by the Court in 1989: *Godínez Cruz v. Honduras*, Inter-Am Ct. H.R. (ser. C) No. 5, Jan. 20, 1989. Both judgments are analyzed in detail in Shelton, "Private Violations, Public Wrongs."

[117] *Velásquez Rodríguez*, at para. 182.

[118] Ibid. at para. 173.

[119] American Convention on Human Rights, at Art. 1(1).

[120] *Velásquez Rodríguez*, at para. 166.

In addition to preventing the violation of protected rights, the State must also attempt to investigate and punish such violations, restore the right violated, and provide appropriate compensation for resulting damages.[121] These heads of responsibility would apply even when the State itself was not the immediate agent of harm. For example, a State could be legally responsible for its lack of due diligence in preventing or responding appropriately to a violation.[122] A State could also incur responsibility by failing to seriously investigate private abuses of rights – thereby aiding in their commission.[123] The doctrine to emerge from *Velásquez Rodríguez* with respect to State responsibility for the acts of private entities is usefully summarized in the following extract from the judgment:

> The State has [under Article 1 of the American Convention] a legal duty to take reasonable steps to prevent human rights violations and to use the means at its disposal to carry out a serious investigation of violations committed within its jurisdiction, to identify those responsible, to impose the appropriate punishment and to ensure the victim adequate compensation.[124]

The decision in *Velásquez Rodríguez* has been described by the UN Special Rapporteur on Violence against Women as "one of the most significant assertions of State responsibility for acts of private individuals" and one which "represents an authoritative interpretation of an international standard on State duty."[125] While acknowledging its importance, it is essential to emphasize that the decision does not mitigate the general rule governing the nonattribution of private conduct. The Court explicitly affirmed that the State is only responsible for those human rights violations that can ultimately be attributed to the act or omission of a public authority under the rules of international law.[126] In this sense, the due diligence standard actually affirms that a State will not be responsible for purely private harm.[127] In

---

[121] Ibid. at para. 177.

[122] Ibid. at para. 172.

[123] Ibid. at para. 166.

[124] Ibid. at para. 174.

[125] UN Commission on Human Rights, "Report of the Special Rapporteur, Ms. Radhika Coomaraswamy, on violence against women, its causes and consequences, on trafficking in women, women's migration and violence against women," UN Doc. E/CN.4/1996/53, Feb. 6, 1996 (Coomaraswamy, "Report," UN Doc. E/CN.4/1996/53), at para. 36.

[126] *Velásquez Rodríguez*, at para. 164.

[127] Shelton, "Private Violations, Public Wrongs," at 22, citing F.V. García-Amador, L. Sohn and R. Baxter, *Recent Codification of the Law of State Responsibility for Injuries to Aliens* (1974), at 28. Shelton points to an important and contextually relevant arbitral decision under the law of State responsibility for injuries to aliens in support of this point: "[t]he mere fact that an alien has suffered at the hands of private persons an aggression, which could have been averted by the presence of a sufficient police force on the spot, does not make a government liable for damages under international law. There must be shown special circumstances from which the responsibility of the authorities arises: either their behaviour in connection with the particular occurrence, or a general failure to comply with their duty to maintain order, to prevent crimes or to … punish criminals," citing *W.A. Noyes Case (Panama v. United States)*, (1933) 6 UNRIAA 308 (General Claims Commission).

cases where responsibility for the initial act does not fall on the State, responsibility can still be imputed because of a subsequent failure on the part of the State to exercise "due diligence" in preventing, responding to, or remedying abuses committed by private persons or entities.[128] Whether or not such imputation is possible depends on the relevant primary rules and the facts of the case. As ILC Rapporteur Crawford has noted, "different primary rules of international law impose different standards, ranging from 'due diligence' to 'strict liability' ... all of those standards are capable of giving rise to responsibility in the event of a breach."[129] In other words, there must be an obligation, within the primary rule, for the State to prevent, respond, or remedy abuses, and the facts must be able to show that the State has failed to discharge that obligation.

Since this decision, there has been increasing evidence that due diligence is becoming the accepted benchmark against which certain types of legal obligations, in particular human rights obligations, are to be interpreted. In *Osman v. UK*,[130] the European Court of Human Rights held that the State could be held responsible for a failure of its police forces to respond to harassment that ultimately resulted in death (although the UK was not found to be responsible in this case). In *Akkoç v. Turkey*, the European Court of Human Rights, in the context of the right to life, explained that the State's primary duty is "to secure the right to life by putting into place effective criminal-law provisions to deter the commission of offences ... [and] law-enforcement machinery for the prevention, suppression and punishment of breaches."[131] The Court continued (citing *Osman v. UK*) that this duty may extend in appropriate circumstances "to a positive obligation on the authorities to take preventive operational measures to protect an individual whose life is at risk from the criminal acts of another individual."[132] The African Commission on Human and Peoples' Rights has similarly explained that:

> the State is obliged to protect right-holders against other subjects by legislation and provision of effective remedies ... Protection generally entails the creation and maintenance of an atmosphere or framework by an effective interplay of laws and regulations so that individuals will be able to freely realize their rights and freedoms.[133]

The connection between trafficking and violence against women has already been noted, and it is in the latter context that the due diligence standard has been repeatedly affirmed by the international community as an appropriate measure of State

---

[128] *Velásquez Rodríguez*, at para. 172.
[129] See Crawford, "Revising the Draft Articles on State Responsibility," at 438.
[130] *Osman v. The United Kingdom*, (2000) 29 EHRR 245 (ECHR, Oct. 28, 1998) (*Osman v. UK*).
[131] *Akkoç v. Turkey*, (2002) 34 EHRR 51 (ECHR, Oct. 10, 2000) (*Akkoç v. Turkey*), at para. 77
[132] Ibid.
[133] *SERAC and CESR v. Nigeria*, at para. 46.

obligation with respect to the conduct of private entities.[134] Decisions of regional courts have confirmed this trend. In *Fernandes v. Brazil*, a case of violence against a woman by her husband, the Inter-American Commission on Human Rights held Brazilian authorities responsible for failing to protect and respond as required under the American Convention of Human Rights.[135] In relation to the disappearances of and attacks on women in Ciudad Juárez, Mexico, the same Commission identified an obligation of due diligence upon Mexico and provided a detailed series of recommendations to "improve the application of due diligence to investigate, prosecute and punish violence against women … and overcome impunity" of the perpetrators, and "to improve the application of due diligence to prevent violence against women … and increase their security."[136] The Ciudad Juárez situation was also also the subject of an inquiry by the CEDAW Committee. The report of that inquiry affirmed the obligation of due diligence and its particular significance in relation to private

[134] The "Declaration on Violence against Women" defines gender-based violence to include all forms of such violence occurring within the family and the general community as well as violence "perpetrated or condoned by the State wherever it occurs" (Art. 2(c)) and requires States to "[e]xercise due diligence to prevent, investigate and … punish acts of violence against women, whether these are perpetrated by the State or private persons" (Art. 4(c)): UN General Assembly, "Declaration on the Elimination of Violence against Women," UN Doc. A/48/49, Dec. 20, 1993 ("Declaration on Violence against Women"). CEDAW General Recommendation No. 19 confirms that discrimination prohibited under CEDAW (defined to include gender-based violence) is "not restricted to action by or on behalf of governments" (para. 9) and requires States to "take appropriate and effective measures to overcome all forms of gender-based violence, whether by private or public act" (para. 24(a)): UN Committee on the Elimination of Discrimination against Women, "General Recommendation No. 19: Violence Against Women," UN Doc. A/47/38, Jan. 29, 1992 (CEDAW General Recommendation No. 19). The Beijing +5 Outcome Document confirms that "it is accepted that States have an obligation to exercise due diligence to prevent, investigate and punish acts of violence against women, whether those acts are perpetrated by the State or by private persons, and provide protection to victims": "Further Actions and Initiatives to Implement the Beijing Declaration and Platform for Action," UN Doc. A/RES/S-23/3, Nov. 16, 2000, at para. 13. The Special Rapporteur on Violence against Women has devoted a full report to a detailed consideration of the due diligence standard in this context: "Report of the Special Rapporteur on Violence against Women, its Causes and Consequences: The Due Diligence Standard as a Tool for the Elimination of Violence against Women," UN Doc. E/CN.4/2006/61, Jan. 20, 2006. For a range of perspectives on the issues raised in this section see C. Benninger-Budel ed., *Due Diligence and its Application to Protect Women from Violence* (2008). See further the discussion on violence against women in Chapter 3 of this book.

[135] The Commission found that ineffective judicial action, impunity for perpetrators, and the inability of victims to obtain compensation all demonstrated that Brazil lacked the commitment to take appropriate action to address domestic violence. The Commission considered Brazil to be liable for failure to meet the standard of due diligence required under Article 7(b) of American Convention on the Prevention, Punishment, and Eradication of Violence against Women, 1438 UNTS 63, done June 9, 1994, entered into force Mar. 5, 1995: *Maria Gives Penha Maia Fernandes v. Brazil*, Case 12.051, Report No. 54/01, Inter-AmCHR Doc. OEA/Ser.L/V/II.111 Doc. 20 rev. at 704 (Inter-Am Comm HR, Apr. 16, 2000), at paras. 56–57.

[136] *The Situation of the Rights of Women in Ciudad Juárez, Mexico: The Right to Be Free from Violence and Discrimination*, Inter-AmCHR Doc. OEA/Ser.L/V/II.117, Doc. 44 (Inter-Am Comm HR, Mar. 7, 2003).

violence against women.[137] In *MC v. Bulgaria*, the European Court of Human Rights held that, under the European Convention on Human Rights, States have an obligation to "enact criminal-law provisions effectively punishing rape and to apply them in practice through effective investigation and prosecution."[138] In *Opuz v. Turkey*, concerning domestic violence, the European Court determined a "crucial question" to be "whether the local authorities displayed due diligence to prevent violence against the applicant and her mother, in particular by pursuing criminal or other appropriate preventive measures,"[139] and ultimately held against the respondent State "since the applicant's husband perpetrated [his attacks] without hindrance and with impunity."[140] While not referring specifically to the obligation of due diligence, the European Court of Human Rights, in *Rantsev v. Cyprus and Turkey*, identified a number of obligations on States with respect to preventing and responding to trafficking, including an obligation to effectively investigate trafficking cases and to engage in effective cross-border cooperation.[141]

The due diligence standard has been adopted by the UN Special Rapporteur on Violence against Women,[142] is repeatedly invoked by the Committee on the Elimination of All Forms of Discrimination against Women,[143] and has been regularly recognized and applied by other UN human rights treaty bodies.[144] In the specific context of trafficking, both the General Assembly and the Commission on

---

[137] UN Committee on the Elimination of All Forms of Discrimination against Women, "Report on Mexico Produced by the Committee on the Elimination of Discrimination against Women under Article 8 of the Optional Protocol to the Convention and Reply from the Government of Mexico," UN Doc. CEDAW/C/2005/OP.8/MEXICO, Jan. 27, 2005, esp at paras. 273–277.

[138] *MC v. Bulgaria*, (2005) 40 EHRR 20 (ECHR, Dec. 4, 2003), at para. 153.

[139] *Opuz v. Turkey*, Dec. No. 33401/02 (unreported) (ECHR, June 9, 2009), at para. 131.

[140] Ibid. at para. 169.

[141] *Rantsev v. Cyprus and Russia*, at paras. 288–289.

[142] UN Commission on Human Rights, "Report of the Special Rapporteur, Ms. Radhika Coomaraswamy, on violence against women, its causes and consequences, on trafficking in women, women's migration and violence against women," UN Doc. E/CN.4/2000/68, Feb. 29, 2000, at paras. 51–53; "Report of the Special Rapporteur on Violence against Women, its Causes and Consequences: The Due Diligence Standard as a Tool for the Elimination of Violence against Women," UN Doc. E/CN.4/2006/61, Jan. 20, 2006.

[143] CEDAW General Recommendation No. 19, at para. 9: "[u]nder general international law and specific human rights covenants, States may also be responsible for private acts if they fail to act with due diligence to prevent violations of rights or to investigate and punish acts of violence, and for providing compensation." See also the decisions of the CEDAW in *Şahide Goekce (deceased) v. Austria*, CEDAW Comm. No. 5/2005, UN Doc. CEDAW/C/39/D/5/2005, decided Aug. 6, 2007; and *Fatma Yildirim (deceased) v. Austria*, CEDAW Comm. No. 6/2005, UN Doc. CEDAW/C/39/D/6/2005, decided Oct. 1, 2007. In both these decisions, the CEDAW Committee found that Austria had breached its obligations of due diligence with respect to preventing and investigating domestic violence.

[144] UN Human Rights Committee, "General Comment No. 31: Nature of the General Legal Obligation Imposed on States Parties to the Covenant," UN Doc. CCPR/C/21/Rev.1/Add.13, May 26, 2004, at para. 8 ("[t]here may be circumstances in which a failure to ensure Covenant rights as required by article 2 would give rise to violations by States Parties of those rights, as a result of States Parties' permitting or failing to take appropriate measures or to exercise due diligence to prevent, punish,

Human Rights/Human Rights Council have, with increasing specificity, recognized the due diligence standard as applicable.[145]

How does "due diligence" apply in practice? The *Velásquez Rodríguez Case* was ultimately concerned with a situation in which the State was tolerating apparently private actions that violated human rights as opposed to merely failing to act (in this case, by enacting appropriate protective legislation). Inferring such "toleration" or the absence of due diligence in the trafficking context will rarely be straightforward. Can "toleration" leading to responsibility be inferred from a systematic or otherwise inexplicable failure to apprehend and prosecute known or suspected traffickers? Can it be inferred from the absence of any legislative, administrative, or social measures to protect trafficked persons from their exploiters? What is the situation with regard to claims that the State is *unable* (as opposed to unwilling) to protect its citizens and others within its territory from trafficking and related violations of human rights?

The due diligence standard provides a starting point but it by no means delivers an authoritative response to such questions. This is not just because of the impact of the primary rules (and their general lack of precision) but also because of an absence of clarity on the point of whether diligence should be assessed with reference to the capacities of the State or an international standard. Should due diligence be analyzed in relation to "means at the disposal of the State"?[146] Would a more appropriate test be whether the breach could have been prevented by reasonable diligence on the part of the State?[147] Is the question of foreseeability (or feasibility of action) relevant? Is the character and importance of the norm in question relevant to determining the standard of care required? These questions cannot be answered in the abstract but must be addressed with reference to the norm in question and the particular facts and circumstances of the case. Ultimately, a decision

investigate or redress the harm caused by such acts by private persons or entities"); Committee on the Elimination of Racial Discrimination, *L.K. v. The Netherlands*, CERD Comm. No. 4/1991, UN Doc. CERD/C/42/D/4/1991, decided Mar. 16, 1993, at para. 6.6 ("[w]hen threats of racial violence are made, and especially when they are made in public and by a group, it is incumbent upon the State to investigate with due diligence and expedition").

[145] See, for example, UN General Assembly, "Trafficking in Women and Girls," UN Doc. A/RES/63/156, Jan. 30, 2009, at Preamble and UN Human Rights Council, "Trafficking in Persons, Especially Women and Children," UN Doc. A/HRC/RES/11/3, June 17, 2009, at Preamble, ("States have an obligation to exercise due diligence to prevent, investigate and punish perpetrators of trafficking in persons, and to rescue victims as well as provide for their protection … not doing so violates and impairs or nullifies the enjoyment of the human rights and fundamental freedoms of the victims"); UN General Assembly, "Improving the Coordination of Efforts against Trafficking in Persons," UN Doc. A/RES/61/180, Mar. 8, 2007, at Preamble ("Member States have an obligation to exercise due diligence to prevent trafficking in persons, to investigate this crime and to ensure that perpetrators do not enjoy impunity").

[146] *Tehran Hostages Case*, at paras. 63, 68(b).

[147] Shelton, for example, argues that due diligence requires "reasonable measures of prevention that a well-administered government could be expected to exercise under similar circumstances": Shelton, "Private Violations, Public Wrongs," at 23.

is likely to come down to an assessment of whether, under the circumstances of the particular case, the State is taking its obligations seriously.[148] In applying the due diligence standard to specific obligations, the present study gives consideration to each of these aspects while focusing, most particularly, on the *ability of the State to influence an alternative, more positive outcome.*

4.3.4. *Conclusion: The Primacy of the Primary Rules*

The ILC rules make clear that acts of private persons (including acts of individuals who have the status of an organ of the State but who, in the relevant circumstance, act in their private capacity) cannot, in general, be attributable to the State and will not, therefore, engage that State's responsibility. This is the starting point for determining responsibility in relation to any situation in which the State is not the direct agent of harm. The development of stricter standards of State responsibility in certain areas of international law (for example, environmental protection) may have led to a modified application of this general rule in certain circumstances, but not to its abandonment.[149] In the specific context of human rights, the State may incur international responsibility in relation to private acts if it can be shown that the State's own organs have omitted to respond appropriately to such acts in terms of both preventing their occurrence and dealing with their consequences. In other words, the State's responsibility under such circumstances derives not from its involvement in or complicity with the original act (which could, if established, constitute an additional head of responsibility) but from the breach of consequential, independent legal obligations. The level of obligation (for example, to prevent and respond) will ultimately depend on the relevant primary rule. However, a finding of responsibility will generally depend upon establishing that the State has failed to secure recognized rights and freedoms in its domestic law or failed to take what, in

---

[148] Writing on the subject of domestic violence, the UN Special Rapporteur on Violence against Women has proposed a seriousness test for deciding whether or not a State has met the due diligence standard: "the test is whether the State undertakes its duties seriously ... If statistics illustrate that existing laws are ineffective in protecting women from violence, States must find other complementary mechanisms to prevent domestic violence. Thus, if education, dismantling of institutional violence, demystifying domestic violence, training of State personnel, the funding of shelters and other direct services for victim-survivors and the systematic documentation of all incidents of domestic violence are found to be effective tools in preventing domestic violence and protecting women's human rights, all become obligations in which the State must exercise due diligence in carrying out." Coomaraswarmy, "Report," UN Doc. E/CN.4/1996/53, at para. 37.

[149] Note that there is some disagreement as to the nature and extent of this modification. Shelton, for example, identifies the due diligence standard as being an *exception* to the general rules of State responsibility: Shelton, "Private Violations, Public Wrongs," at 22. Crawford, however, is emphatic on the point that such refinements relate only to the primary rule and therefore leave intact the validity of the general principle: Crawford, "Revising the Draft Articles on State Responsibility," at 438, 441.

the context of the European Human Rights Convention, have been termed "reasonable and appropriate" measures of protection.[150]

In the case of trafficking, a State may refuse to accept responsibility for the acts of organized criminal groups taking place within its jurisdiction on the basis of the "private" nature of the acts. It may also reject responsibility on the grounds of its inability to exercise effective control over the presence, power, and influence of such groups. Neither claim will be justified if it can be shown that the State did not reasonably use whatever means it had available to prevent the breach in question and, if prevention was not possible, to respond appropriately to it. While a determination on this point will depend heavily on the facts of a particular case and the nature of the obligations in question,[151] the increasingly accepted standard of "due diligence" renders it unlikely that States will be able to avoid responsibility for the acts of private persons or entities when their ability to influence an alternative outcome can be established.

International human rights law has accepted the notion that the State is required, under certain circumstances, to guarantee rights as opposed to simply refraining from intervening.[152] In other words, the effective enjoyment of human rights will often require positive actions on the State including, but not limited to, the provision of a legal infrastructure through which human rights can be secured and violations redressed. This does not mean, however, that developments in international human rights law (for example, with regard to making the State responsible if laws authorize certain action that results in violations, or if it fails to provide proper safeguards against abuses of rights by private persons) have resulted in substantive change to the general law of attribution.[153] The specific requirements for responsibility vary from one primary rule to another.[154] Ultimately, it is these rules that will be determinative: "if the State acts or fails to act, its responsibility is potentially engaged and remaining questions are left to be resolved by the interpretation and application of the relevant primary rules."[155] Accordingly, if the test in a particular case is deemed to be one of "appropriate measures" or "due diligence,"

---

[150] See Lawson, "Out of Control: State Responsibility and Human Rights," at 105. In Lawson's view, the State can only incur international responsibility for a private act in the case of an action or omission of the State's own organs "where they are guilty of not having done everything within their power to prevent the injurious act of the private individual or to punish it suitably if it has occurred despite everything": ibid. at 96.

[151] In his examination of State responsibility under the European Convention on Human Rights, Lawson proposes a presumption along the following lines: "a State is bound to secure the relevant rights and freedoms throughout its territory. The presumption is rebuttable: in exceptional circumstances the State may be able to demonstrate that it has no means whatsoever to secure specific rights and freedoms … to all persons in its territory." Ibid. at 114.

[152] Crawford, "Revising the Draft Articles on State Responsibility," at 439.

[153] This is the position taken by the ILC Rapporteur. See ibid. at 439–440. Crawford also rejects the idea that such developments have created any *lex specialis* in the field of human rights: ibid.

[154] Ibid. at 438.

[155] Ibid. at 440.

reference must be made to the original obligation and not to the rules of State responsibility.

This separation of the primary obligations from the secondary rules of State responsibility allows a much more objective analysis to be made of whether and to what extent international law is moving toward increased accountability of the State for violations that originate in the conduct of private individuals. As noted above, the area of women's human rights has seen perhaps the most significant advancements in this area, and it is now widely accepted that traditionally "private" issues such as domestic violence, harmful cultural practices, discriminatory social traditions, and indeed trafficking are not just matters for international attention and concern but also implicate the responsibility of States. The substantive content of key economic and social rights is also being interpreted so as to require States to control the actions of private individuals and entities that impact negatively on the effective enjoyment of these rights.[156] The increasingly popular notion of corporate responsibility for human rights abuses (that is, that the corporation itself has specific legal obligations vis-à-vis the rights holder) has not overshadowed a growing acceptance of the much more immediately relevant fact that both home and host States may be legally responsible for failing to prevent or respond adequately to abuses that originate in the conduct of business entities, including multinational corporations.[157] Procedural aspects of international human rights law are also revealing. Clapham views the move away from interstate responsibility under international law toward international procedures granting individuals the right to complain about human rights violations as indicative of a growing readiness on the part

---

[156] While the ICESCR (International Covenant on Economic, Social and Cultural Rights, 993 UNTS 3, done Dec. 16, 1966, entered into force Jan. 3, 1976) makes no reference to situations in which the State is not the immediate agent of harm, the relevant treaty body has confirmed the potential responsibility of the State for violation of certain protected rights through the actions of private individuals and entities: for example, UN Committee on Economic, Social and Cultural Rights, "General Comment No. 20: Non-Discrimination in Economic, Social and Cultural Rights," UN Doc. E/C.12/GC/20, July 2, 2009, at para. 11; UN Committee on Economic, Social and Cultural Rights, "General Comment No. 18: The Right to Work," UN Doc. E/C.12/GC/18, Feb. 6, 2006, at para. 35. See also generally, A. Eide, "Promoting Economic, Social and Cultural Rights: Obligations of States and Accountability of Non-State Actors," paper presented to the Second Global Forum on Human Development: Human Rights and Human Development, Oct. 10, 2000, available at http:// hdr.undp.org/docs/events/global_forum/2000/eide.pdf (accessed Nov. 25, 2009). For a detailed examination of the issue of State accountability for the acts of private individuals with specific reference to the right to health, see A. Clapham and M. Garcia Rubio, "The Obligations of States with Regard to Non-State Actors in the Context of the Right to Health," Health and Human Rights Working Paper Series No. 3 (World Health Organization, 2002).

[157] For an overview of the relevant responsibility issues with respect to multinational corporations, see D. Kinley and J. Tadaki, "From Talk to Walk: The Emergence of Human Rights Responsibilities for Corporations at International Law," (2004) 44 *Virginia Journal of International Law* 931 (Kinley and Tadaki, "From Talk to Walk"). On the specific question of whether corporations themselves could or should be recognized as a category of duty holders separate from the State (and thereby held responsible for violations of international human rights law), see Chapter 4.6 below.

of the various international monitoring bodies to accept complaints concerning the inability of the State to control such violations.[158]

In conclusion, therefore, it is possible to confirm that international law offers significant opportunities to invoke State responsibility in respect of the trafficking-related acts of private persons and entities. These opportunities arise, however, largely from the relevant primary rules and not from the secondary rules governing State responsibility. It follows therefore that efforts to improve the effectiveness of international law in this or any other area should focus on refining what constitutes an unlawful act (that is, improving the primary rules) and not on "stretch[ing] the secondary rules unduly."[159]

4.4. CONSEQUENCES OF A FINDING OF STATE RESPONSIBILITY

Once responsibility has been established, it is necessary to examine the consequences that arise from such a finding. Such consequences are inevitable because the commission by a State of an internationally wrongful act creates a new legal relationship between the responsible State and those to whom the obligation is owed. According to the ILC, it is this aspect that "constitutes the substance or content of the international responsibility of a State."[160] The nature of this new legal relationship can arise between the responsible State and another State, a group of States, or the international community as a whole.[161] Identification of the other party to the relationship must be made with reference to the character and content of the obligation (the primary rule) as well as to the circumstances of the breach.[162] The following general principles will nevertheless continue to apply to the extent that they are not displaced by the regime created under a specific system or treaty.

4.4.1. *The Obligations of Cessation and Reparation*

While a new legal relationship arises from the fact of the breach, the old one does not disappear. As a general principle, the legal consequences of an internationally wrongful act do not affect the continued duty of the State to perform the obligation it has breached.[163]

---

[158] Clapham, *Human Rights Obligations of Non-State Actors.*
[159] Lawson, "Out of Control: State Responsibility and Human Rights," at 116. Crawford comes to a similar conclusion: "[i]f international law is not responsive enough to [human rights] problems in the private sector, the answer lies in the further development of the primary rules ... or in exploring what may have been neglected aspects of existing obligations." Crawford, "Revising the Draft Articles on State Responsibility," at 440.
[160] ILC Commentary, at Part Two, Introduction, para. 1.
[161] ILC Draft Articles, at Art. 33(1).
[162] ILC Commentary, at Art. 33, para. 1.
[163] Ibid. at Art. 29. See also the VCLT, at Art. 60: "the mere fact of breach or of repudiation of a treaty does not terminate the treaty."

The immediate obligation of a State found to have committed an internationally wrongful act is the obligation of cessation: The State in breach is obliged to cease the internationally wrongful act (or omission)[164] and, if appropriate under the circumstances, to offer assurances and guarantees of nonrepetition.[165] This obligation, which is immediate and an automatic consequence of the breach,[166] goes to the heart of the State responsibility regime and is directly linked to the overall objective of that regime to restore relations as they existed prior to the occurrence of the breach. In fact, as noted by the ILC in its Commentary to this part, it is cessation, rather than reparation, which is often the central issue in a dispute between States as to questions of responsibility.[167] Cessation protects not just the interests of the immediately affected State, but also the broader interests of the international community in "the preservation of and reliance on the international rule of law."[168] This is clearly the case for human rights matters including those likely to be raised in the trafficking context: While reparation for harm caused will certainly be an important issue, the most immediate concern will almost always be with ensuring that the harm itself is brought to an end and that the underlying rule is thereby protected and preserved. The importance of guarantees of nonrepetition is confirmed by their identification in the human rights context specifically as a form of reparation.[169] Such guarantees are aimed above and beyond the individual victim and focus, in particular, on ensuring prevention of future violations.

The second obligation of a State that has committed an internationally wrongful act is that of reparation. The responsible State is under an obligation to make full reparation for the injury (that is, any damage)[170] caused by the internationally wrongful act.[171] The principle was articulated by the Permanent Court of International Justice in the *Chorzow Factory* case as follows:

> It is a principle of international law that the breach of an engagement involves an obligation to make reparation in an adequate form. Reparation therefore is the indispensable complement of a failure to apply a convention and there is no necessity for this to be stated in the Convention itself.[172]

---

[164] ILC Commentary, at Art. 30, para. 2.

[165] ILC Draft Articles, at Art. 30(1).

[166] Jiménez de Arechaga, "International Responsibility," at 533.

[167] ILC Commentary, at Art. 29, para. 4.

[168] Ibid. at Art. 29, para. 5.

[169] UN General Assembly, "Basic Principles and Guidelines on the Right to a Remedy and Reparation for Victims of Gross Violations of International Human Rights Law and Serious Violations of International Humanitarian Law," UN Doc. A/RES/60/147, Dec. 16, 2005 ("Principles and Guidelines on the Right to a Remedy and Reparation"), at paras. 18, 23.

[170] ILC Draft Articles, at Art. 31(2): "[i]njury includes any damage, whether material or moral, caused by the internationally wrongful act of a State". Further, see ILC Commentary, at Art. 31, para. 5.

[171] ILC Draft Articles, at Art. 31.

[172] *Factory at Chorzow (Germany v. Poland)*, Jurisdiction, [1927] PCIJ Rep, Series A, No. 9, at 21, cited in ILC Commentary, at Art. 31, para.1.

Importantly, the obligation of reparation arises automatically following the commission of an internationally wrongful act. It does not depend on the invocation of a right to reparation on the part of one or more injured States.[173] It also does not depend on the injured State having suffered material harm or damage.[174] In the context of the obligation of reparation, the injury is, in fact, the breach itself. Actual harm (in terms of the damage that flows from the breach itself) will, in the words of the ILC, be "highly relevant to the form and quantum of reparation."[175] The ILC Commentary makes the important point that "while an obligation of reparation exists towards a State, reparation does not necessarily accrue to that State's benefit."[176] This is relevant for many of the primary obligations that relate to trafficking whereby individuals are the holders of certain legal entitlements and thereby the ultimate beneficiaries of any reparations.[177]

In terms of the nature and effect of reparations, the Permanent Court of International Justice subsequently observed, in a later stage of the *Chorzow Factory* case, that reparation "must, as far as possible, wipe out all the consequences of the illegal act and re-establish the situation which would, in all probability, have existed if the act had not been committed."[178] In other words, the purpose and effect of reparations due for an internationally wrongful act should be to reach a situation whereby the consequences of that act have been eliminated and to reestablish the *status quo ante*. The manner in which this situation is to be reached will depend on the content of the primary obligation and will clearly be more straightforward in relation to simple obligations in comparison with those that are composite in nature.

International law has traditionally recognized three means or "forms" that can be used by a State either separately or in combination in discharging its obligation to make full reparation for injury caused by an internationally wrongful act: restitution, compensation, and satisfaction.[179] Restitution refers to the reestablishment of the situation that existed prior to the breach, as far as this is possible through material, juridical, or any other measures. States are under an obligation to make restitution to the extent that this is not impossible or disproportionate.[180] As restitution is most closely linked with the general principle that the responsible State

---

[173] ILC Commentary, at Art. 31, para. 4.

[174] Ibid. at Art. 31, paras. 7–10.

[175] Ibid. at Art. 31, para. 7.

[176] Ibid. at Art. 33, para. 3.

[177] Note that certain primary rules, most particularly international human rights treaties, operate to permit individuals to invoke the responsibility of a State on their own account. The ILC Articles acknowledge this possibility but do not include it within the scope of the rules governing reparation. See also ILC Draft Articles, at Art. 33(2); and ILC Commentary, at Art. 28, para. 3

[178] *Factory at Chorzow (Germany v. Poland), Merits*, [1928] PCIJ Rep, Series A, No. 17, at 47. cited in ILC Commentary, at Art. 31, para. 2.

[179] ILC Draft Articles, at Art. 34.

[180] Ibid. at Art. 35.

is required to wipe out the consequences of its wrongful act by reestablishing the situation that existed prior to its commission, it is considered to be, in principle, the primary form of reparation.[181] The relevant primary obligation will often determine what is required in terms of restitution. Actions to secure restitution in a case of trafficking may include release of an individual from unlawful detention (by a trafficker or other private entity or by the State); recognition of legal identity and citizenship; return of property; and safe return to one's place of residence.[182] Restitution for a failure of protection may be more difficult if the failure has already resulted in harm, such as retrafficking, that cannot be reversed. In such cases, other means of reparation may be required. Rehabilitation, an accepted form of reparation in human rights law,[183] can be considered an aspect of restitution to the extent that it seeks to ensure that the person who has suffered a gross violation of their human rights has his or her status and position "restored" in the eyes of the law as well as of the wider community. Victims of serious violations of human rights, such as trafficking, will inevitably require a range of support services including medical and psychological care as well as legal and social assistance. The rehabilitation element of reparation would impose an obligation on the offending State to provide such services.

Compensation, the second form of reparation, is payable for damage caused by an internationally wrongful act to the extent that "such damage is not made good by restitution."[184] Its function is to "address the *actual losses* incurred as a result of an internationally wrongful act."[185] Compensation covers "any financially assessable damage,"[186] including nonmaterial damage but not extending to punitive or "moral damage," in the sense of "affront or injury caused by a violation of rights not associated with actual damage" (which is more properly the subject of satisfaction).[187] "Moral damage," in this context, is not to be confused with nonmaterial damage such as loss of loved ones, injury to feelings, pain and suffering, loss of social position, or injury to reputation, which may be difficult to quantify but is no less than material injury for the purposes of the law of State responsibility.[188] While restitution retains its primacy as a legal principle, compensation appears to be the most frequently sought

---

[181] ILC Commentary, at Art. 35, para. 3. Restitution will not, however, be required if it is "materially impossible" (ILC Draft Articles, at Art. 35(a)), or where the benefit to be gained from restitution is wholly disproportionate to its cost to the responsible State (ILC Draft Articles, at Art. 35(b)). Shelton refers to restitution as the "preferred or normal remedy" while noting that neither international tribunals nor commentators are consistent on this point: D. Shelton, *Remedies in International Human Rights Law* (2001) (Shelton, *Remedies in International Human Rights Law*), at 94.

[182] These examples are drawn from the "Principles and Guidelines on the Right to a Remedy and Reparation," at para. 19.

[183] Ibid. at paras. 18, 21.

[184] ILC Draft Articles, at Art. 36(1).

[185] ILC Commentary, at Art. 36, para. 4 (emphasis added).

[186] ILC Draft Articles, at Art. 36(2).

[187] ILC Commentary, at Art. 36, para. 1.

[188] Ibid. at Art. 36, para. 16, citing *Lusitania* (1923) 7 UNRIAA 32.

form of reparation.[189] The way in which compensation is to work in a particular situation will depend on a range of factors including the relevant primary rule and "concern to reach an equitable and acceptable outcome."[190] Compensation will be a key aspect of reparation for a victim of trafficking and could be payable for physical and psychological harm, lost opportunities, loss of earnings, and medical, legal, or other costs incurred as a result of the violation.[191]

Satisfaction, the final internationally recognized form of reparation, is an exceptional remedy for injuries in relation to which it is not possible to fully restore the situation that existed previous to the breach and for which compensation will not be an adequate remedy. The obligation of satisfaction is exceptional in the sense that it will exist for the responsible State only "insofar as [the injury] cannot be made good by restitution or compensation."[192] Satisfaction, which must be proportionate to the injury,[193] can take various forms depending on the circumstances of a particular case, but may include "an acknowledgement of the breach, an expression of regret, a formal apology or another appropriate modality."[194] The ILC Commentary also gives the examples of due inquiry into how the wrongful situation arose, a compensation fund for victims, and disciplinary or penal action against the individuals whose conduct caused the internationally wrongful act.[195] In the context of trafficking, satisfaction may be considered an appropriate form of restitution through which to ensure that the violations of the victim's rights are properly acknowledged and dealt with.

The question of whether a State can avoid the full weight of reparations owing for an internationally wrongful act by pointing to contributing factors or other causes falling outside its sphere of control is an important one. In the present context, it is relevant to point out that the "injury" of trafficking is often a cumulative one, caused by a combination of factors, not all of which can necessarily be ascribed to an individual State held responsible for a particular injury. In some cases, a third State will be involved. For example, the failure of a country of origin to prevent individuals from being trafficked is a concurrent cause of the harm they suffer in a country of destination. This reality, however, would be insufficient to reduce or attenuate the

---

[189] Ibid. at Art. 36, paras. 2–3.

[190] Ibid. at Art. 36, para. 7. For examples of types of damage that may be compensable and methods of quantification, see ibid. at paras. 8–34. For a detailed discussion of compensation in the area of international human rights law including the practice of human rights courts and other bodies, see Shelton, *Remedies in International Human Rights Law*, esp. at Chapter 8.

[191] These examples are drawn from the "Principles and Guidelines on the Right to a Remedy and Reparation," at para. 20. See further the discussion on remedies in Chapter 6 of this volume.

[192] ILC Draft Articles, at Art. 37(1). See ILC Commentary, at Art. 37, para. 1.

[193] ILC Draft Articles, at Art. 37(3).

[194] Ibid. at Art. 37(2). See further, ILC Commentary, at Art. 37, para. 5. The issue of appropriateness was raised by the International Court of Justice in the *LaGrand* case in which it held that "an apology would not suffice in cases where the individuals concerned have been subjected to prolonged detention or convicted and sentenced to severe penalties" following a failure of consular notification: *LaGrand (Germany v. United States)*, [2001] ICJ Rep 466, at para. 125.

[195] ILC Commentary, at Art. 37, para. 5.

obligation of reparation owed in a particular case by either the country of origin or the country of destination.[196] Similarly, as shown by the ICJ in the *Tehran Hostages* case, a State that is held responsible for an international wrong cannot lessen its obligation of reparation by pointing to concurrent causes on the part of a private party – such as an organized criminal group.[197] As stated by the ILC in its Commentary:

> unless some part of the injury can be shown to be severable in causal terms from that attributed to the responsible State, the latter is held responsible for all the consequences, not being too remote, of its wrongful conduct.[198]

4.4.2. *Consequences Attached to Serious Breaches of Peremptory Norms*

Is there one uniform set of consequences attached to breaches of international legal rules, or do the consequences vary according to the severity of the breach and/or the relative importance of the primary rule that has been violated? The question of a qualitative distinction between different breaches of international law has occupied international courts, tribunals, and commentators for many years. The ILC, along with much of the international legal community, has long acknowledged the existence of a hierarchy of norms, "ensuing from the recognition, by the international community, of the pre-eminence of certain common interests and values and the consequent necessity of surrounding them with maximum legal protection."[199] The related identification, by the International Court of Justice, of legal obligations *erga omnes* (those that, by virtue of the importance of the rights involved, are owed to the international community as a whole)[200] provides further evidence of the existence of a special class of norms.[201]

---

[196] In the *Corfu Channel* case, for example, the United Kingdom recovered the full amount of its damage claim against Albania based on its wrongful failure to warn of the presence of mines, even though the mines had been laid by a third party: *Corfu Channel (United Kingdom v. Albania), Assessment of the Amount of Compensation*, [1949] ICJ Rep 244, at 250, cited in ILC Commentary, at Art. 31, para. 13.

[197] *Tehran Hostages Case*, at 29–32, cited in ILC Commentary, at Art. 31, para. 12.

[198] ILC Commentary, at Art. 31, para. 13.

[199] G. Abi-Saab, "The Uses of Article 19," (1999) 10 *European Journal of International Law* 339 (Abi-Saab, "The Uses of Article 19"), at 339.

[200] The basis for this doctrine is a statement of the International Court of Justice in the *Barcelona Traction* case: "an essential distinction should be drawn between the obligations of a State towards the international community as a whole, and those arising vis-à-vis another State in the field of diplomatic protection. By their very nature the former are the concern of all States. In view of the importance of the rights involved, all States can be held to have a legal interest in their protection; they are obligations *erga omnes* ... Such obligations derive, for example, in contemporary international law, from the outlawing of acts of aggression, and of genocide, as also from the principles and rules concerning the basic rights of the human person, including protection from slavery and racial discrimination. Some of the corresponding rights of protection have entered into the body of general international law ... others are conferred by international instruments of a universal or quasi-universal character." *Barcelona Traction, Light and Power Company Limited (Belgium v. Spain)*, [1970] ICJ Rep 3, at paras. 33–34.

[201] The relationship between peremptory norms and obligations *erga omnes* (that is, whether they are different concepts or two aspects of a single idea) is not completely clear. The ILC Commentary

While acceptance of this "entrenched legal phenomenon"[202] may be widespread, considerable divisions arose with respect to the way in which the notion of a normative hierarchy could be incorporated into the ILC's work on State responsibility. After much debate, the ILC abandoned its attempt to forge a distinction through the creation of two different categories of wrongs: "international crimes of State" (most serious) and "internationally wrongful acts" or "international delicts" (relatively less serious). In their final version, the Draft Articles omit all reference to "international crimes of State" and instead focus on serious violations of peremptory norms of international law. Such violations are to be identified using the general rules of responsibility but attract a special regime of consequences, described further in this chapter, which involves not just the responsible State but all other States as well. Violations of peremptory norms of international law also impact upon rules regarding entitlement to invoke responsibility. This issue is considered in the following section.

The notion of a peremptory norm of international law was codified in the Vienna Convention on the Law of Treaties as one which is:

> recognised by the international community of States as a whole as a norm from which no derogation is permitted and which can be modified only by a subsequent norm of general international law having the same character.[203]

These "stringent" criteria[204] have served to ensure that very few norms can be conclusively claimed as peremptory. The ILC Commentary notes that those widely accepted and recognized as such "include the prohibitions of aggression, genocide, slavery, racial discrimination, crimes against humanity and torture as well as, more recently, the right to self-determination."[205] The question as to whether certain forms and modalities of trafficking can ever be considered as falling within the peremptory norm prohibiting slavery and the slave trade or the category of "crimes against humanity" has been addressed in some detail in Chapter 3.3. In view of the finding

---

    identifies a substantive overlap and notes that all examples given by the ICJ of obligations owed to the international community as a whole involve obligations arising under peremptory norms of international law: ILC Commentary, at Part II, Introduction, paras. 2–7.

[202] Abi-Saab, "The Uses of Article 19," at 340.

[203] VCLT, at Art. 53. Note that this concept is also included in the Vienna Convention on the Law of Treaties between States and International Organisations or between International Organisations, done Mar. 21, 1986, not yet in force, reprinted in (1986) 25 ILM 543, at Art. 53.

[204] ILC Commentary, at Art. 26, para. 5.

[205] Ibid., citing the ICJ in *East Timor (Portugal v. Australia)*, [1995] ICJ Rep 90, at 102, para. 29. The commentary adds that "[s]o far, relatively few peremptory norms have been recognised as such. But various tribunals, national and international, have affirmed the idea of peremptory norms in contexts not limited to the validity of treaties": ILC Commentary, at Art. 27, para. 5. It cites the decisions of the International Criminal Tribunal for the Former Yugoslavia in *Prosecutor v. Furundzija*, Case IT-95–17/1-T, ICTY Trial Chamber, Dec. 10, 1998, and of the English House of Lords in *R v. Bow Street Metropolitan Stipendiary Magistrate, ex parte Pinochet Ugarte (No. 3)*, [1999] 2 All ER 97, esp. at 108–109, 114–115 (per Lord Browne-Wilkinson). See further, *Legality of the Threat or Use of Nuclear Weapons (Advisory Opinion)*, [1996] ICJ Rep 226, at 257, para. 79. See also ILC Commentary, at Art. 40, paras. 4–5.

that either inclusion could not be ruled out as a contemporary (or future) possibility, it is relevant, in the present context, to consider the responsibility regime established in the ILC Draft Articles for breaches of such peremptory norms.

Under the ILC special responsibility regime, serious breaches of peremptory norms of international law give rise to particular consequences above and beyond those attaching to other breaches of international obligation. In particular, States are under a positive obligation to cooperate in order to end, through lawful means, any serious breach.[206] In addition, States are under a "duty of abstention"[207] that requires, first, that they do not recognize as lawful any situation created by such a breach, and, second, that they not render aid or assistance in maintaining this situation.[208]

The scope of application of this special responsibility regime is highly restricted. For a particular situation to qualify, there must, as noted above, have been "a serious breach by a State of an obligation arising under a peremptory norm of international law."[209] To be considered "serious," the breach in question must involve "a gross or systematic failure by the responsible State to fulfill its obligation."[210] According to the ILC Commentary, a violation would have to be carried out in an organized and deliberate way to be regarded as systematic,[211] and an isolated violation of a peremptory norm would be unlikely to qualify on this point. The term "gross" refers to the intensity of the violation or of its effects: "it denotes violations of a flagrant nature, amounting to a direct and outright assault on the values protected by the rule."[212] Factors that could go toward establishing the seriousness of the breach could include intent, the scope and number of individual violations, and the gravity of their consequences for victims.[213] On this basis, application of the ILC's special responsibility regime to situations of trafficking is likely to be fraught with legal and practical difficulty. First, it will be necessary to establish that the circumstances of the particular case justify its characterization as one of slavery or the slave trade, or otherwise as a crime against humanity for which the State in question is legally responsible. This would involve reference to the primary obligation as well as application of rules of attribution as explored above. It is only following such a finding that the additional hurdle of "seriousness" must be overcome, by showing that the breach involved a gross or systematic failure by the State to fulfill its obligation to prevent the conduct identified as violative of a peremptory norm.

---

[206] ILC Draft Articles, at Art. 41(1). The ILC Commentary notes that the question as to whether general international law prescribes a positive duty of cooperation under such circumstances is not yet settled. This provision may therefore reflect the progressive development of international law. ILC Commentary, at Art. 41, para. 3.

[207] ILC Commentary, at Art. 41, para. 4.

[208] ILC Draft Articles, at Art. 41(2).

[209] Ibid. at Art. 40(1).

[210] Ibid. at Art. 40(2).

[211] ILC Commentary, at Art. 40, para. 8.

[212] Ibid.

[213] Ibid.

4.5. INVOCATION OF RESPONSIBILITY

The term "invocation" refers to the taking of "measures of a relatively formal character" by one State against another State, such as the raising of a claim or the commencement of proceedings in an international court or tribunal.[214] Rules relating to invocation of responsibility thereby govern how State responsibility is actually administered in practice. While State responsibility will exist independently of its invocation by another State, it is important, as a practical matter, to be able to identify what States actually faced with a breach of an international obligation are able to do in terms of securing cessation and/or reparation from the offending State.[215]

Questions surrounding implementation of State responsibility are particularly complex in those areas of law of most relevance to the present study (including human rights law and transnational criminal law), where the post-breach relationship will most commonly be one between the offending State and the other parties to the agreement in question. The opposing party will be extended to include the international community as a whole when the breach relates to rights that are recognized to be of a fundamental nature.[216] In human rights law particularly, there is also another possibility: that a non-State entity could invoke responsibility and thereby claim reparation for injury.[217] This is possible because of the peculiar nature of this branch of law: The primary obligation in human rights treaties is, in fact, owed to the individual and not to his or her State. Certain human rights treaties have taken this theoretical possibility to its logical conclusion by permitting an aggrieved individual to bypass the State completely and to invoke responsibility on his or her own account. Whether and to what extent non-State entities can invoke the responsibility of a State will depend on the content of the relevant primary rule.[218] The following paragraphs will examine the general international legal rules governing invocation of responsibility *between States* before considering the very particular regime created under international human rights treaties.

4.5.1. *General Rules Governing Invocation of Responsibility*

General rules of international law provide that only an "injured State" can invoke responsibility on its own account.[219] Under the ILC regime, a State is entitled, as an

---

[214] Ibid. at Art. 42, para. 2. Mere protest or other "informal" diplomatic contacts do not amount to an invocation of responsibility unless they also include a specific claim (for example, for restitution). The definition of invocation has been criticized as too narrow: see E. Brown Weiss, "Invoking State Responsibility in the Twenty-First Century," (2002) 96 *American Journal of International Law* 798 (Brown Weiss, "Invoking State Responsibility in the Twenty-First Century"), at 800.

[215] ILC Commentary, at Part Three, Introduction.

[216] See above at notes 200 to 201 and the accompanying text.

[217] This possibility is acknowledged in Article 33 of the ILC Draft Articles. See also ILC Commentary, at Art. 33, paras. 1–4.

[218] See Chapter 4.3.2.

[219] See further, Crawford, *The ILC's Articles on State Responsibility*, at 54–260.

injured State, to invoke the responsibility of another State (and is entitled to resort to all stipulated means of redress) if the obligation breached is owed:

- to that State individually[220] (that is, if the invoking State has an individual right to the performance of the relevant obligation[221])
- to a group of States including that State or to the international community as a whole, *providing* that the breach specially affects that State *or* that it is "of such a character as radically to change the position of all the other States to which the obligation is owed with respect to the further performance of the obligation."[222]

According to the ILC Commentary, to be "specially affected" and thereby considered as injured for the purposes of entitlement to invoke responsibility, the State in question must be able to show that it has been affected by the breach "in a way which distinguishes it from the generality of other States to which the obligation is owed."[223] Situations in which the breach of a collective obligation is of a nature to radically affect every other State to which the obligation is owed are most likely to arise under "regimes" created through treaties that establish interdependent obligations for all States Parties.[224] They would not occur in the context of human rights treaties, which "do not operate in an all-or-nothing way."[225]

Because of the nature of the violations involved in trafficking and their location in international norms or treaties of widespread or general applicability, invocation of responsibility by a State against another State in this context is most likely to involve collective obligations. While it is possible to envisage a situation whereby an injured State could claim breach of an obligation owed to it individually (for example, through violation of a bilateral agreement governing matters such as the treatment of migrant workers or the repatriation of victims of trafficking), these situations can be expected to remain the exception. Accordingly, and absent the existence of a special regime referred to above, a State seeking to invoke the responsibility of other

---

[220] ILC Draft Articles, at Art. 42(a).

[221] ILC Commentary, at Art. 42, para. 5.

[222] ILC Draft Articles, at Art. 42(b).

[223] ILC Commentary, at Art. 42, para. 12.

[224] For example, a disarmament treaty or a treaty establishing a military or nuclear-free zone. See further, ILC Commentary, at Art. 42, paras. 5, 13–15.

[225] Crawford, *The ILC's Articles on State Responsibility*, at 41. The same can be said of transnational criminal law treaties such as the Organized Crime Convention and its Protocols: United Nations Convention against Transnational Organized Crime, 2225 UNTS 209, done Nov. 15, 2000, entered into force Sept. 29, 2003; the Trafficking Protocol; Protocol against the Smuggling of Migrants by Land, Sea and Air, supplementing the United Nations Convention against Transnational Organized Crime, done Nov. 15, 2000, GA Res. 55/25, Annex III, UN GAOR, 55th Sess., Supp. No. 49, at 62, UN Doc. A/45/49 (Vol. I) (2001), entered into force Jan. 28, 2004; Protocol against the Illicit Manufacturing of and Trafficking in Firearms, Their Parts and Components and Ammunition, supplementing the United Nations Convention against Transnational Organized Crime GA Res. 255, Nov. 15, 2000, UN Doc. A/RES/55/255 (2001), done May 31, 2001, entered into force July 3, 2005.

States for breaches associated with trafficking on its own account will normally be required to establish its status as "injured" by showing that it has been "specially affected" by the breach in question. Failure of one State to prevent or respond adequately to trafficking could well "specially affect" the nationals of another State. In respect of trafficking-related violations taking place in or through or affecting third States, meeting the "specially affects" criterion is likely to be more difficult.

There may well be situations in which more than one State is "injured" by an internationally wrongful act. In such cases, international law is clear on the point that each of the States injured by this act have an independent and severable right to invoke the responsibility of the offending State.[226] A similar rule applies in situations where several States are responsible for the same wrongful act. An example relevant to the present context would be wrongful acts on the part of both destination and transit countries contributing to the plight of a particular group of trafficked persons originating from the claimant State. Under such circumstances, each State is responsible for the conduct attributable to it, and the responsibility of each State may be invoked.[227] Further, a claim against one State would not operate to prejudice any right of future action by one injured State against the other responsible State(s).[228]

Can a State that has not been "injured" by a breach of international legal obligation under the terms detailed above still invoke the responsibility of another State? This is an essential question in realizing State responsibility for human rights violations – particularly in relation to violations committed by a State against its own citizens. International law appears to be moving to a point whereby direct "injury" is not always an essential precondition to launching a claim. ILC Draft Article 48 (aspects of which are argued to be progressive development and not codification of an established rule[229]) has been described as an attempt to balance the traditional bilateralism of the law of State responsibility with the rise of collective interests.[230] Article 48 foresees a situation whereby a State that is not permitted to invoke responsibility on its own account may nevertheless invoke responsibility in its capacity as a member of a group to which the obligation is owed, or as a member of the international community as a whole. More precisely, responsibility can be invoked by a noninjured State in one of two situations. In the first situation, the obligation whose breach gives rise to the international responsibility must have

---

[226] ILC Draft Articles, at Art. 46. On the practice of international courts and tribunals on this point, see ILC Commentary, at Art. 46, paras. 1–4.

[227] ILC Draft Articles, at Art. 47(1). See also the ILC Commentary on this provision, which notes that the principle of independent responsibility expressed in this Article reflects the position under general international law, absent an agreement to the contrary between the States concerned: ILC Commentary, at Art. 47, para. 3.

[228] ILC Draft Articles, at Art. 47(2)(b).

[229] Brown Weiss, "Invoking State Responsibility in the Twenty-First Century," at 803–815.

[230] I. Scobbie, "The Invocation of Responsibility for the Breach of 'Obligations under Peremptory Norms of General International Law,'" (2002) 13 *European Journal of International Law* 1202, at 1204.

been owed to a group to which the invoking State belongs and must have been established for the collective interest.[231] The nature of an obligation falling within this first category must be such as to "transcend the sphere of bilateral relations of the States parties"[232] and would include, for example, regional systems for the protection of human rights, such as have been established in Europe, the Americas, and Africa.[233]

In the second situation, the relevant obligation must be one that is owed to the international community as a whole.[234] The ILC Commentary attached to this Article confirms that this particular provision is intended to give effect to the concept of obligations *erga omnes* (obligations owed to the international community as a whole and, because of the importance of the rights involved, in whose protection all States have a legal interest) as set out by the ICJ in the *Barcelona Traction* case.[235] The relevance of the provision lies in the fact that many legal obligations relevant to trafficking can be characterized as obligations *erga omnes*.[236] Importantly, the full spectrum of remedies is only available to injured States. The claimant State under Article 48, not having been injured in its own right, is not entitled to claim compensation on its own behalf (and apparently not entitled to engage in countermeasures).[237] The emphasis is accordingly on cessation of the wrongful act; guarantees of noncontinuation as appropriate; and, in the interests of those injured or of the beneficiaries of the obligation, performance of the obligation of reparation.[238] Beyond that, the availability of reparation will depend on a range of factors most easily ascertained with reference to the primary rule and the individual circumstances of the case.

In terms of procedural requirements, international law provides guidance on the modalities to be observed regarding the making and recognition of claims involving

---

[231] ILC Draft Articles, at Art. 48(1).

[232] ILC Commentary, at Art. 48, para. 7.

[233] Ibid.

[234] ILC Draft Articles, at Art. 48(2). On the term "international community as a whole," see ILC Commentary, at Art. 48, para. 7 and Brown Weiss, "Invoking State Responsibility in the Twenty-First Century," at 804.

[235] Further on this doctrine, see Chapter 2 of this volume. On the concept of customary obligations *erga omnes* pre-*Barcelona Traction*, see Meron, *Human Rights and Humanitarian Norms as Customary Law*, at 188–190.

[236] The court in *Barcelona Traction* identified obligations *erga omnes* as deriving, for example, "from the principles and rules governing basic rights of the human person including protection from slavery and racial discrimination": at para. 34. See further, the discussion of obligations *erga omnes* earlier in this chapter. Brown Weiss notes that this category of obligations is likely to grow, especially in relation to human rights and environmental protection. She argues that, through Article 48, the ILC "sets the stage for states to invoke state responsibility for the breach of any obligation owed to the international community": Brown Weiss, "Invoking State Responsibility in the Twenty-First Century," at 804.

[237] ILC Article 54 preserves the right of States invoking responsibility under Article 48 to take "lawful measures" to ensure cessation of the violation and reparation in the interest of the State and beneficiaries of the obligation breached.

[238] ILC Draft Articles, at Arts. 48(2), 54.

State responsibility, which are the same whether or not the claim is being made by an "injured" State.[239] For example, the invoking State is required to give notice of its claim.[240] Such notice may specify the conduct that the responsible State is to take in order to ease the wrongful act as well as the form of reparation it is seeking.[241] General international law also requires the injured State to fulfill the rule relating to nationality of claims[242] as well as, in applicable cases, the customary rule requiring exhaustion of local remedies.[243] Most claims involving violations of international human rights law will be subject to this latter rule whereby the claim itself will be rendered inadmissible if available and effective local remedies have not been exhausted.[244] An injured State can also lose its right to invoke a claim through waiver or acquiescence.[245]

---

[239] ILC Draft Article 48(3) extends the application of the procedural provisions contained in Articles 43 (notice of claim), 44 (admissibility of claims), and 45 (loss of the right to invoke responsibility) to invocation of responsibility by a noninjured State entitled to do so under paragraph 1 of Article 48.

[240] Ibid. at Art. 43(1); VCLT, at Art. 65.

[241] ILC Draft Articles, at Art. 43(2); VCLT, at Art. 65.

[242] ILC Draft Articles, at Art. 44(a): "Admissibility of claims: The responsibility of a State may not be invoked if: (a) The claim is not brought in accordance with any applicable rule relating to the nationality of claims; (b) The claim is one to which the rule of exhaustion of local remedies applies and any available and effective local remedy has not been exhausted."

[243] Ibid. at Art. 44(b). Note that the ILC Commentary identifies this rule as one of customary international law: ILC Commentary, at Art. 44, para. 4. The exhaustion of local remedies rule was an important aspect of the law of State responsibility for injury to aliens. An alien alleging breach of an international obligation was obliged to exhaust all remedies available in the host country before his or her State of nationality could take over the claim. See further, Shaw, *International Law*, at 730–733. On the application of this rule in the specific context of contemporary international human rights law, see S. D'Ascoli and K.M. Scherr, "The Rule of Prior Exhaustion of Local Remedies in the International Law Doctrine and its Application in the Specific Context of Human Rights Protection," European University Institute Working Paper LAW No. 2007/02 (Feb. 19, 2007) (D'Ascoli and Scherr, "The Rule of Prior Exhaustion of Local Remedies").

[244] See, for example, the American Convention on Human Rights, at Art. 46(1)(a); European Human Rights Convention, at Art. 26; African Charter, at Arts. 50, 56(5)-(6); CERD, at Arts. 11(3), 14(7)(a); ICCPR, at Art. 41(1)(c); Optional Protocol to the International Covenant on Civil and Political Rights, 999 UNTS 302, done Dec. 16, 1966, entered into force Mar. 23, 1976 (ICCPR First Optional Protocol), at Art. 5(2)(b); Convention against Torture and Other Cruel, Inhuman or Degrading Treatment or Punishment, 1465 UNTS 85, done Dec. 10, 1984, June 26, 1987 (Convention against Torture), at Art. 21(1)(c); and Optional Protocol to the Convention on the Elimination of All Forms of Discrimination against Women, 2131 UNTS 83, done Dec. 19, 1999, entered into force Dec. 22, 2000 (CEDAW Optional Protocol), at Art. 4(1). Note that customary law does not require the claimant to satisfy this requirement if local remedies can be shown to be unavailable or otherwise ineffective: *Robert E. Brown Case (United States v. Great Britain)*, (1923) 6 UNRIAA 120. Brownlie states that "[t]he best test appears to be that an effective remedy must be available 'as a matter of reasonable possibility'": I. Brownlie, *Principles of Public International Law* (2008), at 495. In most cases, the treaty provisions referred to above specifically exclude the application of the exhaustion of local remedies rule in cases where their exhaustion is unreasonably prolonged, ineffective, or otherwise, unavailable. See further, Shaw, *International Law*; and D'Ascoli and Scherr, "The Rule of Prior Exhaustion of Local Remedies."

[245] ILC Draft Articles, at Art. 45; VCLT, at Art. 45.

4.5.2. *Rules Governing Invocation of Responsibility for Violations of Human Rights Norms*

The ILC provisions on invocation of responsibility "operate in a residual way"[246] and do not affect the international legal rights of individuals and non-State entities under particular treaty regimes. Customary rules governing a particular area of law can also play an important role in determining applicable rules with respect to invocation. In the area of human rights, custom as well as international and regional human rights treaties have together created a set of rules that express the special nature of human rights and that both reflect and differ from the generally applicable rules set out above. Concordance between the general rules and the special regime is high. Human rights law recognizes, for example, the concept of certain internationally wrongful acts offending the international system and international society as a whole; "[a]s such, they injure the 'legal' interest of each and every party to a human rights treaty and, with respect to customary human rights, of all States."[247] The ILC rules that extend a right of invocation to noninjured States are in accordance with international human rights law, which does not require a connection of nationality between the "victim" and the invoking State:

> Unless a treaty provision otherwise provides or implies, a claim alleging violation of human rights may therefore be submitted by one State against another even if the individual victim possesses the nationality of the defendant State and not of the complaining State.[248]

Most of the major international and regional human rights treaties, as well as labor rights conventions, create and regulate systems for the submission and consideration of complaints by one State Party against another.[249] The right to challenge violations is vested in all States Parties, irrespective of the nationality of the victim and of any material injury to the claimant State. While such provisions would appear to offer

---

[246] ILC Commentary, at Art. 55, para. 2.

[247] Meron, *Human Rights and Humanitarian Norms as Customary Law*, at 148. See further, the discussion of obligations *erga omnes* at notes 200–201, 236 and the accompanying text above.

[248] Meron, *Human Rights and Humanitarian Norms as Customary Law*, at 196, citing American Law Institute, *Restatement (Third) of the Foreign Relations Law of the United States* (1987), at § 703(2).

[249] See, for example, European Human Rights Convention, at Arts. 24, 48 (compulsory jurisdiction of the European Court over interstate complaints); ICCPR, at Art. 41 (jurisdiction of the Human Rights Committee over interstate complaints dependent on special acceptance); Convention against Torture, at Art. 21 (jurisdiction of the Committee against Torture over interstate complaints dependent on special acceptance); American Convention on Human Rights, at Art. 45 (jurisdiction of the Inter-American Court of Human Rights dependent on special acceptance); African Charter, at Art. 49 (right of States Parties to refer violations by other States Parties to the African Commission on Human and Peoples' Rights); and the Protocol to the African Charter on the Establishment of the African Court of Human and Peoples' Rights, OAU Doc. OAU/LEG/EXP/AFCHPR/PROT(III), done June 9, 1998, entered into force Jan. 25, 2005, at Art. 5 (permitting both States Parties that have lodged complaints with the Commission and those that have had complaints lodged against them to refer these cases to the Court).

an important avenue for securing State responsibility for violations such as those related to trafficking, they are very rarely used.[250]

Of much more practical significance are the provisions contained in many international and regional human rights treaties that provide for the possibility of individuals to allege violations of human rights by States Parties and to seek remedies on their own behalf.[251] It is relevant to note that, at least at the international level, such procedures almost never form an integral part of the central treaty but require a separate adherence by States Parties prepared to subject themselves to invocation of legal responsibility in this way. Individual complaints procedures have proved to be useful mechanisms for fleshing out the substance of specific human rights provisions and even, on occasion, for prompting legislative and administrative changes that result in a substantial improvement in the protection of rights. However, the treaty bodies responsible for considering such complaints are heavily overcommitted, particularly at the international level. Relatively low and skewed ratification rates for these optional mechanisms mean that they do not offer a secure or consistent avenue for securing accountability and redress in relation to specific cases or situations. It is relevant to note that, to date, only one complaint lodged under an international human rights treaty has related directly to trafficking.[252] Only a small handful of the many more individual complaints considered by regional human rights courts have touched on violations of obligations related to trafficking.[253] The potential of the human rights treaty bodies to contribute to more effective implementation of the international law of trafficking is considered further in Chapter 9.

The rules governing invocation are permissive. States *may* invoke the responsibility of others under certain circumstances. However, they do not appear to be under an obligation to do so. Some have argued that this represents an overly narrow

[250] For a discussion of why interstate complaints are so rare, see P.H. Kooijmans, "Interstate Dispute Settlement in the Field of Human Rights," in M. Brus, A.S. Muller and S. Wiermers eds., *The United Nations Decade of International Law: Reflections on International Dispute Settlement* 87 (1991); S. Leckie, "The Interstate Complaint Procedure in International Human Rights Law: Hopeful Prospects or Wishful Thinking?" (1988) 10 *Human Rights Quarterly* 249; and generally M.T. Kamminga, *Interstate Accountability for Violations of Human Rights* (1992) (describing the formal interstate complaints procedures under most human rights treaties as "a dead letter," at 47). A useful discussion of international State responsibility, the right to a remedy and the rarity of interstate complaints in the context of "the uniqueness of human rights cases" can be found in Shelton, *Remedies in International Human Rights Law*, at 47–49.

[251] ICCPR First Optional Protocol; CEDAW Optional Protocol; Optional Protocol to the International Covenant on Economic, Social and Cultural Rights, UN Doc. A/63/435, done Dec. 10, 2008, not yet in force; Convention against Torture, at Art. 22; CERD, at Art. 14; American Convention on Human Rights, at Art. 90; European Human Rights Convention, at Art. 25; African Charter, at Arts. 55–56.

[252] *Zheng v. The Netherlands*, CEDAW Comm. No. 15/2007, UN Doc. CEDAW/C/42/D/15/2007, decided Oct. 27, 2008.

[253] See, for example, *Rantsev v. Cyprus and Russia*; *Siliadan v. France*, (2006) 43 EHRR 16 (ECHR, July 26, 2005) (slavery, servitude, forced labor); *Koraou v. Republic of Niger*, Judgment No. ECW/CCJ/JUD/06/08, ECOWAS Community Court of Justice, Oct. 27, 2008 (slavery, forced labor, sexual exploitation).

reading of both obligations and responsibilities, particularly with regard to international human rights law. Henkin, for example, asserts that "[e]very State Party [to the major human rights instruments] has a right, and has also assumed responsibility, to seek compliance by other States for *their* undertakings under such treaties,"[254] and that "every State is responsible to seek compliance by all other States with their obligations under the customary international law of human rights."[255] While such an interpretation would add considerably to the strength of international law, a *duty* to invoke international responsibility is not yet widely recognized. Indeed, as noted previously, even the more equivocal "duty to cooperate" in order to end violations of peremptory norms is yet to secure the status of a general norm of international law.[256]

4.5.3. *Countermeasures*

Countermeasures involve actions (or omissions) by an injured State in response to an internationally wrongful act, which, in the absence of this prior wrongful act, would be contrary to the injured State's own international obligations. Countermeasures are not punishment or retaliation; their purpose must always be to induce compliance, to "restore the legal relationship with the responsible State which has been ruptured by the internationally wrongful act."[257] While the issue of countermeasures has not traditionally been of great practical significance to the enforcement of international human rights obligations,[258] it is nevertheless important to acknowledge the central role that countermeasures have played and continue to play in the implementation of the State responsibility regime and to explore their potential application to internationally wrongful acts such as those associated with trafficking.

The capacity for abuse of countermeasures has led to the development of strong procedural rules governing their use. The key rules are contained in Chapter II of the ILC Draft Articles and include a reiteration of the general principle that the purpose of countermeasures is to induce compliance.[259] For this reason, they are to be temporary in nature and, as far as possible, reversible in terms of future legal relations between the two States concerned.[260] Countermeasures must always follow a demand from the injured State for compliance on the part of the responsible State

---

[254] L. Henkin, "Interstate Responsibility for Compliance with Human Rights Obligations," in L.C. Vohrah et al eds., *Man's Inhumanity to Man: Essays on International Law in Honour of Antonio Cassese* 383 (2003), at 383.

[255] Ibid.

[256] ILC Draft Articles, at Art. 4(1); ILC Commentary, at Art. 4, para. 3.

[257] ILC Commentary, at Part Three, Chapter II, Introduction, para. 1.

[258] See further the discussion on countermeasures and human rights in R. Provost, *International Human Rights and Humanitarian Law* (2002), at 201–226.

[259] ILC Draft Articles, at Art. 49(1).

[260] Ibid. at Art. 49.

and an offer to negotiate;[261] they must be proportionate,[262] and must not involve a departure from basic norms of international law including obligations for the protection of fundamental human rights.[263] In other words, States will generally not be entitled to suspend their human rights obligations in response to violations of international law, including human rights law, by another State. The ILC also establishes a clear link between countermeasures and binding dispute settlement procedures with a view to ensuring that a State resorting to countermeasures could be required by the "responsible" State to justify its action before an arbitral tribunal.[264]

Which States may lawfully adopt countermeasures? More specifically, can countermeasures only be taken by "injured" States as these are defined by ILC Draft Article 42? Or are they also an option for a State entitled to invoke responsibility under ILC Draft Article 48, because the breach is of an obligation owed to a group of which it is a member or to the international community as a whole? This is an important question in the present context because, as pointed out above, it is under the latter circumstances that a typical claim of State responsibility for violation of the obligations most commonly associated with trafficking (for example, human rights obligations) is likely to be raised. The relevant provisions of the ILC Draft Articles are, in fact, limited in their application to injured States and do not identify a right of States not directly injured to take countermeasures in the general or collective interest. The ILC Commentary concludes that the current state of international law on this point is uncertain.[265] It is only by way of a savings clause that a potential right of this kind is preserved in the ILC Draft Articles and left to further development of international law.[266] As Crawford has noted, the preservation of a potential right of a noninjured State to take countermeasures is in keeping with the need to ensure that obligations toward the international community or otherwise in the collective interest are not relegated to second-class status in comparison with those under bilateral treaties.[267] It also reflects the reality that States do not appear

---

[261] Ibid. at Art. 52(1).

[262] Ibid. at Art. 51.

[263] Ibid. at Art. 50(1).

[264] Ibid. at Arts. 50(2)(a), 52(3), 52(4). See also J. Crawford, J. Peel and S. Olleson, "The ILC's Articles on Responsibility of States for Internationally Wrongful Acts: Completion of the Second Reading," (2001) 12 *European Journal of International Law* 963 (Crawford, Peel and Olleson, "The ILC's Articles on Responsibility of States for Internationally Wrongful Acts: Completion of the Second Reading"), at 966.

[265] ILC Commentary, at Art. 54, para. 6.

[266] ILC Draft Articles, at Art. 54. See ILC Commentary, at Art. 54, paras. 3–4, for an overview of State practice supporting the ILC's conclusion that "[a]t present, there appears to be no clearly recognized entitlement of States referred to in Article 48 to take countermeasures in the collective interest": ILC Commentary, at Art. 54, para. 6. For an analysis of the "doctrine" of humanitarian intervention from the perspective of countermeasures and State responsibility, see A. Cassese, "*Ex Iniuria Ius Oritur*: Are We Moving Towards International Legitimation of Forcible Humanitarian Countermeasures in the World Community?" (1999) 10 *European Journal of International Law* 23.

[267] Crawford, Peel and Olleson, "The ILC's Articles on Responsibility of States for Internationally Wrongful Acts: Completion of the Second Reading," at 982.

willing to give up all possibility of individual action in the face of collective inaction or apathy.[268]

A final avenue of justification for countermeasures by third States could be identified with respect to conduct that amounts to a "serious breach" of a "peremptory norm of international law."[269] As noted above, such serious breaches place States under a duty not to recognize the legality of the breach *and* to cooperate in bringing the violation to an end.[270] Countermeasures taken in pursuance of this goal may well be permissible.

It is certainly possible to envisage countermeasures in the context of trafficking. States could, for example, refuse to accept the return of their nationals on the basis that those being returned were trafficked persons who had not been correctly identified or treated as such by the returning State and in relation to whom the right to a remedy had been denied. In this case, the violation of an international legal obligation (the right to return to one's country) is in response to an internationally wrongful act (failure to identify, support, protect, or provide remedies). It could be argued that this is a temporary and proportionate response by the State of origin aimed at inducing compliance. However, this example serves as a useful illustration of the restrictive nature of permissible countermeasures. To deny victims the right to return home would likely compound the injury done to them. Such countermeasures would thereby be illegal on the basis that their application affects obligations for the protection of fundamental human rights.[271]

On even less firm ground is the sanctions regime created by the United States' Victims of Trafficking and Violence Protection Act of 2000 (as amended).[272] In accordance with this legislation, the United States Government will not, as a matter of policy, provide nonhumanitarian, non-trade-related assistance to any government that does not comply with its prescribed minimum standards to prevent and punish trafficking and that is not making significant efforts to bring itself into compliance.[273] In addition, such countries will also face U.S. opposition to their seeking and obtaining funds from multilateral financial institutions including the World Bank and the International Monetary Fund.[274] Officials of the administering agency, the U.S. State Department, have occasionally (and imprecisely) referred to "countermeasures" when describing the regime established by the Act.[275] Even

---

[268] Ibid.

[269] ILC Draft Articles, at Art. 40.

[270] Ibid. at Art. 41.

[271] Ibid. at Art. 50(1)(b).

[272] Victims of Trafficking and Violence Protection Act of 2000, 22 USC 7102.

[273] Ibid. at § 10(a). A determination to this effect is to be made by the President.

[274] Ibid. at § 110(d)(1)(B).

[275] See, for example, R.L. Hoffman, "Effective Countermeasures against the Trafficking in Human Beings and Smuggling of Migrants," in UN Asia and Far East Institute for the Prevention of Crime and Treatment of Offenders, *Work Product of the 122nd International Training Course: Effective*

if it could be argued that the minimum standards prescribed by the Act are reflective of existing international obligations, and that a failure on the part of any State to meet these standards is therefore indicative of a breach of that State's international obligation,[276] the sanctions regime does not measure up to the ILC standard of countermeasures. Withdrawal of voluntary aid and lobbying against international financial assistance are certainly unfriendly acts, but it would be extremely difficult to characterize them as contrary to specific treaty rights or otherwise as breaches of international obligations owed by the U.S. Such measures would therefore more accurately be described as "retorsion"[277] and, as such, outside the scope of the State responsibility regime.

4.6. A NOTE ON LEGAL RESPONSIBILITIES OF INTERNATIONAL ORGANIZATIONS, PRIVATE INDIVIDUALS, AND PRIVATE ENTITIES

The discussion in this chapter has focused exclusively on *State* responsibility – both for acts of the State and for acts of private individuals and entities. It does not extend to consider the separate question of whether legal responsibilities for internationally wrongful acts can attach directly to such individuals and entities – or indeed to international governmental organizations. This focus on State responsibility is justified because of the primary position of States in the international legal order. While that position may be changing, it is not yet time to let go of an international legal order that is predicated on the existence of sovereign States. On a more practical level, it is largely (if not exclusively) through the State that trafficked persons may seek protection, and it is against the State that those same individuals may claim reparations or redress for violations. The actions of individual exploiters and indeed of organized criminal groups must ultimately be controlled by and through States. To recognize this situation is not the same as expressing satisfaction with it. Practitioners and guardians of international law are acutely conscious that the essentially Statist nature of its rules and mechanisms is a major weakness in a world where players other than States wield very real power and influence.

International law is not, of course, just for and about States. International human rights law, for example, is based on an acceptance of the idea that individuals have legal personality. They are holders of legal entitlements that can, in some cases, be directly enforced against States by those same individuals. International law has also come some way toward recognizing that it is persons, not abstract entities, who break rules and violate rights. The concept of individual criminal liability, first recognized

---

Administration of Criminal Justice to Tackle Trafficking in Human Beings and Smuggling of Migrants 80 (2002).

[276] See further, the discussion at Chapter 9.4.

[277] The ILC Commentary refers to retorsion as "unfriendly conduct which is not inconsistent with any international obligation of the State engaging in it even though it may be in response to an internationally wrongful act": ILC Commentary, at Part Three, Chapter II, Introduction, para. 3.

at Nuremburg and more recently institutionalized in international law through the Statute of the International Criminal Court,[278] is perhaps the best example of such recognition. International criminal law unambiguously recognizes that individuals can be held legally responsible for a range of internationally wrongful acts including war crimes and crimes against humanity.[279] Beyond international criminal law, international responsibility in relation to individuals remains undeveloped.[280] A similar situation exists with respect to armed opposition groups – some of whom have been implicated in trafficking-related conduct: for example, recruitment of children for soldiering, forced labor, and sexual exploitation. Members of such groups are of course subject to international criminal responsibility. The group itself may, under certain circumstances, also be held responsible for violations of relevant humanitarian law and human rights norms.[281] However, the nature of this responsibility and the way in which it may be invoked remains uncertain.

International organizations have become increasingly important players in international affairs. As their roles and activities expand, there is, in the words of two recent commentators:

> an expansion of responsibility for their interactions with an equally increasing number of other non-state entities like individuals, groups of individuals, transnational corporations, nongovernmental organizations, minorities, and indigenous peoples.[282]

The responsibility of IGOs for internationally wrongful acts[283] is of potential importance to the issue of trafficking. Particularly in situations of conflict and post-conflict, the complicity of military, peacekeeping, humanitarian, and other international personnel in trafficking and related exploitation has been extensively documented.[284] Certain policies and practices of international finance organizations

---

[278] Rome Statute of the International Criminal Court, 2187 UNTS 90, done July 17, 1998, entered into force July 1, 2002.

[279] See further, the discussion of individual criminal liability in Chapter 3 in this book. Another related example is the requirement that those committing genocide be punished "whether they are constitutionally responsible rulers, public officials or private individuals": Convention on the Prevention and Punishment of the Crime of Genocide, 78 UNTS 227, Dec. 9, 1948, entered into force Jan. 12, 1951, at Art. 4.

[280] Crawford and Olleson, "The Nature and Forms of International Responsibility," at 453.

[281] See generally, Clapham, *Human Rights Obligations of Non-State Actors*, at chapter 7.

[282] E. Suzuki and S. Nanwani, "Responsibility of International Organizations: The Accountability Mechanisms of Multilateral Development Banks," (2006) 27 Mi*chigan Journal of International Law* 177 (Suzuki and Nanwani, "Responsibility of International Organizations: The Accountability Mechanisms of Multilateral Development Banks"), at 180.

[283] The International Law Commission has been working on this topic (including the related issue of international responsibility of a State for the internationally wrongful act of an international organization) since 2002. That work confirms that the rules of State responsibility generally apply to international organizations *mutatis mutandis* with some fundamental differences, several of which are discussed below. See further, the series of annual reports produced by ILC Rapporteur Giorgio Gaja since 2003, available at http://untreaty.un.org/ilc/guide/9_11.htm (accessed Nov. 25, 2009).

[284] See further, Chapter 8.1.5 in this volume.

and development assistance agencies have been shown to negatively affect human rights. It is eminently foreseeable that such bodies could be implicated in violations of rights related to trafficking.[285]

International law recognizes the international legal personality of IGOs (conferred by States), including their capacity to enter into and become bound by treaties.[286] International organizations are, in the words of the ICJ, "bound by any obligations incumbent upon them under general rules of international law, under their constitutions or under international agreements to which they are parties."[287] A critical aspect of their legal personality is the capacity of international organizations to be legally responsible for the acts and omissions that violate international law and that can be attributed to them under the secondary rules that govern such responsibility.[288] Importantly, attribution of conduct necessary to establish an internationally wrongful act extends beyond employees of the organization to include the actions of contractors or agents who have been recruited to carry out or help carry out one of the functions of the organization.[289] It would also appear to cover the conduct of State organs (such as military units) placed at the disposal of the organization and under its "effective or factual control."[290]

[285] On international responsibility and the UN's financial institutions, see Clapham, *Human Rights Obligations of Non-State Actors*, at chapter 4. Specifically on multilateral development banks including the World Bank, see Suzuki and Nanwani, "Responsibility of International Organizations: The Accountability Mechanisms of Multilateral Development Banks." On the international responsibility of multilateral development agencies for human rights, see M. Darrow and L. Arbour, "The Pillar of Glass: Human Rights in the Development Operations of the United Nations," (2009) 103 *American Journal of International Law* 406.

[286] See generally, P. Klein and P. Sands eds., *Bowett's Law of International Institutions* (2009), esp. at Part III, "Legal Personality." See also the Vienna Convention on the Law of Treaties between States and International Organisations or between International Organisations, done Mar. 21, 1986, not yet in force, reprinted in (1986) 25 ILM 543.

[287] *Interpretation of the Agreement of 25 March 1951 between the WHO and Egypt (Advisory Opinion)*, [1980] ICJ Rep 73, at 89–90, para. 37.

[288] See ILC Draft Articles on the Responsibility of International Organizations, at Art. 3 (with Commentaries, in International Law Commission, *Report of the International Law Commission on the Work of Its Fifty-Fifth Session*, UNGAOR, 58th Sess., Supp. No. 10, UN Doc. A/58/10, at 45–49) and Art. 8 (with Commentaries, in International Law Commission, *Report of the International Law Commission on the Work of Its Fifty-Seventh Session*, UNGAOR, 60th Sess., Supp. No. 10, UN Doc. A/60/10, at 87–90).

[289] *Reparation for Injuries Case*, at 177. This position is reflected in Article 4(2) of the ILC Draft Articles on the Responsibility of International Organizations: with Commentaries, in International Law Commission, *Report of the International Law Commission on the Work of Its Fifty-Sixth Session*, UNGAOR, 59th Sess., Supp. No. 10, UN Doc. A/59/10, at 103–109.

[290] ILC Draft Articles on the Responsibility of International Organizations, at Art. 5: with Commentaries, in International Law Commission, *Report of the International Law Commission on the Work of Its Fifty-Sixth Session*, UNGAOR, 59th Sess., Supp. No. 10, UN Doc. A/59/10, at 109–115. This issue was considered by the European Court of Human Rights in a recent and controversial judgment in which it held that the actions of armed forces of States acting under UN Security Council authorization were attributable to the UN and not to the States themselves or to NATO (to whom the UN had delegated operational command): *Behrami and Behrami v. France; Saramati v. France, Germany and Norway*, (2007) 45 EHRR 10 (ECtHR, May 2, 2007). The ILC Rapporteur Gaja has noted that

Beyond this narrow field, *the law as it stands* too often morphs into *the law as it could be*. Transnational corporations could be implicated in trafficking through, for example, the use of forced labor. These entities do indeed have certain limited rights and duties under contemporary human rights law in areas such as foreign investment and environmental damage[291] and, in some cases, are even empowered to enforce their rights against others.[292] Arguments for anything more substantial rest largely on the shifting and unstable sands of soft accountability processes that can only optimistically be characterized as "law." For present purposes, it is clear that the nature and quality of the established legal capacities of private corporations fall far short of what would be required to secure any meaningful progress with respect to holding such entities directly liable under international law for breaches of international standards relating to trafficking. The possibility of invoking international legal responsibility against organized criminal groups and other private bodies involved in trafficking appears to be even more remote. While sobering, this verdict serves to highlight the potential value of alternative methods for securing accountability for the actions of non-State entities, for example, through criminal actions and civil suits in national courts.

A realistic assessment of the current situation should not operate to lessen the impetus toward expanding the reach of international law to include private actors and to hold such actors accountable for violations. In trafficking, as in other areas of international law, the impunity that non-State actors continue to enjoy operates to undermine the effectiveness of international legal regulation and denies justice to many.

4.7. SUMMARY OF THE KEY PRINCIPLES OF STATE RESPONSIBILITY RELEVANT TO TRAFFICKING

The task of the present chapter has been to explore the relationship between trafficking and the legal responsibility of States. Of particular interest is the question of whether, and under what circumstances, States can be held responsible for the

---

a different conclusion would have been reached had the Court applied Draft Article 5; he also concluded that: "as a matter of policy, the approach taken by the European Court of Human Rights is unconvincing. It would lead to attributing to the United Nations conduct which the organization has not specifically authorized and of which it may have little knowledge or no knowledge at all": G. Gaja, "Seventh Report on the Responsibility of International Organizations," UN Doc. A/CN.4/610, Mar. 27, 2009, at paras. 26, 30. See further, K.M. Larsen, "Attribution of Conduct in Peace Operations: The 'Ultimate Authority and Control' Test," (2008) 19 *European Journal of International Law* 509; M. Milanović and T. Papić, "As Bad As It Gets: The European Court of Human Rights' *Behrami and Saramati* Decision and General International Law," (2009) 58 *International and Comparative Law Quarterly* 267; and A. Sari, "Jurisdiction and International Responsibility in Peace Support Operations: The *Behrami* and *Saramati* Cases," (2008) 8 *Human Rights Law Review* 151.

[291] Kinley and Tadaki, "From Talk to Walk," at 946–947.
[292] Ibid. at 947.

trafficking-related actions of private persons and entities – and the consequences of those actions. The analysis set out above has provided some important insights and a few preliminary conclusions.

First, international legal responsibility requires that the act or omission be attributable to the State. The key principles of attribution are as follows:

- The "official" (even if unauthorized) conduct of a State organ or of a State official who violates established primary rules will be attributable to the State.
- Whether an act or omission of a government official is determined to be "official" or private depends on whether the conduct in question was carried out by persons acting with apparent governmental authority.
- A legislative, executive, or judicial act will most easily be directly attributable to the State because of the inevitably "official" nature of such acts.
- Examples of other acts potentially attributable to the State (subject to the requirement set out in the second point above) could include: direct involvement of public officials in trafficking through protection or patronage of commercial premises using the services of victims of trafficking; substantial involvement or effective control by public officials or entities over organized criminal groups implicated in trafficking; and corruption of the judicial process through bribery.
- States will generally not be held responsible for the conduct of private entities absent a special circumstance (indicating control and/or approval) linking apparent private behavior to the State itself.

Second, in addition to being attributable to the State, the act or omission must *also* constitute a breach of an international obligation of the State.

- The question of whether there has been a breach of an obligation depends on the content and interpretation of the primary rule.
- In areas of law relevant to trafficking, including human rights, the relevant primary obligation will often extend beyond negative obligations on noninterference to include positive obligations such as legislative reform, provision of remedies, and protection from non-State interference. Breaches of obligation may involve composite acts and omissions.

Third, despite the general rule of nonattribution of private conduct, the primacy of the primary rule means that there will be circumstances under which the State can be held responsible for trafficking-related violations originating in the conduct of private persons or entities.

- In cases where responsibility for the initial act does not fall on the State, responsibility could still be imputed through a concomitant or subsequent failure on the part of the State to prevent, respond to, or remedy abuses committed by private persons or entities. Whether or not responsibility can be imputed in this way in a particular case will always depend on the content of the relevant primary rule.

- Human rights treaties often impose a general obligation on States to, for example, "respect" and "ensure" the rights identified in that instrument. In such cases, States are required to guarantee rights as opposed to merely refraining from interfering with their enjoyment. This will usually require at least some action on the part of the State Party to prevent and respond to non-State interference with established rights.

- The standard of "due diligence" is becoming the accepted benchmark against which State actions to prevent or respond to violations originating in the acts of third parties are to be judged. An assessment of whether a State has met such a standard will depend, once again, on the content of the original obligation as well as the facts and circumstances of the case.

- In relation to trafficking, States will generally not be able to avoid responsibility for the acts of private persons when their ability to influence an alternative, more positive outcome (judged against the primary rule) can be established. In such cases, the source of responsibility is not the act itself but the failure of States to take measures of prevention or response in accordance with the required standard.

Fourth, a finding of State responsibility carries with it certain consequences. International law dictates several governing principles related to both consequences for breach and invocation of responsibility. These apply in all cases to the extent they have not been displaced by a regime created under a specific system or treaty.

- The immediate and automatic consequence of a finding of responsibility is an obligation of cessation. The second, automatic obligation on the offending State is to make full reparation for injury caused by the internationally wrongful act.

- International law recognizes a range of elements within the concept of reparations, namely restitution, compensation, and satisfaction. Subelements of these categories, particularly appropriate for responding to human rights violations and violations associated with trafficking, include rehabilitation and guarantees of nonrepetition.

- International law generally only recognizes the right of an "injured" State to invoke responsibility on its own account. However, direct injury is not always an essential precondition to launching a claim, especially in relation to collective obligations owed to a group of States or to the international community as a whole.

- Rules governing invocation of responsibility for violations of international human rights law differ significantly from those that apply to breaches of international law more generally. In both treaty law and custom, there is usually no damage requirement and no requirement for a connection of nationality between the "victim" and the invoking State. Most of the major human rights treaties, including those considered in the previous two chapters, have developed their own invocation procedures that, in at least several cases, provide for the possibility of individuals to allege violations of human rights and to seek reparation.

Writing about State responsibility almost half a century ago, García-Amador described it as "[o]ne of the most vast and complex [areas] of international law – it would be difficult to find a topic beset with greater confusion and uncertainty."[293] While the finalization of the International Law Commission's work has gone some way toward improving this situation, it remains true that these abstract rules of uneven authority are, as noted in the Introduction to this book, "devilishly difficult to apply."[294] It is unsurprising that State responsibility remains an area where angels (and international lawyers) fear to tread. The challenges must, however, be faced head-on. State responsibility is the heart and soul of international law. Without these secondary rules, the substance of the primary rules would be lost. The inverse is also true. The task of determining responsibility and its consequences in a specific situation can only be undertaken with reference to the primary rules that are, after all, the original source of obligation. The practical implications of this relationship between the primary rules relating to trafficking and those governing responsibility for their breach are explored in detail in the following chapters.

---

[293] F.V. García-Amador, "First Report on International Responsibility," UN Doc. A/CN.4/SER.A/1956/Add.1, reprinted in (1956) 2 *Yearbook of the International Law Commission* 173, at 175, cited in Allott, "State Responsibility and the Unmaking of International Law," at 4.

[294] Caron, "The ILC Articles on State Responsibility: The Paradoxical Relationship between Form and Authority," at 872.

5

Obligations of Protection and Support

What obligations do States owe to victims of trafficking? The answer to this question is far from settled. While there seems to be general agreement on the need for victim protection, the precise contours and limits of that protection have not yet been firmly established. Victim advocates have claimed a wide range of entitlements, from the provision of emergency shelter to a right of permanent residency in the destination country. States have been much more cautious in embracing specific rights of victims and in accepting the corresponding obligations. This reluctance to recognize obligations to victims has been tempered over time by a number of factors. These include a growing acceptance by States of the plight of trafficked persons and of the political importance of being seen to be responding appropriately. Another important factor in shifting attitudes to victim protection and support is the now-widespread recognition among criminal justice practitioners that protection and support are a vital part of ensuring that victims are able to play an effective role in the investigation and prosecution of trafficking cases.[1]

Over the past decade, there has been considerable progress in the articulation of States' obligations to victims. Taking the various international, regional, and national instruments together, and drawing on a broader trend in international law toward recognition and detailed articulation of victims' rights and concomitant State duties, it is now possible to identify an emergent consensus around several core obligations, underscored by a general obligation to identify victims of trafficking in the first place. These include: noncriminalization of victims; provision of immediate protection and support; provision of legal assistance including temporary residency; and safe and voluntary return. In the case of child victims, special obligations have been identified and accepted. Although the various obligations of protection and

---

[1] See, for example, International Criminal Police Organization (Interpol), *Trafficking in Human Beings: Best Practice Guidance Manual for Investigators* (2008); UN Office on Drugs and Crime, *Toolkit to Combat Trafficking in Persons* (2008) (UNODC Toolkit); A.T. Gallagher and P. Holmes, "Developing an Effective Criminal Justice Response to Human Trafficking: Lessons from the Front Line," (2008) 18 *International Criminal Justice Review* 3 (Gallagher and Holmes, "Lessons from the Front Line"). See further Chapter 7, below.

support considered further are closely related to each other, they enjoy differing levels of maturity and persuasive force. This difference is highlighted, where appropriate, throughout the present chapter.

One preliminary matter that deserves to be raised at the outset of this discussion concerns the definition of a "victim of trafficking." While the Trafficking Protocol[2] does not contain such a definition, the European Trafficking Convention addresses this point, stipulating that a victim is "any natural person who is subjected to trafficking in human beings as defined."[3] The issue, however, is not quite so simple. As noted in Chapter 1 and discussed further in this chapter, the process of identifying victims of trafficking is a complicated one. Deciding that a particular situation constitutes trafficking – or that a particular individual is a victim (or indeed a perpetrator) of trafficking – is notoriously complex and time-consuming. If such difficulties and delays result in a withholding of victim status from a person who has indeed been trafficked, this will directly affect the ability of that person to access the rights and protections to which he or she is entitled. Efforts to address this problem have included presumptions of victim status[4] and the introduction of lower-threshold definitions that provide the trigger for certain entitlements.[5]

---

[2] Protocol to Prevent, Suppress and Punish Trafficking in Persons, Especially Women and Children, supplementing the United Nations Convention against Transnational Organized Crime, done Nov. 15, 2000, GA Res. 55/25, Annex II, UN GAOR, 55th Sess., Supp. No. 49, at 53, UN Doc. A/45/49 (Vol. I) (2001), entered into force Dec. 25, 2003 (Trafficking Protocol).

[3] Council of Europe Convention on Action against Trafficking in Human Beings and its Explanatory Report, ETS 197, 16.V.2005, done May 16, 2005, entered into force Feb. 1, 2008 (European Trafficking Convention), at Art. 4(e).

[4] For example, the European Trafficking Convention provides that if there are reasonable grounds to believe that a person is a victim of trafficking, that person is to be provided with immediate support and not to be removed until the formal identification process is completed: ibid. at Art. 10(2). See further, Chapter 5.1.2.

[5] For example, the United Nations Model Law on Trafficking identifies the need for a two-pronged definition of victim of trafficking: United Nations Office on Drugs and Crime, *Model Law on Trafficking in Persons*, UN Sales No. E.09.V.11 (2009) (UNODC Model Law). The first definition, applicable to basic rights and entitlements, is pitched at a relatively low threshold – only requiring a reasonable belief, by the competent authority or organization, that an individual is a victim of trafficking, regardless of whether the perpetrator is identified, apprehended, prosecuted, or convicted. The higher-threshold definition would apply to the more significant rights and entitlements and requires that the person concerned is indeed a victim of the offenses of trafficking set forth in the law. This approach is justified as an attempt to "strike a balance between fulfilling victims' basic and immediate needs upon fleeing a situation of exploitation and a Government's need to regulate the dispensation of services and benefits": ibid. at 21. It also reflects a more general principle that that rights to redress should not be based on a requirement that harm or loss is attributed to a specific perpetrator: UN General Assembly, "Basic Principles and Guidelines on the Right to a Remedy and Reparation for Victims of Gross Violations of International Human Rights Law and Serious Violations of International Humanitarian Law," UN Doc. A/RES/60/147, Dec. 16, 2005 ("Principles and Guidelines on the Right to a Remedy and Reparation"), at para. 9. The UNODC Model Law confirms that "[a] person should be considered and treated as a victim of trafficking in persons, irrespective of whether or not there is already a strong suspicion against an alleged trafficker or an official granting/recognition of the status of victim": UNODC Model Law, at 42. The presumption

In addition to their status as trafficked persons, individuals who have been trafficked are also "victims of crime"[6] and "victims of human rights violations."[7] These two characterizations become important in relation to certain rights, obligations, and responsibilities that are derived from laws that have wider application than the specialized trafficking instruments.

5.1. RAPID AND ACCURATE VICTIM IDENTIFICATION

In many countries, victims of trafficking are never identified and, as a result, are simply invisible. When victims do come to the attention of the State, they are commonly misidentified as illegal or smuggled migrants. Sometimes this is because the State does not wish to accept the existence of trafficked persons within its territory. More commonly, misidentification can be traced to a lack of commitment, understanding, and resources on the part of the State and its agencies. In this respect, it is worth noting that while the additional elements, such as force, deception, coercion, and so on, that distinguish trafficking from illegal migration and migrant smuggling may sometimes be obvious, in many cases they are difficult to prove without active investigation. In other words, many individuals trafficked across international borders, will, *prima facie*, be illegal migrants or victims of migrant smuggling because these characterizations are the easiest for national law enforcement authorities to make. Individuals trafficked internally face different but equally serious obstacles to identification.

5.1.1. *The Importance of Identification*

Why would it matter whether someone is identified as an illegal worker or smuggled migrant rather than as a trafficked person? The difference, in terms of rights and entitlements owed to the trafficked individual, is substantial. As noted earlier in this

---

of victim status in the context of trafficking is most highly developed in relation to children. See further, Chapter 5.5.1.

[6] The Declaration of Basic Principles for Victims of Crime and Abuse of Power defines "victims of crime" as "persons who ... have suffered harm, including physical or mental injury, emotional suffering, economic loss or substantial impairment of their fundamental rights, through acts or omissions that are in violation of criminal laws": UN General Assembly, "Declaration of Basic Principles of Justice for Victims of Crime and Abuse of Power," UN Doc. A/RES/40/34, Nov. 29, 1985 ("Basic Principles for Victims of Crime and Abuse of Power"), at para. 1.

[7] The UN General Assembly's "Basic Principles and Guidelines on the Right to a Remedy and Reparation" defines victims of gross violations of human rights and serious violations of international humanitarian law as "persons who individually or collectively suffered harm, including physical or mental injury, emotional suffering, economic loss or substantial impairment of their fundamental rights, through acts or omissions that constitute gross violations of international human rights law, or serious violations of international humanitarian law. Where appropriate, and in accordance with domestic law, the term 'victim' also includes the immediate family or dependants of the direct victim and persons who have suffered harm in intervening to assist victims in distress or to prevent victimization." "Principles and Guidelines on the Right to a Remedy and Reparation," at para. 8.

book, international law and the national law of many States now recognize that trafficked persons have special rights – and that the State owes a particular duty of protection and support to those persons. An example is provided by contrasting the relevant provisions of the Trafficking Protocol and the Migrant Smuggling Protocol.[8] Under the terms of the latter instrument, States Parties are not required to consider the possibility of permitting victims to remain in their territories temporarily or permanently. When it comes to repatriation, States Parties of origin are to facilitate and accept, without delay, the return of their smuggled nationals and those who have a right of permanent abode within their territories once the nationality or right of permanent residence of the returnee is verified.[9] There is no requirement for either the State of origin or the State of destination to take into account the safety of smuggled migrants in the repatriation process.[10] Smuggled migrants are not entitled to any of the special protections that States Parties are encouraged to grant trafficked persons in relation to their personal safety and physical and psychological well-being. No entitlements are envisaged with respect to legal proceedings against smugglers or the right to a remedy, and there are no special protective measures provided for smuggled children.

The situation is even more calamitous for trafficked persons who are misidentified as illegal or undocumented migrants. While basic rights, applicable to all persons in all circumstances (as considered in detail in Chapter 3), remain at least in theory unaffected, international practice makes clear that illegal migrants do not generally benefit from even the minimal protections afforded to those who are identified as having been smuggled.[11] Without the "resources of citizenship,"[12] illegal migrants are vulnerable to detention and removal. The failure to identify a victim of trafficking and the subsequent deportation of this person as an illegal migrant renders any rights granted to such victims "purely theoretical and illusory."[13] Even if correctly identified as such, trafficked persons may suffer a denial of their rights as a consequence of a subsequent identification failure. A typical example is the failure to identify among trafficked persons those who are entitled to receive

---

[8] Protocol against the Smuggling of Migrants by Land, Sea and Air, supplementing the United Nations Convention against Transnational Organized Crime, done Nov. 15, 2000, GA Res. 55/25, Annex III, UN GAOR, 55th Sess., Supp. No. 49, at 62, UN Doc. A/45/49 (Vol. I) (2001), entered into force Jan. 28, 2004 (Migrant Smuggling Protocol).

[9] Ibid. at Art. 18(1). See further, Chapter 6.1.

[10] The Migrant Smuggling Protocol, at Art. 18(5), does require returning States Parties to "carry out the return in an orderly manner and with due regard for the safety and dignity of the person." It is evident from negotiations that this reference to safety and dignity refers only to the process of return and not to the eventual fate of the individual concerned.

[11] See generally, T.A. Aleinikoff, "International Legal Norms on Migration: Substance Without Architecture," in R. Cholewinski, R. Perruchoud and E. MacDonald eds., *International Migration Law: Developing Paradigms and Key Challenges* 467 (2007).

[12] UNODC Toolkit, at 251.

[13] Council of Europe, *Explanatory Report on the Convention on Action against Trafficking in Human Beings*, ETS 197, 16.V.2005 (European Trafficking Convention Explanatory Report), at para. 131.

international protection. The inadequacy of referral and determination procedures with respect to determining the asylum entitlements of trafficked persons has been well documented.[14]

Those who have been trafficked internally are also greatly disadvantaged by a failure to identify them as such. International obligations described in this chapter and the following ones generally do not distinguish on the basis of whether an international border has been crossed. By not being identified, internally trafficked persons lose access to important rights and protections owed to them by their State.

5.1.2. *An Obligation to Identify Victims*

The major international legal instrument on trafficking does not impose on States Parties an unambiguous obligation to take positive measures to identify individuals who have been trafficked. The failure of the Trafficking Protocol in this respect was not accidental. Throughout the drafting process, States were reminded of the importance of dealing with identification.[15] Those observing the negotiations were also aware of the fact that the regime established by the Organized Crime Convention[16] and its Protocols (whereby trafficked persons are accorded greater protection and therefore impose a greater financial and administrative burden than smuggled migrants) created a clear incentive for national authorities to identify irregular migrants as smuggled rather than trafficked. However, requests to the Drafting Committee to address the issue of identification and provide guidance on the relationship between the two Protocols were not taken up.[17] Supplementary interpretative material related to the Trafficking Protocol provides important

---

[14] See J. Bhabha and C. Alfirev, "The Identification and Referral of Trafficked Persons to Procedures for Determining International Protection Needs" (United Nations High Commissioner for Refugees, 2009) (Bhabha and Alfirev, "The Identification and Referral of Trafficked Persons to Procedures for Determining International Protection Needs").

[15] The obvious question was asked by the Canadian Refugee Council: "[i]f authorities have no means of determining among the intercepted or arrested who is being trafficked, how do they propose to grant them the measures of protection they are committing themselves to?" Canadian Council for Refugees, "Migrant Smuggling and Trafficking in Persons," Feb. 20, 2000, available at http://www.ccrweb.ca//traffick.htm (accessed Dec. 1, 2009).

[16] United Nations Convention Against Transnational Organized Crime, 2225 UNTS 209, done Nov. 15, 2000, entered into force Sept. 29, 2003 (Organized Crime Convention).

[17] The Inter-Agency Group, comprising OHCHR, UNHCR, IOM, and UNICEF made the following plea to the Ad Hoc Committee at its eighth session: "[w]hile work has been done on identifying common provisions [between the two protocols], little or no discussion has taken place on the potential for conflict between them. The distinction that has been made between trafficked persons and smuggled migrants is evidently a useful one. However, the [agencies] are aware that such distinctions are less clear on the ground, where there is considerable movement and overlapping between the two categories. During the informal consultations devoted to consideration of the draft protocols it was determined that trafficked persons are to be granted protections additional to those accorded to smuggled migrants. However, there is little guidance in either instrument regarding how the identification process is to be made and by whom. The [Ad Hoc Committee] may wish to consider the implications of the fact that ... identifying an individual as a trafficked person carries different

guidance on the issue, recommending that legislators consider establishing some process whereby victims or others acting on their behalf can seek the status of victims of trafficking.[18]

The silence of the Trafficking Protocol on the point of victim identification stands in sharp contrast to the explicit provisions of the European Trafficking Convention. Drafters of the Convention recognized that timely and accurate identification of victims is essential for the provision of protection and assistance, and that failure to correctly identify a victim will likely lead to a denial of that person's rights as well as problems in the prosecution process.[19] States Parties are required to ensure the necessary legal framework is in place as well as the availability of competent personnel for the identification process. They are also required to cooperate with each other and, internally, with victim support agencies in this process.[20] Importantly, given the complexities of victim identification, the immediate victim assistance and support

responsibilities for the State Party concerned than in the case when that same person is identified as a smuggled migrant. The [Ad Hoc Committee] may also wish to consider the possible consequences of a State ratifying one but not both instruments." "Note by the Office of the United Nations High Commissioner for Human Rights, the Office of the United Nations High Commissioner for Refugees, the United Nations Children's Fund and the International Organization for Migration on the Draft Protocols Concerning Migrant Smuggling and Trafficking in Persons," UN Doc. A/AC.254/27, Feb. 8, 2000 and UN Doc. A/AC.254/27/Corr.1, Feb. 22, 2000, at para. 2.

[18] "Generally, these might involve any or all of the following: (*a*) Allowing courts or tribunals that convict traffickers or deal with trafficking in civil or other litigation to certify as such any victims who are identified during the proceedings, whether or not they actually participate in those proceedings; (*b*) Allowing a judicial or administrative determination to be made based on the application of law enforcement, border control or other officials who encounter victims in the course of investigations or prosecutions; and/or (*c*) Allowing a judicial or administrative determination to be made based on the application of the alleged victim personally or some representative, such as a representative of a non-governmental organization." UN Office on Drugs and Crime, *Legislative Guides for the Implementation of the United Nations Convention against Transnational Organized Crime and the Protocols Thereto*, UN Sales No. E.05.V.2 (2004) (*Legislative Guide*), Part 2, at 289. See also UNODC Model Law, at Optional Article 18.

[19] European Trafficking Convention Explanatory Report, at para. 127.

[20] European Trafficking Convention, at Arts. 19(1), 19(2). Note that the EU Framework Decision 2009 Proposal also acknowledges the importance of identification in a provision that requires Member States to "take the necessary measures to establish at national and local level appropriate mechanisms aimed at early identification and support to victims, in cooperation with relevant support organisations": Commission of the European Communities, Proposal for a Framework Decision on preventing and combating trafficking in human beings, and protecting victims, repealing Framework Decision 2002/629/JHA, COM(2009) 136 final, Mar. 25, 2009 (Framework Decision 2009 Proposal), at Art. 10(3). Note that this particular draft is no longer active as it was not adopted by the entry into force of the Treaty of Lisbon (Treaty of Lisbon amending the Treaty on European Union and the Treaty establishing the European Community, OJ C 306/1, done Dec. 13, 2007, entered into force Dec. 1, 2009), which abolished the "third pillar" decision-making process for Framework Decisions. However, substantive sections of the lapsed Framework Decision 2009 Proposal have been put forward again as a proposed Directive for adoption by the EU under alternative post-Lisbon decision-making processes. The proposed Directive is, in the words of the European Commission, "essentially identical to the previous Proposal for a Framework Decision": European Commission, Proposal for a Directive of the European Parliament and of the Council on preventing and combating trafficking in human beings, and protecting victims, repealing Framework Decision 2002/629/

provisions of the Convention are applicable, prior to formal identification, to any person who the competent authorities have "reasonable grounds to believe ... has been a victim of trafficking."[21]

For those States Parties not bound by the provisions of the European Trafficking Convention, the obligation of identification can be argued to flow from the fact that any rights accorded to trafficked persons amount to nothing without a corresponding obligation on competent authorities to identify them as such. By failing to identify trafficked persons correctly, States effectively and permanently deny victims the ability to realize the rights and protections to which they are legally entitled. Delays in the identification process can have a similarly deleterious effect. The identification of trafficked persons is never a default position and will always require a level of activity and engagement on the part of the State. Accordingly, the obligation on the State to identify trafficked persons as such can be characterized as an active one. It is also an obligation fundamentally linked to those related to victim protection and repatriation, as detailed further in this chapter. International and regional policy documents confirm the connection between identification and access to rights.[22]

Finally, it is important to acknowledge the great practical difficulties that are associated with the identification of victims of trafficking. Even leaving aside problems related to knowledge, understanding, and attitude on the part of officials responsible for such identification, the obstacles to prompt and accurate identification are daunting.[23] Perhaps most critically, the identification of victims of trafficking will almost always be an *ex post facto* exercise. The definitional requirement of *intention to exploit* is usually no more than a legal nicety. In practice, trafficking is extremely

---

JHA, COM(2010) 95 final, Mar. 29, 2010 (EC Directive 2010 Proposal), at 6. Accordingly, while much discussion of recent EU policy in this volume is conducted in relation to the Framework Decision 2009 Proposal, it remains equally relevant to the new Directive Proposal.

[21] European Trafficking Convention, at Art. 10(2). As noted above, the same Article also prevents a person in relation to whom there are reasonable grounds to suspect he or she has been trafficked from being removed from the country prior to the completion of formal identification procedures. This provision is also reflected in the draft EU Framework Decision, which provides that "[a] person shall be treated as a victim as soon as the competent authorities have an indication that she/he might have been subjected to an offence": Framework Decision 2009 Proposal, at Art. 10(2).

[22] See, for example, UN Economic and Social Council, Office of the United Nations High Commissioner for Human Rights, *Recommended Principles and Guidelines on Human Rights and Human Trafficking*, UN Doc E/2002/68/Add.1, May 20, 2002 (UN Trafficking Principles and Guidelines), at Guideline 2; and the Memorandum of Understanding on Cooperation against Trafficking in Persons in the Greater Mekong Sub-region, adopted on Oct. 29, 2004 in Yangon (Cambodia, China, Lao PDR, Myanmar, Thailand, and Vietnam) (COMMIT MOU) establishing the Coordinated Mekong Ministerial Initiative against Trafficking, or COMMIT.

[23] For a useful summary of the main obstacles to accurate and timely identification, see Bhabha and Alfirev, "The Identification and Referral of Trafficked Persons to Procedures for Determining International Protection Needs," at 10. For a discussion of obstacles as they relate to child victims, see E.M. Goździak, "Identifying Child Victims of Trafficking: Toward Solutions and Resolutions," (2010) 9 *Criminology & Public Policy* 245 (Goździak, "Identifying Child Victims of Trafficking").

difficult to confirm prior to the exploitation phase. In the case of cross-border trafficking, this is because the hallmarks of trafficking – those features that separate trafficking from other forms of migration, including various forms of abusive migration – will usually only be apparent once the exploitation has occurred. In addition to contributing to the problematic nature of victim identification, this feature explains why the obligations detailed in this chapter will weigh more heavily on countries of destination than on countries of origin. It also reinforces the value of provisional identification procedures such as those set out in the European Trafficking Convention.

5.2. NO PROSECUTION OR DETENTION OF VICTIMS

In countries of transit and destination, trafficked persons are often arrested, detained, charged, and even prosecuted for unlawful activities such as entering illegally, working illegally, or engaging in prostitution. Criminalization of trafficked persons is commonplace, even in situations where it would appear obvious that the victim was an unwilling participant in the relevant illegal act. In this latter case, such criminalization is often tied to a related failure by the State to identify the victim as such.[24] In these cases, trafficked persons are detained and, far from being treated as victims of trafficking, are subsequently charged as smuggled or illegal migrants, or illegal migrant workers. Immigration laws may operate to compel the arrest, detention, or summary deportation of all undocumented persons, including those who are recognized as having been trafficked. Countries of origin sometimes also directly criminalize victims upon their return, penalizing them for unlawful or unauthorized departure. It is also not uncommon for victims of trafficking to be detained in police lock-ups, immigration centers, shelters, or other facilities, sometimes for very extended periods. Criminalization is the antithesis of a victim-centered approach, inevitably operating to deny trafficked persons the rights to which they are entitled under international law. The common practice of deportation of foreign victims of trafficking, which invariably results in a denial of a range of rights, including the right to a remedy, is just one example of this link.[25]

The following discussion considers two issues: first, the criminalization of trafficked persons for status-related offenses; and second, the detention of trafficked persons for protection or any other reason. The issue of victim detention is subject to detailed

---

[24] This has been acknowledged by the Conference of Parties to the Organized Crime Convention, which has recommended that "[w]ith regard to ensuring the non-punishment and non-prosecution of trafficked persons, States parties [to the Trafficking Protocol] should ... [e]stablish appropriate procedures for identifying victims of trafficking in persons." Conference of the Parties to the United Nations Convention on Transnational Organized Crime, "Report on the Meeting of the Working Group on Trafficking in Persons held in Vienna on 14 and 15 April 2009," UN Doc. CTOC/COP/WG.4/2009/2, Apr. 21, 2009, at Recommendation 1(H).

[25] See further, Chapter 6.2 of this volume, for a discussion of access to remedies.

consideration in view of the prevalence of this practice an
holds for the rights of trafficked persons, in particular w

5.2.1. *Prosecution for Status*

As noted above, trafficked persons are routine
deported for offenses that relate directly to their
Protocol does not specifically address the issue of prosecution for status-related
offenses; indeed, efforts to encourage States to include a provision on this issue were
not accepted.[26] However, developments since the adoption of the Protocol indicate
that States are moving toward a rejection of status-related criminalization and prosecution. In 2009, the Conference of the Parties to the Organized Crime Convention
recommended that States Parties to the Trafficking Protocol "[c]onsider, in line
with their domestic legislation, not punishing or prosecuting trafficked persons for
unlawful acts committed by them as a direct consequence of their situation as trafficked persons or where they were compelled to commit such unlawful acts."[27] This
recommendation identifies two potential prisms through which nonprosecution for
status offenses can be viewed: the "causation model" (by which the acts in question
were a result of the trafficking situation) and the "compulsion model" (by which the
acts in question were carried out under duress).[28]

Article 26 of the European Trafficking Convention follows the duress model, requiring States Parties, in accordance with the basic principles of their legal systems, to
"provide for the possibility of not imposing penalties on victims for their involvement
in unlawful activities, to the extent that they have been compelled to do so."[29] The
notion of compulsion is linked to the "means" element of the definition of trafficking
and thereby extends to include, at a minimum, involvement in unlawful activities as
the result of coercion, abduction, fraud, deception, or abuse of power or of a position
of vulnerability.[30] This provision does not provide complete protection from prosecution for status offenses. States Parties must only provide for the *possibility* of nonprosecution. Nevertheless, as the first and, at present, only treaty-based standard relating to

[26] United Nations Office on Drugs and Crime, Travaux Préparatoires *of the Negotiations for the Elaboration of the United Nations Convention against Transnational Organized Crime and the Protocols Thereto* (2006) (Travaux Préparatoires *for the Organized Crime Convention and Protocols*), at 368.

[27] Conference of the Parties to the United Nations Convention on Transnational Organized Crime, "Report on the Meeting of the Working Group on Trafficking in Persons held in Vienna on 14 and 15 April 2009," UN Doc. CTOC/COP/WG.4/2009/2, Apr. 21, 2009, at Recommendation 1(H).

[28] See Working Group on Trafficking in Persons, "Non-Punishment and Non-Prosecution of Victims of Trafficking in Persons: Administrative and Judicial Approaches to Offences Committed in the Process of Such Trafficking," UN Doc. CTOC/COP/WG.4/2010/4, Dec. 9, 2009 (Working Group on Trafficking in Persons, "Non-Punishment and Non-Prosecution of Victims").

[29] European Trafficking Convention, at Art. 26; European Trafficking Convention Explanatory Report, at paras. 272–274.

[30] European Trafficking Convention Explanatory Report, at para. 273.

the issue of status-related offenses, the provision represents an important step forward in the recognition of a need to prevent the criminalization of victims.[31]

Outside existing and proposed[32] legal regulation, there is considerable and growing evidence that the *policy preference* for victims of trafficking not to be subject to criminalization is evolving into a widely accepted normative standard.[33] The UN Trafficking Principles and Guidelines provide the most explicit statement on the issue: "[T]rafficked persons shall not be detained, charged or prosecuted for their illegal entry into or residence in countries of transit or destination, or for their involvement in unlawful activities to the extent that such involvement is a direct consequence of their situation as trafficked persons."[34] That articulation of

---

[31] The proposed new EU Framework Decision on Trafficking has also taken up this issue, in even stronger terms. Under the relevant draft position, "each Member State shall provide for the possibility of not prosecuting or imposing penalties on victims of trafficking in human beings for their involvement in unlawful activities as a direct consequence of being subjected to any of the illicit means referred to in [the definition of trafficking]": Framework Decision 2009 Proposal, at Art. 6. The preamble provides further information, stating that "[v]ictims should be protected from prosecution and punishment, following a decision of the competent authority, for unlawful activities they have been involved in as a direct consequence of being subjected to any of the illicit means used by traffickers, such as violations of immigration laws, the use of false documents or offences envisaged by prostitution laws. An additional aim of such protection is to encourage them to act as witnesses in criminal proceedings": ibid. at Preambular para. 6. The formulation reflects an intention to improve on the corresponding provision of the European Trafficking Convention. The Impact Study on the Framework Decision 2009 Proposal sets out this rationale in full: "[s]takeholders have pointed out that victims of trafficking are normally detained or prosecuted or punished for minor offences which are typically connected with the victimisation process, such as violations of immigration laws, use of false documents, and prostitution, in countries where prostitution as such is criminalised. The fear of punishment and/or deportation is considered a major obstacle for victims to come forward, report the crime, and act as witnesses. Therefore the clause must be considered a major element of a successful anti-trafficking legislation. A similar nonpunishment clause has been included in the CoE Convention, but the formulation is not clearly binding; moreover it does not cover all victims, since it only refers to victims who have been compelled to commit a crime, while in some cases they are trafficked by means of deception and abuse, according to the legal definition of trafficking. The added value of the new FD would be a better and binding formulation of the clause. In order to avoid an abuse of the clause, MS could be allowed not to apply the clause in case of extreme gravity of the crime committed by the victim." "Accompanying Document to the proposal for a Council Framework Decision in preventing and combating trafficking in human beings, and protecting victims, repealing Framework Decision 2002/629/JHA, Impact Assessment," Mar. 25, 2009, SEC (2009) 358 at 30 (Framework Decision Impact Assessment). Note that, as discussed at note 20 to this chapter, the Framework Decision 2009 Proposal is no longer an active draft but an "essentially identical" proposal for a Directive was tabled in March 2010: EC Directive 2010 Proposal, at 6. Note further that as this volume was going to press, the latest draft of the EC Directive 2010 Proposal obtained by the author (dated June 28, 2010) contained a much stronger nonprosecution and nonpenalization clause in the form "Member States shall not prosecute or impose penalties on victims" for involvement in such offenses. If it does survive, this provision will be the most emphatic affirmation of the principle that victims of trafficking should not be prosecuted or penalized for status-related offenses.

[32] See the discussion in note 31 immediately preceding.

[33] This conclusion applies, even more strongly, to noncriminalization of child victims of trafficking. See further, Chapter 5.5.3.

[34] UN Trafficking Principles and Guidelines, at Principle 7. Principle 7 is supplemented by Guideline 2.5, which, in the context of the need for trafficked persons to be identified quickly and accurately, calls on States and others to ensure that "trafficked persons are not prosecuted for violations of

the principle of noncriminalization for status offenses has been extensively cited as the accepted standard.[35] Significantly, the relevant United Nations political bodies, including the General Assembly, have affirmed the importance of noncriminalization of victims of trafficking in relation to status-related offenses,[36] as have the Secretary-General[37] and several of the human rights treaty bodies, including the Committee on the Rights of the Child[38] and the Committee on the Elimination of Discrimination against Women.[39] The principle is reiterated in major international[40]

immigration laws or for the activities they are involved in as a direct consequence of their situation as trafficked persons." Guideline 4.5 also considers the issue of prosecution for status-related offenses with reference to the need for an adequate legal framework, requiring States to consider ensuring that "legislation prevents trafficked persons from being prosecuted, detained or punished for the illegality of their entry or residence or for the activities they are involved in as a direct consequence of their situation as trafficked persons."

[35] See, for example, United Nations Office on Drugs and Crime, *Trafficking in Persons, Handbook for Parliamentarians* (2009) (UNODC Handbook for Parliamentarians), at 43–45; UNODC Toolkit, at 253–254.

[36] See, for example, UN General Assembly, "Trafficking in Women and Girls," UN Doc. A/RES/63/156, Jan. 30, 2009, at para. 12 which "*[u]rges* Governments to take all appropriate measures to ensure that victims of trafficking are not penalized for being trafficked and that they do not suffer from revictimization as a result of actions taken by government authorities, and *encourages* Governments to prevent, within their legal framework and in accordance with national policies, victims of trafficking in persons from being prosecuted for their illegal entry or residence." The Commission on Human Rights/ Human Rights Council has also addressed this issue. See, for example, UN Human Rights Council, "Trafficking in Persons, Especially Women and Children," UN Doc. A/HRC/RES/11/3, June 17, 2009, at para. 3, urging States to "take all appropriate measures to ensure that victims of trafficking are not penalized for being trafficked and that they do not suffer from revictimization as a result of actions taken by Government authorities, bearing in mind that they are victims of exploitation."

[37] See, for example, "Trafficking in Women and Girls: Report of the Secretary-General," UN Doc. A/63/215, Aug. 4, 2008, which refers, in para. 62, to "the principle of non-punishment" and states that that "victims should be protected from re-victimization, including protection from prosecution for illegal migration, labour law violations or other acts."

[38] See, for example, UN Committee on the Rights of the Child, "Concluding Observations: Kenya," UN Doc. CRC/C/KEN/CO/2, June 19, 2007, at para. 66. In relation to the CRC Optional Protocol on Sale of Children (Optional Protocol to the Child Convention on the Sale of Children, Child Prostitution and Child Pornography, GA Res. 54/263, Annex I, 54 UN GAOR Supp. (No. 49), 7, UN Doc. A/54/49, Vol. III (2000), done May 25, 2000, entered into force Jan. 18, 2002), the Committee has clearly and consistently maintained the position that child victims of offenses covered by the Optional Protocol should not be either criminalized or penalized, and that all possible measures should be taken to avoid their stigmatization and social marginalization. See, for example, UN Committee on the Rights of the Child, "Concluding Observations: Republic of Korea," UN Doc. CRC/C/OPSC/KOR/CO/1, June 6, 2008, at paras. 40–41.

[39] See, for example, UN Committee on the Elimination of Discrimination Against Women: "Concluding Observations: Lebanon," UN Doc. CEDAW/C/LBN/CO/3, Feb. 1, 2008, at paras. 28–29; "Concluding Observations: Singapore," UN Doc. CEDAW/C/SGP/CO/3, Aug. 10, 2007, at paras. 21–22.

[40] See, for example, "Further Actions and Initiatives to Implement the Beijing Declaration and Platform for Action," UN Doc. A/RES/S-23/3, Nov. 16, 2000 (Beijing +5 Outcome Document), at para. 70(c), which states that governments should consider preventing trafficked persons from being prosecuted for illegal entry or residence into the State, "taking into account that they are victims of exploitation." The "Beijing Declaration and Platform for Action," Fourth World Conference on Women, UN Doc. A/CONF.177/20 and UN Doc. A/CONF.177/20/Add.1, Sept. 15, 1995 (Beijing Declaration and Platform for Action), at para. 124(l) requires the State to create or strengthen institutional

and regional[41] policy instruments and interpretative texts,[42] and has also been recognized in national antitrafficking laws.[43]

With respect to trafficked persons with a valid claim for asylum, it should be noted that international refugee law prevents States, under certain conditions, from imposing penalties on refugees on account of their illegal entry or presence.[44] The

mechanisms so that victims of violence against women can report acts of violence "free from the fear of penalties."

[41] See, for example, "Brussels Declaration on Preventing and Combating Trafficking in Human Beings," adopted by the European Conference on Preventing and Combating Trafficking in Human Beings, Sept. 20, 2002 (Brussels Declaration), at 10, para. 13; European Union and African States, "Ouagadougou Action Plan to Combat Trafficking in Human Beings, Especially Women and Children," adopted by the Ministerial Conference on Migration and Development, Nov. 22–23, 2006 (Ouagadougou Action Plan), at 4; "Conclusions and Recommendations of the Meeting of National Authorities on Trafficking in Persons," adopted by the Organization of American States, Docs. OEA/Ser.K/XXXIX and RTP/doc. 16/06 rev. 1, Mar. 17, 2006 (OAS Recommendations on Trafficking in Persons), at Section IV(7); Memorandum of Understanding between the Royal Government of the Kingdom of Cambodia and the Royal Government of the Kingdom of Thailand on Bilateral Cooperation for Eliminating Trafficking in Children and Women and Assisting Victims of Trafficking, adopted on May 31, 2003 in Siem Reap (Cambodia-Thailand MOU), at Art. 7; Organization for Security and Co-operation in Europe (OSCE) Ministerial Council, "Declaration on Trafficking in Human Beings," OSCE Doc. MC(10).JOUR/2, Annex II, Dec. 7, 2002, at 3, Section II; OSCE Ministerial Council, "Decision on Enhancing the OSCE's Efforts to Combat Trafficking in Human Beings," OSCE Doc. MC(8).DEC/1, Nov. 28, 2000, at para. 9.

[42] For example, the UNODC Model Law, which provides, in Article 10, that "(1) A victim of trafficking in persons shall not be held criminally or administratively liable [punished] [inappropriately incarcerated, fined or otherwise penalized] for offences [unlawful acts] committed by them, to the extent that such involvement is a direct consequence of their situation as trafficked persons. (2) A victim of trafficking in persons shall not be held criminally or administratively liable for immigration offences established under national law. (3) The provisions of this article shall be without prejudice to general defences available at law to the victim. (4) The provisions of this article shall not apply where the crime is of a particularly serious nature as defined under national law."

[43] See, for example, the Victims of Trafficking and Violence Protection Act of 2000, 22 USC 7101 (US Trafficking Victims Protection Act), at § 102(b)(19): "victims of severe forms of trafficking should not be inappropriately incarcerated, fined, or otherwise penalized solely for unlawful acts committed as a direct result of being trafficked, such as using false documents, entering the country without documentation, or working without documentation." The minimum standards used by the U.S. Department of State in its assessment of individual State responses to trafficking include "whether the government of the country … ensures that victims are not inappropriately incarcerated, fined or otherwise penalized solely for unlawful acts as a direct result of being trafficked." United States Department of State, "Trafficking in Persons Report" (2009), at 28. See also, United Nations Interim Administrative Mission in Kosovo, Regulation 2001/14 on the Prohibition of Trafficking in Persons in Kosovo, at § 8 ("[a] person is not criminally responsible for prostitution or illegal entry, presence or work in Kosovo if that person provides evidence that supports a reasonable belief that he or she was the victim of trafficking"). For further examples of State practice in this area, see UNODC Handbook for Parliamentarians, at 43–45; and Working Group on Trafficking in Persons, "Non-Punishment and Non-Prosecution of Victims."

[44] Convention Relating to the Status of Refugees, 189 UNTS 137, July 28, 1951, entered into force Apr. 22, 1954 (Refugee Convention), at Art. 31. Further on the scope of this provision, see J.C. Hathaway, *The Rights of Refugees under International Law* (2005) (Hathaway, *The Rights of Refugees*), at 385–413.

following section should be read in light of the fact that the concept of penalties can be interpreted to include detention.[45]

It is important to emphasize that the notion of protecting trafficked persons from criminalization for status-related offenses is not particularly innovative or radical. Rather, it reflects basic principles recognized in most national legal systems relating to responsibility and accountability for criminal offenses. The principle is not intended to confer blanket immunity on trafficked victims who may commit other non-status-related crimes with the requisite level of criminal intent. For example, if a trafficked person engages in a criminal act such as robbery or unlawful violence, then he or she should be subject to the normal criminal procedure with due attention to available lawful defenses.

5.2.2. *Detention of Trafficked Persons*

Detention of victims of trafficking is common in all parts of the world and can occur under a range of circumstances. Immigration laws of many countries permit an automatic right of detention for unauthorized migrants, and it is under such provisions that many trafficked persons end up in prison or immigration detention facilities pending deportation. In many cases, those who are detained as illegal migrants have not been correctly identified as having been trafficked. Trafficked persons, whether correctly identified or not, are also detained in police lock-ups and prisons as a result of engagement in illegal activities such as illegal entry, presentation of false documentation, or unauthorized work, including prostitution. Even if correctly identified as such, victims of trafficking who are unwilling or unable to cooperate in criminal investigations or to provide information that is deemed useful may be sent to immigration detention pending deportation. Finally, detention can occur when trafficking victims are placed in a shelter or other welfare facility from which they are unable to leave. Common justifications offered for this form of detention include the need to provide shelter and support; the need to protect victims from further harm; and the need to secure victims' cooperation in investigation and prosecution of traffickers.

The specialized international and regional treaties on trafficking do not directly address the issue of victim detention. The drafting history of the Trafficking Protocol reveals that while no State was arguing for recognition of a right to detain victims, most were resistant to an explicit prohibition because of a fear that this would curtail their options in dealing with undocumented or otherwise irregular migrants.[46] The

---

[45] Hathaway, *The Rights of Refugees*, at 411–412.

[46] See further, Travaux Préparatoires *for the Organized Crime Convention and Protocols*, at 368. Note, however, that the UNODC Model Law, at 46, includes an optional provision: "[v]ictims of trafficking in persons shall not be held in any detention facility as a result of their status as victims or their immigration status." The accompanying commentary confirms that such detention could never be considered as "appropriate housing" under the terms of Article 6(3)(a) of the Trafficking Protocol.

European Trafficking Convention is equally silent, and any position on this issue can only be inferred indirectly.[47] In sharp contrast, the UN Trafficking Principles and Guidelines explicitly address detention of victims of trafficking, linking this practice to the broader problem of criminalization of victims and characterizing it as inappropriate and (implicitly) illegal. States are encouraged to ensure that trafficked persons are not, in any circumstances, held in immigration detention or other forms of custody.[48] International and regional policy on this issue is generally more equivocal. One reason may be a desire to preserve those aspects of detention that are considered useful and/or necessary. In Southeast Asia, for example, there has been a clear attempt to preserve a prerogative of the State with respect to shelter detention.[49]

The detention of victims of trafficking implicates a range of international standards. The question of whether such practices are legal under international law requires careful consideration of the full spectrum of potentially applicable standards in light of the particular circumstances of a case and the justifications provided. Of particular relevance are rules protecting the right to freedom of movement and those prohibiting arbitrary detention. The fact that detention affects women, men, and children in very different ways also demands consideration of other norms including those protecting the rights of children and prohibiting sex-based discrimination. These issues are considered briefly below.

Detention and the Right to Freedom of Movement. Does victim detention constitute an unlawful interference with freedom of movement? Can the right to freedom of movement conflict with or modify application of other obligations such as that of the State to protect victims from harm? In terms of its substantive content,

---

[47] The issue of victim detention arises in the European Trafficking Convention indirectly, in the context of victim consent to protective measures. States Parties to the Convention are required to "take due account of the victim's safety and protection needs" (Art. 12(2)). This requirement is supplemented by a detailed provision that sets out the specific measures that must be implemented to provide "effective and appropriate protection" to victims from potential retaliation and intimidation, in particular during and after the investigation and prosecution processes (Art. 28). The Explanatory Report to the Convention is clear on the point of beneficiary consent: The victim's agreement to protective measures is essential except in extreme circumstances such as an emergency in which the victim is physically incapable of giving consent. European Trafficking Convention Explanatory Report, at para. 289.

[48] European Trafficking Convention Explanatory Report, at para. 289; UN Trafficking Principles and Guidelines, at Guidelines 2.6, 6.1.

[49] The six States of the greater Mekong subregion (Cambodia, China, Lao PDR, Myanmar, Thailand, and Vietnam) have committed themselves to "ensuring that persons identified as victims of trafficking are not held in detention *by law enforcement authorities*": COMMIT MOU, at Art. 16 (emphasis added). A bilateral MOU between Cambodia and Thailand states that children and women who have been trafficked shall be considered victims and should not be prosecuted or detained *in immigration detention centers*: Cambodia-Thailand MOU, at Art. 7. The MOU specifies further that victims should stay in safe shelters administered by the ministry responsible for social welfare in each country, which should be responsible for ensuring their security: ibid.

the right to freedom of movement is generally held to refer to a set of liberal rights of the individual, including the right to move freely and to choose a place of residence within a State, the right to cross frontiers in order to both enter and leave the country, and the prohibition on arbitrary expulsion of aliens.[50] The International Covenant on Civil and Political Rights (ICCPR) explicitly recognizes and protects a right to freedom of movement,[51] as do all major regional human rights treaties.[52]

The only direct reference to freedom of movement in the specific context of trafficking is contained in the UN Trafficking Principles and Guidelines, which provide that "States should consider protecting the rights of all persons to freedom of movement and ensuring that anti-trafficking measures do not infringe on this right."[53] The drafters of this provision did not necessarily have in mind the issue of victim detention, but were rather focusing on problematic responses such as confiscation of passports and discriminatory denial of entry and exit visas.[54] There is, nevertheless, a clear link between freedom of movement and victim detention, and several restrictions on this right appear especially relevant to the situation of trafficked persons. In particular, under the terms of the ICCPR, freedom of movement is only guaranteed as a matter of law to those who are *lawfully* within the territory of the relevant State.[55] Trafficked persons without regular migration status (the vast majority of those detained in criminal justice facilities as well as shelters) are therefore unlikely to benefit greatly from the protections afforded by this particular right. The right to freedom of movement will be similarly constrained for those with a valid claim for refugee status but whose presence has not been expressly authorized.[56]

For trafficked persons who are indeed lawfully within the relevant country, it appears that their detention would, without further justification, violate their right to freedom of movement. However, the ICCPR includes freedom of movement among a small group of rights subject to limitations clauses, such that the right can

---

[50] M. Nowak, *UN Covenant on Civil and Political Rights: CCPR Commentary* (2005) (Nowak, *CCPR Commentary*), at 260.

[51] International Covenant on Civil and Political Rights, 999 UNTS 171, done Dec. 16, 1966, entered into force Mar. 3, 1976 (ICCPR), at Art. 12.

[52] Protocol No. 4 to the Convention of 4 November 1950 for the Protection of Human Rights and Fundamental Freedoms, 1496 UNTS 263, done Sept. 16, 1963, entered into force May 2, 1968, at Arts. 2–4, Protocol No. 7 to the Convention of 4 November 1950 for the Protection of Human Rights and Fundamental Freedoms, ETS No. 117, done Nov. 22, 1984, entered into force Nov. 1, 1988, at Art. 1; African Charter on Human And Peoples' Rights, 1520 UNTS 217, done June 27, 1981, entered into force Oct. 21, 1986 (African Charter), at Art. 12; American Convention on Human Rights, 1144 UNTS 123, done Nov. 22, 1969, entered into force 18 July, 1978 (American Convention on Human Rights), at Art. 22.

[53] UN Trafficking Principles and Guidelines, at Guideline 1.5.

[54] For an insight into this and other aspects of the drafting of this instrument, see Office of the United Nations High Commissioner for Human Rights, *Commentary to the Recommended Principles and Guidelines on Human Rights and Human Trafficking* (forthcoming, 2010).

[55] ICCPR, at Art. 12(1).

[56] Refugee Convention, at Art. 31. See generally, Hathaway, *The Rights of Refugees*, at 413–439.

lawfully be restricted by States Parties on grounds of national security, public order, public health or morals, or the rights and freedom of others.[57] This caveat could conceivably be used by States to buttress a claim that detention of victims, irrespective of their legal status, is necessary in order to ensure availability of witnesses, for example, or to protect trafficked persons from retaliation and intimidation. Such a claim would need to be tested on its merits. It would also be important to ascertain independently that the claimed restrictions do not separately violate other rights recognized in the ICCPR, for example, the prohibition on discrimination.[58]

The UN Human Rights Committee, in considering the application of this exception, has noted that freedom of movement is "an indispensable condition for the free development of a person."[59] Any restrictions on this right "must be provided by law, must be necessary ... and must be consistent with all other rights."[60] The Committee has also noted that:

> Restrictive measures must conform to the principle of proportionality; they must be appropriate to achieve their protective function; they must be the least intrusive instrument amongst those which might achieve the desired result; and they must be proportionate to the interest to be protected ... The principle of proportionality has to be respected not only in the law that frames the restrictions, but also by the administrative and judicial authorities in applying the law.[61]

In deciding whether shelter detention violates the right to freedom of movement of an individual who is lawfully within the country, it is therefore necessary to ask whether that detention is: (1) provided for by law; (2) consistent with other rights (such as the prohibition on sex-based discrimination); and (3) necessary to protect that person.

Detention, the Right to Liberty, and the Prohibition on Arbitrary Detention. The international legal standard in relation to liberty and the prohibition on arbitrary detention is set out in Article 9(1) of the ICCPR: "Everyone has the right to liberty and security of person. No one shall be subjected to arbitrary arrest or detention. No one shall be deprived of his liberty except on such grounds and in accordance with such procedures as are established by law."[62] Similar provisions can be found in all major regional human rights treaties.[63] In determining its scope and applicability, it

---

[57] ICCPR, at Art. 12(3).
[58] Ibid. On the issue of compatibility between restrictions on freedom of movement and compatibility with other rights protected in the ICCPR, see Nowak, *CCPR Commentary*, at 273–274.
[59] UN Human Rights Committee, "General Comment No. 27: Freedom of Movement," UN Doc. CCPR/C/21/Rev.1/Add.9, Nov. 2, 1999, at para. 1.
[60] Ibid. at para. 11.
[61] Ibid. at paras. 14–15.
[62] ICCPR, at Art. 9.
[63] Convention for the Protection of Human Rights and Fundamental Freedoms, 213 UNTS 221, done Nov. 4, 1950, entered into force Sept. 3, 1953 (European Human Rights Convention), at Art. 5(1); African Charter, at Art. 6; American Convention on Human Rights, at Art. 7(1).

must be stressed that the right to liberty is not absolute. International law recognizes that States retain the ability to use measures that deprive people of their liberty. Deprivation of liberty only becomes problematic in legal terms when it is unlawful and arbitrary.[64] States should make sure that they define precisely those cases in which deprivation of liberty is permissible. The principle of *legality* is violated if someone is detained on grounds that are not clearly established in a domestic law or are contrary to such law.[65]

The *prohibition on arbitrariness* represents a second, additional requirement for States in relation to deprivation of liberty. In other words, it is not enough that the national law permits detention of victims of trafficking. That law must itself not be arbitrary and its application must not take place arbitrarily.[66] The word *arbitrary* refers to elements of injustice, unpredictability, unreasonableness, capriciousness, and lack of proportionality, as well as the common law principle of due process of law.[67] The UN Human Rights Committee has confirmed that the prohibition on arbitrariness requires legally authorized detention to be reasonable and necessary in all of the circumstances of the case, and to be a proportionate means to achieve a legitimate aim.[68]

Deprivation of liberty provided by law must not be "manifestly disproportional, unjust or unpredictable."[69] The manner in which a decision is taken to deprive someone of his or her liberty must be capable of being deemed appropriate and proportionate in view of the circumstances of the case.[70] Importantly, a detention situation that was originally not arbitrary might become arbitrary if it continues over time without proper justification.[71] Regional human rights courts have confirmed that indefinite detention, particularly that which can be characterized as

[64] Nowak, *CCPR Commentary*, at 211; see also UN Human Rights Committee, "General Comment No. 8: Right to Liberty and Security of Persons," UN Doc. HRI/GEN/1/Rev.6 at 130, June 30, 1982.

[65] Nowak, *CCPR Commentary*, at 224; Y. Dinstein, "Right to Life, Physical Integrity, and Liberty," in L. Henkin ed., *The International Bill of Rights: The Covenant on Civil and Political Rights* 114 (1981), at 130.

[66] Nowak, *CCPR Commentary*, at 224; S. Joseph, J. Schultz and M. Castan, *The International Covenant on Civil and Political Rights: Cases, Materials and Commentary* (2004) (Joseph, Schultz and Castan, *The ICCPR*), at 308.

[67] Nowak, *CCPR Commentary*, at 225; Joseph, Schultz and Castan, *The ICCPR*, at 156, 308–309; see also UN Human Rights Committee, "General Comment No. 16: The Right to Respect of Privacy, Family, Home and Correspondence, and Protection of Honour and Reputation," UN Doc. HRI/GEN/1/Rev.6 at 142, Apr. 8, 1988, at para. 4: "[t]he introduction of the concept of arbitrariness is intended to guarantee that even interference provided for by law should be in accordance with the provisions, aims and objectives of the Covenant and should be, in any event, reasonable in the particular circumstances."

[68] *Van Alphen v. The Netherlands*, UNHRC Comm. No. 305/1988, UN Doc. CCPR/C/39/D/305/1988, decided July 23, 1990, at para. 5.8; *A v. Australia*, UNHRC Comm. No. 560/1993, UN Doc. CCPR/C/59/D/560/1993, decided Apr. 3, 1997, at para. 9.2.

[69] Nowak, *CCPR Commentary*, at 226.

[70] Ibid. at 225.

[71] Ibid.

disproportionate or discriminatory (for example, between nationals and non-nationals), violates the fundamental right to protection from arbitrary detention.[72]

Finally, States are required under international law to ensure that necessary procedural guarantees are in place to identify and respond to situations of unlawful or arbitrary deprivation of liberty. The ICCPR specifies several of these procedural guarantees:

> Anyone who is deprived of his liberty by arrest or detention shall be entitled to take proceedings before a court, in order that the court may decide without delay on the lawfulness of his detention and order his release if the detention is not lawful[73]

and "anyone who has been a victim of unlawful arrest or detention shall have an enforceable right to compensation."[74]

Under this analysis, it is evident that the detention of victims of trafficking could, in certain cases, amount to unlawful deprivation of liberty and violate the prohibition on arbitrary detention. The likelihood of detention being characterized as unlawful or arbitrary is particularly high if it can be shown that such detention: is not specifically provided for in law or is imposed contrary to law; is provided for or imposed in a discriminatory manner; is imposed for a prolonged, unspecified, or indefinite period; is unjust, unpredictable, or disproportionate; or is not subject to judicial or administrative review to confirm its legality and to confirm that it continues to be necessary in the circumstances, with the possibility for release where no grounds for its continuation exist.

Detention and the Prohibition on Sex-based Discrimination. The practice of victim detention is often highly gendered in a way that negatively affects both women and men. For example, the overwhelming majority of trafficked persons detained in welfare shelters are female.[75] One reason for this is that women and girls are more likely to be identified through official channels as trafficked and therefore more likely than men and boys to enter both formal and informal protection systems. Male victims are commonly misidentified as illegal migrants, transferred to immigration detention facilities, and eventually deported. Even when correctly identified as having been trafficked, adult males are often ineligible for public or private shelter and protection.

---

[72] See, for example, *A and Others v. United Kingdom*, Dec. No. 3455/05 (unreported) (ECHR, Feb. 19, 2009), finding a violation of Article 5 of the European Human Rights Convention.

[73] ICCPR, at Art. 9(4).

[74] Ibid. at Art. 9(5).

[75] See the references in A.T. Gallagher and E. Pearson, "The High Cost of Freedom: A Legal and Policy Analysis of Shelter Detention for Victims of Trafficking," (2010) 32 *Human Rights Quarterly* 73.

The arguments commonly advanced in favor of victim detention, particularly shelter or welfare detention, are also gendered. Protection from further harm is one of the most commonly cited justifications for detaining trafficked persons against their will. Female victims of trafficking are widely considered to need this protection much more than their male counterparts. Females, both women and girls, are also perceived as being less competent to make decisions about their own safety.[76]

Is it possible to argue that detention of victims in shelters constitutes unlawful discrimination on the basis of sex? Chapter 3 confirmed that equal treatment and non-discrimination on the basis of sex is a fundamental human right, firmly enshrined in the major international and regional instruments. The prohibition on sex-based discrimination is related to and reinforces the duty of equal application of the law, and it is widely accepted that this prohibition requires States Parties to take action to prevent private as well as public acts of discrimination. On this basis, a determination in relation to a particular situation that (1) victim detention negatively affects the rights of the individual involved, and (2) such detention is overwhelmingly directed to and affecting women and girls, should be sufficient to support a claim of unlawful discrimination on the basis of sex. In addition, as noted directly above, a finding that detention laws or practices discriminate unlawfully against women and girls would likewise be sufficient to support a claim of unlawful deprivation of liberty and/or arbitrary detention.

Detention of Child Victims. In relation to the issue of detention, it is important to recognize some fundamental differences between children and adults. A critical source of vulnerability for children lies in their lack of full agency – in fact and under law.[77] A lack of agency is often made worse by the absence of a parent or legal guardian who is able to act in the child's best interests. Such absence is typical in trafficking cases, since the deliberate separation of children from parents or guardians is a common strategy to facilitate exploitation. In some cases, parents or caregivers are or have been complicit in the trafficking of the child. As explored in more detail elsewhere in this chapter, the obligation to protect from further harm will have different implications for children as compared to adults given their greater vulnerability. Premature release of a child from a secure place of care without individual case assessment (including risk assessment) could greatly endanger the child and expose him or her to further harm, including retrafficking. These dangers are confirmed by recent reports of children being improperly removed from shelters

---

[76] See the in-depth discussion by Gallagher and Pearson of the relative merits of these and other arguments used to justify victim detention: ibid.

[77] This is acknowledged in the ICCPR, which stipulates at Article 24 the right of the child to "such measures of protection as are required by his status as a minor."

by their exploiters.[78] It is for these reasons that the relevant laws, principles, and guidelines emphasize the importance of ensuring that the child is appointed a legal guardian, who is able to act in that child's best interests throughout the entire process until a durable solution is identified and implemented.[79]

These additional considerations do not take away from the fact that children who are placed in safe and secure accommodation are to be considered as subject to detention for the purposes of ascertaining their rights and the obligations of the State towards them. International legal rules on the detention of children are very exacting and are governed by the overriding principle of respect for the child's best interests. The strictness of rules around juvenile detention reflects an acknowledgment of the fact that detained children are highly vulnerable to abuse, victimization, and the violation of their rights. Under the provisions of the Convention on the Rights of the Child (CRC), no child is to be deprived of his or her liberty unlawfully or arbitrarily.[80] This prohibition extends beyond penal detention to include deprivation of liberty on the basis of the child's welfare, health, and protection. It is therefore directly relevant to the situation of child victims of trafficking who are detained in welfare homes and shelters as well as in immigration detention.[81] International law requires any form of juvenile detention to be in conformity with the law, used only as a measure of last resort, and imposed for the shortest appropriate period of time.[82]

In addition to stipulating the circumstances under which a child can be detained, international law also imposes conditions on the conduct of such detention. Once

---

[78] See, for example, United States Department of State, "Trafficking in Persons Report" (2008), at 30 (citing improper removal of children from shelters in China, Ghana, India, the Netherlands, and the United Kingdom).

[79] UN Trafficking Principles and Guidelines; United Nations Children's Fund, *Guidelines for the Protection of Child Victims of Trafficking* (September 2006) (UNICEF Guidelines), esp. at Guideline 4.1. See further, Chapters 5.5.2 and 5.5.3.

[80] Convention on the Rights of the Child, 1577 UNTS 3, done Nov. 20, 1989, entered into force Sept. 2, 1990 (CRC), at Art. 37(b).

[81] The "UN Rules for the Protection of Juveniles Deprived of Their Liberty," at para. 11(b), define a deprivation of liberty as any form of detention or imprisonment or the placement of a person in a public or private custodial setting from which a person under the age of 18 is not permitted to leave at will, by order of any judicial, administrative, or other public authority: "United Nations Rules for the Protection of Juveniles Deprived of Their Liberty," adopted by GA Res. 45/113, UN Doc. A/RES/45/113, Dec. 14, 1990. Note that the Committee on the Rights of the Child has explicitly rejected detention of children in need of protection: "[s]uch deprivation of liberty for children who have been abandoned or abused equates to punishment for children who are victims of crimes, not the offenders." See UN Committee on the Rights of the Child, "General Comment No. 10: Children's Rights in Juvenile Justice," UN Doc. CRC/C/GC/10, Apr. 25, 2007.

[82] CRC, at Art. 37(b); "UN Rules for the Protection of Juveniles Deprived of their Liberty," at para. 2; UN Committee on the Rights of the Child, "General Comment No. 6: Treatment of Unaccompanied and Separated Children Outside Their Country of Origin," UN Doc. CRC/GC/2005/6, June 3, 2005 (CRC General Comment No. 6), at para. 61. See also UN Committee on the Rights of the Child, "Concluding Observations: The Netherlands," UN Doc. CRC/C/15/Add.227, Jan. 30, 2004, at para. 54; "Concluding Observations: Canada," UN Doc. CRC/C/15/Add.215, Oct. 3, 2003, at para. 47.

again, the overriding principle is respect for the best interests of the child including respect for his or her humanity and human dignity.[83] Additional and more detailed rules concern the separation of children detainees from adults;[84] the right of the detained child to maintain contact with his or her family through correspondence and visits;[85] the right of the detained child to prompt access to legal and other appropriate assistance;[86] and the right of the detained child to challenge the legality of the deprivation of his or her liberty before a court or other competent, independent, and impartial authority, and to a prompt decision on any such action.[87] Detained children are further entitled to support for their physical and psychological recovery and social reintegration in an environment that fosters the health, self-respect, and dignity of the child.[88] International law also provides that each case involving a child deprived of his or her liberty should be handled expeditiously without any unnecessary delay.[89] These provisions appear to confirm the need to ensure that decisions impacting on the welfare and well-being of children are made on a case-by-case basis and with a view to ensuring the best interests of that individual child.

Conclusions on Detention of Victims. In evaluating the lawfulness or otherwise of victim detention, it is important to make a distinction between *routine detention*, applied generally and as a matter or policy, law, or practice, and *case-by-case detention*. The earlier analysis confirms that routine detention of victims or suspected victims of trafficking in police lock-ups, prisons, immigration detention centers, or shelters violates a number of fundamental principles of international law and is therefore to be considered, *prima facie*, unlawful. Routine detention of victims of trafficking violates, in some circumstances, the right to freedom of movement and, under most – if not all – circumstances, the prohibitions on unlawful deprivation of liberty and arbitrary detention. International law prohibits discriminatory detention of victims, including detention linked to the sex of the victim. The practice of routine detention for women and girls is inherently discriminatory and therefore unlawful. Routine detention of trafficked children is also directly contrary to international

---

[83]　CRC, at Art. 37(c).

[84]　Ibid; "UN Rules for the Protection of Juveniles Deprived of their Liberty," at para. 29; CRC General Comment No. 6, at para. 63.

[85]　CRC, at Art. 37(c); "UN Rules for the Protection of Juveniles Deprived of their Liberty," at para. 59; CRC General Comment No. 6, at para. 63.

[86]　CRC Optional Protocol, at Art. 8; UNICEF Guidelines, at Guidelines 4.2, 7.1, 9.2.1, 10.1, 10.2; CRC General Comment No. 6, at para. 63.

[87]　CRC, at Art. 37(d). See also UN Committee on the Rights of the Child: "Concluding Observations: Canada," UN Doc. CRC/C/15/Add.215, Oct. 3, 2003, at para. 47.

[88]　CRC, at Art. 39; CRC Optional Protocol, at Art. 8; UNICEF Guidelines, at Guidelines 7.1, 7.2. See also UN Committee on the Rights of the Child: "Concluding Observations: Nepal," UN Doc. CRC/C/15/Add.261, Sept. 21, 2005, at para. 96; "Concluding Observations: Myanmar," UN Doc. CRC/C/15/Add.237, June 30, 2004, at para. 73; "Concluding Observations: Armenia," UN Doc. CRC/C/15/Add.225, Jan. 30, 2004, at para. 67.

[89]　CRC Optional Protocol, at Art. 8(1)(g); UNICEF Guidelines, at Guideline 8.

law and cannot be legally justified on the basis of protection, best interests, or any other grounds.

States may, on a case-by-case basis, be able to successfully defend victim detention in shelters with reference to, for example, criminal justice imperatives, public order requirements, or victim safety needs. The internationally accepted principles of *necessity*, *legality*, and *proportionality* should be used to evaluate the validity of any such defense. Application of these principles would most likely only support a claim of lawful detention in relation to a situation where detention is administered as a last resort and in response to credible and specific threats to an individual victim's safety. However, even when these basic tests are satisfied, a range of protections must be in place to ensure that the rights of the detained person are respected and protected. Such measures would include, but are not limited to, judicial oversight of the situation to determine its ongoing legality and necessity, as well as an enforceable right to challenge the fact of detention. Failure of the State to act to prevent unlawful victim detention by public or private agencies is an internationally wrongful act that, in accordance with the analysis presented in Chapter 4, invokes the international legal responsibility of that State. Victims may be eligible for remedies, including compensation, for this unlawful detention.

In relation to child victims of trafficking, international law recognizes the existence of special needs and special vulnerabilities. While this may impose greater duties on the State when it comes to shelter and protection of children, it does not translate into a legal justification for undifferentiated detention. In cases where children are kept in a shelter or secure accommodation, the detaining authority must be able to demonstrate that the detention is in the child's best interests. The detaining authority must also be able to demonstrate, in relation to each and every case, that there is no reasonable option available to it other than the detention of the child. Specific protections, including the appointment of a guardian, judicial or administrative oversight, and the right of challenge must be upheld in all situations where the fact of detention can be legally justified.

5.3. PROTECTION AND SUPPORT FOR VICTIMS

Victims who break free from their traffickers often find themselves in a situation of great insecurity and vulnerability. They may be physically injured as well as psychologically and/or emotionally traumatized. They may be afraid of retaliation. They are likely to have few, if any, means of subsistence. As detailed below, the responsibility of protecting and caring for victims lies with the State. This responsibility becomes operational when the State knows or should know that an individual within its jurisdiction is a victim of trafficking. The principle is applicable to all countries in whose territory the victim is located. It applies to all trafficked persons, whether victims of internal or transnational trafficking. When considering the protection and support obligations owed to victims of trafficking, it is important to acknowledge that their experience of harm does not necessarily cease when they come to the attention of national authorities. Corruption and complicity of public officials may result in a continuation of an exploitative situation or the emergence of a new one. The harm already done to victims can be compounded by failures to provide medical and other forms of support – or by linking the provision of such services to an obligation of cooperation that victims may not be willing or able to meet.

This section first considers whether the State may lawfully link protection and support to victim cooperation. It then examines the issue of protection from further harm: What does this mean in the context of trafficking, and to what extent is the State required to actively protect victims from further harm? The final part examines the nature and substantive content of the obligation to provide protection and support to victims of trafficking.

5.3.1. *Separating Protection and Support from Victim Cooperation*

The linking of assistance and protection to cooperation with national criminal justice agencies is prevalent in all regions of the world. The legal and regulatory frameworks of many countries explicitly condition any form of support on cooperation.[90] For some of these countries, a victim's willingness to cooperate is insufficient – the relevant authorities are required to make a further determination on the quality and usefulness of that cooperation.[91] Even in the very few countries where nonconditional assistance is guaranteed by law, victims still tend to be pressured into providing information and testimony.[92] The fact that such cooperation may not be optional under some legal systems further complicates this issue.

There are many problems with conditioning the provision of victim protection and support in this way. As detailed further below, victims of trafficking have a legal entitlement to receive assistance commensurate with their status as victims of crime and victims of human rights violations. States are under a corresponding obligation to provide such assistance. Placing conditions on the provision of assistance denies the legal nature of both the entitlement and the obligation. Other problems are more practical in nature. The linking of victim support to cooperation reflects the widely acknowledged importance of victims as a source of intelligence and testimony required to secure convictions against traffickers. However, the compelled victim is unlikely to make a strong witness, particularly in the likely event that this person is still suffering from physical or psychological trauma or fears retaliation.[93]

---

[90] See, for example, US Trafficking Victims Protection Act, at § 107(c).

[91] See, for example, Migration Amendment Regulations 2003 (No. 11) 2003 No. 363 (Australia), at Schedule 8, which provides for Witness Protection (Trafficking) (Temporary) (Class UM) and Witness Protection (Trafficking) (Permanent) (Class DH) visas.

[92] See, for example, case studies provided in Global Alliance Against Trafficking in Women, *Collateral Damage: the Impact of Anti-Trafficking Measures on Human Rights Around the World* (2007).

[93] See Gallagher and Holmes, "Lessons from the Front Line."

Conditional assistance can be expected to exacerbate the high levels of distrust that may already exist between victims and law enforcement. Conditional assistance can also serve to undermine victim credibility in a manner that would be avoided if all identified victims were provided similar levels of assistance and support.

There is growing acceptance of the need to separate protection and support from victim cooperation.[94] While the Trafficking Protocol and its *travaux préparatoires* make no specific reference to this issue, that omission may be explained, at least in part, by the optional nature of most provisions relating to victim assistance and support. Importantly, the Legislative Guide to the Protocol states that "support and protection shall ... not be made conditional upon the victim's capacity or willingness to cooperate in legal proceedings."[95] Other interpretative and guidance documentation produced by the UN provide further support for this principle.[96]

The European Trafficking Convention is more explicit on the need to separate protection and support from legal cooperation. States Parties to the Convention are required to "adopt such legislative or other measures as may be necessary to ensure that assistance to a victim is not made conditional on his or her willingness to act as a witness."[97] The Explanatory Report to the Convention confirms the intention of the drafters that this provision refers to both investigations and criminal proceedings.[98] However, the Report also highlights the fact that in the law of many countries, it is compulsory to give evidence if required to do so. Under such circumstances, it would not be possible to rely on the above provision – or provisions mandating a "recovery and reflection period" (see Chapter 5.4.3) – in refusing to act as a witness when legally compelled to do so.[99]

While State practice still lags some way behind, the position taken by the European Trafficking Convention provides early evidence of a trend toward acknowledging the need to detach protection and support from victim cooperation, particularly during the time immediately following identification, when victims can be expected to be most vulnerable.[100] Several of the UN human rights treaty bodies

---

[94] See, for example, UN Trafficking Principles and Guidelines, at Guideline 6.1.

[95] *Legislative Guide*, at Part 2, para. 62. The Guide cites (at note 23) the UN Trafficking Principles and Guidelines to support this point.

[96] See, for example, UNODC Toolkit, at 351; UNODC Handbook for Parliamentarians, at 49.

[97] European Trafficking Convention, at Art. 12(6).

[98] European Trafficking Convention Explanatory Report, at para. 168.

[99] Ibid, at paras. 170, 176.

[100] The now-elapsed draft victim support provisions of the Framework Decision 2009 Proposal did not establish any link between the provision of assistance and cooperation with national authorities. An accompanying analysis of the draft described the relevant measure as an "[o]bligation on [Member States] to establish adequate victim support schemes for victims based on unconditional assistance since the first stage of the identification process": Framework Decision Impact Assessment, at 27. However, all relevant provisions in the lapsed proposal specifically referred to assistance and support being provided in the context of criminal proceedings. For example, draft Article 10(1) provided that: "[e]ach Member State shall ensure that assistance is provided to victims before, during and after criminal proceedings." Draft Article 10(4) provided that: "[v]ictims shall be granted the

have pointed to the importance of providing assistance on the sole basis of need[101] and expressed concern at the tying of residence permits to victim cooperation.[102] Other UN human rights mechanisms,[103] intergovernmental agencies,[104] and non-governmental organizations[105] have supported the call for nonconditional provision of assistance to victims of trafficking. Growing acceptance of the importance of a "reflection and recovery period" – during which a victim is provided the space,

necessary assistance and support by Member States in the framework of criminal proceedings, to enable them to recover and escape from the influence of the perpetrators, including by providing them with secure accommodation and material assistance, necessary medical treatment including psychological assistance, counselling and information, assistance to enable their rights and interests to be presented and considered in criminal proceedings, and translation and interpretation services where appropriate." This seeming inconsistency is clarified in favor of nonconditionality in the successor instrument to the lapsed Framework Decision Proposal, by the addition of a new clause requiring that "Member States shall take the necessary measures to ensure that assistance and support for a victim are not made conditional on the victim's willingness to act as a witness": EC Directive 2010 Proposal, at Art. 10(3).

[101] UN Human Rights Committee, "Concluding Observations: Belgium," UN Doc. CCPR/CO/81/BEL, Aug. 12, 2004, at para. 15; UN Committee on the Elimination of Discrimination against Women, "Concluding Observations: France," UN Doc. CEDAW/C/FRA/CO/6, Apr. 8, 2008, at paras. 30–31; "Concluding Observations: Australia," UN Doc. CEDAW/C/AUL/CO/5, Feb. 3, 2006, at para. 21.

[102] For example, in its 2008 Concluding Observations on the report of Australia, the UN Committee against Torture requested that State Party "take effective measures to prevent and punish trafficking in persons and provide recovery services to victims on a needs basis *unrelated to whether they collaborate with investigators*": "Concluding Observations: Australia," UN Doc. CAT/C/AUS/CO/1, May 15, 2008, at para. 32 (emphasis added). The UN Committee on the Elimination of Discrimination against Women, in its 2007 Concluding Observations on the report of the Netherlands, called upon the State Party "to provide for the extension of temporary protection visas, reintegration and support services to all victims of trafficking, including those who are unable or unwilling to cooperate in the investigation and prosecution of traffickers": "Concluding Observation: The Netherlands," UN Doc. CEDAW/C/NLD/CO/4, Feb. 2, 2007, at para. 24.

[103] For example, the Special Rapporteur on Trafficking. See Human Rights Council, "Report Submitted by the Special Rapporteur on Trafficking in Persons, Especially Women and Children, Joy Ngozi Ezeilo," UN Doc. A/HRC/10/16, Feb. 20, 2009, at para. 47 ("protection and care shall not be made conditional upon the capacity or willingness of the trafficked person to cooperate in legal proceedings") and UN General Assembly, "Trafficking in Persons, especially Women and Children: Report of the Special Rapporteur on Trafficking in Persons, Especially Women and Children," UN Doc. A/64/290, Aug. 12, 2009, at paras. 50 ("assistance to victims of trafficking should be non-conditional and not based upon their willingness to cooperate with law enforcement or to participate in trials as witnesses. States should refrain from the practice of according conditional assistance to victims and rather build their trust in deciding on the course of action to pursue") and 100(l).

[104] See, for example, UN High Commissioner for Refugees, *Guidelines on International Protection: The application of Article 1(A)(2) of the 1951 Convention and/or 1967 Protocol relating to the Status of Refugees to victims of trafficking and persons at risk of being trafficked*, UN Doc. HCR/GIP/06/07 (Apr. 7, 2006), at para. 50, which note the importance of separating refusal or willingness to provide evidence against traffickers from evaluation of the merits of a claim to asylum.

[105] See, for example, Save the Children, Amnesty International, Anti-Slavery International and Global Alliance Against Traffic in Women, "10 Year Goals for the Global Initiative To Fight Human Trafficking: Submission by Save the Children, Amnesty International, Anti-Slavery International, Global Alliance Against Traffic in Women," submission to the Global Initiative to Fight Human Trafficking (2008), at 2: "[a]ssistance and protection measures should not be conditioned on an individual's cooperation in law enforcement efforts against those responsible for their trafficking."

assistance, information, and support that will allow her or him to make an informed decision about what to do next – provides additional evidence of the value in separating immediate assistance from a decision to cooperate.[106]

5.3.2. *Protection from Further Harm*

Trafficking is only made possible by, and sustained through, high levels of violence and intimidation. Unlike many other crimes, the threat to a victim does not end once she or he has escaped or been rescued from a criminal situation. In some cases, for example, in situations where the victim is in contact with the criminal justice system, freedom from a trafficking situation can actually exacerbate the risks to that person's safety and well-being.

The question of whether States are under an international legal obligation to protect victims of trafficking from further harm is therefore an important one. The Trafficking Protocol requires each State Party to "endeavor to provide for the physical safety of victims of trafficking in persons while they are within its territory."[107] While this provision is limited by the soft nature of the obligation and the specific reference to physical safety, it nevertheless obliges States Parties "to actually take at least some steps that amount to an 'endeavor' to protect safety."[108] Importantly, the provisions of the Protocol on this point are weaker than those contained in its parent instrument, the Organized Crime Convention, which require States Parties to provide witnesses (including those who are victims) with protection from potential retaliation or intimidation.[109] The Convention also requires States Parties to take appropriate measures, within their means, "to provide assistance and protection to victims [of trafficking], in particular in cases of threats of retaliation or intimidation."[110] Measures of protection may include physical protection, domestic or foreign relocation, and special arrangements for giving evidence.[111] It is relevant to note that the protection obligations of the Convention are mandatory for States Parties "but only where appropriate and within the means of the State party concerned."[112]

The European Trafficking Convention contains a general obligation on States Parties to "take due account of the victim's safety and protection needs."[113] This requirement is supplemented by a detailed provision that sets out the specific measures that must be implemented to provide "effective and appropriate protection" to

---

[106] See further, Chapter 5.4.3.
[107] Trafficking Protocol, at Art. 6(5).
[108] *Legislative Guide*, at Part 2, para. 59.
[109] Organized Crime Convention, at Art. 24.
[110] Ibid. at Art. 25(1).
[111] *Legislative Guide*, at Part 1, para. 350.
[112] Ibid. at 167.
[113] European Trafficking Convention, at Art. 12(2). Note that this provision will also apply to victims who have only been provisionally identified as such: ibid. at Art. 10(2).

victims and others (including witnesses, family members, and victim support agencies) from potential retaliation and intimidation, in particular during and after the investigation and prosecution processes.[114] Measures may include physical protection, relocation, identity change, and assistance in obtaining jobs.[115] Protection from harm is an additional aspect of the Convention's provisions on privacy and court proceedings,[116] considered further here and at Chapter 5.4.2. The CRC Optional Protocol on the Sale of Children, Child Prostitution and Child Pornography also contains specific provisions on protection from further harm that would be applicable to certain child victims of trafficking.[117]

Various nontreaty instruments and documents support the existence of an obligation on the part of States in this area. Resolutions of the General Assembly and Human Rights Council have called on governments to ensure the "protection" of victims of trafficking,[118] and more recently identified an obligation to provide such protection.[119] The Human Rights Committee has repeatedly called for victim protection so as to enable victims to testify against the perpetrators of trafficking.[120] The UN Trafficking Principles and Guidelines, for example, specifically refer to the responsibility of States to "protect trafficked persons from further exploitation and harm"[121] as well as the need for States and others to "ensure that trafficked persons are effectively protected from harm, threats or intimidation by traffickers and associated persons."[122]

---

[114] Ibid. at Art. 28.

[115] Ibid.

[116] Ibid. at Arts. 11, 30.

[117] CRC Optional Protocol, at Arts. 8(1)(f), 8(5).

[118] See, for example, UN Human Rights Council, "Trafficking in Persons, Especially Women and Children," UN Doc. A/HRC/RES/11/3, June 17, 2009, at para. 3(c) ("*[u]rges* governments … [t]o ensure protection and assistance to the victims of trafficking with full respect for their human rights, including, where appropriate, through legislation"); UN Human Rights Council, "Rights of the Child," UN Doc. A/HRC/7/L.34, Mar. 26, 2008, at para. 36 ("*[c]alls upon* all States … to address effectively the needs of victims of trafficking … including their safety and protection"); UN General Assembly, "Trafficking in Women and Girls," UN Doc. A/RES/61/144, Dec. 19, 2006, at para. 19 ("*[i]nvites* Governments to take steps to ensure that criminal justice procedures and witness protection programmes are sensitive to the particular situation of trafficked women and girls … and to ensure that during [the criminal justice process] they have access to protection").

[119] See, for example, UN Human Rights Council, "Trafficking in Persons, Especially Women and Children," UN Doc. A/HRC/RES/11/3, June 17, 2009, at Preamble ("all States have an obligation to … rescue victims and to provide for their protection") and UN General Assembly, "Improving the Coordination of Efforts against Trafficking in Persons," UN Doc. A/RES/61/180, Mar. 8, 2007, at Preamble ("Member States have an obligation to provide protection for the victims").

[120] UN Human Rights Committee, "Concluding Observations: Costa Rica," UN Doc. CCPR/C/CRI/CO/5, Nov. 16, 2007, at para. 12; "Concluding Observations: Kosovo (Serbia)," UN Doc. CCPR/C/UNK/CO/1, July 25, 2006, at para. 16; "Concluding Observations: Brazil," UN Doc. CCPR/C/BRA/CO/2, Dec. 1, 2005, at para. 15; "Concluding Observations: Slovenia," UN Doc. CCPR/CO/84/SVN, July 25, 2005, at para. 11; "Concluding Observations: Thailand," UN Doc. CCPR/CO/84/THA, July 8, 2005, at para. 21.

[121] UN Trafficking Principles and Guidelines, at Principle 8. See also Principle 2.

[122] Ibid. at Guideline 6.6.

The precise content of the obligation to protect from further harm will depend on the circumstances of each case. The standard of due diligence, discussed in detail in Chapter 4, will certainly require States to take reasonable measures to this end. In most situations, reasonable protection from harm will require a positive and immediate action on the part of the State to move the trafficked person out of the place of exploitation to a place of safety. It is also likely that protection from further harm will require attention to the immediate medical needs of the victim. Risk assessment may be necessary to determine whether victims are under a particular risk of intimidation or retaliation. Risk assessment should take into account the individual profile of the trafficked person and should also be appropriate to the situation. For example, the nature and level of any risk to a trafficked person may change if and when that person decides or declines to provide a statement, decides or declines to participate as a witness in a criminal trial, and so on. Measures to protect victims from further harm should only be used with the consent of the beneficiary.[123]

The object of protection will also change depending on the stage at which this issue arises. The immediate obligation to protect from further harm relates, of course, to the victim. However, once criminal justice agencies become involved, the obligation will naturally extend to others who could potentially be harmed or intimidated by traffickers and their accomplices. In addition to victims, this list would potentially include informants, those giving testimony, those providing support services to the trafficked person, and family members.[124] Appropriate and effective protection of victims also requires an open and honest assessment of potential sources of harm. For example, detained trafficked persons may be under threat of sexual assault from agents of the State. The UN General Assembly has recently recognized this phenomenon and called on States to penalize persons in authority found guilty of sexually assaulting victims of trafficking in their custody.[125]

5.3.3. *Privacy and Protection from Further Harm*

Protection from further harm is inextricably linked to protection of the trafficked person's privacy. Failure to protect privacy can increase the danger of intimidation and retaliation. It can cause humiliation and hurt to victims and compromise their recovery. In addition, due to the shame and stigmatization often attached to trafficking – for both victims and their families – protection of private life is essential

---

[123] While the Trafficking Protocol is not specific on this point, the Explanatory Report to the European Trafficking Convention explicitly states that consent to protective measures is essential except in extreme circumstances such as an emergency where the victim is physically incapable of giving consent: European Trafficking Convention Explanatory Report, at para. 289. See further the discussion of noncoercion in the provision of support at Chapter 5.3.7.

[124] See, for example, European Trafficking Convention, at Art. 28.

[125] UN General Assembly, "Trafficking in Women and Girls," UN Doc. A/RES/63/156, Jan. 30, 2009, at para. 11.

to preserve victims' chances of social reintegration in the country of origin or the receiving country.[126]

The Trafficking Protocol requires States Parties to protect the privacy and identity of victims of trafficking "in appropriate cases and to the extent possible under its domestic law."[127] The equivocal nature of this provision attracted considerable criticism from observers during the negotiations, but efforts to strengthen its protective language were unsuccessful.[128] It is clear, from the text of the provision as well as from various interpretative texts that followed, that its focus is on the specific issue of privacy in the context of court proceedings.[129] The European Trafficking Convention takes a broader approach to victim privacy, separating the protection of private life from the more specific concern of protecting privacy in the context of judicial proceedings. In relation to the former, the Convention sets out a general obligation on States Parties to "protect the private life and identity of victims,"[130] laying down specific measures to meet that objective, including standards for the storage of personal data and encouraging the media to respect the private life and identity of victims.[131] It sets higher standards in respect of measures required to ensure the privacy of child victims.[132] In relation to judicial proceedings, the Convention requires States Parties to adopt procedures so as to protect victims' privacy as well as to ensure their safety.[133]

References to privacy in other legal and nonlegal texts are not extensive. The South Asian Association for Regional Cooperation (SAARC) Convention specifies that judicial authorities shall ensure that the confidentiality of child and women

---

[126] European Trafficking Convention Explanatory Report, at para. 138.

[127] Trafficking Protocol, at Art. 6(1). Note the same provision highlights the importance of protecting privacy in legal proceedings, an issue that is considered in more detail at Chapter 5.4.2.

[128] Both the UN Special Rapporteur on Violence against Women and the High Commissioner for Human Rights argued that the wording was restrictive and indirect, allowing States Parties an inappropriate measure of discretion over whether or not to ensure the privacy and confidentiality of legal proceedings relating to trafficking in persons. Calls for the deletion of clauses such as "in appropriate cases" were unsuccessful. See further, Travaux Préparatoires *for the Organized Crime Convention and Protocols*, at 368.

[129] Article 6(1) of the Trafficking Protocol reads: "[i]n appropriate cases and to the extent possible under domestic law, each State Party shall protect the privacy and identity of victims of trafficking in persons, including, inter alia, by making legal proceedings relating to such trafficking confidential." See further, *Legislative Guide*, at 283–284. Note that the UNODC Model Law takes a much broader view, referring to the right to privacy in the context of data collection (at 51, 61), repatriation (at 62), and interagency cooperation and information exchange (at 71), as well as in relation to court proceedings (at 43, 45–47).

[130] European Trafficking Convention, at Art. 11.

[131] Ibid. For a detailed explanation of the personal data provision and its link with the European Convention for the Protection of Individuals with Regard to Automatic Processing of Personal Data (1496 UNTS 66, done Jan. 28, 1981, entered into force Oct. 1, 1985), see European Trafficking Convention Explanatory Report, at paras. 140–141.

[132] See further, the discussion at Chapter 5.5.3.

[133] European Trafficking Convention, at Art. 30. See also, European Trafficking Convention Explanatory Report, at paras. 299–300. See further, Chapter 5.5.3.

victims when trying trafficking offenses.[134] The UN Trafficking Principles and Guidelines link the right to privacy to the need to ensure that trafficked persons are protected from their exploiters: "there should be no public disclosure of the identity of trafficking victims and their privacy should be respected to the extent possible, while taking into account the right of an accused person to a fair trial."[135] The UN's human rights treaty bodies[136] and its investigatory mechanisms[137] have also occasionally affirmed the importance of the right to privacy in relation to victims of trafficking.

There are strong indications that the right to privacy is vulnerable to violation in situations of trafficking, in particular when victims are in contact with State apparatus including support services and criminal justice agencies. The provisions cited earlier support the existence of an obligation on the part of the State to take active measures to ensure that victims' right to privacy is protected from unreasonable and unjustifiable interference. Measures to protect the privacy of victims may need to be weighed against the rights of accused persons to a fair trial.[138] The possibility of a conflict between victims' right to privacy and the right of accused persons is considered further at Chapter 5.4.2.

5.3.4. *Physical and Psychological Care and Support*

The nature of the obligation on States to provide care and support of victims of trafficking is inextricably tied up with their status as victims of crime and victims of human rights violations – a status that, as noted above, provides such victims with a right to be treated with humanity and with respect for their dignity and human rights, as well as with an entitlement to measures that ensure their well-being and avoid revictimization.[139] More specifically, victims of crime are entitled to receive "the necessary material, medical, psychological and social assistance through

---

[134] South Asian Association for Regional Cooperation, Convention on Preventing and Combating Trafficking in Women and Children for Prostitution, done Jan. 5, 2002, entered into force Dec. 1, 2005 (SAARC Convention), at Art. V.

[135] UN Trafficking Principles and Guidelines, at Guideline 6, para. 6. Guideline 6 also recognizes the significant practical obstacles facing law enforcement agencies in protecting the privacy of victims: "[t]rafficked persons should be given full warning, in advance, of the difficulties inherent in protecting identities and should not be given false or unrealistic expectations regarding the capacities of law enforcement agencies in this regard."

[136] See, for example, noting the importance of witness protection, UN Committee on the Elimination of Discrimination against Women, "Concluding Observations: Cameroon," UN Doc. CEDAW/C/CMR/CO/3, Feb. 10, 2009, at para. 31; "Concluding Observations: Mongolia," UN Doc. CEDAW/C/MNG/CO/7, Nov. 7, 2008, at para. 27. See also CRC General Comment No. 6, at paras. 29–30.

[137] See, for example, UN General Assembly, "Trafficking in Persons, Especially Women and Children, Report of the Special Rapporteur on Trafficking in Persons, Especially Women and Children," UN Doc. A/64/290, Aug. 12, 2009, at paras. 41–42, 56, 62, 91.

[138] UN Trafficking Principles and Guidelines, at Guideline 6.6; *Legislative Guide*, at Part 2, para. 54.

[139] "Principles and Guidelines on the Right to a Remedy and Reparation," at para. 10.

governmental, voluntary, community-based and indigenous means."[140] Victims of gross violations of human rights have a legal entitlement to rehabilitation, an important component of reparation that includes medical and psychological care.[141]

Certain human rights, such as the right to the highest attainable standard of physical and mental health[142] and the right to adequate food, clothing, and housing,[143] are especially relevant in this context. It is also important to note that trafficked persons may be entitled to additional, status-related rights. For example, as explored further below, specific and additional obligations of care and support are owed by the State to child victims of trafficking. The prohibition on sex-based discrimination is also important when considering issues of access to support and assistance. Women victims of trafficking are victims of gender-based violence and thereby entitled to access help on this basis as well as on the basis of their status as victims of trafficking.[144]

The major trafficking treaties set out varying standards in relation to victim care and support. The Trafficking Protocol requires States Parties to:

[140] "Basic Principles for Victims of Crime and Abuse of Power," at para. 7. The UNODC Model Law, at 43, notes that many countries already have laws and regulations in place to ensure that victims of serious crime have access to certain benefits and services, and that if necessary, such access should be explicitly extended to victims of trafficking.

[141] "Principles and Guidelines on the Right to a Remedy and Reparation," at para. 21. See further the discussion of remedies in Chapter 6 of this volume.

[142] International Covenant on Economic, Social and Cultural Rights, 993 UNTS 3, done Dec. 16, 1966, entered into force Jan. 3, 1976 (ICESCR), at Art. 12; Convention on the Elimination of All Forms of Discrimination Against Women, 1249 UNTS 13, done Dec. 13, 1979, entered into force Sept. 3, 1981 (CEDAW), at Art. 12; International Convention on the Protection of the Rights of All Migrant Workers and Members of Their Families, UN Doc. A/RES/45/158, done Dec. 18, 1990, entered into force July 1, 2003 (Migrant Workers Convention), at Art. 28; Convention on the Elimination of All Forms of Racial Discrimination, 660 UNTS 195, done Dec. 21, 1965, entered into force Jan. 4, 1969 (CERD), at Art. 5(e)(iv); CRC, at Art. 24; The Committee on Economic, Social and Cultural Rights has asserted the obligation of States Parties to respect the right to health of all persons, including especially vulnerable groups such as asylum seekers and illegal immigrants: UN Committee on Economic, Social and Cultural Rights, "General Comment No. 14: The Right to the Highest Attainable Standard of Health," UN Doc. E/C.12/2000/4, Aug. 11, 2000.

[143] ICESCR, at Art. 11; CERD, at Art. 5(e)(iii); Trafficking Protocol, Art. 6(3)(a); Refugee Convention, at Art. 21; Protocol to the African Charter on Human and Peoples' Rights on the Rights of Women in Africa, OAU Doc. CAB/LEG/66.6, done July 11, 2003, entered into force Nov. 25, 2005, at Arts. 15 and 16; SAARC Convention, at Art. IX(3); UN Committee on the Elimination of Discrimination against Women "General Recommendation No. 19: Violence against Women," UN Doc. A/47/38, Jan. 29, 1992 (CEDAW General Recommendation No. 19), at para. 24(t)(iii); Beijing Declaration and Platform for Action, at para. 125(a).

[144] See, for example, CEDAW General Recommendation No. 19, at para. 24(b) ("[a]ppropriate protective and support services should be provided for victims"). See also, UN General Assembly, "Declaration on the Elimination of Violence against Women," UN Doc. A/48/49, Dec. 20, 1993, at Art. 4(g), which makes provision for specialized assistance for women subjected to violence, such as "rehabilitation, assistance in child care and maintenance, treatment, counselling, and health and social services, facilities and programmes, as well as support structures, and ... other appropriate measures to promote their safety and physical and psychological rehabilitation"; Beijing Declaration and Platform for Action, at paras. 99, 106, 107, 122, 125, 130; and Beijing +5 Outcome Document, at para. 97(c).

consider implementing measures to provide for the physical, psychological and social recovery of victims … in particular the provision of (a) appropriate housing; (b) counseling and information in particular as regards their legal rights in a language that the victims … can understand; (c) medical, psychological and material assistance; and (d) employment, education and training opportunities.[145]

In applying these provisions to those victims within its territory,[146] States Parties are required to take into account the age, gender, and special needs of victims of trafficking, in particular the special needs of children.[147]

While victim protection and support is one of the three stated purposes of the Trafficking Protocol,[148] the corresponding provisions reflect a level of reluctance, on the part of States, to tie themselves down to specific obligations in this regard.[149] The Legislative Guide to the Protocol confirms that "requirements to provide assistance and support for victims incorporate some element of discretion."[150] It does also confirm, however, that while *implementation* of these measures is not mandatory, States Parties are required to *consider* implementing these requirements and "urged to do so to the greatest extent possible within resource and other constraints."[151] The Legislative Guide further explains that these support measures are intended to reduce the suffering and harm caused to victims and to assist in their recovery and rehabilitation.[152] It further notes that, while not obligatory, implementation of these provisions can provide important practical benefits including increasing the likelihood of victim cooperation in investigations and prosecutions, and avoiding further harm including revictimization.[153]

The requirements of the European Trafficking Convention with respect to victim support and assistance are much more specific, detailed, and substantive than those of the Trafficking Protocol. States Parties to the European Trafficking Convention are required to provide all victims within their territory or jurisdiction with a range of measures aimed to "assist victims in their physical, psychological and social recovery."[154] Such assistance is also to extend to those who have been provisionally

---

[145] Trafficking Protocol, at Art. 6(3) (emphasis added).

[146] An Interpretative Note relating to Art. 6(3) affirms that: "[t]he type of assistance set forth in this paragraph is applicable to both the receiving State and the State of origin of the victims of trafficking in persons, but only as regards victims who are in their respective territory. Paragraph 3 is applicable to the receiving State until the victim of trafficking in persons has returned to his or her State of origin, and to the State of origin thereafter." Travaux Préparatoires *for the Organized Crime Convention and Protocols*, at 373.

[147] Trafficking Protocol, at Art. 6(4).

[148] Ibid. at Art. 2(b).

[149] See further, Travaux Préparatoires *for the Organized Crime Convention and Protocols*, at 366–373.

[150] *Legislative Guide*, at Part 2, para. 52.

[151] Ibid. This is confirmed in the UNODC Model Law, at 44: "Article 6, paragraph 3, of the Protocol obliges States parties to consider implementing measures to provide for the physical, psychological and social recovery of victims of trafficking."

[152] *Legislative Guide*, at Part 2, para. 62.

[153] Ibid.

[154] European Trafficking Convention, at Art. 12(1). See also European Trafficking Convention Explanatory Report, at para. 148.

identified as victims and, crucially, cannot be reserved only for those agreeing to act as witnesses.[155] It is to include, at the least, appropriate and secure accommodation, psychological and material assistance at subsistence level, access to emergency medical treatment, translation or other services, counseling and information, assistance with legal proceedings, and, for children, access to education.[156] Additional provisions are made for victims lawfully within the territory of the State Party.[157] Obligations to provide assistance and support are linked to and reinforce the related obligation of States Parties to take due account of victims' safety and protection needs.[158]

The SAARC Convention calls on States Parties to establish protective homes and shelters for the rehabilitation of victims, and to make provisions for legal advice, counseling, and health care for victims.[159]

Nontreaty instruments developed at both the international and regional levels point to the development of an emerging consensus on the existence of certain minimum obligations on States with respect to victim support. The UN Trafficking Principles and Guidelines, for example, require States to ensure that victims of trafficking have *access to adequate physical and psychological care.*[160] States and others are requested to consider ensuring, along with NGOs, the availability of "safe and adequate shelter that meets the needs of trafficked persons" and "access to primary health care and counseling."[161] Regional soft law agreements and policy statements affirm the importance of ensuring that victims of trafficking are supported and assisted. In Europe, these include the EU Plan on Best Practices,[162] the European Experts Group Opinion of October 2005,[163] the European Experts Group Opinion

---

[155] European Trafficking Convention, at Arts. 10(2) and 12(6). In contrast, while the draft EU Framework Decision 2009 Proposal also set out substantial obligations on Member States with respect to victim support and assistance at Articles 9 and 10, these provisions were compromised somewhat by their explicit link to criminal proceedings. That proposal has now lapsed (see note 20 to this chapter), and the conditioning of victim support and assistance has been rectified in the successor instrument: EC Directive 2010 Proposal, at Art. 10(3) ("Member States shall take the necessary measures to ensure that assistance and support for a victim are not made conditional on the victim's willingness to act as a witness").

[156] European Trafficking Convention, at Art. 12(1).

[157] Ibid, at Arts. 12(3), 12(4). The extent to which these provisions actually impose specific obligations on States Parties or confer additional rights is unclear. See European Trafficking Convention Explanatory Report, at paras. 165–166.

[158] European Trafficking Convention, at Art. 12(2). See also European Trafficking Convention Explanatory Report, at paras. 153–154 and 164.

[159] SAARC Convention, at Art. IX(3).

[160] UN Trafficking Principles and Guidelines, at Principle 8.

[161] Ibid. at Guidelines 6.1 and 6.2.

[162] European Union, "EU Plan on Best Practices, Standards and Procedures for Combating and Preventing Trafficking in Human Beings," OJ C 2005/C 311/01, Dec. 9, 2005, at para. 4(vii).

[163] Experts Group on Trafficking in Human Beings of the European Commission, "Opinion of 11 October 2005 in connection with the conference 'Tackling human trafficking: Policy and best practices in Europe' and its related documents," at 2.

of May 2004,[164] the OSCE Action Plan,[165] and the Brussels Declaration.[166] In Africa, they include the Ouagadougou Action Plan,[167] the Economic Community of West African States (ECOWAS) Declaration on Trafficking in Persons,[168] and the ECOWAS Initial Plan of Action.[169] In Latin America, they include the Organization of American States (OAS) Recommendations on Trafficking in Persons[170] and Resolution 2348 of the Assembly-General of Organization of American States.[171] In Asia, the COMMIT MOU obliges States to provide all victims of trafficking "with shelter and appropriate physical, psycho-social, legal, educational and health-care assistance."[172] The MOU between the Governments of Thailand and Cambodia requires the parties to "provide trafficked children, women, and their immediate family, if any, with safe shelters, health care, access to legal assistance, and other imperative for their protection."[173]

Several resolutions of the UN General Assembly and Human Rights Council call for the provision of physical and psychological care to victims of trafficking.[174] Various UN human rights treaty bodies have recommended the provision of physical and

---

[164] Experts Group on Trafficking in Human Beings of the European Commission, "Opinion of 18 May 2004 on reflection period and residence permit for victims of trafficking in human beings," at para. 3.

[165] Organization for Security and Co-operation in Europe (OSCE) Permanent Council, "Decision No. 557: OSCE Action Plan to Combat Trafficking In Human Beings," OSCE Doc. PC.DEC/557, July 24, 2003, at Section V.

[166] Brussels Declaration, at para. 13.

[167] Ouagadougou Action Plan, at 4.

[168] Economic Community of West African States, "Declaration A/DC12/12/01 on the Fight Against Trafficking in Persons," adopted by the Twenty-Fifth Ordinary Session of Authority of Heads of State and Government, Dec. 20–21, 2001, at para. 7.

[169] Economic Community of West African States, "ECOWAS Initial Plan of Action against Trafficking in Persons (2002–2003)," adopted by the Twenty-Fifth Ordinary Session of Authority of Heads of State and Government, Dec. 20–21, 2001, at 5.

[170] OAS Recommendations on Trafficking in Persons, at Section IV(1)(2).

[171] OAS General Assembly, "Hemispheric Efforts to Combat Trafficking in Persons: Conclusions and Recommendations of the First Meeting of National Authorities on Trafficking in Persons," OAS Doc. AG/RES. 2256 (XXXVI-O/06), June 6, 2006, at Preamble, para. 1.

[172] COMMIT MOU, at Arts. 17–18.

[173] Cambodia-Thailand MOU, at Art. 9. The MOU between the Governments of Thailand and Lao PDR requires the parties to provide legal assistance, health care, and other necessary measures to protect victims and their families: Memorandum of Understanding Between the Government of the Kingdom of Thailand and the Government of the Lao People's Democratic Republic on Cooperation to Combat Trafficking in Persons, Especially Women and Children, adopted on July 13, 2005 in Bangkok, at Art. 8.

[174] See, for example, UN General Assembly, "Trafficking in Women and Girls," UN Doc. A/RES/63/156, Jan. 30, 2009, at para.15, ("*[c]alls upon* concerned Governments to allocate resources, as appropriate, to provide comprehensive programmes for the physical, psychological and social recovery of victims of trafficking") and UN Human Rights Council, "Trafficking in Persons, Especially Women and Children," UN Doc. A/HRC/RES/11/3, June 17, 2009, at paras. 3(c), 3(d) ("*[u]rges* governments ... [t]o ensure protection and assistance to the victims of trafficking with full respect for their human rights ... [t]o provide resources, as appropriate, for the comprehensive protection and assistance to victims of trafficking, including access to adequate social, necessary medical and psychological care

psychological care and support – specifically, rehabilitation[175] and reintegration[176] programs, medical care,[177] counseling,[178] crisis centers and telephone hotlines,[179] safe houses, and shelters.[180] The Special Rapporteur on Trafficking in Persons has repeatedly referred to an obligation to provide protection and support to victims in her communications with States.[181]

5.3.5. *Consular Access and Support*

As noted throughout this chapter, the criminalization and detention of victims of trafficking, including for status offenses, is widespread in every part of the world.

---

and services, including those related to HIV/AIDS, as well as shelter, legal assistance in a language that they can understand").

[175] See, for example, UN Human Rights Committee, "Concluding Observations: Japan," UN Doc. CCPR/C/JPN/CO/5, Dec. 18, 2008, at para. 23; UN Committee on the Rights of the Child, "Concluding Observations: Democratic Republic of the Congo," UN Doc. CRC/C/COD/CO/2, Feb. 10, 2009, at para. 83; UN Committee Against Torture, "Concluding Observations: Ukraine," UN Doc. CAT/C/UKR/CO/5, May 18, 2007, at paras. 14, 24; UN Committee on the Elimination of Discrimination against Women, "Concluding Observations: El Salvador," UN Doc. CEDAW/C/SLV/CO/7, Nov. 7, 2008, at para. 26; "Concluding Observations: Bolivia," UN Doc. CEDAW/C/BOL/CO/4, Apr. 8, 2008, at para. 27.

[176] UN Committee on the Rights of the Child, "Concluding Observations: United States of America," UN Doc. CRC/C/OPSC/USA/CO/1, June 25, 2008, at para. 39; UN Committee on the Elimination of Discrimination against Women "Concluding Observations: Brazil," UN Doc. CEDAW/C/BRA/CO/6, Aug. 10, 2007, at para. 24;

[177] See, for example, UN Human Rights Committee, "Concluding Observations: Japan," UN Doc. CCPR/C/JPN/CO/5, Dec. 18, 2008, at para. 23; "Concluding Observations: Kosovo (Serbia)," UN Doc. CCPR/C/UNK/CO/1, July 25, 2006, at para. 16; UN Committee Against Torture, "Concluding Observations: Indonesia," UN Doc. CAT/C/IDN/CO/2, May 16, 2008, at para. 20; "Concluding Observations: Ukraine," UN Doc. CAT/C/UKR/CO/5, May 18, 2007, at paras. 14, 24; UN Committee on the Elimination of Discrimination against Women, "Concluding Observations: Myanmar," UN Doc. CEDAW/C/MMR/CO/3, Nov. 27, 2008, at para. 27.

[178] See, for example, UN Human Rights Committee, "Concluding Observations: Japan," UN Doc. CCPR/C/JPN/CO/5, Dec. 18, 2008, at para. 23; "Concluding Observations: Kosovo (Serbia)," UN Doc. CCPR/C/UNK/CO/1, July 25, 2006, at para. 16; UN Committee on the Elimination of Discrimination against Women, "Concluding Observations: Myanmar," UN Doc. CEDAW/C/MMR/CO/3, Nov. 27, 2008, at para. 27; UN Committee against Torture, "Concluding Observations: Belgium," UN Doc. CAT/C/BEL/CO/2, Jan. 19, 2009, at para. 25.

[179] UN Committee on the Elimination of Discrimination against Women, "Concluding Observations: Kyrgyzstan," UN Doc. CEDAW/C/KGZ/CO/3, Nov. 14, 2008, at para. 28; UN Committee on the Rights of the Child, "Concluding Observations: Kazakhstan," UN Doc. CRC/C/OPSC/KAZ/CO/1, Mar. 17, 2006, at para. 22.

[180] UN Committee on the Elimination of Discrimination against Women, "Concluding Observations: Azerbaijan," UN Doc. CEDAW/C/AZE/CO/4, Aug. 7, 2009, at para. 24; "Concluding Observations: Ireland," UN Doc. CEDAW/C/IRL/CO/4–5, July 22, 2005, at para. 31; UN Committee Against Torture, "Concluding Observations: Japan," UN Doc. CAT/C/JPN/CO/1, May 18, 2007, at para. 8.

[181] "Report of the Special Rapporteur on the human rights aspects of the victims of trafficking in persons, especially women and children, Sigma Huda, Addendum 1: Summary of cases transmitted to Governments and replies received," UN Doc E/CN.4/2006/62/Add.1, March 26, 2006, at para. 21 (Cambodia), at para. 50 (India), at para. 66 (Israel), at para. 76 (Democratic People's Republic of Korea).

The right to consular access and support is especially important for trafficked persons who have been arrested, detained, charged with any offense, or threatened with deportation. This right has not been articulated in any of the specialist trafficking treaties, perhaps because of a perceived incompatibility between the need for consular protection and the identification of trafficked persons as victims.[182] Despite being recognized in the UN Trafficking Principles and Guidelines,[183] the issue of consular access and support for detained victims of trafficking is rarely raised in international forums or by human rights mechanisms.[184]

Silence on the issue of consular access and support should not be taken as confirmation that trafficked persons lack specific legal entitlements in this area. The issues are, however, quite complex. The extent to which general international law recognizes a right to consular assistance – and a right to timely *notification* of the right to consular assistance – is both difficult and unresolved. The UN General Assembly has, in the past, recognized aliens' right of consular access, as well as a right to information about this right, through a nonbinding declaration.[185] Under the Vienna Convention on Consular Relations, States Parties are required to assist noncitizens who have been detained in contacting consular officials in their country of citizenship. Specifically:

> if [the individual concerned] so requests, the competent authorities of the receiving State shall, without delay, inform the consular post of the sending State if, within the consular district, a national of that State is arrested or committed to prison or to custody pending trial, or is detained in any other manner. Any communication addressed to the consular post by the person arrested, in prison, custody or detention shall also be forwarded by the said authorities without delay. The said authorities shall inform the person concerned without delay of his rights under this sub-paragraph.[186]

---

[182] This interpretation is borne out by the *travaux préparatoires*. The issue of consular protection was not discussed in the context of the Trafficking Protocol. It was, however, a major concern for drafters of the Migrant Smuggling Protocol, and the final text of that instrument affirms a right of consular access for smuggled migrants in detention (at Art. 16(5)).

[183] The UN Trafficking Principles and Guidelines, at Guideline 6.3, request States and others to consider "ensuring that trafficked persons are informed of their right of access to diplomatic and consular representatives from their State of nationality." It recommends that staff working in consulates and embassies be provided with appropriate training in responding to requests for information and assistance from trafficked persons: ibid.

[184] For example, the General Assembly and the Special Rapporteur on Trafficking have only considered the issue in the narrow context of a need for consular officials to receive appropriate (but otherwise unspecified) training. See UN General Assembly, "Trafficking in Women and Girls," UN Doc. A/RES/63/156, Jan. 30, 2009, at para. 18; and UN General Assembly, "Trafficking in Persons, Especially Women and Children: Report of the Special Rapporteur on Trafficking in Persons, Especially Women and Children," UN Doc. A/64/290, Aug. 12, 2009, at para. 100(c).

[185] UN General Assembly, "Declaration on the Human Rights of Individuals who are not Nationals of the Countries in which They Live," UN Doc. A/RES/40/144, Dec. 13, 1985, at Art. 10.

[186] Vienna Convention on Consular Relations, 596 UNTS 261, done April 24, 1961, entered into force March 19, 1967, at Art. 36(1)(b).

Importantly, the Vienna Convention does not create an obligation on the national's State to provide assistance once it is contacted. In other words, it is up to the notified State to decide whether or not it will provide protection and support – and, if so, the nature and extent of that assistance. The provision on notification extracted above was subject to examination by the Inter-American Court of Human Rights in the context of an advisory opinion issued in 1999.[187] In a "surprisingly bold" and "remarkable" opinion,[188] the Court affirmed that the provision applied "to all cases in which a national of a sending state is deprived of his freedom *regardless of the reason*."[189] The Court found that whenever a foreign national is detained, that person has the fundamental right (recognized in but not created by the Vienna Convention) to be informed of his right to contact consular authorities. It further found that failure to so notify constitutes a violation of the human right to due process, recognized in Article 14 of the ICCPR.[190]

The International Court of Justice has, on several recent occasions, examined the implications of the relevant provision of the Vienna Convention on Consular Relations from the perspective of individual rights.[191] In the *LaGrand* case, the court identified a right to consular notification and held that the Vienna Convention does not just apply to the rights of the sending State but also to those of the detained individual. While not pronouncing directly on whether the right to consular notification was part of the right of due process, the Court did give some indication that this was more than a treaty right.[192] In a subsequent case, it retracted slightly on this position while still avoiding a direct conclusion on the matter of whether, as found by the Inter-American Court, the right to consular notification is a *human* right.[193]

It is relevant to note that several other international human rights treaties contain provisions on consular assistance and protection. The Convention against Torture, for example, provides that any person in custody for a torture-related offense "shall be assisted in communicating immediately with the nearest appropriate representative of the State of which he is a national, or, if he is a stateless person, to the representative

---

[187] *The Right to Information on Consular Assistance in the Framework of the Guarantees of the Due Process of Law*, Advisory Opinion OC-16/99, Inter-American Court of Human Rights (ser. A) No. 16, Oct. 1, 1999 (*Right to Information on Consular Assistance*).

[188] C.M. Cerna, "Impact on the Right to Consular Notification," in M.T. Kamminga and M. Scheinin eds., *The Impact of Human Rights on General International Law* 171 (2009) (Cerna, "Impact on the Right to Consular Notification"), at 180, 186.

[189] *Right to Information on Consular Assistance*, at para. 101 (emphasis added).

[190] For a detailed consideration and critique of the Court's advisory opinion, see Cerna, "Impact on the Right to Consular Notification," at 180–186.

[191] *Case Concerning the Vienna Convention on Consular Relations (Paraguay v. United States), Request for the Indication of Provisional Measures*, [1998] ICJ Rep 248; *LaGrand (Germany v. United States)*, [2001] ICJ Rep 466; *Avena and Other Mexican Nationals (Mexico v. the United States)*, [2004] ICJ Rep 12 (*Avena*).

[192] See Cerna, "Impact on the Right to Consular Notification," at 192.

[193] *Avena*, at para.124.

of the State where he usually resides."[194] The Migrant Workers Convention confirms that migrants falling within its provisions have a right of recourse to consular notification as well as to consular protection and assistance, including in cases of expulsion.[195] This instrument also specifies that where a migrant worker is detained, the consular or diplomatic staff of his or her State of origin shall be informed without delay of the arrest and the reasons therefor.[196]

In summary, trafficked persons who have been arrested and/or detained by (or indeed, in) the country of destination for any reason have the right to be informed of the availability of consular assistance from their country of origin. They have the right to choose whether or not to utilize such access, to communicate freely with the consular post, and to obtain or decline consular protection and support. Failure of a State to meet its international legal obligations in this regard engages the international responsibility of that State.[197]

5.3.6. *Noncoercion in the Provision of Care and Support*

The Trafficking Protocol does not foresee any danger that its nonmandatory victim protection and support provisions would be applied coercively. However, the European Trafficking Convention requires that, in relation to all assistance measures provided for in that instrument, States Parties are to ensure the relevant services "are provided on a consensual and informed basis, taking due account of the special needs of persons in a vulnerable position and rights of children in terms of accommodation, education and appropriate health care."[198] The Explanatory Report to the Convention makes specific reference to the issue of medical testing, noting that "victims must be able to agree to the detection of illness such as HIV/AIDS for [the tests] to be licit."[199]

The issue of mandatory HIV/AIDS testing is a contentious one.[200] It is also of great relevance to the present discussion in view of the fact that HIV/AIDS prevalence can be very high among certain trafficked populations.[201]While international

---

[194] Convention against Torture and Other Cruel, Inhuman or Degrading Treatment or Punishment, 1465 UNTS 85, adopted Dec. 10, 1984, entered into force June 26, 1987, at Art. 6.

[195] Migrant Workers Convention, at Art. 23.

[196] Ibid. at Art. 7(a).

[197] For a more detailed discussion of this aspect, see R. Perruchoud, "Consular Protection and Assistance," in R. Cholewinski, R. Perruchoud and E. MacDonald ed., *International Migration Law: Developing Paradigms and Key Challenges* 71 (2007), at 80–81.

[198] European Trafficking Convention, at Art. 12(7).

[199] European Trafficking Convention Explanatory Report, at para. 171.

[200] For an overview of the relevant human rights issues from two very different perspectives, see E. Durojay, "Addressing Human Rights Concerns Raised by Mandatory HIV Testing of Pregnant Women through the Protocol to the African Charter on the Rights of Women," (2008) 52 *Journal of African Law* 43; and Canadian HIV/AIDS Legal Network, "HIV Testing of UN Peacekeeping Forces: Legal and Human Rights Issues" (2001).

[201] See, for example, J.G. Silverman et al, "Syphilis and Hepatitis B Co-Infection among HIV-Infected, Sex-Trafficked Women and Girls, Nepal," (2008) 14 *Emerging Infectious Diseases* 932. The report at

treaty law does not provide firm guidance, there is abundant soft law support for the position that testing of victims should not be coercive or mandatory. For example, in its General Comment No. 3, the Committee on the Rights of the Child affirmed that:

> States must refrain from imposing mandatory HIV/AIDS testing of children in all circumstances and ensure protection against it. While the evolving capacities of the child will determine whether consent is required from him or her directly or from his or her parent or guardian … States Parties must ensure that, prior to any HIV testing … the risks and benefits of such testing are sufficiently conveyed so that an informed decision can be made.[202]

The Special Rapporteur on Violence against Women has recommended that HIV testing be provided "only if requested by the person concerned."[203] The United Nations has also adopted the standard of informed consent.[204] In the specific context of trafficking, the principle of noncoercion is supported in the Brussels Declaration, which prohibits mandatory HIV/AIDS testing and recommends that the provision of support measures be on a "consensual and fully informed basis."[205] A similar position is taken in the UNODC Model Law.[206]

It is important to note that in this area, as in many others, the circumstances of the case may require a balancing of different rights and responsibilities. In the case of child victims of trafficking, for example, the application of the "best interests" principle (discussed further below) may require the provision of services such as shelter and medical treatment on a nonconsensual basis. Generally, however, and absent special and defined circumstances, the provision of care and support should be both informed and noncoercive. Victims of trafficking should, for example, receive information on their entitlements so they can make an informed decision. As discussed above, care and support should not be made conditional on cooperation with criminal justice authorities. Not all individuals who have been trafficked will want or

---

its outset, briefly and without further comment, notes that the HIV testing, conducted by a large Nepalese NGO, was not dependent on the consent of the victim (all sex trafficking victims at the shelter were "routinely tested," "[u]pon intake and pending verbal consent").

[202] UN Committee on the Rights of the Child, "General Comment No. 3: HIV/AIDS and the Rights of the Child," UN Doc. CRC/GC/2003/3, Mar. 17, 2003, at para. 23.

[203] UN Commission on Human Rights, "Report of the Special Rapporteur, Ms. Radhika Coomaraswamy, on Violence against Women, Its Causes and Consequences, on Trafficking in Women, Women's Migration and Violence against Women," UN Doc. E/CN.4/2000/68, Feb. 29, 2000, at para. 116(c).

[204] See, for example, World Health Organization and UNAIDS, *WHO/UNAIDS Guidance on Provider Initiated HIV Testing and Counselling in Health Facilities* (2007); UNODC Toolkit, at 393–397 (citing the draft *Guidance on Provider-Initiated HIV Testing and Counselling for People Vulnerable to Human Trafficking*).

[205] Brussels Declaration, at para. 13.

[206] UNODC Model Law, at 44 (assistance to include "[h]ealth care and necessary medical treatment, including, where appropriate, free optional confidential testing for HIV and other sexually transmitted diseases").

need to exercise the entitlements set out in this chapter.[207] Victims should also be able to refuse care and support. They should not be forced into accepting or receiving assistance.

5.4. LEGAL ASSISTANCE, PARTICIPATION, AND THE RIGHT TO REMAIN

Victims of trafficking are often in a precarious legal situation. As noted previously, the immigration status of those trafficked across national borders may be in doubt and they may be at risk of prosecution for offenses such as illegal work. Victims are unlikely to have a full understanding of the rights to which they are entitled and will rarely be in a strong position to pursue those rights without help. The provision of legal assistance to trafficked persons can best be viewed as a prerequisite to the realization of other important rights, including the right to protection, the right not to be prosecuted for status-related offenses, and the right to participate in legal proceedings against their exploiters. The following paragraphs explore the nature of rights and obligations associated with legal assistance and participation, including the special needs of victims who are acting as witnesses and the status of victims throughout legal proceedings.

5.4.1. *Legal Information, Support, and Participation*

The Trafficking Protocol requires that trafficked persons be provided with information on relevant court and administrative proceedings.[208] It has been noted that this should include information on the timing and progress of relevant proceedings as well as the disposition of any case in which the victim has an interest.[209] The Trafficking Protocol further recognizes a duty on States to assist in making sure that victims can be present at and have their concerns and views considered during criminal proceedings against traffickers in a manner not prejudicial to the rights of the defense.[210] Both provisions are mandatory, and the latter provision echoes a

---

[207] See, for example, R. Salazar Parrenas, "Sex for Sale: Trafficked? Filipino Hostesses in Tokyo's Nightlife Industry," (2006) 18 *Yale Journal of Law and Feminism* 145, discussing the need, among women trafficked into Japan, for improved conditions of labor and migration rather than "rescue, rehabilitation and repatriation."

[208] Trafficking Protocol, at Art. 6(2)(a). Victim involvement in legal proceedings can take a number of different forms. Individuals who have been trafficked may provide evidence against their exploiters either through written statements or in person as part of a trial. Trafficked persons may also be called upon to provide a victim statement about the impact of the offense that could become part of a sentencing hearing. (This possibility is envisaged in the *Legislative Guide*, at Part 2, para. 56.) In civil proceedings against their exploiters, trafficked persons may be applicants and/or witnesses.

[209] UNODC Model Law, at 45.

[210] Trafficking Protocol, at Art. 6(2)(b). This is an important recognition that even for a trafficked person who is unwilling or unable to testify, she or he still has a legitimate interest in relevant legal proceedings that needs to be accommodated.

similar article of the Organized Crime Convention.[211] The Protocol recognizes that the right of victims to be present and have their views known during legal proceedings is compromised by premature repatriation. It therefore requires States Parties of destination to ensure, *inter alia*, "that such return is undertaken with due regard ... for the status of any legal proceedings related to the fact that the person is a victim of trafficking."[212] This issue is considered further below at Chapter 5.4.3 in reference to temporary residence permits and in the context of the obligation to ensure safe and preferably voluntary return.

The European Trafficking Convention, which also requires any return to be undertaken with due regard for legal proceedings,[213] establishes a range of victim assistance provisions related to the legal process, including an obligation on States Parties to ensure victims are provided counseling and information regarding their legal rights in a language they understand.[214] The SAARC Convention requires Member States to provide women and children victims of trafficking for sexual exploitation with legal assistance.[215]

The right of victims of trafficking to receive legal information as well as legal and other assistance for the duration of any criminal proceedings against their exploiters, and the concomitant obligation on States to facilitate the provision of such assistance, are both affirmed in the UN Trafficking Principles and Guidelines.[216] Additional support for a right of trafficked persons to legal information and assistance can found in the "Declaration of Basic Principles for Victims of Crime and Abuse of Power." Paragraph 6 includes such actions as keeping victims informed as to the scope, timing, and progress of proceedings and of the disposition of their cases and providing victims with proper assistance. A key General Assembly resolution on criminal justice measures to eliminate violence against women urges States to:

---

[211] Organized Crime Convention, at Art. 25(3): "[e]ach State Party shall, subject to its domestic law, enable views and concerns of victims to be presented and considered at appropriate stages of criminal proceedings against offenders in a manner not prejudicial to the rights of the defence."

[212] Trafficking Protocol, at Art. 8(2).

[213] European Trafficking Convention, at Art. 16(2).

[214] Ibid. at Arts. 12(1)(d), 12(1)(e). Also within that region, the EU Framework Decision 2009 Proposal and its successor EC Directive 2010 Proposal have been particularly expansive on victim assistance and protection in the context of criminal proceedings.

[215] SAARC Convention, at Art. V.

[216] UN Trafficking Principles and Guidelines. Principle 9 confirms the right of victims of trafficking to receive legal and other assistance for the duration of any criminal proceedings against their exploiters. This provision is supplemented by several Guidelines that would also apply to any pre- or post-trial period. Guideline 4.8 requests States to consider: "making effective provision for trafficked persons to be given legal information and assistance in a language they understand as well as appropriate social support to meet their immediate needs. States should ensure that entitlement to such information, assistance and support is not discretionary but is available as a right for all persons who have been identified as trafficked." Guideline 6.5 reiterates that trafficked persons should be provided with legal and other assistance in relation to any criminal, civil, or other actions against traffickers/exploiters. It also notes that such information should be provided to victims in a language they understand.

make available to women who have been subjected to violence information on rights and remedies and on how to obtain them, in addition to information about participating in criminal proceedings and the scheduling, progress and ultimate disposition of the proceedings.[217]

Other resolutions of the General Assembly[218] and Human Rights Council,[219] as well as Concluding Observations of the UN treaty bodies,[220] have also recommended the provision of legal assistance to victims of trafficking.

In summary, victims of trafficking should be given a genuine opportunity to consider their legal options. This requires, at a minimum, the provision of information of a type and in a manner that will allow them to make an informed choice. Should victims be involved in or otherwise support any legal action, they have the right to play a meaningful role in that process. Irrespective of such involvement, victims should be kept informed of the progress of legal proceedings.

5.4.2. *Protection and Support for Victim-Witnesses*

Trafficked persons have an important role to play and a legitimate interest in legal proceedings against their exploiters. In fact, as noted throughout this study, investigations and prosecutions are usually difficult and sometimes impossible without the cooperation and testimony of victims. While victim involvement in prosecutions is fraught with dangers and pitfalls, it is also important to acknowledge that trafficked persons are the major (and often only) source of evidence necessary to secure convictions of traffickers for the grave physical, sexual, and psychological abuses that they inflict upon their victims. Accordingly, it is essential that States work toward a situation whereby victims of trafficking are sufficiently informed, supported, and protected to enable those who wish to do so to participate effectively and safely in the criminal justice process on the basis of full information.

---

[217] UN General Assembly, "Crime Prevention and Criminal Justice Measures to Eliminate Violence Against Women," UN Doc. A/RES/52/86, Dec. 12, 1997, Annex, at para. 10(a).

[218] See, for example, UN General Assembly, "Trafficking in Women and Girls," UN Doc. A/RES/61/144, Dec. 19, 2006, at para. 15: "[c]alls upon concerned Governments to allocate resources, as appropriate, to provide comprehensive programmes for the physical, psychological and social recovery of victims of trafficking, including through … legal assistance in a language that they can understand."

[219] See, for example, UN Human Rights Council, "Trafficking in Persons, Especially Women and Children," UN Doc. A/HRC/RES/11/3, June 17, 2009, at para. 3(d): "[u]rges governments … [t]o provide resources, as appropriate, for the comprehensive protection and assistance to victims of trafficking, including … legal assistance in a language that they can understand."

[220] See, for example, UN Committee on the Elimination of Discrimination against Women, "Concluding Observations: Lebanon," UN Doc. CEDAW/C/LBN/CO/3, Apr. 8, 2008, at para. 29; "Concluding Observations: Austria," UN Doc. CEDAW/C/AUT/CO/6, Feb. 2, 2007, at para. 26; UN Committee Against Torture, "Concluding Observations: Indonesia," UN Doc. CAT/C/IDN/CO/2, May 16, 2008, at para. 20; "Concluding Observations: Ukraine," UN Doc. CAT/C/UKR/CO/5, Aug. 3, 2007, at para. 14.

International law is beginning to recognize that victims who are involved, or potentially involved, in legal proceedings have special needs and special vulnerabilities that must be addressed.[221] It is important to acknowledge that in this area, factors such as age and gender can have a significant impact on the nature and level of need and vulnerability, as well as of obligation, that must be taken into account.[222]

Victims of trafficking are often unwilling to assist in criminal investigations for fear of harm to themselves or their families. As the UNODC Model Law notes, refusal, unwillingness, or incapacity to assist should not result in discriminatory treatment:

> those victims who do not want or do not dare to act as witnesses – or are not required as witnesses because they do not possess any relevant information or because the perpetrators cannot be identified or taken into custody – require adequate assistance and protection on an equal footing with victims who are willing and able to testify.[223]

The same source acknowledges, however, that witness protection is therefore an essential aspect of any credible criminal justice response to trafficking.[224] The Organized Crime Convention requires State Parties to take a wide range of "appropriate measures within its means to provide effective protection from potential retaliation or intimidation for witnesses in criminal proceedings who give testimony … and, as appropriate, for their relatives and other persons close to them."[225] The

---

[221] See, for example: Rome Statute of the International Criminal Court, 2187 UNTS 90, done July 17, 1998, entered into force July 1, 2002 (ICC Statute), at Arts. 68(1), 68(5), 69(2), 43(6), 54(1)(b), 57(3), 64(2) and 64(6)(e); Assembly of States Parties to the Rome Statute of the International Criminal Court, "Rules of Procedure and Evidence," contained in the Report of the Assembly of States Parties to the Rome Statute of the International Criminal Court: First Session, Sept. 3–10, 2002, Official Records, UN Doc. ICC-ASP/1/3, at Rules 19, 64, 67, 68, 86, 87(3), 107(3); Statute of the International Criminal Tribunal for the Former Yugoslavia, UN Doc. S/RES/827, May 25, 1993, and amended by UN Doc. S/RES/1166, May 13, 1998, at Arts. 20(1), 22; International Criminal Tribunal for the Former Yugoslavia, Rules of Procedure and Evidence, UN Doc. IT/32/Rev.43, Feb. 11, 1994, as amended July 24, 2009, at Rules 69, 75, 79; Statute of the International Criminal Tribunal for Rwanda, UN Doc. S/RES/955, Nov. 8, 1994, at Arts. 19(1), 21; International Criminal Tribunal for Rwanda, Rules of Procedure and Evidence, UN Doc. ITR/3/Rev.11, June 29, 2005, as amended Mar. 14, 2008, at Rules 69, 75, 79. See also United Nations Office for Drugs and Crime, *Anti-Human Trafficking Manual for Criminal Justice Practitioners* (2009), "Module 12: Protection and Assistance to Victim-Witnesses in Trafficking in Persons Cases" (*UNODC Anti-Trafficking Practitioners' Manual* (2009), Module 12).

[222] Trafficking Protocol, at Art. 6(4).

[223] UNODC Model Law, at 46.

[224] Ibid. at 46–47. "Witness protection" in this context refers to: "any form of physical protection that is provided for a witness or an informant or any body concerned with the supply of vital information (against a criminal group, network or activities) that may activate a criminal justice process against such group or network with a view to dismantling them. The protection may include but is not limited to police and judicial protection during investigation and the trial stage of a case to a full-blown witness protection programme, including measures such as physical relocation of such a witness or informant to a different location, with the identity and vital particulars changed." *UNODC Anti-Trafficking Practitioners' Manual* (2009), Module 12, at 1.

[225] Organized Crime Convention, at Art. 24.

Convention also requires State Parties to "take appropriate measures within its means to provide assistance and protection to victims" of trafficking in persons, "in particular in cases of threat of retaliation or intimidation."[226] The European Trafficking Convention requires States Parties to do all within their power and resources to provide or otherwise ensure effective protection to victims who are cooperating in criminal investigations.[227]

Various soft law sources confirm the need for States to guarantee that protections for witnesses are provided for in law,[228] while ensuring that victims are made to understand the limits of protection and are not lured into cooperating with false or unrealistic promises regarding their safety and that of their families.[229] The UN human rights treaty bodies have repeatedly reaffirmed the need for States to provide witnesses with support and protection to enable them to testify against the perpetrators of trafficking.[230] The strong gender component of victim-witness protection has also been noted.[231]

Witness support and protection must extend to the trial process itself, and States should take measures to ensure that legal proceedings in which trafficked persons are involved are not prejudicial to their rights, dignity, or physical or psychological well-being.[232] An important aspect of this is protection of the victim's privacy. Victims of trafficking will be understandably reluctant to give evidence if this means being identified by the media or standing up in a public courtroom, often in view of their exploiter, and talking about traumatic personal experiences. This can be especially difficult for women and girls who have suffered sexual and other forms of violence at the hands of their exploiters. As noted above, victims can also be at real

---

[226] Ibid. at Art. 25.

[227] European Trafficking Convention, at Art. 28; Organized Crime Convention, at Art. 24. Note also that trafficked persons have a right, through their status as victims of crime, to measures that ensure their safety from intimidation and retaliation: "Basic Principles for Victims of Crime and Abuse of Power," at para. 6(d).

[228] See, for example, UN Trafficking Principles and Guidelines, at Guideline 4.10. See also Guideline 5.8.

[229] Ibid. at Guideline 6.6.

[230] UN Human Rights Committee, "Concluding Observations: Costa Rica," UN Doc. CCPR/C/CRI/CO/5, Nov. 16, 2007, at para. 12; UN Committee on the Elimination of Discrimination against Women, "Concluding Observations: Guatemala," UN Doc. CEDAW/C/GUA/CO/7, Feb. 12, 2009, at para. 24; "Concluding Observations: El Salvador," UN Doc. CEDAW/C/SLV/CO/7, Nov. 7, 2008, at para. 26; UN Committee on the Rights of the Child, "Concluding Observations: Chad," UN Doc. CRC/C/TCD/CO/2, Feb. 12, 2009, at para. 87; "Concluding Observations: Chile," UN Doc. CRC/C/CHL/CO/3, April 23, 2007, at para. 9.

[231] The General Assembly resolution on Crime Prevention and Criminal Justice Measures to Eliminate Violence against Women urges States to ensure that criminal procedure measures can be taken to ensure the safety of victims, including protection against intimidation and retaliation and that victims and witnesses are protected before, during, and after criminal proceedings: UN General Assembly, "Crime Prevention and Criminal Justice Measures to Eliminate Violence against Women," UN Doc. A/RES/52/86, Dec. 12, 1997, Annex, at paras. 8(c), 9(h). On the special needs of child witnesses, see below at Chapter 5.5.

[232] This point is made in the UN Trafficking Principles and Guidelines, at Guideline 6.4.

risk of retaliation and intimidation. It is essential that national criminal justice systems find ways to assist victims of trafficking to participate, safely and meaningfully, in court processes. Potentially useful measures have been identified as including alternatives to direct testimony aimed at protecting the witness's identity, privacy, and dignity, such as video, closed hearings and witness concealment, preliminary or accelerated hearings, and the provision of free legal counsel.[233]

When developing or evaluating systems and processes aimed at encouraging the participation of victims in court processes, it is essential to remain mindful of the rights of accused persons to a fair trial. These include the right to be informed promptly and in detail of the nature and cause of the charges; and the right to examine or have examined the witnesses against them and to obtain the attendance and examination of witnesses on their behalf under the same conditions.[234] As noted in the Explanatory Report to the European Trafficking Convention and elsewhere,[235] this is an especially important consideration to weigh up when endeavoring to protect the victim's right to privacy.

5.4.3. *Right to Remain*

An individual who has been trafficked across international borders may not be in compliance with immigration requirements or may fall out of compliance at some stage during proceedings. Without special provision to remain, this could mean that trafficked persons are deported before they can participate effectively in criminal actions against their exploiters. It could also operate to prevent victims of trafficking from accessing their right to an effective remedy through civil or other legal or administrative action. They may be unable to access important sources of subsistence and support, including housing and work opportunities. They may be vulnerable to further exploitation as well as intimidation and retaliation. Lack of legal status can be used by States to justify detaining victims during legal proceedings, an approach that has been identified elsewhere in this study as incompatible with internationally accepted standards of human rights.

In practice, foreign victims of trafficking may be granted a "right to remain" for a number of reasons and in a number of different ways, including through:

---

[233] See further, *UNODC Anti-Trafficking Practitioners' Manual* (2009), Module 12; UNODC Model Law, at 49–50. See also the draft EU Framework Decision, which sets out a comprehensive range of support measures to be made available to vulnerable victims of trafficking in criminal proceedings including measures aimed at protecting privacy and dignity, witness protection, free legal counsel and legal representation on an equal basis with the defendant: Framework Decision 2009 Proposal, at Art. 9. Although the draft itself has lapsed, its substantive content has been reintroduced in "essentially identical" form in the proposal for a successor instrument: EC Directive 2010 Proposal, at 6. See note 20 to this chapter.

[234] ICCPR, at Art. 14(3).

[235] European Trafficking Convention Explanatory Report, at paras. 299–303; UN Trafficking Principles and Guidelines, at Guideline 6.6.

- granting of a reflection and recovery period during which nonconditional support is given with the aim of providing victims with time and space to decide on their options, including whether they will cooperate with criminal justice agencies in the prosecution of their exploiters (see further the discussion immediately following)
- granting of a temporary residence permit linked to (usually criminal) proceedings against traffickers; such permits usually require the victim's cooperation and terminate once legal proceedings are completed
- granting of a temporary residence permit on social or humanitarian grounds that may be related to, for example, respect for the principle of *non-refoulement*, inability to guarantee a secure return, and risk of retrafficking
- granting of a permanent residence permit on social or humanitarian grounds.

The Trafficking Protocol encourages States to consider adopting legislative or other appropriate measures that permit victims of trafficking to remain in their territory, temporarily or permanently, in appropriate cases.[236] This provision does not constitute a clear legal obligation, and the question of whether such an obligation can be found to exist will depend on the circumstances of a particular case. Certain rights and obligations, explored elsewhere in this study, are relevant to a consideration of whether or not a State should (or indeed is obliged to) grant victims a right of temporary residence. These include the right of victims to participate in legal proceedings against traffickers, their right to receive protection from further harm, their right to access effective remedies, the obligation on States not to return victims when they are at serious risk of harm, and the special rights of child victims of trafficking, including the obligation to take full account of the child's best interests. The legal implications of two common bases for a "right to remain" are explored in more detail below.

Reflection and Recovery Periods. An increasing number of States are offering a "reflection and recovery period" to trafficked persons aimed at providing them with time and space to decide on their options, including whether they will cooperate with criminal justice agencies in the prosecution of their exploiters. The concept of a reflection and recovery period, initially developed within countries of Western Europe, was not incorporated in the Trafficking Protocol. It was taken up by the European Union in 2004[237] and entered international law the following year through the European Trafficking Convention. Under the European model, illegally present victims (and those who may reasonably be presumed to be victims) are granted

---

[236] Trafficking Protocol, at Art. 7.

[237] EU Council Directive 2004/81/EC of 29 April 2004 on the residence permit issued to third-country nationals who are victims of trafficking in human beings or who have been the subject of an action to facilitate illegal immigration, who cooperate with authorities, OJ L 261/19, Aug. 6, 2004. See further discussion of this instrument in Chapter 2.3.1.2 above.

a period of grace (a "reflection period") allowing them to recover and escape the influence of traffickers so that they can make an informed decision as to whether to cooperate with criminal justice agencies in the investigation and prosecution of their exploiters. According to the Explanatory Report to the Convention, victim recovery implies, for example, healing of the wounds and recovery from the physical assault they have suffered, as well as recovery of a minimum of psychological stability.[238] Importantly, granting of the reflection period is *not* conditional on future cooperation with criminal justice authorities.

The reflection period established by the European Trafficking Convention is to be mandated by law and to last at least thirty days. During that time, victims and presumed victims are not to be removed from the territory of the State Party and are entitled to the protection, assistance, and support provisions available under the Convention. There are several important caveats. The reflection period can be refused or terminated on grounds of public order or if it is found that victim status is being claimed improperly. In addition, the granting of a reflection period would not provide a basis for an individual to refuse to testify if that person was legally compelled, by a judge, to do so.[239]

It is perhaps too early to argue that those States outside the European Trafficking Convention and the EU Directive are under an international legal obligation to provide victims of trafficking with a reflection and recovery period.[240] Certainly the more recent calls for a no-strings-attached six-month period of residency, assistance, and support for all identified victims of trafficking are unlikely to garner widespread support.[241] However, when considering the existence and nature of any obligation in this regard, it is important to note the link between: (1) the recovery and reflection mechanism and the realization of certain rights; and (2) the absence of this mechanism and the expected result, summary deportation resulting in denial of rights. It is these links that are promoted in growing calls for States of destination to provide a reflection and recovery period to those victims of trafficking identified in their territory who do not otherwise have a legal right to remain.[242]

---

[238] European Trafficking Convention Explanatory Report, at para. 173.

[239] European Trafficking Convention, at Art. 13(1), and European Trafficking Convention Explanatory Report, at para. 176.

[240] In this regard, note that recent resolutions of the UN Human Rights Council and General Assembly are silent on the issue of reflection and recovery periods.

[241] UNODC Model Law, at 60: "[i]f the competent authorities [name the authority] have identified a person as a victim of trafficking, he or she shall be issued a temporary residence permit for at least a period of six months, irrespective of whether he or she cooperates with the [competent authority], with the possibility of renewal."

[242] See, for example, UN General Assembly, "Trafficking in Persons, Especially Women and Children, Report of the Special Rapporteur on Trafficking in Persons, Especially Women and Children," UN Doc. A/64/290, Aug. 12, 2009, at para. 94: "[t]he Special Rapporteur is concerned that victims of trafficking are sometimes deported without a sufficient period for recovery and reflection. The Special Rapporteur reiterates that victims should not summarily be deported." See also UN Committee on the Elimination of Discrimination against Women: "Concluding Observations: Denmark," UN Doc. CEDAW/C/DEN/CO/6, Aug. 25, 2006, at paras. 22–23; and on temporary protection visas

Right to Remain During Legal Proceedings. The Trafficking Protocol places an obligation on countries of destination to conduct return "with due regard for the safety of the person and for the status of any related legal proceedings."[243] This provision should be read in light of the broader obligation to ensure that victims are provided with an opportunity to participate in legal action against their exploiters as set out in the Organized Crime Convention,[244] as well as the specific obligation in the Protocol to provide victims with an opportunity to present their views.[245] As noted in the UNODC Model Law, "[i]t is in the interest of both the victim and the prosecution to allow the victim at least a temporary residence permit during criminal proceedings."[246] In practice, the right to remain during legal proceedings is often linked to more general provisions regarding the issuing of residency permits for victims of trafficking. In the European Trafficking Convention, for example, the need to remain "for the purpose of cooperation with the competent authorities in investigation or criminal proceedings" is one of two justifications offered to States Parties for issuing of a residence permit to victims.[247] The UN Trafficking Principles and Guidelines also refer to residence permits in the context of the right to remain during legal proceedings.[248] A further and more detailed discussion on the issue of repatriation and legal proceedings is contained in Chapter 6.1.4.

5.5. THE RIGHTS AND NEEDS OF CHILD VICTIMS

Children are naturally included in the rules and standards considered throughout this chapter. However, international law recognizes a distinction between child and adult trafficking, and a consequent need for a different response. The reasons for this are well expressed in the UN Trafficking Principles and Guidelines:

> The particular physical, psychological and psychosocial harm suffered by trafficked children and their increased vulnerability to exploitation requires that they be dealt with separately from adult trafficked persons in terms of laws, policies, programmes and interventions. The best interests of the child must be a primary consideration in all actions concerning trafficked children whether undertaken by public or private welfare institutions, courts of law, administrative authorities or legislative bodies. Child victims of trafficking should be provided with appropriate assistance and protection and full account should be taken of their special rights and needs.[249]

---

for trafficked women: "Concluding Observations: The Netherlands," UN Doc. CEDAW/C/NLD/CO/4, Feb. 2, 2007, at para. 24; "Concluding Observations: Australia," UN Doc. CEDAW/C/AUL/CO/5, Feb. 3, 2006, at para. 21.

[243] Trafficking Protocol, at Art. 8(2).
[244] Organized Crime Convention, at Art. 25(3).
[245] Trafficking Protocol, at Art. 6(2).
[246] UNODC Model Law, at 60.
[247] European Trafficking Convention, at Art. 14(1).
[248] UN Trafficking Principles and Guidelines, at Principle 9, Guideline 4.7.
[249] Ibid. at Guideline 8.

An important source of vulnerability for children lies in their lack of full agency – in fact and under law.[250] A lack of agency is often made worse by the absence of a parent or legal guardian who is able to act in the child's best interests. Such absence is typical: Child victims of trafficking are generally "unaccompanied," with deliberate separation from parents or guardians being a strategy to facilitate exploitation. In some cases, parents or other authority figures are complicit in the trafficking. Many of the care and protection measures outlined in this section – from prioritization of the child's "bests interests" to the appointment of legal guardians – are designed to address the particular vulnerabilities faced by unaccompanied child victims.

5.5.1. *Identification of Child Victims*

As is the case with adult trafficking victims, a trafficked child who is not identified at all or who is incorrectly identified as a criminal or an illegal or smuggled migrant will be unable to access the rights to which she or he is entitled.[251] In this context, it is important to reiterate that the international legal definition of child trafficking is different to the definition of trafficking in adults. The crime of trafficking in children requires only an action (movement, sale, receipt, etc.) for the purposes of exploitation. It is not necessary to show that the child was deceived or coerced. As a result, it should be comparatively easier to establish a trafficking-related crime against a child. Failure to correctly identify a trafficked child as such removes this important distinction and thereby obstructs the successful investigation and prosecution of trafficking-related crimes affecting children. It could also lead to an incorrect charge, conviction, or penalty – for example, in circumstances where trafficking of children is an aggravated offense.[252]

There are several key issues associated with the identification of child victims. The first relates to presumptions of age and of victim status. The second issue concerns the laws, systems, and procedures that need to be in place to ensure that correct and timely identification can take place.

Presumptions of Age and Status. Not all child victims of trafficking will appear as such. They may appear to be eighteen years of age or older. Their passports may have been destroyed or taken away from them. They may be carrying false identity papers that misstate their age. Child victims of trafficking may lie about their age

---

[250] This is acknowledged in the ICCPR, which stipulates the right of the child to "such measures of protection as are required by his status as a minor": at Art. 24.

[251] This is recognized in the UN Trafficking Principles and Guidelines, at Guideline 2. See also Guideline 10.4 and Principle 10: "children who are victims of trafficking shall be identified as such."

[252] See further, the discussion of aggravated offenses at Chapter 7.3.3 in this volume.

because this is what they have been told to do by their exploiters. They may lie because they are afraid of being taken into care or being sent back home.

There is some indication of a growing acceptance of a presumption of age in the case of children to the effect that a victim who *may* be a child is treated as a child unless or until another determination is made. Evidence for the emergence of such a presumption can be found in the Legislative Guide to the Trafficking Protocol, which provides that:

> In a case where the age of a victim is uncertain and there are reasons to believe the victim is a child, a State Party may, to the extent possible under its domestic law, treat the victim as a child in accordance with the Convention on the Rights of the Child until his or her age is verified.[253]

This position is echoed in the European Trafficking Convention, which requires States Parties to presume the victim is a child if there are reasons for believing that this is so and if there is uncertainty about their age.[254] The Explanatory Report to the Convention confirms that the individual presumed to be a child victim of trafficking is to be given special protection measures in accordance with their rights as defined, in particular, in the CRC.[255]

The UNICEF Guidelines for the Protection of the Rights of Child Victims of Trafficking (UNICEF Guidelines) state that where the age of the victim is uncertain and there are reasons to believe that the victim is a child, the presumption shall be that the victim is a child. Pending verification of the victim's age, she or he is to be treated as a child and to be accorded all special protection measures stipulated in those Guidelines.[256] The essence of this provision is reproduced in an optional provision of the UNODC Model Law.[257]

The presumption of age is linked to the presumption of status: A child (or an individual who is presumed to be a child) who *may* be a victim of trafficking is to

---

[253] *Legislative Guide*, at Part 2, para. 65. This provision is also inserted in the UNODC Model Law (at 47–48) as part of a mandatory provision relating protection and support of child victims.

[254] European Trafficking Convention, at Art. 10(3). See also EC Directive 2010 Proposal, at Art. 12(2): "where the age of a person subject to trafficking in human beings is uncertain and there are reasons to believe that the person is a child, the person is presumed to be a child in order to receive immediate access to assistance, support and protection." Note that draft Article 12(2) is a new addition not explicitly included in the previous Framework Decision 2009 Proposal, though Article 11 of that instrument cross-referenced a similar presumption of age provision in another proposed (and now-lapsed) Framework Decision: Commission of the European Communities, Proposal for a Council Framework Decision on combating the sexual abuse, sexual exploitation of children and child pornography, repealing Framework Decision 2004/68/JHA, COM(2009) 135 final, Mar. 25, 2009, at Art. 14(1).

[255] European Trafficking Convention Explanatory Report, at para. 136.

[256] UNICEF Guidelines, at Guideline 3.1.2.

[257] "When the age of the victim is uncertain and there are reasons to believe that the victim is a child, he or she shall be presumed to be a child and shall be treated as such, pending verification of his or her age": UNODC Model Law, at 47.

be presumed to be a victim unless or until another determination is made. The relevant best practice guidance for law enforcement officials in the European Union, for example, states that:

> in any case where there are *any grounds* to suspect that a child is a victim of trafficking, that child *will be presumed* to be a trafficked victim and treated accordingly pending verification of the facts of the case.[258]

The European Trafficking Convention affirms this general approach for both children and adults but shifts the standard to "reasonable grounds."[259]

Requirements for Identification of Child Victims. The identification of victims of trafficking is, as noted elsewhere, a complicated and inexact science.[260] The presumption of age and the related presumption of status are both aimed at addressing the special or additional difficulties that would otherwise complicate identification of child victims. Nevertheless, the particular situation of children necessitates special measures to ensure the quick and accurate identification of those who have been trafficked. The European Trafficking Convention requires States Parties to ensure that trained and qualified individuals are involved in identifying victims including children. It further requires different authorities to collaborate with each other and with relevant support organizations to ensure that victims can be identified in a procedure that duly takes account of the special situation of both women and children.[261]

The UN Trafficking Principles and Guidelines request States and others to ensure that procedures are in place for the rapid identification of child victims of trafficking.[262] The UNICEF Guidelines go further, emphasizing the critical importance of establishing effective identification procedures and of ensuring that different agencies involved in identification are working together and sharing information.[263] The UN Committee on the Rights of the Child has called on States to strengthen their efforts to identify trafficking in children – although not child victims of trafficking per se.[264]

---

[258] International Organization for Migration, *Identification and Protection Schemes for Victims of Trafficking in Persons in Europe: Tools and Best Practices* (2005), at 30 (emphasis added).

[259] European Trafficking Convention, at Art. 10; European Trafficking Convention Explanatory Report, at paras. 132–137.

[260] For a discussion of obstacles to the identification of child victims, see Goździak, "Identifying Child Victims of Trafficking."

[261] European Trafficking Convention, at Art. 10(1).

[262] UN Trafficking Principles and Guidelines, at Guideline 6.2.

[263] UNICEF Guidelines, esp. at Guideline 3.1: "[s]pecial efforts are needed to share information and coordinate interventions between agencies and individuals (including law enforcement, health, education, social welfare agencies, and NGOs), to ensure that child victims are identified and assisted as soon as possible."

[264] See, for example, UN Committee on the Rights of the Child, "Concluding Observations: Oman," UN Doc. CRC/C/OPSC/OMN/CO/1, June 24, 2009, at para. 30; "Concluding Observations: Malaysia," UN Doc. CRC/C/MYS/CO/1, June 25, 2007, at para. 96; "Concluding Observations: Azerbaijan," UN Doc. CRC/C/AZE/CO/2, Mar. 17, 2006, at para. 66.

5.5.2. *Applying the "Best Interests" Principle*

The principle of "best interests of the child" is a legal doctrine, accepted in many countries, that has been enshrined in international law through the CRC.[265] Many other international and regional human rights instruments have adopted and incorporated this principle.[266]

In General Comment No. 6, the Committee on the Rights of the Child considered the application of the "best interests" principle in the context of unaccompanied or separated children (a group that can be expected to include most, if not all child victims of trafficking).[267] In the case of a displaced child,

> the principle must be respected during all stages of the displacement cycle. At any of these stages, a best interests determination must be documented in preparation of any decision fundamentally impacting on the unaccompanied or separated child's life.[268]

Such a determination requires:

> a clear and comprehensive assessment of the child's identity, including her or his nationality, upbringing, ethnic, cultural and linguistic background, particular vulnerabilities and protection needs … The assessment process should be carried out in a friendly and safe atmosphere by qualified professionals who are trained in age and gender-sensitive interviewing techniques.[269]
>
> Subsequent steps, such as the appointment of a competent guardian as expeditiously as possible, serves as a key procedural safeguard to ensure respect for the best interests of an unaccompanied or separated child … In cases where separated or unaccompanied children are referred to asylum procedures or other administrative or judicial proceedings, they should also be provided with a legal representative in addition to a guardian.[270]

The principle also requires that where authorities have placed the child in care, "the State recognizes the right of that child to a 'periodic review' of their treatment."[271]

---

[265] CRC, at Art. 3(1).

[266] See, for example, the African Charter on the Rights and Welfare of the Child, OAU Doc. CAB/LEG/2.49/49, done July 11, 1990, entered into force Nov. 29, 1999 (African Children's Charter), at Art. 4; CEDAW, at Art. 5(b); Inter-American Convention on International Traffic in Minors, OAS Doc. OEA/Ser.K/XXI.5, 79 OASTS, done Mar. 18, 1994, entered into force Aug. 15, 1997, reprinted in (1994) 33 ILM 721, at Art. 1; South Asian Association for Regional Cooperation, Convention on Regional Arrangements for the Promotion of Child Welfare in South Asia, done Jan. 5, 2002, entered into force Sept. 21, 2006, at Art. III(4). CRC Optional Protocol, at Art. 8(3), requires that the best interests of the child be "a primary consideration" in the treatment within the criminal justice system of child victims of offenses under the Protocol.

[267] CRC General Comment No. 6, at paras. 19–22.

[268] Ibid. at para. 19.

[269] Ibid. at para. 20.

[270] Ibid. at para. 21.

[271] Ibid. at para. 22.

The principle of the best interests of the child is included in a number of trafficking-specific legal and policy instruments, including the European Trafficking Convention.[272] The SAARC Convention requires States Parties to uphold the "best interests of the child" as a principle of paramount importance and to adhere to this principle in all actions concerning children.[273] While the Trafficking Protocol does not specifically refer to the principle, it is identified as the appropriate standard in the Legislative Guide in relation to decisions concerning family tracing and reunification and repatriation of children.[274] Both the UN Trafficking Principles and Guidelines and the UNICEF Guidelines identify the best interests of the child as a general principle that is to be borne in mind at all stages of the care and protection of child victims of trafficking in countries of destination, transit, and origin.[275] The principle has also been repeatedly upheld in the context of trafficking in resolutions of the UN Human Rights Council (formerly the Commission on Human Rights).[276] It is proposed as part of the UNODC Model Law.[277]

What does it mean to prioritize the best interests of the child? In the context of trafficking, the following points, largely extrapolated from the CRC, could provide useful guidance. First and foremost, in the case of actions and decisions affecting an individual child, it is the best interests of that individual child that must be taken into account. Second, it is in a child's best interests to enjoy the rights and freedoms provided to it by international law and as set out in the CRC. For example, it is in a child's best interests to maintain contact with both parents in most circumstances (Article 9(3)) and it is in the child's best interests to have access to

---

[272] European Trafficking Convention, at Art. 10(4)(c) (dealing with family tracing). See also the EC Directive 2010 Proposal, Art. 12(1).

[273] SAARC Convention, at Art. III.

[274] *Legislative Guide*, at Part 2, paras. 66–67.

[275] UN Trafficking Principles and Guidelines, at Principle 10, Guideline 8; UNICEF Guidelines, at Guideline 2.

[276] UN Human Rights Council, "Rights of the Child," UN Doc. A/HRC/RES/7/29, Mar. 28, 2008, at para. 36(e), and UN Commission on Human Rights, "Rights of the Child," UN Doc. E/CN.4/RES/2005/44, Apr. 20, 2005, at para. 32(e) (both calling on States to "address effectively the needs of victims of trafficking ... including their safety and protection, physical and psychological recovery and full reintegration into their family and society and bearing in mind the best interest of the child"); UN Commission on Human Rights, "Rights of the Child," UN Doc. E/CN.4/RES/2004/48, Apr. 20, 2004, at para. 37(e), and UN Commission on Human Rights, "Rights of the Child," UN Doc. E/CN.4/RES/2003/86, Apr. 25, 2003, at para. 36(d) (both calling on States to "criminalize and effectively penalize all forms of ... child trafficking ... while ensuring that, in the treatment by the criminal justice system of children who are victims, the best interests of the child shall be a primary consideration").

[277] The UNODC Model Law, at 47, suggests the following general principle be inserted in national legislation: "[a]ll actions undertaken in relation to child victims and witnesses shall be based on the principles set out in the Convention on the Rights of the Child and the Guidelines on Justice in Matters involving Child Victims and Witnesses of Crime, in particular the principle that the best interests of the child must be a primary consideration in all actions involving the child and the principle that the child's view must be considered and taken into account in all matters affecting him or her."

education (Article 28) and to health care (Article 24). Third, a child capable of form-ing a view on his or her best interests must be able to give it freely, and this view must be taken into account (Article 12). However, acting in the best interests of the child may sometimes require that his or her wishes are overridden. Fourth, parents have primary decision-making responsibility on behalf of their children (Articles 5 and 18(1)), but if they fail to make the child's best interests a basic concern, for example, by themselves being complicit in the trafficking of the child, the State may inter-vene to protect those interests (see Article 9(1), for example). Fifth, States should not privilege other considerations, such as those related to immigration control or pub-lic order, over the best interests of the child victim of trafficking.[278]

5.5.3. *Protection and Support for Trafficked Children*

A number of core protections that apply to all trafficked persons deserve to be high-lighted in the context of a discussion of trafficked children. For example, it is critical that the trafficked child not be criminalized in any way. He or she should not be liable for prosecution for any status-related offenses.[279] The trafficked child should never be placed in a law enforcement detention facility including a police cell, prison, or special detention center for children. As detailed at length in Chapter 5.2.2 earlier, any decision relating to the detention of children should be made on a case-by-case basis and with full consideration of the best interests principle, and any detention of a child victim of trafficking should, in all cases, be for the shortest possible time and subject to independent oversight and review.[280] Care and support

---

[278] CRC General Comment No. 6, at paras. 19–22.

[279] Generally on noncriminalization for status-related offenses, see Chapter 5.2.2. On the specific issue of children, see UN Trafficking Principles and Guidelines, at Guideline 8.3 (requesting States and others to ensure "that children who are victims of trafficking are not subjected to criminal pro-ceedings or sanctions for offences related to their situation as trafficked persons"). Note that the UNICEF Guidelines declare that "the involvement of a child victim in criminal activities should not undermine their status as both a child and a victim and his/her related rights to special pro-tection." UNICEF Guidelines, at Guideline 2.1. The UN Committee on the Rights of the Child stated that "in developing policies on unaccompanied or separated children, including those who are victims of trafficking ... States should ensure that such children are not criminalized solely for reasons of illegal entry or presence in the country": CRC General Comment No. 6, at para. 62. The Committee has repeatedly emphasized the noncriminalization of child victims of trafficking in its Concluding Observations relating to both the CRC and the CRC Optional Protocol. The joint Inter-Parliamentary Union and UNICEF publication *Combating Child Trafficking*, Handbook for Parliamentarians No. 9 (2005) unequivocally states, at 34, that "[u]nder no condition should laws criminalize children. Those who have been trafficked or sexually exploited must be treated as vic-tims, not as offenders. The law needs to include specific provisions guaranteeing that children will not face criminal penalty as a result of their being trafficked into illegal industries such as prostitu-tion. Victims are not to be subject to incarceration, detention or other punishment."

[280] See authorities cited at Chapter 5.2.2 from page 294, under "Detention of child victims." See also CRC General Comment No. 6, at para. 61: "[i]n application of article 37 of the Convention and the principle of the best interests of the child, unaccompanied or separated children should not, as a general rule, be detained ... Where detention is exceptionally justified ... it shall ... only be used as a measure of

to trafficked children should be made available as a right. It should never be conditional on the child's cooperation with criminal justice agencies.[281] Children should not be coerced into receiving care and protection, including medical assistance and testing, unless it can be demonstrated, on a case-by-case basis, that this is clearly in the best interests of the individual child victim.[282]

International law generally supports a relatively higher standard of protection and support for trafficked children, a standard that takes into account their special vulnerabilities, rights, and needs.[283] In accordance with the presumptions outlined above, all persons identified as or reasonably presumed to be victims of trafficking, and identified as or reasonably presumed to be under the age of eighteen years, are entitled to this enhanced standard of protection and support. The following are key aspects or components of the obligation to support and protect trafficked children and children at risk of being trafficked.

Nondiscrimination, Right to Information, and Respect for the Views of the Child. Every child under the jurisdiction or control of a State is entitled to care and protection on an equal basis. This means that non-national child victims of trafficking are to enjoy the same rights as national or resident children.[284] Their nationality, as well as their race, sex, language, religion, ethnic or social origin, birth, or other characteristic, is not to impact negatively on their rights and freedoms.[285]

A child victim who is capable of forming his or her own views should enjoy the right to express those views freely in all matters affecting him or her, in particular concerning decisions about his or her possible return to the family. The views of the child should be given due weight in accordance with his or her age and maturity.[286] Those views must be supported by adequate and accurate information. The UNICEF Guidelines highlight the importance of ensuring that child victims are provided information about, for example, their situation, their entitlement, services available, and the family reunification and/or repatriation process.[287] Additional

---

last resort and for the shortest appropriate period of time." The Committee has echoed these views in its Concluding Observations: "Concluding Observations: The Netherlands," UN Doc. CRC/C/15/Add.227, Jan. 30, 2004, at para. 54(d); "Concluding Observations: Canada," UN Doc. CRC/C/15/Add.215, Oct. 3, 2003, at para. 47(c).

[281] See the authorities cited at notes 94 to 105 to this chapter. See also UNICEF Guidelines, at Guideline 11 regarding the right to reparation.

[282] See Chapter 5.3.7.

[283] See, for example, CRC, at Art. 20(1): "a child temporarily or permanently deprived of his or her family environment, or in whose own best interests cannot be allowed to remain in that environment, shall be entitled to special protection and assistance provided by the State." See also African Children's Charter, at Art. 25; UN Trafficking Principles and Guidelines, at Principle 10.

[284] CRC, at Art. 2. See further, the discussion at Chapters 3.1 and 3.2 of this book.

[285] CRC, at Art. 2.

[286] Ibid. at Art. 12. See also African Children's Charter, at Art. 4(2) and UN Trafficking Principles and Guidelines, at Guideline 6.6.

[287] UNICEF Guidelines, at Guideline 2.5

information requirements apply in respect of children who are or may be witnesses in criminal prosecutions. These requirements are considered further below.

Right to Privacy. While all trafficked persons have a right to privacy, this right is a particularly important aspect of providing child victims with the care, support, and protection to which they are legally entitled. Failure to protect the privacy of child victims can increase the danger of intimidation and retaliation. It can also cause humiliation and hurt to victims and compromise their recovery. The Trafficking Protocol focuses on privacy and protection of identity in the particular context of legal proceedings.[288] The European Trafficking Convention, on the other hand, takes a much broader view, recognizing that protection of private life is essential, not just to ensure victims' safety, but also to preserve their chances of social reintegration in the country of origin or the receiving country.[289] The European Trafficking Convention recognizes that "it would be particularly harmful for th[e] identity [of trafficked children] to be disclosed by the media or by other means"[290] and requires States Parties to:

> adopt measures to ensure, in particular, that the identity, or details allowing the identification, of a child victim of trafficking are not made publicly known, through the media or by any other means, except, in exceptional circumstances, in order to facilitate the tracing of family members or otherwise secure the well-being and protection of the child.[291]

More generally, the CRC prohibits arbitrary and unlawful interference with a child's privacy.[292] In General Comment No. 4, the Committee on the Rights of the Child elaborated on this provision, encouraging States Parties to respect strictly children's right to privacy and confidentiality, including with respect to advice and counseling on health matters.[293] In General Comment No. 6, the Committee reaffirmed a child's right to privacy in the context of separated or unaccompanied children.[294] In its consideration of States Parties' reports, the Committee has recommended that law enforcement officials, social workers, and prosecutors must be trained to treat victims of trafficking in a child-sensitive manner that respects the privacy of the victim.[295] Further, the UN Guidelines on Justice in Matters Involving

---

[288] Trafficking Protocol, at Art. 6(1). On this issue, see further, the discussion at Chapters 5.3.3 and 5.4.2.
[289] European Trafficking Convention Explanatory Report, at para. 138.
[290] Ibid. at para. 142.
[291] European Trafficking Convention, at Art. 11(2).
[292] CRC, at Art. 16.
[293] UN Committee on the Rights of the Child, "General Comment No. 4: Adolescent Health and Development in the Context of the Convention on the Rights of the Child," UN Doc. CRC/GC/2003/4, July, 1, 2003, at para. 11.
[294] CRC General Comment No. 6, at para. 29.
[295] UN Committee on the Rights of the Child: "Concluding Observations: Kenya," UN Doc. CRC/C/KEN/CO/2, June 19, 2007, at para. 66; "Concluding Observations: Kyrgyzstan," UN Doc. CRC/C/15/Add.244, Nov. 3, 2004, at para. 61.

Child Victims and Witnesses of Crime[296] specify that child victims and witnesses should have their privacy respected as a matter of primary importance.[297] Key policy instruments provide further evidence of an obligation on States to protect the privacy of child victims.[298]

Appointment of a Guardian. The appointment of a guardian to protect the rights and interests of child victims of trafficking is an important practical means of securing those rights and interests. While the Trafficking Protocol is silent on this point, the Legislative Guide encourages States Parties to consider:

> appointing, as soon as the child victim is identified, a guardian to accompany the child throughout the entire process until a durable solution in the best interests of the child has been identified and implemented. To the extent possible, the same person should be assigned to the child victim throughout the entire process.[299]

The European Trafficking Convention requires States Parties to "provide for representation of [an identified child victim of trafficking] by a legal guardian, organisation or authority, *which shall act in the best interests of the child*."[300] The Committee on the Rights of the Child, in General Comment No. 6, stated that "the appointment of a competent guardian … serves as a procedural safeguard to ensure respect for the best interests of an unaccompanied or separated child"[301] and recommended that States appoint a guardian as soon as an unaccompanied or separated child is identified.[302] The UNICEF Guidelines provide detailed information on the functions and responsibilities of guardianship in the context of the special needs of child victims of trafficking.[303] Typical tasks would include ensuring the child's best interests remain the paramount consideration in all actions or decisions taken in respect of the child; ensuring the provision of all necessary assistance, support, and protection; being present during any engagement with criminal justice authorities; facilitating referral to appropriate services; and assisting in the identification and implementation of a durable solution.[304]

Child Victims in Criminal Proceedings. As noted above, victims of trafficking have a legitimate role to play in criminal or civil actions against their exploiters,

---

[296] "Guidelines on Justice in Matters involving Child Victims and Witnesses of Crime," adopted by ECOSOC Res. 2005/20, July 22, 2005.

[297] Ibid, at para. 26.

[298] See, for example, UN Trafficking Principles and Guidelines, at Guideline 8.9.

[299] *Legislative Guide*, at Part 2, para. 65(a).

[300] European Trafficking Convention, at Art. 10(4)(a) (emphasis added).

[301] CRC General Comment No. 6, at para. 21.

[302] Ibid. at para. 33.

[303] UNICEF Guidelines, at Guideline 3.2.

[304] For a further elaboration on the duties of a guardian, see also CRC General Comment No. 6, at para. 33.

in that they have a right to be heard, a right to information, and a right to be kept informed. All trafficked persons, children as well as adults, are entitled to use the legal system to ensure their own interests are preserved and their own rights protected. However, it is important to be mindful of the precarious position of victims in the criminal justice system and the risk that such involvement will further compromise their rights and/or well-being. These concerns are particularly acute in the case of children who are asked or required to participate in the investigation and prosecution of their exploiters. Child witnesses are especially vulnerable to intimidation and reprisals from traffickers. Their families can also be at serious risk. In addition to safety and protection concerns, the involvement in legal proceedings can cause trauma for the child victim, which may significantly compromise or delay their recovery. In all cases, it will be important for the relevant authorities to consider the best interests of each individual child victim in determining whether that child should be involved in criminal proceedings and, if so, the nature and extent of that involvement. The views of the child should, as noted above, also be taken into account.

While the Trafficking Protocol does not specifically address the issue of child victim involvement in criminal proceedings, the accompanying Legislative Guide provides extensive guidance on this point, requesting States Parties to:

> Ensur[e] that, during investigations, as well as prosecutions and trial hearings where possible, direct contact between the child victim and the suspected offender be avoided. Unless it is against the best interests of the child, the child victim has the right to be fully informed about security issues and criminal procedures prior to deciding whether or not to testify in criminal proceedings. During legal proceedings, the right to legal safeguards and effective protection of child witnesses needs to be strongly emphasized. Children who agree to testify should be accorded special protection measures to ensure their safety.[305]

The UNICEF Guidelines and other policy instruments extend this list of measures to include: granting of a "reflection and recovery" period prior to the child making any decisions about her or his involvement in criminal proceedings; prioritizing family reunification and return over criminal justice proceedings when such reunification/return is in the child's best interests; providing the child witness with legal representation and interpretation services; and providing for alternatives to direct testimony that protect the child witness's identity, privacy, and dignity, such as video, closed hearings, and witness concealment.[306]

Durable Solutions: Family Tracing and Reunification. Family reunification is often an important aspect, especially for younger children, of securing the "best

---

[305] Legislative Guide, at Part 2, para. 65(b). See also UN Trafficking Principles and Guidelines, at Guideline 8.8.

[306] See further, UNICEF Guidelines, at Guideline 3.9.1; "Guidelines on Justice in Matters involving Child Victims and Witnesses of Crime," adopted by ECOSOC Res. 2005/20, July 22, 2005.

interests of the child." The CRC requires States to deal with family reunification requests "in a positive, humane and expeditious manner."[307] The Legislative Guide to the Trafficking Protocol requests the relevant authorities to "take all necessary steps to trace, identify and locate family members and facilitate the reunion of the child victim with his or her family where that is in the best interests of the child."[308] The European Trafficking Convention similarly requires States Parties, following identification of an unaccompanied child as a victim of trafficking, to "make every effort to locate his/her family when this is in the best interests of the child."[309] Key policy instruments confirm this position, further emphasizing that decisions about family reunification should give due weight to the views of the child in accordance with that child's age and level of maturity,[310] and that risk assessment be carried out prior to such reunification.[311]

Durable Solutions: Repatriation of Child Victims of Trafficking. While the repatriation standards explored in detail in the following chapter apply equally to trafficked adults and children, the major specialist international instruments recognize a need for special care in relation to decisions about the repatriation of children who have been trafficked. Article 16 of the European Trafficking Convention, for example, is unequivocal on the point that "child victims shall not be returned to a State if there is an indication, following a risk and security assessment, that such return would not be in the best interests of the child."[312] As noted in both the European Trafficking Convention and the UNICEF Guidelines, a determination to this effect would need to be made on the basis of a comprehensive risk assessment.[313] The purpose of such a risk assessment should be to: (1) collect the information that will enable authorities to understand the implications of returning a child; (2) ensure that no decision is taken that places a child in a situation of foreseeable risk; and (3) reach a meaningful conclusion about which course of action is in the child's best interests.

In General Comment No. 6, the Committee on the Rights of the Child recommended the following factors be taken into account in determining whether repatriation of an unaccompanied or separated child is in that child's best interests: (1) the safety, security, and other conditions, including socioeconomic conditions, awaiting the child upon return, including through home study, where appropriate, conducted by social network organizations; (2) the availability of care arrangements for that particular child; (3) the views of the child expressed in exercise of his or her right to do

---

[307] CRC, at Art. 10(1).
[308] Legislative Guide, at para. 66.
[309] European Trafficking Convention, at Art. 10(4)(c).
[310] UNICEF Guidelines, at Guideline 8.6.
[311] Ibid. at Guideline 8.2.
[312] European Trafficking Convention, at Art. 16(7). See also UN Trafficking Principles and Guidelines, at Guideline 8.5.
[313] UNICEF Guidelines, at Guideline 3.7; European Trafficking Convention, at Art. 16(7).

so under Article 12, and those of the caretakers; (4) the child's level of integration in the host country and the duration of absence from the home country; (5) the child's right "to preserve his or her identity, including nationality, name and family relations" (Article 8); and (6) the "desirability of continuity in a child's upbringing and ... the child's ethnic, religious, cultural and linguistic background" (Article 20).[314]

The Legislative Guide to the Trafficking Protocol is also very specific on the need for special care in the repatriation of child victims:

> In cases where child victims are involved, legislators may also wish to consider not returning those child victims unless doing so is in their best interest and, prior to the return, a suitable caregiver such as a parent, a relative, another adult caregiver, a government agency or a child-care agency in the country of origin has agreed and is able to take responsibility for the child and to provide him or her with appropriate care and protection. Relevant ... authorities ... should be responsible for establishing whether or not the repatriation of a child victim is safe and should ensure the process takes place in a dignified manner and is in the best interests of the child[315] ... In those cases where the return is voluntary or is in the best interests of the child, each State party is encouraged to ensure that the child returns to his or her home country in a speedy and safe manner.[316]

The importance of cooperation and collaboration between countries of origin and destination in relation to safe repatriation of child victims of trafficking is noted in the Legislative Guide to the Trafficking Protocol[317] as well as in the UNICEF Guidelines.[318]

Durable Solutions: Local Integration or Third-country Resettlement. As noted above, international law generally recognizes a need for legal alternatives to repatriation where this is required because of risks to the safety of the victim and/or that person's family.[319] In such cases, States should ensure the establishment of "adequate care arrangements that respect the rights and dignity of the trafficked child."[320] The UNICEF Guidelines provide important information on the key elements of "adequate care arrangements," highlighting access to health care, psychosocial support, social services, and education[321] and identifying the critical aspects of ensuring

---

[314] CRC General Comment No. 6, at para. 84.
[315] Legislative Guide, at Part 2, para. 66.
[316] Ibid. at para. 67.
[317] Ibid.
[318] UNICEF Guidelines, at Guidelines 3.8.2, 3.8.3.
[319] While the Trafficking Protocol does not directly address the situation of children who cannot be safely returned, the Legislative Guide to the Organized Crime Convention and its Protocols notes that "[i]n situations where the safe return of the child to his or her family and/or country of origin is not possible or where such return would not be in the child's best interests, the social welfare authorities should make adequate arrangements to ensure the effective protection of the child *and the safeguarding of his or her human rights*." Legislative Guide, at Part 2, para. 67 (emphasis added).
[320] UN Trafficking Principles and Guidelines, at Guideline 8.5. See also, Principle 11.
[321] UNICEF Guidelines, at Guideline 3.8.1.

the child victim's safe resettlement in a third country where this is the required option.[322] In General Comment No. 6, the Committee on the Rights of the Child outlined local integration, intercountry adoption, and third-country resettlement as alternatives to repatriation and the considerations that should be taken into account in those cases.[323]

5.6. CONCLUSIONS ON OBLIGATIONS OF PROTECTION AND SUPPORT

The reluctance of States to embrace specific and detailed obligations of protection and support to trafficked persons within their jurisdiction is reflected in the ungenerous and equivocal provisions of the Trafficking Protocol. However, in the decade since that instrument was adopted, a significant shift has taken place. The European Trafficking Convention sets much higher and more specific standards – an approach that appears to have been followed in the evolving jurisprudence around the Trafficking Protocol, as well as in more recent instruments and policy documents. As a result, the substantive content of a general obligation of protection and support is becoming increasingly clear. States appear to be moving steadily toward agreement that that they are obliged, as a matter of international law, to accurately and quickly identify victims of trafficking; to avoid criminalizing victims for status offenses; to refrain from detaining victims; to provide at least immediate protection and support to victims that is not conditional on cooperation with criminal justice agencies; to provide additional protection and support to victim-witnesses; and to make special provision for child victims. While the standard is not as high as many victim advocates would prefer, it does represent real and tangible progress over a relatively short period of time.

---

[322] Ibid. at Guideline 3.8.4.
[323] CRC General Comment No. 6, at paras. 89–94.

6

Obligations Related to Repatriation and Remedies

As noted previously, trafficked persons are routinely deported from countries of transit and destination. While States are able to point to a legal entitlement to control their own borders (and the absence of an obligation to permit all persons identified as having been trafficked to stay), there can be no doubt that forced repatriation to the country of origin or to a third country can have serious consequences for victims of trafficking. They may be subject to punishment from national authorities for unauthorized departure or other alleged offenses; they may face social isolation or stigmatization and be rejected by their families and communities; they may be subject to violence and intimidation from traffickers – particularly if they have cooperated with criminal justice agencies or owe money that cannot be repaid. Victims of trafficking who are forcibly repatriated, particularly without the benefit of supported reintegration, are at great risk of retrafficking. From a legal perspective, the issue of repatriation is a controversial one, involving consideration of complex issues such as entitlement to return and the principle of *non-refoulement*. As demonstrated below, a legal determination of the nature and scope of State obligations in this area requires a careful balance of often conflicting rights and interests.

The question of victim entitlement to remedies is equally difficult, if somewhat less politically controversial. The analysis in this chapter seeks to identify and explain the obligation of States to provide remedies to victims of trafficking, as well as the substantive content of that obligation. It focuses on the general right to a remedy in international law, the right to a remedy in the context of violence against women, and the right to a remedy in the specific context of trafficking. The issue of separating remedies from victim cooperation is then discussed along with the appropriate standard of remedy. The chapter concludes with a consideration of factors such as access to information and support that are critical to ensuring victims are able to secure their right to a remedy.

6.1. REPATRIATION OF VICTIMS

In 2009, the Organization for Security and Co-operation in Europe (OSCE) commissioned a series of studies on the issue of repatriation of victims of trafficking. The resulting report focused on laws, policies, and practices in four major destination countries of the OSCE region: the United Kingdom, Germany, Spain, and Italy. It identified serious problems with the repatriation process, including:

> continuing difficulties with the identification of trafficked persons resulting in possibly significant numbers of trafficked persons not being given the opportunity to establish their status during proceedings to remove them; the detention of vulnerable people; the failure to conduct risk assessments to ensure the safety of the return and the application of re-entry bans. At the same time legal advice and sometimes emergency medical assistance are not available during the return process.[1]

After examining systems and procedures in place for the repatriation of victims of trafficking from all four countries, the report concluded that:

> No country examined provided for permanent residency for identified victims. Trafficked persons are ultimately always obliged to return to their country of origin. Programmes to assist in their 'voluntary' return, which some argue would better be referred to as 'mandatory' return, were in place in all countries. Failing voluntary return, trafficked persons could be forcibly returned. No country examined had developed clear procedures to ensure that the return was conducted with due regard for the rights and safety of the person concerned. Instead issues of safety were only systematically considered in countries where the person had applied for asylum or other forms of international protection. The prevalence of re-trafficking, although not the focus of the papers, was referenced in all, which was seen to result in some measure from failed return policies.[2]

This extract neatly encapsulates the major issues related to repatriation of trafficked persons. For example, it serves to highlight the link between repatriation and identification. In many cases, it is a failure to correctly identify victims that provides a cover for routine deportation policies and practices.[3] The quality of procedures in place for timely and accurate victim identification will directly influence the capacity of the destination State to make correct and transparent decisions about victim

---

[1] Organization for Security and Co-operation in Europe, "Report of the Expert Group Meeting on Human Rights Protection in the Return of Trafficked Persons to Countries of Origin," Warsaw, June 24–25, 2009, at 1.

[2] Ibid.

[3] This is recognized in UN Office on Drugs and Crime, *Toolkit to Combat Trafficking in Persons* (2008), at 350: "[v]ictims of human trafficking may be facing deportation before they have had a chance to establish that they are victims of trafficking. In many countries, apart from criminal proceedings against offenders, there are often no formal judicial or administrative proceedings in which a person's status as a 'victim of trafficking' can be determined."

repatriation. Generally, legal obligations with regard to repatriation will fall most heavily on the country of destination. However, as the following discussion makes clear, countries of origin have a key role to play, particularly in respect of identification, family tracing, risk assessment, issuing necessary documentation, and ensuring safe and successful reintegration. Third countries may also be involved if resettlement outside the countries of destination and origin is the necessary or preferred option.

6.1.1. *The Standard of Safe and Preferably Voluntary Return*

From the earliest stages of its drafting, the Trafficking Protocol has been concerned with the issue of repatriation of victims.[4] The final text identifies specific obligations for countries of destination and of origin. In relation to the first group, the Protocol requires repatriation to "preferably be voluntary" and to be conducted "with due regard for the safety of the person and for the status of any related legal proceedings."[5] The *travaux préparatoires* reveal that many States were uncomfortable with the reference to voluntary repatriation,[6] and an Interpretative Note indicates that the words "shall preferably be voluntary" are to be understood as not placing any obligation on the repatriating State Party.[7] Countries of origin are required to accept the return of a trafficked national or resident without undue delay and with due regard for their safety.[8] They are further required to cooperate in return, including through verifying victim nationality or residence and issuing necessary travel documents.[9] The

---

[4] The first draft of the Protocol, submitted by Argentina, identified, as a primary purpose of the Protocol: "the prompt return of children or women victims of trafficking to their country of habitual residence." United Nations Office on Drugs and Crime, Travaux Préparatoires *of the Negotiations for the Elaboration of the United Nations Convention against Transnational Organized Crime and the Protocols Thereto* (2006) (Travaux Préparatoires *for the Organized Crime Convention and Protocols*), at 331.

[5] Trafficking Protocol, at Art. 8(2): "[w]hen a State Party returns a victim of trafficking in persons to a State Party of which that person is a national or in which he or she had, at the time of entry into the territory of the receiving State Party, the right of permanent residence, such return shall be with due regard for the safety of that person and for the status of any legal proceedings related to the fact that the person is a victim of trafficking and shall preferably be voluntary."

[6] Travaux Préparatoires *for the Organized Crime Convention and Protocols*, at 397, note 19.

[7] Ibid. at 388.

[8] Trafficking Protocol, at Art. 8(1): "the State Party of which a victim of trafficking in persons is a national or in which the person had the right of permanent residence at the time of entry into the territory of the receiving State Party shall facilitate and accept, with due regard for the safety of that person, the return of that person without undue or unreasonable delay." An Interpretative Note states that "[t]he words 'permanent residence' in this paragraph mean long-term residence, but not necessarily indefinite residence. The paragraph should be understood as being without prejudice to any domestic legislation regarding either the granting of the right of residence or the duration of residence." Travaux Préparatoires *for the Organized Crime Convention and Protocols*, at 388.

[9] Trafficking Protocol, at Arts. 8(3), 8(4). The Legislative Guide notes that the obligation relating to the issuing of travel documents is primarily administrative but may require legislation to ensure that the appropriate officials or agencies are both able and obliged to issue the documents when the conditions set out in Article 8 are met: UN Office on Drugs and Crime, *Legislative Guides for the*

Legislative Guide to the Protocol confirms the scope of application of the Protocol's requirement that repatriation must be with due regard to the safety of the victim: This provision applies to all victims, including those who have not participated in the investigation and prosecution of their exploiters. It also applies to any country to which the victim is repatriated as a national or permanent resident, even where the victim has not testified or has done so in another country.[10] The Protocol is careful to characterize its provisions on repatriation as supplementary to standards and agreements that may be in place within or between countries. It specifies that the repatriation provisions outlined above are without prejudice to any right afforded to victims of trafficking by any domestic law of the receiving State Party, or to any agreement governing the return of trafficked persons,[11] including obligations under customary international law regarding the return of migrants.[12]

The Explanatory Report to the European Trafficking Convention confirms that its provisions on repatriation are inspired, in part, by the Protocol.[13] There is, however, a noticeably stronger emphasis on both rights and dignity. States Parties to the Convention are required to facilitate and accept the return of a trafficked national or resident "with due regard for the rights, safety and dignity" of the victim and without undue delay.[14] The Explanatory Report notes that this provision upholds the right to return that is, as explored further in this chapter, well established in international human rights law.[15] All countries involved in repatriation are required to conduct return "with due regard for the rights, safety and dignity" of the victim and for the status of any related legal proceedings.[16] States Parties are further required to ensure

---

Implementation of the United Nations Convention Against Transnational Organized Crime and the Protocols Thereto, UN Sales No. E.05.V.2 (2004) (*Legislative Guide*), at para. 61(d). An Interpretative Note confirms the understanding of the Ad Hoc Committee that "a return under this article shall not be undertaken before the nationality or right of permanent residence of the person whose return is sought has been duly verified": Travaux Préparatoires *for the Organized Crime Convention and Protocols*, at 388.

[10] *Legislative Guide*, at Part 2, para. 61(c).

[11] Trafficking Protocol, at Arts. 8(5), 8(6).

[12] Travaux Préparatoires *for the Organized Crime Convention and Protocols*, at 389.

[13] Council of Europe, *Explanatory Report on the Convention on Action against Trafficking in Human Beings*, ETS 197, 16.V.2005 (European Trafficking Convention Explanatory Report), at para. 200.

[14] Council of Europe Convention on Action against Trafficking in Human Beings and its Explanatory Report, ETS 197, 16.V.2005, done May 16, 2005, entered into force Feb. 1, 2008 (European Trafficking Convention), at Art. 16(1).

[15] European Trafficking Convention Explanatory Report, at para. 210, referencing the Universal Declaration of Human Rights, adopted by UNGA Res. 217A (III), UN Doc. A/810 at 71, Dec. 10, 1948 (UDHR), at Art. 13(2); Protocol No. 4 to the Convention of 4 November 1950 for the Protection of Human Rights and Fundamental Freedoms, 1496 UNTS 263, done Sept. 16, 1963, entered into force May 2, 1968 (European Convention, Protocol No. 4), at Art. 3(2); and International Covenant on Civil and Political Rights, 999 UNTS 171, done Dec. 16, 1966, entered into force Mar. 3, 1976 (ICCPR), at Art. 12(4).

[16] European Trafficking Convention, at Art. 16(2). The two references to rights of the victim would, according to the Explanatory Report, include the right not to be subject to inhuman or degrading treatment, the right to protection of private and family life, and the right to privacy: European Trafficking Convention Explanatory Report, at paras. 202–203.

that such return "shall preferably be voluntary."[17] As with the Trafficking Protocol, the European Trafficking Convention requires countries of origin to cooperate in return, including through verification of victim nationality or residence and issuing of necessary travel documents.[18] The Explanatory Report clarifies these provisions as imposing a standard of due diligence on the requested State Party.[19] Importantly, the European Trafficking Convention also imposes, on States Parties, an obligation not to return child victims of trafficking "if there is an indication, following a risk and security assessment, that such return would not be in the best interests of the child."[20]

The standard of safe and preferably voluntary return appears to be well established in international law and policy. That standard, along with many of the related guarantees set out above, is affirmed in the UN Trafficking Principles and Guidelines,[21] echoed in a wide range of international and regional policy documents,[22] and

---

[17] European Trafficking Convention, at Art. 16(2).

[18] Ibid. at Arts. 16(3), 16(4).

[19] European Trafficking Convention Explanatory Report, at para. 204.

[20] European Trafficking Convention, at Art. 16(7). This obligation is echoed in United Nations Children's Fund, *Guidelines for the Protection of Child Victims of Trafficking* (September 2006) (UNICEF Guidelines), at Guideline 3.7, as well as in the UNODC Model Law, which cites CRC General Comment No. 6 in noting that "children who are at risk of being re-trafficked should not be returned to their country of origin unless it is in their best interest and appropriate measures for their protection have been taken." United Nations Office on Drugs and Crime, *Model Law on Trafficking in Persons*, UN Sales No. E.09.V.11 (2009) (UNODC Model Law), at 65, citing UN Committee on the Rights of the Child, "General Comment No. 6: Treatment of Unaccompanied and Separated Children Outside Their Country of Origin," UN Doc. CRC/GC/2005/6, June 3, 2005 (CRC General Comment No. 6). Further on the "best interests" standard, see the discussion at Chapter 5.5.2 of this volume.

[21] UN Economic and Social Council, Office of the United Nations High Commissioner for Human Rights, *Recommended Principles and Guidelines on Human Rights and Human Trafficking*, UN Doc. E/2002/68/Add.1, May 20, 2002 (UN Trafficking Principles and Guidelines), at Principle 11 and Guidelines 4.6, 6.7.

[22] See, for example, UNICEF Guidelines, at 29, Guideline 9.2 ("[t]he competent authority shall establish agreements and procedures for the safe voluntary return of child victims to their country"); Organization for Security and Co-operation in Europe (OSCE) Permanent Council, "Decision No. 557: OSCE Action Plan to Combat Trafficking in Human Beings," OSCE Doc. PC.DEC/557, July 24, 2003 (OSCE Action Plan), at 15 ("[a]ssisting the victims … in – preferably – voluntary repatriation to the country of origin with due regard for their safety and that of their families"); "Brussels Declaration on Preventing and Combating Trafficking in Human Beings," adopted by the European Conference on Preventing and Combating Trafficking in Human Beings, Sept. 20, 2002 (Brussels Declaration), at 12 ("[i]n view of the increased level of risk that will exist after the provision of evidence by a victim, there should be no forced return unless the victim has expressed a desire to return or a thorough risk assessment has been conducted that concludes that it is safe to do so"). On the rights of victims of trafficking related to the issue of repatriation, see also European Union and African States, "Ouagadougou Action Plan to Combat Trafficking in Human Beings, Especially Women and Children," adopted by the Ministerial Conference on Migration and Development, Nov. 22–23, 2006 (Ouagadougou Action Plan), at 4 ("[a]dopt appropriate measures for the protection of victims of trafficking and provide them with information on their legal and other rights in the country of destination as well as the country of origin in case of repatriation") and 5 ("[e]nsure … that the status of [relevant legal] proceedings are considered [sic] prior to any repatriation of the

affirmed by UN human rights treaty bodies[23] and other human rights mechanisms.[24] However, several of the more difficult questions remain unanswered. The reference to "preferably voluntary" in both specialist trafficking treaties is especially problematic. While it is easy to understand why States wished to qualify the obligation in

victim"); Economic Community of West African States, "ECOWAS Initial Plan of Action against Trafficking in Persons (2002–2003)," adopted by the Twenty-Fifth Ordinary Session of Authority of Heads of State and Government, Dec. 20–21, 2001 (ECOWAS Initial Plan of Action), at paras. 7 ("States shall ensure … that the status of [relevant legal] proceedings are considered [sic] prior to any repatriation of the victim") and 8 ("States shall consider adopting legislative or other appropriate measures that permit victims of trafficking in persons to remain in their territory, temporarily or permanently, in appropriate cases; and shall give appropriate consideration to humanitarian and compassionate factors"); European Union, "EU Plan on Best Practices, Standards and Procedures for Combating and Preventing Trafficking in Human Beings," OJ C 2005/C 311/01, Dec. 9, 2005 (EU Plan on Best Practices), at para. 5(iii) ("[r]egional solutions … to ensure the safe return and to ensure the effective, and secure reintegration of victims are essential"). For a less than satisfactory approach to the manner of repatriation, see Memorandum of Understanding between the Royal Government of the Kingdom of Cambodia and the Royal Government of the Kingdom of Thailand on Bilateral Cooperation for Eliminating Trafficking in Children and Women and Assisting Victims of Trafficking, adopted on May 31, 2003 in Siem Reap (Cambodia-Thailand MOU), at Art. 16(b) ("[r] epatriation of trafficked children and women shall be arrange [sic] and conducted in their best interest"); Memorandum of Understanding Between the Government of the Kingdom of Thailand and the Government of the Lao People's Democratic Republic on Cooperation to Combat Trafficking in Persons, Especially Women and Children, adopted on July 13, 2005 in Bangkok (Thailand-Lao PDR MOU), at Arts. 14–15 (which mention "ensuring the safety of the victims, especially women and children in the execution of their return and acceptance" at Art. 15(b)(3), but make no mention of the will of victims); and Cooperation Agreement between the Royal Government of the Kingdom of Cambodia and the Government of the Socialist Republic of Vietnam on Standard Operating Procedures (SOPs) for the Identification and Repatriation of Trafficked Victims, done in Phnom Penh on Dec. 3, 2009 (which makes no reference to safe and/or preferably voluntary return).

[23] See, for example, UN Committee on the Rights of the Child, "Concluding Observations: Austria," UN Doc. CRC/C/OPSC/AUT/CO/1, Oct. 22, 2008, at para. 30 ("ensure that the best interests of the child is the primary consideration in the case of a decision to repatriate a child [victim of sale or trafficking]") "Concluding Observations: Mali," UN Doc. CRC/C/MLI/CO/2, May 3, 2007, at para. 69(f) ("[e]nsure the return of the [trafficked] child to its country and its family, *if this is in the best interests of the child*" (emphasis added)). On the factors involved in assessing a child's best interests, which include consideration of the views and wishes of the child, see UNICEF Guidelines, at 29. See also, UN Committee on the Elimination of All Forms of Discrimination against Women, "Concluding Observations: Guatemala," UN Doc. CEDAW/C/GUA/CO/7, Feb. 12, 2009, at para. 23 ("[t]he Committee is … concerned about the human rights principles related to the deportation of migrants who have been trafficked"); "Concluding Observations: Denmark," UN Doc. CEDAW/C/ DEN/CO/6, Aug. 25, 2006, at para. 22 ("[the Committee] is also concerned about the vulnerability of trafficked women, who after a so-called 'reflection period' that has been prolonged to 30 days, are deported to their countries of origin unless an exception is made"). See also, on the safe and voluntary return of displaced persons, UN Human Rights Committee: "Concluding Observations: Chad," UN Doc. CCPR/C/TCD/CO/1, Aug. 11, 2009, at para. 13 ([c]reate conditions that offer lasting solutions to displaced persons, including their voluntary and safe return"); "Concluding Observations: Sudan," UN Doc. CCPR/C/SDN/CO/3, Aug. 29, 2007, at para. 23 ("[r]edouble its efforts to guarantee the safe, voluntary return of displaced persons").

[24] See, for example, UN General Assembly, "Note by the Secretary-General Transmitting the Report of the Special Rapporteur on Trafficking in Persons Especially Women and Children," UN Doc. A/64/290, Aug. 12, 2009, at paras. 64–65; UN Human Rights Council, "Report of the Special Rapporteur on the Human Rights of Migrants, Jorge Bustamante," UN Doc. A/HRC/7/12, Feb. 25,

this way, it is much less simple to identify the nature and quality of the implied obligation. It could be argued, for example, that States are required to make at least some effort to avoid repatriation that goes against the will of the victim. It is equally possible to sustain an argument that the qualification renders the notion of obligation meaningless in both practical and legal terms. The Interpretative Note to the relevant provision of the Trafficking Protocol appears to support this latter interpretation, at least in regard to that instrument.[25] The OSCE has recently weighed in, pointing out that "repatriation can only be called voluntary where people have a legal basis for remaining in a third country and have made an informed choice and consented to repatriate."[26]

One way to consider the standard is to focus on its more tangible element of "safe return." In other words, nonvoluntary return could be viewed as permissible only under circumstances where it is possible to demonstrate that the proposed repatriation is "safe."[27] The obligation to provide safe and, as far as possible, voluntary return implies that the repatriating State has the appropriate information at its disposal and is under some obligation to consider that information when making decisions about repatriation.[28] Many of the instruments and policy documents cited above confirm the importance of the repatriating State, presumably with the assistance and support of the receiving State, conducting pre-return risk assessments for all persons who have been trafficked.[29] Such assessments should preferably be undertaken on an individual basis and take into account the particular circumstances of each case. The way in which a person was trafficked; the extent to which they have cooperated in the prosecution of their exploiters; whether or not they owe money to traffickers; their age, gender, and family situation; and the capacity of the country of return to

---

2008, at para. 71 (calling on States to make "all efforts ... to provide assistance to irregular migrants in their safe return"). See also UN Human Rights Council, "Report of the Special Rapporteur on the Human Rights of Migrants: Mission to the Republic of Korea," UN Doc. A/HRC/4/24/Add.2, Mar. 14, 2007, at para. 58 (encouraging "incentives for voluntary return rather than expulsion").

[25] Travaux Préparatoires *for the Organized Crime Convention and Protocols*, at 388: "The words 'and shall preferably be voluntary' are understood not to place any obligation on the State party returning the victims."

[26] Organization for Security and Cooperation in Europe, "Report of the Expert Group Meeting on Human Rights Protection in the Return of Trafficked Persons to Countries of Origin," Warsaw, June 24–25, 2009, at 3.

[27] This interpretation finds support in the UNODC Model Law, which notes that while the Trafficking Protocol does envisage involuntary return, its provisions "clearly limit involuntary returns to those which are safe and are carried out with due regard for legal proceedings." UNODC Model Law, at 64.

[28] This point is made in the *Legislative Guide*, at Part 2, para. 91.

[29] See, for example, the UNODC Model Law, which identifies, as a mandatory requirement for full implementation of the Trafficking Protocol, a national legal provision to the effect that "[w]hen a victim of trafficking raises a substantial allegation that he or she or his or her family may face danger to life, health or personal liberty if he or she is returned to his or her country of origin, the competent authority shall conduct a risk and security assessment before returning the victim." UNODC Model Law, at 64. See also, United Nations Office for Drugs and Crime, *Anti-Human Trafficking Manual for Criminal Justice Practitioners* (2009), at "Module 5: Risk Assessment in Trafficking in Persons Cases."

provide effective protection are all important factors that should contribute to a consideration of whether safe return is possible.[30] Risk assessment should be explicitly connected to the obligation of *non-refoulement*, considered further in this chapter.[31]

The importance of a pre-repatriation risk assessment has been particularly highlighted in the case of children. As noted above, the European Trafficking Convention mandates pre-return risk assessment in the case of child victims of trafficking. In its General Comment No. 6, the UN Committee on the Rights of the Child specified that repatriation should not occur where there is a "reasonable risk" that the return would result in the violation of fundamental human rights of the child. The Committee recommended that the decision to return should take into account the "safety, security and other conditions, including socio-economic conditions, awaiting the child upon return."[32] The UNICEF Guidelines echo and expand on these recommendations.[33]

6.1.2. *Entitlement to Return*

All victims of trafficking, children as well as adults, who are not residents of the country in which they find themselves are entitled to return to their country of origin. The right to return, a corollary of the right to leave and part of the broader right to freedom of movement, is protected in international human rights treaty law.[34] It

---

[30] Further on the substantive content of risk assessment, see the UNODC Model Law at 64: "risk assessment should take into consideration factors such as the risk of reprisals by the trafficking network against the victim and his or her family, the capacity and willingness of the authorities in the country of origin to protect the victim and his or her family from possible intimidation or violence, the social position of the victim on return, the risk of the victim being arrested, detained or prosecuted by the authorities in his or her home country for trafficking related offences (such as the use of false documents and prostitution), the availability of assistance and opportunities for long-term employment. Non-governmental organizations and other service agencies working with victims of trafficking should have the right to submit information on these aspects, which should be taken into account in any decision about the return or deportation of victims by the competent authorities."

[31] Article 33 of the Model Law connects this issue to risk assessment by providing that "[a]ny decision to return a victim of trafficking in persons to his or her country shall be considered in light of the principle of non-refoulement and of the prohibition of inhuman and degrading treatment": ibid.

[32] CRC General Comment No. 6, at para. 84.

[33] UNICEF Guidelines, at 26, Guideline 8.2.

[34] See UDHR, at Art. 13(2) ("[e]veryone has the right to … return to his country"); ICCPR, at Art. 12(4) ("[n]o-one shall be arbitrarily deprived of the right to enter his own country"). Similar provisions can be found in the major regional human rights instruments: European Convention, Protocol No. 4, at Art. 3(2); American Convention on Human Rights, 1144 UNTS 123, done Nov. 22, 1969, entered into force 18 July, 1978 (American Convention), at Art. 22(5); African Charter on Human And Peoples' Rights, 1520 UNTS 217, done June 27, 1981, entered into force Oct. 21, 1986 (African Charter), at Art. 12(2). Generally, on the right to return, see H. Hannum, *The Right to Leave and Return in International Law and Practice* (1987); G.S. Goodwin-Gill, "The Right to Leave, the Right to Return and the Question of a Right to Remain," in V. Gowland-Debbas ed., *The Protection of Refugees in the Light of Contemporary International Legal Issues* 93 (1995).

has also been identified as a norm of customary international law.[35] In the specific context of trafficking, this right has been linked to an obligation on the part of the country of origin to receive its returning nationals without undue or unreasonable delay.[36] As noted in the relevant instruments cited above, the effective discharge of this obligation is likely to involve the State of origin conducting checks in order to verify whether the victim is a national or does indeed hold a right of permanent residence,[37] and, if so, ensuring that the individual is in possession of the documentation required to travel to and re-enter its territory.[38] The obligation to facilitate and accept return must be also be discharged with due regard to the safety of the person being returned.[39] The UN has taken the position that, in relation to the Trafficking Protocol, this provision:

> imposes a positive obligation upon Governments to ensure that there is no danger of retaliation or other harm the trafficked person could face upon returning home, such as arrest for leaving the country or working in prostitution abroad, when these are actions criminalized in the country of origin.[40]

The right to return also imposes an obligation on the country of destination to permit those victims who wish to return to do so – again without undue or unreasonable delay. Detention of trafficked persons in shelters, prisons, or immigration detention facilities is one way in which the right to return can be interfered with.[41] Compelling victims to remain for the duration of lengthy criminal proceedings can also constitute an interference with the right of return. The International Covenant on Civil and Political Rights (ICCPR) prohibits *arbitrary* deprivation of the right to return. Accordingly, a State preventing the return of a trafficked person must be able to show, in relation to each individual case, that its actions are in accordance with law and are not arbitrary or unreasonable.[42] The obligation on States to consider the best interests of the child (discussed at Chapter 5.5.2 of this volume) will also be a

---

[35] See, for example, W.T. Mallison and S. Mallison, "The Right to Return," (1980) 9(3) *Journal of Palestine Studies* 125 ("[f]or most individuals the actual practice of returning to one's home or country is so commonplace a part of every day living that the right of return as a legal concept is given little attention. The great majority of people in the world are able to exercise the customary right of return based upon state practice," at 125) and J. Quigley, "Mass Displacement and the Individual Right of Return," (1997) 68 *British Yearbook of International Law* 122.

[36] Trafficking Protocol, at Art. 8(3); European Trafficking Convention, at Art. 16(1).

[37] Note that under Article 8(1) of the Trafficking Protocol, return must be facilitated and accepted in relation to all victims who are nationals or *who had the right of permanent residence at the time of entry into the receiving country*. This means that a trafficked person who had the right of permanent residency in the country of origin but subsequently lost it could still be repatriated under this provision.

[38] Trafficking Protocol, at Art. 8(4); European Trafficking Convention, at Arts. 16(3), 16(4).

[39] Trafficking Protocol, at Arts. 8(1), 8(2); European Trafficking Convention, at Arts. 16(1), 16(2).

[40] UNODC Model Law, at 62.

[41] See further, Chapter 5.2.2.

[42] See further, the discussion of this standard in the context of victim detention at Chapter 5.2.2.

major consideration when it comes to upholding this important right in relation to child victims of trafficking.

6.1.3. *Expulsion, Due Process, and the Obligation of* Non-refoulement

The return of trafficked persons cannot operate to violate their established rights.[43] One key aspect of this important principle relates to the right to due process. Repatriation that is not voluntary effectively amounts to expulsion from a State. International human rights law rejects arbitrary expulsion and is clear on the point that aliens lawfully within the country can only be expelled in accordance with the law.[44] An alien lawfully present is entitled to present reasons why she or he should not be expelled, and these reasons must be reviewed by the competent authority.[45]

For trafficked persons who are not lawfully within the country, substantive and procedural guarantees against expulsion are much less clear, and States generally retain a considerable degree of discretion in deciding whether and when to remove unlawful immigrants. The precise nature of a State's obligations in this regard may relate, at least in part, to specific treaty obligations of that State.[46] However, one of the most important protections, potentially applicable to all non-nationals, relates to the principle of *non-refoulement*.

---

[43] This is recognized in the savings clause of the Trafficking Protocol (Art. 14) and the European Trafficking Convention (Art. 40).

[44] ICCPR, at Art. 13.

[45] See generally, the recent series of reports on the expulsion of aliens produced for the International Law Commission by Rapporteur Maurice Kamto, available at http://untreaty.un.org/ilc/guide/9_12. htm (accessed Dec. 4, 2009). See also the discussion of the rights of noncitizens at Chapter 3.1 in this book, particularly the references contained in notes 15 and 16 of that chapter and the accompanying text.

[46] States Parties to the Migrant Workers Convention, for example, may be held to a higher standard with regard to the expulsion of non-nationals: International Convention on the Protection of the Rights of All Migrant Workers and Members of Their Families, UN Doc. A/RES/45/158, done Dec. 18, 1990, entered into force July 1, 2003 (Migrant Workers Convention), at Arts. 22, 67. The Inter-American Court of Human Rights has recognized that "the State may grant a distinct treatment to documented migrants with respect to undocumented migrants, or between migrants and nationals, provided that this differential treatment is reasonable, objective, proportionate and does not harm human rights": *Juridical Conditions and Rights of Undocumented Migrants*, Advisory Opinion OC=18/03, Inter-American Court of Human Rights (ser. A) No. 18, Sept. 17, 2003, at para. 119. Thus States may apply their immigration laws and require the exit of undocumented migrants, including trafficked persons. However, any such process "must always be applied with strict regard for the guarantees of due process and respect for human dignity": ibid. The African Commission on Human and Peoples' Rights has adopted a similar approach in saying that it "does not wish to call into question ... the right of any State to take legal action against illegal immigrants and deport them to their countries of origin, if the competent courts so decide. It is however of the view that it is unacceptable to deport individuals without giving them the possibility to plead their case before the competent national courts": *Union Inter Africaine des Droits de l'Homme, Fédération Internationale des Ligues des Droits de l'Homme and Others v. Angola*, ACHPPHR Comm. No. 159/96 (African Commission on Human and Peoples' Rights, Nov. 11, 1997), at para. 20.

The obligation of *non-refoulement* (nonreturn), a central principle of refugee law,[47] is widely, but not uniformly, recognized as a norm of customary international law – at least in the specific context of asylum from persecution.[48] However, as a means of protection, *non-refoulement* is much broader than asylum.[49] For example, under the Convention against Torture, States are prevented from returning or extraditing a person to another State where there are substantial grounds for believing that the individual in question would be subject to torture or other forms of ill treatment.[50] The prohibition on torture and inhuman or degrading treatment or punishment contained in the European Convention on Human Rights (which does not specifically refer to the obligation of *non-refoulement*) has also been interpreted as prohibiting return in circumstances where an individual faces a real risk of torture or inhuman or degrading treatment or punishment.[51] A similar interpretation

[47] Convention Relating to the Status of Refugees, 189 UNTS 137, July 28, 1951, entered into force Apr. 22, 1954 (Refugee Convention) as amended by the Protocol Relating to the Status of Refugees, 606 UNTS 267, done Jan. 31, 1967, entered into force Oct. 4, 1967 (Refugee Convention), at Art. 33(1): "[n]o contracting State shall expel or return ('refouler') a refugee in any manner whatsoever to the frontiers of territories where his life or freedom would be threatened on account of his race, religion, nationality, membership of a particular social group, or political opinion."

[48] See Office of the High Commissioner for Refugees, "The Principle of Non-Refoulement as a Norm of Customary International Law: Response to the Questions Posed to UNHCR by the Federal Constitutional Court of the Federal Republic of Germany in Cases 2 BvR 1938/93, 2 BvR 1953/93, 2 BvR 1954/93" (Jan. 31, 1994); Office of the High Commissioner for Refugees, "Summary Conclusions: The Principle of Non-Refoulement: Expert Roundtable organized by the UNHCR and the Lauterpacht Research Centre for International Law, University of Cambridge, UK, 9–10 July 2001," in E. Feller, V. Türk and F. Nicholson eds., *Refugee Protection in International Law: UNHCR's Global Consultations on International Protection* 178 (2003); E. Lauterpacht and D. Bethlehem, "The Scope and Content of the Principle of Non-Refoulement," also in E. Feller, V. Türk and F. Nicholson eds., *Refugee Protection in International Law: UNHCR's Global Consultations on International Protection* 78 (2003); N. Coleman, "Renewed Review of the Status of the Principle of Non-Refoulement as Customary International Law," (2003) 5 *European Journal of Migration and Law* 23; and "Declaration of States Parties to the 1951 Convention and/or its 1967 Protocol Relating to the Status of Refugees," UN Doc. HCR/MMSP/2001/09, Dec. 13, 2001, at para. 4. See also, however, J.C. Hathaway, *The Rights of Refugees under International Law* (2005), at 363–370 (challenging the view that *non-refoulement* of refugees is an established principle of customary international law and lamenting, at 365, "the persistent overstatement of the reach of custom"). Hathaway expands on this position in J.C. Hathaway, "Leveraging Asylum," (2010) 45 *Texas International Law Journal* 503.

[49] Ibid.

[50] Convention against Torture and Other Cruel, Inhuman or Degrading Treatment or Punishment, 1465 UNTS 85, adopted Dec. 10, 1984, entered into force June 26, 1987 (Torture Convention), at Art. 3(1); See also, Refugee Convention, at Art. 33; ICCPR, at Art. 7; Convention on the Rights of the Child, 1577 UNTS 3, done Nov. 20, 1989, entered into force Sept. 2, 1990 (CRC), at Art. 22. Note that the UN Special Rapporteur on Torture has recently linked torture and related harms to gender-based violence including trafficking: "Report of the Special Rapporteur on Torture and Other Cruel, Inhuman or Degrading Treatment or Punishment, Manfred Nowak," UN Doc. A/HRC/7/3, Jan. 15, 2008, at paras. 44, 56–58.

[51] See, for example, *Soering v. UK*, (1989) 11 EHRR 439 (ECHR, July 7, 1989). In this case, the European Court of Human Rights found no express duty of *non-refoulement* under Article 3 of the Convention for the Protection of Human Rights and Fundamental Freedoms, 213 UNTS 222, done Nov. 4, 1950, entered into force Sept. 3, 1953 (European Human Rights Convention). However, in considering whether the extradition of a suspect would violate the European Convention on Human Rights'

has been made by the UN Human Rights Committee with respect to the prohibitions on arbitrary deprivation of life and cruel, inhuman, or degrading treatment or
punishment contained in Articles 6 and 7 of the ICCPR.[52] Of particular relevance
to the present context is the extension, by regional courts and human rights bodies,
of the prohibition on *refoulement* to certain situations where the fear of persecution
or ill treatment emanates from non-State actors, and the relevant State is unable to
provide appropriate or effective protection.[53]

prohibition on torture, or inhuman or degrading treatment or punishment, the Court held, at para.
88, that "[i]t would hardly be compatible with the underlying values of the Convention … were a
Contracting State knowingly to surrender a fugitive to another State where there were substantial
grounds for believing that he would be in danger of being subjected to torture, however heinous
the crime allegedly committed. Extradition in such circumstances, while not explicitly referred
to in the brief and general wording of Article 3 would plainly be contrary to the spirit and intend-
ment of the Article, and in the Court's view this inherent obligation not to extradite also extends to
cases in which the fugitive would be faced in the receiving State by a real risk of exposure to inhuman or degrading treatment or punishment proscribed by that Article." The European Trafficking
Convention Explanatory Report's commentary to the relevant provision cites (at para. 203) other
jurisprudence of the European Court of Human Rights, including *D v. UK*, (1997) 24 EHRR 423
(ECHR, May 2, 1997) (violation of Article 3 possible through potential omission rather than positive action by the receiving State as the individual would, if returned, no longer be able to receive
life-saving medical treatment); *Cruz Varas and Others v. Sweden*, (1991) 14 EHRR 1 (ECHR, Mar.
20, 1991) (extending these principles to deportation). See also *Saadi v. Italy*, Dec. No. 37201/06 (unreported) (ECHR, Feb. 28, 2008) (requirement of real risk of ill treatment, not mere possibility; risk of
ill treatment not to be weighed up against reason for expulsion; risk to be assessed on facts known/
ought to have been known at time of expulsion). Further on the potential application of Article 3
of the European Human Rights Convention to trafficked persons, see A.L. Seaman, "Permanent
Residency for Human Trafficking Victims in Europe: The Potential Use of Article 3 of the European
Convention as a Means of Protection," *Columbia Journal of Transnational Law* (forthcoming), available at SSRN: http://ssrn.com/abstract=1503739 (accessed Feb. 8, 2010).

52 "[T]he article 2 obligation requiring that States parties respect and ensure the Covenant rights for
all persons in their territory and all persons under their control entails an obligation not to extradite,
deport, expel or otherwise remove a person from their territory, where there are substantial grounds
for believing that there is a real risk of irreparable harm, such as that contemplated by articles 6 and
7 of the Covenant, either in the country to which removal is to be effected or in any country to which
the person may subsequently be removed": United Nations Human Rights Committee, "General
Comment No. 31: The Nature of the General Legal Obligation Imposed on States Parties to the
Covenant," UN Doc. CCPR/C/21/Rev.1/Add.13, May 26, 2004 (HRC General Comment No. 31), at
para. 12.

53 See European Council Directive 2004/83/EC of 29 April 2004 on minimum standards for the qualification and status of third-country nationals or stateless persons as refugees or as persons who otherwise need international protection and the content of the protection granted, OJ L 304/12, Sept. 30,
2004. See also *Salah Seekh v. The Netherlands*, (2007) 45 EHRR 50 (ECHR, Jan. 11, 2007), at para.
137 (danger emanating from persons or groups other than public officials); *HLR v. France*, (1997) 26
EHRR 29 (ECHR, Apr. 29, 1997), at para. 40. In *HLR v. France*, the applicant challenged his deportation to Colombia because he feared the threats allegedly presented to him from the actions by drug
traffickers there. The Court held, at para. 40, that "where the danger emanates from persons … who
are not public officials," there was still a potential breach of Article 3 of the European Human Rights
Convention where the risk is real and the State authorities cannot provide appropriate protection.
The UN Committee against Torture has also concluded that in some exceptional circumstances
there should be no return where the fear of torture on return is through the actions of non-State

Major specialist trafficking treaties acknowledge the principle of *non-refoulement* and its relevance to individuals who have been trafficked. The Trafficking Protocol specifically refers to this obligation in its general savings clause, as does the European Trafficking Convention in its equivalent provision.[54] Notably, both instruments reference the principle in specific connection with the Refugee Convention.

The importance of *non-refoulement* in the context of trafficking has been repeatedly affirmed in policy documents, international guidelines, and other nonlegal texts. The UN Trafficking Principles and Guidelines, for example, are clear on the point that:

> [States should ensure] that procedures and processes are in place for receipt and consideration of asylum claims for both trafficked persons and smuggled asylum seekers and that the principle of *non-refoulement* is respected and upheld at all times.[55]

The UNHCR Guidelines also address this issue, highlighting the particular risks (such as reprisals, social exclusion, and retrafficking) that may face trafficked persons upon their return. The UNICEF Guidelines note the potential relevance of the principle of *non-refoulement* to trafficked children with a valid claim to asylum while also pointing out that other trafficked children may also be entitled to complementary forms of protection that include *non-refoulement*.[56] Notably, however, UN General Assembly and Human Rights Council resolutions on trafficking typically refrain from any reference to either repatriation or the principle of *non-refoulement*.

6.1.4. *Repatriation and Legal Proceedings*

As noted in Chapter 5.4.3, the right to remain during legal proceedings, asserted in a range of soft law texts,[57] is confirmed in treaty law. The Trafficking Protocol places an obligation on countries of destination to conduct return "with due regard for ... the

---

actors. See, for example, *Sadiq Shek Elmi v. Australia*, UNCAT Comm. No. 120/1998, UN Doc. CAT/C/22/D/120/1998, decided May 14, 1999, at para. 6.5 (where non-State actors are exercising *de facto* governmental powers).

[54] Trafficking Protocol, at Art. 14(1); European Trafficking Convention, at Art. 40(3). Note these respective savings clauses are subject to detailed consideration in Chapter 8.4, below.

[55] UN Trafficking Principles and Guidelines, at Guideline 2.7.

[56] UNICEF Guidelines, at 23.

[57] See, for example, UN Trafficking Principles and Guidelines, at Principle 9. Principle 9 articulates the right of trafficked persons to remain in the country during legal proceedings against traffickers and refers to the granting of temporary residence permits for this purpose. Principle 9 is supplemented by Guideline 4.7 that requests States to consider "[p]roviding legislative protection for trafficked persons who voluntarily agree to cooperate with law enforcement authorities *including protection of their right to remain lawfully within the country of destination for the duration of any legal proceedings*" (emphasis added).

status of any related legal proceedings."[58] This obligation should be read in light of the requirement, set out in both the Organized Crime Convention and Trafficking Protocol, that participation by victims in criminal justice proceedings against their exploiters be facilitated.[59] As noted above, the European Trafficking Convention also obliges States Parties that are countries of destination to conduct return "with due regard for … the status of any related legal proceedings":[60] "in order not to affect the rights that the victim could exercise in the course of the proceedings as well as in the proceedings themselves."[61] It can be convincingly argued that involuntary return that operates to deprive a victim of the opportunity to participate effectively in legal proceedings (both criminal and civil) violates the obligations of States Parties to these two instruments.

There are also practical considerations at play in ensuring that the right to remain during legal proceedings is protected. As noted in the UNODC Model Law:

> it is in the interest of both the victim and the prosecution to allow the victim at least a temporary residence permit during criminal proceedings. Without the presence of the victim it will be impossible or very difficult to prosecute the suspects successfully. Moreover, the victim should be enabled to initiate a civil procedure for damages or to bring his or her case before any other relevant court, for example, a labour court.[62]

States should therefore be careful to ensure that their return of trafficked persons does not jeopardize the initiation and/or successful completion of any legal proceedings involving or implicating the victim. As has been noted previously, the term "legal proceedings" extends beyond criminal actions against exploiters to include civil actions such as for recovery of wages. In this context, it is relevant to note the intersection between this obligation and the right of trafficked persons to remedies. The presence of the trafficked person in the country in which remedies are being sought is often a practical – and sometimes a legal – requirement for that person to secure remedial action. In some countries, civil action to recover damages cannot

---

[58] Trafficking Protocol, at Art. 8(2). As noted in Chapter 5.4, this provision should be read in light of the broader obligation to ensure victims are provided with an opportunity to participate in legal proceedings as set out in Article 25(3) of the Organized Crime Convention (United Nations Convention against Transnational Organized Crime, 2225 UNTS 209, done Nov. 15, 2000, entered into force Sept. 29, 2003) as well as the specific obligation in the Trafficking Protocol to provide victims with an opportunity to present their views under Article 6(2). The Legislative Guide to the Protocol affirms the importance of ensuring that there are "adequate links between law enforcement and prosecution officials who may be developing a criminal case against traffickers and immigration authorities responsible for deporting and repatriating victims to ensure that victims are not removed before they can participate effectively in the criminal process": *Legislative Guide*, at Part 2, para. 91.

[59] Organized Crime Convention, at Art. 25(3); Trafficking Protocol, at Art. 6(2)(b).

[60] European Trafficking Convention, at Art. 16(2).

[61] European Trafficking Convention Explanatory Report, at para. 202.

[62] See further, UNODC Model Law, at 60–61.

commence until criminal proceedings have been concluded. Repatriation that does not take account of the victim's right of access to remedies will inevitably obstruct the free and effective exercise of that right.[63] At the very least, there should be a deferral of deportation, accompanied by a temporary regularization of legal status, until the victim has been able to participate in the relevant legal proceedings. The connection between a right to remain and the right to access remedies is considered further at Chapters 5.4.3 and 6.2.

6.1.5. *Alternatives to Repatriation*

In some cases, repatriation of the victim to her or his country of origin, even in the longer term, will not be the preferred course of action. This may be due to ongoing safety and security concerns, including the risk of retrafficking. It may also be due to humanitarian considerations that relate, for example, to the victim's health or the links and relationships that she or he has established in the destination country. The Trafficking Protocol does not specifically address alternatives to repatriation except through indirect references in its parent instrument to certain forms of witness protection including relocation.[64] The European Trafficking Convention takes a different approach. By recognizing the possibility of temporary visas and even permanent residency, this treaty does not automatically assume that repatriation is the immediate or even ultimate outcome of a trafficking event. States Parties are encouraged to provide victims with residence permits "for the purpose of their cooperation with the competent authorities in investigation or criminal proceedings" *or* to do so owing to their personal situation.[65]

Soft law sources tend toward the standard set out in the European Trafficking Convention. The UN Trafficking Principles and Guidelines, for example, identify the need for "legal alternatives to repatriation" in situations where return would pose unacceptable risks to the victim and/or the victim's family.[66] The UNICEF Guidelines identify both local and third-country integration as appropriate options for a durable solution in cases where return to the country of origin is not in the

---

[63] The Explanatory Report to the European Trafficking Convention notes that "it is ... essential that victims who are illegally present in the country be informed of their rights as regards the possibility of obtaining a residence permit under Article 14 of the Convention, as it would be very difficult for them to obtain compensation if they were unable to remain in the country where the proceeding is taking place": European Trafficking Convention Explanatory Report, at para. 192.

[64] Organized Crime Convention, at Art. 24, requiring each State Party to "take appropriate measures within its means to provide effective protection from potential retaliation or intimidation for witnesses in criminal proceedings who give testimony concerning offences covered by this Convention and, as appropriate, for their relatives and other persons close to them [including by] [e]stablishing procedures for the physical protection of such persons, such as, to the extent necessary and feasible, relocating them and permitting, where appropriate, non-disclosure or limitations on the disclosure of information concerning the identity and whereabouts of such persons."

[65] European Trafficking Convention, at Art. 14(1).

[66] UN Trafficking Principles and Guidelines, at Principle 11. See also Guideline 6.7.

child's best interests.[67] The UN Committee on the Rights of the Child has also affirmed that repatriation is not an option "if it would lead to a 'reasonable risk' that such return would result in the violation of fundamental human rights of the child."[68] It too recommends local integration, intercountry adoption, or resettlement in a third country as alternatives.[69] The Special Rapporteur on Trafficking has also called attention to the principle that trafficked persons should be offered legal alternatives to repatriation in cases where it is reasonable to conclude that such repatriation would pose a serious safety risk to them or their families.[70]

6.1.6. *Reintegration of Victims*

Supported reintegration is a critical aspect of safe repatriation. As noted above, victims of trafficking who are provided with reintegration assistance are much less likely to be retrafficked. They may also, depending on the nature and quality of support provided, be less vulnerable to intimidation, retaliation, social isolation, and stigmatization. Supported reintegration is a right owed to trafficked persons by virtue of their status as victims of crime and victims of human rights violations. It must be accompanied by respect for the repatriated individuals' rights, including their right to privacy and right not to be discriminated against. As discussed above, international treaty law generally supports repatriation when such repatriation is safe and preferably voluntary and, in the case of children, in that child's best interests.

The Trafficking Protocol does not refer to reintegration. A provision on victim rehabilitation was included in the first drafts of the Protocol, but not incorporated as a separate provision into the final text. That provision would have required State Parties to:

> consider implementing measures to provide for the physical, psychological and social recovery of victims of and witnesses to crimes covered by this Protocol, in order to foster their health, self respect and dignity, in a manner appropriate to their age, gender and special needs.[71]

While aspects of this provision have been picked up in Article 6(3), the absence of any specific reference to reintegration is a significant weakness in the Trafficking Protocol.

The European Trafficking Convention requires States Parties to:

---

[67] UNICEF Guidelines, at Guideline 3.8.
[68] CRC General Comment No. 6, at para. 84.
[69] Ibid. at paras. 89–94.
[70] UN Human Rights Council, "Report of the Special Rapporteur on the human rights aspects of the victims of trafficking in persons, especially women and children, Sigma Huda, Addendum: Summary of cases transmitted to Governments and replies received," UN Doc. A/HRC/4/23/Add.1, May 30, 2007, at para. 62.
[71] Travaux Préparatoires *for the Organized Crime Convention and Protocols*, at 374.

adopt such legislative or other measures as may be necessary to establish repatriation programmes … [that] aim at avoiding re-victimization. Each party should
make its best effort to favour the reintegration of victims into the society of the
State of return, including reintegration into the education system and the labour
market, in particular through the acquisition and improvement of their professional skills. With regard to children, these programmes should include enjoyment of the right to education and measures to secure adequate care or receipt by
the family or appropriate care structures.[72]

The Convention further requires States Parties to adopt measures necessary to
ensure the availability of contact information for structures that can assist returned
victims in the country to which they are repatriated.[73] While not referring specifically to reintegration, the South Asian Association for Regional Cooperation
(SAARC) Convention identifies a range of "rehabilitation" measures such as legal
advice, counseling, job training, and health care.[74]

The need for repatriation that avoids revictimization is also emphasized in key
international and regional policy instruments.[75] There is growing appreciation of
what is required for reintegration to work well[76] and this improved understanding

---

[72] European Trafficking Convention, at Art. 16(6).

[73] Ibid. at Art. 16(7).

[74] South Asian Association for Regional Cooperation, Convention on Preventing and Combating
Trafficking in Women and Children for Prostitution, done Jan. 5, 2002, entered into force Dec. 1,
2005 (SAARC Convention), at Art. IX(3).

[75] UN Trafficking Principles and Guidelines, at Guideline 6.8; UNICEF Guidelines, at Guideline
3.8.3; COMMIT MOU, at Art. 21. The Beijing Platform for Action requires States to develop strategies that ensure the revictimization of victims of violence against women does not occur through
gender insensitive laws or judicial or other practices: "Beijing Declaration and Platform for Action,"
Fourth World Conference on Women, UN Doc. A/CONF.177/20 and UN Doc. A/CONF.177/20/
Add.1, Sept. 15, 1995 (Beijing Declaration and Platform for Action), at para.124(d). The Beijing +5
Outcome Document, directed at governments and regional and international organizations, proposes measures to facilitate the return of trafficked persons to their State of origin and to support
their reintegration there: "Further Actions and Initiatives to Implement the Beijing Declaration
and Platform for Action," UN Doc. A/RES/S-23/3, Nov. 16, 2000 (Beijing +5 Outcome Document),
at para. 97(c). The UN General Assembly has urged States "to support comprehensive, practical
approaches by the international community to assist women and children victims of transnational
trafficking to return home and be reintegrated into their home societies": UN General Assembly,
"Traffic in Women and Girls," UN Doc. A/RES/51/66, Dec. 12, 1996, at para. 8; UN General
Assembly, "Traffic in Women and Girls," UN Doc. A/RES/50/167, Dec. 22, 1995, at para. 5. See also
the Ouagadougou Action Plan, at 4 ("[a]dopt appropriate measures for the protection of victims of
trafficking and provide them with information on their legal and other rights in the country of destination as well as the country of origin in case of repatriation … Adopt specific measures to avoid
criminalisation of victims of trafficking, as well as stigmatisation and the risk of re-victimisation");
Brussels Declaration, at 10 ("[t]rafficking victims must be recognised as victims of serious crime.
Therefore they should not be re-victimised, further stigmatised, criminalised, prosecuted or held in
detention centres for offences that may have been committed by the victim as part of the trafficking
process").

[76] See, for example, International Organization for Migration, *Handbook on Direct Assistance for
Victims of Trafficking*, available at http://www.iom.int/jahia/webdav/site/myjahiasite/shared/shared/
mainsite/published_docs/books/CT%20handbook.pdf (accessed Feb. 9, 2010).

is likely, over time, to add substance to the general obligation outlined above. For example, it is becoming clear that successful reintegration requires active cooperation between repatriating and receiving countries.[77] The importance of such cooperation is recognized in relevant regional treaties[78] as well as in key international and regional policy documents.[79]

6.2. ACCESS TO REMEDIES

Victims of trafficking have often been exploited for little or no payment over long periods of time. They may have suffered injuries or contracted illnesses that require medical attention. They may have incurred debts as a result of their trafficking experiences. While remedies (or, more precisely, reparations) for trafficking are still very rare, there is a clear trend toward making this a legal and practical possibility. For example, some countries have expressly granted victims of trafficking the right to private action against their traffickers and have included mandatory restitution to trafficked persons as part of the criminal sentencing of traffickers. Other countries grant victims the right to bring civil action against their traffickers, regardless of their nationality or migration status.[80]

Remedies confirm the status of trafficked persons as victims of crime and victims of human rights abuse. They are a practical means by which victims can both access and receive justice. Remedies are strongly linked to rules of responsibility, and the present section should be read in conjunction with those parts of Chapter 4 dealing with the obligation of reparation. As discussed more fully in that chapter, the obligation to provide remedies and the right to access remedies in the context of trafficking can arise either directly or indirectly. In the first case, the obligation will be a consequence of the State being responsible for the violation of a human right or other obligation protected under international law through either custom or treaty. In the second case, the State is not directly implicated in the initial harm, but has failed to discharge its obligation to prevent the harm and/or to respond appropriately (for example, failure to investigate and prosecute trafficking to the required standard

---

[77] See the UNODC Model Law, at 62: "[i]t is good practice for countries of origin and countries of destination to enter into bilateral or regional agreements/arrangements that provide for the reintegration of repatriated victims of trafficking in persons and minimize the risk of such victims being re-trafficked."

[78] European Trafficking Convention, at Art. 16(6); SAARC Convention, at Preamble, Art. II.

[79] See, for example, UN Trafficking Principles and Guidelines, at Guidelines 11.11, 11.12; COMMIT MOU, at Arts. 20–21; Ouagadougou Action Plan, at 3, 7; EU Plan on Best Practices, at para. 5(i), Annex, 6, Objective 1; OSCE Action Plan, at Section VI(3); Brussels Declaration, at paras. 4, 13, 15.

[80] For a useful overview of State practice within the OSCE region (specifically, Albania, France, Moldova, Romania, Russian Federation, Ukraine, United Kingdom, United States of America), see Organization for Security and Co-operation in Europe, *Compensation for Trafficked and Exploited Persons in the OSCE Region* (2008), esp. at 53–152.

of due diligence). It is in relation to this subsequent failure that the State incurs an obligation to provide remedies. The investigation and prosecution of violations, as well as the provision of assistance and support, can also be important forms of remedy to which a victim is entitled. Reference should therefore be made to Chapters 5 and 7 where these issues are considered in detail.

It is useful to reiterate that the obligation on *States* to provide remedies for violations originating in the conduct of private persons must generally be linked to a distinct internationally wrongful act on the part of that State, such as a failure to protect or respond. A State's duty to provide reparation for violations by non-State actors in the absence of such a distinct wrong has been described as, at best, "an emerging norm."[81] Another important limitation lies in the fact that any international legal right to remedies arises only as a consequence of the establishment of responsibility for the harm produced. In other words, "the idealistic notion of providing compensation, reparations, and redress to a victim on the basis of human or social solidarity is not yet part of mainstream legal thinking, particularly in connection with criminal proceedings."[82]

It has been stated that "[t]rafficked persons, as victims of human rights violations, have an international legal right to adequate and appropriate remedies."[83] This standard is considered and evaluated below with reference to international human rights law as well as the law specific to trafficking. The section considers the substantive content of the standard of "effective, adequate, and appropriate remedies." It concludes with an examination of the practical aspects of realizing the right to a remedy in the case of trafficking.

6.2.1. *Obligation to Remedy Violations of Human Rights Law*

This study has confirmed that trafficking will invariably involve multiple violations of human rights that are protected in treaties and, in some cases, through customary international law. It is a well established rule of international law that States have a duty to provide a domestic legal remedy to victims of human rights violations (and violations of international humanitarian law) committed in their territory.[84] In human rights law, the first formal articulation of this obligation was in the Universal Declaration of Human Rights.[85] Most international and regional human rights treaties, with the notable exceptions of the International Covenant on Economic,

---

[81] M.C. Bassiouni, "International Recognition of Victims' Rights," (2006) 6 *Human Rights Law Review* 203 (Bassiouni, "International Recognition of Victims' Rights"), at 223.

[82] Ibid. at 206.

[83] UN Trafficking Principles and Guidelines, at Guideline 9.

[84] See generally, D. Shelton, *Remedies in International Human Rights Law* (1999). See also Bassiouni, "International Recognition of Victims' Rights," at 213.

[85] UDHR, at Art. 8: "[e]veryone has the right to an effective remedy by the competent national tribunals for acts violating the fundamental rights granted him by the constitution or by law."

Social and Cultural Rights (ICESCR)[86] and the Convention on the Elimination of All Forms of Discrimination against Women (CEDAW),[87] recognize a substantive right to remedy for violations as well as a procedural right of access to remedies. The ICCPR, for example, requires States Parties to ensure "that any person whose rights or freedoms as herein recognized are violated shall have an effective remedy."[88] Similar provisions are found in the European Convention on Human Rights[89] and the American Convention on Human Rights.[90] The African Charter provides every individual with "the right to appeal to competent national organs against acts violating his fundamental rights."[91] The Convention on the Elimination of All Forms of Racial Discrimination requires States to provide effective remedies and upholds the right of all persons to seek from national tribunals "just and adequate reparation or satisfaction for any damage suffered as a result of ... discrimination."[92] The Convention against Torture is also explicit in providing victims with an "enforceable right to fair and adequate compensation including the means for as full rehabilitation as possible."[93] The Convention on the Rights of the Child includes a similar provision.[94] The Migrant Workers Convention's provision on remedies is identical to that of the ICCPR.[95] The Rome Statute of the International Criminal Court grants the Court broad powers to order convicted persons to make symbolic or financial reparations to victims.[96]

---

[86] International Covenant on Economic, Social and Cultural Rights, 993 UNTS 3, done Dec. 16, 1966, entered into force Jan. 3, 1976.

[87] Convention on the Elimination of All Forms of Discrimination against Women, 1249 UNTS 13, done Dec. 13, 1979, entered into force Sept. 3, 1981 (CEDAW).

[88] The relevant provision reads in full as follows: "[e]ach State Party to the present Covenant undertakes: (a) To ensure that any person whose rights or freedoms as herein recognized are violated shall have an effective remedy, notwithstanding that the violation has been committed by persons acting in an official capacity; (b) To ensure that any person claiming such a remedy shall have his right thereto determined by competent judicial, administrative or legislative authorities, or by any other competent authority provided for by the legal system of the State, and to develop the possibilities of judicial remedy; (c) To ensure that the competent authorities shall enforce such remedies when granted." ICCPR, at Art. 2(3). The UN Human Rights Council's General Comment No. 29 states that Article 2(3): "requires a State party to the Covenant to provide remedies for any violation of the provisions of the Covenant. This clause ... constitutes a treaty obligation inherent in the Covenant as a whole." UN Human Rights Council, "General Comment No. 29: States of Emergency," UN Doc. CCPR/C/21/Rev.1/Add.11, Aug. 31, 2001, at para. 14. See also HRC General Comment No. 31. Note further ICCPR, at Arts. 9(5) (granting victims of unlawful arrest or detention an enforceable right to compensation) and 14(6) (dealing with compensation for miscarriage of justice).

[89] "Everyone whose rights and freedoms as set forth in this Convention are violated shall have an effective remedy before a national authority": European Human Rights Convention, at Art. 13.

[90] American Convention on Human Rights, at Art. 25.

[91] African Charter, at Art. 7(1)(a).

[92] International Convention on the Elimination of All Forms of Racial Discrimination, 660 UNTS 195, done Dec. 21, 1965, entered into force Jan. 4, 1969, at Art. 6.

[93] Torture Convention, at Art. 14.

[94] CRC, at Art. 39.

[95] Migrant Workers Convention, at Art. 83. Note that the Convention also provides for an "enforceable right to compensation" with respect to unlawful detention or arrest: ibid. at Art. 16(9).

[96] Rome Statute of the International Criminal Court, 2187 UNTS 90, done July 17, 1998, entered into force July 1, 2002, at Art. 73. The Court itself may establish principles related to reparations and, in

Once a treaty-based right to a remedy can be found to apply to a particular factual situation, then failure of the State to provide such remedies itself becomes an independent breach of that instrument. In the human rights context, this can mean that the State will be held responsible for a series of violations including the individual violation that gives rise to the right to a remedy as well as the breach of that right.

The obligation to provide a remedy for human rights violations may be present even when not specifically articulated in a treaty. One approach identifies this obligation as itself a norm of customary international law.[97] Cited evidence includes the previously mentioned reference in the Universal Declaration of Human Rights to the right of everyone to "an effective remedy by the competent national tribunals for acts violating the fundamental rights granted him by the constitution or by law,"[98] as well as reiterations of the right to a remedy in numerous other soft law instruments,[99] conforming State practice,[100] and the decisions of international courts and tribunals.[101] Under a slightly different approach, the duty on a State Party to provide a remedy for violations "is perhaps implicit in human rights treaties which require national implementation and whose effectiveness depends on the availability of municipal remedies."[102]

The first (and, until recently, the only) international instrument to deal specifically with the right to a remedy was the 1985 UN Declaration of Basic Principles of Justice for Victims of Crime and Abuse of Power.[103] The drafting history of the Declaration reveals its links with the nascent victim movement, as well as growing concern over the lack of recompense for those who have suffered harm not necessarily attributed to a criminal act.[104] The Declaration, which focuses on the victims

---

certain cases, may award reparations to, or in respect of, victims including restitution, compensation, and rehabilitation (Art. 75). Note that the Statute contains a range of other provisions designed to secure justice for victims including measures to facilitate their protection as well as their participation in proceedings (Arts. 43, 68).

[97] Bassiouni, "International Recognition of Victims' Rights," at 218.

[98] UDHR, at Art. 8.

[99] See, for example, "Vienna Declaration and Programme of Action," UN Doc. A/CONF.157/23, July 12, 1993, at para. 27: "[e]very State should provide an effective framework of remedies to redress human rights grievances or violations."

[100] See Bassiouni's examination of State practice in Bassiouni, "International Recognition of Victims' Rights," at 218–223.

[101] See, for example, the Inter-American Court of Human Rights in the *Velásquez Rodríguez* case: "the State has a legal duty to take reasonable steps to prevent human rights violations and to ... ensure the victim adequate compensation." *Velásquez Rodríguez v. Honduras*, Inter-Am Ct. H.R. (ser. C) No. 4, July 29, 1988 (*Velásquez Rodríguez*), at para. 174.

[102] T. Meron, *Human Rights and Humanitarian Norms as Customary Law* (1989), at 138. It has also been contended, in the case of CEDAW, that certain of its Articles, taken together, constitute such a right. See R. Cook, "State Responsibility for Violations of Women's Human Rights," (1995) 7 *Harvard Human Rights Journal* 125, at 168–169.

[103] UN General Assembly, "Declaration of Basic Principles of Justice for Victims of Crime and Abuse of Power," UN Doc. A/40/53, Nov. 29, 1985 ("Basic Principles for Victims of Crime and Abuse of Power").

[104] For an overview of the drafting history of the Declaration, see R.S. Clarke, *The United Nations Crime Prevention and Criminal Justice Program: Formulation of Standards and Efforts at Their*

of *domestic* crimes committed by *individuals,* affirms that such persons[105] are to be treated with compassion and with respect for their dignity and are entitled to access to justice and fair treatment, including judicial and administrative processes that are responsive to the needs of victims.[106] In respect of remedies, the Declaration affirms that those responsible for the harm (including the State where it can be deemed responsible for the harm inflicted) should make fair restitution to the victims, their families, or their dependants. Such restitution should include the return of property or payment for the harm or loss suffered, reimbursement of expenses incurred as a result of the victimization, the provision of services, and the restoration of rights.[107] Where compensation is not fully available from the offender or other sources, the State should endeavor to provide compensation to victims and their families.[108] The establishment of national funds for compensation to victims is encouraged.[109] While these provisions are identified as applying only to victims of crime, they would be relevant to victims of violations of international norms (for example, the prohibition on trafficking or the prohibition on sex-based discrimination) to the extent that these have been incorporated into national criminal law.

The Declaration includes a short section on victims of "abuse of power," defined as:

> persons who, individually or collectively, have suffered harm, including physical or mental injury, emotional suffering, economic loss or substantial impairment of their fundamental rights, through acts or omissions that do not yet constitute violations of national criminal laws but of internationally recognized norms relating to human rights.[110]

The very limited provisions on victims of abuse of power include a short and qualified reference to the issue of remedies:

> States should consider incorporating into the national law norms proscribing abuses of power and providing remedies to victims of such abuses. In particular, such remedies should include restitution and/or compensation, and necessary material, medical, psychological and social assistance and support.[111]

Implementation (1994). See also G.M. Kerrigan, "Historical Development of the United Nations Declaration," in M.C. Bassiouni ed., *International Protection of Victims* (1998) 7 *Nouvelles Etudes Pénales* 91; and *Guide for Policy Makers on the Implementation of the United Nations Declaration of Basic Principles of Justice for Victims of Crime and Abuse of Power,* UN Doc. E/CN.15/1998/CRP.4, Apr. 17, 1988.

[105] "Victims of crime" are defined as "persons who, individually or collectively, have suffered harm, including physical or mental injury, emotional suffering, economic loss or substantial impairment of their fundamental rights, through acts or omissions that are in violation of criminal laws ... including those laws proscribing criminal abuse of power." "Basic Principles for Victims of Crime and Abuse of Power," at para. 1.

[106] Ibid. at paras. 4–6.

[107] Ibid. at paras. 8–11.

[108] Ibid. at para. 12.

[109] Ibid. at para. 13.

[110] Ibid. at para. 18. Further on this unclear category of victims, see L.L. Lamborn, "The United Nations Declaration on Victims: Incorporating 'Abuse of Power,'" (1987) 19 *Rutgers Law Journal* 59.

[111] "Basic Principles for Victims of Crime and Abuse of Power," at para. 19.

The rules on remedies and reparation applicable to human rights violations committed by or implicating States have been clarified with the adoption, by the General Assembly in 2005, of the Basic Principles and Guidelines on the Right to a Remedy and Reparation for Victims of Gross Violations of International Human Rights Law and Serious Violations of International Humanitarian Law (Principles and Guidelines on the Right to a Remedy and Reparation).[112] This instrument has been described as an international bill of rights for victims of international crimes.[113] It does not create new obligations for States – rather, it seeks to "identify mechanisms, modalities, procedures and methods for the implementation of existing legal obligations under international human rights law and international humanitarian law."[114]

While applicable only to the worst human rights and humanitarian law violations, the Principles and Guidelines on the Right to a Remedy and Reparation serve to reaffirm some of the most important principles relating to remedies for all violations. For example, it confirms that the general obligation on States to ensure respect for and to implement human rights law includes an obligation to ensure equal and effective access to justice and the availability of remedies.[115] It also confirms that the right to a remedy for gross violations of human rights, a term that would incorporate egregious cases of trafficking,[116] includes the rights of access to justice, reparation for harm suffered, and access to information concerning violations and reparation mechanisms.[117] Access to justice is seen as including protection of victims' privacy and safety in the course of any legal proceedings as well as measures to ensure that victims can actually exercise their rights to a remedy.[118]

The Principles and Guidelines on the Right to a Remedy and Reparation identify the purpose of reparations as being to promote justice by redressing violations.[119] Reparations are, as noted above, linked to responsibility: A State is required to

---

[112] UN General Assembly, "Basic Principles and Guidelines on the Right to a Remedy and Reparation for Victims of Gross Violations of International Human Rights Law and Serious Violations of International Humanitarian Law," UN Doc. A/RES/60/147, Dec. 16, 2005 ("Principles and Guidelines on the Right to a Remedy and Reparation"). For a detailed analysis of the drafting history and substantive provisions of this instrument, see Bassiouni, "International Recognition of Victims' Rights," at 247–278; and Redress Trust, "Implementing Victims' Rights: A Handbook on the Basic Principles and Guidelines on the Right to a Remedy and Reparations" (2006).

[113] Bassiouni, "International Recognition of Victims' Rights," at 203.

[114] "Principles and Guidelines on the Right to a Remedy and Reparation," at Preambular para. 7.

[115] Ibid. at para. 3.

[116] The term "gross violations of human rights" is not defined in the "Principles and Guidelines on the Right to a Remedy and Reparation." Late in the drafting process, it was proposed to be defined as meaning "unlawful deprivation of the right to life, torture or other cruel, inhuman treatment or punishment, enforced disappearance, slavery, slave trade and related practices, deprivation of the rights of persons before the law and similar serious violations of fundamental rights and freedoms and norms guaranteed under applicable international law." Bassiouni, "International Recognition of Victims' Rights," at 251.

[117] "Principles and Guidelines on the Right to a Remedy and Reparation," at paras. 12, 15, 24.

[118] Ibid. at para. 12–14.

[119] Ibid. at para. 15.

provide reparation for those acts or omissions that can be attributed to it. In relation to acts that cannot be attributed to the State, the responsibility for reparation falls on the perpetrator, and judgments to this effect should be effectively enforced by the State.[120] If it is not possible to secure reparations for victims in this way, then the State itself should endeavor to ensure the provision of reparations and other assistance.[121] This instrument confirms that reparation for victims of gross violations of human rights should be full and effective while respecting the principles of appropriateness and proportionality.[122] Reparation covers the accepted range of remedial elements including restitution, compensation, and rehabilitation.[123] Guarantees of nonrepetition are also highlighted as an additional, important element that aims above and beyond the individual victim and focus, in particular by ensuring prevention of future violations.[124]

6.2.2. *Right to a Remedy for Violence against Women*

The relationship between trafficking and violence against women was explored and confirmed in Chapter 3.4, as was the obligation on States to respond effectively to violence against women. An essential part of that general obligation is a concurrent legal duty to provide just and effective remedies for women subjected to such violence. All major legal and policy instruments relating to violence against women affirm the importance of remedies. These include the Inter-American Convention on Violence against Women,[125] the UN Declaration on Violence against Women,[126] CEDAW General Recommendation No. 19,[127] and the Beijing Platform for Action.[128]

---

[120] Ibid.

[121] Ibid. at para. 16.

[122] Ibid. at para. 18.

[123] Ibid.

[124] Ibid. at para. 23.

[125] American Convention on the Prevention, Punishment and Eradication of Violence against Women, 1438 UNTS 63, done June 9, 1994, entered into force Mar. 5, 1995 (Inter-American Convention on Violence against Women), at Art. 7(g): women victims of violence to have "effective access to restitution, reparations or just and effective remedies."

[126] UN General Assembly, "Declaration on the Elimination of Violence against Women," UN Doc. A/RES/48/104, Dec. 20, 1993, at para. 4(d) (States to provide women subjected to violence with "access to the mechanisms of justice and, as provided for by national legislation, to just and effective remedies for the harm that they have suffered; States should also inform women of their rights in seeking redress through such mechanisms").

[127] UN Committee on the Elimination of Discrimination against Women, "General Recommendation No. 19: Violence against Women," UN Doc. A/47/38, Jan. 29, 1992, at para. 24(i) (provision of effective complaints procedures and remedies, including compensation). See also UN General Assembly, "Crime Prevention and Criminal Justice Measures to Eliminate Violence against Women," UN Doc. A/RES/52/86, Dec. 12, 1997, Annex, at para. 10(c) (urging States to ensure women victims of violence receive "prompt and fair redress" including restitution or compensation).

[128] Beijing Declaration and Platform for Action, at paras. 124(d) (States to provide victims of violence against women, including trafficked persons, "access to just and effective remedies, including

A notable nonlegal instrument that deals specifically with this issue is the Nairobi Declaration on Women's and Girls' Right to a Remedy and Reparation, adopted at a regional meeting of women's rights activists and advocates in 2007.[129] The Declaration, which focuses particularly on the right to a remedy for conflict-related violations, explicitly recognizes the particular challenges involved in developing and applying remedies for violence against women. It affirms, for example, that the particular circumstances in which women and girls are made victims of crimes and human rights violations in situations of conflict require approaches specially adapted to their needs, interests, and priorities. It identifies basic principles related to women and girls' right to a remedy and reparation, the issue of access to reparation, and key aspects of reparation for women and girls. Importantly, the Declaration recognizes that reparation should extend beyond the immediate reasons and consequences of the crimes and violations: "they must aim to address the political and structural inequalities that negatively shape women's and girls' lives."[130]

As with all other human rights violations, the form and extent of remedies required for trafficking as violence against women will depend on the nature and circumstances of the breach and may include access to justice, reparation for harm suffered, restitution, compensation, satisfaction, rehabilitation, and guarantees of nonrepetition and prevention. Civil remedies such as protection orders, civil laws to sue perpetrators, and victim compensation funds can be an important adjunct to remedies available under criminal and administrative law.[131] The Committee on the Elimination of Discrimination against Women has clarified that reparation should be proportionate to the physical and mental harm undergone and to the gravity of the violations suffered.[132] Other international human rights mechanisms have

---

compensation and indemnification and healing of victims") and 124(h) (victims of violence against women to have access to the mechanisms of justice and effective remedies for the harms they have incurred, and to be informed of their legal rights). Note also the Beijing +5 Outcome Document, at paras. 69(b) (governments to take measures to provide victims with avenues for redress) and 98(a) (governments and international organizations should "improve knowledge and awareness of the remedies available" for violations of women's human rights).

[129] "Nairobi Declaration on Women's and Girls' Right to a Remedy and Reparation," adopted at the International Meeting on Women's and Girls' Right to a Remedy and Reparation, held in Nairobi, Mar. 19–21, 2007.

[130] Ibid. at Principle 3(H).

[131] See further, "In-Depth Study on All Forms of Violence against Women: Report of the Secretary-General," UN Doc. A/61/122/Add.1, July 6, 2006, at 87.

[132] *AT v. Hungary*, CEDAW Comm. No. 2/2003, UN Doc. CEDAW/C/32/D/2/2003, decided Jan. 26, 2005, at para. 9.6(II)(vi). Note also *Fernandes v. Brazil*, in which the Inter-American Commission on Human Rights recommended that a victim of domestic violence receive "appropriate symbolic and actual compensation" for the violence that she had suffered, as well as for the failure of the State to "provide rapid and effective remedies, for the impunity that has surrounded the case for more than 15 years, and for making it impossible, as a result of that delay, to institute timely proceedings for redress and compensation in the civil sphere": *Fernandes v. Brazil*, Case No. 12.051, Report No. 54/01, Inter-AmCHR Doc. OEA/Ser.L/V/II.111 Doc. 20 rev. (Inter-Am Comm HR, Apr. 16, 2001), at para. 61, Recommendation 3.

noted the particular issues and concerns that will arise with regard to remedies for violence against women.[133]

6.2.3. *The Right to a Remedy in the Specific Context of Trafficking*

To what extent has the general international legal right to a remedy been affirmed, or even expanded, through treaties and other legal and nonlegal instruments dealing specifically with trafficking?

The Organized Crime Convention requires States Parties to "establish appropriate procedures to provide access to compensation and restitution for victims of offences covered by the Convention."[134] While this provision does not *require* that victims be guaranteed compensation or restitution, it is evident that the State's legislative or other measures must provide procedures whereby it can be sought or claimed.[135] The Trafficking Protocol, drafted concurrently with Organized Crime Convention, is more specific. In one of its very few mandatory victim support provisions, the Protocol requires States Parties to ensure that their domestic legal systems contain measures that offer victims of trafficking the possibility of obtaining compensation for damage suffered.[136] Crucially, this provision does not amount to an obligation to provide remedies. To discharge their obligation under the Protocol, States Parties need only offer the *legal possibility* of compensation.[137] According to the Legislative Guide, the compensation requirement under both the Organized Crime Convention and the Trafficking Protocol would be satisfied by the State establishing one or more of three options: provisions allowing victims to sue offenders for civil damages; provisions allowing criminal courts to award criminal damages (paid by offenders) or to impose orders for compensation or restitution against persons convicted of trafficking offenses; or provisions establishing dedicated funds or schemes to allow victims to claim compensation from the State for injuries or

---

[133] For example, the Special Rapporteur on Torture has noted that stigma is a central obstacle hindering justice for victims of sexual violence: "Report of the Special Rapporteur on Torture and Other Cruel, Inhuman or Degrading Treatment or Punishment, Manfred Nowak," UN Doc. A/HRC/7/3, Jan. 15, 2008, at para. 65.

[134] Organized Crime Convention, at Art. 25(2). Note that Article 25 is subject to a curious Interpretative Note: "[w]hile the purpose of this article is to concentrate on the physical protection of victims, the Ad Hoc Committee was cognizant of the need for protection of the rights of individuals as accorded under applicable international law." Travaux Préparatoires *for the Organized Crime Convention and Protocols*, at 224.

[135] *Legislative Guide*, at Part 1, at 170.

[136] Trafficking Protocol, at Art. 6(6). Note that this provision represents a retreat from earlier drafts in which the obligation was formulated in more precise terms as follows: "States Parties shall ensure that their legislative frameworks contain measures that provide victims of trafficking in persons with access to adequate procedures for seeking: (a) Compensation for damages, including compensation coming from fines, penalties or, where possible, forfeited proceeds or instrumentalities of perpetrators of trafficking in persons; and (b) Restitution from the offenders." See Travaux Préparatoires *for the Organized Crime Convention and Protocols*, at 365–373.

[137] *Legislative Guide*, at Part 1, para. 368.

damages.[138] The offense of trafficking should be capable of forming the basis of a claim under at least one of these options.[139] Other interpretative materials support this position.[140]

The European Trafficking Convention takes a much more comprehensive approach than the Trafficking Protocol to the issue of victim compensation and legal redress. The provision on remedies commences with a requirement that victims be provided with information on relevant judicial and administrative proceedings[141] (relating, *inter alia*, to possibilities for obtaining compensation and regularization of immigration status)[142] as well as access to legal assistance.[143] The Explanatory Report highlights the crucial link between legal status and remedies, noting that "it would be very difficult for [victims] to obtain compensation if they were unable to remain in the country where the proceedings take place."[144] The Convention confirms that victims have a right to monetary compensation from convicted traffickers in respect of both material injury (such as the cost of medical treatment) and nonmaterial injury (such as emotional suffering).[145] The Explanatory Report notes that a victim's right to compensation consists in a claim against the perpetrator of harm. If criminal courts are not empowered to determine civil liability toward victims, "it must be possible for victims to submit their claims to civil courts with jurisdiction in the matter and powers to award damages with interest."[146] The Convention confronts the reality that the State will not always be able to enforce compensation orders against traffickers. It thereby requires States Parties to take steps to guarantee the compensation of victims. The means of guaranteeing compensation are not mandated, although the Convention suggests several examples including the establishment of a special fund or initiatives aimed at social assistance or reintegration of victims.[147] The possibility of State compensation schemes being funded by the seized proceeds of trafficking is specifically noted.[148]

The obligation to provide effective and appropriate remedies to victims of trafficking is referred to or otherwise confirmed by UN organs,[149] human rights

---

[138] Ibid. at Part 1, at 170, and Part 2, at 285–286.

[139] Ibid. at Part 1, at 170.

[140] See, for example, UNODC Model Law, at 53–58.

[141] European Trafficking Convention, at Art. 15(1).

[142] European Trafficking Convention Explanatory Report, at para. 192.

[143] European Trafficking Convention, at Art. 15(2). On the extent of required assistance and whether it includes a right to free legal aid, see European Trafficking Convention Explanatory Report, at para. 196.

[144] European Trafficking Convention Explanatory Report, at para. 192.

[145] European Trafficking Convention, at Art. 15(3).

[146] European Trafficking Convention Explanatory Report, at para. 197.

[147] European Trafficking Convention, at Art. 15(4).

[148] Ibid. On this point, see the discussion on use of confiscated assets to support victims of trafficking at Chapter 7.4.2 of this volume.

[149] See, for example, UN General Assembly, "Trafficking in Women and Girls," UN Doc. A/RES/63/156, Jan. 30, 2009, at para. 19, referring (in the context of support and assistance measures for trafficked

bodies,[150] and through a range of regional and international policy instruments.[151] The UN Trafficking Principles and Guidelines are particularly strong on this point, declaring that "States should ensure that trafficked persons are given access to effective and appropriate remedies."[152]

6.2.4. *Standards and Forms of Remedy*

The substantive content of the obligation to provide "effective remedies" has been extensively considered by international and regional treaty bodies. It is generally accepted that remedies or reparation should be proportionate to the gravity of harm suffered[153] as well as "accessible, affordable, timely and effective."[154] Other terms that are commonly used in the context of remedies for trafficking include "adequate" and "appropriate."[155] The precise nature of the required remedy will, of course, depend on the primary obligation and the nature of the violation. In relation to violations of the ICCPR, for example, the UN Human Rights Committee has referred to the need to take account of the special vulnerability of certain categories of persons;

women and girls) to "the possibility of obtaining compensation for damages suffered"; and UN Human Rights Council, "Trafficking in Persons, Especially Women and Children," UN Doc. A/HRC/RES/11/3, June 17, 2009, at para. 1 ("[a]ffirms that it is essential to place the protection of human rights at the centre of measures taken to prevent and end trafficking in persons, and to protect, assist and provide access to adequate redress to victims, including the possibility of obtaining compensation from the perpetrators"). Note that these references, typical of those incorporated in General Assembly and Human Rights Council resolutions of the past several years, refer only to compensation and do not pronounce directly on the issue of a victim right to a remedy.

[150] See, for example, UN Human Rights Committee, "Concluding Observations: Japan," UN Doc. CCPR/C/JPN/CO/5, Dec. 18, 2008, at para. 23; UN Committee on Economic, Social and Cultural Rights, "Concluding Observations: Latvia," UN Doc. E/C.12/LVA/CO/1, Jan. 7, 2008, at para. 47; UN Committee against Torture, "Concluding Observations: Serbia," UN Doc. CAT/C/SRB/CO/1, Jan. 19, 2009, at para. 21; UN Committee on the Elimination of Discrimination against Women, "Concluding Observations: Singapore," UN Doc. CEDAW/C/SGP/CO/3, Aug. 10, 2007, at para. 22; "Promotion and Protection of All Human Rights, Civil, Political, Economic, Social and Cultural Rights, Including the Right to Development: Report submitted by the Special Rapporteur on trafficking in persons, especially women and children, Joy Ngozi Ezeilo," UN Doc. A/HRC/10/16, Feb. 20, 2009, at para. 44.

[151] See, for example, Association of Southeast Asian Nations (ASEAN), *Criminal Justice Responses to Trafficking in Persons – ASEAN Practitioner Guidelines* (Jakarta, 2007), at Part 1.A.6: "[t]o the extent possible, the legal framework should enable victims to seek and receive remedies including compensation from appropriate sources including those convicted guilty of trafficking and related offences." See also the Brussels Declaration, at para. 16; ECOWAS Initial Plan of Action, at 3, para. 6; OAS Recommendations on Trafficking in Persons, at Section IV(8).

[152] UN Trafficking Principles and Guidelines, at Principle 17. See also Guideline 9: "[t]rafficked persons, as victims of human rights violations, have an international legal right to adequate and appropriate remedies."

[153] "Principles and Guidelines on the Right to a Remedy and Reparation," at Principle 15.

[154] UN Committee on Economic, Social and Cultural Rights, "General Comment No. 9: The Domestic Application of the Covenant," UN Doc. E/C.12/1998/24, Dec. 3, 1998 (CESCR General Comment No. 9), at para. 9.

[155] See the references contained in notes 126 to 133 in this chapter.

the importance of States Parties establishing appropriate judicial and administrative mechanisms for addressing claims of rights violations under domestic law; the key role of the judiciary in assuring rights and remedies; and the importance of administrative mechanisms giving effect to the remedies-related obligation to investigate allegations of violations promptly, thoroughly, and effectively through independent and impartial bodies.[156] In relation to violations of the ICESCR, the relevant treaty body has noted that the right to an effective remedy may require administrative action as well as – or instead of – judicial remedies. The selection of appropriate remedies must depend on what kind of action is required to make the relevant Covenant right fully effective.[157] Other human rights treaty bodies have affirmed the need for adequate and appropriate remedies that take into account the circumstances of the breach.[158]

As noted in Chapter 4, the international law of State responsibility identifies a range of generally required actions for reparation of an international wrong, including restitution, compensation, rehabilitation, satisfaction, and guarantees of nonrepetition.[159] The Principles and Guidelines on the Right to a Remedy and Reparation affirm the relevance of these elements for serious violations of human rights.[160] The following paragraphs define and briefly explore each of these elements with reference to the specific situation and needs of trafficked persons.

Compensation is the most common form of remedy and is payable for damage caused by an internationally wrongful act to the extent that such damage is economically assessable and "not made good by restitution."[161] In other words, monetary compensation should be intended to remedy the damage caused by the breach to the extent that this is possible.[162] Compensation should be "appropriate and

---

[156] HRC General Comment No. 31.

[157] CESCR General Comment No. 9, at para. 9.

[158] See, for example, UN Committee on the Elimination of Racial Discrimination, "General Recommendation No. 23: Indigenous Peoples," UN Doc. A/52/18, Annex V, at 122, Aug. 18, 1997, at para. 5 (noting that restitution is the appropriate remedy for dispossession of land and that "[o]nly when this is for factual reasons not possible, the right to restitution should be substituted by the right to just, fair and prompt compensation"); and UN Committee on the Rights of the Child, "General Comment No. 5: General Measures of Implementation of the Convention on the Rights of the Child," UN Doc. CRC/GC/2003/5, Oct. 3, 2003, at para. 24 ("[c]hildren's special and dependent status creates real difficulties for them in pursuing remedies for breaches of their rights. So States need to give particular attention to ensuring that there are effective, child-sensitive procedures available to children and their representatives ... Where rights are found to have been breached, there should be appropriate reparation, including compensation, and, where needed, measures to promote physical and psychological recovery, rehabilitation and reintegration, as required by article 39.").

[159] See Chapter 4.4.1 in this book.

[160] "Principles and Guidelines on the Right to a Remedy and Reparation," at paras. 18–23.

[161] International Law Commission (ILC), *Draft Articles on Responsibility of States for Internationally Wrongful Acts, Report of the International Law Commission on the Work of Its Fifty-third Session*, UN GAOR, 56th Sess., Supp. No. 10, at 43, UN Doc. A/56/10 (2001), at Art. 36(1).

[162] In *Godínez Cruz*, the Inter-American Court of Human Rights held that "it is appropriate to fix the payment of 'fair compensation' in sufficiently broad terms in order to compensate, to the extent

proportional to the gravity of the violation and the circumstances of each case."[163] It can, as acknowledged in the relevant provision of the European Trafficking Convention, cover both material losses and nonmaterial or so-called moral suffering. In the case of trafficking, an effective, adequate, and appropriate remedy could include compensation payable (by the offender or by the State) under a range of heads identified by the Principles and Guidelines on the Right to a Remedy and Reparation, including physical and psychological harm, lost opportunities, loss of earnings, moral damage, and medical, legal, or other costs incurred as a result of the violation.[164] The UNODC Model Law extends this generic list by noting that court-ordered compensation could include payment for or toward: (1) costs of medical, physical, psychological, or psychiatric treatment required by the victim; (2) costs of physical and occupational therapy or rehabilitation required by the victim; (3) costs of necessary transportation, temporary childcare, temporary housing, or the movement of the victim to a place of temporary safe residence; (4) lost income and due wages according to national law and regulations regarding wages; (5) legal fees and other costs or expenses incurred, including costs incurred related to the participation of the victim in the criminal investigation and prosecution process; (6) payment for nonmaterial damages resulting from moral, physical, or psychological injury, emotional distress, pain, and suffering suffered by the victim as a result of the crime committed against him or her; and (7) any other costs or losses incurred by the victim as a direct result of being trafficked and reasonably assessed by a court.[165]

Restitution involves material, judicial, or other measures aimed at restoring the situation that existed prior to the violation, as far as this is possible. Restitution can be especially important in relation to violations of a continuing character. Effective, adequate, and appropriate actions to secure restitution in a case of trafficking may include release of the victim from detention (imposed by traffickers, the State, or any other entity), recognition of legal identity and citizenship, return of property, and safe return to the individual's place of residence.[166] It is important to note that in the context of a complex violation such as trafficking, restitution can often be problematic. For example, the pre-violation situation of many victims could itself be dangerous and restoring that situation could conceivably place the individual at risk of retrafficking or other violations of his or her rights.

Rehabilitation is a victim-centered notion that recognizes a need to ensure that persons who have suffered a violation of their human rights have their status and position "restored" in the eyes of the law as well as of the wider community.

---

possible, for the loss suffered": *Godínez Cruz v. Honduras, Interpretation of the Compensatory Damages*, Inter-Am Ct. H.R. (ser. C) No. 10, Aug. 17, 1990, at para. 27.

[163] "Principles and Guidelines on the Right to a Remedy and Reparation," at para. 20.

[164] Ibid.

[165] UNODC Model Law, at 55.

[166] Several of these examples are drawn from the "Principles and Guidelines on the Right to a Remedy and Reparation," at para. 19.

Rehabilitation should include the provision of medical and psychological care as well as legal and social services.[167] The present study has confirmed that victims of serious violations of human rights such as trafficking will inevitably require a range of support services. The rehabilitation element of reparation would impose an obligation on the offending State to provide such services.

Satisfaction and *guarantees of nonrepetition*: Satisfaction is a remedy for injuries that are not necessarily financially assessable but that can be addressed by ensuring that the violations of the victim's rights are properly acknowledged and dealt with. Measures aimed at cessation of violations, verification of the facts, and full and public disclosure of the truth (to the extent that this will not cause further harm) are examples of remedies aimed at providing satisfaction to the victim.[168] Guarantees of nonrepetition are a similarly important component of the right to a remedy in the case of trafficking due to the danger of and harm caused by retrafficking. Measures to prevent future trafficking[169] would be relevant to a discharge of this aspect of the remedies obligation, as would the effective investigation, prosecution, and sanctioning of traffickers,[170] explored in detail in the following chapter. In relation to trafficking that disproportionately affects women and girls, measures aimed at modifying legal, social, and cultural practices that sustain or promote tolerance of such violence would be an important aspect of a guarantee of nonrepetition.[171]

As noted above, the form and extent of remedies required will depend on the nature and circumstances of the breach as well as on the content of the relevant primary obligation. In all cases, however, the form or forms must reflect and advance the obligation on the offending State to, as far as possible, wipe out the consequences of the breach and reestablish the situation that existed prior to its occurrence.[172] It is important to note that States providing remedies do not have an unfettered discretion in deciding the appropriateness of various options. In the *LaGrand Case*, for example, the International Court of Justice ruled that satisfaction in the form of an apology for failure to discharge an obligation of consular notification was insufficient in a situation whereby the individual involved had been subject to prolonged detention or convicted and sentenced to severe penalties.[173] The Court has further ruled, in a different case, that an obligation to review and reconsider potential breaches of

---

[167] Ibid. at Principle 21.

[168] "Principles and Guidelines on the Right to a Remedy and Reparation," at Principles 22(a) and 22(b).

[169] Discussed further, at Chapter 8 of this volume.

[170] Bassiouni, "International Recognition of Victims' Rights," at 271.

[171] This obligation to work toward modification of discriminatory or otherwise harmful practices and traditions is contained in the CEDAW, at Arts. 2(f), 5(a); Inter-American Convention on Violence against Women, at Art. 7(e); and the Protocol to the African Charter on Human and Peoples' Rights on the Rights of Women in Africa, OAU Doc. CAB/LEG/66.6, done July 11, 2003, entered into force Nov. 25, 2005, at Arts. 2(2), 5.

[172] *Factory at Chorzow (Germany v. Poland), Merits*, [1928] PCIJ Rep, Series A, No. 17, at 47.

[173] *LaGrand (Germany v. United States)*, [2001] ICJ Rep 466, at para. 123.

the relevant treaty could not be done through informal means but must engage the judicial process.[174]

6.2.5. *Information and Other Means of Accessing Remedies*

The right to a remedy is often not effectively available to trafficked persons. Sometimes this is because they are incorrectly identified, arrested, and deported. Even when identified as such, trafficked persons are often removed from the country of destination before they have a chance to seek remedies for the harm they have suffered. As noted by the UN Human Rights Committee, such a failure by the State "effectively prevents women [and equally all trafficked persons] from pursuing a remedy for the violation of their rights."[175] Sometimes national laws prevent noncitizens, including those unlawfully present, from accessing certain forms of remedies such as criminal compensation. Even without such restrictive laws, it is clear that in most situations, the presence of the victim in the country where the remedy is being sought is, in practice, an additional and important corequisite for realizing the right to a remedy. The need for specific provisions enabling trafficked persons to remain safely in the country in which the remedy is being sought for the duration of any criminal, civil, or administrative proceedings is noted in the Explanatory Report to the European Trafficking Convention as a natural corollary to the right to a remedy.[176] The right of victims to be involved in legal proceedings (recognized in the Trafficking Protocol and discussed in Chapter 5.4 of this volume) is also relevant in this context. The availability of remedies is tied up with other rights and violations. For example, victims who are denied assistance on the basis of their inability or unwillingness to cooperate with legal authorities will generally find that they are also unable to access remedies.

Often victims of trafficking will be denied their rights in this area simply because they lack information on the possibilities and processes for accessing remedies. A right of access to effective remedies means that in addition to making such remedies available under criminal or civil law, States should ensure that victims are provided with information and assistance that will enable them to actually secure the compensation or restitution to which they are entitled. As noted in the Explanatory Report to the European Trafficking Convention, "people cannot claim their rights if they do not know about them."[177] States Parties to that Convention are required to

---

[174] *Avena and Other Mexican Nationals (Mexico v the United States)*, [2004] ICJ Rep 12, at para. 143.
[175] UN Human Rights Committee, "Concluding Observations: Israel," UN Doc. CCPR/C/79/Add.93, Aug. 18, 1998, at para. 16.
[176] European Trafficking Convention Explanatory Report, at para. 192. See also UN Trafficking Principles and Guidelines, at Guideline 9.3 and the discussion at Chapter 5.4.3 of this volume on the right to remain during legal proceedings.
[177] European Trafficking Convention Explanatory Report, at para. 192. The report also notes that provision of information on the possibility of obtaining a residency permit will be very important for

ensure that victims are provided with both information and legal assistance for the purpose of pursuing the remedies to which they are entitled.[178] A similar entitlement is proposed in the UN Trafficking Principles and Guidelines.[179] The Principles and Guidelines on the Right to a Remedy are even more specific in identifying the steps to be taken by States toward ensuring access to justice for victims of serious human rights violations. These include: dissemination of information about all available remedies; development of measures to minimize inconvenience to victims and their representatives; protection against unlawful interference with victims' privacy and ensuring their safety from intimidation and retaliation before, during, and after judicial, administrative, or other proceedings that affect their interests; provision of proper assistance to victims seeking access to justice; and ensuring availability of all appropriate legal, diplomatic, and consular means to ensure that victims can exercise their rights to a remedy.[180]

Increasing attention to confiscation of assets in the context of trafficking in persons should also help assist in the enforcement of criminal or civil compensation claims against their exploiters. This is particularly the case where States follow international and regional policy direction with respect to ensuring that confiscated assets are made available for the purposes of victim support and compensation.[181]

In conclusion, if a State is directly or indirectly involved in the violation of an individual's right then that same State must make a genuine attempt to provide the injured person with some measure of reparation or redress. In the present context, this could involve the State ensuring the possibility of compensation and actively assisting a victim of trafficking to pursue a civil claim for damages and/or lost earnings against a trafficker. It could also require the State itself to provide compensation, particularly in situations where the State has fallen short of the due diligence standard when it comes to preventing trafficking, investigating and prosecuting traffickers, and protecting victims. The obligation on States to provide remedies to victims of trafficking requires a genuine effort on the part of individual States to address the legal, procedural, and attitudinal obstacles that commonly thwart access to remedies.[182]

---

victims who are illegally in the country, as it would be very difficult for a victim to obtain compensation if she is unable to remain in the country.

[178] European Trafficking Convention, at Arts. 15(1), 15(2).

[179] UN Trafficking Principles and Guidelines, at Guideline 9.2.

[180] "Principles and Guidelines on the Right to a Remedy and Reparation," at Principle 12.

[181] On this issue, see the discussion at Chapter 7.4.2 in this book.

[182] For a consideration of these obstacles within a domestic context, see J. Lam and K. Skrivankova, *Opportunities and Obstacles: Ensuring Access to Compensation for Trafficked Persons in the UK* (Anti-Slavery International, 2009).

7

Obligations of an Effective Criminal Justice Response

The existence of a general culture of impunity for those involved in the exploitation of trafficking victims is beyond dispute. Traffickers and their accomplices are seldom arrested, investigated, prosecuted, or convicted. As noted elsewhere in this book, victims of trafficking are rarely identified and too often criminalized. Despite being the key to successful prosecutions, victims are rarely brought into the criminal justice process as witnesses. Criminal justice responses to trafficking have been subject to severe criticism, with many commentators viewing such an approach as unsuitable to the nature of the trafficking phenomenon and inevitably damaging to the rights of victims.[1] The present chapter takes a different position: A criminal justice response to trafficking that prioritizes rights and seeks both to end impunity for traffickers and to secure justice for victims is in full conformity with international law and deserves to take its rightful place as a critical component of any lasting solution to trafficking.

The international community has acknowledged the need for an effective criminal justice response to trafficking and, through legal and policy developments detailed in this chapter, confirmed a number of important "markers" or indicators of such a response. It is widely agreed, for example, that trafficking, as defined in international law, should be criminalized; that traffickers should be investigated, prosecuted, and appropriately punished; that proceeds of trafficking crimes should be confiscated; and, in cases of trafficking across national borders, that international legal and operational collaboration should aim to ensure that there are no safe havens for traffickers. The following analysis seeks to examine these standards from the perspective of international law with a view to determining, as precisely as possible, their substantive content and normative value.

---

[1] See, for example, H. Askola, *Legal Responses to Trafficking in Women for Sexual Exploitation in the European Union* (2007), esp. at chapter 5; and M. Segrave, "Order at the Border," 32 (2009) *Women's Studies International Forum* 251.

7.1. THE OBLIGATION OF CRIMINALIZATION

Criminalization of trafficking is widely considered an essential component of a comprehensive national response to trafficking, providing the basis for efforts aimed at ending impunity for traffickers and securing justice for victims. From an international perspective, an obligation to criminalize defined conduct promotes efficient international cooperation in the investigation and prosecution of trafficking cases,[2] and prevents the development of legislative "safe havens."[3]

While the present section identifies a separate and independent obligation to criminalize trafficking, the issue of criminalization should also be considered in connection with the discharge of other obligations. For example, it could be argued that States failing to fully and effectively criminalize trafficking are not meeting their obligations to protect victims of trafficking[4] and to prevent future trafficking.[5] In addition, they may also be failing to provide the necessary structures within which State agencies can investigate, prosecute, and adjudicate cases of trafficking in persons to the required standard of due diligence.[6] Failure to criminalize in accordance with the international legal definition could also impact on the ability of States to effectively discharge their obligations with respect to legal and other forms of cooperation. The specific contours of the criminalization obligation are discussed below, along with the related issue of jurisdiction.

An obligation to criminalize trafficking is well established in international treaty law. The criminalization provision of the Trafficking Protocol[7] has been described as "a central and mandatory obligation of all States Parties to [that instrument]."[8] The European Trafficking Convention contains an identical provision.[9] The

---

[2] UN Office on Drugs and Crime, *Legislative Guides for the Implementation of the United Nations Convention against Transnational Organized Crime and the Protocols Thereto*, UN Sales No. E.05.V.2 (2004) (*Legislative Guide*), at Part 2, para. 35. The *Legislative Guide* further notes that "[t]he requirement (in the Trafficking Protocol) to criminalize trafficking was intended as an element of a global counterstrategy that would also include the provision of support and assistance for victims and that would integrate the fight against trafficking into the broader efforts against transnational organized crime": ibid.

[3] The Explanatory Report to the European Trafficking Convention further notes the need to harmonize national laws as a way of "avoiding a criminal preference for committing offences in a Party which previously had less strict rules": Council of Europe, *Explanatory Report on the Convention on Action against Trafficking in Human Beings*, ETS 197, 16.V.2005 (European Trafficking Convention Explanatory Report), at para. 216.

[4] See further, Chapter 5 in this volume.

[5] See further, Chapter 8 in this volume.

[6] See further, Chapter 4 in this volume.

[7] Protocol to Prevent, Suppress and Punish Trafficking in Persons, Especially Women and Children, supplementing the United Nations Convention against Transnational Organized Crime, done Nov. 15, 2000, GA Res. 55/25, Annex II, UN GAOR, 55th Sess., Supp. No. 49, at 53, UN Doc. A/45/49 (Vol. I) (2001), entered into force Dec. 25, 2003 (Trafficking Protocol), at Art. 5.

[8] *Legislative Guide*, at Part 2, para. 36.

[9] Council of Europe Convention on Action against Trafficking in Human Beings and its Explanatory Report, ETS 197, 16.V.2005, done May 16, 2005, entered into force Feb. 1, 2008 (European Trafficking

Convention on Preventing and Combating Trafficking in Women and Children for Prostitution (SAARC Convention) also requires criminalization of trafficking and related offenses as defined in that instrument.[10] A requirement to criminalize trafficking in women can be inferred from the Convention on the Elimination of All Forms of Discrimination against Women (CEDAW),[11] and an equivalent requirement in respect of children can be inferred from the Convention on the Rights of the Child (CRC).[12] International[13] and regional[14] policy instruments confirm the

Convention), at Art. 18. A similar obligation is set forth in the draft EU Framework Decision 2009 Proposal: Commission of the European Communities, Proposal for a Framework Decision on preventing and combating trafficking in human beings, and protecting victims, repealing Framework Decision 2002/629/JHA, COM(2009) 136 final, Mar. 25, 2009, at Art. 1. Although this is no longer an active draft following the recent entry into force of the Treaty of Lisbon (Treaty of Lisbon amending the Treaty on European Union and the Treaty establishing the European Community, OJ C 306/1, done Dec. 13, 2007, entered into force Dec. 1, 2009), its substantive provisions have recently been reintroduced for negotiation. In the words of the European Commission, the new Proposal for a Directive on Trafficking "is, to its content, essentially identical to the previous Proposal for a Framework Decision": European Commission, Proposal for a Directive of the European Parliament and of the Council on preventing and combating trafficking in human beings, and protecting victims, repealing Framework Decision 2002/629/JHA, COM(2010) 95 final, Mar. 29, 2010 (EC Directive 2010 Proposal), at 6.

[10] South Asian Association for Regional Cooperation, Convention on Preventing and Combating Trafficking in Women and Children for Prostitution, done Jan. 5, 2002, entered into force Dec. 1, 2005 (SAARC Convention), at Art. III. Note that the scope of this provision is narrowed by the fact that the Convention applies only to trafficking in children and women for the purposes of prostitution.

[11] Convention on the Elimination of All Forms of Discrimination Against Women, 1249 UNTS 13, done Dec. 13, 1979, entered into force Sept. 3, 1981 (CEDAW), at Art. 6: "States Parties shall take all appropriate measures, including legislation, to suppress all forms of traffic in women." Article 2 also spells out States' obligation to use legislative and other measures to achieve CEDAW rights.

[12] Convention on the Rights of the Child, 1577 UNTS 3, done Nov. 20, 1989, entered into force Sept. 2, 1990 (CRC), at Art. 35. Articles 34 and 36 contain more general provisions requiring States to protect children from sexual exploitation, and all other forms of exploitation respectively.

[13] See, for example, UN Economic and Social Council, Office of the United Nations High Commissioner for Human Rights, *Recommended Principles and Guidelines on Human Rights and Human Trafficking*, UN Doc. E/2002/68/Add.1, May 20, 2002 (UN Trafficking Principles and Guidelines), at Principle 12. See also a range of United Nations resolutions including UN General Assembly, "Trafficking in Women and Girls," UN Doc. A/RES/63/156, Jan. 30, 2009, at para. 11 ("[c]alls upon all Governments to criminalize all forms of trafficking in persons") and UN Human Rights Council, "Trafficking in Persons, Especially Women and Children," UN Doc. A/HRC/RES/11/3, June 17, 2009, at para. 3(b) ("[u]rges governments … [t]o criminalize trafficking in persons in all its forms and to condemn and penalize traffickers, facilitators and intermediaries, including, where applicable, by imposing sanctions against legal entities involved in the process of trafficking").

[14] See, for example, European Union, "EU Plan on Best Practices, Standards and Procedures for Combating and Preventing Trafficking in Human Beings," OJ C 2005/C 311/01, Dec. 9, 2005 (EU Plan on Best Practices), at para. 3(iii); Organization for Security and Co-operation in Europe (OSCE) Permanent Council, "OSCE Action Plan to Combat Trafficking in Human Beings," OSCE Doc. PC.DEC/557, July 24, 2003 (OSCE Action Plan), at Recommendation III(1); European Union, "Brussels Declaration on Preventing and Combating Trafficking in Human Beings," EU Doc. 14981/02, Nov. 29, 2002 (Brussels Declaration), at para. 16; Economic Community of West African States, "ECOWAS Initial Plan of Action against Trafficking in Persons (2002–2003)," Dec. 21, 2001 (ECOWAS Initial Plan of Action), at 2, para. 4; Organization of American States, "Conclusions and Recommendations of the First Meeting of National Authorities on Trafficking in Persons,"

importance of the obligation to criminalize trafficking. The international human rights treaty bodies and UN special procedures have also noted criminalization as both an obligation of States in itself and a critical component of an effective national response to trafficking in persons.[15] The key elements of the obligation to criminalize trafficking are considered further below.

7.1.1. *The Conduct to be Criminalized*

The following section considers what conduct, specifically, must be criminalized. First and foremost, States are obliged to ensure the criminalization of trafficking in accordance with its international definition. The obligation of criminalization extends to the attempting of and complicity in trafficking offenses. However, the extent of any obligation of criminalization in relation to trafficking-related conduct and use of the services of a trafficking victim is not so straightforward.

Applying the International Definition. The relevant international legal obligation identified above requires States to criminalize trafficking as it has been defined by international law. This requirement is implicit in the major treaties that include the definition along with the obligation to criminalize.[16] States are not necessarily obliged to reproduce the fairly complex international legal definition as set out in the Trafficking Protocol, the European Trafficking Convention, and other instruments.[17] However, certain core features of the international definition would

OEA/Ser. K/XXXIX, Mar. 17, 2006 (OAS Recommendations on Trafficking in Persons), at Section I(3); Memorandum of Understanding on Cooperation against Trafficking in Persons in the Greater Mekong Sub-Region, adopted on Oct. 29, 2004 in Yangon (Cambodia, China, Lao PDR, Myanmar, Thailand, and Vietnam) (COMMIT MOU), at Art. 7.

[15] See, for example, UN Human Rights Committee: "Concluding Observations: Barbados," UN Doc. CCPR/C/BRB/CO/3, May 11, 2007, at para. 8; "Concluding Observations: Kenya," UN Doc. CCPR/CO/83/KEN, Apr. 29, 2005, at para. 25; UN Committee on the Elimination of All Forms of Discrimination against Women: "Concluding Observations: Guatemala," UN Doc. CEDAW/C/GUA/CO/7, Feb. 12, 2009, at para. 24; "Concluding Observations: Lebanon," UN Doc. CEDAW/C/LBN/CO/3, Apr. 8, 2008, at para. 29; UN Committee on the Rights of the Child: "Concluding Observations: Antigua and Barbuda," UN Doc. CRC/C/15/Add.247, Sept. 3, 2004, at para. 67; UN Committee against Torture, "Concluding Observations: South Africa," UN Doc. CAT/C/ZAF/CO/1, Dec. 7, 2006, at para. 24; UN Committee on the Protection of the Rights of All Migrant Workers and Members of Their Families, "Concluding Observations: Mexico," UN Doc. CMW/C/MEX/CO/1, Dec. 20, 2006, at para. 40; "Report of Special Rapporteur on the human rights aspects of the victims of trafficking in persons, especially women and children, Sigma Huda, Addendum 1: Summary of cases transmitted to Governments and replies received," UN Doc. E/CN.4/2006/62/Add.1, March 26, 2006, at para. 90 (Malawi).

[16] The Legislative Guide to the Trafficking Protocol provides a useful insight into the importance of the definition by noting that it was intended to contribute to a standardization of the concept which in turn would "form the basis of domestic criminal offences that would be similar enough to support efficient international cooperation in investigating and prosecuting cases": *Legislative Guide*, at Part 2, para. 35.

[17] Indeed the Legislative Guide cautions against incorporation of the language of the Protocol verbatim: "[i]n drafting the domestic offences, the language used should be such that it will be

need to be included to satisfy the obligation of criminalization. A law that did not distinguish between trafficking in children and in adults, that only criminalized trafficking for sexual exploitation, or that only criminalized trafficking in women and children would not meet the international legal standard. It is also relevant to highlight two important features of the international definition: First, that definition does not require that exploitation actually take place;[18] and second, the consent of the victim does not alter the offender's criminal liability.[19]

As noted above, the central and mandatory obligation of all States Parties to the Trafficking Protocol is to criminalize trafficking in their domestic legal systems.[20] The Protocol's parent instrument, the Organized Crime Convention, requires the offense of trafficking to be established in the domestic law of every State Party independently of its transnational nature[21] or the involvement of an organized criminal group.[22] Similarly, in relation to the European Trafficking Convention, a trafficking offense under national law does not require a "transnational" element or the involvement of an organized criminal group.[23] Under all the major

---

interpreted by domestic courts and other competent authorities in a manner consistent with the meaning of the Protocol and the apparent intention of its drafters." *Legislative Guide*, at Part Two, 277.

[18] On this point, see European Trafficking Convention Explanatory Report, at para. 225: "[t]he offence [of trafficking] is constituted at an early stage: a person does not have to be exploited for there to be trafficking in human beings. It is sufficient that they have been subjected to one of the acts in the definition by one of the means in the definition for the purpose of exploitation. There is thus trafficking of human beings before any actual exploitation of the individual." See also *Legislative Guide*, at Part 2, 269: "[t]he offence defined in Article 3 of the Protocol is completed at a very early stage. No exploitation needs to take place."

[19] Trafficking Protocol, at Art. 3; European Trafficking Convention, at Art. 3(b). See also the SAARC Convention, at Art. I(3). See also the discussion of consent in Chapter 1.2.1 of this volume.

[20] *Legislative Guide*, at Part 2, 269–270.

[21] United Nations Convention against Transnational Organized Crime, 2225 UNTS 209, done Nov. 15, 2000, entered into force Sept. 29, 2003 (Organized Crime Convention), at Art. 34(2). See also *Legislative Guide*, at Part 2, 275–276: "transnationality must not be required as a proof in a domestic prosecution ... transnationality is not required as an element of domestic offences." See also the Interpretative Note on Article 34 included in the *travaux préparatoires*: "[t]he purpose of this paragraph is, without altering the scope of application of the convention ... to indicate unequivocally that the transnational element and the involvement of an organized criminal group are not to be considered elements of those offences for criminalization purposes." United Nations Office on Drugs and Crime, Travaux Préparatoires *of the Negotiations for the Elaboration of the United Nations Convention against Transnational Organized Crime and the Protocols Thereto* (2006) (Travaux Préparatoires *for the Organized Crime Convention and Protocols*), at 285. Further on this aspect of the criminalization obligation, see A.T. Gallagher, "Human Rights and Human Trafficking: Quagmire or Firm Ground? A Response to James Hathaway," (2009) 49(4) *Virginia Journal of International Law* 789, at 812–814.

[22] See *Legislative Guide*, Part 2, at 276: "[a]s with transnationality, the involvement of an organized criminal group must not be required as a proof in a domestic prosecution. Thus, offences established in accordance with the Protocol should apply equally, regardless of whether they were committed by individuals or by individuals associated with an organized criminal group and regardless of whether this can be proved or not."

[23] European Trafficking Convention, at Art. 18.

instruments, the offense must be committed intentionally for there to be criminal liability.[24]

Criminalizing Attempt and Complicity, Liability of Legal Persons. The obligation to criminalize trafficking extends to criminalization of organizing, directing, or being an accomplice in the commission of trafficking offenses and attempting to commit such offenses.[25] The nature of the trafficking phenomenon makes it especially important that liability for trafficking offenses, including, where possible under domestic law, criminal liability, covers both natural and legal persons. Legal persons, in this context, might include commercial companies and corporations operating in a range of different sectors such as tourism, entertainment, hospitality, labor recruitment, adoption, and the provision of medical services. Carriers, such as airlines, are another important group of legal persons whose potential complicity and liability are specifically identified in the Trafficking Protocol.[26]

The Organized Crime Convention and European Trafficking Convention both require States to consider enacting legislation to provide for the administrative, civil, and criminal liability of legal persons for trafficking offenses in addition to the criminal liability of natural persons.[27] The European Trafficking Convention provides additional detail: It envisages corporate liability for trafficking-related offenses, including aiding and abetting, committed on behalf of an entity and for its benefit by "a person who has a leading position within the legal person."[28] The Convention

---

[24] Trafficking Protocol, at Art. 5(1). The *Legislative Guide* to the Protocol confirms that States are obliged only to criminalize intentional conduct and not conduct involving lower standards such as negligence. The commentary cautions however that "the element of intention refers only to the conduct or action that constitutes each criminal offence and should not be taken as a requirement to excuse cases, in particular where persons may have been ignorant or unaware of the law establishing the offence": *Legislative Guide*, Part 2, at 276. The European Trafficking Convention (at Art. 18) also extends the obligation of criminalization to offenses committed intentionally. The Explanatory Report to the Convention notes that while interpretation of the word "intentionally" in Article 18 is left to domestic law, Article 4(a) of the Convention also provides for a specific element of intention in the types of conduct that comprise "purposes of exploitation." Accordingly, "there is trafficking in human beings only when that specific intention is present": European Trafficking Convention Explanatory Report, at para. 228.

[25] See Organized Crime Convention, at Art. 5; Trafficking Protocol, at Art. 5(2); European Trafficking Convention, at Art. 21; SAARC Convention, at Art. III. Note that the *Legislative Guide* to the Trafficking Protocol affirms that "mere preparation for an offence generally does not constitute an attempt": at Part Two, 272. The Interpretative Notes attached to Article 5 of the Trafficking Protocol state that references to attempting to commit the offenses established under domestic law are understood in some countries to include both acts perpetrated in preparation for a criminal offense and those carried out in an unsuccessful attempt to commit the offense, where those acts are also punishable under domestic law. *Travaux Préparatoires for the Organized Crime Convention and Protocols*, at 364.

[26] Trafficking Protocol, at Arts. 11(3), 11(4).

[27] Organized Crime Convention, at Art. 10; European Trafficking Convention, at Art. 22. See further, European Trafficking Convention Explanatory Report, at para. 251.

[28] European Trafficking Convention, at Art. 22(1).

further requires States Parties to impose liability on a legal entity where the crime is committed for the benefit of the entity by an employee or agent under circumstances in which commission of the offense was made possible by the failure of a "leading person" to supervise the employee or agent.[29] International and regional policy instruments reflect a growing recognition of the need for corporate liability in trafficking in persons cases.[30]

Criminalizing Related Conduct. The international legal definition of trafficking comprises several distinct elements, raising the question of whether an obligation to criminalize *trafficking* extends to criminalizing some or all of those separate elements. International treaty law is clear on this point. A requirement to criminalize component acts is not supported by either the Trafficking Protocol or the European Trafficking Convention. Their respective commentaries are explicit on the point that the criminalization obligation relates to the constitutive acts taken together and not to the individual elements.[31]

The broader question of whether States are under an obligation to criminalize offenses commonly associated with trafficking (which may also be component acts identified in the definition) is more complex. As noted in earlier chapters, trafficking implicates a wide range of acts prohibited under international law. Certain trafficking-related practices (including slavery and servitude, debt bondage, forced labor, the worst forms of child labor, and forced marriage) implicate rights and prohibitions generally recognized under customary law and therefore applicable to all States in all situations. A failure on the part of any State to criminalize (and, subsequently, to investigate and prosecute) such acts would represent a failure of the State to effectively implement the corresponding customary right or obligation. A State may also be under an international legal obligation through a treaty or other recognized source of law with respect to additional practices implicated in trafficking such as discrimination, torture, violence against women, violations of the rights of noncitizens and migrant workers, and violations of economic, social, and cultural

---

[29]   Ibid. at Art. 22(2). The commentary to the Convention notes that in this context, "failure to supervise should be interpreted to include not taking appropriate and reasonable steps to prevent employees or agents from engaging in criminal activities on the entity's behalf. Such appropriate and reasonable steps could be determined by various factors such as the type of business, its size and the rules and good practices in force": European Trafficking Convention Explanatory Report, at para. 249.

[30]   See, for example, UN Trafficking Principles and Guidelines, at Guideline 4.1.

[31]   *Legislative Guide*, Part 2, at 268: "[t]he obligation is to criminalize trafficking as a combination of constituent elements and not the elements themselves … Individual elements such as abduction or the exploitation of prostitution need not be criminalized, although in some cases supplementary offences may support the purposes of the protocol and States are free to adopt or maintain them if they wish to do so." European Trafficking Convention Explanatory Report, at para. 224: "[t]rafficking in human beings is a combination of ingredients that have to be made a criminal offence and not the ingredients taken in isolation. Thus, for example, the Convention does not create any obligation to make *abduction, deception, threats, forced labour, slavery or exploitation of the prostitution of others*, taken individually" (sic, emphasis in original).

rights. As with the well-established customary rules cited above, a failure on the part of a State to criminalize, investigate, and prosecute to the required standard would amount to a failure of that State to implement its legal obligation.[32] Importantly, obligations to criminalize related conduct must be sourced from outside trafficking-specific agreements. As explained above, failure to criminalize related offenses would not, on its own, constitute a violation of a trafficking-specific agreement such as the Trafficking Protocol or European Trafficking Convention.

There is also a practical aspect to the criminalization of a broader range of offenses as part of a comprehensive national or transnational strategy to deal with trafficking. From a criminal justice perspective, the definition of trafficking is complex, and the separate elements of the crime are often difficult to prove. Recent, field-based studies have indicated that it may be easier to investigate and prosecute more established and better understood offenses (such as debt bondage, sexual assault, forced labor, and even money laundering and corruption) rather than the complex and resource-intensive crime of trafficking.[33] This approach, which is widely supported,[34] can be particularly useful in situations and in countries where a distinct criminal offense of trafficking does not yet exist; where the penalties for trafficking do not sufficiently reflect the nature of the crime; or where the available evidence in the particular case is not sufficient to support a prosecution for trafficking but may be sufficient to prosecute for such related offenses.[35] Prosecuting for related offenses rather than for trafficking may be appealing in the short term but has a number of potentially significant long-term consequences that should be taken into consideration. For example, a trafficking charge may trigger an entitlement on the part of victims to secure access to support services, protection, and assistance that would not otherwise be available. As noted previously, these support services can include the possibility of a reflection period and temporary or even permanent residence status in the destination country.

Criminalization of the Use of the Services of a Victim of Trafficking. Does international law require States to criminalize those who use or otherwise benefit from

---

[32] This is the position taken by the UN Trafficking Principles and Guidelines which encourage criminalization of component acts (as defined under the Trafficking Protocol) and related conduct or offenses, referring specifically to those practices covered by the definition of trafficking such as sexual exploitation, forced labor or services, slavery or practices similar to slavery and servitude: UN Trafficking Principles and Guidelines, at Guideline 4.1.

[33] A.T. Gallagher and P. Holmes, "Developing an Effective Criminal Justice Response to Human Trafficking: Lessons from the Front Line," (2008) 18 *International Criminal Justice Review* 3 (Gallagher and Holmes, "Lessons from the Front Line"), at 322.

[34] See, for example, United Nations Office on Drugs and Crime, *Model Law on Trafficking in Persons*, UN Sales No. E.09.V.11 (2009) (UNODC Model Law), at Preamble: "[r]ecognizing that, in order to deter traffickers and bring them to justice, it is necessary to appropriately criminalize trafficking in persons and related offences."

[35] See, for example, *R v. Tang*, in which the High Court of Australia upheld the convictions of a brothel owner for slavery: *R v. Tang*, (2008) 249 ALR 200 (Aus. HC, Aug. 28, 2008).

the services of victims of trafficking? For example, should an individual (or corporate entity) purchasing or otherwise obtaining goods produced through trafficked labor be held criminally responsible? Should the "client" of an individual trafficked into sexual exploitation ever be held criminally responsible? Should the owner of a business that uses trafficked workers or the buyer of goods produced through trafficked labor be liable for criminal prosecution? Does it make a difference whether or not the individual had or should have had knowledge of the trafficking?

The Trafficking Protocol does not pronounce directly on whether the use of the services of victims of trafficking should be criminalized, and it is to be presumed that this instrument places no specific obligation on States Parties to that end. However, the European Trafficking Convention requires States Parties to consider criminalizing "the use of services which are the object of [trafficking-related] exploitation … with the knowledge that the person is a victim of trafficking in human beings."[36] The Explanatory Report to the Convention emphasizes its narrow application: To be liable for punishment under this provision, the user must be aware that the person is a trafficking victim.[37] The Explanatory Report acknowledges the potential difficulties in securing evidence of a nonmaterial element such as knowledge. However, it notes that this is not a conclusive counterargument and suggests that the perpetrator's intention can be inferred from the objective, factual circumstances.[38]

There is growing acknowledgment that the end "users" of the services of trafficking victims are a critical part of the problem and should be held accountable.[39] Should this view become more widely accepted, it may be possible to sustain an argument to the effect that failure to criminalize this essential step in the trafficking chain equates to a failure to fully discharge the broader obligation of criminalization. However, as a more detailed consideration of this issue in the following chapter makes clear, criminalization of the use of the services of a trafficking victim while either knowing or recklessly disregarding the fact that the individual involved is a trafficking victim is not currently an established international legal obligation.

---

[36] European Trafficking Convention, at Art. 19. Note that the SAARC Convention, which was concluded several years before the European Trafficking Convention, indirectly touches on the issue of liability of end users by requiring States Parties to provide for the punishment of any person "who keeps, maintains or manages or knowingly finances or takes part in the financing of a place used for the purpose of trafficking [for prostitution] and knowingly lets or rents a building or other place or any part thereof for the purpose of trafficking [for prostitution]": SAARC Convention, at Art. III(2).

[37] European Trafficking Convention Explanatory Report, at para. 234.

[38] Ibid, at paras. 234–235. See also Working Group on Trafficking in Persons, "Good Practices and Tools in Reducing the Demand for Exploitative Service: Background Paper Prepared by the Secretariat," UN Doc. CTOC/COP/WG.4/2010/3, Dec. 9, 2009 (noting, at para. 4, the need for: "[e]xamination of the standard of knowledge required of a person before they can be prosecuted for having used the services of a trafficked person"). The UNODC Model Law, in discussing an optional provision criminalizing the use of a person's services or labor with the prior knowledge of trafficking, notes that "[t]he mens rea required here is 'knowingly' to ensure that once a person learns that he or she will be using the services of a victim of trafficking, and nevertheless decides to go ahead and benefit from the exploitation of another person, he or she will be punished": UNODC Model Law, at 34–35.

[39] See references at Chapter 8 in this volume.

7.1.2. *Exercise of Criminal Jurisdiction*

The rules related to the exercise of criminal jurisdiction (which form part of customary international law) are an important aspect of the criminalization obligation. These rules identify the circumstances under which a State is required – or permitted – to assert its criminal justice authority over a particular situation. Jurisdictional authority under international law has traditionally been construed quite narrowly as being primarily territorial. This is changing as States and intergovernmental organizations grapple with the challenges presented by transnational crimes, dysfunctional national legal systems, and increasingly mobile offenders.[40]

Jurisdictional rules are more complicated for trafficking than for many other crimes because trafficking often involves the commission of multiple offenses in two or more countries, in particular across different States of origin, transit, and destination. The international legal rules on jurisdiction in trafficking situations are set out in the major international and regional treaties. Their objective is to reduce or eliminate jurisdictional safe havens for traffickers by ensuring that all parts of the crime can be punished wherever they took place.[41] Another concern is to ensure coordination mechanisms in cases where more than one country may have grounds to assert jurisdiction.[42] The main rules[43] extracted from the major specialist trafficking treaties are as follows. First, a State is *required* to exercise jurisdiction over trafficking offenses when the offense is committed in the territory of that State or onboard a vessel flying its flag or on an aircraft registered under its laws

---

[40] The International Court of Justice, for example, has observed "a gradual movement towards bases of jurisdiction other than territoriality … This slow but steady shifting to a more extensive application of extraterritorial jurisdiction by States reflects the emergence of values which enjoy an ever-increasing recognition in international society. One such value is the importance of the punishment of the perpetrators of international crimes": *Arrest Warrant of 11 April 2000 (Democratic Republic of the Congo v. Belgium)*, [2002] ICJ Rep 3, at para. 73 (Joint Separate Opinion of Judges Higgins, Kooijmans and Buergenthal). See generally, M. Inazumi, *Universal Jurisdiction in Modern International Law: Expansion of National Jurisdiction for Prosecuting Serious Crimes under International Law* (2005). In relation to the CEDAW Convention, it has been noted that while jurisdiction under this instrument remains primarily territorial, "in some cases the State will be obliged to fulfil its obligations under the Convention in relation to territory outside because of the nature of its control over that territory or the persons affected. For example, the obligations of States parties under the Convention apply where a State party is in effective control of a territory outside its borders. Similarly, the obligations of States parties under Article 2 (c) and (e) of the Convention also extend to acts of national corporations operating extraterritorially. Obligations of States parties may also extend to regulating the acts of its nationals when they are outside the territory of the State party (for example, in situations where nationals are perpetrators of trafficking)": International Women's Rights Action Watch Asia Pacific, "Possible Elements for Inclusion in a General Recommendation on Article 2 of CEDAW: Outcome Document of the Expert Group Meeting on CEDAW Article 2: National and International Dimensions of State Obligation" (2007), at 4, available at http://www.iwraw-ap.org/aboutus/pdf/Elements_paper_final_version_Jan9.pdf (accessed Jan. 29, 2010).

[41] *Legislative Guide*, Part 1, at 104.

[42] Ibid.

[43] The jurisdictional rules in the specialist trafficking treaties draw on the general jurisdictional rules of international law. For a discussion of the general rules of jurisdictional competence, see I. Brownlie, *Principles of Public International Law* (2008), at 299–322.

(territoriality principle).[44] Second, a State *may* exercise jurisdiction over trafficking offenses when such offenses are committed outside the territorial jurisdiction of that State against one of its nationals (principle of passive personality).[45] Third, a State *may* exercise jurisdiction over trafficking offenses when such offenses are committed outside the territorial jurisdiction of that State by one of its nationals (principle of active personality).[46] Fourth, a State *may* exercise jurisdiction over trafficking offenses when such offenses are committed outside the territorial jurisdiction of that State but are linked to serious crimes or money laundering planned to be conducted in the territory of that State.[47] Fifth, a State *must* establish jurisdiction over trafficking offenses when the offender is present in the territory of the State and the State does not extradite the offender on grounds of nationality or any other grounds[48] (principle of "extradite or prosecute").[49] Related treaties, such as those dealing with the exploitation of children and trafficking in children for adoption, generally reiterate these rules.[50] Intergovernmental organizations have repeatedly emphasized the importance of coordinating jurisdictional requirements and thereby eliminating gaps.[51]

---

[44] Organized Crime Convention, at Art. 15(1); European Trafficking Convention, at Arts. 31(1) (a)-(c).

[45] Organized Crime Convention, at Art. 15(2)(a); European Trafficking Convention, at Art. 31(1)(e).

[46] Organized Crime Convention, at Art. 15(2)(b); European Trafficking Convention, at Art. 31(1) (d). This form of jurisdiction based on nationality of the offender is being increasingly used by States to criminalize and punish nationals involved in the sexual exploitation of children abroad. For an overview and critique see ECPAT International, "Extraterritorial Laws: Why They Are Not Really Working and How They Can Be Strengthened" (2008), available at http:// www.ecpat.net/worldcongressIII/PDF/Journals/EXTRATERRITORIAL_LAWS.pdf (accessed Feb. 14, 2010).

[47] Organized Crime Convention, at Art. 15(2)(c).

[48] Ibid. at Arts. 15(3), 15(4); European Trafficking Convention, at Art. 31(3).

[49] For a full discussion of this rule, see Chapter 7.5 in this book.

[50] See, for example, Optional Protocol to the Child Convention on the Sale of Children, Child Prostitution and Child Pornography, GA Res. 54/263, Annex I, 54 UN GAOR Supp. (No. 49), 7, UN Doc. A/54/49, Vol. III (2000), done May 25, 2000, entered into force Jan. 18, 2002 (CRC Optional Protocol), at Art. 4, which provides that jurisdiction may be exercised over those accused of sale of children, child prostitution, or child pornography by the territorial State; the State of registration of ship and aircraft where offenses occurred; where the victim is a national of or has habitual residence in the State; where the alleged perpetrator is a national; and where the alleged offender is present within the territory. The same Article requires that jurisdiction be established over the relevant offenses "when the alleged offender is present in [the territory of the State Party] and it does not extradite him or her to another State Party on the ground that the offence has been committed by one of its nationals." See also, Inter-American Convention on International Traffic in Minors, OAS Doc. OEA/Ser.K/XXI.5, 79 OASTS, done Mar. 18, 1994, entered into force Aug. 15, 1997, reprinted in (1994) 33 ILM 721 (Inter-American Convention on International Traffic in Minors), at Art. 9 (territoriality; habitual residence of victim; presence of alleged offender within territory; presence of victim within territory).

[51] The UN General Assembly, for example, has also called upon Governments to penalize all offenders involved in trafficking, whether local or foreign, though the competent national authorities, either in the country of origin or in the country in which the abuse occurs. See, for example, UN General Assembly, "Trafficking in Women and Girls," UN Doc. A/RES/63/156, Jan. 30, 2009, at

As noted above, it is possible that more than one country will be in a position to assert jurisdiction over a particular trafficking case or even in respect of the same offenders. This is called "concurrent jurisdiction." Consultation and cooperation are important from the outset in order to coordinate actions, and more specifically, to determine the most appropriate jurisdiction within which to prosecute a particular case.[52] In some cases, it will be most effective for a single State to prosecute all offenders, whereas in other cases it may be preferable for one State to prosecute some participants, while one or more other States pursue the remainder. Issues such as nationality, the location of witnesses, the applicable legal framework, resource availability, and the location of offender when apprehended will need to be taken into consideration.[53] The Organized Crime Convention provides that where several jurisdictions are involved, States Parties are to consider transferring the case to the best forum in the "interests of the proper administration of justice" and "with a view to concentrating the prosecution."[54] Other recent instruments impose on States a binding obligation to consult when parallel investigations arise relating to the same

para. 11; and UN General Assembly, "Trafficking in Women and Girls," UN Doc. A/RES/61/144, Dec. 19, 2006, at para. 7. The ASEAN Practitioner Guidelines note that "where possible, extra-territorial provisions should be attached to trafficking in persons laws and related statutes as a further measure to remove safe havens for traffickers": Association of Southeast Asian Nations (ASEAN), *Criminal Justice Responses to Trafficking in Persons – ASEAN Practitioner Guidelines* (Jakarta, 2007) (ASEAN Practitioner Guidelines), at Part 2.B.2.

[52] Such consultation is required under Article 15(5) of the Organized Crime Convention and Article 31(4) of the European Trafficking Convention.

[53] These issues are explored further in P. David, F. David and A.T. Gallagher, "International Legal Cooperation in Trafficking in Persons Cases" (ASEAN, United Nations Office on Drugs and Crime, Asia Regional Cooperation to Prevent People Trafficking; forthcoming, 2010). See also the discussion of international legal cooperation in Chapter 7.5, below.

[54] Organized Crime Convention, at Art. 21. The ASEAN Practitioner Guidelines at Part 2.C.3 reiterate this requirement: "[i]n appropriate transnational cases where traffickers could be prosecuted in two or more States, alternative means at the international, regional or bilateral levels could be considered to assess and coordinate criminal proceedings and, where appropriate, consider the transfer of criminal proceedings to the most appropriate State in the interests of the proper administration of justice." The draft EU Framework Decision 2009 Proposal, in addition to including a broader and more binding extraterritorial jurisdiction rule (at Art. 8), requires cooperation between Member States "in order to decide which of them will prosecute the offenders with the aim, if possible, of centralising proceedings in a single Member State." It adds that in deciding which State will prosecute the offender, "special account shall be taken of the following factors: the Member State is that in the territory of which the acts were committed, the Member State is that of which the perpetrator is a national or resident, the Member State is the Member State of origin of the victim, the Member State is that in the territory of which the perpetrator was found." Framework Decision 2009 Proposal, at Art. 8(4). The accompanying Explanatory Memorandum stated that these provisions on coordination of prosecution "may be superseded once the Proposal for a Framework Decision on conflicts of jurisdiction in criminal proceedings is adopted": ibid. at 6. That Framework Decision was indeed adopted in late 2009: Council Framework Decision 2009/948/JHA of 30 November 2009 on prevention and settlement of conflicts of exercise of jurisdiction in criminal proceedings, OJ L 328/42, Dec. 15, 2009. Note that the Framework Decision 2009 Proposal recently lapsed (see note 9 to this chapter), and its proposed successor instrument, the EC Directive 2010 Proposal, does not address coordination of prosecution.

person and the same facts – thereby creating a possible situation of "international" *ne bis in idem* (double jeopardy).[55]

7.2. EFFECTIVE INVESTIGATION, PROSECUTION, AND ADJUDICATION

Specialist trafficking treaties do not explicitly require States Parties to investigate and prosecute trafficking cases. However, the *combating* of trafficking is one of the key purposes of all three major instruments.[56] In addition, the investigation and prosecution of offenses established under the Trafficking Protocol is expressly included in the scope of its application.[57] In the case of the SAARC and European Trafficking Conventions, detailed provisions are included relating to criminal procedure in the investigation and prosecution of trafficking offenses.[58] On the basis of this and other evidence presented below, it can be convincingly argued that States have an obligation to give effect to their criminal laws by appropriately investigating allegations of trafficking, prosecuting those against whom there is adequate evidence, and subjecting them to trial.

7.2.1. *Practical Application of the Due Diligence Standard*

The analysis set out in Chapter 4 confirmed that international law places a responsibility on States to investigate, prosecute, and adjudicate trafficking to the required standard of "due diligence." Chapter 4 also confirmed that this standard imposes a positive duty on States to ensure the effectiveness of their criminal law through effective investigation and prosecution. The duty to investigate and prosecute is applicable both when there is an allegation of violation by State officials and when the alleged perpetrator is a non-State actor. In relation to the latter case, a State will become responsible under international law if it fails to seriously investigate private abuses of rights and to punish those responsible, thereby aiding in the commission of those private acts.[59]

How does one measure whether a State is taking seriously its obligation to investigate and prosecute trafficking cases? The worst case will generally be the easiest

---

[55] See, for example, Council Framework Decision 2009/948/JHA of 30 November 2009 on prevention and settlement of conflicts of exercise of jurisdiction in criminal proceedings, OJ L 328/42, Dec. 15, 2009. Further on the principle of *ne bis in idem*, see Chapter 7.5.1 of this volume.

[56] Trafficking Protocol, at Art. 2(a); European Trafficking Convention, at Art. 1(1)(a); SAARC Convention, at Art. II. See also, Framework Decision 2009 Proposal, at Preambular para. 3; EC Directive 2010 Proposal, at Preambular para. 3.

[57] Trafficking Protocol, at Art. 4.

[58] European Trafficking Convention, at chapter V; SAARC Convention, at Arts. III-VIII.

[59] See further references in Chapter 4.4 of this volume. Note the position of the Inter-American Court that investigations "must be conducted in serious manner and not as a mere formality preordained to be ineffective": *Velásquez Rodríguez v. Honduras*, Inter-Am Ct. H.R. (ser. C) No. 4, July 29, 1988, at para. 177.

to decide. A State that does not criminalize trafficking, that fails to investigate any cases of trafficking, that fails to protect any victims or to prosecute any perpetrators when there is reliable evidence available of the existence of a trafficking problem, will clearly not pass the due diligence test. In less egregious cases, it is necessary to evaluate whether the steps taken evidence seriousness on the part of the State to investigate and prosecute trafficking. A decision as to whether or not a State has taken seriously its obligation to investigate and prosecute trafficking requires consideration of a myriad of factors, only some of which can be dealt with in the present chapter.

At a general level, it is useful to look to the broad requirements of effective criminal investigation. For example, the European Court of Human Rights has, in another context, provided rudimentary indicia of an effective criminal investigation that include factors such as the independence of the investigators; the promptness of the investigation; whether the investigation is capable of leading to a determination on whether the unlawful act was committed and the identification and punishment of those responsible; whether reasonable steps are taken to secure evidence concerning the incident; and whether there is a sufficient element of public scrutiny of the investigation or its results.[60] In its recent decision of *Rantsev v. Cyprus and Russia*, the Court reiterated these factors in the context of a trafficking-related death.[61] The Court also emphasized that investigations into trafficking must cover "all aspects of trafficking allegations *from recruitment to exploitation*,"[62] and to this end found violations by both the State of origin[63] and the State of destination.[64] Regarding the likelihood of disparate witnesses and evidence located in multiple States, the Court affirmed that: "member States are also subject to a duty in cross-border trafficking cases to cooperate effectively with the relevant authorities of other States concerned in the investigation of events which occurred outside their territories."[65]

In evaluating the extent to which a State has met the due diligence standard, it is essential to recall that trafficking is a crime whose investigation and prosecution rely heavily on the cooperation of victims. If victims are prevented or discouraged from making complaints then this will have a direct impact on the ability of the criminal justice system to investigate and prosecute trafficking cases. Accordingly, it is important to ascertain how easy (or difficult) it is for victims to make complaints

---

[60] *Finucane v. United Kingdom*, (2003) 37 EHRR 29 (ECHR, July 1, 2003) (*Finucane v. UK*), at paras. 68–71. See also see *McCann v. United Kingdom*, (1995) 21 EHRR 97 (ECHR, Sept. 27, 1995), at para. 161.

[61] *Rantsev v. Cyprus and Russia*, Dec. No. 25965/04 (not yet reported) (ECHR, Jan, 7, 2010) (*Rantsev v. Cyprus and Russia*), at para. 233 and the discussion which follows at paras. 234–242.

[62] Ibid. at para. 307 (emphasis added).

[63] Ibid. at para. 309.

[64] Ibid. at para. 300, finding the obligation to investigate trafficking allegations to be subsumed under the obligation to investigate the trafficking-related death of the deceased.

[65] Ibid. at para. 289.

to police. Questions pertinent to this inquiry include: Are there provisions for them to be protected and supported, or are they criminalized and deported? Are there genuine incentives in place for victims to cooperate (for example, the provision of short-term residency permits and/or reflection periods to allow an informed decision on cooperation)? How active is law enforcement in investigating trafficking? What happens further up the criminal justice hierarchy? When police are doing their job and investigating trafficking cases, do prosecutors or judges take such cases seriously? Do they understand the crime of trafficking and are they able to apply the national legal framework? Is there real and effective cooperation between the various criminal justice agencies on this issue or are prosecutions thwarted through competing agendas, corruption, or inefficiency? To what extent does the criminal justice system guarantee free and fair trials including respect for the rights of suspects?

Due diligence may also require that investigators do not just rely on complaints from victims but actually go out and investigate on their own. The European Trafficking Convention specifically requires States Parties to:

> ensure that investigations into or prosecution of offences established in accordance with th[e] Convention shall not be dependent on the report or accusation made by a victim, at least when the offence was committed in whole or in part on its territory.[66]

It is noted that this provision seeks to avoid traffickers subjecting victims to pressure and threats in attempting to deter them from complaining to the authorities[67] or to withdraw a complaint already made. An obligation to move beyond reactive investigation of trafficking in persons cases is supported by European case law as well as the pronouncements of human rights treaty bodies.[68]

---

[66] European Trafficking Convention, at Art. 27(1).

[67] European Trafficking Convention Explanatory Report, at para. 277.

[68] See, for example, *Sánchez v. Honduras*, Inter-Am Ct. H.R. (ser. C) No. 99, June 7, 2003, at para. 144 (an investigation "must have an objective and be assumed by the State as its own legal duty, not as a step taken by private interests that depends upon the *initiative of the victim or his family or upon their offer of proof*" (emphasis added)); *Rantsev v. Cyprus and Russia*, at para. 288 ("[t]he requirement to investigate does not depend on a complaint from the victim or next-of-kin: once the matter has come to the attention of the authorities they must act of their own motion"); *Finucane v. UK*, at para. 67 ("the authorities must act of their own motion, once the matter has come to their attention. They cannot leave it to the initiative of the next-of-kin either to lodge a formal complaint or to take responsibility for the conduct of any investigative procedures"). Note that the UN Human Rights Council has recently urged States to not make "accusations by, or the participation of, the victims of trafficking a precondition to the prosecution of trafficking": "Trafficking in Persons, Especially Women and Children," UN Doc. A/HRC/RES/11/3, June 17, 2009, at para. 3. The draft Framework Decision 2009 Proposal also reiterated that obligation at Art. 7(1): "[e]ach Member State shall ensure that investigation into or prosecution of [trafficking] offences ... is not be dependent on the report or accusation made by a victim and that criminal proceedings may continue even if the victim has withdrawn his or her statement." See, similarly, EC Directive 2010 Proposal, at Art. 8(1).

Critically, is it even possible to know what is happening? In many countries, criminal justice data on trafficking is nonexistent, unavailable, or seriously compromised in terms of quality and reliability. States should be able to produce the necessary data on investigations, arrests, prosecutions, and convictions for trafficking and related offenses that will either confirm or call into question their adherence to the standard of due diligence.

As well as the factual question of what the State actually did (or did not do) in relation to a particular situation, issues of mandate, organization, and capacity are also relevant. For example: Is there an adequate legislative framework within which the criminal justice system can function effectively in relation to such cases? Have law enforcement agencies been given the powers required to investigate this crime? Do these same agencies possess the necessary technical capacity and can they access the required resources? Are they organized in such a way as to ensure that investigations can and do take place? Technical capacity is another issue that goes to the heart of whether a State is fully discharging its obligation to investigate and prosecute trafficking cases.

For most national criminal justice agencies, trafficking is a relatively new crime and the relevant indicators of an effective response are yet to be definitively settled. However, there is growing consensus around what constitutes an appropriate discharge of the State's duty of due diligence. For example, it is generally recognized (in specialist international[69] and regional[70] trafficking treaties, as well as through

[69] Trafficking Protocol, at Art. 10(2): "States Parties shall provide or strengthen training for law enforcement, immigration and other relevant officials in the prevention of trafficking in persons. The training should focus on methods used in preventing such trafficking, prosecuting the traffickers and protecting the rights of victims, including protecting the victims from the traffickers. The training should also take into account the need to consider human rights and child and gender-sensitive issues and should encourage cooperation with non-governmental organizations, other relevant organizations and other elements of civil society." The body established to provide recommendations on the effective implementation of the Trafficking Protocol affirms that: "States parties should provide training to front-line law enforcement officials ... soldiers involved in peacekeeping missions, consular officers, prosecutorial and judicial authorities, medical services providers and social workers ... in order to enable national authorities to respond effectively to trafficking in persons, especially by identifying the victims of such trafficking." Conference of the Parties to the United Nations Convention against Transnational Organized Crime, "Report on the Meeting of the Working Group on Trafficking in Persons held in Vienna on 14 and 15 April 2009," UN Doc. CTOC/COP/WG.4/2009/2, Apr. 21, 2009, at para. 9.

[70] European Trafficking Convention, at Art. 29(3) ("[e]ach Party shall provide or strengthen training for relevant officials in the prevention of and fight against trafficking in human beings including Human Rights training. The training may be agency-specific and shall, as appropriate, focus on methods used in preventing such trafficking, prosecuting the traffickers and protecting the rights of victims, including protecting victims from the traffickers"); SAARC Convention, at Art. VIII(2) ("[t]he States Parties to the Convention shall sensitize their law enforcement agencies and the judiciary in respect of the offences under this Convention and other related factors that encourage trafficking in women and children"). Note also European Trafficking Convention, at Art. 10(1), on the need to ensure the provision of persons trained and qualified in preventing and combating trafficking in identifying and helping victims.

intergovernmental policy[71] and the work of human rights bodies[72]) that an effective criminal justice response to trafficking requires trained and competent officials. These sources reveal general agreement on several key points. First, training should be provided to all officials involved in the identification, investigation, prosecution, and adjudication of trafficking cases, including specialist and frontline law enforcement officials, immigration officials, prosecutors, and judges. Second, training should adopt a human rights approach.[73] It should, for example, seek to sensitize

---

[71] See, for example, UN Trafficking Principles and Guidelines, at Guideline 5.2; OSCE Action Plan, at Recommendation III(5); Brussels Declaration, at para. 9; ECOWAS Initial Plan of Action, at 7–8, paras. 1–3; OAS Recommendations on Trafficking in Persons, at Sections II(9), II(13); COMMIT MOU, at Art. 8; ASEAN Practitioner Guidelines, at Part 1.B. See also, UN General Assembly, "Trafficking in Persons, Especially Women and Children, Report of the Special Rapporteur on Trafficking in Persons, Especially Women and Children," UN Doc. A/64/290, Aug. 12, 2009, at para. 100(c) ("[l]aw enforcement officials (police, immigration, including embassy staff, staff of health and social services, and labour inspectors) should be adequately trained in respect of the national and international legal and policy framework for identification and protection of and assistance to victims, with clear emphasis on respect for the human rights of victims of trafficking. Such capacity-building should be institutionalized through the provision of regular training and retraining that is human rights, child and gender sensitive"); and UN Human Rights Council, "Trafficking in Persons, Especially Women and Children," UN Doc. A/HRC/RES/11/3, June 17, 2009, at para. 3 ("[u]rges governments ... [t]o provide or strengthen training for law enforcement, immigration, criminal justice and other relevant officials, including personnel participating in peacekeeping operations, in preventing and responding effectively to trafficking in persons, including the identification and treatment of victims with full respect for their human rights"); and UN General Assembly, "Trafficking in Women and Girls," UN Doc. A/RES/63/156, Jan. 30, 2009, at para. 18 ("[u]rges Governments to provide or strengthen training for law enforcement, judicial, immigration and other relevant officials in the prevention and combating of trafficking in persons").

[72] See, for example, UN Human Rights Committee: "Concluding Observations: Costa Rica," UN Doc. CCPR/C/CRI/CO/5, Nov. 16, 2007, at para. 12; "Concluding Observations: Bosnia and Herzegovina," UN Doc. CCPR/C/BIH/CO/1, Nov. 22, 2006, at para. 16; UN Committee on the Rights of the Child, "Concluding Observations: Kenya," UN Doc. CRC/C/KEN/CO/2, June 19, 2007, at para. 66(h); UN Committee against Torture, "Concluding Observations: Latvia," UN Doc. CAT/C/LVA/CO/2, Feb. 19, 2008, at para. 21; "Concluding Observations: Japan," UN Doc. CAT/C/JPN/CO/1, Aug. 3, 2007, at para. 25; UN Committee on Economic, Social and Cultural Rights, "Concluding Observations: Cambodia," UN Doc. E/C.12/KHM/CO/1, June 12, 2009, at para. 26; UN Committee on the Elimination of Discrimination against Women, "Concluding Observations: Mozambique," UN Doc. CEDAW/C/MOZ/CO/2, June 11, 2007, at para. 32; "Concluding Observations: Austria," UN Doc. CEDAW/C/AUT/CO/6, Feb. 2, 2007, at para. 26; *Şahide Goekce (deceased) v. Austria*, CEDAW Comm. No. 5/2005, UN Doc. CEDAW/C/39/D/5/2005, decided Aug. 6, 2007, at para. 12.3; "Report of Special Rapporteur on the human rights aspects of the victims trafficking in persons, especially women and children, Sigma Huda: Addendum 2: Mission to Bosnia and Herzegovina," UN Doc. E/CN.4/2006/62/Add.2, Nov. 30, 2005, at paras. 80, 82, 86; UN Commission on Human Rights, "Report of the Special Rapporteur, Ms. Radhika Coomaraswamy, on violence against women, its causes and consequences, on trafficking in women, women's migration and violence against women," UN Doc. E/CN.4/2000/68, Feb. 29, 2000, at para. 122(a).

[73] The concept of a "human rights-based approach" to trafficking has recently been explained in the UN Commentary to the Trafficking Principles and Guidelines: "A human rights-based approach is a conceptual framework for dealing with a phenomenon such as trafficking that is *normatively based* on international human rights standards and that is *operationally directed* to promoting and protecting human rights. Such an approach requires analysis of the ways in which human rights violations

participants to the needs of trafficked persons, in particular those of women and children. Third, training should aim to provide criminal justice officials with the technical skills they require to identify, investigate, prosecute, and adjudicate trafficking cases. Fourth, training should also aim to strengthen the capacity of criminal justice officials to protect victims and to respect and promote their rights. Fifth, training should encourage cooperation between criminal justice agencies and nongovernmental agencies, especially those working to support victims of trafficking. Sixth, consideration should be given to the involvement of relevant nongovernmental agencies in such training as a means of increasing its relevance and effectiveness; and, finally, the quality of training should be evaluated. Following training, trainee performance should be monitored and training impact assessment should take place.

In addition to receiving skills and awareness training, criminal justice officials and agencies also need to be organized, empowered, and funded in a manner that enables them to respond appropriately and effectively to the crime of trafficking. A skilled, empowered, and adequately resourced law enforcement response provides a powerful disincentive for traffickers by increasing the risks and costs associated with their activities. The position taken on this by relevant treaty law[74] finds considerable additional authority elsewhere.[75] The major points of agreement in this area relate to specialization and coordination. For example, it is widely accepted that a dedicated and specialized investigatory capacity is an essential component

arise throughout the trafficking cycle and of States' obligations under international human rights law. It seeks to both identify and redress the discriminatory practices and unjust distributions of power that underlie trafficking, that maintain impunity for traffickers, and that deny justice to victims of trafficking. Under a human rights-based approach, every aspect of the national, regional and international response to trafficking is anchored in the rights and obligations established by international human rights law." Office of the UN High Commissioner for Human Rights, *Commentary to the United Nations Recommended Principles and Guidelines on Human Rights and Human Trafficking* (forthcoming, 2010), citing Office of the UN High Commissioner for Human Rights, *Frequently Asked Questions on a Human Rights-Based Approach to International Development Cooperation*, UN Sales No. HR/PUB/06/8 (2006).

74 For example, Organized Crime Convention, at Art. 20 (special investigative techniques); Trafficking Protocol, at Art. 10 (information exchange and training); European Trafficking Convention, at Art. 29 (specialized authorities and coordinating bodies); SAARC Convention, at Art. VIII(1) ("[t]he States Parties ... shall provide sufficient means, training and assistance to their respective authorities to enable them to effectively conduct enquiries, investigations and prosecutions of offences under this Convention").

75 See, for example, ASEAN Practitioner Guidelines, at Part 1.B.1 ("[a] specialist investigation capacity within national police forces is key to a strong and effective criminal justice response to trafficking in persons"); UN Trafficking Principles and Guidelines, at Guidelines 5.3, 5.4; OSCE Action Plan, at Recommendation III(2.2) (special antitrafficking units); ECOWAS Initial Plan of Action, at 7, para. 1 ("special units, within existing law enforcement structures, with a specific mandate to develop and effectively target operational activities to combat trafficking of persons"). The Committee on the Elimination of All Forms of Discrimination against Women has praised States on the establishment of specialist law enforcement trafficking units: "Concluding Observations: Luxembourg," UN Doc. CEDAW/C/LUX/CO/5, Apr. 8, 2008, at para. 31; "Concluding Observations: Kenya," UN Doc. CEDAW/C/KEN/CO/6, Aug. 10, 2007, at para. 29.

of an effective criminal justice response.[76] The specialist investigatory capacity should be mandated to supervise as well as advise on all the trafficking investigations undertaken within the country. It should be granted and enjoy the legal and procedural powers that are required to conduct trafficking investigations using the full range of available investigative techniques. The specialist capacity should have the necessary independence, capacity, resources, and gender profile to carry out its work. Consideration should also be given to the specialization of other functions, such as the prosecution and adjudication of trafficking cases – to the extent that the caseload requires.[77] Coordination between various criminal justice agencies (for example, between frontline police agencies and specialist investigation units; and between specialist units and prosecutorial agencies) is equally essential. Such coordination should cover both policies and action. It may require the establishment of coordinating bodies.[78] Specialist criminal justice agencies dealing with trafficking should work closely with victim support agencies, including nongovernmental organizations, to ensure that the rights of victims are upheld and that they receive protection and support appropriate to their needs.[79] Legislative or other measures should be in place to ensure that judicial proceedings protect victims' privacy and safety to the extent that this is compatible with the right to a fair trial.[80] The rights

[76] European Trafficking Convention, at Art. 29; ASEAN Practitioner Guidelines, at Guideline B.1; International Criminal Police Organization (Interpol), *Trafficking in Human Beings: Best Practice Guidance Manual for Investigators* (2008), at chapter 2.7; Gallagher and Holmes, "Lessons from the Front Line."

[77] The ASEAN Practitioner Guidelines propose specialization of both the prosecutorial and adjudicatory functions: at Guideline 1.B.2 ("[p]rosecution agencies should ... develop a specialist response capacity. A number of prosecutors – appropriate to the current and anticipated caseload – should be specially trained and designated to undertake the preparation and presentation of TIP and related prosecutions") and at Guideline 1.B.5 ("[a] number of judges, appropriate to the current and anticipated caseload, should be specially prepared and designated to undertake the management and adjudication of TIP related trials"). The Brussels Declaration recommends the establishment of "specialized, joint investigative teams of investigators and prosecutors": at para. 17.

[78] European Trafficking Convention, at Art. 29(2). See also UN General Assembly, "Trafficking in Women and Girls," UN Doc. A/RES/63/156, Jan. 30, 2009, at para. 13. The UN Committee on the Elimination of All Forms of Discrimination against Women has repeatedly praised States for the establishment of national groups to coordinate actions to combat trafficking: "Concluding Observations: Luxembourg," UN Doc. CEDAW/C/LUX/CO/5, Apr. 8, 2008, at para. 31; "Concluding Observations: Greece," UN Doc. CEDAW/C/GRC/CO/6, Feb. 2, 2007, at para. 21; "Concluding Observations: Kazakhstan," UN Doc. CEDAW/C/KAZ/CO/2, Feb. 2, 2007, at para. 6; "Concluding Observations: Austria," UN Doc. CEDAW/C/AUT/CO/6, Feb. 2, 2007, at para. 25; "Concluding Observations: Georgia," UN Doc. CEDAW/C/GEO/CO/3, Aug. 25, 2006, at para. 6; "Concluding Observations: Thailand," UN Doc. CEDAW/C/THA/CO/5, Feb. 3, 2006, at para. 5.

[79] Trafficking Protocol, at Arts. 6(3), 9(3); European Trafficking Convention, at Art. 35. Resolutions of the UN General Assembly, UN Commission on Human Rights, and UN Human Rights Council have repeatedly called for closer collaboration between Governments and nongovernment organizations to provide support for victims. See, for example, UN General Assembly, "Trafficking in Women and Girls," UN Doc. A/RES/63/156, Jan. 30, 2009, at Preamble, paras. 1, 13, 15, 16, 17, 23; UN Human Rights Council, "Trafficking in Persons, Especially Women and Children," UN Doc. A/HRC/RES/11/3, June 17, 2009, at para. 3(k).

[80] See further, the references at Chapter 5.3.3 in this volume.

and needs of child victims should be given the highest priority in the context of judicial proceedings.[81]

7.2.2. *Gender in the Investigation, Prosecution, and Adjudication of Trafficking Cases*

International and regional treaty law notes the importance of ensuring the integration of a gender perspective into responses to trafficking.[82] This need is particularly acute in the context of criminal justice responses. Men and boys are often overlooked as victims of trafficking. The harm done to them may be underreported and criminal justice agencies may be less willing to investigate and prosecute such cases.[83] Women and girls have often been trafficked in ways that are specific to their gender and with impacts that can also be very gender-specific. Criminal justice systems are often ill-equipped to deal with this reality. Failure of national criminal justice agencies to integrate a gender perspective into their work may aggravate the harm done to victims and render responses less effective in terms of both ending impunity and securing justice.

While the serious problem of underinvestigation of trafficking of men and boys must be addressed, discrimination and associated harms in the criminal justice response to trafficking are most obvious in relation to trafficked women and girls. Examples of actual or potential harm may include arbitrary detention of women and girl victims;[84] discriminatory and inappropriate investigatory responses that criminalize women and girls, especially vulnerable groups including migrants and prostitutes;[85] failure to acknowledge gender-specific violence such as sexual abuse, and to provide or facilitate access to appropriate medical, psychological, and psychosocial support;[86] failure to acknowledge the impact that concerns about loss of

---

[81] See further, the references and citations under the heading "Right to privacy" at Chapter 5.5.3 of this volume.

[82] For example, Trafficking Protocol, at Art. 10(2); European Trafficking Convention, at Art. 17.

[83] See, for example, R. Surtees, "Trafficked Men as Unwilling Victims," (2008) 4(1) *St Antony's International Review* 16; United Nations Inter-Agency Project on Human Trafficking, "Exploitation of Cambodian Men at Sea: Facts about the Trafficking of Cambodian Men onto Thai Fishing Boats" (2009), available at http://www.no-trafficking.org/reports_docs/siren/siren_cb3.pdf (accessed Nov. 30, 2009).

[84] See further, Chapter 5.2.2 in this book.

[85] The UN Trafficking Principles and Guidelines provide several examples of discriminatory and inappropriate criminal justice response that would have a disproportionate effect on women and girls. Guideline 5.5 calls on States to guarantee "that traffickers are and will remain the focus of anti-trafficking strategies and that law enforcement efforts do not place trafficked persons at risk of being punished for offences committed as a consequence of their situation." Guideline 5.6 calls upon States to implement measures "to ensure that rescue operations [such as raids on brothels and factories] do not further harm the rights and dignity of trafficked persons. Such operations should only take place once appropriate and adequate procedures for responding to the needs of trafficked persons released in this way have been put in place."

[86] On the need to acknowledge trafficking as gender-based violence and to provide appropriate support, see UN Human Rights Council, "Trafficking in Persons, Especially Women and Children,"

privacy and the prospect of humiliation may have on women and girl victims during the criminal justice process;[87] and interviewing and examining of female victims of trafficking by personnel who have not been trained in gender-sensitive methods of securing and recording evidence.[88] Even apparently gender-neutral rules of procedure and rules of evidence can operate to compound the harm experienced by trafficked women and girls. A useful example is provided by rules that unreasonably require evidence of force or restraint; this is particularly problematic in light of a growing understanding that victims can be denied liberty and freedom of movement without being physically detained, for example, through threats or the withholding of identity documents.[89] Another example is provided by rules of procedure

UN Doc. A/HRC/RES/11/3, June 17, 2009, at Preamble, para. 3; UN General Assembly, "Trafficking in Women and Girls," UN Doc. A/RES/63/156, Jan. 30, 2009, at Preamble, paras. 3, 4, 5, 6, 17, 18, 19, 27; UN Human Rights Council, "Special Rapporteur on Trafficking in Persons, Especially Women and Children," UN Doc. A/HRC/RES/8/12, June 18, 2008, at Preamble, para. 4.

[87] "Report of the Special Rapporteur on Torture and Other Cruel, Inhuman or Degrading Treatment or Punishment, Manfred Nowak," UN Doc. A/HRC/7/3, Jan. 15, 2008, at para. 61; *V.L. v. Switzerland*, CAT Comm. No. 262/2005, UN Doc. CAT/C/37/D/262/2005, decided Jan. 22, 2007, at para. 8.8.

[88] "Report of the Special Rapporteur on Torture and Other Cruel, Inhuman or Degrading Treatment or Punishment, Manfred Nowak," UN Doc. A/HRC/7/3, Jan. 15, 2008, at para. 61. The UN General Assembly and Commission on Human Rights have recommended that training take into account gender-sensitive issues and perspectives: UN General Assembly, "Trafficking in Women and Girls," UN Doc. A/RES/59/166, Dec. 20, 2004, at para. 24; UN Commission on Human Rights, "Trafficking in Women and Girls," UN Doc. E/CN.4/RES/2004/45, Apr. 19, 2004, at para. 23. See also, World Health Organization, *Ethical and Safety Recommendations on Interviewing Women Victims of Trafficking* (2003).

[89] This is particularly pertinent in the case of trafficking where the issue of consent is, by definition, irrelevant. International criminal law has also acknowledged that consent cannot be inferred from any words or conduct of a victim where force, threat of force, coercion, or taking advantage of a coercive environment undermined the victim's ability to give voluntary and genuine consent, nor from the silence of, or lack of resistance by, a victim: Assembly of States Parties to the Rome Statute of the International Criminal Court, "Rules of Procedure and Evidence," contained in the Report of the Assembly of States Parties to the Rome Statute of the International Criminal Court: First Session, Sept. 3–10, 2002, Official Records, UN Doc. ICC-ASP/1/3 (ICC Rules of Procedure and Evidence), at Rule 70. See also, Rules of Procedure and Evidence of the Special Court for Sierra Leone, first adopted by the Plenary of Judges on Jan. 16, 2002, as amended (SCSL Rules of Procedure and Evidence), at Rule 96. On the irrelevance of consent to slavery and enslavement, see generally the discussion of trafficking as slavery at Chapter 3.3, above. Note that the Special Rapporteur on systematic rape, sexual slavery, and slavery-like practices during armed conflict stated: "[a]s a *jus cogens* crime, neither a State or its agents, including government or military officials, can consent to the enslavement of any person under any circumstances. Likewise, a person cannot, under any circumstances, consent to be enslaved or subjected to slavery." UN Sub-Commission on the Promotion and Protection of Human Rights, "Systematic Rape, Sexual Slavery and Slavery-like Practices during Armed Conflict: Update to the Final Report, Submitted by Gay J. McDougall, Special Rapporteur," UN Doc. E/CN.4/Sub.2/2000/21, June 6, 2000, at para. 51. The Appeals Chamber of the ICTY has held that consent is not an element of the crime against humanity (enslavement) as it is "often rendered impossible by a series of influences such as detention, captivity or psychological oppression": *Prosecutor v. Kunarac, Kovac and Vukovic*, Case IT-96-23-T and IT-96-23/1-T, ICTY Appeals Chamber, June 12, 2002, at para. 113. This interpretation was upheld by the Special Court for Sierra Leone in *Prosecutor v. Brima, Kamara and Kanu (the AFRC Accused)*, Case SCSL-04–16-T, SCSL Trial Chamber, June 20, 2007, at paras. 709, 746.

and rules of evidence that permit or require evidence of the prior sexual conduct of the victim.[90] As noted elsewhere in this study, States are required to ensure that their responses to trafficking, including their criminal justice responses, do not discriminate against any person on any of the prohibited grounds and that such responses do not result in a violation of any other established rights.[91] Practices such as those outlined above should be considered in light of this obligation.

7.2.3. *Rights of Suspects and the Right to a Fair Trial*

The danger that suspects' rights will be trampled on in the "war against trafficking" is not a remote one. Recent international events have confirmed that even those States most attached to the rule of law may be tempted into compromising the rights of individuals suspected of certain crimes.[92] Terrorism and organized crime both appear particularly susceptible to this trend as States seek to protect themselves from vague or specific threats. External and internal pressures on criminal justice agencies to be seen to be responding to a particular crime present an additional risk factor that is particularly acute in the trafficking context.[93] Such pressures can have especially unfortunate consequences in States with underdeveloped criminal justice systems, where rules of evidence and procedure already fall short of international standards. Of course, the rights of a perpetrator cannot supersede an individual's right to life and to physical and mental integrity.[94] A balancing of rights may also be

---

[90] The Special Rapporteur on torture has noted that the admission of this type of evidence increases the trauma of testifying as women may be humiliated in having to expose aspects of their private life that are irrelevant to ascertaining the fact of having been trafficked: "Report of the Special Rapporteur on Torture and Other Cruel, Inhuman or Degrading Treatment or Punishment, Manfred Nowak," UN Doc. A/HRC/7/3, Jan. 15, 2008, at para. 62. Note that the International Criminal Court prohibits the admission of evidence related to the prior sexual conduct of the victim: ICC Rules of Procedure and Evidence, at Rule 71. See also SCSL Rules of Procedure and Evidence, at Rule 96. The Trial Chamber of the ICTY has held that the exclusion of evidence of the prior sexual conduct of a witness, adduced during cross-examination, was in the "interests of justice" and that "due regard was given to the fact that in rape or other sexual assault cases, evidence of prior sexual conduct of the victims mainly serves to call the reputation of the victim into question. Moreover, it was considered that the value, if any, of information about the prior sexual conduct of a witness in the context of trials of this nature was nullified by the potential danger of further causing distress and emotional damage to the witnesses": *Prosecutor v. Delalic et al.*, Case IT-96–21-T, ICTY Trial Chamber, Decision on the Prosecution's Motion for the Redaction of the Public Record, June 5, 1997, at paras. 48, 50.

[91] See further, Chapter 8.4 in this volume.

[92] UN Human Rights Council, "Report of the Special Rapporteur on the Promotion and Protection of Human Rights and Fundamental Freedoms While Countering Terrorism," UN Doc. A/HRC/4/26, Jan. 29, 2007; "Report of the United Nations High Commissioner for Human Rights on the Protection of Human Rights and Fundamental Freedoms While Countering Terrorism," UN Doc. A/HRC/4/88, Mar. 9, 2007 (specifically addressing the procedural obligations of States towards terrorism suspects, the principle of *non-refoulement*, and the human rights aspects of individual sanctions implemented against terrorism suspects by States).

[93] Gallagher and Holmes, "Lessons from the Front Line," at 338.

[94] This position has been affirmed by the UN CEDAW Committee. See, for example, *AT v. Hungary*, CEDAW Comm. No. 2/2003, UN Doc. CEDAW/C/32/D/2/2003, decided Jan. 26, 2005, at para. 9.3;

required under special circumstances. For example, a trial involving an organized criminal group may require that relatively greater attention be given to the rights of victims and the interests of the community at large. Generally, however, victim and suspect rights are not incompatible.

International law imposes certain obligations on States with respect to their treatment of individuals suspected (and indeed convicted) of offenses related to trafficking. In short, States are required to ensure that their pursuit of traffickers is never at the expense of the international rules governing human rights and the administration of justice. Failure to observe these rules invokes the international legal responsibility of that State. Such failures also risk compromising the integrity and reputation of the criminal justice response and can lead to an erosion of community support for the investigation and prosecution of traffickers.

7.3. EFFECTIVE AND PROPORTIONATE SANCTIONS

Sanctions are an essential component of a comprehensive response to trafficking. Sanctions that are disproportionate to the harm caused and the potential benefits derived from trafficking will create distortions that can only hinder effective criminal justice responses. Inconsistent penalties across different jurisdictions risk contributing to the development of safe havens. Inadequate penalties for trafficking can also impair the effectiveness of international cooperation procedures, such as extradition, which are triggered by a severity test linked to the gravity of sanctions. Conversely, rigid or extremely severe sanctions such as mandatory minimum custodial terms or provision for capital punishment may not meet the required human rights and criminal justice standards for reasons explored more fully below.

7.3.1. *Obligation to Impose Sanctions*

International law requires that effective and proportionate sanctions be applied to those convicted of trafficking, as well as of component or related offenses such as sexual exploitation, forced labor or services, slavery or practices similar to slavery and servitude, debt bondage, the worst forms of child labor, and forced marriage. This obligation is linked and gives effect to a range of other obligations including those related to criminalization, investigation, and prosecution. The obligation to impose effective and proportionate sanctions is confirmed through international treaty law. The Organized Crime Convention, for example, requires that offenses established

and *Fatma Yildirim (deceased) v. Austria*, CEDAW Comm. No. 6/2005, UN Doc. CEDAW/C/39/ D/6/2005, decided Oct. 1, 2007, at para. 12.1.5. The view of the CEDAW Committee was cited with approval by the European Court of Human Rights in *Opuz v. Turkey*, Dec. No. 33401/02 (unreported) (ECHR, June 9, 2009), at para. 147.

under that instrument (and, by extension, the Trafficking Protocol)[95] be liable to sanctions that take into account the gravity of the offenses.[96] The Convention also requires that discretionary legal powers with regard to sentencing be exercised in a way that maximizes the effectiveness of law enforcement measures and gives due regard to the need to deter the commission of trafficking-related offenses.[97] The European Trafficking Convention requires trafficking and other offenses established under that instrument to be punishable by "effective, proportionate and dissuasive sanctions," including custodial penalties that can give rise to extradition.[98]

Both the Organized Crime Convention and the European Trafficking Convention further require that in cases of trafficking involving legal persons (companies, business enterprises, charitable organizations, etc.), that such legal persons be made subject to effective, proportionate, and dissuasive criminal or noncriminal sanctions, including monetary sanctions.[99] Punishment for the crime of trafficking may, in relation to both individuals and legal persons, involve noncustodial sanctions or "measures" directed at individuals or legal persons. The confiscation of assets, discussed further in Chapter 7.4, is an example of such a measure. The European Trafficking Convention envisages several others, including the closure of any establishment used to carry out trafficking in human beings and the banning of a perpetrator from carrying out the activity in the course of which the offense was committed.[100] This provision is aimed at enabling States to act against establishments that might be used as a cover for trafficking, such as matrimonial agencies, placement agencies, travel agencies, hotels, or escort services.[101] It is also intended to:

> reduce the risk of further victims by closing premises on which trafficking victims are known to have been recruited or exploited (such as bars, hotels, restaurants or textile workshops) and banning people from carrying on activities which they used to engage in trafficking.[102]

---

[95] A State that is party to the Organized Crime Convention and not the Trafficking Protocol would be required to establish that trafficking is, under its law, a "serious crime" as defined in the Convention for these provisions to apply to trafficking offenses: Organized Crime Convention, at Arts. 2(b), 3(1)(b); *Legislative Guide*, at Part 1, para. 302.

[96] Organized Crime Convention, at Art. 11(1).

[97] Ibid. at Art. 11. Note that Convention also requires: the need to ensure the presence of offenders to be borne in mind in connection with decisions on release pending trial or appeal (at Art. 11(3)); the grave nature of the offenses to be borne in mind when considering the eventuality of early release or parole (at Art. 11(4)); and a long statute of limitations to be established for trafficking offenses with provision for a longer period where the alleged offender has evaded the administration of justice (at Art. 11(5)).

[98] European Trafficking Convention, at Art. 23(1). As noted in the European Trafficking Convention Explanatory Report, at para. 252, this would require provision for custodial penalties of at least one year.

[99] Organized Crime Convention, at Art. 10(4); European Trafficking Convention, at Art. 23(2).

[100] European Trafficking Convention, at Art. 23(4).

[101] European Trafficking Convention Explanatory Report at para. 257.

[102] Ibid. at para. 256. On this point, see also the UN Trafficking Principles and Guidelines, at Guideline 4.2.

International and regional treaties on related issues, such as the exploitation of children and migrant workers, identify an obligation on States Parties to sanction violations of the rights protected by those instruments.[103] On the particular issue of trafficking, the UN General Assembly,[104] the UN Human Rights Council,[105] and a number of UN human rights treaty bodies[106] as well as key policy documents[107] have emphasized the importance of punishing those involved in the trafficking and exploitation of human beings. Also relevant are the sanctioning provisions of a large number of instruments dealing with violence against women.[108]

[103] CRC, at Art. 32(c) (economic exploitation of children); CRC Optional Protocol, at Art. 3(3) (sale of children, child prostitution, and child pornography). The Migrant Workers Convention requires States Parties to sanction those who use violence, threats or intimidation against migrant workers or members of their families in an irregular situation: International Convention on the Protection of the Rights of All Migrant Workers and Members of Their Families, UN Doc. A/RES/45/158, done Dec. 18, 1990, entered into force July 1, 2003 (Migrant Workers Convention), at Art. 68(1)(c).

[104] See, for example, UN General Assembly, "Trafficking in Women and Girls," UN Doc. A/RES/63/156, Jan. 30, 2009, at Preamble ("all States have an obligation to exercise due diligence to prevent, investigate and punish perpetrators of trafficking in persons, and to rescue victims as well as provide for their protection ... not doing so violates and impairs or nullifies the enjoyment of the human rights and fundamental freedoms of the victims) and paras. 3 ("[c]alls upon all Governments to ... strengthe[n] existing legislation with a view to ...punishing perpetrators") and 11 ("[c]alls upon all Governments to ... bring to justice and punish the offenders and intermediaries involved").

[105] See, for example, UN Human Rights Council, "Trafficking in Persons, Especially Women and Children," UN Doc. A/HRC/RES/11/3, June 17, 2009, at Preamble ("all States have an obligation to exercise due diligence to prevent, investigate and punish perpetrators of trafficking in persons, and to rescue victims as well as provide for their protection ... not doing so violates and impairs or nullifies the enjoyment of the human rights and fundamental freedoms of the victims").

[106] The UN treaty bodies have repeatedly called on States to punish those who engage in trafficking, for example: UN Human Rights Committee, "Concluding Observations: Czech Republic," UN Doc. CCPR/C/CZE/CO/2, Aug. 9, 2007, at para. 12; UN Committee against Torture, "Concluding Observations: Italy," UN Doc. CAT/C/ITA/CO/4, July 16, 2007, at para. 22; "Concluding Observations: Hungary," UN Doc. CAT/C/HUN/CO/4, Feb. 6, 2007, at para. 21; UN Committee on the Elimination of All Forms of Discrimination against Women, "Concluding Observations: Azerbaijan," UN Doc. CEDAW/C/AZE/CO/4, Aug. 7, 2009, at para. 24; "Concluding Observations: Lebanon," UN Doc. CEDAW/C/LBN/CO/3, Apr. 8, 2008, at para. 29; UN Committee on the Rights of the Child, "Concluding Observations: Niger," UN Doc. CRC/C/NER/CO/2, June 18, 2009, at para. 77.

[107] See, for example, UN Trafficking Principles and Guidelines, at Principle 15, Guideline 4.3.

[108] CEDAW, at Art. 2(b); Protocol to the African Charter on Human and Peoples' Rights on the Rights of Women in Africa, OAU Doc. CAB/LEG/66.6, done July 11, 2003, entered into force Nov. 25, 2005, at Art. 4(2)(e); "Beijing Declaration and Platform for Action," Fourth World Conference on Women, UN Doc. A/CONF.177/20 and UN Doc. A/CONF.177/20/Add.1, Sept. 15, 1995 (Beijing Declaration and Platform for Action), at para. 125(c) (States to "enact and/or reinforce penal, civil, labour and administrative sanctions in domestic legislation to punish and redress the wrongs done to women and girls who are subjected to any form of violence") and para. 131(b) (States to strengthen "existing legislation with a view to ... punishing perpetrators"); "Further Actions and Initiatives to Implement the Beijing Declaration and Platform for Action," UN Doc. A/RES/S-23/3, Nov. 16, 2000 (Beijing +5 Outcome Document), at paras. 69(a) (States to criminalize all forms of violence against women), 69(b) (States to prosecute and sentence appropriately the perpetrators of violence against women) and 97(c) (proposing the strengthening of "national legislation by further defining the crime of trafficking in all its elements and by reinforcing the punishment accordingly"); UN General Assembly, "Crime Prevention and Criminal Justice Measures to Eliminate Violence against Women," UN

7.3.2. *The Standard: "Effective and Proportionate" Sanctions*

As noted above, the Organized Crime Convention (and, by extension, the Trafficking Protocol) requires penalties that take into account the gravity of the offense and give due regard to deterrence. The European Trafficking Convention standard for sanctions is that they be "effective, proportionate, and dissuasive." Various "soft law" sources confirm the general tenor of these provisions.[109] Sanctions must be generally consistent with the harm caused and the benefits derived from trafficking and related exploitation. They must, in short, "clearly outweigh the benefits of the crime."[110]

A standard of "effective and proportionate" requires consideration of many factors. As noted above, inappropriately light sentences that do not reflect the harm caused or the benefits derived will compromise the criminal justice task and may even impair the effectiveness of international cooperation procedures, such as extradition. Such sentences also fail the victims by not offering them protection from further harm. At the same time, as has been noted in relation to penalties for violence against women, draconian sanctions can have the unintended consequence of decreasing reporting and convictions and placing victims in greater danger.[111]

When considering whether penalties meet the generally accepted standard, it is important to keep in mind the particularities of this crime-type. A typical trafficking case may involve recruiters and brokers as defendants as well as individuals more directly involved in the exploitation of the victim. The benefits that each party derives from the exploitation are likely to be starkly different, as will be their contribution to the harm caused to victims. It could be argued, on this basis, that legislatively mandated minimum penalties, particularly if set very high, do not satisfy the

---

Doc. A/RES/52/86, Dec. 12, 1997, Annex, at para. 9(a)(i); UN General Assembly, "Declaration on the Elimination of Violence against Women," UN Doc. A/48/49, Dec. 20, 1993, at Art. 4(d) (States should "develop penal, civil, labour and administrative sanctions in domestic legislation to punish and redress the wrongs caused to women who are subjected to violence"); UN Committee on the Elimination of Discrimination against Women, "General Recommendation No. 19: Violence against Women," UN Doc. A/47/38, Jan. 29, 1992, at paras. 24(g), 24(t)(i).

[109] See, for example, UN Trafficking Principles and Guidelines, at Principle 15; ASEAN Practitioner Guidelines, at Part 1.A.2 ("[p]enalties for those convicted of the crime of trafficking in persons and related crimes should be appropriate to the gravity of the crime and ... reflect aggravating circumstances"). The UN human rights treaty bodies have in some cases specifically called on States to ensure that penalties are commensurate with the seriousness of the acts. See, for example, UN Human Rights Committee, "Concluding Observations: Costa Rica," UN Doc. CCPR/C/CRI/CO/5, Nov. 16, 2007, at para. 12; UN Committee against Torture, "Concluding Observations: Philippines," UN Doc. CAT/C/PHL/CO/2, May 29, 2009, at para. 26; UN Committee on the Elimination of All Forms of Discrimination against Women, "Concluding Observations: Morocco," UN Doc. CEDAW/C/MAR/CO/4, Apr. 8, 2008, at para. 23; UN Committee on Economic, Social and Cultural Rights, "Concluding Observations: Nicaragua," UN Doc. E/C.12/NIC/CO/4, Nov. 28, 2008, at para. 28.

[110] *Legislative Guide*, at Part 1, 130.

[111] UN General Assembly, "In-depth Study on All Forms of Violence against Women: Report of the Secretary General," UN Doc. A/61/122/Add.1, July 6, 2006, at para. 360.

"effective and proportionate" standard because they remove the measure of judicial discretion necessary for its proper application.[112] The death penalty is also problematic, and not just from a human rights perspective. While international law does not yet categorically reject capital punishment,[113] it is unlikely that provision for such a sanction for trafficking offenses would easily meet the "effective and proportionate" standard given the complexity of the trafficking crime, inevitable investigatory difficulties, and highly variable levels of complicity among offenders.[114] Imposition of the death penalty may also be an obstacle to extradition under the major extradition treaties.[115]

7.3.3. *Aggravated Offenses and Previous Convictions*

The concept of aggravated offenses is an aspect of the proportionality requirement discussed above. It accepts that a crime such as trafficking can be made worse under certain circumstances and should therefore attract a different, presumably harsher penalty. The Organized Crime Convention and its Trafficking Protocol do not refer to aggravated offenses,[116] and the drafting history confirms that the issue was never under consideration. However, subsequent interpretative materials make clear that States Parties remain free, under those instruments, to develop a system of sanctions that includes aggravated offenses.[117] The European Trafficking Convention explicitly

---

[112] See further, Gallagher and Holmes, "Lessons from the Front Line," at 323.

[113] See generally, W. Schabas, *The Abolition of the Death Penalty in International Law* (2002); and M. Nowak, *UN Covenant on Civil and Political Rights: CCPR Commentary* (2005), at 133–153.

[114] Gallagher and Holmes, "Lessons from the Front Line," at 323.

[115] Some extradition treaties specify that States shall not grant extradition when the offense in question is punishable in the requesting State by death penalty: Inter-American Convention on Extradition, 1752 UNTS 190, done Feb. 25, 1981, entered into force Mar. 28, 1992 (Inter-American Convention on Extradition), at Art. 9; or at least that States may refuse extradition in such circumstances: European Convention on Extradition, 359 UNTS 273, done Dec. 13, 1957, entered into force Apr. 18, 1960 (European Convention on Extradition), at Art. 11; Economic Community of West African States Convention on Extradition, ECOWAS Convention A/P.1/8/94, done Aug. 6, 1994, entered into force Aug. 1995 (ECOWAS Convention on Extradition), at Art. 17.

[116] The only reference to aggravated offenses is in Article 6 of the Migrant Smuggling Protocol which requires State Parties to "adopt such legislative and other measures as may be necessary to establish as aggravating circumstances [to the offense of migrant smuggling] ... circumstances: (a) That endanger, or are likely to endanger, the lives or safety of the migrants concerned; or (b) That entail inhuman or degrading treatment, including for exploitation of such migrants." Protocol against the Smuggling of Migrants by Land, Sea and Air, supplementing the United Nations Convention against Transnational Organized Crime, done Nov. 15, 2000, GA Res. 55/25, Annex III, UN GAOR, 55th Sess., Supp. No. 49, at 62, UN Doc. A/45/49 (Vol. I) (2001), entered into force Jan. 28, 2004 (Migrant Smuggling Protocol), at Art. 6.

[117] See, for example, the UNODC Model Law, which, at 31–32, proposes the following circumstances as suitable for designation as aggravated offenses: "(a) Where the offence involves serious injury or death of the victim or another person, including death as a result of suicide; (b) Where the offence involves a victim who is particularly vulnerable, including a pregnant woman; (c) Where the offence exposed the victim to a life-threatening illness, including HIV/AIDS; (d) Where the victim is physically or mentally handicapped; (e) Where the victim is a child; (f) Where the offence involves more

requires that certain circumstances be regarded as aggravating circumstances in the determination of penalties for trafficking-related offenses. These include: when the offense deliberately or by gross negligence endangered the life of the victim or was committed against a child; when the offense was committed by a public official in the performance of his or her duties; or when the offense was committed within the framework of a criminal organization.[118]

The SAARC Convention also contains an aggravated offenses provision in respect of each of the above grounds, as well as in respect of the involvement of the offender in an organized criminal group or in organized criminal activities, and the commission of offenses in a custodial, educational, or social institution or facility for children.[119] Other related international and regional legal and policy instruments recognize the concept of aggravated offenses,[120] and the sentencing judgments of international tribunals provide important guidance on this point.[121] Crimes against

than one victim; (g) Where the crime was committed as part of the activity of an organized criminal group; (h) Where drugs, medications or weapons were used in the commission of the crime; (i) Where a child has been adopted for the purpose of trafficking; (j) Where the offender has been previously convicted for the same or similar offences; (k) Where the offender is a [public official] [civil servant]; (l) Where the offender is a spouse or the conjugal partner of the victim; and (m) Where the offender is in a position of responsibility or trust in relation to the victim."

[118] European Trafficking Convention, at Art. 24. Note that "criminal organization" is not defined in the Convention. The European Trafficking Convention Explanatory Report (at para. 264) cites, as applicable, the very broad definition set out in the Organized Crime Convention.

[119] SAARC Convention, at Art. IV.

[120] UN Trafficking Principles and Guidelines, at Guideline 4.3 (requesting States to consider, where appropriate, making legislative provision for additional penalties to be applied to persons found guilty of trafficking in aggravating circumstances, including offenses involving trafficking in children or offenses committed or involving complicity by State officials); ASEAN Practitioner Guidelines, at Part 1.A.2 ("[p]enalties for those convicted of the crime of trafficking in persons and related crimes should be appropriate to the gravity of the crime and to reflect aggravating circumstances"). The Brussels Declaration calls on States to consider trafficking offenses involving children as aggravated offenses deserving of more severe penalties: at para. 16. The Organization for Security and Co-operation in Europe has recommended that "legislation should provide for additional penalties to be applied to persons found guilty of trafficking in aggravating circumstances": OSCE Action Plan, at Recommendation III(1.4). Statutes of the various international criminal tribunals require the Court, when sentencing for violations of international humanitarian law, to take into account the gravity of the offense and the individual circumstances of the convicted person: Rome Statute of the International Criminal Court, 2187 UNTS 90, done July 17, 1998, entered into force July 1, 2002 (ICC Statute), at Art. 78; Statute of the International Criminal Tribunal for the Former Yugoslavia, UN Doc. S/RES/827, May 25, 1993, and amended by UN Doc. S/RES/1166, May 13, 1998 (ICTY Statute), at Art. 24(2); Statute of the International Tribunal for Rwanda, UN Doc. S/RES/955, Nov. 8, 1994, as amended, at Art. 23(2).

[121] *Prosecutor v. Erdemovic*, Case No. IT-96-22, ICTY Trial Chamber II, Mar. 5, 1998 (Sentencing Judgment), at para. 15; *Prosecutor v. Tadic*, Case No. IT-94-1, ICTY Trial Chamber II, Nov. 11, 1999 (Sentencing Judgment), at paras. 19–24; *Prosecutor v. Sikirica et al.*, Case No. IT-95-8, ICTY Trial Chamber III (Sentencing Judgment), Nov. 13, 2001, at para. 109; *Prosecutor v. Todorovic*, Case No. IT-95-9/1, ICTY Trial Chamber I, July 3, 2001 (Sentencing Judgment), at paras. 50–95; *Prosecutor v. Simic*, Case No. IT-95-9/2, ICTY Trial Chamber II, Oct. 17, 2002 (Sentencing Judgment), at paras. 40–43; *Prosecutor v. Plavsic*, Case Nos. IT-00-39 & 40/1-S, ICTY Trial Chamber III, Feb. 27, 2003 (Sentencing Judgment), at paras. 53–60; *Prosecutor v. Rajic*, Case No. IT-95-12-S, ICTY Trial Chamber I, May 8, 2006 (Sentencing Judgment), at paras. 97–165.

children and crimes committed by public officials in the performance of their duties are the most commonly cited grounds for imposing relatively harsher penalties in relation to trafficking and comparable crimes.[122]

Trafficking is often conducted across national borders by criminal organizations whose members may have been tried and convicted in more than one country. While prior convictions in national courts are often taken into account in deciding penalties, previous convictions in foreign courts are not generally made known or considered for sentencing purposes. The European and SAARC Trafficking Conventions both recognize the principle of "international recidivism" by providing that previous convictions in other countries, particularly for similar offenses, can be taken into account when determining penalties.[123] This provision addresses both the "effectiveness" and "proportionality" requirements discussed earlier.

To date, there has been very little acknowledgement of suspects' rights or of the existence of a potential conflict between those rights and protection of victims.[124] A number of core principles and rights, enshrined in international law, must be upheld to ensure that trafficking cases are prosecuted and adjudicated fairly and in accordance with international human rights and criminal justice standards. These include the principles that all persons are considered equal before courts and tribunals; that everyone is entitled to and receives a fair and public hearing by a competent, independent, and impartial court or tribunal established by law; and that all accused persons are presumed innocent until proven guilty according to law. Additional procedural guarantees for accused persons, as set out in the ICCPR and other instruments, will apply in the determination of any criminal charges. These include the rights of the accused to be informed promptly and in detail of the nature and cause of the charge; to adequate time and facilities for preparation of the defense and to communicate in private with counsel of his or her choosing; to be tried without undue delay; to be present at trial; to legal assistance where required in the interests of justice; to examine or have examined the witnesses against him or her and to obtain the attendance and examination of witnesses on his or her behalf under the same conditions as witnesses against him or her; to the services of an

---

[122] European Trafficking Convention, at Art. 24(b); SAARC Convention, at Art. IV(1)(e); Brussels Declaration, at para. 16; OSCE Action Plan, at Recommendation III (1.4).

[123] European Trafficking Convention, at Art. 25; SAARC Convention, at Art. IV. The Explanatory Report to the European Trafficking Convention notes that the drafters had in mind only convictions in respect of offenses related to trafficking in human beings (Article 18) and the forging of travel or identity documents for purposes of trafficking (Article 20(a)); other offenses (related to use of the services of a victim of trafficking (Article 19) or other document-related offenses (Articles 20(b) and 20(c)) could be taken into account in cases of reciprocal criminalization: European Trafficking Convention Explanatory Report, at para. 271.

[124] Limited exceptions include the Organized Crime Convention, at Art. 24(2); UN Trafficking Principles and Guidelines, at Guideline 6.6; and the *Legislative Guide* to the Organized Crime Convention and its Protocols, which briefly notes (at Part 1, paras. 345, 362–363; and Part 2, para. 54) the need to ensure that provisions protecting victim's identity and privacy do not compromise suspects' rights.

interpreter if required; and not to be compelled to testify against himself or herself or to confess guilt.[125]

In the specific context of a criminal trial, it is the responsibility of both the prosecutor and the judge to ensure that a fair trial takes place in accordance with applicable international standards.[126] The due diligence standard would also require that oversight mechanisms are in place to ensure the transparency and accountability of the criminal justice process.[127]

---

[125] See for example, International Covenant on Civil and Political Rights, 999 UNTS 171, done Dec. 16, 1966, entered into force Mar. 3, 1976 (ICCPR), at Art. 14; African Charter on Human And Peoples' Rights, 1520 UNTS 217, done June 27, 1981, entered into force Oct. 21, 1986, at Art. 7; African Charter on the Rights and Welfare of the Child, OAU Doc. CAB/LEG/2.49/49, done July 1990, entered into force Nov. 29, 1999, at Art. 17 (the administration of juvenile justice: the right to special treatment of young offenders); American Convention on Human Rights, 1144 UNTS 123, done Nov. 22, 1969, entered into force 18 July, 1978, at Art. 8 (right to a fair trial); Convention for the Protection of Human Rights and Fundamental Freedoms, 213 UNTS 222, done Nov. 4, 1950, entered into force Sept. 3, 1953, at Art. 6 (right to a fair trial); Protocol No. 7 to the Convention of 4 November 1950 for the Protection of Human Rights and Fundamental Freedoms, ETS No. 117, done Nov. 22, 1984, entered into force Nov. 1, 1988, at Arts. 2 (right to appeal against a criminal conviction), 3 (right to compensation in case of miscarriage of justice), and 4 (right not to be tried again for the same offense within the jurisdiction of the same State).

[126] This responsibility is noted in the ASEAN Practitioner Guidelines, at Part 1.F.5.

[127] The UN CEDAW Committee has recommended sanctions for failure by State officials to act with due diligence to prevent and respond to violence against women: *Şahide Goekce (deceased) v. Austria*, CEDAW Comm. No. 5/2005, UN Doc. CEDAW/C/39/D/5/2005, decided Aug. 6, 2007, at paras. 12.3(a) and 12.3(c); *Fatma Yildirim (deceased) v. Austria*, CEDAW Comm. No. 6/2005, UN Doc. CEDAW/C/39/D/6/2005, decided Oct. 1, 2007, at paras. 12.3(a) and 12.3(c). In Kenya, the Special Rapporteur on Extrajudicial, Summary or Arbitrary Executions has called for transparent, merits-based judicial appointment procedures and the establishment of a complaints procedure on judicial conduct: "Report of the Special Rapporteur on Extrajudicial, Summary or Arbitrary Executions, Philip Alston, Addendum: Mission to Kenya," UN Doc. A/HRC/11/2/Add.6, May 26, 2009, at para. 95. See also, generally, UN Committee on the Elimination of Racial Discrimination, "General Recommendation 31: The Prevention of Racial Discrimination in the Administration and Functioning of the Criminal Justice System," UN Doc. A/60/18, at 98, Aug. 17, 2005. Additionally, various bodies have emphasized the necessity of oversight by members of the public. The European Court of Human Rights has indicated that where State agents are implicated, an effective investigation requires "the persons responsible for and carrying out the investigation to be independent from those implicated in the events ... not only a lack of hierarchical or institutional connection but also a practical independence": *Paul and Audrey Edwards v. UK*, (2002) 35 EHRR 487 (ECHR, Mar. 14, 2002) at para. 70. Further, "there must be a sufficient element of public scrutiny of the investigation or its results to secure accountability in practice as well as in theory. The degree of public scrutiny required may well vary from case to case. In all cases, however, the next-of-kin of the victim must be involved in the procedure to the extent necessary to safeguard his or her legitimate interests": ibid. at para. 73. In that case, the *in camera* inquiry into the death of a prison inmate was found to fall below the level of public scrutiny required under the European Convention on Human Rights. Similarly, the Special Rapporteur on Extrajudicial, Summary or Arbitrary Executions has recommended that "[t]he international forces present in Afghanistan should respect the principles of accountability and transparency ... they should ensure that, despite the complexity of multiple mandates and disparate national criminal justice systems, directly affected persons can go to a military base and promptly receive answers with regard to ... the status of any investigation or prosecution": "Report of the Special Rapporteur on Extrajudicial, Summary or Arbitrary Executions, Philip Alston, Addendum: Preliminary Note on the Mission to Afghanistan," UN Doc. A/HRC/8/3/Add.6, May 29, 2008, at para. 35.

7.4. ASSET CONFISCATION AND USE OF CONFISCATED ASSETS

Trafficking in persons is widely recognized as a highly lucrative and relatively risk-free crime. Criminals involved in organizing and financing trafficking activities often distance themselves from direct involvement in the trafficking activity. This makes it difficult for investigators to gather sufficient evidence against them to secure convictions. Even if arrested and punished, traffickers will often be able to enjoy their illegal gains for personal use and for maintaining the operation of their trafficking enterprises. Given the large financial interests involved and the difficulties experienced in securing convictions, it is important for States to take steps to ensure that trafficking does not reward its financers, organizers, and beneficiaries. An obligation to pursue the proceeds of trafficking can be considered part of the broader obligation on States to develop and implement an effective criminal justice response. In this respect, a functioning asset recovery regime becomes part of the due diligence standard against which State performance of this broader obligation is to be measured.

Asset recovery for any crime is usually a three-step process: (1) investigative measures to trace the assets in question; (2) preventative measures (namely freezing and seizing) to immobilize the assets identified as related to the crime in question; and (3) confiscation, return, and disposal.[128] In the context of trafficking, effective asset recovery renders such an activity less lucrative and increases the risks, thereby acting as an important means of preventing future trafficking. In the context of identifying obligations, it is also relevant to note the links between asset recovery and prosecution. A strong confiscation and recovery regime can operate to support the criminal conviction of traffickers by providing evidence to substantiate or corroborate a case of human trafficking, for example by demonstrating to the court that the income of an individual or of a legal person far exceeds that which can be explained by legitimate sources.

Criminals involved in trafficking may organize their affairs so that the proceeds derived from trafficking-related crime are located in a State other than the one in which they live or in which the crime takes place. The goal of ensuring that there are no safe havens for traffickers must be applied in respect of the assets accrued through the exploitation of their victims. International cooperation mechanisms that enable countries to give effect to foreign freezing and confiscation orders and that allow countries to work together in recovering criminal assets are a crucial part of effective asset recovery. The assets and proceeds of trafficking could include property and monies such as: profits from the services and exploitation of the victim;

---

[128] The term "freezing" (or seizure) in the context of asset recovery is defined by the Organized Crime Convention as "temporarily prohibiting the transfer, conversion, disposition, or movement of property or temporarily assuming custody or control of property on the basis of an order issued by a court or other competent authority": at Art. 2(f). The term "confiscation" is defined in the same instrument as "the permanent deprivation of property by order of a court or other competent authority": ibid. at Art. 2(g).

costs paid by victims (including for passports, visas, or transport), for example where the victim has paid for illegally facilitated migration and subsequently becomes a victim of trafficking; vehicles used to transport victims; factories, brothels, boats, and farms where the exploitation took place; profits from the sale or resale of a person from one trafficker to another; and the value of unpaid services and salaries that would have otherwise been paid to the persons exploited.

The legal basis of a national confiscation and recovery regime can be domestic law, bilateral or multilateral treaties, or, most commonly, a combination of the above. States generally develop their own national laws that specify a range of matters, such as: which "proceeds" can be a target of confiscation; criminal and civil evidentiary standards; institutions and tools and orders for obtaining financial information; and procedures for recovery of proceeds. In relation to cooperation with other countries, recovery of proceeds is a form of mutual legal assistance. States will, therefore, rely on provisions of their national mutual legal assistance laws as well as any treaties that may exist between them and the cooperating State.[129] Domestic money laundering laws and extradition treaties may also contain provisions on international cooperation in the recovery of the proceeds of crime. Provisions for the most appropriate use of confiscated assets are another important aspect. Some treaties specify how confiscated funds and property are to be used. Often, States have a wide discretion in this matter and regulate the disposal of confiscated proceeds or property through a combination of domestic law and administrative procedures. This issue is considered further below.

7.4.1. *Obligation to Seize and Confiscate Proceeds of Trafficking*

The existence of an obligation on States to seize and confiscate assets of trafficking is supported by relevant treaty law. The Organized Crime Convention sets out detailed rules and procedures for identification, tracing, freezing, and seizure of assets and confiscation of proceeds of designated crimes, including trafficking.[130] States Parties to the Convention and to the Trafficking Protocol[131] are required to create adequate powers (relating to both substantive and procedural law) to enable and support confiscation and seizure.[132] The Convention also sets forth a number of mechanisms to enhance international cooperation with respect to confiscation, in order to eliminate advantages to criminals presented by national borders and

---

[129] See further, the discussion on mutual legal assistance at Chapter 7.5.2.

[130] Organized Crime Convention, at Arts. 12–14.

[131] A State that is party to the Convention and not the Protocol would be required to establish that trafficking is, under its law, a "serious crime" as defined in the Convention for these provisions to apply to trafficking offenses: ibid. at Arts. 2(b), 3(1)(b); *Legislative Guide*, at Part 1, para. 302.

[132] Organized Crime Convention, at Art. 12. See further, *Legislative Guide*, at Part One, 145–147. Note however that the UNODC Model Law on Trafficking contains no reference to asset recovery – an indication, perhaps, of a broader failure to link the Trafficking Protocol with its parent Organized Crime Convention.

differences in legal systems.[133] States Parties are required to comply with requests for confiscation presented by another State Party.[134] Mutual legal assistance obligations under the Convention (explored further below) are to apply to such international cooperation.[135]

The European Trafficking Convention requires States Parties to "adopt such legislative and other measures as may be necessary to enable it to confiscate or otherwise deprive the instrumentalities and proceeds of [trafficking-related] criminal offences or property the value of which corresponds to such proceeds."[136] The Explanatory Report notes the link[137] between this provision and the European Convention on Laundering, Search, Seizure and Confiscation of the Proceeds from Crime,[138] which identifies confiscation of proceeds as an effective anticrime weapon.

International and regional treaties on related issues such as corruption and sale of children, child prostitution, and child pornography identify an obligation on States Parties to confiscate the assets and proceeds of relevant crimes.[139] On the particular issue of trafficking, the UN General Assembly has emphasized the importance of asset confiscation,[140] as have regional organizations[141] and various soft law instruments including the UN Trafficking Principles and Guidelines.[142]

---

[133] Organized Crime Convention, at Arts. 12, 13.

[134] Ibid. at Art. 13.

[135] Ibid. at Art. 13(3).

[136] European Trafficking Convention, at Art. 23(3). Note this provision applies only to offenses related to trafficking in human beings (Art. 18) and the forging of travel or identity documents for purposes of trafficking (Art. 20(a)).

[137] European Trafficking Convention Explanatory Report, at para. 254.

[138] Convention on Laundering, Search, Seizure and Confiscation of the Proceeds from Crime, 1862 UNTS 69, ETS No. 141, done Nov. 8, 1990, entered into force Sept. 1, 1993.

[139] CRC Optional Protocol, at Art. 7; United Nations Convention against Corruption, 2349 UNTS 41, done Oct. 31, 2003, entered into force Dec. 14, 2005 (Convention against Corruption), at Art. 31; Inter-American Convention against Corruption, OAS Treaties Register B-58, 35 ILM 724, done Mar. 29, 1996, entered into force Mar. 6, 1997, at Art. XV; Criminal Law Convention on Corruption, 2216 UNTS 225, ETS No. 173, done Jan. 27, 1999, entered into force July 1, 2002, at Art. 23; African Union Convention on Preventing and Combating Corruption, 43 ILM 5, adopted by the 2nd Ordinary Session of the Assembly of the Union on July 11, 2003, entered into force Aug. 5, 2006, at Art. 16.

[140] UN General Assembly, "Trafficking in Women and Girls," UN Doc. A/RES/63/156, Jan. 30, 2009, at para. 11; and UN General Assembly, "Trafficking in Women and Girls," UN Doc. A/RES/61/144, Dec. 19, 2006, at para. 10; UN General Assembly, "Trafficking in Women and Girls," UN Doc. A/RES/59/166, Dec. 20, 2004, at para. 9; UN General Assembly, "Strengthening International Cooperation in Preventing and Combating Trafficking in Persons and Protecting Victims of Such Trafficking," UN Doc. A/RES/58/137, Feb. 4, 2004, at para. 1.

[141] See, for example, the ASEAN Practitioner Guidelines, at Parts 1.A.3 ("[o]ffences of trafficking in persons, together with trafficking related crimes are recommended to be predicate offences in respect of money laundering legislation and assets confiscation provisions") and 2.D.6 ("[c]onsideration should be given to amending domestic legislation to ensure that measures are taken to identify, trace and freeze or seize proceeds of crime derived from trafficking in persons for the purpose of eventual confiscation"). See also the Brussels Declaration, at para. 16; EU Plan on Best Practices, at para. 4(v); OSCE Action Plan, at Recommendation III(1.5); OAS Recommendations on Trafficking in Persons, at Section III(3).

[142] UN Trafficking Principles and Guidelines, at Principle 16 and Guideline 4.4.

7.4.2. *Using Confiscated Assets to Compensate or Support Victims*

As noted above, States generally regulate the disposal of confiscated assets through domestic law and administrative procedures. The linking of a criminal justice measure such as confiscation of proceeds to victim support is an important step forward in both ending impunity for traffickers and securing justice for victims. This position finds considerable support in relevant treaty law. While the Organized Crime Convention does not contain any mandatory provisions with respect to disposal of confiscated proceeds or property, States Parties are required to consider specific disposal options. The priority option relates to victim compensation. Under the terms of the Convention, when a State Party has responded to a request from another State Party with regard to asset confiscation, then the requested State shall, if requested and legally able, "give priority to returning the confiscated proceeds or property to the requesting State Party so that it can give compensation to the victim of the crime or return such proceeds of crime or property to their legitimate owners."[143] The European Trafficking Convention's provisions on this point are also advisory rather than mandatory. States Parties are required to guarantee pecuniary compensation for victims "for instance through the establishment of a fund for victim compensation or measures or programmes aimed at social assistance and social integration of victims, *which could be funded by the assets resulting from the application of [confiscation] measures.*"[144]

International and regional policy instruments and the pronouncements of human rights bodies provide some indication that States are beginning to accept the notion that confiscated proceeds of trafficking crimes should be returned, in some form or another, to the victims whose exploitation has made such profits possible.[145] Importantly, it has

---

[143] Organized Crime Convention, at Art. 14(2). Other options proposed under Article 14 include contributing proceeds or property to a special UN fund for use against organized crime and sharing confiscated funds with other States Parties in order to encourage enhanced cooperation among law enforcement agencies.

[144] European Trafficking Convention, at Art. 15(4) (emphasis added). In addition, at the time that the present volume was going to press, the latest draft of a forthcoming European Parliament Directive on trafficking obtained by the author contained the much stronger, mandatory language that "Member States shall take the necessary measures to ensure that the proceeds and profits seized and confiscated under this Directive are used to support victim assistance and protection, including compensation of victims": draft of June 28, 2010 on file with author. If this provision survives, it will be the first such mandatory provision in a major binding instrument. At the time of publication, the latest publicly available draft of the forthcoming Directive was European Commission, Proposal for a Directive of the European Parliament and of the Council on preventing and combating trafficking in human beings, and protecting victims, repealing Framework Decision 2002/629/JHA, COM(2010) 95 final, Mar. 29, 2010.

[145] UN Trafficking Principles and Guidelines, at Principle 16 and Guideline 4.4; ASEAN Practitioner Guidelines, at Part 1.A.4 ("[a]s far as possible, confiscated assets should be used to fund both victim compensation claims and, where appropriate, other forms of counter-trafficking initiatives"); OSCE Action Plan, at Recommendation III(1.5); "Report of the Special Rapporteur on the human rights aspects of the victims of trafficking in persons, especially women and children, Sigma Huda, Addendum 2: Mission to Bosnia and Herzegovina," UN Doc. E/CN.4/2006/62/Add.2, Nov. 30, 2005, at para. 78. See also, UN General Assembly, "Declaration of Basic Principles of Justice for Victims of Crime and Abuse of Power," UN Doc. A/RES/40/34, Nov. 29, 1985, at para. 4(h), encouraging States "to co-operate with other States, through mutual judicial and administrative assistance, in such

been noted that these measures are not generally sustainable and should only ever be considered an adjunct to an institutionalized, adequately funded victim support and protection program.[146] Reference should also be made to the discussion of compensation within the broader context of a right to a remedy in the previous chapter.

7.5. INTERNATIONAL COOPERATION

It is possible for all elements of the crime of trafficking to take place within national borders and for offenders, victims, and evidence to be co-located. However, trafficking cases are typically much more complicated than this. Alleged offenders, victims, and evidence can be located in two or more countries. The same factual situation can justify and give rise to criminal investigations and prosecutions in multiple jurisdictions. Informal cooperation mechanisms as well as more traditional legal tools are important means of eliminating safe havens for traffickers and thereby enabling States to meet their obligations with respect to criminalization, investigation, and prosecution of trafficking cases. The nature and scope of States' obligations to cooperate in the investigation and prosecution of traffickers and their accomplices is considered below. Additional and more detailed consideration is given to the specific obligations related to the most important vehicles for such cooperation: extradition and mutual legal assistance.

7.5.1. *Obligations Related to Extradition*

The term "extradition" refers to one of the oldest of all forms of international legal cooperation in criminal matters: a process whereby one State (the Requesting State) asks another State (the Requested State) to return an individual to face criminal charges or punishment in the Requesting State. Because of the nature of human trafficking, suspects wanted for prosecution in one State will often be in another State. This may be because they are nationals of that other State or because they have deliberately taken steps to avoid prosecution or sentencing by fleeing to another State. Extradition will, therefore, sometimes be essential for the successful prosecution of trafficking cases.

Traditionally, extradition was based on pacts, courtesy, or good will between heads of States. Today, the legal basis for extradition at the national level is generally domestic law, bilateral or multilateral treaties, or a combination of the above. Extradition based on domestic law is increasingly common, providing for extradition with countries in the absence of specific treaty-based agreements. Some States today use domestic law exclusively as their basis for extradition. Others have adopted a blended system in which extradition is permitted on a treaty basis and also on the basis of domestic law. With the emergence of international courts and tribunals exercising

---

matters as the detection and pursuit of offenders, their extradition and the seizure of their assets, to be used for restitution to the victims." See also UNODC Model Law, at 58.

[146] Gallagher and Holmes, "Lessons from the Front Line," at 330.

criminal jurisdiction, treaties also provide for extradition to these non-State bodies.[147] In the past, extradition laws and treaties would usually contain a list of offenses covered. More recent treaties and national laws are based on the principle of *dual criminality*, which allows extradition in relation to an offense if it is criminalized in both the requested and the requesting countries and the penalties provided for are above a defined threshold, for example, a defined period of imprisonment. The principle of dual criminality provides an additional, compelling reason for States to criminalize trafficking as it has been defined by international law.[148]

Making Trafficking an Extraditable Offense. International treaty law generally supports the existence of an obligation on States to ensure that trafficking and related offenses prohibited under international law (defined above to include, at a minimum, sexual exploitation, forced labor or services, slavery or practices similar to slavery and servitude, debt bondage, the worst forms of child labor, and forced marriage) constitute extraditable offenses under national law and extradition treaties. While the Trafficking Protocol does not deal with extradition, its parent instrument, the Organized Crime Convention, sets out a basic minimum standard. The Organized Crime Convention requires States Parties to treat offenses established in accordance with the Protocol (limited to trafficking, offenses related to documents, etc.)[149] as extraditable offenses under their laws and to ensure that such offenses are included as extraditable offenses in every current and future extradition treaty.[150] Other relevant international and regional treaties identify trafficking and related conduct as extraditable offenses.[151]

The European Trafficking Convention requires States Parties to impose penalties that give rise to extradition.[152] Also, in the European context, trafficking in persons falls within the categories of extraditable offenses covered by the European Convention on Extradition.[153] Similar umbrella extradition treaties have been

---

[147] See further C. Nicholls, C. Montgomery and J. Knowles, *The Law of Extradition and Mutual Assistance: Practice and Procedure* (2007) (Nicholls et al., *The Law of Extradition*).

[148] See further, the discussion of the obligation of criminalization at Chapter 7.1.

[149] Note that the obligation to make trafficking an extraditable offense would only apply to offenses constituting a "serious" transnational crime under the Convention and Protocol, and involving an organized criminal group: *Legislative Guide*, at Part 1, paras. 403, 414–417. States Parties may, however, apply the extradition provisions to other offenses (such as trafficking that does not involve an organized criminal group) and, under Art. 16(2), are encouraged to do so.

[150] Organized Crime Convention, at Art. 16.

[151] SAARC Convention, at Art. VII; Inter-American Convention on International Traffic in Minors, at Art. 10; CRC Optional Protocol, at Art. 4.

[152] European Trafficking Convention, at Art. 23(1). Under Article 2 of the European Convention on Extradition, this would require Parties to provide for a custodial penalty of at least one year: European Trafficking Convention Explanatory Report, at para. 252.

[153] Note the Council of Europe Convention Relating to the Simplified Extradition Procedure between Member States of the European Union, adopted March 10, 1995, to supplement the European Convention on Extradition, OJ C 78/1, Mar. 30, 1995. Note also the introduction of a European Arrest Warrant through the Council Framework Decision of 13 June 2002 on a European Arrest Warrant and the Surrender Procedures between Member States (2002/284/JHA), OJ L 190/1, July 18, 2002, at Art. 2(2). Human trafficking is one of the crimes for which surrender procedures are possible pursuant to the European arrest warrant.

concluded for the Americas and West Africa.[154] International and regional policy around trafficking is also beginning to recognize the importance of ensuring that trafficking offenses are subject to extradition.[155]

The Organized Crime Convention encourages States to adopt a range of measures designed to streamline the extradition process by expediting requests and simplifying evidentiary procedures.[156] Other trafficking-specific policy instruments echo this request.[157] These provisions reflect an understanding that extradition is generally a very complicated and time-consuming process that is subject to numerous obstacles and restrictions. Unless States make a positive effort to streamline their extradition procedures in cases of trafficking, it is unlikely that this tool of international legal cooperation will contribute greatly to ending impunity for traffickers who move across borders to escape prosecution or punishment for their crimes.

Sovereignty, Fair Treatment, and Human Rights in Extradition. An effective criminal justice response to trafficking, as with any other crime, requires that the human rights of suspects and offenders are respected and protected. This requirement extends to the extradition process. The importance of fair treatment and human rights in extradition is confirmed by the Organized Crime Convention[158] as well as by regional extradition treaties.[159] International policy documents refer specifically to

---

[154] Inter-American Convention on Extradition; ECOWAS Convention on Extradition.

[155] See, for example, UN Trafficking Principles and Guidelines, at Principle 14; ASEAN Practitioner Guidelines, at Part 1.A.4 ("[i]n order to ensure that there are no safe havens for traffickers, States are encouraged to either extradite or prosecute alleged offenders"); OSCE Action Plan, at Recommendation III(1.6) ("trafficking, its constitutive acts and related offences constitute extraditable offences under national law and extradition treaties"). The UN General Assembly has called on States to "consider establishing coordination and cooperation mechanisms at the national and international levels on extradition, mutual legal assistance and sharing police intelligence information": UN General Assembly, "Improving the Coordination of Efforts against Trafficking In Persons," UN Doc. A/RES/61/180, Dec. 20, 2006, at para. 7.

[156] Organized Crime Convention, at Art. 16(8).

[157] Under the ASEAN Practitioner Guidelines, for example, "States should accord high priority to and expedite requests relating to trafficking cases": at Guideline 2.D.4. More generally, the Brussels Declaration has requested States, "with the aim to speed up exchange of information in criminal investigations and mutual legal assistance" to establish "direct contacts between law enforcement services and judicial authorities": at para. 16. The OAS Recommendations on Trafficking in Persons call on States to "introduce expeditious mechanisms ... to enable information to be exchanged and political dialogue to be strengthened among the countries of origin, transit, destination within and outside the hemisphere": at Section V(2). See also UN Trafficking Principles and Guidelines, at Guideline 9.

[158] The Organized Crime Convention, at Article 16(13), provides that "[a]ny person [involved in an extradition request or process] ... shall be guaranteed fair treatment at all stages of the proceedings including enjoyment of the rights and guarantees provided by the domestic law of the State Party in the territory of which that person is present." Article 16(14) provides that an obligation to extradite will not exist under the Convention: "if the requested State Party has substantial grounds for believing that the request has been made for the purpose of prosecuting or punishing a person on account of that person's race, sex, religion, nationality, ethnic origin or political opinions or that compliance with the request would cause prejudice to that person's position for any of these reasons."

[159] For example, the Inter-American Convention on Extradition, at Article 16(1), provides that "[t]he person sought shall enjoy in the requested State all the legal rights and guarantees granted by the laws of that State." See also the ECOWAS Convention on Extradition, at Arts. 5, 14.

the need to ensure extradition in trafficking cases meets international human rights and criminal justice standards.[160]

A number of principles and rules have been developed to guard against unfair treatment in extradition – as well as to protect State sovereignty.[161] For example, extradition laws and regimes including those that govern trafficking require that the conduct constituting the extradition offense be recognized as a criminal offense in both the Requesting and the Requested State. This is often referred to as the principle of *dual criminality*.[162] The requirement of dual criminality in relation to trafficking offenses can be satisfied by States both ratifying the Organized Crime Convention and Trafficking Protocol, which stipulate and define the relevant offenses, and ensuring that domestic legislation incorporates the offenses and definitions under those treaties.[163] A Requested State may also deny cooperation if the person sought has already been tried and acquitted or punished for the conduct underlying the extradition request. This derives from the principle of *double jeopardy (ne bis in idem)* under international human rights law. While the prohibition against double jeopardy under international human rights law is generally restricted to double prosecution within the same jurisdiction, it has been widened to a principle of so-called "international" double jeopardy under several major extradition treaties.[164] Further, under the rule of *speciality* (or *specialty*), a Requesting State must not, without the

---

[160] See, for example, the UN Trafficking Principles and Guidelines, at Principle 14.

[161] In addition to the cited sources, these points draw on the UN General Assembly, "Model Treaty on Extradition," annexed to UN General Assembly, "Model Treaty on Extradition," UN Doc. A/RES/45/116, Dec. 14, 1990, subsequently amended by UN General Assembly, "International Cooperation in Criminal Matters," UN Doc. A/RES/52/88, Dec. 12, 1997. See also, J. Dugard and C. Van den Wyngaert, "Reconciling Extradition with Human Rights," (1998) 92 *American Journal of International Law* 187.

[162] See Organized Crime Convention, at Art. 16(1); European Convention on Extradition, at Art. 2; Inter-American Convention on Extradition, at Art. 3; ECOWAS Convention on Extradition, at Art. 3.

[163] The dual criminality requirement will be automatically satisfied with respect to offenses established under Articles 6, 8 and 23 of the Convention (money laundering, corruption, obstruction of justice) but not necessarily in relation to offenses established under Article 5 (criminalization of participation in an organized criminal group) or "serious crime" where States Parties are not required to criminalize exactly the same conduct: *Legislative Guide*, at Part One, 200.

[164] See, for example, ICCPR, at Art. 14(7) ("[n]o one shall be liable to be tried or punished again for an offence for which he has already been finally convicted or acquitted in accordance with the law and penal procedure of each country"). Note that in human rights law, double jeopardy has traditionally applied only to double prosecution within the same jurisdiction. See, for example, *AP v. Italy*, UNHRC Comm. No. 204/1986, UN Doc. CCPR/C/31/D/204/1986, decided Nov. 2, 1987: "[t]he [Human Rights] Committee observes that this provision [Art. 14(7) of the ICCPR] prohibits double jeopardy only with regard to an offence adjudicated in a given State." However, under the regime established by the major extradition treaties, an expanded double jeopardy principle can operate to exclude extradition notwithstanding that the prior adjudication occurred in a jurisdiction other than that of the Requesting State: see European Convention on Extradition, at Art. 9; Inter-American Convention on Extradition, at Art. 4(1); ECOWAS Convention on Extradition, at Art. 13. For a thorough discussion of so-called international double jeopardy, see C. Van den Wyngaert and G. Stessens, "The International *Non Bis in Idem* Principle: Resolving Some of the Unanswered Questions," (1999) 48 *International and Comparative Law Quarterly* 779.

consent of the Requested State, try or punish the suspect for an offense not referred to in the extradition request and alleged to have been committed before the person was extradited.[165] Speciality supports the rule of double jeopardy and prevents abuse of the extradition process by States that might otherwise secure the extradition of a person for one offense and then prosecute him or her for another.

Many States will not extradite their nationals. The *nationality* exception recognizes the right to decline to extradite a person who is a national of the Requested State. Refusal on these grounds is sometimes provided for in treaties and often in domestic laws. It is also enshrined within the constitutions of some countries. Depending on the relevant legal framework, the application of this principle might be mandatory or discretionary. Under some laws and treaties, if a country refuses to extradite an individual because of nationality, then the Requested State must prosecute the person in their own jurisdiction. This is known as the "extradite or prosecute" principle (*aut dedere aut judicare*). This principle is considered in more detail below.

The *political offense exception* recognizes a right of the Requested State to decline to extradite a person because he or she is accused or has been convicted of a political offense.[166] The political offense exception is not absolute and it can be expected to narrow further as States develop stronger responses to crimes such as terrorism that often have a strong political dimension. Importantly, violent crimes such as genocide, crimes against humanity, and war crimes are regarded by the international community as so heinous that perpetrators cannot be permitted to rely on the political offense exception.[167] Under international treaty law, the political offense exception has also been removed in relation to prosecutions for corruption.[168]

International law recognizes a right of States (amounting to an obligation) to refuse an extradition request that is discriminatory in its purpose or if the person sought for extradition may be persecuted or otherwise prejudiced because of one of the recognized grounds such as race, sex, religion, nationality, ethnic origin, or political opinion.[169] States also have the right to refuse extradition on the basis that: (1) the offense for which extradition is being sought carries the death penalty

---

[165] See European Convention on Extradition, at Art. 14; Inter-American Convention on Extradition, at Art. 13; ECOWAS Convention on Extradition, at Art. 20.

[166] See European Convention on Extradition, at Art. 3(1); Inter-American Convention on Extradition, at Art. 4(4); ECOWAS Convention on Extradition, at Art. 4(1).

[167] For example, the Additional Protocol to the European Convention on Extradition provides that for the purposes of the Convention, "political offences" shall not include crimes against humanity specified in the Convention on the Prevention and Punishment of the Crime of Genocide, certain violations of the Geneva Conventions, and any comparable violations of the laws of war: 1161 UNTS 449, ETS 86, done Oct. 15 1975, entered into force Aug. 20, 1979, at Art. 1. See also the ICC Statute, at Articles 6–8, defining the crimes of genocide, crimes against humanity, and war crimes.

[168] Convention against Corruption, at Art. 44(4): if a State uses this convention as the legal basis for extradition, it "shall not consider any of the offences established in accordance with this Convention to be a political offence."

[169] Authority for the contention that such refusal would be obligatory under international law is provided by the antidiscrimination clauses of all major international and regional human rights treaties. See

(unless the Requesting State provides an assurance not to impose the death penalty or not to carry it out if it is imposed);[170] or (2) the person sought would be subjected to torture or cruel, inhuman, or degrading treatment or punishment. Requested States may also refuse extradition if there are reasonable grounds to believe the individual concerned will not benefit from minimum guarantees in criminal proceedings[171] or otherwise not receive a fair trial.[172]

An Obligation to Extradite or Prosecute? As outlined above, States may be entitled to refuse extradition on certain grounds. While respecting such entitlements, international law places an obligation on States refusing extradition to nevertheless prosecute certain offenses. This obligation to either extradite or prosecute (also referred to as extradite or adjudicate, *aut dedere aut judicare*, or *aut dedere aut prosequi*) has a long history in international law, particularly international humanitarian law. It is part of all four Geneva Conventions of 1949 in relation to the commission of "grave breaches" of those Conventions.[173] The Torture Convention contains a similar obligation,[174] as does the Statute of the International Criminal Court.[175] When it comes to violations of *jus cogens* norms (including those related to slavery and the slave trade), it is accepted that the obligation to extradite or prosecute applies to all States as a matter of customary international law.[176] Importantly, however,

also European Convention on Extradition, at Art. 3(2); Inter-American Convention on Extradition, at Art. 4(5); ECOWAS Convention on Extradition, at Art. 4(2). See also Trafficking Protocol, at Art. 14 and European Trafficking Convention, at Art. 40 and the discussion of *non-refoulement* in Chapter 6.1.3, above.

[170] See European Convention on Extradition, at Art. 11; Inter-American Convention on Extradition, at Art. 9; ECOWAS Convention on Extradition, at Art. 17 (unless the death penalty is also imposed in Requested State).

[171] Authority for the contention that such refusal would be obligatory under international law is provided by ICCPR, at Art. 7 and Convention against Torture and Other Cruel, Inhuman or Degrading Treatment or Punishment, 1465 UNTS 85, done Dec. 10, 1984, June 26, 1987 (Convention against Torture), at Art. 3.

[172] UN General Assembly, "Protection of Human Rights and Fundamental Freedoms While Countering Terrorism: Note by the Secretary General," UN Doc. A/63/223, Aug. 6, 2008, at 6, para. 8.

[173] For example, the Fourth Geneva Convention states that "[e]ach High Contracting Party shall be under the obligation to search for persons alleged to have committed or have ordered to be committed, such grave breaches, and shall bring such persons, regardless of their nationality, before its own courts. It may also, if it prefers, and in accordance with the provisions of its own legislation, hand such persons over for trial to another High Contracting Party concerned, provided such High Contracting Party has made out a *prima facie* case": Geneva Convention Relative to the Protection of Civilian Persons in Time of War, 75 UNTS 287, done Aug. 12, 1949, entered into force Oct. 21, 1950 (Fourth Geneva Convention), at Art. 146.

[174] "The State Party in the territory under whose jurisdiction a person alleged to have committed any offence referred to in Article 4 is found shall, in the cases contemplated in Article 5, if it does not extradite him, submit the case to its competent authorities for the purpose of prosecution": Convention against Torture, at Art. 7(1).

[175] ICC Statute, particularly at Part 2, Arts. 5, 8(1), 11, 12, 13, 17, 19, and Part 3, Art. 26.

[176] M.C. Bassiouni and E.M. Wise, Aut Dedere Aut Judicare: *The Duty to Extradite or Prosecute in International Law* (1995). See also, C. Enache-Brown and A. Fried, "Universal Crime, Jurisdiction

when the relevant trafficking-related offense does not involve violations of *jus cogens* norms, the obligation is not customary and will only apply if imposed by treaties. The Organized Crime Convention extends the principle of "extradite or prosecute" to trafficking offenses.[177] States Parties to the European Trafficking Convention are similarly obliged to prosecute if they refuse a request for extradition for an offense established under that instrument.[178] Other relevant international treaties reiterate the importance of this principle.[179] Currently, the obligation to extradite or prosecute is under consideration by the International Law Commission, under the leadership of Special Rapporteur Zdzislaw Galicki.[180]

7.5.2. *Mutual Legal Assistance in Trafficking Cases*

Successful investigation and prosecution of trafficking cases will often involve cooperation between States in securing evidence that is located in a country other than that in which the prosecution is to take place. When such cooperation involves evidence required to be admissible in court, or relates to outcomes that can only be secured through coercive means, it is generally governed by strict "mutual legal assistance" rules set out in international and domestic laws. Common types of mutual legal assistance include: taking evidence or statements from persons; locating and identifying witnesses and suspects; effecting service of judicial documents; executing searches and seizures; freezing assets; providing originals or certified copies of relevant documents and records; identifying or tracing proceeds of crime; facilitating the voluntary appearance of persons in the Requesting State; transfer of proceedings, investigation, or prisoners, including transfer of prisoners to give evidence; and video recording of testimony.[181]

Mutual legal assistance regimes are often established through bilateral or multilateral treaties. Such regimes may cover a single issue such as terrorism, money laundering, or organized crime. Treaties can also be concluded for the purpose of providing a general framework of rules within which mutual legal assistance matters are dealt with between two or more countries. The Inter-American Convention on Mutual Legal Assistance in Criminal Matters[182] and the Convention on Mutual

---

and Duty: The Obligation of *Aut Dedere Aut Judicare* in International Law," (1998) 43 *McGill Law Journal* 613.

[177] Organized Crime Convention, at Arts. 15(3), 16(10). Note that the *aut dedere aut judicare* rule is limited, in this convention, to cases where refusal relates to nationality of the suspect.

[178] European Trafficking Convention, at Art. 31(3). Note that the provision is limited to cases where refusal relates to nationality of the suspect.

[179] SAARC Convention, at Art. VII(4); CRC Optional Protocol, at Art. 4(3); Inter-American Convention on Extradition, at Art. 8.

[180] See the reports available at http://untreaty.un.org/ilc/guide/gfra.htm (accessed Feb. 9, 2010).

[181] See, for example, Organized Crime Convention, at Art. 18(3).

[182] Inter-American Convention on Mutual Legal Assistance in Criminal Matters, OASTS 75, done May 23, 1992, entered into force Apr. 14, 1996.

Legal Assistance between Like-Minded ASEAN Countries[183] are examples of this latter approach. Mutual legal assistance treaties generally indicate the kinds of assistance to be provided, the rights of the Requesting and Requested States, the rights of alleged offenders, and the procedures to be followed in making, receiving, and executing requests. States can also deal with mutual legal assistance matters through their domestic law. Many countries have passed legislation enabling them to provide various forms of assistance to other States without the need for treaty relations. The legislation usually prescribes the preconditions and the procedure for making, transmitting, and executing incoming and outgoing requests. Some laws designate the foreign States to which they will provide assistance and some provide that assistance will be extended on a case-by-case basis.

The Organized Crime Convention, as the parent instrument to the Trafficking Protocol, obliges States Parties to afford one another the widest measure of such assistance in investigations, prosecutions, and judicial proceedings in relation to offenses covered by that instrument, including trafficking.[184] It also sets out a detailed legal and procedural framework for mutual legal assistance between States Parties.[185] There are no provisions on mutual legal assistance in the European Trafficking Convention in deference to an already established regime.[186] The SAARC Convention contains an obligation of mutual legal assistance in respect of offenses established under that treaty.[187] The importance of mutual legal assistance in trafficking cases is reiterated in international and regional policy documents.[188] Indeed, seeking mutual legal assistance where necessary may be vital to fulfilling the obligation of due diligence: In a recent decision considering a trafficking-related death, the European Court of Human Rights criticized the State of destination for failing to avail itself of a mutual legal assistance regime established under treaty with the State of origin.[189]

Most of the exceptions outlined above in relation to extradition including the principles of dual criminality, double jeopardy, and speciality also apply to mutual

---

[183] Convention on Mutual Legal Assistance between Like-Minded ASEAN Countries, done Nov. 29, 2004, entered into force from June 1, 2005.

[184] Organized Crime Convention, at Art. 18.

[185] Ibid.

[186] European Trafficking Convention Explanatory Report, at para. 337.

[187] SAARC Convention, at Art. VI.

[188] For example, the UN General Assembly has called on States to "address the problem of trafficking in persons through, inter alia … mutual legal assistance": "Trafficking in Women and Girls," UN Doc. A/RES/63/156, Jan. 30, 2009, at para. 10. See also, UN General Assembly, "Improving the Coordination of Efforts against Trafficking in Persons," UN Doc. A/RES/63/194, Jan. 23, 2009, at para. 7; Brussels Declaration, at para. 16; OAS Recommendations on Trafficking in Persons, at Section III(6); UN Trafficking Principles and Guidelines, at Guideline 11.8; and ASEAN Practitioner Guidelines, at Parts 1.A.1 and 2.B.3.

[189] *Rantsev v. Cyprus and Russia*, at para. 241. The criticism was made in the context of finding a violation of the obligation to carry out an effective investigation, under the right to life.

legal assistance requests. Human rights guarantees apply as much to mutual legal assistance as they do to extradition. States must ensure that nothing in the terms of a mutual legal assistance request would constitute an actual or potential infringement of the human rights of either the subject of the request or of any third parties. Particularly in relation to coercive measures, it is important to ensure that these requests are reasonable and necessary, taking into account the evidence sought and the seriousness of the offense under investigation. Cooperation may be refused when Requesting States do not respect basic rights and procedural guarantees as set out in major human rights instruments such as the Universal Declaration of Human Rights and the ICCPR.

7.5.3. *Informal Cooperation*

Informal cooperation is a separate, less rule-bound international crime cooperation tool, which is available outside the formal mutual assistance regime. Informal cooperation enables law enforcement and regulatory agencies (such as taxation and revenue authorities or companies and financial service regulators) to directly share information and intelligence with their foreign counterparts without any requirement to make a formal mutual assistance request. In this sense, informal cooperation complements mutual legal assistance regimes. This international cooperation tool can be used prior to an investigation becoming official and prior to the commencement of court proceedings, for example to conduct surveillance or take voluntary witness statements. In circumstances where coercive measures are not required, it is usually faster, cheaper, and easier to obtain information or intelligence on an informal basis rather than via formal mutual assistance channels.

The Organized Crime Convention and the Trafficking Protocol both recognize the value of police-to-police cooperation. The Convention lists a range of objectives for such cooperation including early identification of offenses and exchange of information and intelligence.[190] It encourages States Parties to enter into bilateral or multilateral agreements or arrangements with a view to enhancing cooperation between law enforcement agencies.[191] The Protocol emphasizes cooperation through information exchange for purposes such as victim and perpetrator identification in transit, document verification, and proactive intelligence gathering.[192] The importance of law enforcement cooperation in the investigation of trafficking-related crimes has been recognized widely outside these two treaties.[193]

---

[190] Organized Crime Convention, at Art. 27(1).
[191] Ibid, at Art. 27(2).
[192] Trafficking Protocol, at Art. 10(1).
[193] The UN Trafficking Principles and Guidelines encourage informal cooperation in the criminal justice process with a particular focus on law enforcement cooperation: see Guidelines 11.6 and 11.7. The Beijing Platform for Action requires States to "[s]tep up cooperation and concerted action by all relevant law enforcement authorities and institutions" aimed at dismantling trafficking networks at the national, regional, and international levels: Beijing Declaration and Platform for Action, at

The Organized Crime Convention encourages joint investigations in trafficking cases;[194] a form of agency-to-agency assistance that enables direct exchange of information between concerned countries. Such investigations could be envisaged for a case that is to be tried in a single jurisdiction. It would also be a useful tool when more than one State has jurisdiction over the offenses involved. Joint investigations can be undertaken on a bilateral basis or can be coordinated through an international or regional police agency such as Interpol or Europol or a regional prosecutorial agency such as Eurojust.[195] The possibility of coordinated specialist investigator-prosecutor investigation teams being deployed at the regional level has been raised in Africa,[196] Europe,[197] and Southeast Asia.[198]

para. 130(c). The UN General Assembly has encouraged States to implement the Organized Crime Convention and Trafficking Protocol by "promoting cooperation among law enforcement authorities in combating trafficking in persons": "Strengthening International Cooperation in Preventing and Combating Trafficking in Persons and Protecting Victims of Such Trafficking," UN Doc. A/RES/58/137, Dec. 22, 2003, at para. 4(b). The Organization of American States has recommended that Member States "introduce expeditious mechanisms … to enable information to be exchanged … among the countries of origin, transit, destination" and that "regional and international cooperation networks should be created to enable competent authorities, in particular judicial and police authorities, to combat the crime of trafficking in persons": OAS Recommendations on Trafficking in Persons, at Section V(2). See also OSCE Action Plan, at Recommendations III(2.5), III(3). See also UN Trafficking Principles and Guidelines, at Guidelines 11.6 and 11.7.

[194] Organized Crime Convention, at Art. 19. See also UN Trafficking Principles and Guidelines, at Guideline 11.8.

[195] See further, Gallagher and Holmes, "Lessons from the Front Line," at 328. The UN General Assembly has encouraged States to consider "sharing police intelligence information … taking into account the information and communication tools offered by Interpol": "Improving the Coordination of Efforts against Trafficking in Persons," UN Doc. A/RES/61/180, Dec. 20, 2006, at para. 7. The Council of the European Union has also recommended that Member States "should ensure that national law enforcement agencies regularly involve Europol in the exchange of information, in joint operations and joint investigative teams and use the potential of Eurojust to facilitate the prosecution of traffickers": EU Plan on Best Practices, at para. 4(viii).

[196] See ECOWAS Initial Plan of Action, at 7–8, which recommends the development of joint investigation units with input from government law enforcement agencies, government personnel and training agencies, Interpol, and other law enforcement agencies.

[197] The Brussels Declaration also recommends the establishment of "specialized, joint investigative teams of investigators and prosecutors": at para. 17.

[198] ASEAN Practitioner Guidelines, at Part 2.A.1.

8

Obligations to Prevent Trafficking and Respond Lawfully

The principles of State responsibility set out in Chapter 4 confirm that States bear some responsibility for preventing the occurrence of internationally wrongful acts. The standard implied in this obligation is one of due diligence: The State is required to take "all reasonable and necessary measures to prevent a given event from occurring."[1] A decision on what is "reasonable or appropriate" in a particular situation will require consideration of the facts of the case and surrounding circumstances, including the capacities of the State, as well as the relevant primary rules.

In the context of trafficking in persons, prevention refers to positive measures to stop future acts of trafficking from occurring. Policies and activities identified as "prevention" are generally those considered to be addressing the *causes* of trafficking. While there is not yet universal agreement on the complex matter of causes of trafficking, the most commonly cited causative factors are those that: (1) increase vulnerability of victims and potential victims; (2) create or sustain demand for the goods and services produced by trafficked labor; and (3) create or sustain an environment within which traffickers and their accomplices can operate with impunity. From this perspective, prevention can be seen to include a wide range of measures – from providing women with fair and equal migration opportunities, to strengthening the criminal justice response in order to end impunity and deter future trafficking-related crimes. The present chapter considers prevention under three main headings that generally correspond to the categories identified above: addressing the factors that increase vulnerability to trafficking; reducing demand for trafficking; and identifying and eradicating public sector involvement in, and corruption related to, trafficking. The prevention aspects of other obligations and responses are dealt with as they arise at various points throughout this book.

---

[1] "[B]ut without warranting that the event will not occur": International Law Commission (ILC), *Draft Articles on Responsibility of States for Internationally Wrongful Acts, Report of the International Law Commission on the Work of Its Fifty-Third Session*, UN GAOR, 56th Sess., Supp. No. 10, at 43, UN Doc. A/56/10 (2001) (ILC Articles on State Responsibility), at Art. 14, para. 14.

An approach to trafficking that derives its legitimacy from international law will inevitably recognize constraints on the responses of States. The key restriction in this regard is provided by the rule that responses to trafficking should not violate established rights. The nature and practical implications of this rule are considered in the final section of this chapter.

8.1. PREVENTION THROUGH ADDRESSING VULNERABILITY

While current understandings of the dynamics of trafficking are incomplete, it is nevertheless evident that certain environmental or contextual factors help shape the vulnerability of an individual, a social group, a community, or a society to trafficking. These factors include, while not being limited to, human rights violations such as poverty, inequality, discrimination, and gender-based violence – all of which contribute to creating economic deprivation and social conditions that limit individual choice and make it easier for traffickers and exploiters to operate. Factors that shape vulnerability to trafficking tend to impact differently and disproportionately on groups that already lack power and status in society, including women, children, migrants, refugees, and the internally displaced. Certain occupations such as prostitution and domestic service can produce, nurture, or exacerbate vulnerabilities through factors such as low visibility, lack of legal protection, or inappropriate regulation.

These intuitively sensible conclusions have been generally borne out in studies of trafficking patterns and victim profiles. However, vulnerability to trafficking is certainly not fixed, predetermined, or even fully "known." A multitude of factors operate to shape the environment within which trafficking takes place, and genuine understanding of vulnerability will almost always require situation-specific analysis.[2]

This section will first provide an overview of the legal obligation to address vulnerability to trafficking, before considering the obligation in relation to specific factors giving rise to vulnerability.

---

[2] An example is provided by a 2009 Europol analysis of trafficking from Central and Eastern Europe, which notes that "[i]t is not necessarily the case that a victim of trafficking can be described as having a 'typical' background. Although there are thousands of examples of individuals who have been targeted by traffickers because of their adverse personal circumstances, there are countless numbers of individuals who do not fit the stereotyped background; for example a lack of formal or secondary education, escaping abusive family or personal relationships, or unemployed with no future prospects. Individuals with a higher education, including university qualifications and with second and third languages, that are in employment and stable relationships are now considered to be almost as vulnerable but for different reasons. Greater freedom of movement and travel, low cost international transport and global communication links, combined with previously unavailable opportunities to work overseas and self confidence are all contributory factors in the recruitment by traffickers of persons who would not normally be thought of as vulnerable." Europol, "Trafficking in Human Beings in the European Union: A Europol Perspective," June 2009, at 3.

8.1.1. A Legal Obligation to Address Vulnerability to Trafficking

Relevant treaty law confirms the existence of certain obligations with respect to preventing trafficking through addressing vulnerability. The Trafficking Protocol, for example, requires States Parties to establish comprehensive policies, programs, and measures to prevent and combat trafficking and to protect victims from revictimization.[3] States Parties are also required to take positive steps to address the underlying causes of trafficking, specifically to "take or strengthen measures … to alleviate the factors that make persons, especially women and children, vulnerable to trafficking, such as poverty, underdevelopment and lack of equal opportunity."[4] It is relevant to note that unlike other, "softer" victim protection provisions, the prevention obligations of the Protocol are framed in mandatory and not merely hortative language. Accordingly, States are required to take at least some positive action to discharge these obligations.

The prevention obligations of the Trafficking Protocol are linked to and reinforced by the prevention obligations of its parent Organized Crime Convention. States Parties to that instrument are, for example, required to address the adverse social and economic conditions believed to contribute to the desire to migrate, and hence to the vulnerability of victims of cross-border trafficking.[5] Both treaties highlight the need for education and awareness raising aimed at improving understanding of trafficking, mobilizing community support for action against trafficking, and providing advice and warning to specific groups and individuals that may be at high risk of victimization.[6]

The European Trafficking Convention affirms an obligation to prevent trafficking through addressing the factors that create or increase vulnerability.[7] States Parties to that instrument are required to establish or strengthen effective and rights-based policies and programs to prevent trafficking for persons vulnerable to trafficking, including measures such as information, awareness raising, and educational

---

[3] Protocol to Prevent, Suppress and Punish Trafficking in Persons, Especially Women and Children, supplementing the United Nations Convention against Transnational Organized Crime, done Nov. 15, 2000, GA Res. 55/25, Annex II, UN GAOR, 55th Sess., Supp. No. 49, at 53, UN Doc. A/45/49 (Vol. I) (2001), entered into force Dec. 25, 2003 (Trafficking Protocol), at Art. 9(1).

[4] Ibid. at Art. 9(4).

[5] United Nations Convention against Transnational Organized Crime, 2225 UNTS 209, done Nov. 15, 2000, entered into force Sept. 29, 2003 (Organized Crime Convention), at Art. 31(7). See also UN Office on Drugs and Crime, *Legislative Guides for the Implementation of the United Nations Convention against Transnational Organized Crime and the Protocols Thereto*, UN Sales No. E.05.V.2 (2004) (*Legislative Guide*), at Part 2, 296.

[6] Trafficking Protocol, at Art. 9(2), Organized Crime Convention, at Art. 31(5). See also *Legislative Guide*, at Part 2, 296. Note that the provisions on prevention have not been prioritized in the Legislative Guide, which contains very little information on their nature, scope, and attendant obligations.

[7] Council of Europe Convention on Action against Trafficking in Human Beings and its Explanatory Report, ETS 197, 16.V.2005, done May 16, 2005, entered into force Feb. 1, 2008 (European Trafficking Convention), at Art. 5.

campaigns. States Parties are also required to take appropriate measures to enable legal migration, including through the dissemination of accurate information,[8] and to take specific measures to reduce children's vulnerability to trafficking, notably by creating a protective environment for them.[9] All such measures must promote human rights and use an approach that recognizes both gender concerns and the special needs of children.[10]

An obligation on States to address trafficking-related vulnerabilities finds support in the pronouncements of UN political organs,[11] UN human rights bodies,[12] and through a range of regional and international policy instruments.[13] The UN

---

[8]   Ibid. at Arts. 5(2), 5(4),

[9]   Ibid. at Art. 5(5). See also the Council of Europe, *Explanatory Report on the Convention on Action against Trafficking in Human Beings*, ETS 197, 16.V.2005 (European Trafficking Convention Explanatory Report), at para. 106. The Explanatory Report explains that the concept of a *protective environment*, as promoted by UNICEF, has eight key components: protecting children's rights from adverse attitudes, traditions, customs, behavior, and practices; government commitment to and protection and realization of children's rights; open discussion of, and engagement with, child protection issues; drawing up and enforcing protective legislation; the capacity of those dealing and in contact with children, families, and communities to protect children; children's life skills, knowledge, and participation; putting in place a system for monitoring and reporting abuse cases; programs and services to enable child victims of trafficking to recover and reintegrate.

[10] European Trafficking Convention, at Arts. 1(1)(a), 5(3).

[11] See, for example, UN Human Rights Council, "Trafficking in Persons, Especially Women and Children," UN Doc. A/HRC/RES/11/3, June 17, 2009, at para. 3 ("*[u]rges* Governments ... [t]o take appropriate measures to address the root factors, including external factors, that encourage trafficking in persons"); and UN General Assembly, "Trafficking in Women and Girls," UN Doc. A/RES/63/156, Jan. 30, 2009, at Preamble, paras. 3, 4 ("*[c]alls upon* Governments to take appropriate measures to address the factors that increase vulnerability to being trafficked, including poverty and gender inequality": at para. 3).

[12] For example, the Special Rapporteur on trafficking in persons has repeatedly referred to the need to address vulnerabilities to trafficking: UN General Assembly, "Trafficking in Persons, Especially Women and Children, Report of the Special Rapporteur on Trafficking in Persons, Especially Women and Children," UN Doc. A/64/290, Aug. 12, 2009, at paras. 30, 34 and 96 ("[t]he Special Rapporteur is concerned that the root causes of trafficking, namely, growing poverty, high youth unemployment, gender inequalities and the demand for cheap labour, are not being sufficiently addressed and trafficking continues to thrive as potential victims become more desperate to escape their unfavourable situations": at para. 96). See also UN Committee on the Elimination of Discrimination against Women: "Concluding Observations: Cameroon," UN Doc. CEDAW/C/CMR/CO/3, Feb. 10, 2009, at para. 31; "Concluding Observations: Mozambique," UN Doc. CEDAW/C/MOZ/CO/2, June 11, 2007, at para. 27; "Concluding Observations: Romania," UN Doc. CEDAW/C/ROM/CO/6, June 2, 2006, at para. 23; "Concluding Observations: Thailand," UN Doc. CEDAW/C/THA/CO/5, Feb. 3, 2006, at para. 28; UN Committee on the Rights of the Child, "Concluding Observations: Mauritania," UN Doc. CRC/C/MRT/CO/2, June 17, 2009, at para. 78; "Concluding Observations: Democratic Republic of the Congo," UN Doc. CRC/C/COD/CO/2, Feb. 10, 2009, at para. 83; UN Committee on the Elimination of Racial Discrimination, "Concluding Observations: Azerbaijan," UN Doc. CERD/C/AZE/CO/6, Sept. 7, 2009, at para. 7.

[13] See, for example, "Conclusions and Recommendations of the Meeting of National Authorities on Trafficking in Persons," adopted by the Organization of American States, Docs. OEA/Ser.K/XXXIX and RTP/doc. 16/06 rev. 1, Mar. 17, 2006 (OAS Recommendations on Trafficking in Persons), at Section II, para. 17; European Union and African States, "Ouagadougou Action Plan to Combat Trafficking in Human Beings, Especially Women and Children," adopted by the Ministerial

Trafficking Principles and Guidelines are particularly strong on this point, highlighting the need for States to take specific measures to reduce vulnerability, including through the provision of genuine livelihood options to traditionally disadvantaged groups, improving access of children to education, compulsory birth registration, review of policies that may compel people to take dangerous migration decisions, provision of accurate information to potential migrants, development of realistic information campaigns to inform communities about trafficking, and expansion of opportunities for legal, gainful, and nonexploitative labor migration.[14]

None of the instruments cited above specifically addresses the question of which State is to deliver on the obligation to prevent or ameliorate vulnerability to trafficking. It is reasonable to argue that in relation to certain measures, the relative ability of an individual State to take effective action should provide a guide as to the expectation generated by the obligation.[15] For example, the obligation on States Parties to the Trafficking Protocol to "take or strengthen measures ... to alleviate the factors that make persons, especially women and children, vulnerable to trafficking, such as poverty, underdevelopment and lack of equal opportunity"[16] should weigh more heavily on those States that have the capacity to address such vulnerabilities in a meaningful way. This does not mean that a poor country of origin is freed of any obligation to prevent and respond to vulnerabilities. It does, however, imply that the obligation will, in most cases, be a shared one.

8.1.2. *Addressing Vulnerability Related to Inequality and to Poverty*

A UN study on the link between poverty and human rights identifies restricted opportunities to pursue well-being as a defining feature of a "poor person."[17] In this

Conference on Migration and Development, Nov. 22–23, 2006 (Ouagadougou Action Plan), at 2–3; Memorandum of Understanding on Cooperation against Trafficking in Persons in the Greater Mekong Sub-region, adopted on Oct. 29, 2004 in Yangon (Cambodia, China, Lao PDR, Myanmar, Thailand, and Vietnam) (COMMIT MOU), at Art. 22; Organization for Security and Co-operation in Europe (OSCE) Permanent Council, "OSCE Action Plan To Combat Trafficking In Human Beings," OSCE Doc. PC.DEC/557, July 24, 2003 (OSCE Action Plan), at Recommendation IV(3); European Union, "Brussels Declaration on Preventing and Combating Trafficking in Human Beings," EU Doc. 14981/02, Nov. 29, 2002 (Brussels Declaration), at para. 7; Economic Community of West African States, "ECOWAS Initial Plan of Action against Trafficking in Persons (2002–2003)," adopted by the Twenty-Fifth Ordinary Session of Authority of Heads of State and Government, Dec. 20–21, 2001 (ECOWAS Initial Plan of Action), at 6, para. 2.

[14] UN Economic and Social Council, Office of the United Nations High Commissioner for Human Rights, *Recommended Principles and Guidelines on Human Rights and Human Trafficking*, UN Doc. E/2002/68/Add.1, May 20, 2002 (UN Trafficking Principles and Guidelines), at Principle 5, Guideline 7.

[15] This notion is explored from a range of legal, political, and philosophical perspectives in A. Kuper ed., *Global Responsibilities: Who Must Deliver on Human Rights?* (2005).

[16] Trafficking Protocol, at Art. 9(4).

[17] Office of the UN High Commissioner for Human Rights, *Human Rights and Poverty Reduction: A Conceptual Framework*, UN Sales No. HR/PUB/04/1 (2004) (*Human Rights and Poverty Reduction*), at 10.

sense, well-being refers not just to income level but to basic capabilities common to everyone and inherent to human dignity – for example, being adequately nourished, being adequately clothed and sheltered, being able to avoid preventable morbidity, taking part in the life of a community, and being able to appear in public with dignity. This expanded view of poverty identifies its defining feature as an *inadequate command over economic resources.* If an individual lacks command over economic resources and this leads to a failure of the kind of basic capacities previously described, then that person would be counted as poor.[18] This analysis is very important in the present context because it acknowledges that poverty limits life choices. Specifically, it can lead to individuals taking risks and making decisions about their life and their future in a way that they would never have done if their basic capabilities were being met.

The Explanatory Report to the European Trafficking Convention explicitly recognizes the link between poverty and increased vulnerability to trafficking:

> It is widely recognized that improvement of economic and social conditions in countries of origin and measures to deal with extreme poverty would be the most effective way of preventing trafficking. Among social and economic initiatives, improved training and more employment opportunities for people liable to be traffickers' prime targets would undoubtedly help to prevent trafficking in human beings.[19]

Inequality (which can relate to opportunity as well as wealth and income) is another factor contributing to trafficking-related vulnerability.[20] In that connection it is relevant to note that trafficking inevitably involves the movement of individuals from regions and countries of relatively less wealth, income, and opportunity to regions and countries of relatively greater wealth, income, and opportunities. In other words, this is not simply a North-South issue: the inequalities that impact upon trafficking exist *within* as well as *between* countries, and *within* regions as well as *between* regions. Several human rights treaties are of particular importance in addressing the link between poverty and vulnerability to trafficking. The key international instrument in this regard is the International Covenant on Economic, Social and Cultural Rights (ICESCR).[21] Several of the specialized international human rights treaties, including the CEDAW Convention[22] and the Convention on the Rights of the Child,[23] are also highly relevant. At the regional level, the European Social

---

[18] Ibid. at 5–12.

[19] European Trafficking Convention Explanatory Report, at para. 104.

[20] This point is made in the UN Trafficking Principles and Guidelines, at Principle 5.

[21] International Covenant on Economic, Social and Cultural Rights, 993 UNTS 3, done Dec. 16, 1966, entered into force Jan. 3, 1976 (ICESCR).

[22] Convention on the Elimination of All Forms of Discrimination against Women, 1249 UNTS 13, done Dec. 13, 1979, entered into force Sept. 3, 1981 (CEDAW).

[23] Convention on the Rights of the Child, 1577 UNTS 3, done Nov. 20, 1989, entered into force Sept. 2, 1990 (CRC).

Charter[24] is another important source of both authority and guidance, guaranteeing a range of economic and social rights including nondiscrimination, education, housing, health, education, and social and legal protection.

Both poverty and inequality have strong gender dimensions.[25] In the context of trafficking, the gender determinant can be particularly detrimental. For example, as noted by the CEDAW Committee's General Recommendation No. 19, poverty and unemployment increase opportunities for trafficking in women and force many women, including young girls, into prostitution.[26] Women working in prostitution are especially vulnerable to violence and exploitation for a range of reasons, including because their status, inevitably low and often unlawful, tends to marginalize them.[27] Social and cultural attitudes toward women working in prostitution can also operate to increase their vulnerability. The CEDAW Committee has repeatedly identified a link between poverty and gendered forms of trafficking in its Concluding Observations on State reports,[28] as have other international human rights mechanisms.[29] The responsibility on States to review and change laws and

---

[24] European Social Charter, 529 UNTS 89, ETS 35, done Oct. 18, 1961, entered into force Feb. 26, 1965; European Social Charter (revised), 2151 UNTS 277, ETS 163, done May 3, 1996, entered into force July 1, 1999.

[25] See, for example, the Beijing Platform for Action which notes that "[i]n addition to economic factors, the rigidity of socially ascribed gender roles and women's limited access to power, education, training and productive resources" contribute to the disproportionate number of women living in poverty: "Beijing Declaration and Platform for Action," Fourth World Conference on Women, UN Doc. A/CONF.177/20 and UN Doc. A/CONF.177/20/Add.1, Sept. 15, 1995 (Beijing Declaration and Platform for Action), at para. 47.

[26] UN Committee on the Elimination of Discrimination against Women, "General Recommendation No. 19: Violence against Women," UN Doc. A/47/38, Jan. 29, 1992 (CEDAW General Recommendation No. 19), at paras. 14–15. See also the Beijing Platform for Action, at para. 51 (noting that poverty forces women into situations "in which they are vulnerable to sexual exploitation").

[27] CEDAW General Recommendation No. 19, at para. 15.

[28] See, for example, UN Committee on the Elimination of All Forms of Discrimination against Women, "Concluding Observations: Armenia," UN Doc. CEDAW/C/ARM/CO/4/REV.1, Feb. 2, 2009, at paras. 24–25; "Concluding Observations: Ecuador," UN Doc. CEDAW/C/ECU/CO/7, Nov. 7, 2008, at para. 23; "Concluding Observations: Niger," UN Doc. CEDAW/C/NER/CO/2, June 11, 2007, at para. 26; "Concluding Observations: Cambodia," UN Doc. CEDAW/C/KHM/CO/3, Jan. 25, 2006, at para. 20.

[29] See, for example, UN General Assembly, "Trafficking in Persons, Especially Women and Children, Report of the Special Rapporteur on Trafficking in Persons, Especially Women and Children," UN Doc. A/64/290, Aug. 12, 2009, at para. 34 ("traffickers exploit persons who are trapped in conditions of poverty and subordinated by conditions, practices or beliefs, such as gender discrimination, gender violence and armed conflict"); and UN Commission on Human Rights, "Report of the Special Rapporteur, Ms. Radhika Coomaraswamy, on Violence against Women, Its Causes and Consequences, on Trafficking in Women, Women's Migration and Violence against Women," UN Doc. E/CN.4/2000/68, Feb. 29, 2000, esp. at paras. 56 ("[t]he failure of the State to guarantee women's rights leads to sexual and economic exploitation of women in both the home and the community and within local, national and global economies. Economic, political and social structures and the models of development that arise from such structures have failed women. They have failed in their attempts to provide basic economic and social rights to all people, particularly to women, and have further entrenched sex-based divisions of education, labour and migration. Basic rights, such as to food, shelter, education, employment, a sustainable living and peace have been denied to a large percentage of the world's population, of which women comprise a large portion"), 57

practices that fuel gender-based discrimination and inequalities leading to or exacerbating trafficking has also been extensively acknowledged.[30]

Addressing poverty and inequality has been identified as a priority for all countries, as well as for the intergovernmental organizations (IGOs) that represent them and promote their interests.[31] While this is a broad and long-term goal that goes well beyond the specific issue of trafficking, States, IGOs and human rights mechanisms have identified certain steps that could specifically address those aspects of poverty and inequality of most relevance to trafficking. These include the following: improved education opportunities, especially for women and children;[32] improved access to credit, finance, and productive resources, especially for women;[33] elimination of any

("[t]rafficking in women flourishes in many less developed countries because the vulnerabilities arising from women's lack of access to resources, poverty and gender discrimination are maintained through the collusion of the market, the State, the community and the family unit"), 58 ("[t]he failure of existing economic, political and social structures to provide equal and just opportunities for women to work has contributed to the feminisation of poverty, which in turn has led to the feminisation of migration, as women leave their homes in search of viable economic options"), and 60 ("[i]n the absence of equal opportunities for education, shelter, food, employment, relief from unpaid domestic and reproductive labour, access to structures of formal state power, and freedom from violence, women will continue to be trafficked").

[30]　See, for example, UN Trafficking Principles and Guidelines, at Guideline 7.6; Beijing Platform on Action, at para. 131(b); UN Commission on Human Rights, "Report of the Special Rapporteur, Ms. Radhika Coomaraswamy, on Violence against Women, Its Causes and Consequences, on Trafficking in Women, Women's Migration and Violence against Women," UN Doc. E/CN.4/2000/68, Feb. 29, 2000, at paras. 42–48, 54–60 ("[i]n the absence of strong measures to protect and promote the rights of women, trafficking thrives … Policies and practices that further curtail women's rights and freedom, such as those that restrict women's movement and limit safe and legal modes of immigration, serve only to entrench trafficking. Therefore, the responsibility for the existence and perseverance of trafficking rests squarely with the State. The State is ultimately responsible for protecting and promoting the rights and freedoms of all women": at para. 60).

[31]　See, for example, UN General Assembly, "United Nations Millennium Declaration," UN Doc. A/RES/55/2 (Sept. 18, 2000) and the Millennium Development Goals set out therein which identify the ending of extreme poverty and the promotion of gender equality and empowerment of women as priorities.

[32]　See, for example, UN Committee on the Elimination of All Forms of Discrimination against Women, "Concluding Observations: Viet Nam," UN Doc. CEDAW/C/VNM/CO/6, Feb. 2, 2007, at para. 19; "Concluding Observations: Nicaragua," UN Doc. CEDAW/C/NIC/CO/6, Feb. 2, 2007, at para. 22; "Concluding Observations: The Philippines," UN Doc. CEDAW/C/PHI/CO/6, Aug. 25, 2006, at para. 20; UN Committee on the Rights of the Child, "Concluding Observations: Mauritania," UN Doc. CRC/C/MRT/CO/2, June 17, 2009, at para. 78; "Concluding Observations: Qatar," UN Doc. CRC/C/OPSC/QAT/CO/1, June 2, 2006, at para. 38; OSCE Action Plan, at Recommendations IV(3.1) ("[i]mproving children's access to educational and vocational opportunities and increasing the level of school attendance, in particular by girls and minority groups"), IV(3.2) ("[c]onsidering the liberalisation by governments of their labour markets with a view to increasing employment opportunities for workers with a wide range of skills levels"), and IV(3.3) ("[d]eveloping programmes that offer livelihood options and include basic education, literacy, communication and other skills, and reduce barriers to entrepreneurship").

[33]　See OSCE Action Plan, at Recommendation IV(3.3) ("[e]nsuring that policies are in place which allow women equal access to and control over economic and financial resources … Promoting flexible financing and access to credit, including micro-credit with low interest"). See also, on the importance of economic opportunities generally, UN Committee on the Elimination of All Forms

de jure or *de facto* barriers to employment for vulnerable groups, including women;[34] legal and social measures to ensure rights in employment including a minimum wage that enables an adequate standard of living;[35] and the provision of technical and other assistance to countries of origin to enable them to address inequalities that contribute to trafficking-related vulnerabilities.[36] A rights-based approach to poverty

of Discrimination against Women, "Concluding Observations: Armenia," UN Doc. CEDAW/C/ ARM/CO/4/REV.1, Feb. 2, 2009, at para. 24; "Concluding Observations: Ecuador," UN Doc. CEDAW/C/ECU/CO/7, Nov. 7, 2008, at para. 22; "Concluding Observations: Nigeria," UN Doc. CEDAW/C/NGA/CO/6, July 8, 2008, at para. 26; "Concluding Observations: Indonesia," UN Doc. CEDAW/C/IDN/CO/5, Aug. 10, 2007, at para. 25; "Concluding Observations: Mozambique," UN Doc. CEDAW/C/MOZ/CO/2, June 11, 2007, at para. 27; "Concluding Observations: Kazakhstan," UN Doc. CEDAW/C/KAZ/CO/2, Feb. 2, 2007, at para. 18; "Concluding Observations: Viet Nam," UN Doc. CEDAW/C/VNM/CO/6, Feb. 2, 2007, at para. 19; UN Committee on the Elimination of Racial Discrimination, "Concluding Observations: Azerbaijan," UN Doc. CERD/C/AZE/ CO/6, Sept. 7, 2009, at para. 7. See also UN Committee on Economic, Social and Cultural Rights, "Concluding Observations: Nicaragua," UN Doc. E/C.12/NIC/CO/4, Nov. 28, 2008, at para. 24; "Concluding Observations: India," UN Doc. E/C.12/IND/CO/5, Aug. 8, 2008, at para. 29.

[34] See, for example, UN Commission on Human Rights, "Report of the Special Rapporteur, Ms. Radhika Coomaraswamy, on Violence against Women, Its Causes and Consequences, on Trafficking in Women, Women's Migration and Violence against Women," UN Doc. E/CN.4/2000/68, Feb. 29, 2000, at para. 4: "[t]he failure of existing economic, political and social structures to provide equal and just opportunities for women to work has contributed to the feminisation of poverty, which in turn has led to the feminisation of migration as women leave homes in search of viable options." See also OSCE Action Plan, at Recommendation IV(3.3) ("[t]aking appropriate measures to eliminate discrimination against women in the field of employment in order to ensure, on a basis of gender equality, the right to equal pay for equal work and the right to equality in employment opportunities"); Ouagadougou Action Plan, at 3 ("States should endeavour to provide viable employment or other livelihood opportunities for youth in general and in particular for young women at risk, especially in regions prone to trafficking").

[35] See, for example, "Report of the Special Rapporteur on Trafficking in Persons, Especially Women and Children, Sigma Huda, Addendum: Mission to Bahrain, Oman and Qatar," UN Doc. A/HRC/4/23/Add.2, Apr. 25, 2007, esp. at paras. 69–82; "Report of the Special Rapporteur on the Human Rights of Migrants, Jorge Bustamante, Addendum: Mission to Indonesia," UN Doc. A/HRC/4/24/ Add.3, Mar. 2, 2007, at para. 64; UN Committee on the Elimination of All Forms of Discrimination against Women, "Concluding Observations: Saudi Arabia," UN Doc. CEDAW/C/SAU/CO/2, Apr. 8, 2008, at paras. 23–24; "Concluding Observations: Mauritania," UN Doc. CEDAW/C/MRT/CO/1, June 11, 2007, at paras. 30–32; "Concluding Observations: The Philippines," UN Doc. CEDAW/C/ PHI/CO/6, Aug. 25, 2006, at para. 21; UN Committee on Economic, Social and Cultural Rights, "Concluding Observations: Cambodia," UN Doc. E/C.12/KHM/CO/1, June 12, 2009, at paras. 22–24; "Concluding Observations: Nepal," UN Doc. E/C.12/NPL/CO/2, Jan. 16, 2008, at para. 11.

[36] *Human Rights and Poverty Reduction*, at 27–30. See also UN General Assembly, "United Nations Millennium Declaration," UN Doc. A/RES/55/2, Sept. 18, 2000, and the Millennium Development Goals set out therein (resolving to provide development assistance and technology transfers to assist countries in poverty reduction: at paras. 15, 27–28); and for follow-up to these goals, UN General Assembly, "Follow-Up to the Development Outcome of the 2005 World Summit, including the Millenium Development Goals and Other Internationally Agreed Development Goals," UN Doc. A/RES/60/265, July 12, 2006. See further, UN General Assembly, "The Right to Development," UN Doc. A/RES/63/178, Mar. 26, 2009 (stressing the inter-related nature of all human rights, including the right to development (at Preamble) and noting the importance of official development assistance (at para. 24), market access (at para. 25), trade liberalization and technical assistance (at paras. 26, 28), and international assistance against HIV/AIDS (at para. 31)); UN Development Programme, *Human Development Report 2000: Human Rights and Human Development* (2000), at 12 ("[h]uman rights and human development cannot be realized universally without stronger international action, especially

reduction, an essential ingredient of preventative measures against trafficking, requires such measures to be implemented in a particular way. For example, it requires implementation, without discrimination, of the guarantees to economic and social rights as well as civil and political rights.[37] It also requires the inclusion of gender analysis and human rights criteria in the development, implementation, and evaluation of poverty reduction strategies and programs.[38]

8.1.3. *Addressing Vulnerability Related to Discrimination and to Violence against Women*

Racial and gender-based discrimination, including in the recognition and application of economic and social rights, are critical factors in rendering individuals and groups susceptible to trafficking.[39] The impact of both racial and gender-based discrimination, particularly in relation to access to education, resources, and employment opportunities, results in fewer and poorer life choices. It is the lack of genuine choice that, in turn, renders women and girls more vulnerable than men to certain forms of trafficking, and particular nationalities and races more vulnerable than

to support disadvantaged people and countries to offset growing global inequalities and marginalization … Aid, debt relief, access to markets, access to private financial flows and stability in the global economy are all needed for the full realization of rights in the poorest and least developed countries"); World Bank, *World Development Report 2000/2001: Attacking Poverty* (2001), at 11 ("[t]here are many areas that require international action – especially by industrial countries – to ensure gains to poor countries and to poor people within the developing world. An increased focus on debt relief and the associated move to make development cooperation through aid more effective are part of the story. Of equal importance are actions in other areas – trade, vaccines, closing the digital and knowledge divides – that can enhance the opportunity, empowerment, and security of poor people"). See also, generally, UN Committee on Economic, Social and Cultural Rights, "General Comment No. 2: International Technical Assistance Measures," UN Doc. E/1990/23, Feb. 2, 1990.

[37] *Human Rights and Poverty Reduction*, at 17.

[38] Beijing Platform for Action, at paras. 47, 67–68; *Human Rights and Poverty Reduction*, at 10–11. See also, for example, UN Committee on Economic, Social and Cultural Rights, "Concluding Observations: Latvia," UN Doc. E/C.12/LVA/CO/1, Jan. 7, 2008, at para. 49: "ensure the full integration of economic, social and cultural rights in its social development and poverty reduction strategies … develop indicators and benchmarks on an annual basis, disaggregated by gender, age, urban/rural population and ethnic background for the purpose of specifically assessing the needs of disadvantaged and marginalized individuals and groups."

[39] On the link between racial discrimination and trafficking, see United Nations Department of Public Information, "The Race Dimensions of Trafficking in Persons, Especially Women and Children," background paper for the World Conference against Racism, Racial Discrimination, Xenophobia and Related Intolerance, Aug. 31 to Sept. 7, 2001, available at http://www.un.org/WCAR/e-kit/trafficking_e.pdf (accessed Jan. 31, 2010): "[t]here has been little discussion of whether race … contribute[s] to the likelihood of women and girls becoming victims of trafficking. However, when attention is paid to which women are most at risk of being trafficked, the link of this risk to their racial and social marginalization becomes clear. Moreover, race and racial discrimination may not only constitute a risk factor for trafficking, it may also determine the treatment that women experience in countries of destination. In addition, racist ideology and racial, ethnic and gender discrimination may create a demand in the region or country of destination which could contribute to trafficking in women and girls": ibid. at 2. See also UN Trafficking Principles and Guidelines, at Principle 3.

others. States are under a clear legal obligation to ensure that their laws, systems, and practices do not promote, reward, or tolerate discrimination. The link between discrimination and vulnerability to trafficking, and the obligations that flow from this link, have been recognized by the UN's policy organs,[40] its treaty bodies,[41] and other human rights mechanisms.[42]

Chapter 3 discussed and confirmed the link between trafficking and violence against women as a form of prohibited discrimination. In the present context, it is relevant to note that violence directed against or primarily affecting women can also be a factor increasing vulnerability to trafficking. For example, women may accept dangerous migration arrangements in order to escape the consequences of entrenched gender discrimination, including family violence and lack of security against such violence. In such cases, even unsafe migration may be perceived as providing the best available opportunity to break free from a dangerous and oppressive environment. Women and girls may also be more vulnerable than men to violence, including coercion and force at the recruitment stage, increasing their susceptibility to being trafficked in the first place.

There is growing understanding of what is required for States and others to address increases in vulnerability to trafficking that are related to racial and gender-based discrimination and violence against women.[43] Practical measures to this end that have been identified by the international community, including international

---

[40] See, for example, UN General Assembly, "Trafficking in Women and Girls," UN Doc. A/RES/63/156, Jan. 30, 2009, at Preamble ("*[r]ecognizing* that victims of trafficking are particularly exposed to racism, racial discrimination, xenophobia and related intolerance and that women and girl victims are often subject to multiple forms of discrimination and violence, including on the grounds of their gender, age, ethnicity, culture and religion, as well as their origins, and that these forms of discrimination themselves may fuel trafficking in persons"). An identical statement is included in the preamble to UN Human Rights Council, "Trafficking in Persons, Especially Women and Children," UN Doc. A/HRC/RES/11/3, June 17, 2009,

[41] See, for example, UN Committee on the Elimination of All Forms of Discrimination against Women, "Concluding Observations: Ecuador," UN Doc. CEDAW/C/ECU/CO/7, Nov. 7, 2008, at paras. 22–23; UN Committee on the Rights of the Child, "Concluding Observations: Colombia," UN Doc. CRC/C/COL/CO/3, June 8, 2006, at para. 35; "Concluding Observations: Turkmenistan," UN Doc. CRC/C/TKM/CO/1, June 2, 2006, at para. 67; UN Committee on the Elimination of All Forms of Racial Discrimination, "Concluding Observations: Belgium," Apr. 11, 2008, at para. 20; "Concluding Observations: South Africa," UN Doc. CERD/C/ZAF/CO/3, Oct. 19, 2006, at para. 17; UN Committee on Economic, Social and Cultural Rights, "Concluding Observations: India," UN Doc. E/C.12/IND/CO/5, Aug. 8, 2008, at para. 27; "Concluding Observations: Nepal," UN Doc. E/C.12/NPL/CO/2, Jan. 16, 2008, at para. 11.

[42] See, for example, UN Commission on Human Rights, "Report of the Special Rapporteur, Ms. Radhika Coomaraswamy, on Violence against Women, Its Causes and Consequences, on Trafficking in Women, Women's Migration and Violence against Women," UN Doc. E/CN.4/2000/68, Feb. 29, 2000, at para. 43: "policies and practices that either overtly discriminate against women or that sanction or encourage discrimination against women tend to increase women's chances of being trafficked."

[43] See, for example, "In-depth Study on All Forms of Violence against Women: Report of the Secretary General," UN Doc. A/61/122/Add.1, July 6, 2006, esp. at 81–100.

human rights bodies, include provision of safe shelter for women experiencing trafficking-related violence,[44] the establishment of crisis hotlines,[45] and victim support centers equipped with medical, psychological, and legal facilities.[46] Longer-term measures that seek to address the social, cultural, and structural causes of violence are also important. These may include: reforming legislation that either discriminates against women or fails to address violence against women;[47] ensuring

[44] See, for example, UN Committee on the Elimination of All Forms of Discrimination against Women, "Concluding Observations: Azerbaijan," UN Doc. CEDAW/C/AZE/CO/4, Aug. 7, 2009, at para. 24; "Concluding Observations: Portugal," UN Doc. CEDAW/C/PRT/CO/7, Nov. 7, 2008, at para. 35; UN Human Rights Committee, "Concluding Observations: Japan," UN Doc. CCPR/C/JPN/CO/5, Dec. 18, 2008, at para. 23; UN Committee on the Rights of the Child, "Concluding Observations: United Kingdom of Great Britain and Northern Ireland," UN Doc. CRC/C/GBR/CO/4, Oct. 20, 2008, at para. 75; UN Committee against Torture, "Concluding Observations: Japan," UN Doc. CAT/C/JPN/CO/1, Aug. 3, 2007, at para. 25; "Report of the Special Rapporteur on Trafficking in Persons, Especially Women and Children, Sigma Huda, Addendum: Mission to Bahrain, Oman and Qatar," UN Doc. A/HRC/4/23/Add.2, Apr. 25, 2007, at para. 95; "Report of the Special Rapporteur on the Human Rights Aspects of the Victims of Trafficking in Persons, Especially Women and Children, Sigma Huda, Addendum: Mission to Lebanon," UN Doc. E/CN.4/2006/62/Add.3, Feb. 20, 2006, at para. 94.

[45] See, for example, "Report Submitted by the Special Rapporteur on the Sale of Children, Child Prostitution and Child Pornography, Juan Miguel Petit, Addendum: Mission to Mexico," UN Doc. A/HRC/7/8/Add.2, Jan. 28, 2008, at para. 80; UN Committee on the Rights of the Child, "Concluding Observations: Kazakhstan," UN Doc. CRC/C/OPSC/KAZ/CO/1, Mar. 11, 2006, at para. 22; UN Human Rights Committee, "Concluding Observations: Albania," UN Doc. CCPR/CO/82/ALB, Dec. 2, 2004, at para. 10.

[46] See, for example, "Report of the Special Rapporteur on Violence against Women, Its Causes and Consequences, Yakin Ertürk, Addendum: Mission to the Republic of Moldova," UN Doc. A/HRC/11/6/Add.4, May 8, 2009, at para. 86; UN Committee on the Elimination of All Forms of Discrimination against Women, "Concluding Observations: The Philippines," UN Doc. CEDAW/C/PHI/CO/6, Aug. 25, 2006, at para. 20; UN Human Rights Committee, "Concluding Observations: Japan," UN Doc. CCPR/C/JPN/CO/5, Dec. 18, 2008, at para. 23; UN Committee on the Rights of the Child, "Concluding Observations: United States of America," UN Doc. CRC/C/OPSC/USA/CO/1, June 25, 2008, at para. 39; UN Committee on Economic, Social and Cultural Rights, "Concluding Observations: Bosnia and Herzegovina," UN Doc. E/C.12/BIH/CO/1, Jan. 24, 2006, at para. 24.

[47] See, for example, UN Committee against Torture, "Concluding Observations: Kenya," UN Doc. CAT/C/KEN/CO/1, Jan. 19, 2009, at para. 26; "Concluding Observations: Japan," UN Doc. CAT/C/JPN/CO/1, Aug. 3, 2007, at para. 25; UN Committee on the Elimination of All Forms of Discrimination against Women, "Concluding Observations: Indonesia," UN Doc. CEDAW/C/IDN/CO/5, Aug. 10, 2007, at para. 28; "Concluding Observations: Kenya," UN Doc. CEDAW/C/KEN/CO/6, Aug. 10, 2007, at para. 30; "Concluding Observations: Syrian Arab Republic," UN Doc. CEDAW/C/SYR/CO/1, June 11, 2007, at para. 24; "Concluding Observations: Mauritius," UN Doc. CEDAW/C/MAR/CO/5, Aug. 25, 2006, at para. 21; "Concluding Observations: Cambodia," UN Doc. CEDAW/C/KHM/CO/3, Jan. 25, 2006, at para. 19; "Report of the Special Rapporteur on Violence against Women, Its Causes and Consequences, Yakin Ertürk, Addendum: Mission to Mexico," UN Doc. E/CN.4/2006/61/Add.4, Jan. 13, 2006, at para. 69; UN Commission on Human Rights, "Report of the Special Rapporteur, Ms. Radhika Coomaraswamy, on Violence against Women, Its Causes and Consequences, on Trafficking in Women, Women's Migration and Violence against Women," UN Doc. E/CN.4/2000/68, Feb. 29, 2000, esp. at paras. 42–48. See also UN General Assembly, "In-depth Study on All Forms of Violence against Women: Report of the Secretary General," UN Doc. A/61/122/Add.1, July 6, 2006, at paras. 262–265.

the prompt investigation and prosecution of complaints related to violence against women;[48] providing access to effective remedies for gender-based violence;[49] implementing education initiatives aimed at educating the public about violence against women and removing negative attitudes toward women[50] (including, in some countries, the association of rape allegations with the crime of adultery[51]); and training police, immigration, judicial, and medical personnel and social workers on the sensitivities involved in cases of violence against women.[52]

[48] See, for example, "Report of the Special Rapporteur on Violence against Women, Its Causes and Consequences, Yakin Ertürk, Addendum: Mission to the Republic of Moldova," UN Doc. A/HRC/11/6/Add.4, May 8, 2009, at para. 86; "Report of the Special Rapporteur on Violence against Women, Its Causes and Consequences, Yakin Ertürk, Addendum: Mission to Sweden," UN Doc. A/HRC/4/34/Add.3, Feb. 6, 2007, at para. 71; "Report of the Special Rapporteur on Violence against Women, Its Causes and Consequences, Yakin Ertürk, Addendum: Mission to Mexico," UN Doc. E/CN.4/2006/61/Add.4, Jan. 13, 2006, at para. 69; UN Committee against Torture, "Concluding Observations: Honduras," UN Doc. CAT/C/HND/CO/1, June 23, 2009, at para. 21; "Concluding Observations: Japan," UN Doc. CAT/C/JPN/CO/1, Aug. 3, 2007, at para. 25; UN Human Rights Committee, "Concluding Observations: Georgia," UN Doc. CCPR/C/GEO/CO/3, 15 November 2007, para. 8(b); UN Committee on the Elimination of All Forms of Discrimination against Women, "Concluding Observations: China," UN Doc. CEDAW/C/CHN/CO/6, Aug. 25, 2006, at para. 22. See also UN General Assembly, "In-depth Study on All Forms of Violence against Women: Report of the Secretary General," UN Doc. A/61/122/Add.1, July 6, 2006, at paras. 266–268.

[49] See, for example, UN Committee on the Elimination of All Forms of Discrimination against Women, "Concluding Observations: Colombia," UN Doc. CEDAW/C/COL/CO/6, Feb. 2, 2007, at para. 18; "Concluding Observations: Netherlands," UN Doc. CEDAW/C/NLD/CO/4, Feb. 2, 2007, at para. 20; "Concluding Observations: Peru," UN Doc. CEDAW/C/PER/CO/6, Feb. 2, 2007, at para. 21; "Concluding Observations: Mexico," UN Doc. CEDAW/C/MEX/CO/6, Aug. 26, 2006, at para. 16; "Concluding Observations: China," UN Doc. CEDAW/C/CHN/CO/6, Aug. 25, 2006, at para. 22; UN General Assembly, "In-depth Study on All Forms of Violence against Women: Report of the Secretary General," UN Doc. A/61/122/Add.1, July 6, 2006, at para. 269; "Report of the Special Rapporteur on Violence against Women, Its Causes and Consequences, Yakin Ertürk, Addendum: Mission to Algeria," UN Doc. A/HRC/7/6/Add.2, Feb. 13, 2008, at para. 103, "Report of the Special Rapporteur on Violence against Women, Its Causes and Consequences, Yakin Ertürk, Addendum: Mission to Mexico," UN Doc. E/CN.4/2006/61/Add.4, Jan. 13, 2006, at para. 69.

[50] See, for example, UN Human Rights Committee, "Concluding Observations: Sudan," UN Doc. CCPR/C/SDN/CO/3, Aug. 29, 2007, at para. 14; "Concluding Observations: Mexico," UN Doc. CEDAW/C/MEX/CO/6, Aug. 26, 2006, at para. 15; "Concluding Observations: Cambodia," UN Doc. CEDAW/C/KHM/CO/3, Jan. 25, 2006, at para. 18; UN Committee on the Rights of the Child, "Concluding Observations: Ghana," UN Doc. CRC/C/GHA/CO/2, Mar. 17, 2006, at para. 45. See also "In-depth Study on All Forms of Violence against Women: Report of the Secretary General," UN Doc. A/61/122/Add.1, July 6, 2006, at paras. 271–272.

[51] See, for example, UN Human Rights Committee, "Concluding Observations: Sudan," UN Doc. CCPR/C/SDN/CO/3, Aug. 29, 2007, at para. 14; "Report of the Special Rapporteur on Violence against Women, Its Causes and Consequences, Yakin Ertürk, Addendum: Mission to the Islamic Republic of Iran," UN Doc. E/CN.4/2006/61/Add.3, Jan. 27, 2006, at para. 73.

[52] See, for example, UN Committee on the Elimination of All Forms of Discrimination against Women, "Concluding Observations: Burundi," UN Doc. CEDAW/C/BDI/CO/4, Apr. 8, 2008, at para. 24; "Concluding Observations: Pakistan," UN Doc. CEDAW/C/PAK/CO/3, June 11, 2007, at para. 23; "Concluding Observations: Greece," UN Doc. CEDAW/C/GRC/CO/6, Feb. 2, 2007, at para. 20; "Concluding Observations: China," UN Doc. CEDAW/C/CHN/CO/6, Aug. 25, 2006, at para. 36; "Concluding Observations: Guatemala," UN Doc. CEDAW/C/GUA/CO/6, June 2, 2006, at para. 26; "Report of the Special Rapporteur on Violence against Women, Its Causes and

8.1.4. *Addressing the Special Vulnerabilities of Children*

International law recognizes that children, because of their reliance on others for security and well-being, are vulnerable to trafficking and related exploitation. In recognition of this vulnerability, children are accorded special rights of care and protection.[53] Appropriate responses to child vulnerability must be built on a genuine understanding of that vulnerability – specifically, why some children are trafficked and others are not. All measures taken to reduce the vulnerability of children to trafficking should aim to improve their situation – rather than to just prevent behaviors such as migration for work which, while not desirable, especially for young children, may not necessarily be exploitative or lead to trafficking.[54] It is also important to accept that children are not a homogenous group: Older children have different needs, expectations, and vulnerabilities from younger children; girls and boys can be similarly disaggregated.

That States have a specific obligation to address the special vulnerabilities of children to trafficking is beyond question. There is, however, less clarity with regard to the substantive content of that obligation. It is nevertheless possible to use international legal instruments, policy documents, and the recommendations of human rights mechanisms to identify certain actions that would contribute to States meeting their international legal duty to reduce the vulnerability of children to trafficking. States should, for example, ensure that appropriate legal documentation (including for birth, citizenship, and marriage) is in place and available.[55] States should tighten

---

Consequences, Yakin Ertürk, Addendum: Mission to Mexico," UN Doc. E/CN.4/2006/61/Add.4, Jan. 13, 2006, at para. 69. See also, "In-depth Study on All Forms of Violence against Women: Report of the Secretary General," UN Doc. A/61/122/Add.1, July 6, 2006, at para. 273.

[53] Details of the relevant standards, including of the "best interests" principle that is required to be applied to all decisions affecting children, are provided in Chapter 5 and referred to at appropriate points throughout this volume.

[54] See further, M. Dottridge, *A Handbook on Planning Projects to Prevent Child Trafficking* (2007). See also International Labour Organization, *Training Manual to Fight Trafficking in Children for Labour, Sexual and Other Forms of Exploitation, Textbook 1: Understanding Child Trafficking* (2009), at 15–16; and generally J. O'Connell Davidson and C. Farrow, "Child Migration and the Construction of Vulnerability" (Save the Children, 2007) (O'Connell Davidson and Farrow, "Child Migration and the Construction of Vulnerability"), available at: http://www.childtrafficking.com/Docs/savechild_07_cmcv_0108.pdf (accessed Jan. 31, 2010). O'Connell Davidson and Farrow note that "the factors identified in this literature as leaving children vulnerable to 'trafficking' are almost identical to the factors that have more generally been identified as triggering children's independent migration. This should alert us to the very real definitional and political problems presented by efforts to distinguish between 'trafficked children' and independent child migrants": ibid at 35.

[55] See, for example, UN Trafficking Principles and Guidelines, at Guideline 7.9; Brussels Declaration, at para. 12. In that regard it noted that effective implementation of a system of compulsory birth registration is likely to reap a range of rewards in terms of improving a child's access to his or her rights including reducing that child's vulnerability to trafficking and related exploitation. See United Nations Children's Fund, *Birth Registration: Right from the Start*, Innocenti Digest No. 9 (March 2002). The right to birth registration is protected in the Convention on the Rights of the Child ("[t]he child shall be registered immediately after birth and shall have the right from birth to a name, the right to acquire a nationality and, as far as possible, the right to know and be

passport, visa, birth certificate, and other identity document regulations in relation to children, particularly unaccompanied minors and minors accompanied but not by an immediate family member.[56] States should improve children's access to educational opportunities and increase the level of school attendance, in particular by girls.[57] They should protect children from violence, including family and sexual violence.[58] States should act to combat discrimination against girls.[59] They should

cared for by his or her parents"): CRC, at Art. 7(1). On the connection between lack of access to birth registration and trafficking, see Plan International, *Count Every Child: the Right to Birth Registration* (2009), available at http://plancanada.ca/downloads/CountEveryChildReport.pdf (accessed Jan. 31, 2010).

[56] See Brussels Declaration, at para. 12 ("[s]pecific action should be implemented such as in the field of passport and visa regulations, including the possibility to require that all children over the age of five must be in possession of their own passport and the extension of submission times for visa applications in respect of children to allow for background enquiry in the origin and destination countries. The inclusion of biometrics in issued travel documents will contribute to better identification of trafficked and missing children. Another important measure is to require carrier agents to retain the identity and travel documents of unaccompanied minors and those of children that are accompanied, but not by an immediate family member that can then be handed into the possession of the immigration authorities at the point of arrival"); ECOWAS Initial Plan of Action, at 9, para. 3 ("States shall take such measures as may be necessary, within available means: (a) to ensure that the birth certificates, and travel and identity documents, they issue are of such quality that they cannot easily be misused and cannot readily be falsified or unlawfully altered, replicated, or issued; and (b) to ensure the integrity and security of travel or identity documents they issue, and to prevent their unlawful creation, issuance, and use"). See also, for example, UN Committee on the Rights of the Child, "Concluding Observations: Bangladesh," UN Doc. CRC/C/OPSC/BGD/CO/1, July 5, 2007, at para. 25.

[57] See UN Trafficking Principles and Guidelines, at Guideline 7.3; UN Commission on Human Rights, "Rights of the Child," UN Doc. E/CN.4/RES/2005/44, Apr. 19, 2005, at para. 32(g) ("take the necessary measures to eliminate the sale of children, child prostitution and child pornography by adopting a holistic approach and addressing the contributing factors, including … lack of education"); OSCE Action Plan, at Recommendation IV(3.1) ("[i]mproving children's access to educational and vocational opportunities and increasing the level of school attendance, in particular by girls and minority groups"). See also UN Committee on the Rights of the Child, "Concluding Observations: Mauritania," UN Doc. CRC/C/MRT/CO/2, June 17, 2009, at para. 78; "Concluding Observations: Ethiopia," UN Doc. CRC/C/ETH/CO/3, Nov. 1, 2006, at para. 65; "Concluding Observations: Colombia," UN Doc. CRC/C/COL/CO/3, June 8, 2006, at para. 35; UN Committee on the Elimination of All Forms of Discrimination against Women, "Concluding Observations: The Philippines," UN Doc. CEDAW/C/PHI/CO/6, Aug. 25, 2006, at para. 20.

[58] See, for example, CRC, at Art. 19(1); UN Committee on the Rights of the Child, "Concluding Observations: Democratic Republic of the Congo," UN Doc. CRC/C/COD/CO/2, Feb. 10, 2009, at paras. 67, 77; "Concluding Observations: Malaysia," UN Doc. CRC/C/MYS/CO/1, June 25, 2007, at para. 57; "Concluding Observations: Kenya," UN Doc. CRC/C/KEN/CO/2, June 19, 2007, at paras. 9, 63; UN Committee on Economic, Social and Cultural Rights, "Concluding Observations: Netherlands Antilles," UN Doc. E/C.12/NLD/CO/3/Add.1, Jan. 31, 2008, at para. 40.

[59] For example, UN human rights treaty bodies have linked responding to trafficking to the need to improve educational and economic opportunities for girls: UN Committee on the Elimination of All Forms of Discrimination against Women, "Concluding Observations: Viet Nam," UN Doc. CEDAW/C/VNM/CO/6, Feb. 2, 2007, at para. 19; UN Committee on the Rights of the Child, "Concluding Observations: Bangladesh," UN Doc. CRC/C/OPSC/BGD/CO/1, July 5, 2007, at para. 20 (in relation to sale of children); "Concluding Observations: Turkmenistan," UN Doc. CRC/C/TKM/CO/1, June 2, 2006, at para. 67.

raise public awareness of the unlawful nature and effects of child trafficking and exploitation.[60] Strategies to address the vulnerability of children to trafficking should acknowledge special needs. Children who may be especially vulnerable to trafficking include girls; abandoned, orphaned, homeless, and displaced children; children in conflict zones; and children who belong to a racial or ethnic minority.[61]

The UN human rights system has recognized that unaccompanied or separated children outside their country of origin are especially susceptible to exploitation and abuse, including through trafficking.[62] The Committee on the Rights of the Child has noted that:

> trafficking of such a child, or "re-trafficking" in cases where a child was already a victim of trafficking, is one of many dangers faced by unaccompanied or separated

---

[60] "Report Submitted by the Special Rapporteur on the Sale of Children, Child Prostitution and Child Pornography, Juan Miguel Petit," UN Doc. A/HRC/7/8, Jan. 9, 2008, at para. 39 ("[c]hildren will also be less vulnerable to abuse when they are aware of their right not to be exploited, or of services available to protect them, which means the need for permanent and massive preventive campaigns in the mass media and also in schools and on the streets"); ECOWAS Initial Plan of Action, at 6, para. 2; OSCE Action Plan, at Recommendation IV(4.7); UN Committee on the Rights of the Child, "Concluding Observations: Democratic Republic of the Congo," UN Doc. CRC/C/COD/CO/2, Feb. 10, 2009, at para. 83; "Concluding Observations: Kenya," UN Doc. CRC/C/KEN/CO/2, June 19, 2007, at para. 66(g); "Concluding Observations: Lithuania," UN Doc. CRC/C/LTU/CO/2, Mar. 17, 2006, at para. 67; "Concluding Observations: Nepal," UN Doc. CRC/C/15/Add.261, Sept. 21, 2005, at para. 96(c).

[61] See, for example, UN Committee on the Rights of the Child, "Concluding Observations: Niger," UN Doc. CRC/C/NER/CO/2, June 18, 2009, at para. 68 (children in conflict situations, children from chronically poor and vulnerable nomadic populations); "Concluding Observations: Democratic Republic of the Congo," UN Doc. CRC/C/COD/CO/2, Feb. 10, 2009, at para. 7 ("street children, refugee and displaced children"); "Concluding Observations: Serbia," UN Doc. CRC/C/SRB/CO/1, June 20, 2008, at para. 69 (Roma children); "Concluding Observations: Georgia," UN Doc. CRC/C/GEO/CO/3, June 23, 2008, at para. 68 ("orphans, children working and living in the street and internally displaced children"); "Concluding Observations: Colombia," UN Doc. CRC/C/COL/CO/3, June 8, 2006, at paras. 35 ("displaced children, Afro-Colombian and indigenous children, and children living in rural and remote areas") and 86 ("internally displaced children and children living in poverty"); "Report Submitted by the Special Rapporteur on the Sale of Children, Child Prostitution and Child Pornography, Juan Miguel Petit, Addendum: Mission to Ukraine," UN Doc. A/HRC/4/31/Add.2, Jan. 24, 2007, at para. 69 ("children from dysfunctional and poor families with a low level of education, street children, victims of sexual abuse and domestic violence, children in State institutions for minors or who recently left such institutions").

[62] UN Committee on the Rights of the Child, "General Comment No. 6: Treatment of Unaccompanied or Separated Children outside Their Country of Origin," UN Doc. CRC/GC/2005/6, Sept. 1, 2005 (CRC General Comment No. 6), at para. 50: "[u]naccompanied or separated children in a country outside their country of origin are particularly vulnerable to exploitation and abuse. Girls are at particular risk of being trafficked including for purposes of sexual exploitation." The Committee on the Rights of the Child defines these two terms as follows: "'[u]naccompanied children' (also called unaccompanied minors) are children, as defined in Article 1 of the Convention, who have been separated from both parents and other relatives and are not being cared for by an adult who, by law or custom, is responsible for doing so. 'Separated children' are children, as defined in Article 1 of the Convention, who have been separated from both parents, or from their previous legal or customary primary caregiver, but not necessarily from other relatives. These may, therefore, include children accompanied by other adult family members": ibid. at paras. 7–8

children. Trafficking in children is a threat to the fulfilment of their right to life, survival and development.[63]

In accordance with Article 35 of the Convention on the Rights of the Child, the Committee and the Special Rapporteur on the Sale of Children, Child Prostitution and Child Pornography have called upon States Parties to take appropriate measures to prevent such trafficking, including identifying unaccompanied and separated children,[64] regularly inquiring as to their whereabouts, the appointment of guardians,[65] and conducting information campaigns that are age-appropriate, gender-sensitive, and in a language and medium that is understandable to the child.[66] The Committee has also noted a need for adequate legislation as well as effective mechanisms of enforcement with respect to labor regulations and border crossing.[67]

8.1.5. *Addressing Increases in Vulnerability in Conflict and Postconflict Situations*

Trafficking is a feature of armed conflict as well as of postconflict situations.[68] During conflict, individuals may be abducted or otherwise trafficked by military or armed groups to provide labor, military, and sexual services. Even after a cessation of hostilities, civilian populations may be under extreme economic or other pressure to move and thereby become particularly vulnerable to threats, coercion, and deception. War and postwar economies are often built on criminal activities, which can quickly be expanded to include trafficking. Weak or dysfunctional criminal justice systems ensure that traffickers and their accomplices can operate with impunity. Violent and lawless war zones often become source, transit, or destination points

---

[63] Ibid. at para. 52.

[64] For example, "Report of the Special Rapporteur on Sale of Children, Child Prostitution and Child Pornography, Juan Miguel Petit, Addendum: Mission to Greece," UN Doc. E/CN.4/2006/67/Add.3, Mar. 27, 2006, at para. 112. See also CRC General Comment No. 6.

[65] For example, UN Committee on the Rights of the Child, "Concluding Observations: Nepal," UN Doc. CRC/C/15/Add.261, Sept. 21, 2005, at para. 53. See also CRC General Comment No. 6.

[66] See generally CRC General Comment No. 6.

[67] Ibid.

[68] See generally, S. Wolte, "Armed Conflict and Trafficking in Women" (Deutsche Gesellschaft für Technische Zusammenarbeit (GTZ) GmbH, 2004), available at http://www2.gtz.de/dokumente/bib/04–5304.pdf (accessed Feb. 1, 2010); and E. Rehn and E. Johnson Sirleaf, *Women, War and Peace, The Independent Experts' Assessment on the Impact of Armed Conflict on Women and Women's Role in Peace-Building* (UNIFEM, 2002) (Rehn and Johnson Sirleaf, *Women, War and Peace*). See also, UN General Assembly, "Trafficking in Women and Girls," UN Doc. A/RES/63/156, Jan. 30, 2009, at para. 4 (calling upon "[g]overnments, the international community and all other organizations and entities that deal with conflict and post-conflict, disaster and other emergency situations to address the heightened vulnerability of women and girls to trafficking and exploitation, and associated gender-based violence").

for victims of trafficking. The presence of international military or peacekeeping forces – and attendant factors such as income disparities and a climate of impunity – can present an additional threat of trafficking and related exploitation, with women and girls being at particular risk.[69]

As with conflict-related violence more generally,[70] trafficking during and after armed conflict usually has a very strong gender dimension. For example, conflict-related trafficking of men and boys is often aimed at supplying combatants to supplement fighting forces. Women and children are trafficked for a wider range of purposes, some of which are specific to their gender. As noted in a major international study of women and conflict:

> Women are trafficked out of one country into another to be used in forced labour schemes that often include forced prostitution. They are pushed into marriage with members of opposing groups either directly, through abduction, or in order to protect their families. They are abducted by armed groups and forced to accompany them on raids and to provide everything from food to sexual services. Many sexual slaves are also used for dangerous work like demining contested areas, forced to risk their lives to make a field or a hillside safe for soldiers.[71]

The factors that create or increase vulnerability to such trafficking are also highly gendered. Armed conflict destroys communities as a traditional means of support. During and after wars, women are often left behind. In order to secure family survival, they may need to move to another part of the country or even abroad, invariably under extremely risky circumstances. The special vulnerabilities of internally displaced persons (IDPs) and refugees have already been outlined (see Chapter 3.5). Women and children constitute the overwhelming majority of IDPs and refugees resulting from armed conflict. On the move, in refugee camps or other temporary shelters, they are highly vulnerable to violence and exploitation, including through trafficking.

International law requires States and the international community to take action to protect the rights and address the particular vulnerabilities of individuals caught up in conflict.[72] Additional obligations may be applicable in relation to particularly vulnerable groups including women, refugees or internally displaced persons,[73] and

---

[69] Particular issues relating to peacekeeping and other international officials are further explored at Chapter 8.3.3.

[70] See generally, Rehn and Johnson Sirleaf, *Women, War and Peace*; and C. Cockburn, "Gender, Armed Conflict and Political Violence" (World Bank, 1999).

[71] Rehn and Johnson Sirleaf, *Women, War and Peace*, at 12.

[72] See generally Volume 1, "Rules," of J.-M. Henckaerts and L. Doswald-Beck, *Customary International Humanitarian Law* (ICRC, 2005). On the obligations of international forces, see S. Wills, *Protecting Civilians: The Obligations of Peacekeepers* (2009).

[73] See Office of the UN High Commissioner for Refugees, *Sexual and Gender-Based Violence against Refugees, Returnees and Internally Displaced Persons: Guidelines for Prevention and Response* (May, 2003).

children.[74] To the extent that the situation, its cause, or its consequences have a gender dimension, it is essential to ensure that responses integrate an appropriate gender perspective.[75] International legal obligations relevant to trafficking identified throughout the present work apply and should be implemented during and after situations of conflict.[76]

8.2. PREVENTION THROUGH ADDRESSING DEMAND

Trafficking feeds into a global market that seeks out cheap, unregulated, and exploitable labor and the goods and services that such labor can produce. Sex tourism (including child sex tourism), the recruitment of domestic labor from developing countries, internet pornography, and organized marriages between women from developing countries and foreign nationals are examples of newer forms of actual or potential exploitation made possible through trafficking. It is this realization, coupled with a broader concern that end users of the goods and services produced by trafficked persons have not been sufficiently targeted, that has prompted calls for States and others to consider demand as part of the problem of trafficking and to acknowledge demand reduction as an important prevention strategy.

8.2.1 *Understanding Demand in the Context of Trafficking*

Demand, in this context, generally refers to two quite different things: *employer* demand for cheap and exploitable labor; and *consumer* demand for the goods or services produced or provided by trafficked persons.[77] Demand may also be generated by exploiters and others involved in the trafficking process such as recruiters, brokers, and transporters who rely on trafficking and victims of trafficking to generate income.[78] It is possible to extend this list even further to include corrupt public officials who receive direct benefit from trafficking, as well as "legitimate" businesses (for example

---

[74] For a comprehensive overview of the issue including relevant international standards, see "The Impact of Armed Conflict on Children: Report of the Expert of the Secretary-General, Ms. Graça Machel," UN Doc. A/51/306, Aug. 26, 1996.

[75] Rehn and Johnson Sirleaf, *Women, War and Peace*, especially the recommendations at 136–142.

[76] See, for example, ibid. at 18: "[t]hose complicit must be held accountable for trafficking women and girls in or through conflict areas. Existing international laws on trafficking must be applied in conflict situations and national legislation should criminalize trafficking with strong punitive measures, including such actions as freezing the assets of trafficking rings. Victims of trafficking should be protected from prosecution."

[77] B. Anderson and J. O'Connell Davidson, *Trafficking: A Demand-Led Problem? A Multi-Country Pilot Study* (Save the Children, 2002) (Anderson and O'Connell-Davidson, *Trafficking: A Demand-Led Problem?*), at 18, 54. See also E. Pearson, *The Mekong Challenge – Human Trafficking: Redefining Demand* (International Labour Organization, 2005) (Pearson, *Human Trafficking: Redefining Demand*).

[78] Pearson, *Human Trafficking: Redefining Demand*, at 4. See also International Labour Organization, *The Demand Side of Human Trafficking in Asia: Empirical Findings* (2006).

in the entertainment, tourism, and travel industries) that indirectly profit from the exploitation associated with trafficking.[79]

While accepting the need to address demand, it is important to acknowledge the limits of a term that is not properly defined, underresearched, and still subject to debate and confusion. More generally, use of the economic terminology of "supply and demand" in the trafficking context, including in the present analysis, is not without problems and potential pitfalls. Trafficking networks and flows are still poorly understood, and the extent to which they mirror more traditional economic exchanges is not yet completely clear. In addition, there is no international consensus on the central question behind any economic analysis of trafficking: how, if at all, "the various areas of social and economic life within which trafficking and related abuses occur should be regulated by the State, or whether market relations should apply in these areas."[80] This is a crucial point: Discussion of demand in the context of trafficking is often highly ideological – linked to, and used to reinforce, political or moral positions on controversial issues such as the regulation or prohibition of prostitution.[81] The widespread failure of mainstream actors, including IGOs, to acknowledge these realities compromises the identification of legal obligations with respect to demand.[82] Such omissions also lessen the value and persuasive force of arguments aimed at placing demand at the center of mainstream trafficking discourse.

Within the limits noted above, it is both possible and useful to identify a distinction between the *causes or factors* that shape demand and the *demand itself*. This distinction becomes highly relevant when considering the roles and responsibilities of different actors including countries of origin, countries of destination, and individuals. As noted by the authors of a major study on this issue:

> to explore "the demand side of trafficking" is not simply to enquire about the individuals who exploit or consume the labour/services of trafficked persons, but

---

[79] See L.L. Lim, "Trafficking, Demand and the Sex Market," paper presented at the International Symposium on Gender at the Heart of Globalization, Mar. 12, 2007 (Lim, "Trafficking, Demand and the Sex Market"), at 6, available at http://www.gtm.cnrs-bellevue.fr/site-gtm/Clq%20Mond%2007/Lin%20Lean%20Lim.pdf (accessed Feb. 1, 2010).

[80] Anderson and O'Connell Davidson, *Trafficking: A Demand-Led Problem?*, at 54.

[81] See generally, G. Chang and K. Kim, "Reconceptualizing Approaches to Human Trafficking: New Directions and Perspectives from the Field(s)," (2007) 3 *Stanford Journal of Civil Rights and Civil Liberties* 317. For two different perspectives on demand that illustrate this point, see Lim, "Trafficking, Demand and the Sex Market" and D.M. Hughes, *The Demand for Victims of Sex Trafficking* (2005). See also K. Bales, *Understanding Global Slavery: A Reader* (2005), at chapter 8, "Understanding the Demand behind Human Trafficking."

[82] An example of failure to acknowledge such problems is provided by a UNODC paper on the issue of demand presented to the January 2010 session of the Working Group of Trafficking in Persons established under the Conference of Parties to the Convention against Transnational Organized Crime (Working Group on Trafficking in Persons, "Good Practices and Tools in Reducing the Demand for Exploitative Service: Background paper prepared by the Secretariat," UN Doc. CTOC/COP/WG.4/2010/3, Dec. 9, 2009. See also the almost identical analysis of demand in the joint UNODC and Inter-Parliamentary Union publication, *Combating Trafficking in Persons: A Handbook for Parliamentarians* (2009), at 70–72.

also to question the way in which states – through a combination of action and inaction – construct conditions under which it is possible or profitable to consume or exploit such labour/services.[83]

States can of course play a more direct part of the demand cycle. Many countries of destination derive great benefit from cheap foreign labor that, deliberately unprotected by law, can be moved on if and when circumstances require. Some countries that maintain a strong policy position against prostitution are nevertheless comfortable with a marginalized and closeted sex industry comprised principally of exploited foreigners. Countries of origin may rely heavily on the remittances of their overseas workers and be reluctant to interfere with a system that brings economic benefits – even in the face of abundant evidence that some of their citizens are being severely exploited.

Finally, demand cannot be considered separately from supply – not least because supply may well generate its own demand. For example, the availability of a cheap and exploitable domestic labor force (made possible through the factors considered throughout the present chapter) can itself contribute to generating demand for exploitative domestic labor at a level that may not otherwise have existed. Similarly, it is not difficult to sustain an argument that the internationalization and growth of the global sex industry, itself made possible by changes in transport, communication, and technology, have fueled the market for persons trafficked into prostitution.[84] However, the broader question – of whether or not an abundant supply of vulnerable individuals has fueled a demand that would otherwise not exist – is more difficult to answer.

8.2.2. *Is There an International Legal Obligation to Address Demand for Trafficking?*

Both the Trafficking Protocol and the European Trafficking Convention directly address the issue of demand in a manner that goes some way toward explaining what the drafters understood as "demand." Article 9(5) of the Trafficking Protocol requires States Parties to:

> adopt or strengthen legislative or other measures, such as educational, social or cultural measures, including through bilateral and multilateral cooperation, to discourage the demand that fosters all forms of exploitation of persons, especially women and children, that leads to trafficking.[85]

This provision builds on a proposal, introduced very late into the negotiations, by the United States.[86] As noted in the Legislative Guide to the Protocol, the relevant

---

[83] Anderson and O'Connell Davidson, *Trafficking: A Demand-Led Problem?*, at 5.

[84] See, for example, Rehn and Johnson Sirleaf, *Women, War and Peace*, at 70–71. See also S. Dillon, "What Human Rights Law Obscures: Global Sex Trafficking and the Demand for Children," (2008) 17 *UCLA Women's Law Journal* 121, esp. at 173–183.

[85] Trafficking Protocol, at Art. 9(5).

[86] United Nations Office on Drugs and Crime, Travaux Préparatoires *of the Negotiations for the Elaboration of the United Nations Convention against Transnational Organized Crime and the*

obligation is mandatory – States Parties to the Protocol are required to take at least some measures toward reducing demand that leads to trafficking.[87] The Conference of the Parties to the Organized Crime Convention[88] recently issued a recommendation urging States Parties to take active steps to this end.[89]

The European Trafficking Convention requires States Parties to adopt or strengthen legislative, administrative, educational, social, cultural, or other measures "to discourage demand that fosters all forms of exploitation of persons, especially women and children, that leads to trafficking."[90] The Convention includes a list of what its Explanatory Report refers to as "minimum measures":[91] research on best practices, methodologies, and strategies; raising awareness of the responsibility and important role of media and civil society in identifying demand as a root cause of trafficking; information campaigns involving public authorities and policy makers; and preventative measures including education programs for children that integrate a gender perspective and focus on the problem of sex-based discrimination.[92] The Explanatory Report to the European Trafficking Convention confirms that this provision places a positive obligation on States to adopt or reinforce measures for discouraging demand for all forms of trafficking. It further notes that by devoting a separate, free-standing article to this issue, the drafters sought to "underline the importance of tackling demand in order to prevent and combat the traffic itself."[93] The aim of the measures is to achieve "effective dissuasion."[94]

Protocols Thereto (2006) (Travaux Préparatoires *for the Organized Crime Convention and Protocols*), at 395. Note that the original US proposal for this provision was worded slightly differently to the final text: "States Parties, whether they are countries of origin, transit or destination, shall take measures, such as educational, social or cultural measures, to discourage the demand that nurtures the exploitation of persons." UN General Assembly, Ad Hoc Committee on the Elaboration of a Convention against Transnational Organized Crime, "Proposals and Contributions Received from Governments: United States of America: amendments to article 10 of the revised draft Protocol to Prevent, Suppress and Punish Trafficking in Persons, Especially Women and Children, supplementing the United Nations Convention against Transnational Organized Crime," UN Doc. A/AC.254/5/Add.33, Sept. 25, 2000.

[87] *Legislative Guide*, at Part Two, 297. The Legislative Guide further notes that the Trafficking Protocol does not specify in detail the exact actions required, leaving States Parties some flexibility to apply the measures that they think are most likely to be effective: ibid.

[88] See further, Chapter 9.2.1 in this volume.

[89] Conference of Parties to the United Nations Convention on Transnational Organized Crime, Decision 3/3, "Implementation of the Protocol to Prevent, Suppress and Punish Trafficking in Persons, Especially Women and Children, and the Protocol against the Smuggling of Migrants by Land, Sea and Air, supplementing the United Nations Convention against Transnational Organized Crime," reproduced in Conference of Parties to the United Nations Convention on Transnational Organized Crime, "Report of the Conference of Parties to the United Nations Convention on Transnational Organized Crime on its third session, held in Vienna from 9 to 18 October 2006," UN Doc. CTOC/COP/2006/14, Dec. 22, 2006, at 7, at para. (g).

[90] European Trafficking Convention, at Art. 6.

[91] European Trafficking Convention Explanatory Report, at para. 110.

[92] European Trafficking Convention, at Art. 6.

[93] European Trafficking Convention Explanatory Report, at para. 108.

[94] Ibid. at para. 109.

The role of demand in fueling trafficking, and the importance of addressing demand as part of a comprehensive response to trafficking and related exploitation, have been repeatedly recognized in other contexts. The UN General Assembly has called upon governments to:

> discourage, with a view to eliminating, the demand that fosters the trafficking of women and girls for all forms of exploitation, and in this regard to enhance preventive measures, including legislative measures, to deter exploiters of trafficked persons, as well as ensure their accountability.[95]

The UN Human Rights Council has made similar recommendations.[96] The preamble to the Optional Protocol to the Convention on the Rights of the Child refers to "the efforts that are needed to raise public awareness and reduce consumer demand for the sale of children."[97] The CEDAW Committee has increasingly dealt with demand (including demand for prostitution) in the context of its broader consideration of trafficking and related exploitation.[98] Several of the other UN human rights

---

[95]   UN General Assembly, "Trafficking in Women and Girls," UN Doc. A/RES/63/156, Jan. 30, 2009, at para. 2.

[96]   UN Human Rights Council, "Trafficking in Persons, Especially Women and Children," UN Doc. A/HRC/RES/11/3, June 17, 2009, at Preamble ("*[n]oting* that some of the demand for prostitution and forced labour is met by trafficking in persons in some parts of the world") and para. 3(g) ("*[u]rges* governments ... To adopt or strengthen legislative or other measures to discourage the demand that fosters all forms of exploitation of persons and leads to trafficking in persons, including the demand created by sex tourism, especially in children, and forced labour").

[97]   Optional Protocol to the Child Convention on the Sale of Children, Child Prostitution and Child Pornography, GA Res. 54/263, Annex I, 54 UN GAOR Supp. (No. 49), 7, UN Doc. A/54/49, Vol. III (2000), done May 25, 2000, entered into force Jan. 18, 2002, at Preamble. Note that Article 10(3) requires international cooperation in addressing the root causes of offenses addressed within the Optional Protocol.

[98]   See, for example, UN Committee on the Elimination of All Forms of Discrimination against Women, "Concluding Observations: Rwanda," UN Doc. CEDAW/C/RWA/CO/6, Feb. 12, 2009, at para. 27 ("concerned at the lack of awareness of the scope of the phenomenon ... further concerned at the criminalization of women and girls involved in prostitution, while the demand is not being addressed"); "Concluding Observations: Libyan Arab Jamahiriya," UN Doc. CEDAW/C/LBY/CO/5, Feb. 6, 2009, at para. 28 ("calls upon the State party to take all appropriate measures to suppress the exploitation of prostitution of women, including discouraging male demand"); "Concluding Observations: Mexico," UN Doc. CEDAW/C/MEX/CO/6, Aug. 26, 2006, at paras. 25, 27 ("recommends that the State party conduct nationwide awareness-raising campaigns on risks and consequences of trafficking targeted at women and girls"; "urges the State party to take all appropriate measures, including the adoption and implementation of a comprehensive plan to suppress the exploitation of prostitution of women and girls, child pornography and child prostitution, through, inter alia ... discouraging the demand for prostitution"); "Concluding Observations: Denmark," UN Doc. CEDAW/C/DEN/CO/6, Aug. 25, 2006, at para. 23) ("requests the State party to intensify its efforts to combat trafficking in women, including measures to prevent trafficking, minimize the demand for prostitution"); "Concluding Observations: Philippines," UN Doc. CEDAW/C/PHI/CO/6, Aug. 25, 2006, at para. 20 ("calls on the State party to take appropriate measures to suppress the exploitation of prostitution of women, including through the discouragement of the demand for prostitution"); "Concluding Observations: Australia," UN Doc. CEDAW/C/AUL/CO/5, Feb. 3, 2006, at paras. 20–21 ("concerned about the absence of effective strategies or programmes to ...

treaty bodies[99] and Special Procedures[100] have taken up this issue, in particular on the need to raise public awareness of the unlawful and exploitative nature of human trafficking. International and regional policy documents provide further confirmation of a growing understanding of the need for States to consider demand as a root cause of trafficking and a key factor in any effective prevention strategy.[101] The UN

address the demand for prostitution ... recommends the formulation of a comprehensive strategy to combat the trafficking of women and exploitation resulting from prostitution, which should include the development of strategies to discourage the demand for prostitution").

[99] The UN human rights treaty bodies have repeatedly called for States to generate public awareness of the unlawful nature, risks, and effects of trafficking and related practices as well as to reduce demand for trafficking. See, for example, UN Human Rights Committee, "Concluding Observations: Ireland," UN Doc. CCPR/C/IRL/CO/3, July 30, 2008, at para. 16 ("continue to reinforce its measures to combat trafficking in human beings particularly by reducing the demand for trafficking"); "Concluding Observations: Costa Rica," UN Doc. CCPR/C/CRI/CO/5, Nov. 16, 2007, at para. 12 ("reinforce measures to combat trafficking of women and children and, in particular ... continue its efforts to generate public awareness of the unlawful nature of the sexual exploitation of women and children"); "Concluding Observations: Thailand," UN Doc. CCPR/CO/84/THA, July 8, 2005, at para. 21 ("take action to implement policies and legislation for eradication of child labour, inter alia through public-awareness campaigns and education of the public on protection of rights of children"). Similarly, see UN Committee on the Rights of the Child, "Concluding Observations: Chad," UN Doc. CRC/C/TCD/CO/2, Feb. 12, 2009, at para. 80 ("urges the State party to carry out awareness-raising activities in order to make both parents and children aware of the dangers of trafficking"); "Concluding Observations: United States of America," UN Doc. CRC/C/OPSC/USA/CO/1, June 25, 2008, at para. 23 ("recommends that demand for sexual services involving the exploitation of children be addressed through both prevention and prosecution measures. Preventive measures should include, among others, public awareness campaigns aimed at the individuals and groups creating demand for sexual exploitation of children").

[100] See, for example, "Report of the Special Rapporteur on Torture and Other Cruel, Inhuman or Degrading Treatment or Punishment, Manfred Nowak, Addendum: Mission to Denmark," UN Doc. A/HRC/10/44/Add.2, Feb. 18, 2009, at para. 76; "Report Submitted by the Special Rapporteur on the Sale of Children, Child Prostitution and Child Pornography, Juan Miguel Petit, Addendum: Mission to Ukraine," UN Doc. A/HRC/4/31/Add.2, Jan. 24, 2007, at para. 79; "Report of the Special Rapporteur on the Human Rights Aspects of the Victims of Trafficking in Persons, Especially Women and Children, Sigma Huda," UN Doc. E/CN.4/2006/62, Feb. 20, 2006, at Section II; "Report of the Special Rapporteur on Sale of Children, Child Prostitution and Child Pornography, Juan Miguel Petit," UN Doc. E/CN.4/2006/67, Jan. 12, 2006, at Section III.

[101] See, for example, UN General Assembly, "Trafficking in Women and Girls," UN Doc. A/RES/63/156, Jan. 30, 2009, at Preamble ("*[n]oting* that some of the demand for prostitution and forced labour is met by trafficking in persons in some parts of the world"), para. 2 ("*[c]alls upon* Governments to discourage, with a view to eliminating, the demand that fosters the trafficking of women and girls for all forms of exploitation, and in this regard to enhance preventive measures, including legislative measures, to deter exploiters of trafficked persons, as well as ensure their accountability"), para. 7 ("*[e]ncourages* Governments to take appropriate measures to eliminate sex tourism demand, especially of children, through all possible preventive actions") and para. 14 ("*[e]ncourages* Governments and relevant United Nations bodies, within existing resources, to take appropriate measures to raise public awareness of the issue of trafficking in persons, particularly women and girls; to discourage, with a view to eliminating, the demand that fosters all forms of exploitation, including sexual exploitation and forced labour"). See also UN Human Rights Council, "Trafficking in Persons, Especially Women and Children," UN Doc. A/HRC/RES/11/3, June 17, 2009, at Preamble and para. 3(g). On regional responses to the issue of demand, see, for example, Brussels Declaration, at para. 7 ("[i]t should be an essential and common goal for the fight against trafficking to address the reduction of the demand for sexual services and cheap labour"); European Union, "EU Plan on Best Practices,

Trafficking Principles and Guidelines deserve particular mention in this context as one of the very first international policy documents to address demand for the goods and services produced by trafficked persons.[102]

Improvements in understanding of the dynamics of trafficking and of the factors that increase vulnerability to trafficking have been helpful in fleshing out the substantive content of the obligation on States to address demand for trafficking. For example, in terms of its scope, it is evident that the obligation to address demand rests primarily with the country within which the exploitation takes place, because it is within these countries that both consumer and employer demand is principally generated. However, the links between demand and supply noted above also imply certain obligations on countries of origin, in particular in relation to addressing factors increasing vulnerability. Importantly, demand reduction required under the Trafficking Protocol and the UN Trafficking Principles and Guidelines is not restricted to demand for exploitative sexual services but encompasses demand for the full range of exploitative practices identified in the international definition of trafficking.

The link between demand and discrimination (most particularly racial and sex-based discrimination) is an important one. Demand in the context of trafficking is often shaped by discriminatory attitudes (including cultural attitudes) and beliefs. Women may be preferred for certain forms of exploitation because they are perceived as weak and less likely to assert themselves or claim the rights to which they are entitled. Certain ethnic or racial groups may be targeted for trafficking-related exploitation on the basis of racist or culturally discriminatory assumptions relating to, for example, their sexuality, servility, or work capacities.[103] Demand for prostitution (often supplied through trafficking) may reflect discriminatory attitudes and

Standards and Procedures for Combating and Preventing Trafficking in Human Beings," OJ C 2005/C 311/01, Dec. 9, 2005 (EU Plan on Best Practices), at para. 3(vi) ("eliminating demand for all forms of exploitation, including sexual exploitation and domestic labour exploitation"); OSCE Action Plan, at Recommendation IV(3.3) ("[a]dopting or strengthening legislative, educational, social, cultural or other measures, and, where applicable, penal legislation … to discourage the demand that fosters all forms of exploitation of persons, especially women and children, and that leads to trafficking"); ECOWAS Initial Plan of Action, at 6, para. 1 ("States … shall develop and disseminate public awareness materials focusing on … discouraging the demand that leads to trafficking, particularly by addressing those who might exploit victims of trafficking, for example as child domestics or farm labourers"); Ouagadougou Action Plan, at 3 ("[t]ake measures to reduce the demand for services involving the exploitation of victims of trafficking in human beings"); OAS Recommendations on Trafficking in Persons, at Sections II(2), V(1); COMMIT MOU, at Art. 26.

[102] Within the UN Trafficking Principles and Guidelines, Principle 4 identifies demand as a *root cause of trafficking* and requires States to address demand in their response to trafficking. It is reinforced by Guideline 7.1, which requires States and others to "analys[e] the factors that generate demand for exploitative commercial sexual services and exploitative labour and tak[e] strong legislative, policy and other measures to address these issues."

[103] Anderson and O'Connell Davidson, *Trafficking: A Demand-Led Problem?*, at 42 (noting also that racism, xenophobia, and prejudice against ethnic minority groups make it easier for consumers of trafficked persons' exploitation to justify the practice).

beliefs based on both race and gender. In seeking to discharge their obligation to address demand, States should focus on addressing discriminatory attitudes and beliefs, particularly those directed against women and migrants.

States should also recognize their role in shaping demand for the goods and services produced by trafficking through laws and policies on a range of matters, including immigration, employment, welfare, and economic development. For example, failure to provide legislative protection to certain individuals such as domestic workers, "entertainers," or migrant workers creates an environment in which exploitation of these persons becomes both "possible and worthwhile."[104] Laws and policies that institutionalize discrimination can also shape demand as can a failure on the part of the State to effectively challenge discriminatory social attitudes, practices, and beliefs. Failure on the part of the State to effectively investigate, prosecute, and punish trafficking and related exploitation can contribute to demand generated by traffickers and exploiters by maintaining trafficking as a low-risk, high-profit crime. A more general failure on the part of the State to protect the rights of certain persons including women, children, and migrants can further contribute to constructing demand by exacerbating vulnerability and thereby exploitability.

Labor protection must be a central element of any strategy to address demand for trafficking and related exploitation. As noted by the International Labour Organization:

> A major incentive for trafficking in labour is the lack of application and enforcement of labour standards in countries of destination as well as origin … Tolerance of restrictions on freedom of movement, long working hours, poor or non-existent health and safety protections, non-payment of wages, substandard housing, etc. all contribute to expanding a market for trafficked migrants who have no choice but to labour in conditions simply intolerable and unacceptable for legal employment.[105]

Research confirms that demand for trafficked persons' labor or services is absent or markedly less where workers are organized and where labor standards regarding wages, working hours and conditions, and health and safety are monitored and enforced.[106] Rights-based strategies to address demand for cheap and controllable labor should therefore aim to secure adequate labor protection, including through

[104] Ibid. at 41. See also *Rantsev v. Cyprus and Russia*, Dec. No. 25965/04 (not yet reported) (ECHR, Jan, 7, 2010) (*Rantsev v. Cyprus and Russia*), in which weaknesses in legislative and administrative frameworks and immigration policy facilitated the exploitation of foreign cabaret artistes. The regime of artiste visas itself was found to violate the prohibition on slavery, servitude, and forced labor: ibid. at para. 293.

[105] P.A. Taran and G. Moreno-Fontes Chammartin (International Labour Organization), "Getting at the Roots: Stopping Exploitation of Migrant Workers by Organized Crime," paper presented at the International Symposium on the UN Convention against Transnational Organized Crime: Requirements for Effective Implementation, Turin, Feb. 22–23, 2002, at 8.

[106] Anderson and O'Connell Davidson, *Trafficking: A Demand-Led Problem?*, at 54.

properly monitored regulatory frameworks, that also extends to migrants and those working in the informal economy.[107]

Finally, demand in the context of trafficking is still poorly understood, often leading to inappropriate responses that may violate established rights.[108] Research is an essential aspect of understanding demand. This is recognized in the European Trafficking Convention, which explicitly calls on States Parties to undertake research on best practices, methodologies, and strategies to discourage demand.[109]

The question of whether certain aspects of "demand" for trafficking should be criminalized (addressed in the previous chapter in the context of a discussion on criminalization of the use of the services of a victim of trafficking) is a relatively recent one, reflecting, as previously noted, a growing realization that some individuals involved in trafficking-related exploitation do not fall within the parameters of existing legislation and, for this and other reasons, are escaping justice. As with the issue of demand more generally, the criminalization question is a controversial one – largely because of its association with the deeply divisive prostitution debate. As noted in Chapter 7, the Trafficking Protocol does not refer specifically to criminalization of demand, and the *travaux préparatoires* do not identify any discussion on this issue during the drafting process. However, the Legislative Guide to the implementation of the Protocol notes that demand reduction "could be achieved in part through legislative or other measures targeting those who knowingly use or take advantage of the services of a victim of exploitation."[110] The UNODC Model Law on Trafficking acknowledges that there is no obligation in the Protocol to criminalize demand in this way, but nevertheless proposes a provision to that effect.[111]

The European Trafficking Convention does address the issue of criminalization of demand in an Article entitled: "Criminalization of the use of the services of a victim."[112] This Article requires States Parties to consider:

---

[107] The Inter-American Court of Human Rights has held that "States are obliged to ensure that, within their territory, all the labour rights stipulated in its laws – rights deriving from international instruments or domestic legislation – are recognized and applied. Likewise, States are internationally responsible when they tolerate actions and practices of third parties that prejudice migrant workers, either because they do not recognize the same rights to them as to national workers or because they recognize the same rights to them but with some type of discrimination": *Juridical Conditions and Rights of Undocumented Migrants*, Advisory Opinion OC=18/03, Inter-American Court of Human Rights (ser. A) No. 18, Sept. 17, 2003, at para. 153.

[108] See further, Chapter 8.4.

[109] European Trafficking Convention, at Art. 6(a).

[110] *Legislative Guide*, at Part 2, 297.

[111] UNODC Model Law, at 34: "[a]nyone who makes use of the services or labour of a person or profits in any form from the services or labour of a person with the prior knowledge that such labour or services are performed or rendered under one or more of the conditions described in article 8, paragraph 1, shall be guilty of an offence and, upon conviction, shall be liable to imprisonment for … and/or a fine of/up to …."

[112] European Trafficking Convention, at Art. 19.

adopting such legislative or other measures as may be necessary to establish as criminal offences under its internal law the use of services [of a victim of trafficking] with the knowledge that the person is a victim of trafficking in human beings.[113]

The Explanatory Report to the European Trafficking Convention confirms that this provision was prompted by a desire to discourage the demand for exploitable people that drives trafficking[114] by, *inter alia*, punishing those who, by buying the services exploited, play a part in exploiting the victim.[115] It also seeks to secure the potential criminalization of individuals involved in trafficking against whom the requisite elements of the crime may be difficult to prove. For example, the owner of business premises used for trafficking may not have undertaken any of the "actions" set out in the definition or used any of the required "means" such as deception or coercion. Article 19 would enable criminal prosecution of that individual if it could be shown that he or she knowingly made those premises available for the use of a trafficker.[116] The Explanatory Report provides additional examples of situation in which Article 19 could apply:

> the client of a prostitute who knew full well that the prostitute had been trafficked could likewise be treated as having committed a criminal offence as could someone who knowingly used a trafficker's services to obtain an organ.[117]

Intent is the key element in the offense proposed under Article 19.[118] While noting that evidence of a nonmaterial ingredient such as intent may be difficult to prove, the Explanatory Report envisages that the perpetrator's intention can indeed be inferred from objective factual circumstances.[119]

In conclusion, criminalization of the use of the services of a trafficking victim while either knowing or recklessly disregarding the fact that the individual involved is a trafficking victim is not currently an established international legal obligation. Nor is there sufficient evidence available to support its status as an emerging norm. However, such criminalization addresses a critical link in the trafficking chain and could be considered a key aspect of a comprehensive strategy to address demand for

---

[113] Ibid.
[114] European Trafficking Convention Explanatory Report, at para. 230.
[115] Ibid. at para. 233.
[116] Ibid. at para. 232.
[117] Ibid.
[118] This is confirmed in the UNODC Model Law, at 35, in the context of its proposed optional provision on this issue: "[t]he mens rea required here is 'knowingly' to ensure that once a person learns that he or she will be using the services of a victim of trafficking, and nevertheless decides to go ahead and benefit from the exploitation of another person, he or she will be punished."
[119] Note that Article 6(2)(f) of the Organized Crime Convention states, in reference to criminalizing laundering of the proceeds of crime, that "[k]nowledge, intent or purpose required as an element of an offence set forth in paragraph 1 of this article may be inferred from objective, factual circumstances." The European Trafficking Convention Explanatory Report, at para. 235, cites this provision in connection with its discussion of Article 19.

the goods and services produced through the exploitation of trafficked persons. The legal and policy parameters of this strategy remain to be established.

8.3. PREVENTION THROUGH ADDRESSING CORRUPTION AND COMPLICITY

While an internationally accepted definition continues to be elusive, corruption is generally understood to refer to the misuse of public power for personal benefit or gain. As used in the present context, the term does not extend to embrace corporate crime in which public officials are not involved. Complicity, a concept found in a number of international conventions,[120] denotes responsibility or liability for the actions of another that is incurred, for example, through knowledge, tacit consent, or acquiescence. An individual who is complicit in a trafficking-related offense may or may not also be an accomplice to that same offense.[121] Complicity involving a public official will invariably fall within the definition of corruption.

It is only recently that corruption has been explicitly linked to human rights violations[122] and to the capacity of States to meet their human rights obligations.[123] Available information appears to confirm that human rights violations associated with corruption invariably afflict the poorest and most vulnerable including women, children, migrants, and minorities[124] – groups that are also overrepresented among victims of trafficking. The link between corruption and trafficking appears to be an obvious one, notwithstanding the lack of scholarly research or official data available to corroborate the widely held assumption that corruption plays a major role in trafficking.[125] It is certainly clear that traffickers require the active involvement or

---

[120] See, for example, Convention on the Prevention and Punishment of the Crime of Genocide, 78 UNTS 227, Dec. 9, 1948, entered into force Jan. 12, 1951, at Art. 3; Convention against Torture and Other Cruel, Inhuman or Degrading Treatment or Punishment, 1465 UNTS 85, adopted Dec. 10, 1984, entered into force June 26, 1987, at Art. 6.

[121] On obligations of criminalization relating to accomplices of trafficking offenses, see the discussion at Chapter 7.1.1, particularly under "Criminalizing Attempt, Complicity, and Corporate Liability," and also note 129 to this chapter.

[122] See International Council on Human Rights Policy and Transparency International, *Corruption and Human Rights: Making the Connection* (2009) (ICHRP and Transparency International, *Corruption and Human Rights*), available at http://www.ichrp.org/files/reports/40/131_web.pdf (accessed Feb. 1, 2010).

[123] See, for example, UN Committee on Economic, Social and Cultural Rights, "Concluding Observations: Moldova," UN Doc. E/C.12/1/ADD.91, Dec. 12, 2003, at para. 12 ("states face serious problems of corruption, which have negative effects on the full exercise of rights covered by the [ICESCR]"), cited in ICHRP and Transparency International, *Corruption and Human Rights*, at 23. The UN Human Rights Committee has repeatedly raised the issue of corruption and the noted its impact on the ability of States to meet their human rights obligations. See, for example, UN Human Rights Committee, "Concluding Observations: Kenya," UN Doc. CCPR/Co/83/KEN, Apr. 29, 2005, at para. 20.

[124] ICHRP and Transparency International, *Corruption and Human Rights*, at 7–10.

[125] A report prepared for a 2009 meeting of States Parties to the UN Convention against Corruption confirms the current poor state of knowledge in this area. That report essentially comprises a review

at least the acquiescence of public officials to move individuals across international borders and, in relation to both internal and international trafficking, to deliver them into and maintain them in situations of exploitation. The high level of impunity enjoyed by traffickers and their accomplices appears due, in large part, to public sector corruption involving enforcement officials, prosecutors, and the judiciary. Corruption also compromises victim safety and the provision of support, assistance, and remedies.[126] One recent analysis of the relationship between corruption and the prevalence of trafficking concludes, albeit on the basis of very limited evidence, that "corruption is probably the most important factor in explaining human trafficking" and "[c]ountries that make the least effort to fight human trafficking also tend to be those with high levels of official corruption."[127]

8.3.1. *An Obligation to Address Trafficking-related Corruption*

The need to identify and eradicate public sector involvement in trafficking is widely accepted in international law and policy. The drafters of the Organized Crime Convention and its Protocols were aware of the strong link between organized criminal activities, such as trafficking, and corruption.[128] The Convention reflects that awareness, requiring States to take strong measures to criminalize all forms of corrupt practices when committed by public officials and to ensure that their laws are harmonized so as to facilitate cooperation.[129] There is no need for the criminalized

---

of the limited available literature, personal information, anonymous sources, and the results of a survey completed by only eight individuals. Anti-Slavery International, Transparency International and United Nations Office on Drugs and Crime "The Role of Corruption in Trafficking in Persons," Background Paper for the Side Event "The Role of Corruption in Trafficking in Persons" at the Third Session of the Conference of State Parties to the United Nations Convention against Corruption, Nov. 11, 2009 (Anti-Slavery International, Transparency International and UNODC, "The Role of Corruption in Trafficking"), at 4, available at http://www.unodc.org/documents/human-trafficking/ Corruption_and_trafficking_Doha_final.pdf (accessed Feb. 1, 2010). For another analysis of the link between trafficking and corruption, see L. Holmes, "Human Trafficking & Corruption: Triple Victimization?" in C. Friesendorf ed., *Strategies against Human Trafficking: The Role of the Security Sector* 83 (2009) (Holmes, "Human Trafficking & Corruption").

[126] Holmes, "Human Trafficking & Corruption."

[127] S.X. Zhang and S.L. Pineda, "Corruption as a Causal Factor in Human Trafficking," in D. Siegel and H. Nelen eds., *Organized Crime: Culture, Markets and Policies* 41 (2008), at 52–53. This conclusion is based on an analysis of, *inter alia*, the extent of trafficking (as measured by the somewhat compromised United States Department of State, "Trafficking in Persons Report" (2005)) and the Transparency International Corruption Perception Index.

[128] See the introduction to Travaux Préparatoires *for the Organized Crime Convention and Protocols.* See also the Interpretative Note on Article 3 of the Convention ("[t]he Ad Hoc Committee was also strongly convinced that the convention would constitute an effective tool and the necessary legal framework for international cooperation in combating, inter alia, such criminal activities as … corruption"): ibid. at 32. See also UN General Assembly, "Action against Corruption," UN Doc. A/ RES/54/128, Dec. 17, 1999, in which the General Assembly directed the Ad Hoc Committee to incorporate into the draft convention measures against corruption linked to organized crime, including provisions regarding the sanctioning of acts of corruption involving public officials: cited, ibid. at 75.

[129] Organized Crime Convention, at Art. 8. Note that while the Convention does not define corruption, States Parties are required to take action against three forms of conduct when committed

conduct to be transnational in commission or effect, or to involve an organized criminal group.[130] In addition to the obligation of criminalization, States Parties are required, to the extent appropriate and consistent with their legal system, to adopt "legislative, administrative or other effective measures to promote integrity and to prevent, detect and punish corruption of public officials."[131] States Parties must also take measures to ensure effective action by domestic authorities in the prevention, detection, and punishment of corruption of public officials, including providing such authorities with adequate independence to deter the exertion of inappropriate influence on their actions.[132] In accordance with the Convention's general provisions on sanctions, the relevant corruption offenses should be liable to penalties that take into account their grave nature.[133]

The use of force, threats, and intimidation against, for example, judges, prosecutors, jurors, victims, and witnesses is a serious obstacle to the development of an effective criminal justice response to trafficking. It is also directly related to public sector corruption. As noted in the Legislative Guide to the Organized Crime Convention and its Protocols:

> No justice can be done if judges, jurors, witnesses or victims are intimidated, threatened or corrupted. No effective national and international cooperation can be hoped for, if such crucial participants in the investigation and law enforcement process are not sufficiently protected to perform their roles and provide their accounts unimpeded. No serious crimes can be detected and punished, if the evidence is prevented from reaching investigators, prosecutors and the court.[134]

The Organized Crime Convention requires criminalization of "obstruction of justice."[135] States Parties are further required to criminalize and take steps to

---

[130]   intentionally: first, active bribery, being "the promise, offering or giving to a public official, directly or indirectly, of an undue advantage, for the official himself or herself or another person or entity, in order that the official act or refrain from acting in the exercise of his or her official duties" (Art. 8(1)); second, passive bribery, or "the solicitation or acceptance by a public official, directly or indirectly, of an undue advantage, for the official himself or herself or another person or entity, in order that the official act or refrain from acting in the exercise of his or her official duties" (Art. 8(1)); and third, participation as an accomplice to bribery (Art. 8(3)). Note that States Parties are only required to "consider" criminalizing such conduct involving a foreign public official or international civil servant or other forms of corruption: ibid. at Art. 8(2).

[130]   *Legislative Guide*, at Part One, 84.

[131]   Organized Crime Convention, at Art. 9(1).

[132]   Ibid. at Art. 9(2).

[133]   Ibid. at Art. 11(1).

[134]   *Legislative Guide*, at Part One, para. 195.

[135]   Organized Crime Convention, at Art. 23. The provision establishes two offenses: first, use of physical force, threats, or intimidation or the promise, offering, or giving of an undue advantage either to induce false testimony or to interfere in the giving of testimony or the production of evidence in proceedings in relation to offenses covered by the Convention (Art. 23(a)); and, secondly, use of physical force, threats, or intimidation to interfere with the exercise of official duties by a justice or law enforcement official in relation to offenses covered by the Convention (Art. 23(b)).

prevent money laundering, another form of conduct commonly associated with corruption.[136]

The European Trafficking Convention does not refer to public sector corruption, save for a provision requiring States Parties to recognize public sector complicity in trafficking as an aggravating circumstance in the determination of penalties.[137] The SAARC Convention contains a similar provision.[138] Many international and regional policy documents confirm the link between trafficking and corruption, the importance of addressing corruption as a means of preventing trafficking, and the need for States to respond effectively.[139] Outside the specialist trafficking treaties, legal and policy instruments dealing with violence against women affirm an obligation on States to investigate acts or omissions of public officials.[140]

The sources and authorities cited above are compatible with and reinforce a growing body of international law that seeks to address corruption more generally, particularly those corrupt practices with transnational reach or effect. The most important instrument in this regard is the UN Convention against Corruption,

---

[136] Ibid. at Arts. 6, 7.

[137] European Trafficking Convention, at Art. 24(c).

[138] South Asian Association for Regional Cooperation, Convention on Preventing and Combating Trafficking in Women and Children for Prostitution, done Jan. 5, 2002, entered into force Dec. 1, 2005 (SAARC Convention), at Art. IV.

[139] See, for example, UN General Assembly, "Trafficking in Women and Girls," UN Doc. A/RES/63/156, Jan. 30, 2009, at para. 11; Brussels Declaration, at para. 19; EU Plan on Best Practices, at para. 4(x); UN Trafficking Principles and Guidelines, at Principles 6, 13, Guideline 4.3; OSCE Action Plan, at Recommendation III(1.7); Ouagadougou Action Plan, at para 2; OAS Recommendations on Trafficking in Persons, at Section II(18). Note that the UN General Assembly has also addressed, specifically, the issue of sexual assaults by public officials directed against trafficking persons in custody. See, for example, UN General Assembly, "Trafficking in Women and Girls," UN Doc. A/RES/63/156, Jan. 30, 2009, at para. 11 ("[c]alls upon all Governments to … penalize persons in authority found guilty of sexually assaulting victims of trafficking in their custody"). See, additionally, "Report Submitted by the Special Rapporteur on the Sale of Children, Child Prostitution and Child Pornography, Juan Miguel Petit, Addendum: Mission to Mexico," UN Doc. A/HRC/7/8/Add.2, Jan. 28, 2008, at para. 77 ("the testimonies gathered overwhelmingly point to corruption and police negligence as one of the main causes of exploitation and trafficking"); "Report Submitted by the Special Rapporteur on the Sale of Children, Child Prostitution and Child Pornography, Juan Miguel Petit, Addendum: Mission to Ukraine," UN Doc. A/HRC/4/31/Add.2, Jan. 24, 2007, at para. 76; UN Committee on the Rights of the Child, "Concluding Observations: Sierra Leone," UN Doc. CRC/C/SLE/CO/2, June 20, 2008, at paras. 74–75; "Concluding Observations: Kyrgyzstan," UN Doc. CRC/C/OPSC/KGZ/CO/1, May 4, 2007, at para. 25; UN Human Rights Committee, "Concluding Observations: Bosnia and Herzegovina," UN Doc. CCPR/C/BIH/CO/1, Nov. 22, 2006, at para. 16.

[140] See, for example, CEDAW General Recommendation No. 19, at para. 9; UN General Assembly, "Declaration on the Elimination of Violence against Women," UN Doc. A/48/49, Dec. 20, 1993, at para. 4(c); Beijing Platform for Action, at para. 124; "Further Actions and Initiatives to Implement the Beijing Declaration and Platform for Action," UN Doc. A/RES/S-23/3, Nov. 16, 2000, at para. 13; American Convention on the Prevention, Punishment, and Eradication of Violence against Women, 1438 UNTS 63, done June 9, 1994, entered into force Mar. 5, 1995, at Art. 7(b).

which was drafted several years after the Organized Crime Convention and entered into force in 2005.[141] The Convention against Corruption seeks to promote and strengthen measures to combat public sector and private corruption at both domestic and international levels. Its scope is wider and its provisions, which would apply to the various forms of trafficking-related corruption identified above, are much more detailed than those of the Organized Crime Convention. For example, States Parties are required to criminalize a range of corruption-related conduct including bribery, embezzlement of funds, abuse of functions, trading in influence, and the concealment and "laundering" of the proceeds of corruption.[142] States Parties are further required to establish "obstruction of justice" – defined as the use of corrupt or coercive means to interfere with potential witnesses or to interfere with the actions of judicial and law enforcement officials – as a criminal offense.[143] They are also required to put in place a range of preventative measures directed at both public and private sectors. These include preventative anticorruption policies, systems, procedures, and institutions that promote the participation of society and reflect basic principles of the rule of law, proper management of public affairs and public property, integrity, transparency, and accountability.[144] States Parties are to cooperate with one another in every aspect of the fight against corruption including prevention, investigation, and prosecution of offenders. Countries are bound to render specific forms of mutual legal assistance in gathering and transferring evidence for use in prosecutions, to extradite offenders, and to support the tracing, seizure, and confiscation of the assets of corruption.[145]

The UN Convention against Corruption builds on and reinforces a number of regional agreements on these issues, including the African Union Convention on Preventing and Combating Corruption;[146] the Inter-American Convention against Corruption;[147] the OECD Convention on Combating Bribery of Foreign Public Officials in International Business Transactions;[148] the Council of Europe Criminal Law Convention on Corruption (criminalizing acts of corruption);[149] and the

---

[141] United Nations Convention against Corruption, 2349 UNTS 41, done Oct. 31, 2003, entered into force Dec. 14, 2005 (Convention against Corruption)

[142] Ibid. at Arts. 16–19, 23, 24.

[143] Ibid. at Art. 25. Note that Article 23 of the Organized Crime Convention also requires criminalization of the obstruction of justice in a context that would directly cover proceedings related to trafficking in persons cases.

[144] Convention against Corruption, at chapter II.

[145] Ibid. at chapter IV, esp. Arts. 43–44.

[146] African Union Convention on Preventing and Combating Corruption, 43 ILM 5, done July 11, 2003, entered into force Aug. 5, 2006.

[147] Inter-American Convention against Corruption, OAS Treaties Register B-58, 35 ILM 724, done Mar. 29, 1996, entered into force Mar. 6, 1997.

[148] OECD Convention on Combating Bribery of Foreign Public Officials in International Business Transactions, 37 ILM 1, done Dec. 17, 1997, entered into force Feb. 15, 1999.

[149] Criminal Law Convention on Corruption, 2216 UNTS 225, ETS No. 173, done Jan. 27, 1999, entered into force July 1, 2002.

Council of Europe Civil Law Convention on Corruption (providing for compensation for victims of corruption).[150]

8.3.2. *Practical Application of the Due Diligence Standard*

When considering the issue of State responsibility for trafficking-related corruption, it is useful to summarize the main points of the relevant doctrine, previously explored at greater length in Chapter 4. Legal responsibility will be incurred by a State for acts and omissions that are: (1) attributable to that State; and (2) a breach of its international legal obligation. International law is clear that the conduct of any organ of the State, such as a court or legislature, will always be regarded as an act of that State for which the State is directly responsible. Attribution for acts of officials who are part of a State organ (such as police, prosecutors, immigration officials) will depend on whether the individual concerned is acting in an apparently official capacity or under the color of authority. Importantly, "it is irrelevant for this purpose that the person concerned may have had ulterior or improper motives or may be abusing public power."[151] That the act in question was unauthorized, or *ultra vires*, is also irrelevant in determining whether or not it is to be characterized as an act of the State. These are both important principles in the present context. As noted in Chapter 4, States may not defend themselves against allegations of public sector involvement in trafficking by pointing out that such involvement is contrary to national law and policy. Under the rules of attribution, "conduct carried out by persons cloaked with governmental authority" will be attributed to the State as an act of that State. The task of distinguishing between "official" conduct and "private" conduct will, in the case of trafficking-related corruption, generally be relatively straightforward: Corruption by governmental authorities that is enabled by their official position – as it so often is – is necessarily imbued with the color of authority.

The due diligence standard is commonly used to identify the obligations of States in relation to acts by private entities that interfere with established rights. The relevant principles confirm that failure to meet this standard, in terms of preventing an anticipated human rights abuse by a private entity or responding effectively to such an abuse, will invoke the international responsibility of the State. Due diligence is also the appropriate standard to be applied in considering: (1) whether the State has taken sufficient steps to prevent involvement in trafficking by its officials; (2) whether the State has discharged its obligation to identify, investigate, and punish public sector complicity in trafficking; and (3) whether the State has discharged its obligation to remedy violations resulting from such corruption.[152] The discussion on

---

[150] Civil Law Convention on Corruption, 2246 UNTS 3, ETS No. 174, done Nov. 4, 1999, entered into force Nov. 1, 2003.

[151] ILC Articles on State Responsibility, at Art. 4, para. 13.

[152] Note that some commentators have argued that the due diligence standard does not have a role to play in determining State responsibility for harm directly caused by the State and its agents; in

due diligence in Chapter 4 confirmed that deciding whether or not a State is meeting the due diligence standard ultimately comes down to an assessment of whether that State is taking its obligations to prevent, respect, protect, and fulfill human rights seriously. In the present context, those obligations include preventing and responding to public sector involvement in the human rights violations associated with trafficking.

International law, including case law, provides some guidance on the actions that may be required by States to meet the due diligence standard with respect to trafficking-related corruption. For example, the national legal framework should provide an appropriate framework for the identification, investigation, and prosecution of trafficking-related offenses, including those committed by or with the complicity of public officials. States should further ensure that the involvement of public officials in trafficking or related offenses is grounds for an aggravated offense, attracting relatively harsher penalties.[153] Procedures should be in place for receiving and effectively investigating complaints of trafficking involving or implicating public officials. These procedures should aim to ensure accountability, maintain public confidence, and alleviate legitimate concerns. Investigation into trafficking-related corruption should commence promptly and be conducted with expedience. An investigation must not be a mere formality but must be one that is capable of leading to identification and punishment of culprits. It should also be independent and public. Effective measures should be in place to establish the truth of a victim's allegations or to obtain corroborating evidence. States should cooperate with each other to ensure that there are no safe havens for corrupt officials or their assets.[154] Due diligence also requires attention to the rights of victims of trafficking-related

---

other words, that the standard should be reserved for assessment of State responsibility for harm that originated in private acts. See further C. Benninger-Budel, "Introduction," in C. Benninger-Budel ed., *Due Diligence and Its Application to Protect Women from Violence* 1 (2008), at 14.

[153] See further the discussion of aggravated offenses at Chapter 7.3.3 in this book.

[154] These procedural requirements are distilled from the instruments cited at Chapter 8.3.1, above, and a body of case law of the European Court of Human Rights, including: *Rantsev v. Cyprus and Russia*, at para. 233; *Ahmet Ozkan and Others v. Turkey*, [2004] ECHR 133 (ECHR, Apr. 6, 2004), at paras. 310–314; *Paul and Audrey Edwards v. UK*, (2002) 35 EHRR 487 (ECHR, Mar. 14, 2002), at paras. 69–73; *Assenov and Others v. Bulgaria*, [1998] ECHR 98 (ECHR, Oct. 28, 1998), esp. at para. 102; and a series of cases involving actions of the Turkish security forces including: *Timurtas v. Turkey*, [2000] ECHR 222 (ECHR, June 13, 2000), at paras. 87–90; *Ertak v. Turkey*, [2000] ECHR 193 (ECHR, May 9, 2000), at paras. 134–135; *Çakici v. Turkey*, [1999] ECHR 43 (ECHR, July 8, 1999), at para. 87; *Tanrikulu v. Turkey*, [1999] ECHR 55 (ECHR, 8 July 1999), at paras. 101–111; *Yasa v. Turkey*, (1999) 28 EHRR 408 (ECHR, Sept. 2, 1998), at paras. 102–104; *Ergi v. Turkey*, [1998] ECHR 59 (ECHR, July 28, 1998), at paras. 82–86; *Tekin v. Turkey*, [1998] ECHR 53 (ECHR, June 9, 1998), at paras. 62–69; *Kurt v. Turkey*, [1998] ECHR 44, (ECHR, May 25, 1998), at paras. 135–142; *Selçuk and Asker v. Turkey*, [1998] ECHR 36 (ECHR, April 24, 1998), at paras. 93–98; *Kaya v. Turkey*, [1998] ECHR 10 (ECHR, Feb. 19, 1998), at paras. 86–92; *Aksoy v. Turkey*, [1996] ECHR 68 (ECHR, Dec. 18, 1996), at paras. 95–100; and *Mentes and Others v. Turkey*, [1997] ECHR 98 (ECHR, Nov. 28, 1997), at paras. 89–92. The elements of an effective investigation have also been confirmed through several cases of the Inter-American Commission/Court of Human Rights including: *Villagrán Morales et al. v. Guatemala (The Street Children Case)*, Inter-American Court of Human Rights (ser. C) No. 63, Nov. 19, 1999, esp. at para. 226; *Raquel Martín de Mejía v. Peru*,

corruption. Victims of trafficking that involves or implicates public officials should have access to justice including remedies.[155]

8.3.3. *Due Diligence in Preventing Trafficking-related Corruption by International Officials*

The involvement of military, peacekeeping, humanitarian, civilian contractors, and other international personnel in trafficking and related exploitation has been extensively documented.[156] Studies into this aspect of the trafficking phenomenon confirm that such involvement can be both direct and indirect. Patronage of a brothel that exploits trafficked persons is an example of indirect involvement. The buying, selling, or exchange of women and girls for the purpose of their sexual exploitation are examples of more direct involvement.

The participation of international personnel in trafficking is a complex issue and one that is not yet fully understood. Certainly, a large, highly militarized, and predominantly male international presence creates an artificial and highly gendered economy that can actually fuel the demand for goods and services produced through trafficking and exploitation, in particular prostitution.[157] International personnel are generally deployed to situations of conflict or immediate postconflict in which populations are vulnerable and basic institutions, including law enforcement, are fragile or nonexistent.[158] In impoverished, postconflict economies, extreme income disparities

---

Case No. 10.970, Report No. 5/96, Inter-AmCHR Doc. OEA/Ser.L/V/II.91 Doc. 7 (Inter-Am Comm HR, Mar. 1, 1996), at 157.

[155] See the case law cited at note 154 to this chapter. See further the discussion of remedies in Chapter 6 of this volume.

[156] See, for example, K. Allred, "Peacekeepers and Prostitutes: How Deployed Forces Fuel the Demand for Trafficked Women and New Hope for Stopping It," in C. Friesendorf ed., *Strategies against Human Trafficking: The Role of the Security Sector* (2009), at 299–328; S.E. Mendelson, *Barracks and Brothels: Peacekeepers and Human Trafficking in the Balkans* (2005); and H.M. Smith and C. Smith, "Human Trafficking: The Unintended Effects of United Nations Intervention," paper prepared for the Annual Meeting of the Midwest Political Science Association, Chicago, Illinois, April 2010.

[157] For example, during the presence of the UN Transitional Authority in Cambodia from 1992 to 1993, some NGOs reported that the number of prostitutes in Cambodia increased from 6,000 to 25,000: S. Whitworth, *Men, Militarism and UN Peacekeeping* (2004), at 67. For a discussion of the role of "hypermilitarized masculinities," see V.K. Vojdik, "Sexual Abuse and Exploitation of Women and Girls by UN Peacekeeping Troops," (2007) 15 *Michigan State Journal of International Law* 157, esp. at 163–166. For a nuanced critique of "the conflation of military masculinities with exploitation" (at 99), see P. Higate, "Peacekeepers, Masculinities and Sexual Exploitation," (2007) 10 *Men and Masculinities* 99. For a detailed analysis of the nature and impact of the gendered economies created through peacekeeping operations in Bosnia-Herzegovina, Kosovo, Liberia, and Haiti, see K.M. Jennings and V. Nicolić-Ristanović, "UN Peacekeeping Economies and Local Sex Industries: Connections and Implications," MICROCON Research Working Paper 17 (2009) (Jennings and Nicolić-Ristanović, "UN Peacekeeping Economies and Local Sex Industries").

[158] A major UN report on peacekeeper sexual exploitation and abuse named as a primary cause "factors external to the Mission, such as the erosion of the social fabric because of the conflict, which results in a high number of children with little or no family support; a high level of extreme poverty; lack of income-generation possibilities; a high incidence of sexual violence against women and

between locals and international personnel[159] render the former, especially women and children, vulnerable to exploitation. Conflict-related demographic changes can mean that there are more civilian women than men. The absence of male family members, destruction of property or problems in accessing property, and emphasis on rehabilitation of former combatants can all contribute to increasing the vulnerability of women in conflict and postconflict situations. In addition, the legal framework governing engagement may be unclear and lines of responsibility and control blurred, not least by provisions guaranteeing many official personnel *prima facie* immunity from prosecution by the host State. The growing privatization of conflict, characterized by the increased involvement of private corporations as contractors and subcontractors, has exacerbated problems of responsibility and control. These various factors can combine to create a climate of impunity – a legal and procedural vacuum in which international personnel involved in criminal exploitation and trafficking are very rarely investigated, apprehended, or prosecuted.[160]

The question of responsibility and accountability for international personnel is problematic and yet to be resolved. It is nevertheless clear that both the deploying organization and the State of nationality of the alleged perpetrator are under legal and moral responsibility to exercise due diligence in preventing and responding to trafficking and related violations by international personnel.[161] Over the past decade, some limited steps have been taken to close this responsibility gap, to identify the obligations and responsibilities of States and intergovernmental organizations, and to ensure that international military, peacekeeping, and humanitarian operations do not become safe havens for traffickers and their accomplices. The following is a summary of the main points extracted from key policy documents as well as reports,

> children during civil conflict coupled with discrimination against women and girls, leading to a degree of local acceptance of violent and/or exploitative behaviour against them; and the lack of a well-functioning legal and judicial system, which creates an environment of de facto impunity": "A Comprehensive Strategy to Eliminate Future Sexual Exploitation and Abuse in United Nations Peacekeeping Operations," UN Doc. A/59/710, Mar. 24, 2005, at 10.

[159] For example, in postconflict Democratic Republic of Congo and Liberia, local poverty is exacerbated by the comparative wealth of UN peacekeepers, who receive 500 to 1,000 times the average income of the locals they protect: P. Higate and M. Henry, "Engendering (In)security in Peace Support Operations," (2004) 35 *Security Dialogue* 481, at 485. See also Jennings and Nicolić-Ristanović, "UN Peacekeeping Economies and Local Sex Industries."

[160] In its major study addressing peacekeeper sexual exploitation and abuse, the UN identified as a key problem "a widespread perception that peacekeeping personnel … who commit acts of sexual exploitation and abuse rarely if ever face disciplinary charges for such acts": "A Comprehensive Strategy to Eliminate Future Sexual Exploitation and Abuse in United Nations Peacekeeping Operations," UN Doc. A/59/710, Mar. 24, 2005, at 24. Trainers in UN gender training sessions have reported that peacekeepers "are acutely aware of their immunity which they understand as exempting them from being prosecuted for acts they commit while abroad": J. Murray, "Who Will Police the Peace-Builders? The Failure to Establish Accountability for the Participation of United Nations Civilian Police in the Trafficking of Women in Post-Conflict Bosnia and Herzegovina," (2003) 34 *Columbia Human Rights Law Review* 475, at 520.

[161] See F. Hampton and A. Kihara-Hunt, "Accountability of Personnel," in C. Aoi, C. de Coning and R. Thakur eds., *Unintended Consequences of Peacekeeping Operations* 196 (2007).

recommendations, commitments, and initiatives of the major intergovernmental organizations, including the UN General Assembly,[162] the UN Security Council,[163] and the North Atlantic Treaty Organization;[164] coalitions of UN and private agencies involved in humanitarian work;[165] and informed commentators.[166]

Training, personnel procedures and leadership are widely identified as essential aspects of an effective response to trafficking-related corruption involving international personnel. States and IGOs should ensure that predeployment and postdeployment training programs for international personnel adequately address the issue of trafficking and related exploitation and clearly set out the expected standard of behavior. All such training should be developed within a human rights framework and be conducted by experienced trainers. States and IGOs should also ensure that recruitment, placement, and transfer procedures (including those of private contractors and subcontractors) are rigorous and transparent.

The importance of clear rules reflecting international standards of human rights and procedures for responding to violations has also been highlighted. States and IGOs should develop regulations and codes of conduct setting out expected standards of behavior; they should also require all international personnel to report on any instances of trafficking or related exploitation that come to their attention.[167] At

---

[162] See, for example, the report to the UN General Assembly entitled "A Comprehensive Strategy to Eliminate Future Sexual Exploitation and Abuse in United Nations Peacekeeping Operations," UN Doc. A/59/710, Mar. 24, 2005. The UN General Assembly debate on this report, held in April 2005, led to the adoption of a two-year package of reforms for peacekeeping on sexual exploitation and abuse: UN General Assembly, "Comprehensive Review of a Strategy to Eliminate Future Sexual Exploitation and Abuse in United Nations Peacekeeping Operations," UN Doc. A/RES/59/300, June 22, 2005, adopting the recommendations of the "Report of the Special Committee on Peacekeeping Operations and its Working Group," UN Doc. A/59/19/Rev.1 (2005). In December 2007, the UN General Assembly adopted the "Comprehensive Strategy on Assistance and Support to Victims of Sexual Exploitation and Abuse by United Nations Staff and Related Personnel," UN Doc. A/RES/62/214, Dec. 21, 2007.

[163] For example, UN Security Council, "Women and Peace and Security," UN Doc. S/RES/1820, June 19, 2008.

[164] North Atlantic Treaty Organization, "NATO Policy on Combating Trafficking in Human Beings," NATO Policy Document adopted 29 June 2004. See also K.J. Allred, "Combating Human Trafficking," (2006, Summer Issue) *NATO Review* (Allred, "Combating Human Trafficking"), available at http://www.nato.int/docu/review/2006/issue2/english/Analysis.html (accessed Feb. 2, 2010).

[165] "Statement of Commitment on Eliminating Sexual Exploitation and Abuse by UN and Non-UN Personnel," adopted in December 2006 by 22 UN agencies and 24 non-UN entities, available at http://www.un.org/en/pseataskforce/docs/statement_of_commitment_on_eliminating_sexual%20_exploitation.doc (accessed Feb. 2, 2010). For a discussion of recent steps taken by the UN Department of Peacekeeping Operations and its Conduct and Discipline Unit, as well as case studies of sexual exploitation and abuse in Haiti, Lebanon, and Kosovo, see C. Lutz, M. Gutmann and K. Brown, "Conduct and Discipline in UN Peacekeeping Operations: Culture, Political Economy and Gender," Report submitted to the Conduct and Discipline Unit, Department of Peacekeeping Operations, United Nations (Oct. 19, 2009).

[166] In particular, Allred, "Combating Human Trafficking."

[167] All UN peacekeeping personnel – whether civilian or uniformed – are bound to report concerns or suspicions of sexual exploitation or sexual abuse by a fellow worker, as outlined in

a minimum, international personnel should be prohibited from engaging in sexual exploitation and trafficking and using the services of individuals in relation to which there are reasonable grounds to suspect they may be in a situation of exploitation.[168] The relevant organizations should take responsibility for ensuring compliance with rules and regulations, as should managers and commanders.[169] Strong leadership in this area may include declaring "off-limits" any establishment suspected of being involved in trafficking or related exploitation. Mechanisms should be established for the systematic investigation of trafficking and related exploitation by international personnel. States and IGOs should consistently apply appropriate criminal, civil, and administrative penalties to those shown to have engaged or been complicit in trafficking and related exploitation. Importantly, privileges and immunities attached to the status of an employee (such as an employee of a diplomatic mission or of an IGO) should not be invoked in order to shield that person from sanctions for trafficking and related offenses. If waiver of immunity is not possible or desirable (for example, because the host country is not able to guarantee a fair trial), then steps should be taken to ensure that offenders are otherwise prosecuted; to this end, mechanisms should be put in place to ensure that the rules of evidence of the prosecuting State (such as the State of nationality) can be observed. Finally, States and deploying organizations should accept and respond to their legal obligation to provide remedies, including compensation to victims of trafficking and related exploitation implicating international personnel.

Significant progress has recently been made, particularly by intergovernmental organizations and agencies, in identifying and responding to trafficking and related abuses by their international personnel. The willingness of contributing Member States to support effective implementation will be a key measure of success. It is also important to acknowledge that not all international operations are undertaken under the umbrella of an IGO. In such cases, personnel in the field will be beyond the reach of these newly developed standards and procedures. Accordingly, it will be up to the controlling State to ensure that measures are in place to prevent the

"Secretary-General's Bulletin: Special Measures for Protection from Sexual Exploitation and Sexual Abuse," UN Doc. ST/SGB/2003/13, Oct. 9, 2003.

[168] Note that all UN peacekeeping personnel – whether civilian or uniformed – are prohibited from committing acts of sexual exploitation and abuse, including exchange of money, employment, goods, or services for sex: ibid. On the implications of this policy, see D. Otto, "Making Sense of Zero Tolerance Policies in Peacekeeping Sexual Economies," in V. Munro and C.F. Stychin eds., *Sexuality and the Law: Feminist Engagements* 259 (2007) and Jennings and Nicolić-Ristanović, "UN Peacekeeping Economies and Local Sex Industries." On complications and contradictions in identifying what constitutes "sexual exploitation," see O. Simic, "Rethinking 'Sexual Exploitation' in UN Peacekeeping Operations," (2009) 32 *Women's Studies International Forum* 288 and N. Quénivet, "The Dissonance between the United Nations Zero-Tolerance Policy and Criminalisation of Sexual Offences on the International Level," (2007) 7(4) *International Criminal Law Review* 657.

[169] This important point on organizational, managerial, and command responsibility is explicitly included in the UN's "A Comprehensive Strategy to Eliminate Future Sexual Exploitation and Abuse in United Nations Peacekeeping Operations," UN Doc. A/59/710, Mar. 24, 2005.

involvement of their personnel in trafficking and other forms of exploitation, and to identify and deal with any such involvement.

8.4. OBLIGATION TO RESPOND LAWFULLY

Measures taken in the name of preventing or otherwise addressing trafficking and related exploitation often have a highly adverse impact on individual rights and freedoms that are protected under international law. Evidence-based examples of such "negative human rights externalities" include many of the practices identified in this book such as: detention of trafficked persons in immigration or shelter facilities; prosecution of trafficked persons for status-related offenses including illegal entry, illegal stay, and illegal work; denial of exit or entry visas or permits; entry bans; compulsory medical examinations; raids, rescues, and "crackdowns" that do not include full consideration of and protection for the rights of individuals involved; forced repatriation of victims in danger of reprisals or retrafficking; conditional provision of support and assistance; denial of a right to a remedy; and violations of the rights of persons suspected or convicted of involvement in trafficking and related offenses, including unfair trials and inappropriate sentencing. These practices, still commonplace in many countries, underscore the strong relationship between trafficking and human rights, as well as the fundamental importance of the international guardians of the relevant instruments, including the human rights treaty bodies, using the full range of tools at their disposal to hold States accountable for their actions and omissions.

This section considers the question of whether States are under a general obligation to ensure that their responses to trafficking do not violate established rights. It then examines, in detail, the prohibition of nondiscrimination – one area in relation to which response-based violations are particularly problematic. Further consideration is not given here to response-based violations that have been discussed in previous chapters, for example: Chapter 3 (response-based denial of rights of noncitizens including migrant workers); Chapter 5 (prosecution and detention of victims of trafficking); Chapter 6 (violations related to victim repatriation and victim remedies); and Chapter 7 (violation of rights of victims, witnesses, and suspects in criminal justice responses).

8.4.1. *Obligation to Avoid Violations of Established Rights when Responding to Trafficking*

The Vienna Convention on the Law of Treaties states that "[w]hen a treaty specifies that it is subject to, or that it is not to be considered as incompatible with, an earlier or later treaty, the provisions of that other treaty prevail."[170] While not

---

[170] Vienna Convention on the Law of Treaties, 1155 UNTS 331, done May 23, 1969, entered into force Jan. 27, 1980, at Art. 30(2). For a detailed consideration of this provision, see M.E. Villiger,

specifically addressing the risks and implications of violation of established rights, the Trafficking Protocol affirms the principle that States cannot breach established rights while seeking to fulfill another obligation, holding that:

> nothing in this Protocol shall affect the rights, obligations and responsibilities of States and individuals under international law, including international humanitarian law and international human rights law and, in particular, where applicable, the 1951 Convention and the 1967 Protocol relating to the Status of Refugees and the principle of non-refoulement as contained therein.[171]

An additional savings clause, referring specifically to obligations of nondiscrimination, is explored further in this chapter.

The general savings clause of the Protocol is the subject of an Interpretative Note, which makes clear the intention of the drafters to not legislate beyond the Protocol. The Note affirms that in addition to not covering the status of refugees, the Protocol:

> is without prejudice to the existing rights, obligations or responsibilities of States Parties under other international instruments, such as those referred to in this paragraph. Rights, obligations and responsibilities under another instrument are determined by the terms of that instrument and whether the State concerned is a party to it, not by this protocol. Therefore, any State that becomes a party to this protocol but is not a party to another international instrument referred to in the protocol would not become subject to any right, obligation or responsibility under that instrument.[172]

The European Trafficking Convention contains a similar savings clause.[173] The Explanatory Report to that instrument confirms that, as with the Protocol's savings clause, the purpose of this provision is not to confer additional rights but rather

---

Commentary on the 1969 Vienna Convention on the Law of Treaties (2009) at 395–412 (chapter entitled "Application of Successive Treaties Relating to the Same Subject-Matter").

[171] Trafficking Protocol, at Art. 14(1).

[172] *Travaux Préparatoires for the Organized Crime Convention and Protocols*, at 421. The *travaux préparatoires* reveal that a similar confirmation was required with respect to the equivalent Article of the Protocol against the Smuggling of Migrants by Land, Sea and Air, supplementing the United Nations Convention against Transnational Organized Crime, done Nov. 15, 2000, GA Res. 55/25, Annex III, UN GAOR, 55th Sess., Supp. No. 49, at 62, UN Doc. A/45/49 (Vol. I) (2001), entered into force Jan. 28, 2004 (Migrant Smuggling Protocol): "[a]t the eighth session of the Ad Hoc Committee, some delegations expressed concerns about the implications of this provision for States that were not parties to the instruments referred to. In particular, Saudi Arabia and the United Arab Emirates were concerned that, as a result of this wording, their Governments might be subject to obligations under those instruments, to which they were not parties, should they become parties to the convention and the protocol. It was pointed out that the opening words protected the integrity of existing obligations, but could not be interpreted as creating new ones. Thus, a State that was not already subject to such an obligation would not become subject to it simply by becoming a party to the protocol. Saudi Arabia and the United Arab Emirates asked for this fact to be noted in the *travaux préparatoires*." *Travaux Préparatoires for the Organized Crime Convention and Protocols*, at 554.

[173] European Trafficking Convention, at Art. 40(3).

to ensure that the exercise of fundamental rights is not prevented on the pretext of taking action against trafficking in human beings.[174] However, the European Trafficking Convention goes one important step further by specifying that the Convention is intended to develop the standards contained in, and enhance the protections afforded by, the Trafficking Protocol, and that nothing in the Convention is to affect rights and obligations derived from that instrument.[175] The same rule is to apply to any other instrument "to which Parties to the present Convention are parties or shall become Parties and which contain provisions on matters governed by this Convention and which ensure greater protection and assistance for victims of trafficking."[176] The Explanatory Report to the European Trafficking Convention links these provisions to the overall aim of the Convention: "to protect and promote the Human Rights of victims of trafficking and to ensure the highest level of protection to them."[177]

The problem of response-based violations to trafficking has been widely recognized. An obligation on State to ensure that measures taken to address trafficking do not deliberately or inadvertently violate established rights is affirmed by international and regional policy instruments,[178] as well as through recommendations

---

[174] European Trafficking Convention Explanatory Report, at para. 377.

[175] European Trafficking Convention, at Art. 39.

[176] Ibid. at Art. 40.

[177] European Trafficking Convention Explanatory Report, at para. 373. A situation envisaged under this provision could well arise in the event that an EU Framework Decision or similar instrument along the lines of that proposed in 2009 (see further, Chapter 2.3 in this volume) is adopted. States Parties to the European Trafficking Convention who are bound by the EU instrument would also be bound to any higher victim protection standards contained in the latter instrument.

[178] See, for example, UN Trafficking Principles and Guidelines, at Principle 3 ("[a]nti-trafficking measures should not adversely affect the human rights and dignity of persons, in particular the rights of those who have been trafficked, and of migrants, internally displaced persons, refugees and asylum seekers"); Guideline 1.9 (States and others to "ensure that bilateral, regional and international cooperation agreements and other laws and policies concerning trafficking in persons do not affect the rights, obligations or responsibilities of States under international law, including human rights law, humanitarian law and refugee law"). The Principles and Guidelines also direct States to: protect the right of freedom of movement and ensure that antitrafficking measures do not infringe on this right (at Guideline 1.5); establish mechanisms and procedures to monitor and evaluate the impact of antitrafficking laws, policies, and programs (at Guideline 1.7); ensure legal proceedings involving trafficked persons are not prejudicial to their rights or well-being (at Guideline 6.4); ensure that trafficked persons are not required to accept medical treatment or counseling and are not subject to mandatory testing including for HIV/AIDS (at Guideline 6.2); and ensure that privacy considerations are not prejudicial to the rights of an accused person to a fair trial (at Guideline 6.6). See also, Brussels Declaration, at 9 (provision of support measures by "on a consensual and fully informed basis," no imposition of mandatory sexual health testing), 10 (trafficking victims not to be revictimized or further stigmatized or criminalized, etc.), and 11–12 (provisions for victim-witnesses); OSCE Action Plan, at III(4) (provisions for victim-witnesses), and V(7.4) (right to privacy); Ouagadougou Action Plan, at 2 (general principle that measures to prevent and combat trafficking should not adversely affect the rights of victims), 5 (safety and security of victim-witnesses); OAS Recommendations on Trafficking in Persons, at 5 (provision of assistance to victims "bearing in mind the age and gender to avoid further exploitation and damage"); and COMMIT MOU, at

and pronouncements of human rights treaty bodies[179] and other human rights mechanisms.[180]

8.4.2. Obligation to Ensure Antitrafficking Measures Do Not Violate the Prohibition on Discrimination

As noted at several points throughout this book, all major human rights instruments, both international and regional, prohibit discrimination on a number of grounds including race, sex, language, religion, property, birth, or other status.[181] Discrimination can be linked to trafficking in a number of ways. It is no coincidence that those most likely to be trafficked, including irregular migrants, stateless persons, noncitizens, asylum seekers, and members of minority groups, are especially susceptible to discrimination and intolerance based on their race, ethnicity,

---

Art. 16 ("[e]nsuring that persons identified as victims of trafficking are not held in detention by law enforcement authorities").

[179] See, for example, UN Committee on the Elimination of All Forms of Discrimination against Women, "Concluding Observations: Iceland," UN Doc. CEDAW/C/ICE/CO/6, July 18, 2008, at para. 23 (lack of witness protection measures); "Concluding Observations: China," UN Doc. CEDAW/C/CHN/CO/6, Aug. 25, 2006, at para. 20 (preventing detention without due process); UN Committee on Economic, Social and Cultural Rights, "Concluding Observations: Ukraine," UN Doc. E/C.12/UKR/CO/5, Jan. 4, 2008, at para. 20 (access to witness protection programs); UN Committee on the Rights of the Child, "Concluding Observations: Lebanon," UN Doc. CRC/C/LBN/CO/3, June 8, 2006, at para. 81 (victims criminalized and sentenced to detention); "Concluding Observations: Qatar," UN Doc. CRC/C/OPSC/QAT/CO/1, June 2, 2006, at para. 27 (protection of child victims during criminal investigation and justice processes, especially when acting as plaintiffs or called to testify).

[180] See, for example, "Promotion and Protection of All Human Rights, Civil, Political, Economic, Social and Cultural Rights, Including the Right to Development: Report submitted by the Special Rapporteur on trafficking in persons, especially women and children, Joy Ngozi Ezeilo," UN Doc. A/HRC/10/16, Feb. 20, 2009, at paras. 32, 39 (need to ensure antitrafficking legislation complies with international human rights law; concern over deportation before identification as victims); "Report of the Special Rapporteur on trafficking in persons, especially women and children, Sigma Huda, Addendum: Mission to Bahrain, Oman and Qatar," UN Doc. A/HRC/4/23/Add.2, Apr. 25, 2007, at paras. 95(m)-95(p) (recommending alternative measures other than deportation or detention centers to house victims; calling for a guarantee to an accessible and fair system of justice with reasonable if any court fees, expeditious proceedings, available interpretation services, and legal aid, with special attention to the needs of women and children; protection of victims, including confidentiality; no mandatory HIV/AIDS testing); "Integration of the Human Rights of Women and a Gender Perspective: Report of the Special Rapporteur on the Human Rights Aspects of the Victims of Trafficking in Persons, Especially Women and Children, Sigma Huda, Addendum: Summary of cases transmitted to Governments and replies received," UN Doc. E/CN.4/2006/62/Add.1, Mar. 27, 2006, at paras. 63, 68, 70, 94, 158 (citing examples of conditional support, detention, forced repatriation, prosecution, denial of a remedy); "Report of the Special Rapporteur on Violence against Women, Ms. Radhika Coomaraswamy, on Trafficking in Women, Women's Migration and Violence against Women," UN Doc. E/CN.4/2000/68, Feb. 29, 2000, at paras. 42–48 (restrictions on mobility, nationality laws, equal protection, labor rights).

[181] See further the discussion of discrimination in Chapter 3 of this volume.

religion, and other distinguishing factors. Some groups, such as migrant women and girls, are vulnerable to intersectional and multiple discriminations.[182] In addition to increasing the risk of trafficking, discriminatory attitudes, perceptions, and practices contribute to shaping and fueling the demand for trafficking.[183]

Discrimination is not just implicated in the causes of trafficking or in the factors that increase vulnerability. Measures taken by States and others to prevent or respond to trafficking can perpetuate discrimination and even violate the legal prohibition against discrimination. This danger, already raised at various points in the previous chapters, is explicitly recognized in the savings clause of the Trafficking Protocol, which states that:

> the measures set forth in this Protocol shall be interpreted and applied in a way that is not discriminatory to persons on the grounds that they are victims of trafficking in persons. The interpretation and application of those measures shall be consistent with internationally recognized principles of non-discrimination.[184]

The Protocol's nondiscrimination provision was hard-won. Despite intense lobbying by observers including United Nations agencies,[185] it was only very late in the negotiations that a draft provision was introduced, discussed, and incorporated into the rolling text of both this instrument and the Migrant Smuggling Protocol.[186]

---

[182] UN Committee on the Elimination of All Forms of Discrimination against Women, "General Recommendation No. 25: Temporary Special Measures," UN Doc. CEDAW/C/2004/I/WP.1/Rev.1, Jan. 30, 2004; C. Chinkin and F. Banda, *Gender, Minorities, Indigenous People and Human Rights* (2004). The Human Rights Committee has noted that "racism, racial discrimination, and xenophobia contribute to discrimination against women and other violations of their rights, including cross-border trafficking of women and children, and enforced trafficking and other forms of forced labour disguised *inter alia* as domestic or other kinds of personal services": UN Human Rights Committee, "Contributions to the World Conference against Racism, Racial Discrimination, Xenophobia and Related Intolerance," UN Doc. A/CONF.189/PC.2/14, Mar. 13, 2001, at para. 18. The UN General Assembly and Human Rights Council have both recently recognized that "victims of trafficking are particularly exposed to racism, racial discrimination, xenophobia and related intolerance and that women and girl victims are often subject to multiple forms of discrimination and violence, including on the grounds of their gender, age, ethnicity, culture and religion, as well as their origins, and that these forms of discrimination themselves may fuel trafficking in persons": "Trafficking in Women and Girls," UN Doc. A/RES/63/156, Jan. 30, 2009, at Preamble; "Trafficking in Persons, Especially Women and Children," UN Doc. A/HRC/RES/11/3, June 17, 2009, at Preamble.

[183] See further, Chapter 8.3.

[184] Trafficking Protocol, at Art. 14(1).

[185] See, for example, UN General Assembly, Ad Hoc Committee on the Elaboration of a Convention against Transnational Organized Crime, "Informal Note by the United Nations High Commissioner for Human Rights," UN Doc. A/AC.254/16, June 1, 1999; UN General Assembly, Ad Hoc Comm. on the Elaboration of a Convention against Transnational Organized Crime, "Note by the Office of the United Nations High Commissioner for Human Rights, the Office of the United Nations High Commissioner for Refugees, the United Nations Children's Fund and the International Organization for Migration on the draft protocols concerning migrant smuggling and trafficking in persons," UN Doc. A/AC.254/27, Feb. 8, 2000 and UN Doc. A/AC.254/27/Corr.1, Feb. 22, 2000.

[186] Travaux Préparatoires *for the Organized Crime Convention and Protocols*, at 354, 420. See also Migrant Smuggling Protocol, at Art. 19(2).

While the second part of the clause amounts to a generalized prohibition on discrimination, there is less clarity around the implications of prohibiting discrimination on the basis of a person's status as a victim of trafficking. The Legislative Guide to the Protocol notes, somewhat obscurely, that:

> This focuses on the interpretation of the Protocol and not the national law that implements it; however, drafters may wish to consider the principle of non-discrimination in drafting specific provisions, particularly where they deal with victims.[187]

It can be presumed that the provision would prevent States from negatively altering or withdrawing entitlements on the basis of an individual's status as a trafficked person. The right to asylum provides a useful example. The nondiscrimination provision would prevent States from applying different rules to trafficked persons that are intended or otherwise operate to negatively affect their right to seek and receive asylum from persecution. The practice of imposing reentry bans on trafficked persons would be similarly circumscribed.[188]

The nondiscrimination provision of the European Trafficking Convention is stronger and more detailed than its international equivalent, providing some additional clarity on the substantive content of the obligation to ensure antitrafficking measures do not unlawfully discriminate. Article 3 of that instrument states that:

> implementation of the provisions of this Convention by parties, in particular the enjoyment of measures to protect and promote the rights of victims, shall be secured without discrimination on any ground such as sex, race, colour, language, religion, political or other opinion, national or social origin, association with a national minority, property, birth or other status.[189]

---

[187] *Legislative Guide*, at Part 2, 256.

[188] Many countries impose reentry bans on individuals who have breached immigration laws. Some major States of destination, such as Australia and the UK, have recently clarified that such bans would not apply to individuals who were trafficked into the country. Article 11(3) of the European Parliament legislative resolution of 18 June 2008 on the proposal for a directive of the European Parliament and of the Council on common standards and procedures in Member States for returning illegally staying third-country nationals (COM(2005)0391 – C6–0266/2005 – 2005/0167(COD)), OJ C 286 E/104, Nov. 27, 2009, states that "[v]ictims of trafficking in human beings who have been granted a residence permit pursuant to Council Directive 2004/81/EC of 29 April 2004 on the residence permit issued to third-country nationals who are victims of trafficking in human beings or who have been the subject of an action to facilitate illegal immigration, who cooperate with the competent authorities shall not be subject of an entry ban without prejudice to [an obligation on Member States to ensure that return decisions are accompanied by a reentry ban if the obligation to return has not been complied with] and provided that the third-country national concerned does not represent a threat to public policy, public security or national security."

[189] European Trafficking Convention, at Art. 3. The Explanatory Report notes that the list of prohibited grounds is identical to that contained in the European Convention of Human Rights and Protocol No. 12 to that instrument. It points out that the list is not exhaustive and that failure to include other grounds that could possibly be relevant to trafficking, such as disability and sexual orientation, may well be relevant and have indeed been recognized in European case law as included within the general prohibition on discrimination. European Trafficking Convention Explanatory Report, at paras. 63, 66.

The Explanatory Report to the Convention refers to the (identical) definition of discrimination in the European Convention on Human Rights and notes that European case law is clear that not every difference or distinction amounts to discrimination. Concepts such as "legitimate aim" and "reasonable relationship of proportionality between the means employed and the aims sought to be realized" are cited to illustrate this point.[190] The specific reference to discrimination in the enjoyment of measures for the protection and promotion of the rights of victims is highlighted. Under Article 3, States Parties are required to apply such measures without discrimination. Different application of the relevant provisions of the Convention in respect of particular categories of persons (for example, depending on their age, sex, or nationality) would violate the nondiscrimination principle if such difference in treatment could not be reasonably justified.[191]

Significantly, the Explanatory Report to the European Trafficking Convention raises the issue of discrimination between nationals and non-nationals, noting that domestic laws generally permit certain distinctions based on nationality with respect to particular rights or entitlement to benefits.[192] Provided there is objective and reasonable justification, such distinctions will not be held to be unlawful, and States are generally provided a measure of discretion "in assessing whether and to what extent differences in otherwise similar situations justify different treatment in law."[193] The extended discussion of trafficked persons as non-nationals in Chapter 3 should be referred to in this context.

In practice, discriminatory responses to trafficking often extend beyond differences in support and assistance to include specific actions that impact, negatively and disproportionately, on particular groups such as women and children. As noted in the discussion on victim detention in Chapter 5 and on investigation, prosecution, and adjudication of trafficking cases in Chapter 7, the problem of gender-based discrimination is particularly acute in respect of antitrafficking measures. This is recognized in the UN Trafficking Principles and Guidelines, which enjoin States and others to "[t]ak[e] particular care to ensure that the issue of gender-based discrimination is addressed systematically when anti-trafficking measures are proposed with a view to ensuring that such measures are not applied in a discriminatory manner."[194]

Certain rights are especially vulnerable to discriminatory application in relation to antitrafficking measures. As recognized in major policy instruments, the right to freedom of movement is notable in this respect.[195] For example, as noted in

---

[190] Ibid. at para. 64.

[191] Ibid. at paras. 67–69.

[192] Ibid. at para. 65.

[193] Ibid.

[194] UN Trafficking Principles and Guidelines, at Guideline 1.4.

[195] See, for example, UN Trafficking Principles and Guidelines, at Guideline 1.6: "States should consider protecting the rights of all persons to freedom of movement and ensuring that anti-trafficking measures do not infringe on this right."

Chapter 3, many States have taken legislative, administrative, or other measures to prevent individuals from emigrating in search of work. Invariably, such emigration restrictions are discriminatory in both intent and impact, being limited to a group defined by its sex (always female) and often also age.[196] The detention of victims of trafficking in shelters and welfare facilities is invariably directed against women and girls, compromising not just the right to freedom of movement but also the prohibition on discrimination.[197] The analysis undertaken in Chapter 5 with respect to victim detention confirmed that in deciding whether a restriction on freedom of movement is lawful, it is necessary to consider whether the relevant restriction is: (1) provided for by law; (2) consistent with other rights (such as the prohibition on sex-based discrimination); and (3) necessary to protect the individual concerned. These requirements must all be fulfilled. For example, even if a State is able to argue that its emigration restrictions are based on a need to preserve public order or public morals through preventing trafficking and that the measures taken are both necessary and in proportion to their stated aim, that same State must also be able to show that its restriction is nondiscriminatory. There appears to be little evidence to suggest that emigration restrictions protect potential migrants from traffickers. Indeed it has been argued that the opposite is true and that such restrictions force migrants into more dangerous migration arrangements.[198] Since almost all emigration restrictions related to trafficking are limited to women and girls, it would be difficult for any State to convincingly argue for their lawfulness under current international legal standards.

---

[196] See generally, N. Oishi, *Women in Motion: Globalization, State Policies and Labour Migration in Asia* (2005) (Oishi, *Women in Motion*), especially at chapter 3, including the table "Emigration restrictions on female migration in Asia, Circa 2000" at 60. On the particular issue of trafficking-related emigration restrictions affecting women, see "Report of the Special Rapporteur on Violence against Women, Ms. Radhika Coomaraswamy, on Trafficking in Women, Women's Migration and Violence against Women," UN Doc. E/CN.4/2000/68, Feb. 29, 2000, at paras. 47–48. See further, the discussion on the right to leave at Chapter 3.2.1 in this volume.

[197] See further, the extended discussion of detention of victims of trafficking in Chapter 5 of this book.

[198] See generally, Oishi, *Women in Motion*; and International Labour Office, *ILO Action against Trafficking in Human Beings* (2008), at 17.

9

Issues of Compliance, Implementation, and Effectiveness

The international legal framework around trafficking includes a range of institutions and processes established for the specific purpose of overseeing and thereby promoting national implementation of the applicable international legal rules. The web of formal compliance mechanisms is dense and expanding – a reflection of the complexity of the trafficking phenomenon, its cross-cutting nature, and the increasing commitment of States and others to be doing (or to be seen to be doing) something about trafficking. It includes institutions and mechanisms set up under the specialist trafficking treaties, as well as the human rights bodies that exercise monitoring authority over certain aspects of the legal framework. Supplementing (and sometimes supplanting) these mechanisms are less traditional structures and processes. This category extends to encompass the controversial but highly influential unilateral reporting and sanctions system established by the U.S. government, as well as transnational networks operating within and between national government agencies, IGOs, and NGOs.

The present chapter commences with a brief consideration of compliance theory and of some of the factors or variables that may help explain and even predict the impact of international legal rules relating to trafficking on the behavior of States. The chapter then examines the structure, functioning, and potential of the major compliance mechanisms identified above: international bodies established under specialist treaties; international human rights mechanisms; the U.S. reporting and sanctions system; and transnational networks.

9.1. COMPLIANCE THEORIES AND VARIABLES

Compliance, in the present context, is generally understood to refer to "a state of conformity or identity between an actor's behavior and a specified rule."[1] In relation

---

[1] K. Raustiala and A.-M. Slaughter, "International Law, International Relations and Compliance," in W. Carlnaes, T. Risse and B.A. Simmons eds., *The Handbook of International Relations* 538 (2002) (Raustiala and Slaughter, "International Law, International Relations and Compliance"), at 539.

to international law, the "actor" is almost always the State and the rule is a legal one. While the concepts are different and not necessarily codependent, there is usually a high level of correlation between compliance with international legal rules and *implementation*, understood as the process of putting legal commitments into effect. Compliance is also related to effectiveness – the extent to which the rule induces change with respect to or otherwise addresses the underlying problem.[2] The present chapter assumes that improving compliance with the international legal framework around trafficking requires implementation of obligations, *and* that such compliance will contribute to the broader goals of that legal framework.[3]

Compliance theory seeks to explain when and why States obey international law; the field is a complex and contested one.[4] For example, many theorists emphasize compliance as the product of a rational cost-benefit calculation of national interests. In short, States obey international rules if and when it is perceived to be in their immediate or longer-term interest. Perceptions of national self-interest may be influenced by considerations of reputation as well as the consequences for noncompliance. Other theorists see compliance as linked to the legitimacy of a rule and the process by which it was generated: Rules that are perceived as clear and fair and emanating from accepted processes will be obeyed more readily than those that fail to meet these standards. A "managerial" approach to compliance takes this one step further by assuming certain norms of behavior, specifically that States will generally comply with rules they have bothered to make the effort of articulating, out of a sense of obligation and also because this is a rational (and usually cost-effective) way to behave. Some have argued that such considerations do not hold up for all rules – that a genuine enforcement capacity is essential to deterring noncompliance and securing cooperation in those difficult and critical areas where compliance matters the most. Many international relations theorists and international lawyers link compliance with domestic politics and domestic enforcement: Compliance is secured through a process of socialization, whereby an international norm is internalized (transformed into a domestic one). More recent research has refined and extended earlier theories, identifying acculturation ("the general process by which actors adopt the beliefs and behavioral patterns of the surrounding culture") as a key force for compliance,[5] or examining more

---

2 Ibid.
3 Of course, this will not always be the case. Compliance with international rules can be accidental. Also, as explored in the epilogue to this book, there may be a discord between the rule and what is required to secure the stated goal of that rule.
4 For a comprehensive overview of compliance theories and the relevant literature see W.C. Bradford, "International Legal Compliance: Surveying the Field," (2005) 36 *Georgetown Journal of International Law* 495; and M. Burgstaller, *Theories of Compliance with International Law* (2005). See also Raustiala and Slaughter, "International Law, International Relations and Compliance."
5 R. Goodman and D. Jinks, "Incomplete Internationalization and Compliance with Human Rights Law," (2008) 19 *European Journal of International Law* 725 (Goodman and Jinks, "Incomplete Internationalization and Compliance with Human Rights Law"), at 726.

specifically the impact of cultural diversity[6] and domestic political coalitions[7] on State behavior with respect to international legal obligations. It is evident, even from this cursory summary, that the lack of an agreed or unified theory as to why States obey international rules reflects broader philosophical divisions regarding the very nature and function of international law and the international legal process.

While a compliance-based analysis of the international law of human trafficking is unnecessary to secure the objectives of this study, several preliminary and informal observations are offered that may help explain and critically appraise the developments outlined below. These observations are not derived from a single or even an integrated theory of compliance. Rather, they are based more modestly on an acceptance of the general proposition that the extent to which – and the way in which – States meet their international commitments is always subject to a range of factors or variables. These include the characteristics of the problem itself, the structure of the legal "solution," and the way in which that solution is developed, as well as broader international factors and factors specific to an individual State.[8] The following section will examine a number of factors particularly relevant to compliance among States with their trafficking obligations.

The Nature of the Problem. Taking the first element, the problem structure, it can be expected that securing compliance in the area of trafficking is likely to be relatively difficult in comparison with other problems that are more easily identified, isolated, and dealt with, and where the behavior to be changed is solely that of States and their agents. In other words, the complexity of the trafficking phenomenon and its essential origins in the actions of non-State parties complicate the task of both securing and measuring compliance. An added difficulty is presented by the complexity of the "solution". The issue of stratospheric ozone depletion provides a

---

[6] A. Alkoby, "Theories of Compliance with International Law and the Challenge of Cultural Difference," (2008) 4 *Journal of International Law and International Relations* 151 (Alkoby, "Theories of Compliance with International Law and the Challenge of Cultural Difference").

[7] J.P. Trachtman, "International Law and Domestic Political Coalitions: The Causes of Compliance with International Law," July 9, 2009, available at SSRN: http://ssrn.com/abstract=1431956 (accessed Feb. 2, 2010).

[8] This list of variables generally follows the "components of compliance" identified in Raustiala and Slaughter, "International Law, International Relations and Compliance," at 545–548. Brown Weiss and Jacobsen propose a similar analytical model: "[f]our broad categories of interrelated factors ... affect the extent to which, and the way in which, countries meet their commitments; the characteristics of the activity involved; the characteristics of the accord; the international environment; and factors involving the country." E. Brown Weiss and H.K. Jacobsen, "Getting Countries to Comply with International Agreements," (1999) 41 *Environment* 16, at 18, cited in G. Auth, "Understanding Compliance with International Law" (a book review of M. Zürn and C. Joerges eds., *Law and Governance in Postnational Europe: Compliance Beyond the Nation State* (2005)), at note 18, available at http://www.europeanlawbooks.org/reviews/getFile.asp?id=231 (accessed Feb. 2, 2010).

useful contrast. In that case, the solution was relatively straightforward: All States were required to phase out certain chemicals that were identified as directly contributing to the problem and to replace these with inexpensive and readily available alternatives. Compliance with the agreed international legal regime has proved to be relatively easy to secure. In the case of trafficking, it has become evident that the "problem" is not amenable to quick, one-off, standardized, or low-cost solutions, but rather requires extensive and ongoing cooperation and active intervention on a wide range of fronts and on the part of many States.

Not all aspects of trafficking militate against compliance. The extent to which States meet their international commitments in this area may be positively influenced by the fact that initial identification of the problem largely took place at the international level: The international legal and policy framework around trafficking has driven and shaped domestic responses, rather than the other way around. As a result, there appears to be relatively little underlying conflict between the two spheres (as evidenced by widespread acceptance of the international legal definition and high use of international agreements as a template for domestic legislation), a situation that should contribute to greater and more uniform internalization of international norms.

Clarity and Legitimacy of Rules. To what extent do the rules themselves operate to contribute to or otherwise influence compliance? The present study is predicated on an assumption that clarity and specificity of obligations is crucial: States will be more motivated and better equipped to conform to international legal rules that are clear and unambiguous and that specify with sufficient detail the actions required to meet an identified obligation. These features also contribute to compliance by making monitoring easier and more transparent. It follows that compliance with an obligation to criminalize trafficking, for example, will be both higher and more easily ascertainable than compliance with a more generalized obligation to protect and support victims, the parameters of which remain to be firmly established. The manner in which the "solution" is constructed is also important. As Raustiala and Slaughter observe, "[t]he inclusiveness, fairness and perceived legitimacy of the process of creating collective rules may influence the degree that states or other actors accept and internalize those rules."[9] Broad acceptance of the legitimacy of the rules contained in the Trafficking Protocol[10] is undoubtedly linked to a widespread appreciation of the negotiation process as fair and inclusive. By contrast, the general view of the U.S. reporting and sanctioning system as intrusive, unfair, and even

---

[9] Raustiala and Slaughter, "International Law, International Relations and Compliance," at 546.

[10] Protocol to Prevent, Suppress and Punish Trafficking in Persons, Especially Women and Children, supplementing the United Nations Convention against Transnational Organized Crime, done Nov. 15, 2000, GA Res. 55/25, Annex II, UN GAOR, 55th Sess., Supp. No. 49, at 53, UN Doc. A/45/49 (Vol. I) (2001), entered into force Dec. 25, 2003 (Trafficking Protocol).

illegitimate[11] can be expected to influence the nature and extent of compliance with that mechanism and the standards which it seeks to uphold. However, that assumption may need to be balanced by other considerations. For example, a real threat of sanctions can operate as a powerful force for compliance. Even absent such a threat, it is apparent that on this particular issue, States appear to care deeply about their own reputations and about what other States think of them. Few governments are indifferent to being identified as "non-compliers," and those who care may thereby be spurred into action, even if that offending label is affixed by another State rather than by an internationally sanctioned mechanism.

Other Factors of Norm Socialization: Normative Convergence and Compliance and Monitoring Machinery. Other forces are also at work when it comes to compliance with the international norms around trafficking. The convergence of legal norms around trafficking, made possible by a broad, if not universal, consensus on the nature of the problem, has been rapid and substantial. In theory, this convergence should operate to both promote and support the internalization of norms – a process that leads States to accept certain responses, attitudes, and behaviors as correct or preferable. Norm socialization/internalization in the present case is aided by the perception of legitimacy referred to previously in this chapter. It may also be facilitated by the peculiar and multilayered nature of relevant compliance machinery, which, particularly in its unilateral form,[12] compels at least some level of engagement from every State and permits no State to forge its own, separate path. On a more practical level, compliance will likely be influenced by the frequency and extent to which State performance is monitored – as well as the strength and sanctioning capacity of the monitoring body itself. Effective monitoring, whether by international institutions, unilateral mechanisms, or even transnational networks, contributes to compliance on a number of levels. It can improve the enforcement of international legal rules by increasing understanding of obligations and how they can be fulfilled. It can also help identify genuine obstacles to effective implementation and assist in crafting technical or other solutions. Monitoring can also operate to expose (if not close) the often-considerable gap between international rhetoric and domestic practice. It is no coincidence that those committed to the effective implementation of the Trafficking Protocol are pushing for a change in the international monitoring regime, from self-reporting and generic, often anodyne, analysis, to an ongoing system of review that will help secure greater transparency and accountability with respect to States Parties' performance of their international treaty obligations.[13]

---

[11] See further, Chapter 9.4.
[12] See Chapter 9.4.
[13] See further, Chapter 9.2.1.

9.2. FORMAL COMPLIANCE MECHANISMS UNDER
THE SPECIALIST TREATIES

The two major specialist trafficking treaties, the Trafficking Protocol and the European Trafficking Convention,[14] both establish or are otherwise connected to a range of compliance bodies.[15] Rather than providing a full account and analysis of these mechanisms, the following paragraphs seek to draw out the most important features of their structure and functioning, with a specific focus on their current and potential contribution to clarifying and promoting the effective implementation of State Party obligations.

9.2.1. *The Organized Crime Convention and Trafficking Protocol*

Article 32(1) of the Organized Crime Convention establishes a Conference of the Parties "to improve the capacity of States to combat transnational organized crime and to promote and review the implementation of [the] Convention."[16] To that end, the Convention envisages that the Conference of Parties (COP) will facilitate training, technical assistance, and related activities; facilitate information exchange between States Parties on patterns and trends in organized crime and successful responses; and cooperate with relevant intergovernmental and nongovernmental organizations.[17] The COP is also entrusted with an oversight function. It is to review, periodically, implementation of the Convention and

---

[14] Council of Europe Convention on Action against Trafficking in Human Beings and its Explanatory Report, ETS 197, 16.V.2005, done May 16, 2005, entered into force Feb. 1, 2008 (European Trafficking Convention).

[15] Note that the SAARC Convention does not establish any form of monitoring or oversight: South Asian Association for Regional Cooperation, Convention on Preventing and Combating Trafficking in Women and Children for Prostitution, done Jan. 5, 2002, entered into force Dec. 1, 2005 (SAARC Convention). At the time of adoption it was envisaged that this issue would be dealt with subsequently. Article 13 of the 2009 draft European Framework Decision required Member States to "take the necessary measures to establish National Rapporteurs or other equivalent mechanisms. The tasks of such mechanisms shall include, at a minimum, monitoring of the implementation of the measures envisaged in this Framework Decision": Commission of the European Communities, Proposal for a Framework Decision on preventing and combating trafficking in human beings, and protecting victims, repealing Framework Decision 2002/629/JHA, COM(2009) 136 final, Mar. 25, 2009, at Art. 13. This draft has now lapsed, as it was not adopted by the entry into force of the Treaty of Lisbon (Treaty of Lisbon amending the Treaty on European Union and the Treaty establishing the European Community, OJ C 306/1, done Dec. 13, 2007, entered into force Dec. 1, 2009), which abolished the decision-making process for Framework Decisions. At the time of writing, many provisions of the draft were in substance under discussion again as part of a proposed Directive of the European Parliament on trafficking: European Commission, Proposal for a Directive of the European Parliament and of the Council on preventing and combating trafficking in human beings, and protecting victims, repealing Framework Decision 2002/629/JHA, COM(2010) 95 final, Mar. 29, 2010.

[16] United Nations Convention against Transnational Organized Crime, 2225 UNTS 209, done Nov. 15, 2000, entered into force Sept. 29, 2003 (Organized Crime Convention), at Art. 32(1).

[17] Ibid. at Art. 32(3)(a)–32(3)(c).

make recommendations to improve both the Convention and its implementa-tion.[18] To these ends, the COP is to:

> acquire the necessary knowledge of the measures taken by States Parties in imple-menting this Convention and the difficulties encountered by them in doing so through information provided by them and through such supplemental review mechanisms as may be established by the Conference of the Parties.[19]

Each State Party is obliged to assist in this process by "provid[ing] the Conference of the Parties with information on its programmes, plans and practices, as well as legislative and administrative measures to implement [the] Convention."[20] An Interpretative Note clarifies that the Conference of the Parties should take into account the need to foresee some regularity in the provision of information required. It further stipulates that the term "administrative measures" is to be understood broadly and as including information about the extent to which legislation, policies, and other relevant measures have been implemented.[21]

None of the Convention's three Protocols (including the Trafficking Protocol) foresee any form of oversight or monitoring or otherwise require States Parties to report on implementation. As the mandate of the mechanism established under Article 32 applies only to the Convention, this created a potential gap whereby only those matters under the Protocols that could be brought within the provisions of the Convention would fall within the purview of the COP.[22] At its inaugural session in July 2004, the COP decided to extend its monitoring, information exchange, cooperation, and other functions to the Trafficking Protocol.[23] The COP is thus now empowered to request and receive information on States Parties' implementa-tion of the Protocol and to make recommendations to improve the Protocol and its implementation.

---

[18] Ibid. at Art. 32(3)(d)-32(3)(e).

[19] Ibid. at Art. 32(4).

[20] Ibid. at Art. 32(5).

[21] United Nations Office on Drugs and Crime, Travaux Préparatoires *of the Negotiations for the Elaboration of the United Nations Convention against Transnational Organized Crime and the Protocols Thereto* (2006) (Travaux Préparatoires *for the Organized Crime Convention and Protocols*), at 277.

[22] A close reading of the *travaux préparatoires* does not reveal any concern on the part of States with this potential gap. The *travaux préparatoires* also do not indicate whether the stipulation that the provisions of the Convention apply, *mutatis mutandis*, to the Protocol unless otherwise provided (Organized Crime Convention, at Art. 37; Trafficking Protocol, at Art. 1(2)) would or should result in an automatic extension of the mandate of the Conference of Parties to cover the Protocol.

[23] Conference of Parties to the United Nations Convention on Transnational Organized Crime, Decision 1/5, "Protocol to Prevent, Suppress and Punish Trafficking in Persons, Especially Women and Children, supplementing the United Nations Convention against Transnational Organized Crime," reproduced in Conference of Parties to the United Nations Convention on Transnational Organized Crime, "Report of the Conference of Parties to the United Nations Convention on Transnational Organized Crime on its first session, held in Vienna from 28 June to 8 July 2004," UN Doc. CTOC/COP/2004/6, Sept. 23, 2004, at 5.

At the time of writing, the COP had met four times (in 2004, 2005, 2006, and 2008), with its next meeting scheduled to take place in October 2010 and a sixth session in 2012. At its first meeting, the COP decided to establish, in respect of the Trafficking Protocol, a program of work that it would review at regular intervals.[24] In both 2004 and 2005, a list of topics was flagged for consideration at the next meeting, and the Secretariat requested to collect information from States Parties and signatories on those topics using an approved questionnaire. For its second session in 2005, the COP decided to undertake a review of the basic adaptation of national legislation to the Protocol as well as initial examination of Article 5 (criminalization obligations), Articles 6 to 9 (protection of victims and prevention measures), and the broader question of international cooperation and technical assistance to overcome implementation difficulties.[25] For its third session in 2006, the program of work was extended to consideration of Article 6 (assistance and protection of victims), Article 7 (status of victims in receiving States), Article 8 (repatriation of victims), Article 11 (border measures), Articles 12 and 13 (document security and legitimacy), and consideration of the value of developing, in cooperation with the International Labour Organization, indicators for forced labor.[26] An initial report, considering implementation issues related to criminalization and international cooperation (the "first reporting cycle") and based on replies received from 43 percent of States, was considered at the 2005 meeting.[27] Updated versions of the same report, incorporating additional responses received to the same questionnaire, were submitted to the 2006 and 2008 meetings.[28] An initial report for

---

[24] Ibid.

[25] Ibid.

[26] Conference of Parties to the United Nations Convention on Transnational Organized Crime, Decisions 2/3, "Implementation of the Protocol to Prevent, Suppress and Punish Trafficking in Persons, Especially Women and Children, supplementing the United Nations Convention against Transnational Organized Crime," and 2/6, "Technical Assistance Activities," reproduced in Conference of Parties to the United Nations Convention on Transnational Organized Crime, "Report of the Conference of Parties to the United Nations Convention on Transnational Organized Crime on its second session, held in Vienna from 10 to 21 October 2005," UN Doc. CTOC/COP/2005/8, Dec. 1, 2005, at 7 and 11.

[27] Conference of the Parties to the United Nations Convention on Transnational Organized Crime, "Implementation of the Protocol to Prevent, Suppress and Punish Trafficking in Persons, Especially Women and Children, supplementing the United Nations Convention against Transnational Organized Crime," UN Doc. CTOC/COP/2005/3, Sept. 14, 2005.

[28] Conference of the Parties to the United Nations Convention on Transnational Organized Crime, "Implementation of the Protocol to Prevent, Suppress and Punish Trafficking in Persons, Especially Women and Children, supplementing the United Nations Convention against Transnational Organized Crime," UN Doc. CTOC/COP/2005/3/Rev.1, Aug. 8, 2006; and Conference of the Parties to the United Nations Convention on Transnational Organized Crime, "Implementation of the Protocol to Prevent, Suppress and Punish Trafficking in Persons, Especially Women and Children, supplementing the United Nations Convention against Transnational Organized Crime," UN Doc. CTOC/COP/2005/3/Rev.2, Aug. 25, 2008. The additional responses received by the time of the 2008 report brought the reporting rate only up to "less than half" of all States Parties: ibid. at para. 37.

the "second reporting cycle" (covering issues related to victim protection and assistance, legal status, repatriation, information exchange, and training), reflecting information received from 35 percent of States Parties, was presented in 2006.[29] An updated version of the same report, incorporating additional information received, was submitted to the 2008 COP meeting.[30]

A review of the voluminous and somewhat repetitive documentation produced for the COP between 2004 and 2008 and for its various working groups up to mid-2010 confirms that the reporting procedure is a relatively crude mechanism for promoting or measuring compliance. Reporting rates are low and the information received is uneven, shallow, and often ambiguous. There is no opportunity to seek clarification from, or for dialogue with, States Parties. The analytical compilations of responses provide, at best, a highly generalized picture of compliance patterns and trends and do not amount to even a cursory review of State Party performance. Perhaps as a consequence of these rather disappointing results, the COP decided in 2008 to take a different approach. A working group was established with the purpose of advising and assisting the COP in the implementation of its responsibilities with regard to the Trafficking Protocol. The Working Group is mandated to: (1) facilitate implementation through the exchange of experience and practices between experts and practitioners; (2) make recommendations to the COP on how States Parties can better implement the provisions of the Protocol; (3) assist the COP in providing guidance to UN Office on Drugs and Crime (UNODC) on its implementation-related activities; and (4) advise the COP on implementation-related coordination with other bodies.[31] The first meeting of the Working Group, involving 40 of the then 127 States Parties, the European Community (also party to the Convention), and six signatories, was held in April 2009.[32] The second meeting was held in January 2010. Seventy-one of the then 135

---

[29] Conference of the Parties to the United Nations Convention against Transnational Organized Crime, "Implementation of the Protocol to Prevent, Suppress and Punish Trafficking in Persons, Especially Women and Children, Supplementing the United Nations Convention against Transnational Organized Crime: Consolidated Information Received from States for the Second Reporting Cycle," UN Doc. CTOC/COP/2006/6, Aug. 16, 2006.

[30] Conference of the Parties to the United Nations Convention against Transnational Organized Crime, "Implementation of the Protocol to Prevent, Suppress and Punish Trafficking in Persons, Especially Women and Children, Supplementing the United Nations Convention against Transnational Organized Crime: Consolidated Information Received from States for the Second Reporting Cycle," UN Doc. CTOC/COP/2006/6/Rev.1, Sept. 9, 2008.

[31] Conference of Parties to the United Nations Convention on Transnational Organized Crime, Decision 4/4, "Trafficking in Human Beings," reproduced in Conference of Parties to the United Nations Convention on Transnational Organized Crime, "Report of the Conference of Parties to the United Nations Convention on Transnational Organized Crime on its fourth session, held in Vienna from 8 to 17 October 2008," UN Doc. CTOC/COP/2008/19, Dec. 1, 2008, at 11.

[32] See Conference of the Parties to the United Nations Convention on Transnational Organized Crime, Working Group on Trafficking in Persons, "Report on the meeting of the Working Group on Trafficking in Persons held in Vienna on 14 and 15 April 2009," UN Doc. CTOC/COP/WG.4/2009/2, Apr. 21, 2009, at paras. 35–37.

States Parties, along with the European Union and seven signatories participated in that meeting.[33]

The new structure appears to have resulted in a more careful consideration of implementation priorities and challenges than was possible under the COP. Significantly, the Working Group has begun to take on a modest role in clarifying and, in some cases, fleshing out the substantive content of key obligations. For example, it has noted that, with respect to victims, States Parties should "[e]nsure victims are provided with immediate support and protection, irrespective of their involvement in the criminal justice process,"[34] and more specifically that "[t]he absence of testimony will not rule out the provision of assistance."[35] These recommendations, which go beyond the strict requirements of the Protocol, make an important contribution to bringing that instrument in line with emerging international consensus on this issue.[36] Another example is provided by the Working Group's recommendation to States Parties that they "[e]nsure that responses to child trafficking at all levels are always based on the best interest of the child."[37] As noted in Chapter 2 of this study, failure of the Protocol to include a specific reference to the best interests of the child principle was considered by many to be a major weakness. While not remedying this omission, the recommendation by the Working Group helps strengthen the link between this principle and the Protocol's protection and support provisions. A third example relates to the contentious issue of nonpunishment and nonprosecution for status-related offenses and the link between criminalization and identification failures. The Working Group issued, at its first session, a recommendation that:

> [w]ith regard to ensuring the non-punishment and non-prosecution of trafficked persons, States parties should: (a) Establish appropriate procedures for identifying victims of trafficking in persons and for giving such victims support; (b) Consider, in line with their domestic legislation, not punishing or prosecuting trafficked persons for unlawful acts committed by them as a direct consequence of their

---

[33] See Conference of the Parties to the United Nations Convention on Transnational Organized Crime, Working Group on Trafficking in Persons, "Report on the meeting of the Working Group on Trafficking in Persons held in Vienna, 27–29 January 2010," UN Doc. CTOC/COP/WG.4/2010/6, Feb. 16, 2010, at paras.70–72.

[34] Conference of the Parties to the United Nations Convention on Transnational Organized Crime, Working Group on Trafficking in Persons, "Report on the meeting of the Working Group on Trafficking in Persons held in Vienna on 14 and 15 April 2009," UN Doc. CTOC/COP/WG.4/2009/2, Apr. 21, 2009, at para. 13(c).

[35] Conference of the Parties to the United Nations Convention on Transnational Organized Crime, Working Group on Trafficking in Persons, "Report on the meeting of the Working Group on Trafficking in Persons held in Vienna, 27–29 January 2010," UN Doc. CTOC/COP/WG.4/2010/6, Feb. 16, 2010, at para. 31.

[36] See further, the discussion of this issue in Chapter 5.3 of this volume.

[37] Conference of the Parties to the United Nations Convention on Transnational Organized Crime, Working Group on Trafficking in Persons, "Report on the meeting of the Working Group on Trafficking in Persons held in Vienna on 14 and 15 April 2009," UN Doc. CTOC/COP/WG.4/2009/2, Apr. 21, 2009, at para. 13(h).

situation as trafficked persons or where they were compelled to commit such unlawful acts.[38]

Once again, while the recommendation of the Working Group does not operate to substantially alter the nature of State obligations under the Protocol with respect to identification and criminalization, it does provide important guidance on how certain provisions should be interpreted and implemented.[39]

While the establishment of a dedicated mechanism has gone some way toward improving oversight of State obligations under the Trafficking Protocol, the need for more rigorous compliance mechanisms that can complement the extensive array of interpretative and implementation guidance currently available[40] has been widely

---

[38] Ibid. at para. 12.

[39] It should be noted, however, that the matter of nonprosecution and nonpunishment remains far from settled. The report of the Working Group's January 2010 meeting notes that "[d]iscussions in relation to the issue of non-punishment and non-prosecution of victims of trafficking were wide ranging, with strongly differing viewpoints expressed on aspects of the issue. The Working Group was unable to reach agreement on an additional recommendation on non-prosecution to that agreed in its first meeting, while a few delegations did not support the decision to restate that recommendation as an outcome of this second meeting": Conference of the Parties to the United Nations Convention on Transnational Organized Crime, Working Group on Trafficking in Persons, "Report on the meeting of the Working Group on Trafficking in Persons held in Vienna, 27–29 January 2010," UN Doc. CTOC/COP/WG.4/2010/6, Feb. 16, 2010, at para. 113. The same report, at para. 45, does in fact affirm the previous recommendation.

[40] Available materials include the *Legislative Guide* (UN Office on Drugs and Crime, *Legislative Guides for the Implementation of the United Nations Convention against Transnational Organized Crime and the Protocols Thereto*, UN Sales No. E.05.V.2 (2004)) and UNODC Model Law (United Nations Office on Drugs and Crime, *Model Law on Trafficking in Persons*, UN Sales No. E.09.V.11 (2009)), used extensively in Chapters 5 to 8 of the present book; an "Anti-Trafficking Assessment Tool" (United Nations Office on Drugs and Crime, "Anti-Trafficking Assessment Tool," July 2, 2003, available at http://www.legislationline.org/download/action/download/id/941/file/0ce323a bbc58994be7445b35b08.pdf (accessed Feb. 2, 2010)); as well as a range of toolkits, handbooks, and manuals for parliamentarians and criminal justice officials. In 2009, following a review of States Parties' reports and complementary mechanisms and resources, the UN Office on Drugs and Crime produced the *International Framework for Action to Implement the Trafficking in Persons Protocol*, available at http://www.unodc.org/documents/human-trafficking/Framework_ for_Action_TIP.pdf (accessed Feb. 2, 2010), a technical assistance instrument aimed at assisting States Parties in the effective implementation of the Protocol. The Framework for Action identifies key implementation challenges and proposes detailed measures to address these challenges. Other resources supporting Protocol oversight and compliance include: Office of the UN High Commissioner for Human Rights, *Commentary to the United Nations Principles and Guidelines on Human Rights and Human Trafficking* (forthcoming, 2010); and American Bar Association, Rule of Law Initiative, *Human Trafficking Assessment Tool* (2005), available at http://www.abanet. org/rol/publications/human_trafficking_assessment_tool.shtml (accessed Feb. 2, 2010). See also UN Economic and Social Council, Office of the United Nations High Commissioner for Human Rights, *Recommended Principles and Guidelines on Human Rights and Human Trafficking*, UN Doc. E/2002/68/Add.1, May 20, 2002 (UN Trafficking Principles and Guidelines); Office UN of the High Commissioner for Human Rights, UN High Commissioner for Refugees, *Guidelines on International Protection: The application of Article 1(A)(2) of the 1951 Convention and/or 1967 Protocol relating to the Status of Refugees to victims of trafficking and persons at risk of being trafficked*, UN Doc. HCR/GIP/06/07, Apr. 7, 2006; United Nations Children's Fund, *Guidelines for the Protection of Child Victims of Trafficking* (September 2006).

acknowledged. The UNODC, for example, in its capacity as COP Secretariat, has drawn attention to the superior monitoring mechanisms established under related treaties such as the Convention against Corruption[41] and the European Trafficking Convention, concluding that in order to secure the objectives of the Convention and its Protocols:

> it may be necessary to establish an effective mechanism, under the authority of the Conference, to review the implementation of the instruments, comprehensively assess progress and gaps in the capacity of States and provide information in order to take informed decisions on the provision of technical assistance.[42]

The COP subsequently agreed to explore possible options for a strengthened review procedure, and a decision on the way forward is expected at its fifth session in 2010.[43]

The prospect of States Parties to the Organized Crime Convention and its Trafficking Protocol being made subject to a rigorous oversight mechanism – or even a procedure capable of evaluating their performance of key obligations – appears to be remote. States involved in the review of current arrangements have made clear that while they are willing to consider establishing a mechanism that is "transparent and efficient," there are limits on what would be acceptable; for example, the focus of any such mechanism should not be on compliance *per se*, but rather on helping to develop national policies for implementation as well as technical assistance and international cooperation initiatives.[44] In what appears to be a direct reaction to the unilateral monitoring and sanctioning regime established by the United States,[45] States Parties have also declared that any oversight mechanism established under the Convention must also be "non-intrusive, impartial,

---

[41] United Nations Convention against Corruption, 2349 UNTS 41, done Oct. 31, 2003, entered into force Dec. 14, 2005 (Convention against Corruption).

[42] Conference of the Parties to the United Nations Convention against Transnational Organized Crime, "Possible Mechanisms to Review Implementation of the United Nations Convention against Transnational Organized Crime and the Protocols thereto," UN Doc. CTOC/COP/2008/3, Aug. 26, 2008, at para. 35.

[43] Conference of Parties to the United Nations Convention on Transnational Organized Crime, Decision 4/1, "Possible Mechanisms to Review Implementation of the United Nations Convention against Transnational Organized Crime and the Protocols thereto," reproduced in Conference of Parties to the United Nations Convention on Transnational Organized Crime, "Report of the Conference of Parties to the United Nations Convention on Transnational Organized Crime on its fourth session, held in Vienna from 8 to 17 October 2008," UN Doc. CTOC/COP/2008/19, Dec. 1, 2008, at 4 (establishing a group of experts to consider possible options for strengthening the review procedures for the Organized Crime Convention and its Protocols. The group of experts held its first meeting in September 2009 and a second meeting in January 2010).

[44] Conference of the Parties to the United Nations Convention against Transnational Organized Crime, "Report on the Meeting of Experts on Possible Mechanisms to Review Implementation of the United Nations Convention against Transnational Organized Crime held in Vienna on 30 September 2009," UN Doc. CTOC/COP/WG.1/2009/3, Oct. 14, 2009, at para. 21.

[45] See further, the discussion at Chapter 9.3.

non-adversarial, non-punitive and flexible. In addition, it should not criticize or rank States or regions but rather contribute to problem-solving. It should furthermore respect the sovereignty of States."[46] This statement echoed a sentiment expressed by China and the Group of 77 to the UN Crime Commission several months previously.[47] It remains to be seen whether experiences generated close to home (for example, with respect to the UN Convention against Corruption,[48] also developed under auspices of the UN Crime Commission and with a structure very similar to that of the Protocol's parent instrument, the Organized Crime Convention) or further afield (for example, with respect to the European Trafficking Convention) will contribute to an evolution of these views.

9.2.2. *The European Trafficking Convention*

The monitoring mechanism established under the European Trafficking Convention is considered by its founding institution to be one of the great strengths of that instrument.[49] The Convention establishes a system comprising two bodies: a technically oriented Group of Experts against trafficking in human beings (GRETA), and

---

[46] Conference of the Parties to the United Nations Convention against Transnational Organized Crime, "Report on the Meeting of Experts on Possible Mechanisms to Review Implementation of the United Nations Convention against Transnational Organized Crime held in Vienna on 30 September 2009," UN Doc. CTOC/COP/WG.1/2009/3, Oct. 14, 2009, at para. 22. This position is stronger than the one adopted by States Parties with respect to a possible improved review mechanism for the United Nations Convention against Corruption, in relation to which it was agreed that such a mechanism should be "transparent, efficient, non-intrusive, inclusive and impartial [and] not produce any form of ranking": see Conference of the States Parties to the United Nations Convention against Corruption, Decision 1/1, "Review of Implementation," reproduced in "Report of the Conference of the States Parties to the United Nations Convention against Corruption on its first session, held in Amman from 10 to 14 December 2006," UN Doc. CAC/COSP/2006/12, Dec. 27, 2006, at 3. Note that the view of the meeting of experts is shared by those who, without the experience of the U.S. mechanism, might have been expected to support a more rigorous approach to the monitoring of State Party performance. See, for example, Global Alliance against Trafficking in Women and Others, "Statement on a Monitoring Mechanism for the United Nations Convention against Transnational Organized Crime and Each of the Protocols Thereto with Specific Attention to the Protocol to Prevent, Suppress and Punish Trafficking in Persons (the Human Trafficking Protocol)," Oct. 13, 2009, available at http://www.gaatw.org/statements/ Statement_on_a_Monitoring_Mechanism-COPS08.pdf (accessed Feb. 2, 2010) ("[a review mechanism should be] non-punitive, non-adversarial, non-conditional and non-ranking"). See further, the discussion on the impact of the U.S. reporting and sanctioning mechanism at Chapter 9.2.3.

[47] Group of 77 (G77) and China, "Statement of the G77 and China at the Eighteenth Session of the Commission on Crime Prevention and Criminal Justice," Apr. 16–24, 2009, available at http://www. g77.org/vienna/UNODCCCPCJ18th.htm (accessed June 9, 2010).

[48] See further, Conference of the Parties to the United Nations Convention against Transnational Organized Crime, "Possible Mechanisms to Review Implementation of the United Nations Convention against Transnational Organized Crime and the Protocols Thereto," UN Doc. CTOC/ COP/2008/3, Aug. 26, 2008, at paras. 28–34.

[49] Council of Europe, *Explanatory Report on the Convention on Action against Trafficking in Human Beings*, ETS 197, 16.V.2005 (European Trafficking Convention Explanatory Report), at para. 354.

a more politically oriented Committee of the Parties, which is linked directly to the Council of Europe's Committee of Ministers.

The Convention mandates that the primary monitoring body, GRETA, is to be composed of ten to fifteen independent technical experts elected by the Committee of the Parties on the basis of their expertise, with attention given to gender balance, geographical balance, and the need to ensure representation from the main legal systems.[50] Members sit in their individual capacity and are to be impartial and independent.[51] The Convention sets out the monitoring procedure in considerable detail, supplemented by Rules of Procedure adopted by GRETA in June 2009.[52] In brief, the evaluation procedure is divided into four-year rounds, with GRETA specifying those provisions of the Convention that are to be the focus of that particular round. A questionnaire aimed at ascertaining compliance with the relevant provisions is developed and distributed to States Parties in accordance with a set schedule.[53] That questionnaire is made public. Once it receives a response, GRETA may contact a State Party requesting additional information. Initial responses and replies to requests for additional information are confidential unless otherwise stipulated by the State Party. GRETA may also request information from civil society[54] or even conduct an on-site visit if this is considered necessary "to complement the information received or to evaluate the implementation of the measures taken."[55] The information collected through these various sources is incorporated into a draft report together with recommendations for how identified problems could be addressed. Other means of evaluation, such as hearings and consultations with experts, may also be used if considered necessary. The Convention makes clear that a dialogue must be established between GRETA and the State Party concerned. A draft report, comprising a descriptive part, an analytical part, and suggestions and proposals, is examined, discussed, and approved by GRETA in plenary. The draft is then sent to the State Party for comment, and any feedback taken into account in

---

[50] European Trafficking Convention, at Art. 36.

[51] Ibid.

[52] Council of Europe, Group of Experts on Action against Trafficking in Human Beings (GRETA), "Rules of Procedure for Evaluating Implementation of the Council of Europe Convention on Action against Trafficking in Human Beings by the Parties," THB-GRETA 2009/3, June 17, 2009 (GRETA, Evaluation Rules of Procedure).

[53] The first evaluation round for a State Party is initiated by a questionnaire sent between one and two years after entry into force of the Convention for that State Party. Subsequent evaluation rounds are initiated by addressing the questionnaire for each round four years from the date that the State Party received the previous questionnaire: ibid. at Rule 3.

[54] The Evaluation Rules of Procedure stipulate that the civil society organization so contacted "shall be active in the field of action against trafficking in human beings and preferably national coalitions of organizations or national branches of international non-governmental organizations. Moreover they shall have access to reliable sources of information and be capable of carrying out the necessary verifications of this information": ibid. at Rule 7.

[55] Ibid. at Rule 8.

its finalization. The final report and conclusions are then adopted[56] and sent to the State Party. GRETA's reports are not left to languish but are also forwarded to the Committee of the Parties for any necessary follow-up, which can include a request to States to take certain measures to implement GRETA's conclusions. Within a month of being adopted, the report and conclusions are made public, together with eventual comments by the State Party concerned.[57]

The Committee of Parties is composed of one representative ("member") from each State Party.[58] Meetings are held *in camera* and convened whenever one-third of parties, the President of GRETA, or the Secretary-General of the Council of Europe so requests.[59] The Rules of Procedure allow for nonvoting "participants" and "observers."[60] The Committee's task is essentially to add political weight to the work of GRETA. It cannot modify or change the reports produced by GRETA,[61] but, as previously noted, may request States Parties to take certain measures to implement GRETA's conclusions.[62] The Explanatory Report to the European Trafficking Convention observes that the intention behind the inclusion of this additional step was to "ensure the respect of the independence of GRETA in its monitoring function, while introducing a 'political' dimension into the dialogue between the parties."[63] In its Rules of Procedure, the Committee has decided to function as an "official Observatory on the prevention and combating of trafficking in human beings and the protection of the human rights of victims of trafficking"; to this end, it may, in addition to its other functions, "hold debates on different aspects of trafficking in human beings" as well as hearings and consultations with experts.[64]

---

[56] By a two-thirds majority of the votes cast: ibid. at Rule 14.

[57] European Trafficking Convention, at Art. 38. See also European Trafficking Convention Explanatory report, at paras. 363–369; Council of Europe, Directorate General of Human Rights and Legal Affairs, "Workflow of the Monitoring Mechanism of the Council of Europe Convention on Action against Trafficking in Human Beings," THB-INF(2009)3, available at http://www.coe.int/t/dghl/monitoring/trafficking/Source/Workflow_en.pdf (accessed Feb. 2, 2010); and GRETA, Evaluation Rules of Procedure.

[58] European Trafficking Convention, at Art. 37(1). For those State Parties who are members of the Council of Europe, their representative is to be the national representative within the Committee of Ministers: ibid.

[59] Committee of the Parties, Council of Europe Convention on Action against Trafficking in Human Beings, "Rules of Procedure of the Committee of the Parties," THB-CP(2008)2, Dec. 5, 2008 (European Trafficking Convention Committee of the Parties, Rules of Procedure).

[60] "Participants" include representatives of States that have signed but not ratified the Convention and States that have ratified or acceded to the Convention but for which it has not yet entered into force, as well as various official bodies of the European system. "Observers," who are to be separately authorized by the Committee, may include States not otherwise eligible to be "participants," representatives of intergovernmental organizations and of non-governmental organizations "in particular Amnesty International, Anti-Slavery International, La Strada International and the International Federation Terre des Hommes": ibid. at Rule 2(b).

[61] European Trafficking Convention Explanatory Report, at para. 368.

[62] European Trafficking Convention, at Art. 38(7).

[63] European Trafficking Convention Explanatory Report, at para. 369.

[64] European Trafficking Convention Committee of the Parties, Rules of Procedure, at Rules 1(c) and 15.

The implementation mechanism of the European Trafficking Convention formally commenced with the first meeting of the Committee of Parties in December 2008. At that meeting, the first group of GRETA members was elected,[65] in accordance with the provisions of the Convention and rules laid down by the Committee of Ministers.[66] GRETA held its first meeting in February 2009 and three further meetings throughout the same year. It is scheduled to meet every three months thereafter,[67] a total of approximately sixteen meeting days per year. It is foreseen that GRETA will undertake approximately ten evaluations per year, although doubts have already been expressed with regard to whether the proposed timetable for evaluations is feasible in light of available resources.[68]

It is too early to evaluate the effectiveness of the implementation machinery established under the European Trafficking Convention. Neither of the two monitoring bodies has yet developed a clear identity separate to the other,[69] and the task of formally evaluating State Party compliance is yet to begin. In terms of the broader impact of the Convention and its implementation machinery, much will depend on whether the Convention (which is open to all States) can attract a significant number and range of States Parties. With a sufficiently broad base of support, it is likely that GRETA in particular will emerge as a key player in terms of developing, articulating, and applying international law to the problem of trafficking. Certainly the architecture, as laid down by the Convention and fleshed out by GRETA and the Committee of Parties, appears sufficiently robust to support real and effective monitoring of State Party performance. The dual implementation mechanism, comprising a technical pillar and a higher-level political pillar, is likely to advance the mechanism's overall credibility and authority. Several other features that separate GRETA from comparable treaty bodies – its capacity to conduct country visits (without requiring additional permission from the State Party) and its ability to formally link with and receive information from third parties including informed NGOs – can also be expected to contribute to its effective functioning. The agreed method of work, which will see GRETA focus on only a few issues or obligations at a time, should give that body the opportunity and time to flesh out those aspects of the treaty that most require

---

[65] Committee of the Parties, Council of Europe Convention on Action against Trafficking in Human Beings, "1st meeting of the Committee of the Parties (Strasbourg, 5 and 8 December 2008): List of Items Discussed and Decisions Taken," THB-CP(2008)LD1, Dec. 8, 2008.

[66] Council of Europe, Committee of Ministers, Resolution CM/Res(2008)7 on rules on the election procedure of the members of the Group of Experts on Action against Trafficking in Human Beings (GRETA), June 11, 2008.

[67] Council of Europe, Group of Experts against Trafficking in Human Beings (GRETA), "2nd meeting of GRETA (Strasbourg, 16–19 June 2009): List of Items Discussed and Decisions Taken," THB-CP(2009)LD2, June 19, 2008, at para. 6.

[68] Council of Europe, Group of Experts against Trafficking in Human Beings (GRETA), 3rd meeting of GRETA (Strasbourg, 22–25 September 2009): List of Items Discussed and Decisions Taken," THB-CP(2009)LD3, Sept. 25, 2009, at para. 4.

[69] This is demonstrated through the high level of overlap between reports generated by both bodies during their first year of operation.

clarification. In this regard it is relevant to note the high degree of convergence between the Trafficking Protocol and the European Trafficking Convention in terms of legal obligations. The work of GRETA in clarifying the substantive content of key obligations contained in both instruments could partly offset the weak implementation structure around the Trafficking Protocol.

9.3. PROMOTING COMPLIANCE THROUGH THE INTERNATIONAL HUMAN RIGHTS SYSTEM

Trafficking was a matter for international human rights law long before it became an issue of migration or of transnational organized crime.[70] However, trafficking and the forms of exploitation with which it is most commonly associated have traditionally not been served well by the international human rights system. In fact, as noted in Chapter 2, it was the chronic inability of human rights law and the human rights mechanisms to deal effectively with contemporary forms of exploitation, including trafficking, that provided a number of States with the incentive to move outside that system for a more effective response. Along with many other "soft" human rights issues, trafficking was, for most of the past fifty years, relegated to the fringes of international human rights discourse and action. In terms of implementation, responsibility for issues related to trafficking, including oversight of the troubled 1949 Trafficking Convention,[71] fell largely to a minor working group that exercised almost no influence on the policies or actions of States during its lackluster tenure. The insignificance of the Working Group on Contemporary Forms of Slavery within the broader international system is brought home through the manner of its passing. Whether that particular body limped along or died a slow death did not, in the end, matter very much to States, to international law, or indeed to those whose interests it was established to promote. That its eventual abolition went unnoticed is compelling evidence of its deep irrelevance.[72]

Historical factors and political preferences were more influential than law in maintaining the marginalization of trafficking as an international human rights issue. Chapters 2 and 3 of the present study exposed the full range of rights that are potentially implicated in this issue. The ICCPR, for example, prohibits slavery, servitude, and forced labor (including debt bondage).[73] These provisions give structure and substance to a range of rights protected in other instruments, including the

---

[70] See further Chapters 2 and 3 above.

[71] Convention for the Suppression of the Traffic in Persons and of the Exploitation of the Prostitution of Others, 96 UNTS 271, done Dec. 2, 1949, entered into force July 25, 1951 (1949 Trafficking Convention).

[72] UN Human Rights Council Resolution 6/14 quietly ended the mandate of the Working Group on Contemporary Forms of Slavery: "Special Rapporteur on Contemporary Forms of Slavery," UN Doc. A/HRC/RES/6/14, Sept. 28, 2007.

[73] International Covenant on Civil and Political Rights, 999 UNTS 171, done Dec. 16, 1966, entered into force Mar. 3, 1976, at Art. 8.

right to employment that is freely chosen and accepted, the right to just and favorable conditions of work, and the right to an adequate standard of living. Several of the specialized human rights treaties (for example, the Convention on the Rights of the Child[74]) provide additional substance to the human rights framework within which trafficking and related forms of contemporary exploitation can and should be considered. The prohibition of discrimination found in all major international and regional human rights treaties, and particularly the prohibition of discrimination on the basis of race and sex, furnishes another example of the intersection between international human rights law and contemporary forms of exploitation including trafficking. While many individuals are subject to trafficking and related forms of exploitation within their own countries, there is no denying the very particular and acute vulnerabilities – including cultural and linguistic isolation as well as likely irregularity in immigration status – that are particular to situations of private exploitation across national borders. The extension of human rights protections to noncitizens is another aspect of international human rights law, enshrined in most of the major treaties, which is of particular relevance to individuals who find themselves in such situations, as is the right to leave and return, the prohibition on arbitrary expulsion, and norms related to the right to a remedy for victims of human rights violations. In this connection, identifying trafficking itself as a violation of human rights provides an additional legal basis for protection for those who are subject to exploitation both within and outside their own borders.

There is, in short, no lack of international human rights standards that address both the rights and obligations of States in relation to the issue of trafficking. However, the system's capacity to both monitor and promote compliance has been extremely limited, even when the particular challenges involved in securing compliance with international human rights law[75] are taken into account. Despite the plethora of relevant standards, there have been few concrete examples of serious engagement with this issue on the part of the international human rights system. Even the most clearcut and uncontested provisions of human rights law that would appear to relate most directly to trafficking (such as the prohibition on slavery or on forced labor – or indeed the specific reference to trafficking in the CEDAW Convention[76]) have rarely been advanced or explored in this context. When such connections are made, their purpose is often rhetorical and generally lacking in

---

[74] Convention on the Rights of the Child, 1577 UNTS 3, done Nov. 20, 1989, entered into force Sept. 2, 1990.

[75] For an introduction to two recent strands of thought on the particular challenges involved in securing compliance with international human rights law, see O.A. Hathaway, "Do Human Rights Treaties Make a Difference?" (2002) 111 *Yale Law Journal* 1935; O.A. Hathaway, "Why Do Countries Commit to Human Rights Treaties?" (2007) 51 *Journal of Conflict Resolution* 588; and R. Goodman and D. Jinks, "Incomplete Internalization and Compliance with Human Rights Law," (2008) 19 *European Journal of International Law* 725.

[76] Convention on the Elimination of All Forms of Discrimination against Women, 1249 UNTS 13, done Dec. 13, 1979, entered into force Sept. 3, 1981 (CEDAW), at Art. 6.

legal analysis or justification. The approach of the human rights treaty bodies is illustrative of a broader trend: While trafficking is raised with increasing frequency in work of the treaty bodies, recommendations made to States Parties are invariably vague and nonspecific. None of the relevant committees has yet managed to tie trafficking to a violation of a specific right in a specific treaty. In this area as in many others, lack of normative clarity and substance has directly impacted on the capacity of the international human rights system to call States to account for violations of their legal obligations.

This situation is slowly changing, a reflection of shifts within the human rights system as a whole as well as of legal and political developments around the specific issue of trafficking. Particularly over the past decade, the international human rights mechanisms have demonstrated a growing willingness to consider issues of private exploitation such as trafficking, debt bondage, forced labor, forced marriage, child sexual exploitation, and child labor, occurring within as well as between countries. Setting an example for others, the human rights bodies have also shown an admirable capacity to adjust to the fact that some of the most important standards on these issues have been generated elsewhere. For example, all relevant parts of that system have adopted the Trafficking Protocol's definition of trafficking,[77] and all have taken up the very specific obligations established under that regime to strengthen their position that governments have an obligation to prevent trafficking and related exploitation,[78] prosecute those responsible,[79] and protect victims.[80]

In a similar vein, the establishment of special procedures of the UN Human Rights Council, including Special Rapporteurs on trafficking, on the sale of children, child prostitution and child pornography, on contemporary forms of slavery, on the rights of migrants, and on violence against women, provide a welcome – and much overdue – indication of an increased acceptance on the part of States that severe exploitation, even that which takes place within the private sphere, is indeed a matter for public concern and international regulation. The significance of this

---

[77] See, for example, "Report Submitted by the Special Rapporteur on the Sale of Children, Child Prostitution and Child Pornography, Najat M'jid Maalla, Addendum: Mission to Estonia," UN Doc. A/HRC/12/23/Add.2, July 10, 2009, at para. 84(e); UN Committee on the Rights of the Child, "Concluding Observations: United States of America," UN Doc. CRC/C/OPSC/USA/CO/1, June 25, 2008, at para. 8; "Concluding Observations: Chile," UN Doc. CRC/C/OPSC/CHL/CO/1, Feb. 18, 2008, at para. 24; UN Committee on the Elimination of All Forms of Discrimination against Women, "Concluding Observations: Hungary," UN Doc. CEDAW/C/HUN/CO/6, Aug. 10, 2007, at para. 23; "Concluding Observations: Singapore," UN Doc. CEDAW/C/SGP/CO/3, Aug. 10, 2007, at para. 22; "Concluding Observations: Poland," UN Doc. CEDAW/C/POL/CO/6, Feb. 2, 2007, at para. 21; UN Committee against Torture, "Concluding Observations: Poland," UN Doc. CAT/C/POL/CO/4, July 25, 2007, at para. 18. The definition has also been adopted by the European Trafficking Convention, at Art. 4; and in the UN Trafficking Principles and Guidelines, at 3, note 1.

[78] See the references in Chapter 8 of this book.

[79] See the references in Chapter 7 of this book.

[80] See the references in Chapter 5 of this volume.

development in terms of its contribution to the erosion of the public/private split in international human rights law should not be underestimated.[81] It is no longer credible for any State to deny an obligation to deal with trafficking simply because those responsible are bad people, not bad governments. At the very least, this development warrants a cautious optimism that the historical marginalization of these issues, in law and in practice, may be coming to an end.

Scrutiny by the international human rights system of rights and obligations relating to trafficking remains uneven. The tendency of the various oversight mechanisms to indulge in vague condemnations at the expense of a rigorous analysis of obligation and responsibility is endemic in this area of law as it is in many others. However, there are signs that this will change over time for the better. Human rights bodies' improved literacy with regard to contemporary exploitation, and the existence of additional rules on which they may rely, are likely to help in this regard, as is the growing range of strong supplementary and interpretative material[82] including jurisprudence generated by the regional human rights courts.[83] The establishment of complementary monitoring and evaluation structures outside the international human rights system (most particularly the mechanisms established under the Trafficking Protocol and European Trafficking Convention, discussed in detail in Chapter 9.2) can also be expected to contribute to more and better oversight of core rights and obligations. In short, the international human rights system has now been given new and better tools with which to work. The real test of its effectiveness, relevance, and resilience will lie in the way it responds to this challenge.

9.4. UNILATERAL COMPLIANCE MACHINERY: THE U.S. EVALUATION AND REPORTING SYSTEM

The developments detailed above are already being overshadowed by an alternative, unilateral monitoring and compliance regime conceived and implemented by the United States. The 2000 Victims of Trafficking and Violence Protection Act (Trafficking Victims Protection Act)[84] required the U.S. Department of State to

---

[81]   In the legal context, the "public/private distinction" operates to define what is an appropriate (public) and inappropriate (private) object of law. According to its critics, this dichotomy is not organic or inevitable but rather politically constructed. Those who have examined the operation of the public/private distinction in international human rights law charge that its influence is reflected in a general inability and unwillingness on the part of States and others to engage on issues of fundamental concern to the rights and dignity of those whose lives are lived within the private spheres of work, community, home, and family – individuals who are most often women. See, for example, H. Charlesworth and C. Chinkin, *The Boundaries of International Law: A Feminist Analysis* (2000).

[82]   See, for example, the sources cited in note 40 to this chapter.

[83]   That jurisprudence is still very limited but can be expected to grow. See, for example, the recent decision of the European Court of Human Rights in *Rantsev v. Cyprus and Russia*, Dec. No. 25965/04 (not yet reported) (ECHR, Jan, 7, 2010) (*Rantsev v. Cyprus and Russia*).

[84]   Victims of Trafficking and Violence Protection Act of 2000, 22 USC 7102 (US Trafficking Victims Protection Act).

issue annual reports describing "the nature and extent of severe forms of trafficking in persons"[85] in countries experiencing a significant trafficking problem and assessing governmental efforts to combat such trafficking against criteria established by U.S. law. From 2009, the assessment procedure has been extended to cover all countries, not just those deemed to have "a significant trafficking problem."[86]

The Trafficking Victims Protection Act establishes "minimum standards" for the elimination of trafficking as well as the criteria for evaluating the performance of States. These are both set out in Table 9.1.

Under the Trafficking Victims Protection Act, governments are required, at a minimum, to (1) prohibit and appropriately punish trafficking and (2) make serious and sustained efforts to eliminate such trafficking.[87] In evaluating governmental efforts in this latter regard, consideration is given to a range of factors, including: whether the government vigorously investigates and punishes trafficking; whether it protects victims and encourages their participation in the investigation and prosecution process; whether it has adopted preventative measures such as public education; whether it cooperates with other governments in investigations and prosecutions; whether it extradites (or is attempting to permit extradition of) traffickers; whether it monitors migration patterns for evidence of trafficking and responds to such evidence; whether it investigates, prosecutes, and takes appropriate measures against the involvement of public officials in trafficking; whether it has taken measures to address demand for trafficking related to sexual exploitation; and whether it has monitored and provides information to the U.S. government on its national response to trafficking. A full comparison between the U.S. criteria and the international legal rules identified and explored in the previous chapters is beyond the scope of the present section. It is nevertheless relevant to note a high degree of overlap that does not reach a point of full symmetry. For example, as explained in Chapter 2, there are important differences between the U.S. definition of "trafficking in persons" and that which has made its way into international law.

The first U.S. "Trafficking in Persons Report" (TIP report) instituted a system of rankings based on three tiers.[88] Tier One was for countries in full compliance with the required standards, Tier Two for countries making an effort but not yet fully compliant, and Tier Three for those countries that were failing on both counts. The U.S. government subsequently created an additional category, "Tier Two Watch List," which applies to countries whose governments do not fully comply with the Trafficking Victims Protection Act's minimum standards but are making significant

---

[85]   Ibid. at § 110.

[86]   William Wilberforce Trafficking Victims Protection Reauthorization Act of 2008, Pub. L. No. 110–457, 122 Stat. 5044 (2008), 5048–49, at §§ 106, 108 (overturning the requirement that there be "a significant number of" victims of severe forms of trafficking for a country to be considered to have a "significant trafficking problem").

[87]   US Trafficking Victims Protection Act, at § 108.

[88]   United States Department of State, "Trafficking in Persons Report" (2001), at 7–8.

TABLE 9.1. *United States Trafficking Victims Protection Act: Minimum Standards for the Elimination of Trafficking in Persons*

Trafficking Victims Protection Act of 2000, Div. A of Pub. L. No. 106–386, § 108, as amended. *Adapted from* US "Trafficking in Persons Report" (2009), at 314–315.

A. Minimum standards

The minimum standards for the elimination of trafficking applicable to the government of a country of origin, transit, or destination for victims of severe forms of trafficking are the following:

(1) The government of the country should prohibit severe forms of trafficking[i] in persons and punish acts of such trafficking.

(2) For the knowing commission of any act of sex trafficking involving force, fraud, coercion, or in which the victim of sex trafficking is a child incapable of giving meaningful consent, or of trafficking which includes rape or kidnapping or which causes a death, the government of the country should prescribe punishment commensurate with that for grave crimes, such as forcible sexual assault.

(3) For the knowing commission of any act of a severe form of trafficking in persons, the government of the country should prescribe punishment that is sufficiently stringent to deter and that adequately reflects the heinous nature of the offense.

(4) The government of the country should make serious and sustained efforts to eliminate severe forms of trafficking in persons.

B. Criteria

In determinations under subsection (a)(4) of this section, the following factors should be considered as indicia of serious and sustained efforts to eliminate severe forms of trafficking in persons:

(1) Whether the government of the country vigorously investigates and prosecutes acts of severe forms of trafficking in persons, and convicts and sentences persons responsible for such acts, that take place wholly or partly within the territory of the country, including, as appropriate, requiring incarceration of individuals convicted of such acts. For purposes of the preceding sentence, suspended or significantly reduced sentences for convictions of principal actors in cases of severe forms of trafficking in persons shall be considered, on a case-by-case basis, whether to be considered as an indicator of serious and sustained efforts to eliminate severe forms of trafficking in persons. After reasonable requests from the Department of State for data regarding investigations, prosecutions, convictions, and sentences, a government which does not provide such data, consistent with the capacity of such government to obtain such data, shall be presumed not to have vigorously investigated, prosecuted, convicted or sentenced such acts. During the periods prior to the annual report submitted on June 1, 2004, and on June 1, 2005, and the periods afterwards until September 30 of each such year, the Secretary of State may disregard the presumption contained in the preceding sentence if the government has provided some data to the Department of State

Note[i]: "Severe forms of trafficking" as well as the acts described in the following paragraph generally equate to the forms of trafficking that would fall within the definition set out in the Trafficking Protocol. See further the discussion in Chapter 1 of both definitions.

Trafficking Victims Protection Act of 2000, Div. A of Pub. L. No. 106–386, § 108, as amended. *Adapted from* US "Trafficking in Persons Report" (2009), at 314–315.

regarding such acts and the Secretary has determined that the government is making a good faith effort to collect such data

(2) Whether the government of the country protects victims of severe forms of trafficking in persons and encourages their assistance in the investigation and prosecution of such trafficking, including provisions for legal alternatives to their removal to countries in which they would face retribution or hardship, and ensures that victims are not inappropriately incarcerated, fined, or otherwise penalized solely for unlawful acts as a direct result of being trafficked, including by providing training to law enforcement and immigration officials regarding the identification and treatment of trafficking victims using approaches that focus on the needs of the victims.

(3) Whether the government of the country has adopted measures to prevent severe forms of trafficking in persons, such as measures to inform and educate the public, including potential victims, about the causes and consequences of severe forms of trafficking in persons, measures to establish the identity of local populations, including birth registration, citizenship, and nationality, measures to ensure that its nationals who are deployed abroad as part of a peacekeeping or other similar mission do not engage in or facilitate severe forms of trafficking in persons or exploit victims of such trafficking, and measures to prevent the use of forced labor or child labor in violation of international standards.

(4) Whether the government of the country cooperates with other governments in the investigation and prosecution of severe forms of trafficking in persons.

(5) Whether the government of the country extradites persons charged with acts of severe forms of trafficking in persons on substantially the same terms and to substantially the same extent as persons charged with other serious crimes (or, to the extent such extradition would be inconsistent with the laws of such country or with international agreements to which the country is a party, whether the government is taking all appropriate measures to modify or replace such laws and treaties so as to permit such extradition).

(6) Whether the government of the country monitors immigration and emigration patterns for evidence of severe forms of trafficking in persons and whether law enforcement agencies of the country respond to any such evidence in a manner that is consistent with the vigorous investigation and prosecution of acts of such trafficking, as well as with the protection of human rights of victims and the internationally recognized human right to leave any country, including one's own, and to return to one's own country.

(7) Whether the government of the country vigorously investigates, prosecutes, convicts, and sentences public officials who participate in or facilitate severe forms of trafficking in persons, including nationals of the country who are deployed abroad as part of a peacekeeping or other similar mission who engage in or facilitate severe forms of trafficking in persons or exploit victims of such trafficking, and takes all appropriate measures against officials who condone such trafficking. After reasonable requests
from the Department of State for data regarding such investigations, prosecutions, convictions, and sentences, a government which does not provide such data consistent with its resources shall be presumed not to have vigorously investigated, prosecuted,

(continued)

Table 9.1 (continued)

Trafficking Victims Protection Act of 2000, Div. A of Pub. L. No. 106–386, § 108, as amended. *Adapted from* US "Trafficking in Persons Report" (2009), at 314–315.

convicted, or sentenced such acts. During the periods prior to the annual report submitted on June 1, 2004, and on June 1, 2005, and the periods afterwards until September 30 of each such year, the Secretary of State may disregard the presumption contained in the preceding sentence if the government has provided some data to the Department of State regarding such acts and the Secretary has determined that the government is making a good faith effort to collect such data.

(8) Whether the percentage of victims of severe forms of trafficking in the country that are non-citizens of such countries is insignificant.

(9) Whether the government of the country, consistent with the capacity of such government, systematically monitors its efforts to satisfy the criteria described in paragraphs (1) through (8) and makes available publicly a periodic assessment of such efforts.

(10) Whether the government of the country achieves appreciable progress in eliminating severe forms of trafficking when compared to the assessment in the previous year.

(11) Whether the government of the country has made serious and sustained efforts to reduce the demand for (A) commercial sex acts; and (B) participation in international sex tourism by nationals of the country.

efforts to bring themselves into compliance with those standards.[89] Under the Act and its various amendments, the U.S. President is authorized to deny the provision of nonhumanitarian, non-trade-related assistance to any Tier Three country, that is, any State that does not comply with the minimum standards and that is not making significant efforts to bring itself into compliance.[90] In addition, such countries will also risk U.S. opposition to their seeking and obtaining funds from multilateral financial institutions, including the World Bank and the International Monetary

---

[89] The US Trafficking Victims Protection Act, at § 110(b)(3)(A)(iii) (as amended by the Trafficking Victims Protection Reauthorization Act of 2003, Pub. L. 103–193), lists three factors by which to determine whether a country should be on Tier 2 or Tier 2 Watch List as opposed to Tier 3: "(a) the absolute number of victims of severe forms of trafficking is very significant or is significantly increasing; or (b) there is a failure to provide evidence of increasing efforts to combat severe forms of trafficking in persons from the previous year; or (c) the determination that a country is making significant efforts to bring themselves into compliance with minimum standards was based on commitments by the country to take additional future steps over the next year." Tier Two Watch List countries are subject to special scrutiny and, subject to special presidential exemption, are moved down to Tier Three after two consecutive years on the Watch List: ibid. at § 110(b)(3)(D) (as amended by the William Wilberforce Trafficking Victims Protection Reauthorization Act of 2008, Pub. L. No. 110–457, 122 Stat. 5044).

[90] Ibid. at § 110(a).

Fund.[91] The annual reports are used as a basis for determining whether, and to what extent, sanctions are to be imposed.[92]

The TIP reports have been subject to criticism on a range of fronts. Some object to the very fact of the U.S. becoming the self-appointed supervisor and arbiter of a complex international issue that remains both contested and controversial.[93] The politicization of the reports (for example, the link they have established between trafficking and prostitution) has been identified as especially unhelpful.[94] Other critiques have questioned the empirical basis of the reports and their findings, identifying serious quality concerns with regard to both methodology and data.[95] The vague and subjective standards used to assess compliance have also been criticized.[96] While accepting the validity of many such objections, it is nevertheless important to acknowledge that the TIP reports have produced some unsettling results for the committed multilateralist. Their contribution to the evolution of a global consensus on the nature of the problem of trafficking is indisputable. Perhaps even more significant has been the impact of the reports on the response of States to trafficking and the various forms of exploitation with which it is associated. In her work with Member States of the Association of Southeast Asian Nations between 2003 and 2010, for example, the author directly observed multiple instances in which the open threat of a negative grade in the U.S. TIP Report provided the impetus for major reform initiatives, including the criminalization of trafficking, decriminalization of victims, changes in the penalty structure for trafficking and related offenses, and the opening of shelters. As explored at various points throughout this book, some of these responses have been highly problematic in human rights terms, a side effect that is not explored or even acknowledged in the U.S. Department of State's reports themselves. Other responses appear to have resulted in more and better prosecutions of traffickers, as well as improvements in both victim identification procedures and victim treatment. Thus far, however, available evidence of impact is

---

[91] Ibid. at § 110(d)(1)(B).

[92] Ibid. at § 110. For a discussion of sanctions and compliance, see S.H. Cleveland, "Norm Internalization and U.S. Economic Sanctions," (2001) 26 *Yale Journal of International Law* 1.

[93] See, for example, J. Chuang, "The United States as Global Sheriff: Using Unilateral Sanctions to Combat Human Trafficking," (2006) 27 *Michigan Journal of International Law* 437.

[94] See, for example, the letter from the Global Alliance Against Trafficking in Women to the United States Secretary of State, July 15, 2008, available at http://www.gaatw.org/statements/TIP_Letter_FINAL.pdf (accessed Feb. 2, 2010).

[95] See, for example, US Government Accountability Office, "Human Trafficking: Better Data, Strategy and Reporting Needed to Enhance UN Antitrafficking Efforts Abroad," July 2006, available at http://www.gao.gov/new.items/d06825.pdf (accessed Nov. 22, 2009).

[96] See generally, H.R. Friman, "Numbers and Certification: Assessing Foreign Compliance in Combating Narcotics and Human Trafficking, in P. Andreas and K.M. Greenhill, *Sex, Drugs and Body Counts: the Politics of Numbers in Global Crime and Conflict* (forthcoming 2010) (Friman, "Numbers and Certification") and K.B. Warren, "The Illusiveness of Counting 'Victims' and the Concreteness of Ranking Countries: Trafficking in Persons from Colombia to Japan," in P. Andreas and K.M. Greenhill eds., *Sex, Drugs and Body Counts: The Politics of Numbers in Global Crime and Conflict* (forthcoming 2010).

largely anecdotal, and the influence of the U.S. compliance machinery on national responses to trafficking is yet to be fully documented and analyzed.[97]

Whatever one's view on their value and impact, there can be no doubt that the TIP reports have radically altered the terms of any discussion on compliance with the international law of human trafficking. Each and every State, irrespective of its relative power, position, or adherence to a particular treaty, is subject to close and continuing scrutiny. A verdict, with potentially serious consequences, is then pronounced. States are working hard to prepare themselves for this annual examination and, almost without exception, appear to care very deeply about the outcome. In many respects this is a welcome development. The international machinery available to monitor and evaluate the performance of States is, as noted earlier, weak and compromised. The U.S. mechanism explicitly recognizes that governments bear a responsibility to prevent trafficking, to prosecute traffickers, and to protect victims. Attempts to persuade governments to take these obligations seriously deserve support and encouragement. At the same time, it is not unreasonable to be concerned that the U.S. approach will end up compromising the legitimacy of the international regime as a whole. Certainly, it is difficult for the international lawyer to be overly enthusiastic about an external compliance mechanism that rejects established international legal rules in favor of an internally generated yardstick for measuring the performance of all States.

9.5. TRANSNATIONAL COMPLIANCE NETWORKS

Scholars and practitioners of international law and international relations have come to recognize the crucial role played by transnational networks in shaping international rules and affecting their implementation.[98] The most prominent transnational compliance networks are governmental in composition and currently operate in areas requiring a high degree of coordinated regulation, such as banking, securities, and environmental protection.[99] Network members usually have some degree of autonomy (or at least discretion) that enables them to engage directly with foreign counterparts, thereby bypassing the traditional and often cumbersome structures

---

[97] For preliminary studies on the impact of the reports, see, for example, Friman, "Numbers and Certification"; L.S. Wyler and A. Siskin, "Trafficking in Persons: U.S. Policy and Issues for Congress," Congressional Research Service (2010), available at http://www.fpc.state.gov/documents/organization/139278.pdf (accessed June 9, 2010); M.G. Freidrich, A.N. Myer and D.G. Perlman, "The Trafficking in Persons Report: Strengthening a Diplomatic Tool," UCLA School of Public Affairs (May 8, 2006);

[98] See K. Raustiala, "The Architecture of International Cooperation: Transgovernmental Networks and the Future of International Law," (2002) 43 *Virginia Journal of International Law* 1 (Raustiala, "The Architecture of International Cooperation"); A.-M. Slaughter, *A New World Order* (2004) (Slaughter, *A New World Order*).

[99] Ibid. See also the growing literature on global administrative law, which takes up many of the same themes; for example, B. Kingsbury, N. Krisch and R.B. Stewart, "The Emergence of Global Administrative Law," (2005) 68 *Law and Contemporary Problems* 15.

of formal State-to-State interaction. It has been argued that such networks are well suited to address the "paradox of globalization" – a clear and urgent need for more international governance on the one hand, and unease about the growth of global governance on the other.[100] Advocates of global network theory identify several characteristics of transnational networks – their relatively greater inclusiveness, flexibility, and domestic acceptability – as making them more amenable to the task of global governance than higher-level compliance mechanisms, which are often weighed down by rigidity, formality, and heavy political baggage.[101] The following analysis accepts this generally positive view of the potential value of transnational networks, while acknowledging that they are not a quick fix for the compliance problem of international law. Their coverage is uneven and capricious and depends heavily on common perceptions of need and benefit. Even more easily than international institutions, they can be dominated by one or more powerful States or by a particular interest group. They can facilitate or perhaps even encourage inconsistent application of international rules. They often lack transparency and accountability.[102] The same flexibility, specialization, and informality that gives these networks their identity intrinsically weakens them as a force for compliance where State interests are not in perfect convergence.[103] These limitations apply to the examples cited below and should not be discounted, even as one accepts the growing influence of such networks on the domestic implementation of international law.

At first glance, trafficking may not appear to trigger the necessary impetus for intergovernmental networking, not least because it is rarely perceived as producing direct negative impacts on the strategic or commercial interests of powerful States. However, a number of other factors have worked in favor of such networks. The elevation of trafficking as an international political issue, and the decision of the U.S. to encourage and, if necessary, enforce compliance with its vision of an appropriate response, have proved instrumental in generating the energy and commitment required to create and sustain cross-border networks. The link between trafficking and organized crime was also decisive, serving to confirm cross-border consequences of trafficking and bringing the issue within the mandate of what has been called "an ever tighter and wider net of criminal justice controls designed by states to detect, deter and interdict criminalized transnational actors and activities."[104] Transgovernmental cooperation has also been encouraged – and in some cases facilitated – by the strong and sustained involvement of NGOs, intergovernmental

---

[100] Slaughter, *A New World Order*, at 8–12.

[101] See Raustiala, "The Architecture of International Cooperation"; Slaughter, *A New World Order*.

[102] For a consideration of these dangers in the context of a study of international criminal law networks, see J.I. Turner, "Transnational Networks and International Criminal Justice," (2007) 105 *Michigan Law Review* 985, at 1020–1030.

[103] See further P.-H. Verdier, "Transnational Regulatory Networks and Their Limits," (2009) 34 *Yale Journal of International Law* 113.

[104] P. Andreas and E. Nadelmann, *Policing the Globe: Criminalization and Crime Control in International Relations* (2006) (Andreas and Nadelmann, *Policing the Globe*), at 3.

organizations, and even aid agencies in this issue. Perhaps most critical has been the development of the international legal framework itself and the cross-national homogenization of laws that it has engendered. Transgovernmental networks cannot operate in a vacuum. Their effective functioning rests, at least in great part, on a shared understanding of the nature of the problem and general agreement on preferred solutions. In addition to encouraging and even mandating cooperation, international law has provided the foundation for this understanding, delivering to States a common definition of trafficking as well as a set of basic obligations from which to work. In that sense, such networks generally operate parallel to, if not directly within, the normative and institutional structures created by international treaty law.

Of course, international cooperation and networking is not the exclusive domain of government officials. Some networks, such as those that have evolved around development cooperation and technical assistance, comprise officials and practitioners from government aid agencies, IGOs, and international NGOs. In the area of trafficking, these partnerships have been instrumental in capturing and disseminating international law-compliant good practice, as well as in facilitating the development of tools, resources, and training programs aimed at operationalizing international law and policy around trafficking.[105] Transnational human rights networks are generally conceived more narrowly as comprising domestic and international NGOs working on a range of fronts, including advocacy and development, but united in their promotion of universal norms. Such networks have long been identified as major sources of influence over the behavior of States and governments and thereby as an essential part of the machinery for compliance with international

---

[105] See, for example, the *International Framework for Action to Implement the Trafficking in Persons Protocol*, developed under the leadership of the UNODC but with the active participation of Anti-Slavery International; Council of Europe; End Child Prostitution, Child Pornography and Trafficking of Children for Sexual Purposes (ECPAT); International Organization for Migration (IOM); International Labour Organization (ILO); Intervention Centre for Victims of Trafficking in Women (LEFOE-IBF); Organization of American States (OAS); Organization for Security and Co-operation in Europe (OSCE); Terre des Hommes International Federation (TDHIF); The Protection Project, Johns Hopkins University School of Advanced International Studies; United Nations Division for the Advancement of Women/Department of Economic and Social Affairs (UNDAW/DESA); United Nations Children's Fund (UNICEF); United Nations Development Fund for Women (UNIFEM); United Nations High Commissioner for Refugees (UNHCR); United Nations Interregional Crime and Justice Research Institute (UNICRI); and the Office of the United Nations High Commissioner for Human Rights (OHCHR): available at http://www.unodc.org/documents/human-trafficking/Framework_for_Action_TIP.pdf (accessed Feb. 2, 2010). See also UN Office on Drugs and Crime, *Toolkit to Combat Trafficking in Persons*, UN Sales No. E.08.V.14 (2nd ed., 2009) (developed under UNODC leadership by a group of expert practitioners drawn from government agencies, NGOs, and intergovernmental organizations), available at http://www.unodc.org/documents/human-trafficking/Toolkit-files/07-89375_Ebook[1].pdf (accessed Feb. 2, 2010); and International Centre for Migration Policy Development, *Anti-Trafficking Training Materials for Judges and Prosecutors* (2006) (developed by a group of prosecutors and judges from eight European States with input from national and international NGOs and intergovernmental agencies), available at http://www.coehelp.org/mod/resource/view.php?inpopup=true&id=1650 (accessed Feb. 2, 2010).

human rights law.[106] In relation to trafficking, human rights networks played a critical role in shaping the international political and legal discourse. As explored further in this chapter, they have also taken on a leading role in promoting effective implementation of the international legal framework.

This section briefly considers the most prominent transnational networks in the area of trafficking: intergovernmental cooperation mechanisms focusing on criminal justice aspects of trafficking, and nongovernmental networks focusing on human rights aspects. While a full consideration of the functioning and prospects of these networks is beyond the scope of the present study, it is relevant to point out that the dualist criminal justice/human rights nature of the trafficking issue and the applicable legal framework is reflected in their structure and focus. At the informal as well as the formal level, there remains a strong sense of discord between the (State-preferred) criminal-justice-moderated-by-human-rights approach and the (NGO-preferred) approach that places human rights at the center of any response. While some hybrid networks have managed to bridge this divide, the perception of mutual incompatibility remains strong.

9.5.1. *Criminal Justice Networks*

Horizontal intergovernmental networks operating across national borders are becoming a prominent important feature of the criminal justice response to trafficking, with the potential to exercise considerable influence over normative development as well as in the socialization of key actors to international rules and standards. The impetus for the development of such networks is strong for reasons that go beyond the general incentives discussed above. First, cooperation with another State is often essential to the domestic investigation and prosecution of trafficking cases. Networks facilitate such cooperation by providing a safe forum for the exchange of information and intelligence between operational level officials who may otherwise have no chance to interact with each other. Second, from the perspective of national criminal justice agencies, trafficking is essentially a new crime, often involving new and untested laws. Even in the most responsive States, the number of investigations and prosecutions, although increasing, is still very low relative to the agreed size of the problem. Failure to implement international rules effectively can often say more about lack of capacity than lack of political will. No State can yet lay claim to genuine, extensive experience in dealing with trafficking as a criminal phenomenon. Most are developing and adapting their responses on the run, often under strong political pressure, and principally through trial and error. Cooperation

---

[106] The seminal text on transnational human rights networks is M.E. Keck and K. Sikkink, *Activists Beyond Borders: Advocacy Networks in International Politics* (1998). For a comprehensive review of scholarship in this area, see H.P. Schmitz, "Transnational Human Rights Networks: Significance and Challenges" (International Studies Association, 2009), available at http://www.isacompss.com/info/samples/transnationalhumanrightsnetworks_sample.pdf (accessed Feb. 2, 2010).

and cross-fertilization of ideas across national borders is an attractive proposition for many national criminal justice agencies, including those that require the additional resources that such networks can often attract.

In some cases, existing networks, such as the International Criminal Police Organization (Interpol), and mechanisms operating in related areas such as transnational organized crime have identified trafficking as an issue of focus or concern; accordingly, they have worked to promote coordination between States as well as to strengthen domestic law enforcement capacity in this area.[107] International law and policy around trafficking has also done much to encourage the establishment of dedicated criminal justice networks, in some cases, providing the framework within which they are established and operate. For example, the Organized Crime Convention and Trafficking Protocol both contain detailed provisions on international law enforcement and judicial cooperation.[108] While such cooperation has generally been low-level and sporadic, that situation is changing, particularly in the area of cross-border investigations. The emergence of specialist trafficking units within national police forces, widely identified as essential to the diligent investigation of trafficking cases,[109] has provided both a focal point and impetus for direct bilateral and multilateral contacts between investigators. In southeast Asia, for example, a region that generally shuns regional solutions to shared crime threats, the heads of the specialist trafficking investigation units (HSU) of ASEAN Member States have been meeting regularly since 2004 to review and progress specific operational investigations and to share case-based intelligence.[110] This development, characterized by the formation of strong interpersonal relationships nurtured through repeated interactions, has strengthened the capacity of the linked units to work together in identifying and effecting the rescue of previously unidentified victims, detaining suspects both in the country of origin and destination, and securing high-quality evidence relating to these crimes.[111]

More importantly from the present perspective, the HSU network has developed or contributed to a range of tools and resources that incorporate, actively promote,

---

[107] See, for example, International Criminal Police Organization (Interpol), "Trafficking in Human Beings," OM/FS/2009–12/THB-02 (2009), available at http://www.interpol.int/Public/ICPO/FactSheets/THB02.pdf (accessed Feb. 3, 2010).

[108] Organized Crime Convention, at Arts. 19, 27–28; Trafficking Protocol, at Art. 10.

[109] See, for example, European Trafficking Convention, at Art. 29; UN Trafficking Principles and Guidelines, at Guideline 5.4; Association of Southeast Asian Nations (ASEAN), *Criminal Justice Responses to Trafficking in Persons – ASEAN Practitioner Guidelines* (Jakarta, 2007) (ASEAN Practitioner Guidelines), at Guideline B.1; International Criminal Police Organization (INTERPOL), *Trafficking in Human Beings: Best Practice Guidance Manual for Investigators* (2nd ed. 2007), at chapter 2.7.

[110] Association of Southeast Asian Nations (ASEAN), *ASEAN Responses to Trafficking in Persons: Ending Impunity for Traffickers and Securing Justice for Victims: Update and Supplement* (2007) (2008), available at http://www.artipproject.org/artip-tip-cjs/resources/specialised_publications/ASEAN%20Responses%20to%20TIP%20Study_Supplement_2007.pdf (accessed Feb. 2, 2010).

[111] See further, A.T. Gallagher and P. Holmes, "Law Enforcement Cooperation in Anti-Trafficking Cases," presentation given at Crossing Borders: Promoting Regional Law Enforcement Cooperation,

and occasionally extend the reach of international norms related to trafficking, including: the use of the internationally agreed-upon definition; due diligence in investigations and prosecutions; protection of victims and victim-witnesses; no prosecution for status-related offenses; and adequate and proportionate sanctions.[112] The HSU network has also influenced ASEAN policy on trafficking including its endorsement of many of these norms in softer but much more specific form. An example is provided by the ASEAN Practitioner Guidelines on an Effective Criminal Justice Response to Trafficking in Persons, developed by an *ad hoc* network of criminal justice officials from all ten ASEAN Member States in 2007 (which subsequently morphed into a standing committee of practitioners and policy makers)[113] and endorsed by ASEAN itself later that same year.[114] HSU members have recently been requested by ASEAN Member States to provide their views on a proposal for an ASEAN treaty on trafficking.[115]

Unlike other regions, criminal justice networks in Europe have a long history and are well established.[116] The unique political geography of Europe and the convergence of crime control laws, policies, and practices have been especially important factors in promoting the development of professional networks, particularly at the level of law enforcement. The European Trafficking Convention and the EU Framework Decision on Trafficking together provide a robust framework for the extension of this strong tradition to the area of trafficking in persons.[117] The European Police Office (Europol), the European police network created to provide a central mechanisms for cooperation and communication among EU police agencies and recently upgraded to a formal entity of the European Union,[118] is mandated to prevent and combat, among other crime types, "trafficking in human beings" as defined in international law.[119] Europol plays a significant role in cross-border investigations of trafficking as well as contributing to the development of common operational standards.[120] The establishment of a network of prosecutors through the

Australian National University, Canberra, Apr. 8, 2009, available at http://works.bepress.com/anne_gallagher/8 (accessed Feb. 2, 2010).

[112] Ibid.

[113] ASEAN, Working Group on Trafficking in Persons, Senior Officials Meeting on Transnational Crime (SOMTC).

[114] ASEAN Practitioner Guidelines.

[115] ASEAN, Minutes of the First Meeting of the Working Group on Trafficking in Persons, Senior Officials Meeting on Transnational Crime (SOMTC), Kuala Lumpur, June 16, 2008.

[116] See Andreas and Nadelmann, *Policing the Globe*, esp. at 59–104, 174–188 and 237–240.

[117] Generally on these instruments, see Chapter 2.3 in this volume. Specifically on their provisions with respect to international criminal justice cooperation, see Chapter 7.5 of this volume.

[118] Council Decision of 6 April 2009 establishing the European Police Office (Europol) (2009/371/JHA), OJ L 121/37, May 15, 2009.

[119] Ibid. at Art. 4(1) and Annex.

[120] See generally, European Police Office (Europol), *Annual Report 2008* (2009), at 18–19, available at http://www.europol.europa.eu/publications/Annual_Reports/Annual%20Report%202008.pdf (accessed Feb. 3, 2010); and European Police Office (Europol), "Trafficking in Human Beings in the EU: A Europol Perspective," June 2009, available at http://www.europol.europa.eu/publications/

Eurojust entity with a mandate to deal with trafficking in persons,[121] the creation of a Europe-wide arrest warrant which is valid throughout the European Union and applicable to people-trafficking cases,[122] and the abolition of the principle of dual criminality in relation to human trafficking offenses[123] have all provided further impetus to the development of specialized professional networks within Europe that work to translate international norms related to trafficking into operational directives and to promote their effective implementation.

It is relevant to note that given the often complex transnational nature of trafficking and related offenses, functional and effective criminal justice networks can play a key part in fulfilling international legal obligations (including those derived from human rights standards), such as the obligation to conduct effective investigations. This point was highlighted in a recent decision of the European Court of Human Rights, which held that "member States are ... subject to a duty in cross-border trafficking cases to cooperate effectively with the relevant authorities of other States concerned in the investigation of events which occurred outside their territories."[124] In that case, the Court found that the obligation to investigate a trafficking-related death had been violated because, *inter alia*, the State of destination failed to seek assistance from the State of origin under an existing mutual legal assistance regime.[125]

9.5.2. *Human Rights Networks*

As noted at various points in this book, the role of international human rights networks in promoting international awareness, shaping international attitudes, and generating trafficking-related norms has been substantial.[126] Their potential capacity to contribute to the effective implementation of the international legal framework around this issue (and less positively, to distort that same framework for their own policy ends)[127] is equally significant. Already, specialist and generalist human rights

---

Serious_Crime_Overviews/Trafficking%20in%20Human%20Beings%20June%202009.pdf (accessed Feb. 3, 2010).

[121] Established by Council Decision of 28 February 2002 setting up Eurojust with a view to reinforcing the fight against serious crime (2002/187/JHA), OJ L 063/1, Mar. 6, 2002. For an overview of the Eurojust mission and its mandate with respect to trafficking, see Eurojust, *Trafficking in Human Beings: The State of Affairs* (2005),

[122] Council Framework Decision of 13 June 2002 on the European arrest warrant and the surrender procedures between Member States (2002/584/JHA), OJ L 190/1, July 18, 2002; see further R. Blextoon and W. van Ballegooij eds., *Handbook on the European Arrest Warrant* (2005).

[123] Council Framework Decision of 19 July 2002 on combating trafficking in human beings (2002/629/JHA), OJ L 203/1, Aug. 1, 2002, at Art. 2(2).

[124] *Rantsev v. Cyprus and Russia*, at para. 289.

[125] Ibid. at para. 241.

[126] For a more detailed analysis of this aspect in the context of legal and policy developments related to trafficking the European Union, see B. Locher, *Trafficking in the European Union: Norms, Advocacy-Networks and Policy-Change* (2007).

[127] An example is provided by transnational networks committed to the elimination of prostitution. Commentators have persuasively argued that these networks have operated to distort the

organizations are actively involved in exposing trafficking-related violations – utilizing international rules and standards to identify failures on the part of States to discharge their legal obligations, particularly with regard to victim protection, support and noncriminalization.[128] In some cases, these networks have moved beyond reactive shaming strategies by involving themselves in the development of "solutions" at both national and international levels such as legislative reform, institutional capacity development, support to victims, and activism aimed at addressing vulnerabilities to trafficking.[129] NGOs and human rights activists have even begun to play an important role in international adjudication around trafficking.[130] Interaction with intergovernmental networks that base their work on the international legal framework agencies can operate to increase the capacity of transnational human rights networks to promote accountability, as well as to contribute, more directly, to improving compliance with international rules and standards.[131]

One relatively unexplored variety of transnational human rights network is that comprised of national human rights institutions. Particularly since the late 1990s, many States have established statutory bodies such as commissions and ombudsman offices to promote implementation of international human rights obligations. In most cases, these institutions are granted a measure of independence from the government that directly contributes to their ability to monitor and promote human rights. In addition, the majority of functioning national institutions are also empowered to undertake investigations into violations of human rights, either on

international legal framework around trafficking in an effort to support a global prohibition on trafficking. See, for example, J. Chuang, "Rescuing Trafficking from Ideological Capture: Anti-Prostitution Reform and Its Influence on U.S. Anti-Trafficking Law and Policy," forthcoming, draft paper presented at the Columbia Law School, Center for Gender and Sexuality Law, Feminist Theory Workshops, Dec. 8, 2009, http://www2.law.columbia.edu/faculty_franke/FTW2009/Chuang%20Paper.pdf (accessed Feb. 2, 2010).

[128] See, for example, Global Alliance Against Trafficking in Women, *Collateral Damage: The Impact of Anti-Trafficking Measures on Human Rights Around the World* (2007).

[129] An international example is provided by the mandated involvement of international NGOs in the implementation machinery of the European Trafficking Convention (see Chapter 9.2.2). A further international example is provided by the involvement of an NGO coalition in debates on a potential monitoring mechanism for the Trafficking Protocol: Global Alliance Against Trafficking in Women and Others, "Statement on a Monitoring Mechanism for the United Nations Convention against Transnational Organized Crime and Each of the Protocols Thereto with Specific Attention to the Protocol to Prevent, Suppress and Punish Trafficking in Persons (the Human Trafficking Protocol)," Oct. 13, 2009, available at http://www.gaatw.org/statements/Statement_on_a_Monitoring_Mechanism-COPS08.pdf (accessed Feb. 2, 2010).

[130] For example, both Interights and the AIRE Centre were third party interveners in *Rantsev v. Cyprus and Russia*. Their submissions were quoted extensively in the judgment. The Litigation Director of Interights was co-counsel in a case involving consideration of slavery before the ECOWAS Court. (*Koraou v. Republic of Niger*, Judgment No. ECW/CCJ/JUD/06/08, ECOWAS Community Court of Justice, Oct. 27, 2008). See her analysis of the decision: H. Duffy, "*Hadijatou Mani Koroua v Niger*: Slavery Unveiled by the ECOWAS Court," (2009) 9 *Human Rights Law Review* 151. A representative of the French NGO *Comité Contre L'Esclavage Moderne* was co-counsel in *Siliadan v. France*, (2006) 43 EHRR 16 (ECHR, July 26, 2005)

[131] See, for example, the agencies at note 105 to this chapter.

the basis of individual complaints or on their own initiative.[132] The former UN High Commissioner for Human Rights, Mary Robinson, identified national commissions as "an under-utilized resource in the fight against trafficking"[133] and urged these bodies to take a more active role in promoting State responsibility and account-ability for trafficking and related exploitation. This theme was picked up in the UN Trafficking Principles and Guidelines. The Principles and Guidelines highlight the important role of national institutions in monitoring the human rights impact of antitrafficking laws, policies, programs, and interventions as well as in the develop-ment, adoption, implementation, and review of antitrafficking legislation, policies, and programs that are in conformity with international legal standards.[134]

The capacity of national human rights institutions to promote effective implemen-tation of international law has been strengthened by the establishment of networks at both international and regional levels. The International Coordinating Committee of National Institutions for the Protection and Promotion of Human Rights (ICC) brings together leaders and practitioners from all national institutions that have been "accredited" as complying with the relevant standards of independence, mandate, and competence.[135] Full accreditation enables individual institutions and their net-work representatives to participate in the UN Human Rights Council, with privi-leges that go well beyond those granted to other non-State bodies.[136] While the ICC network has not engaged deeply on the issue of trafficking, its high-profile regional partner, the Asia Pacific Forum of National Human Rights Institutions (APF), has been extremely active.[137] Even before the issue gained true international currency,

---

[132] For an overview of the nature and structure of national human rights institutions, including their role in monitoring the implementation of international human rights law, see B. Burdekin and A.T. Gallagher, "The United Nations and National Human Rights Institutions," in G. Alfredsson et al. eds., *International Human Rights Monitoring Mechanisms: Essays in Honour of Jakob Th. Moller* 815 (2001). On the specific issue of cooperation between national human rights institutions and the UN human rights treaty bodies, see A.T. Gallagher, "Making Human Rights Treaty Obligations a Reality at the National Level: Identifying and Working with New Actors and Partners," in P. Alston and J. Crawford eds., *The Future of UN Human Rights Treaty Monitoring* 201 (1999). For an analysis of the impact of national human rights institutions on regional policy and institution-building, see A. Durbach, C. Renshaw and A. Byrnes, "'A Tongue But No Teeth'? The Emergence of a Regional Human Rights Mechanism in the Asia-Pacific," (2009) 31 *Sydney Law Review* 211.

[133] United Nations High Commissioner for Human Rights, address to the International Coordinating Committee of National Institutions for the Promotion and Protection of Human Rights, Geneva, 1999 (copy on file with the author).

[134] UN Trafficking Principles and Guidelines, at Guideline 1.

[135] Those standards are set out in the Principles relating to the Status of National Institutions for the Protection and Promotion of Human Rights (the Paris Principles), endorsed by the United Nations General Assembly in "National Institutions for the Promotion and Protection of Human Rights," UN Doc. A/RES/48/134, Dec. 20, 1993.

[136] For example, the right to submit documentation to the Council, to make oral interventions and to organize parallel events. See further references at UN Human Rights Council, "Information for National Human Rights Institutions," http://www2.ohchr.org/english/bodies/hrcouncil/nhri.htm (accessed Feb. 2, 2010).

[137] For an analysis of the Asia Pacific Forum's composition, work, and impact, see A. Byrnes, A. Durbach and C. Renshaw, "Joining the Club: the Asia Pacific Forum of National Human Rights Institutions,

the APF and its members were working on identifying ways in which national institutions could influence the domestic political agenda on trafficking using international human rights law. In 2000, APF referred the issue of trafficking and international law for consideration to its Advisory Council of Jurists.[138] The resulting report paved the way for APF to articulate a position that affirms trafficking as a violation of human rights and confirms the international legal responsibility of States to take action to prevent and suppress trafficking. The report identifies specific obligations of States under international law, including the obligations to criminalize trafficking and provide for appropriate penalties; to investigate and prosecute trafficking with due diligence; to assist and protect trafficked persons; to provide trafficked persons with access to remedies; and to provide special measures for the identification and treatment of trafficked children. APF has also asserted that States are under an obligation to ensure that their responses to trafficking do not violate established rights of both victims and accused persons, including the right to a fair trial, the prohibition on arbitrary detention, and the prohibition on discrimination.[139] As with the work of other networks, it is not easy to identify those changes in State behavior that are directly attributable to the APF.[140] It is nevertheless not unreasonable to suggest that APF has likely made a substantial contribution to the socialization of its members to relevant international norms, and thereby enhanced the internalization of those norms at the level of national law and policy. Anecdotal information may support this: National responses to trafficking in APF-member countries appear to reflect a relatively higher level of understanding of and compliance with international standards.[141]

the Paris Principles, and the Advancement of Human Rights Protection in the Region," (2008) 14 *Australian Journal of Human Rights* 63.

[138] The Advisory Council of Jurists (ACJ) was formally established by Asia Pacific Forum of National Human Rights Institutions (APF) in 1998 to serve as an international human rights law advisory panel to the APF. In 2001, APF member institutions decided to refer the issue of trafficking to the APF. The terms of reference specifically focused on the nature and scope of States' obligations under international law with regard to trafficking, including the issue of State responsibility. The ACJ's final report, "Consideration of the Issue of Trafficking: Final Report," Dec. 2002, is available at http://www.asiapacificforum.net/acj/references/trafficking/downloads/reference-on-trafficking/final_report.pdf (accessed Feb. 2, 2010). See also the background paper prepared on the issue: A.T. Gallagher, "Consideration of the Issue of Trafficking: Background Paper," Nov. 2002, available at http://www.asiapacificforum.net/acj/references/trafficking/downloads/reference-on-trafficking/background.pdf (accessed Feb. 2, 2010).

[139] In addition to the ACJ report cited above, see "Concluding Statement and Plan of Action," Regional Workshop on Human Trafficking and National Human Rights Institutions: Cooperating to End Impunity for Traffickers and to Secure Justice for Trafficked People, Sydney, Nov. 20–23, 2005, esp. at paras. 5, 10–11, available, with related documentation on trafficking, at http://www.asiapacificforum.net/services/training/regional-workshops/trafficking (accessed Feb. 2, 2010).

[140] For an overview of APF member institution responses to trafficking, see Global Alliance Against Trafficking in Women, *Rights in Practice: A Report on National Human Rights Institution's (NHRIs) work to Evaluate and Monitor State Anti-Trafficking Responses in the Association of South-East Asian Nations (ASEAN) Area* (2009) (Global Alliance Against Trafficking in Women, *Rights in Practice*).

[141] See Global Alliance Against Trafficking in Women, *Rights in Practice*. See also the country analyses of Indonesia, Malaysia, Philippines, and Thailand in Association of Southeast Asian Nations

9.6. IMPROVING COMPLIANCE: ISSUES AND PROSPECTS

The compliance environment around trafficking reflects the complexity and elusiveness of the problem, and is driven by forces similar to those that have shaped the antitrafficking movement as a whole: different and often conflicting agendas; power imbalances; and strong competition for influence and control. This is cogently illustrated by the following extract from the September 2009 report of the expert body established to oversee implementation of the European Trafficking Convention:

> GRETA expressed concern regarding the recent tendency, developed by different international organisations to carry out monitoring of the implementation of national measures in the field of trafficking in human beings. In this respect GRETA pointed out that there was a need to safeguard the effectiveness of the monitoring machinery established by the Council of Europe Convention, a binding international instrument imposing strict legal obligations on State Parties. GRETA also pointed out that unnecessary duplication of monitoring operations might lead to inconsistent or contradictory conclusions with detrimental effects on the monitoring process: "forum shopping" and relinquishment of peer pressure. Above all, it may create confusion as to the binding or non-binding nature of the obligations of States in the field of trafficking in human beings and was likely to generate monitoring fatigue on the part of national authorities.[142]

It is possible that some of these grievances, for example those relating to duplication of effort and dilution of pressure, will be resolved over time as GRETA establishes itself as a source of authority capable of meeting the strong regional demand for accountability mechanisms. Normative confusion, while more difficult to deal with, is to be expected in an area as new and politicized as trafficking. Rather than inveighing against this situation, GRETA would be well advised to view it as an opportunity. A supervisory body committed to authoritative identification of obligation and responsibility, rather than vague pronouncements and inoffensive analysis, would provide a novel and much-needed addition to the existing compliance inventory.

(ASEAN), ASEAN *Responses to Trafficking in Persons: Ending Impunity for Traffickers and Securing Justice for Victims: Update and Supplement* (2007) (2008), available at http://www.artipproject.org/artip-tip-cjs/resources/specialised_publications/ASEAN%20Responses%20to%20TIP%20Study_Supplement_2007.pdf (accessed Feb. 2, 2010). For a perhaps overly optimistic view of the impact of the APF and its member institutions on national law and policy on trafficking, see C. Renshaw, "The Globalisation Paradox and the Implementation of International Human Rights: The Function of Transnational Networks in Combating Human Trafficking in the ASEAN Region," paper presented to the Law and Society Association Australia and New Zealand (LSAANZ) Conference: W(h)ither Human Rights, Sydney, Dec. 10–12, 2008.

[142] Committee of the Parties, Council of Europe Convention on Action against Trafficking in Human Beings, "3rd Meeting of the Committee of the Parties (Strasbourg, 22–25 September 2008): List of Items Discussed and Decisions Taken," THB-CP(2009)LD3, Sept. 25, 2009, at para. 8.

It is of course important to acknowledge that in this area of international law as in many others, the situation in western Europe is different from the rest of the world. The States Parties to the European Trafficking Convention will shortly be subject to ongoing performance review of the most constructive and supportive variety. The existence of other European bodies with jurisdiction and capacity to engage on the issue of trafficking (for example, the European Court of Human Rights) could well exert a further compliance "pull" on Member States of the European Union. In contrast, formal compliance mechanisms operating at the international level can be expected to remain limited in scope and severely constrained in their capacity to actively encourage conformity with international legal rules.

As noted throughout this chapter, formal treaty-based mechanisms are just one part of the picture and the compliance effects of less structured groupings and processes must also be taken into account. Transnational networks and domestic constituencies have already contributed substantially to the socialization process through which States internalize trafficking-related norms that have been generated at the international level. That process will likely continue and gain momentum as networks grow and diversify. Indeed, it is not impossible to imagine that the space created by the absence of strong monitoring and evaluation structures at the international level will provide these less traditional compliance forces with new opportunities for leverage and influence. That same gap may also encourage intergovernmental organizations, aid agencies, and others to generate innovative strategies aimed at building the capacity of States to improve their compliance with international legal rules.[143]

By choosing its words very carefully, GRETA adroitly avoided any mention of the elephant in the room – the U.S. Department of State. As noted above, the reporting and sanctioning system created and administered by the U.S. government has fundamentally altered the rules of the compliance game. For example, by choosing to apply its own standards rather than internationally accepted legal norms, the United States has been able to determine the criteria against which international compliance for all States is being measured. This may well contribute to a global and national-level acculturation of norms that are qualitatively distinct from those established by international law. Other effects are likely to be even more profound: A mechanism of this strength and influence cannot exist outside the international system without fundamentally altering that system at every level. Scholars of compliance in the area of international environmental law have noted that external enforcement of this variety may enhance the effectiveness of an international regime by preventing damaging violations, but could just as easily (and even at the same time) undermine

---

[143] This is already apparent with respect to the Trafficking Protocol. The lack of a performance review mechanism for that instrument has led to the development of a range of assessment tools for the use of States, IGOs, and NGOs (see note 40 to this chapter). Technical assistance to States aimed at promoting compliance with the Trafficking Protocol is also extensive and growing rapidly.

that regime's legitimacy. Critically, the determinative factor seems to be the level of congruence between international law and the enforcement actions:

> If external enforcement takes place within the boundaries set by international law, while at the same time adding significantly to the deterrent effect of a regime's internal consequences, it is likely to enhance compliance without necessarily being detrimental to the regime's legitimacy. Although the best option of all is likely to be an internal system that is both effective and fair, a second best option may be external enforcement in accordance with the dictates of international law.[144]

In relation to trafficking, neither choice appears to be within easy reach. It remains to be seen whether any of the alternative structures and processes identified in this chapter will be able to mount a serious challenge to the current situation.

---

[144] J. Hovi, "The Pros and Cons of External Enforcement," in O.S. Stokke, J. Hovi and G. Ulfstein eds., *Implementing the Climate Regime: International Compliance* 129 (2005), at 141.

Epilogue

In January 2010, the European Court of Human Rights found that Cyprus and Russia had incurred international legal responsibility with respect to the death, in Cyprus, of a Russian national and probable victim of trafficking, and that they were therefore liable in damages.[1] Although the victim's death and likely exploitation were not attributed to Cyprus or Russia, both States were held to have violated related human rights obligations, specifically through failure to regulate employment and through inaction in the face of private conduct. These violations arose through failure to carry out an effective investigation into the death (including securing the relevant evidence from overseas as well as domestically, and investigating whether there had been any trafficking-related corruption); failure to ensure that the migration regime itself afforded protection against trafficking; and failure to investigate trafficking. The Court held that "national legislation must be adequate to ensure the practical and effective protection of the rights of victims or potential victims of trafficking."[2] It explained that in addition to criminal law measures to punish traffickers, Member States are also required to "put in place adequate measures regulating businesses often used as a cover for human trafficking,"[3] and to ensure their immigration rules "address relevant concerns relating to encouragement, facilitation or tolerance of trafficking."[4] In reaching its decision, the Court went beyond the European Convention on Human Rights[5] to examine the provisions of a range of specialist instruments including the Trafficking Protocol,[6] the European Trafficking Convention,[7] and the European Convention on Mutual Assistance in Criminal Matters.[8]

---

[1] *Rantsev v. Cyprus and Russia*, Dec. No. 25965/04 (not yet reported) (ECHR, Jan. 7, 2010).

[2] Ibid. at para 284.

[3] Ibid.

[4] Ibid.

[5] Convention for the Protection of Human Rights and Fundamental Freedoms, 213 UNTS 222, done Nov. 4, 1950, entered into force Sept. 3, 1953.

[6] Protocol to Prevent, Suppress and Punish Trafficking in Persons, Especially Women and Children, supplementing the United Nations Convention against Transnational Organized Crime, done Nov. 15, 2000, GA Res. 55/25, Annex II, UN GAOR, 55th Sess., Supp. No. 49, at 53, UN Doc. A/45/49 (Vol. I) (2001), entered into force Dec. 25, 2003 (Trafficking Protocol).

[7] Council of Europe Convention on Action against Trafficking in Human Beings and its Explanatory Report, ETS 197, 16.V.2005, done May 16, 2005, entered into force Feb. 1, 2008.

[8] European Convention on Mutual Assistance in Criminal Matters, 472 UNTS 185, ETS No. 30, done April 20, 1959, entered into force June 12, 1962.

This book has sought to document and analyze the significant body of law that now applies to the issue of human trafficking. It has demonstrated that States are obliged, as a matter of law, to take particular steps with respect to preventing trafficking, protecting and supporting victims, and prosecuting perpetrators. It has shown how and why a failure to fulfill those obligations will incur the international legal responsibility of the delinquent State. Like the judgment of the European Court summarized in the opening, this is not a book that could have been written even as recently as ten years earlier. In 2000, the year the Trafficking Protocol was adopted, there was no international legal definition of trafficking and no political consensus on the nature of the problem. Apart from a few vague and rarely invoked treaty references, there was very little in the way of tangible obligation. At the national level, only a small handful of States specifically prohibited the process by which individuals were moved into and maintained in situations of exploitation at home or abroad. Slavery and related practices were certainly outlawed in almost every State, but these laws, like their international equivalents, were almost never invoked – certainly not against the exploitative practices such as forced labor, child labor, or debt bondage that are the hallmarks of contemporary exploitation. International scrutiny of State actions with respect to such exploitation was extremely limited and ineffectual.

In the short space of a decade, this situation has changed dramatically and irreversibly. The overwhelming majority of States are now parties to one or more treaties that set out, with an exceptional level of particularity and detail, their obligations with respect to the prevention of trafficking, the protection of victims, and the investigation and prosecution of perpetrators. In response to their new international legal obligations and associated pressures, most States have now enacted comprehensive anti-trafficking laws. The majority of these laws are modeled on the definition of trafficking provided by the Trafficking Protocol and, accordingly, most now cover the full range of exploitative purposes set out in that instrument. As such, they provide an additional avenue through which existing human rights prohibitions of related practices, such as those on slavery, servitude, forced labor, and child sexual exploitation, taking place within as well as across national borders, can be implemented. Even though most, if not all, of these laws fall short of the standards identified in this book, certain positive trends can be identified. For example, many laws now mandate the provision of protection and support to victims, including, at least in principle, access to remedies. Often, statutory reforms have been undertaken in the context of a broader national plan that seeks to address the various factors that contribute to trafficking-related vulnerabilities; to strengthen criminal justice institutions and procedures; and to secure justice for those who have been exploited. International, regional, and even unilateral monitoring of responses to trafficking and related exploitation has never been as widespread or as intense. Every State, including those few that have remained outside the major specialist treaties, is now subject to comprehensive scrutiny.

Although remarkable when viewed in historical perspective, these advances are nevertheless fundamentally constrained in terms of both vision and effect. Compliance theory usefully reminds us that compliance is not, in the end, the same thing as effectiveness. States are able to record relatively high and improving levels of conformity with international legal rules related to trafficking in large part because those rules, in the end, do not demand a great deal. They request but do not demand that States take positive action to address the root causes of trafficking, not least "the merciless Moloch of capitalism that fattens on underpaid labour."[9] They acknowledge the link between trafficking and the labor migration that greases the wheels of the global economy without requiring States to provide individuals with safe and legal avenues through which to move. They affirm the principle of non-discrimination without insisting that the rules, attitudes, and practices that render women, children, and migrants most vulnerable to trafficking-related exploitation be immediately and comprehensively dismantled. It is currently possible for a State to find itself within the letter, if not the spirit, of its international legal obligations merely by criminalizing trafficking, diligently investigating cases that come to its attention, cooperating with other States when requested, and taking at least some measures to support and protect identified victims. While the present study has succeeded in fleshing out these basic obligations, they do not, even in expanded form, amount to terribly much. Like a commitment to halt anthropogenic climate change by imposing emission reductions that have, in truth, no hope of meeting that goal, there is a fatal gap between what is legally required of States and what is actually needed to reach the stated objective. A genuine commitment to ending trafficking requires one to both acknowledge and challenge the limitations of the contemporary international legal imagination.

Other obstacles and difficulties are of a more immediate and earthly variety. Even from the narrow perspective of vastly improved international minimum standards, it is clear that responses to trafficking and related exploitation continue to be inadequate, incomplete, and sometimes, particularly from the perspective of human rights, immensely problematic. For example, measures taken in the name of addressing trafficking and related exploitation often have highly adverse impact on individual rights and freedoms. Evidence-based examples identified throughout this book include detention of trafficked persons in immigration or shelter facilities; prosecution of trafficked persons for status-related offenses including illegal entry, illegal stay, and illegal work; denial of exit or entry visas or permits; raids, rescues, and "crackdowns" without full consideration of and protection for the rights of individuals involved; forced repatriation of victims in danger of reprisals or retrafficking; conditional provision of support and assistance; denial of a right to a remedy; and violations of the rights of persons suspected or convicted of involvement in

9   E. Goldman, "The Traffic in Women," in E. Goldman, *Anarchism and other Essays* 183 (1917), at 184.

trafficking and related offenses, including unfair trials and inappropriate sentencing. Responses to trafficking and related practices such as forced labor and commercial sexual exploitation can also operate to reinforce detrimental gender-based – and
even racial – stereotypes, setting back efforts to counter entrenched discrimination.
Oversight of such "collateral damage" by the major compliance mechanisms is generally very poor. In this area of international law, as in many others, the *existence* or
intention of policies and laws is invariably judged to be more important than their
impact.

Even where strong laws and institutions are in place, the attitudinal shifts required
to deliver justice, protection, and support to those who have been exploited are often
frustratingly slow. Criminal justice officials, for example, find it difficult to change
the way they think about and act toward individuals who have traditionally been
identified more as criminals than as victims of crime. Governments are uniformly
reluctant to engage in what must inevitably be an uncomfortable and confront-
ing discussion about the demand that nurtures trafficking. These challenges are,
of course, part of a much broader problem. Many States experience great difficulty
in maintaining and fulfilling a legal and policy commitment to supporting and
protecting victims of trafficking when, as a matter of reality, the beneficiaries of that
commitment exist at the margins of social acceptability and political relevance. In
other words, whereas international commitment is cheap, implementation of international legal obligations can be much more expensive in domestic political terms.
This situation exacerbates the rhetoric/reality gap that is already such a problem
in international human rights law. Of course, there sometimes also exists a genuine incompatibility between different policy goals. Conflicting State interests – for
example, in maintaining a largely foreign and compliant sex industry, or a cheap and
disempowered sector of the labor market – can be inimical to effective action. Such
conflicts and their impact on the nature and level of States' engagement with the
international law of trafficking are rarely spoken of and even more rarely explored.

These difficulties are fundamentally connected to the controversial and politicized environment within which the international legal framework around trafficking has developed. It should come as no surprise to discover that some States, aided
and abetted by civil society groups and activists, have taken advantage of the global
momentum against trafficking to wage their own wars against perceived social
harms such as illegal migration or prostitution. Trafficking has also proved useful to
States, criminal justice agencies, and others interested in extending their power and
influence within and across national borders and, more generally, to the growing
industry involved in combating transnational organized crime. Many commentators have decried such rampant and unselfconscious opportunism, some even to the
point of rejecting any "international law" of trafficking on the basis of its dangerous
vulnerability to unfavorable manipulation. Such views are unnecessarily parochial
and defeatist. The inevitability of special interests and hidden agendas (and even

of unintended consequences) is a poor reason to reject the corpus of rules that has developed around trafficking. It is also disingenuous in the extreme to deny the link between trafficking and migration, or trafficking and the global sex industry. A scholarship of integrity, questioning, and genuine inquiry will not be afraid to acknowledge and explore these links, confident that the legal framework is strong enough to withstand attempts at misrepresentation or distortion.

Such a scholarship will also be open to the possibility that misuse of the legal framework is not just a problem involving recalcitrant States and reactionary NGOs. As noted in the introduction to this book, legal writers and practitioners all too often fall into the trap of confusing moral and legal claims, ignoring the distinction between the "is" and the "ought" of international law. Any short-term gains secured this way are likely to be heavily compromised, their worth outweighed by the damage inevitably wreaked on the predictability, authority, and utility of international law.

The highly charged environment around trafficking should, on balance, be considered more as an opportunity than a liability. This environment has, after all, provided the impetus for a suite of legal and institutional developments that are unprecedented, not just in terms of the speed and scale of their evolution, but also in the extent of their impact on the behavior of States. The elaboration of a conceptual and legal framework around trafficking has, in turn, been crucial in shifting the parameters of the debate around private exploitation, providing both space and structure for the development of new ideas and the constructive challenging of old, tired ones. Of course, this framework remains fragile and incomplete. In looking toward the future, a consent-based vision of international law cannot ignore the overriding challenge of political will. States are unwilling to commit themselves to the level of change required to fundamentally alter the trafficking dynamic because they do not perceive such changes to be in their interest. It is therefore necessary to accept that at least for the foreseeable future, improvements to the international legal framework will likely be slow and incremental. This should not be reason for despair. This book has shown that international law in its present state of development is eminently capable of being used to identify obligations and hold States to account for violation of established rules. One can hope that, over the longer term, it may also play a "civilizing" role in shaping State perception of obligation, responsibility, and self-interest.[10]

---

[10] This concept of international law as a "gentle civilizer of national self-interest" is taken from M. Koskenniemi, *The Gentle Civilizer of Nations: The Rise and Fall of International Law 1870–1960* (2001).

Select Bibliography

1. Books

Allain, J., *The Slavery Conventions: The* Travaux Préparatoires *of the 1926 League of Nations Convention and the 1956 United Nations Convention* (2008, Martinus Nijhoff).

Andreas, P., and E. Nadelmann eds., *Policing the Globe: Criminalisation and Crime Control in International Relations* (2006, Oxford University Press).

Askola, H., *Legal Responses to Trafficking in Women for Sexual Exploitation in the European Union* (2007, Oxford University Press).

Bales, K., *Disposable People: New Slavery in the Global Economy* (2004, University of California Press).

   Ending Slavery: How We Free Today's Slaves (2007, University of California Press).

   The Slave Next Door: Human Trafficking and Slavery in America Today (2009, University of California Press).

   Understanding Global Slavery: A Reader (2005, University of California Press).

Barry, K., *Female Sexual Slavery* (1979, rev. 1984, New York University Press).

Bassiouni, M.C. and E.M. Wise, Aut Dedere Aut Judicare: *The Duty to Extradite or Prosecute in International Law* (1995, Martinus Nijhoff).

Beare, M.E. ed., *Critical Reflections on Transnational Organized Crime, Money Laundering and Corruption* (2003, University of Toronto Press).

Beeks, K.D., and D. Amir eds., *Trafficking and the Global Sex Industry* (2006, Lexington Books).

Benninger-Budel, C. ed., *Due Diligence and Its Application to Protect Women from Violence* (2008, Martinus Nijhoff).

Birnie, P., A. Boyle and C. Redgwell, *International Law and the Environment* (2009, Oxford University Press).

Blextoon, R., and W. van Ballegooij eds., *Handbook on the European Arrest Warrant* (2005, Cambridge University Press).

Bossuyt, M.J., *Guide to the* Travaux Préparatoires *of the International Covenant on Civil and Political Rights* (1987, Martinus Nijhoff).

Brownlie, I., *Principles of Public International Law* (2008, Oxford University Press).

de Brouwer, A.-M. *Supranational Criminal Prosecution of Sexual Violence: The ICC and the Practice of the ICTY and ICTR* (2005, Intersentia).

Burgstaller, M., *Theories of Compliance with International Law* (2005, Martinus Nijhoff).

Butler, J.E., *Personal Reminisces of a Great Crusade* (1911, Hyperion Press).

Cassese, A., *International Criminal Law* (2003, Oxford University Press).

Chang, G., *Disposable Domestics: Immigrant Women Workers in the Global Economy* (2002, South End Press).

Charlesworth, H., and C. Chinkin, *The Boundaries of International Law: A Feminist Analysis* (2000, Juris Publishing).

Cheng, B., *General Principles of Law as Applied by International Courts and Tribunals* (1987, Cambridge University Press).

Chinkin, C., and F. Banda, *Gender, Minorities, Indigenous People and Human Rights* (2004, Minority Rights Group).

Cholewinski, R., *Migrant Workers in International Human Rights Law: Their Protection in Countries of Employment* (1997, Clarendon Press).

Cholewinski, R., P. de Guchteneire and A. Pécoud eds., *Migration and Human Rights: The United Nations Convention on Migrant Workers' Rights* (2009, Cambridge University Press).

Cholewinski, R., R. Perruchoud and E. MacDonald eds., *International Migration Law: Developing Paradigms and Key Challenges* (2007, T.M.C. Asser).

Clapham, A., *Human Rights in the Private Sphere* (1996, Oxford University Press).

Human Rights Obligations of Non-State Actors (2006, Oxford University Press).

Clarke, R.S., *The United Nations Crime Prevention and Criminal Justice Program: Formulation of Standards and Efforts at Their Implementation* (1994, University of Pennsylvania Press).

Clawson, H., N. Dutch and M. Cummings, *Law Enforcement Responses to Human Trafficking and the Implications for Victims: Current Practices and Lessons Learned* (2006, Caliber).

Cohen, S., *Folk Devils and Moral Panics: The Creation of the Mods and Rockers* (2002, Routledge).

Connelly, M., *The Response to Prostitution in the Progressive Era* (1980, University of North Carolina Press).

Coomans, F., and M.T. Kamminga eds., *Extraterritorial Application of Human Rights Treaties* (2004, Intersentia).

Crawford, J., *The International Law Commission's Articles on State Responsibility: Introduction, Text and Commentaries* (2002, Cambridge University Press).

D'Amato, A., *The Concept of Custom in International Law* (1971, Cornell University Press).

Dauvergne, C., *Making People Illegal: What Globalization Means for Migration and Law* (2008, Cambridge University Press).

van Dijk, P., and G.J.H. van Hoof, *Theory and Practice of the European Convention on Human Rights* (1990, Kluwer Law International).

Dixon, M., *Textbook on International Law* (2007, Blackstone).

Doezema, J., *Sex Slaves and Discourse Masters: The Construction of Trafficking* (2010, Zed Books).

Dolgopol, U., and S. Paranjape, *Comfort Women: An Unfinished Ordeal* (1994, International Commission of Jurists).

Dorman, K., *Elements of War Crimes under the Rome Statute of the International Criminal Court: Sources and Commentary* (2003, Cambridge University Press).

Ehrenreich, B., and A. Hochschild eds., *Global Women: Nannies, Maids, and Sex Workers in the New Economy* (2003, Metropolitan Books).

Elias, T.O., *The International Court of Justice and Some Contemporary Problems: Essays on International Law* (1983, Martinus Nijhoff).

Feller, E., V. Türk and F. Nicholson eds., *Refugee Protection in International Law: UNHCR's Global Consultations on International Protection* (2003, Cambridge University Press).

Foster, M.M., *International Refugee Law and Socio-Economic Rights: Refuge from Deprivation* (2007, Cambridge University Press).

García-Amador, F. V., L. Sohn and R.R. Baxter, *Recent Codification of the Law of State Responsibility for Injuries to Aliens* (1974, Harvard University Press).

Ghosh, B. ed., *Managing Migration: Time for a New International Regime?* (2000, Oxford University Press).

Gibney, M.J., *The Ethics and Politics of Asylum: Liberal Democracy and the Response to Refugees* (2004, Cambridge University Press).

Grittner, F.K., *White Slavery: Myth, Ideology and American Law* (1990, Garland).

Guild, E., and P. Minderhoud eds., *Security of Residence and Expulsion: Protection of Aliens in Europe* (2001, Kluwer Law International).

Hannum, H., *The Right to Leave and Return in International Law and Practice* (1987, Martinus Nijhoff).

Harris, D.J., *Cases and Materials on International Law* (1991, Sweet & Maxwell).

Hathaway, J.C., *The Law of Refugee Status* (1991, Butterworths).
 The Rights of Refugees under International Law (2005, Cambridge University Press).

Henckaerts, J.-M., *Mass Expulsion in Modern Law and Practice* (1998, Martinus Nijhoff).

Henckaerts, J.-M., and L. Doswald-Beck, *Customary International Humanitarian Law* (2005, ICRC, Cambridge University Press).

Henkin, L., *International Law, Politics and Values* (1995, Martinus Nijhoff).

Higgins, R., *Problems and Process: International Law and How We Use It* (1994, Clarendon Press).

Inazumi, M., *Universal Jurisdiction in Modern International Law: Expansion of National Jurisdiction for Prosecuting Serious Crimes under International Law* (2005, Intersentia).

Jacobs, F.G., and R.C.A. White, *The European Convention on Human Rights* (1996, Oxford University Press).

Janis, M., *An Introduction to International Law* (2003, Little Brown).

Jeffries, S., *The Idea of Prostitution* (1997, Spinifex).

Jennings, R., and A. Watts eds., *Oppenheim's International Law* (1992, Longman Publishers).

Joseph, S., J. Schultz and M. Castan, *The International Covenant on Civil and Political Rights: Cases, Materials and Commentary* (2004, Oxford University Press).

Kälin, W., *The Annotations to the Guiding Principles on Internal Displacement* (2000, American Society of International Law, Brookings Project).

Kamminga, M.T., *Inter-State Accountability for Violations of Human Rights* (1992, University of Pennsylvania Press).

Keck, M.E., and K. Sikkink, *Activists Beyond Borders: Advocacy Networks in International Politics* (1998, Cornell University Press).

Klein, P., and P. Sands eds., *Bowett's Law of International Institutions* (2009, Sweet & Maxwell).

Kontou, N., *The Termination and Review of Treaties in the Light of New Customary International Law* (1994, Oxford University Press).

Koskenniemi, M., *The Gentle Civilizer of Nations: The Rise and Fall of International Law 1870–1960* (2001, Cambridge University Press).

Kuper, A. ed., *Global Responsibilities: Who Must Deliver on Human Rights?* (2005, Routledge).

Kyle, D., and R. Koslowski, *Global Human Smuggling: Comparative Perspectives* (2001, Johns Hopkins University Press).

Lillich, R. ed., *International Law of State Responsibility for Injury to Aliens* (1983, University Press of Virginia).

Locher, B., *Trafficking in the European Union: Norms, Advocacy-Networks and Policy-Change* (2007, VS Verlag).

McClean, D., *Transnational Organized Crime: A Commentary on the UN Convention and Protocols* (2007, Oxford University Press).

McKean, W., *Equality and Discrimination under International Law* (1983, Clarendon Press).

Mendelson, S.E., *Barracks and Brothels: Peacekeepers and Human Trafficking in the Balkans* (2005, Center for Strategic and International Studies).

Meron, T., *Human Rights and Humanitarian Norms as Customary Law* (1989, Clarendon Press).

Human Rights Law-Making in the United Nations (1986, Clarendon Press).

The Humanization of International Law (2006, Martinus Nijhoff).

Miers, S., *Britain and the Ending of the Slave Trade* (1975, Longman).

Slavery in the Twentieth Century: the Evolution of a Global Problem (2003, Altamira Press).

Montgomery, H., *Modern Babylon? Prostituting Children in Thailand* (2001, Berghahn Books).

Nicholls, C., C. Montgomery and J. Knowles, *The Law of Extradition and Mutual Assistance: Practice and Procedure* (2007, Oxford University Press).

Nowak, M., *UN Covenant on Civil and Political Rights: CCPR Commentary* (2005, N.P. Engel).

Obokata, T., *Trafficking of Human Beings from a Human Rights Perspective: Towards a Holistic Approach* (2006, Martinus Nijhoff).

Off, C., *Bitter Chocolate: Investigating the Dark Side of the World's Most Seductive Sweet* (2006, New Press).

Oishi, N., *Women in Motion: Globalization, State Policies and Labor Migration in Asia* (2005, Stanford University Press).

O'Connell Davidson, J., *Children in the Global Sex Trade* (2005, Polity).

O'Neill Richard, A., *International Trafficking in Women to the United States: A Contemporary Manifestation of Slavery and Organized Crime* (2000, Center for Study of Intelligence).

Oppenheim, L., *International Law: A Treatise* (1955, Longman Publishers).

Piper, N. ed., *New Perspectives on Gender and Migration: Livelihood, Rights and Entitlements* (2007, Routledge).

Provost, R., *International Human Rights and Humanitarian Law* (2002, Cambridge University Press).

Quirk, J., *Unfinished Business: A Comparative Survey of Historical and Contemporary Slavery* (2008, UNESCO).

Ragazzi, M., *The Concept of International Obligations Erga Omnes* (2000, Oxford University Press).

Rehof, L.A., *Guide to the Travaux Préparatoires of the Convention on the Elimination of All Forms of Discrimination against Women* (1993, Martinus Nijhoff).

Reichel, P. ed., *Handbook of Transnational Crime and Justice* (2005, Age Publications).

Rijken, C., *Trafficking in Persons: Prosecution from a European Perspective* (2003, T.M.C. Asser).

Savona, E.U., and S. Stefanizzi eds., *Measuring Human Trafficking* (2007, Springer).

Scarpa, S., *Trafficking in Human Beings: Modern Slavery* (2008, Oxford University Press).

Schabas, W., *The Abolition of the Death Penalty in International Law* (2002, Cambridge University Press).

The UN International Criminal Tribunals: The Former Yugoslavia, Rwanda and Sierra Leone (2006, Cambridge University Press).

Sepúlveda, M.M., *The Nature of the Obligations under the International Covenant on Economic, Social and Cultural Rights* (2003, Intersentia).

Shaw, M., *International Law* (2003, Cambridge University Press).

Shelton, D. ed., *Commitment and Compliance: The Role of Non-Binding Norms in the International Legal Process* (2003, Oxford University Press).

Shelton, D., *Remedies in International Human Rights Law* (2001, Oxford University Press).

Slaughter, A.-M., *A New World Order* (2004, Princeton University Press).

Tiburcio, C., *The Human Rights of Aliens under International and Comparative Law* (2001, Martinus Nijhoff).

Valticos, N., *International Labour Law* (1979, Kluwer Law International).

de Vattel, E., *The Law of Nations: Book III* (reprinted 1974, AMS Press).

Verzijl, J.H.W., *International Law in Historical Perspective* (1976, A.W. Sijthoff).

Villiger, M.E., *Commentary on the 1969 Vienna Convention on the Law of Treaties* (2009, University of California Press).

Walkowitz, J., *Prostitution and Victorian Society: Women, Class and the State* (1980, Cambridge University Press).

Walvin, J., *Black Ivory: A History of British Slavery* (2001, Blackwell).

Whitworth, S., *Men, Militarism and UN Peacekeeping* (2004, Lynne Rienner Publishers).

Wijers, M., and L. Lap-Chew, *Trafficking in Women, Forced Labour and Slavery-Like Practices in Marriage, Domestic Labour and Prostitution* (1997, The Foundation Against Trafficking in Women (STV)/The Global Alliance Against Trafficking in Women (GAATW)).

Wille, C., *Thailand-Laos People's Democratic Republic and Thailand-Myanmar Border Areas: Trafficking in Children into the Worst Forms of Child Labour, A Rapid Assessment* (2000, International Labour Organization, International Programme on the Elimination of Child Labour).

Williams, P. ed., *Illegal Immigration and Commercial Sex: The New Slave Trade* (1999, Frank Cass).

Wills, S., *Protecting Civilians: The Obligations of Peacekeepers* (2009, Oxford University Press).

2. Articles and Book Chapters

Abi-Saab, G., "The Uses of Article 19," (1999) 10 *European Journal of International Law* 339.

Akehurst, M., "Custom as a Source of International Law," (1975) 47 *British Yearbook of International Law* 1.

Akhavan, P., "The Crime of Genocide in the ICTR Jurisprudence," (2005) 3 *Journal of International Criminal Justice* 989.

Aleinikoff, T.A., "International Legal Norms on Migration: Substance Without Architecture," in R. Cholewinski, R. Perruchoud and E. MacDonald ed., *International Migration Law: Developing Paradigms and Key Challenges* 467 (2007, Cambridge University Press).

Ali, H.M., "Data Collection on Victims of Human Trafficking: An Analysis of Various Sources," (2010) 6(1) *Journal of Human Security* 55.

Alkoby, A., "Theories of Compliance with International Law and the Challenge of Cultural Difference," (2008) 4 *Journal of International Law and International Relations* 151.

Allain, J., "On the Curious Disappearance of Human Servitude from General International Law," (2009) 11 *Journal of the History of International Law* 25.

"Slavery – Positive Obligations – Nonapplicability of the Rule of Exhaustion of Domestic Remedies (*Koraou v. Republic of Niger*)," (2009) 103 *American Journal of International Law* 311.

Allott, P., "State Responsibility and the Unmaking of International Law," (1988) 29 *Harvard International Law Journal* 1.

Allred, K.J., "Combating Human Trafficking," (2006, Summer Issue) *NATO Review.*

"Peacekeepers and Prostitutes: How Deployed Forces Fuel the Demand for Trafficked Women and New Hope for Stopping It," in C. Friesendorf ed., *Strategies against Human Trafficking: The Role of the Security Sector* 299 (2009, Geneva Centre for the Democratic Control of Armed Forces).

Askin, K.D., "Prosecuting Wartime Rape and Other Gender-Related Crimes under International Law: Extraordinary Advances, Enduring Obstacles," (2003) 21 *Berkeley Journal of International Law* 288.

"Sexual Violence in Decisions and Indictments of the Yugoslav and Rwandan Tribunals: Current Status," (1999) 93 *American Journal of International Law* 97.

d'Aspremont, J., "Softness in International Law: A Self-Serving Quest for New Legal Materials," (2008) 19 *European Journal of International Law* 1075.

Ausserer, C., "'Control in the Name of Protection': A Critical Analysis of the Discourse of International Human Trafficking as a Form of Forced Migration," (2008) 4 *St Antony's International Review* 96.

Baker, R.B., "Customary International Law in the 21st Century: Old Challenges and New Debates," (2010) 21 *European Journal of International Law* 173.

Bales, K., and P.T. Robbins, "No One Shall Be Held in Slavery or Servitude: A Critical Analysis of International Slavery Agreements and Concepts of Slavery," (2001) 2 *Human Rights Review* 18.

Bassiouni, M.C., "Enslavement as an International Crime," (1991) 234 *New York Journal of International Law and Politics* 445.

"A Functional Approach to General Principles of International Law," (1990) 11 *Michigan Journal of International Law* 786.

"International Crimes: *Jus Cogens* and *Obligatio Erga Omnes*," (1996) 59 *Law and Contemporary Problems* 63.

"International Recognition of Victims' Rights," (2006) 6 *Human Rights Law Review* 203.

Bederman, D.J., "What's Wrong With International Legal Scholarship?" (2000) 1 *Chicago Journal of International Law* 75.

Bedont, B., "Gender Specific Provisions in the Statute of the International Criminal Court," in F. Lattanzi and W.A. Schabas eds., *Essays on the Rome Statute of the International Criminal Court: Volume 1* 183 (1999, Il Sirente).

Benninger-Budel, C., "Introduction," in C. Benninger-Budel ed., *Due Diligence and its Application to Protect Women from Violence* 1 (2008).

Berdal, M.R., and M. Serrano, "Introduction," in M.R. Berdal and M. Serrano eds., *Transnational Organized Crime and International Security: Business as Usual?* 1 (2002, Lynne Rienner Publishers).

Berman, J., "(Un)Popular Strangers and Crises (Un)Bounded: Discourses of Sex Trafficking, the European Political Community and the Panicked State of the Modern State," (2003) 9 *European Journal of International Relations* 37.

Beyers, M., "Conceptualizing the Relationship between *Jus Cogens* and *Erga Omnes* Rules," (1997) 66 *Nordic Journal of International Law* 211.

Bhabha, J., "Internationalist Gatekeepers? The Tension Between Asylum Advocacy and Human Rights," (2002) 15 *Harvard Human Rights Journal* 155.

Bohning, R., "The ILO and the New UN Convention on Migrant Workers: The Past and the Future," (1991) 25 *International Migration Review* 698.

Bosniak, L., "Human Rights, State Sovereignty and Protection of Undocumented Migrants under the International Migrant Workers Convention," (1991) 25 *International Migration Review* 737.

Bracka, J.M., "Past the Point of No Return? The Palestinian Right of Return in International Human Rights Law," (2005) 6 *Melbourne Journal of International Law* 272.

Bradford, W.C., "International Legal Compliance: Surveying the Field," (2005) 36 *Georgetown Journal of International Law* 495.

Brolan, C., "An Analysis of the Human Smuggling Trade and the Protocol Against the Smuggling of Migrants by Land, Air and Sea (2000) from a Refugee Protection Perspective," (2002) 14 *International Journal of Refugee Law* 561.

Brown Weiss, E., "Invoking State Responsibility in the Twenty-First Century," (2002) 96 *American Journal of International Law* 798.

Brown Weiss, E., and H.K. Jacobsen, "Getting Countries to Comply with International Agreements," (1999) 41 *Environment* 16.

Brownlie, I., "To What Extent are the Traditional Categories of Lex Lata and Lex Ferenda Still Viable?" in A. Cassese and J.H. Weiler eds., *Change and Stability in International Law-Making* 62 (1988, Oxford University Press).

Buckland, B.S., "Human Trafficking & Smuggling: Crossover & Overlap," in C. Friesendorf ed., *Strategies Against Human Trafficking: The Role of the Security Sector* 132 (2009, Geneva Centre for the Democratic Control of Armed Forces).

Burdekin, B., and A.T. Gallagher, "The United Nations and National Human Rights Institutions," in G. Alfredsson et al. eds., *International Human Rights Monitoring Mechanisms: Essays in Honour of Jakob Th. Moller* 815 (2001, Martinus Nijhoff).

Byrne, R., "Changing Paradigms in Refugee Law," in R. Cholewinski, R. Perruchoud and E. MacDonald eds., *International Migration Law: Developing Paradigms and Key Challenges* 163 (2007, T.M.C. Asser).

Byrnes, A., A. Durbach and C. Renshaw, "Joining the Club: The Asia Pacific Forum of National Human Rights Institutions, the Paris Principles, and the Advancement of Human Rights Protection in the Region," (2008) 14 *Australian Journal of Human Rights* 63.

Caron, D.D., "The ILC Articles on State Responsibility: The Paradoxical Relationship Between Form and Authority," (2002) 96 *American Journal of International Law* 857.

Cassese, A., "*Ex Iniuria Ius Oritur*: Are We Moving Towards International Legitimation of Forcible Humanitarian Countermeasures in the World Community?" (1999) 10 *European Journal of International Law* 23.

"The *Nicaragua* and *Tadic* Tests Revisited in Light of the ICJ Judgment on Genocide in Bosnia," (2007) 18 *European Journal of International Law* 649.

Cerna, C.M., "Impact on the Right to Consular Notification," in M.T. Kamminga and M. Scheinin eds., *The Impact of Human Rights on General International Law* 171 (2009, Oxford University Press).

Charlesworth, H., and C. Chinkin, "The Gender of *Jus Cogens*," (1993) 15 *Human Rights Quarterly* 63.

Chesterman, S., "Altogether Different Order: Defining the Elements of Crimes against Humanity," (2000) 10 *Duke Journal of Comparative and International Law* 307.

Chou, M.-H., "The European Union and the Fight against Human Trafficking: Comprehensive or Contradicting?" (2008) 4 *St Antony's International Review* 76.

Chang, G., and K. Kim, "Reconceptualizing Approaches to Human Trafficking: New Directions and Perspectives from the Field(s)," (2007) 3 *Stanford Journal of Civil Rights and Civil Liberties* 317.

Chuang, J., "Beyond a Snapshot: Preventing Human Trafficking in the Global Economy," (2006) 13 *Indiana Journal of Global Legal Studies* 137.

"CEDAW Article 6," in C. Chinkin, M. Freeman and B. Rudolf eds., *Commentary to the Convention on the Elimination of All Forms of Discrimination against Women* (2010, Oxford University Press, forthcoming).

"Redirecting the Debate over Trafficking in Women: Definitions, Paradigms and Contexts," (1998) 11 *Harvard Human Rights Journal* 65.

"The United States as Global Sheriff: Using Unilateral Sanctions to Combat Human Trafficking," (2006) 27 *Michigan Journal of International Law* 437.

Cleveland, S.H., "Norm Internalization and U.S. Economic Sanctions," (2001) 26 *Yale Journal of International Law* 1.

Coleman, N., "Renewed Review of the Status of the Principle of *Non-Refoulement as* Customary International Law," (2003) 5 *European Journal of Migration and Law* 23.

Conaghan, J., "Extending the Reach of Human Rights to Encompass Victims of Rape: M.C. v. Bulgaria," (2005) 13 *Feminist Legal Studies* 145.

Cook, R.J., "State Responsibility for Violations of Women's Human Rights," (1995) 7 *Harvard Human Rights Journal* 125.

Copelon, R., "Gender Crimes as War Crimes: Integrating Crimes Against Women into International Criminal Law," (2000) 46 *McGill Law Journal* 217.

"Surfacing Gender: Re-Engraving Crimes against Women in International Humanitarian Law," (1994) 5 *Hasting Women's Law Journal* 243.

Crawford, J., "Revising the Draft Articles on State Responsibility," (1999) 10 *European Journal of International Law* 435.

Crawford, J., J. Peel and S. Olleson, "The ILC's Articles Responsibility of States for Internationally Wrongful Acts: Completion of the Second Reading," (2001) 12 *European Journal of International Law* 963.

Crawford, J., and S. Olleson, "The Continuing Debate on a UN Convention on State Responsibility," (2005) 54 *International and Comparative Law Quarterly* 959.

"The Nature and Forms of International Responsibility," in M.D. Evans ed., *International Law* 451 (2006, Oxford University Press).

Cullen, H., "*Siliadin v. France*: Positive Obligations under Article 4 of the European Convention of Human Rights," (2006) 6 *Human Rights Law Review* 585.

Darrow, M., and L. Arbour, "The Pillar of Glass: Human Rights in the Development Operations of the United Nations," (2009) 103 *American Journal of International Law* 406.

Demleitner, N.V., "Forced Prostitution: Naming an International Offence," (1994) 18 *Fordham International Law Journal* 163.

Dillon, S., "Making Legal Regimes for Intercountry Adoption Reflect Human Rights Principles: Transforming the United Nations Convention on the Rights of the Child with the Hague Convention on Intercountry Adoption," (2003) 21 *Boston University International Law Journal* 179.

"What Human Rights Law Obscures: Global Sex Trafficking and the Demand for Children," (2008) 17 *UCLA Women's Law Journal* 121.

Dinstein, Y., "Right to Life, Physical Integrity, and Liberty," in L. Henkin ed., *The International Bill of Rights: The Covenant on Civil Political Rights* 114 (1981, Columbia University Press).

Doezema, J., "Loose Women or Lost Women? The Re-Emergence of the Myth of 'White Slavery' in Contemporary Discourses of 'Trafficking in Women,'" (2000) 18(1) *Gender Issues* 23.

"Who Gets to Choose? Coercion, Consent and the U.N. Trafficking Protocol," (2002) 10 *Gender and Development* 20.

Dorevitch, A., and M. Foster, "Obstacles on the Road to Protection: Assessing the Treatment of Sex-Trafficking Victims under Australia's Migration and Refugee Law," (2008) 9 *Melbourne Journal of International Law* 1.

Duffy, H., "*Hadijatou Mani Koroua v Niger*: Slavery Unveiled by the ECOWAS Court," (2009) 9 *Human Rights Law Review* 151.

Dugard, J., and C. Van den Wyngaert, "Reconciling Extradition with Human Rights," (1998) 92 *American Journal of International Law* 187.

Dupuy, P.M., "The International Law of State Responsibility: Revolution or Evolution?" (1989) 11 *Michigan Journal of International Law* 105.

"Reviewing the Difficulties of Codification: On Ago's Classification of Obligation of Means and Obligation of Result in Relation to State Responsibility," (1999) 10 *European Journal of International Law* 371.

Durbach, A., C. Renshaw and A. Byrnes, "'A Tongue but No Teeth'? The Emergence of a Regional Human Rights Mechanism in the Asia-Pacific," (2009) 31 *Sydney Law Review* 211.

Durojay, E., "Addressing Human Rights Concerns Raised by Mandatory HIV Testing of Pregnant Women through the Protocol to the African Charter on the Rights of Women," (2008) 52 *Journal of African Law* 43.

Edelenbos, C., "Committee on Migrant Workers and Implementation of the ICRMW," in R. Cholewinski, P. de Guchteneire and A. Pécoud eds., *Migration and Human Rights: The United Nations Convention on Migrant Workers' Rights* 100 (2009, Cambridge University Press).

Eide, A., "Economic, Social and Cultural Rights as Human Rights," in A. Eide, C. Krause and A. Rosas eds., *Economic, Social, and Cultural Rights: A Textbook* 21 (1995, Kluwer Law International).

Enache-Brown, C., and A. Fried, "Universal Crime, Jurisdiction and Duty: The Obligation of *Aut Dedere Aut Judicare* in International Law," (1998) 43 *McGill Law Journal* 613.

Farrell, A., J. McDevitt and S. Fahy, "Where Are All the Victims? Understanding the Determinants of Official Identification of Human Trafficking Incidents," (2010) 9 *Criminology & Public Policy* 201.

Farrior, S., "The International Law on Trafficking in Women and Children for Prostitution: Making It Live Up to Its Potential," (1997) 10 *Harvard Human Rights Journal* 213.

Feingold, D.A., "Trafficking in Numbers: The Social Construction of Human Trafficking Data," in P. Andreas and K.M. Greenhill eds., *Sex, Drugs and Body Counts: The Politics of Numbers in Global Crime and Conflict* (2010, Cornell University Press, forthcoming).

Feve, S., and C. Finzel, "Trafficking of People," (2001) 38 *Harvard Journal on Legislation* 279.

Freamon, B.K., "Slavery, Freedom and the Doctrine of Consensus in Islamic Jurisprudence," (1998) 11 *Harvard Human Rights Journal* 31.

Friman, H.R., "Numbers and Certification: Assessing Foreign Compliance in Combating Narcotics and Human Trafficking, in P. Andreas and K.M. Greenhill eds., *Sex, Drugs and Body Counts: The Politics of Numbers in Global Crime and Conflict* (2010, Cornell University Press, forthcoming).

Gallagher, A.T., "Human Rights and Human Trafficking: Quagmire or Firm Ground? A Response to James Hathaway," (2009) 49 *Virginia Journal of International Law* 789.

"Human Rights and the New UN Protocols on Trafficking and Migrant Smuggling: A Preliminary Analysis," (2001) 23 *Human Rights Quarterly* 975.

"Making Human Rights Treaty Obligations a Reality at the National Level: Identifying and Working with New Actors and Partners," in P. Alston and J. Crawford eds., *The Future of UN Human Rights Treaty Monitoring* 201 (1999, Cambridge University Press).

"Recent Legal Developments in the Field of Human Trafficking: A Critical Review of the 2005 European Convention and Related Instruments," (2006) 8 *European Journal of Migration and Law* 163.

"Using International Human Rights Law to Better Protect Victims of Trafficking: The Prohibitions on Slavery, Servitude, Forced Labor and Debt Bondage," in L. Sadat and M.P. Scharf eds., *Coming of Age in International Criminal Law: An Intellectual Reflection on the Work of M. Cherif Bassiouni* 397 (2008, Martinus Nijhoff).

"A Shadow Report on Human Trafficking in Lao PDR: The US Approach vs. International Law," (2006) 15 *Asian and Pacific Migration Journal* 525.

Gallagher, A.T., and P. Holmes, "Developing an Effective Criminal Justice Response to Human Trafficking: Lessons from the Front Line," (2008) 18 *International Criminal Justice Review* 318.

Gallagher, A.T., and E. Pearson, "The High Cost of Freedom: A Legal and Policy Analysis of Shelter Detention for Victims of Trafficking," (2010) 32 *Human Rights Quarterly* 73.

Gattini, A., "Breach of the Obligation to Prevent and Reparation Thereof in the ICJ's Genocide Judgment," (2007) 19 *European Journal of International Law* 695.

"Smoking/No Smoking: Some Remarks on the Current Place of Fault in the ILC Draft Articles on State Responsibility," (1999) 10 *European Journal of International Law* 397.

Gibney, M., "Genocide and State Responsibility," (2007) 7 *Human Rights Law Review* 760.

Gjerdingen, E., "Suffocation inside a Cold Storage Truck and Other Problems with Trafficking as 'Exploitation' and Smuggling as 'Choice' along the Thai-Burmese Border," (2009) 26 *Arizona Journal of International & Comparative Law* 699.

Goździak, E.M., "Identifying Child Victims of Trafficking: Toward Solutions and Resolutions," (2010) 9 *Criminology & Public Policy* 245.

Goldman, E., "The Traffic in Women," in E. Goldman, *Anarchism and other Essays* 183 (1917, Mother Earth Publishing Association).

Goodman, R., and D. Jinks, "Incomplete Internationalization and Compliance with Human Rights Law," (2008) 19 *European Journal of International Law* 725.

Goodwin-Gill, G.S., "Article 31 of the 1951 Convention Relating to the Status of Refugees: Non-Penalization, Detention, and Protection," in E. Feller, V. Türk and F. Nicholson eds., *Refugee Protection in International Law: UNHCR's Global Consultations on International Protection* 183 (2003, Cambridge University Press).

"The Right to Leave, the Right to Return and the Question of a Right to Remain," in V. Gowland-Debbas ed., *The Problem of Refugees in the Light of Contemporary International Legal Issues* 93 (1995, Martinus Nijhoff).

Grover, S., "Denying the Right of Trafficked Minors to be Classified as Convention Refugees: the Canadian Case Example," (2006) 14 *International Journal of Children's Rights* 235.

Hainsfurther, J.S., "A Rights-Based Approach: The Utilization of CEDAW to Protect the Human Rights of Migrant Workers," (2009) 24 *American University International Law Review* 843.

Halley, J., et al., "From the International to the Local in Feminist Legal Responses to Rape, Prostitution/Sex Work, and Sex Trafficking: Four Studies in Contemporary Governance Feminism," (2006) 29 *Harvard Journal of Law and Gender* 335.

Hamim, A., "Provincial Assessments: Riau Islands," in K.L. Sugiarti, J. Davis and A. Dasgupta eds., *When They Were Sold: Trafficking of Women and Girls in 15 Provinces of Indonesia* 79 (2006, International Catholic Migration Commission and the American Center for International Labor Solidarity).

Hammer, L.M., "Migrant Workers in Israel: Towards Proposing a Framework of Enforceable Customary International Human Rights," (1999) 17 *Netherlands Quarterly of Human Rights* 5.

Hampton, F., and A. Kihara-Hunt, "Accountability of Personnel," in C. Aoi, C. de Coning and R. Thakur eds., *Unintended Consequences of Peacekeeping Operations* 196 (2007, United Nations University Press).

Harvey, C., and R.P. Barnidge, Jr., "Human Rights, Free Movement and the Right to Leave in International Law," (2007) 19 *International Journal of Refugee Law* 1.

Hasenau, M., "ILO Standards on Migrant Workers: The Fundamentals of the UN Convention and Their Genesis," (1991) 25 *International Migration Review* 693.

"Setting Norms in the United Nations System: The Draft International Convention on the Rights of All Migrant Workers and Members of their Families in Relation to ILO Standards on Migrant Workers," (1990) 28 *International Migration Review* 133.

Hathaway, J.C., "The Human Rights Quagmire of Human Trafficking," (2008) 49 *Virginia Journal of International Law* 1.

"Leveraging Asylum," (2010) 45 *Texas International Law Journal* 503.

Hathaway, O.A., "Do Human Rights Treaties Make a Difference?" (2002) 111 *Yale Law Journal* 1935

"Why Do Countries Commit to Human Rights Treaties?" (2007) 51 *Journal of Conflict Resolution* 588.

Henkin, L., "Inter-State Responsibility for Compliance with Human Rights Obligations," in L.C. Vohrah et al. eds., *Man's Inhumanity to Man: Essays on International Law in Honour of Antonio Cassese* 383 (2003, Kluwer Law International).

Higate, P., "Peacekeepers, Masculinities and Sexual Exploitation," (2007) 10 *Men and Masculinities* 99.

Higate, P., and M. Henry, "Engendering (In)security in Peace Support Operations," (2004) 35 *Security Dialogue* 481.

Holmes, L., "Human Trafficking & Corruption: Triple Victimization?" in C. Friesendorf ed., *Strategies against Human Trafficking: The Role of the Security Sector* 83 (2009).

Hovi, J., "The Pros and Cons of External Enforcement," in O.S. Stokke, J. Hovi and G. Ulfstein eds., *Implementing the Climate Regime: International Compliance* 129 (2005, Earthscan).

Hune, S., "Migrant Women in the Context of the International Convention on the Rights of all Migrant Workers and Members of their Families," (1991) 25 *International Migration Review* 809.

Hunt, D., "The International Criminal Court: High Hopes, Creative Ambiguity, and an Unfortunate Mistrust in Judges," (2004) 2 *Journal of International Criminal Justice* 56.

Irwin, M.A., "'White Slavery' as Metaphor: Anatomy of a Moral Panic," (1996) 5 *Ex-Post Facto: the History Journal* 1.

Jiménez de Arechaga, E., "International Responsibility," in M. Sorensen ed., *Manual of Public International Law* 531 (1976, St Martin's Press).

Jinks, D., "State Responsibility for the Acts of Private Armed Groups," (2003) 4 *Chicago Journal of International Law* 83.

Kälin, W., "The Guiding Principles on Internal Displacement as International Minimum Standard and Protection Tool," (2005) 24 *Refugee Survey Quarterly* 27.

Kangaspunta, K., "Measuring the Immeasurable: Can the Severity of Human Trafficking Be Ranked?" (2010) 9 *Criminology & Public Policy* 257.

Kelly, J., "The Twilight of Customary International Law," (2000) 40 *Virginia Journal of International Law* 449.

Kelly, L., "'You Can Find Anything You Want': A Critical Reflection on Research on Trafficking in Persons within and into Europe," (2005) 43 *International Migration* 235.

Kerrigan, G.M., "Historical Development of the United Nations Declaration," in M.C. Bassiouni ed., "International Protection of Victims," (1998) 7 *Nouvelles Etudes Pénales* 91.

King, H., "The Extraterritorial Rights Obligations of States," (2009) 9 *Human Rights Law Review* 521.

Kingsbury, B., N. Krisch and R.B. Stewart, "The Emergence of Global Administrative Law," (2005) 68 *Law and Contemporary Problems* 15.

Kinley, D., and J. Tadaki, "From Talk to Walk: The Emergence of Human Rights Responsibilities for Corporations at International Law," (2004) 44 *Virginia Journal of International Law* 931.

Kooijmans, P.H., "Inter-State Dispute Settlement in the Field of Human Rights," in M. Brus, A.S. Muller and S. Wiermers eds., *The United Nations Decade of International Law: Reflections on International Dispute Settlement* 87 (1991, Martinus Nijhoff).

Lamborn, L.L., "The United Nations Declaration on Victims: Incorporating 'Abuse of Power,'" (1987) 19 *Rutgers Law Journal* 59.

Larsen, K.M., "Attribution of Conduct in Peace Operations: The 'Ultimate Authority and Control' Test," (2008) 19 *European Journal of International Law* 509.

Lassen, N., "Slavery and Slavery-like Practices: United Nations Standards and Implementation," (1998) 57 *Nordic Journal of International Law* 197.

Lauterpacht, E., and D. Bethlehem, "The Scope and Content of the Principle of Non-Refoulement," in E. Feller, V. Türk and F. Nicholson eds., *Refugee Protection in International Law: UNHCR's Global Consultations on International Protection* 78 (2003, Cambridge University Press).

Lawson, R., "Out of Control: State Responsibility and Human Rights: Will the ILC's Definition of the 'Act of State' Meet the Challenges of the 21st Century?" in M. Castermans-Holleman, R. van Hoof, and J. Smith eds., *The Role of the Nation-State in the 21st Century: Human Rights, International Organisations and Foreign Policy: Essays in Honour of Peter Baehr* 91 (1998, Kluwer Law International).

Leckie, S., "The Inter-State Complaint Procedure in International Human Rights Law: Hopeful Prospects or Wishful Thinking?" (1988) 10 *Human Rights Quarterly* 249.

Limoncelli, S.A., "Paths to the Abolition of Regulated Prostitution in Europe, 1875–1950: International Voluntary Associations, Local Social Movements and State," (2006) 21 *International Sociology* 31.

de Londras, F., "Prosecuting Sexual Violence in the Ad Hoc International Criminal Tribunals for Rwanda and the Former Yugoslavia," in M. Fineman ed., *Transcending the Boundaries of Law* (2010, Routledge, forthcoming).

Lonnroth, J., "The International Convention on the Rights of all Migrant Workers and Members of their Families in the Context of International Migration Policies: An Analysis of Ten Years of Negotiation," (1991) 24 *International Migration Review* 721.

Lyon, B., "The Unsigned United Nations Migrant Worker Rights Convention," (2010) 42 *New York Journal of International Law and Politics* (forthcoming).

McCorquodale, R., "Impact on State Responsibility," in M.T. Kamminga and M. Scheinin eds., *The Impact of Human Rights on General International Law* 235 (2009, Oxford University Press).

McCreight, M.V., "Smuggling of Migrants, Trafficking in Human Beings and Irregular Migration on a Comparative Perspective," (2006) 12 *European Law Journal* 106.

McDougal, M.M., H.D. Lasswell, and L.-C. Chen, "The Protection of Aliens from Discrimination and World Public Order: Responsibility of States Conjoined with Human Rights," (1976) 70 *American Journal of International Law* 432.

Mackinnon, C.A., "Pornography as Trafficking," (2004) 26 *Michigan Journal of International Law* 993.

Mallison, W.T., and S. Mallison, "The Right to Return," (1980) 9 *Journal of Palestine Studies* 125.

Malone, L.A., "Economic Hardship as Coercion under the Protocol on International Trafficking in Persons by Organized Crime Elements," (2001) 25 *Fordham International Law Journal* 54.

Mantouvalou, V., "Servitude and Forced Labour in the 21st Century: the Human Rights of Domestic Workers," (2006) 35 *Industrial Law Journal* 395.

Martin, S., "Internal Trafficking," (2006) 25 *Forced Migration Review* 12.

Martinez, J.S., "Anti-Slavery Courts and the Dawn of International Human Rights Law," (2007) 117 *Yale Law Journal* 550.

Meron, T., "Rape as a Crime Under International Humanitarian Law," (1993) 87 *American Journal of International Law* 424.

Mertus, J., "The Prosecution of Rape under International Law: Justice that is Long Overdue," (2002) 35 *Vanderbilt Journal of Transnational Law* 1269.

Milanović, M., "State Responsibility for Genocide: A Follow-Up," (2007) 18 *European Journal of International Law* 669.

Milanović, M., and T. Papić, "As Bad As It Gets: The European Court of Human Rights' *Behrami and Saramati* Decision and General International Law," (2009) 58 *International and Comparative Law Quarterly* 267.

Miller, A., and A. Stewart, "Report from the Roundtable on the Meaning of 'Trafficking in Persons': A Human Rights Perspective," (1998) 20 *Women's Rights Law Reporter* 11.

Mitsilegas, V., "From National to Global, From Empirical to Legal: The Ambivalent Concept of Transnational Organized Crime," in M.E. Beare ed., *Critical Reflections on Transnational Organized Crime, Money Laundering and Corruption* 55 (2003, University of Toronto Press).

Morokvasic, M. ed., "Women in Migration" (1984) 18 *International Migration Review*.

Murray, J., "Who Will Police the Peace-Builders? The Failure to Establish Accountability for the Participation of United Nations Civilian Police in the Trafficking of Women in Post-Conflict Bosnia and Herzegovina," (2003) 34 *Columbia Human Rights Law Review* 475.

Nadelmann, E.A., "Global Prohibition Regimes: The Evolution of Norms in International Society," (1990) 44 *International Organisation* 479.

Nafziger, J., and B.C. Bartel, "The Migrant Workers Convention: Its Place in Human Rights Law," (1991) 25 *International Migration Review* 771.

Nkamleu, G.B., and A. Kielland, "Modeling Farmers' Decisions on Child Labor and Schooling in the Cocoa Sector: A Multinomial Logit Analysis in Côte d'Ivoire," (2006) 35 *Agricultural Economics* 319.

Office of the High Commissioner for Refugees, "Summary Conclusions: The Principle of *Non-Refoulement*: Expert Roundtable organized by the UNHCR and the Lauterpacht Research Centre for International Law, University of Cambridge, UK, 9–10 July 2001," in E. Feller, V. Türk and F. Nicholson eds., *Refugee Protection in International Law: UNHCR's Global Consultations on International Protection* 178 (2003, Cambridge University Press).

Otto, D., "Making Sense of Zero Tolerance Policies in Peacekeeping Sexual Economies," in V. Munro and C.F. Stychin eds., *Sexuality and the Law: Feminist Engagements* 259 (2007, Routledge).

Outshoorn, J., "The Political Debates on Prostitution and Trafficking in Women," (2005) 12 *International Studies in Gender, State and Society* 142.

Pearson, E., "Preventing What?" (2004) 21 *Prevention of Trafficking: Alliance News* 15.

Perruchoud, R., "Consular Protection and Assistance," in R. Cholewinski, R. Perruchoud and E. MacDonald eds., *International Migration Law: Developing Paradigms and Key Challenges* 71 (2007, T.M.C. Asser).

Piotrowicz, R., "The UNHCR's Guidelines on Human Trafficking," (2008) 20 *International Journal of Refugee Law* 242.

Piper, N., "A Problem by a Different Name: A Review of Research on Trafficking in South East Asia and Oceania," in International Organization for Migration ed., *Data and Research on Human Trafficking* 203 (2005, International Organization for Migration).

Pitea, C., "Rape as a Human Rights Obligation and a Criminal Offence: The European Court's Judgement in M.C. v. Bulgaria," (2005) 3 *Journal of International Criminal Justice* 447.

Pocar, F., "Human Trafficking: A Crime against Humanity," in E.U. Savona and S. Stefanizzi eds., *Measuring Human Trafficking: Complexities and Pitfalls* 5 (2007, Springer).

Quigley, J., "Mass Displacement and the Individual Right of Return," (1997) 68 *British Yearbook of International Law* 122.

Quénivet, N., "The Dissonance between the United Nations Zero-Tolerance Policy and Criminalisation of Sexual Offences on the International Level," (2007) 7(4) *International Criminal Law Review* 657.

Quirk, J., "The Anti-Slavery Project: Linking the Historical and Contemporary," (2006) 28 *Human Rights Quarterly* 565.

Raffaelli, R., "The European Approach to the Protection of Trafficking Victims: The Council of Europe Convention, the EU Directive and the Italian Experience," (2009) 10 *German Law Journal* 205.

Rassam, A.Y., "Contemporary Forms of Slavery and the Evolution of the Prohibition of Slavery and the Slave Trade under Customary International Law," (1999) 39 *Virginia Journal of International Law* 303.

"International Law and Contemporary Forms of Slavery: An Economic and Social Rights-Based Approach," (2005) 23 *Penn State International Law Review* 809.

Raustiala, K., "The Architecture of International Cooperation: Transgovernmental Networks and the Future of International Law," (2002) 43 *Virginia Journal of International Law* 1.

Raustiala, K., and A.-M. Slaughter, "International Law, International Relations and Compliance," in W. Carlnaes, T. Risse and B.A. Simmons eds., *The Handbook of International Relations* 538 (2002, Sage).

Reanda, L., "Prostitution as a Human Rights Question," (1991) 13 *Human Rights Quarterly* 202.

Roberts, A.E., "Traditional and Modern Approaches to Customary International Law: A Reconciliation," (2001) 95 *American Journal of International Law* 757.

Robinson, D., "Defining 'Crimes against Humanity' at the Rome Conference," (1999) 93 *American Journal of International Law* 43.

Rosenstock, R., "The ILC and State Responsibility," (2002) 96 *American Journal of International Law* 792.

Salt, J., and J. Stein, "Migration as a Business: The Case of Trafficking," (1997) 35 *International Migration* 467.

Salazar Parrenas, R., "Sex for Sale: Trafficked? Filipino Hostesses in Tokyo's Nightlife Industry," (2006) 18 *Yale Journal of Law and Feminism* 145.

Sanghera, J., "Unpacking the Trafficking Discourse," in K. Kempadoo ed., *Trafficking and Prostitution Reconsidered: New Perspectives on Migration, Sex Work, and Human Rights* 3 (2005, Paradigm Publishers).

Sari, A., "Jurisdiction and International Responsibility in Peace Support Operations: The *Behrami* and *Saramati* Cases," (2008) 8 *Human Rights Law Review* 151.

Satterthwaite, M., "Crossing Borders, Claiming Rights: Using Human Rights Law to Empower Women Migrant Workers," (2005) 8 *Yale Human Rights and Development Law Journal* 1.

Saunders, P., "Working on the Inside: Migration, Sex Work and Trafficking in Persons," (2000) 11(2) *Legal Link* 44.

Scheper-Hughes, N., "Illegal Organ Trade: Global Justice and the Traffic in Human Organs," in R.W.G. Gruessner and E. Benedetti eds., *Living Donor Organ Transplantation* 106 (2008, McGraw-Hill Professional).

Scobbie, I., "The Invocation of Responsibility for the Breach of 'Obligations under Peremptory Norms of General International Law,'" (2002) 13 *European Journal of International Law* 1202.

Seaman, A.L., "Permanent Residency for Human Trafficking Victims in Europe: The Potential Use of Article 3 of the European Convention as a Means of Protection," (2010) 48 *Columbia Journal of Transnational Law* (forthcoming).

Segrave, M., "Order at the Border," 32 (2009) *Women's Studies International Forum* 251.

Shelton, D., "Private Violations, Public Wrongs and the Responsibilities of States," (1989) 23 *Fordham International Law Journal* 13.

Silferberg, K., "Suppression of Trafficking in Persons and Exploitation of the Prostitution of Others," (1991) 2 *Finnish Yearbook of International Law* 66.

Silverman, J.G., et al., "Syphilis and Hepatitis B Co-infection among HIV-Infected, Sex-Trafficked Women and Girls, Nepal," (2008) 14 *Emerging Infectious Diseases* 932.

Simic, O., "Rethinking 'Sexual Exploitation' in UN Peacekeeping Operations," (2009) 32 *Women's Studies International Forum* 288.

Simma, B., "Bilateralism and Community Interest in the Law of State Responsibility," in Y. Dinstein ed., *International Law at a Time of Perplexity: Essays in Honour of Shabtai Rosenne* 821 (1989, Martinus Nijhoff).

Slaughter, A.-M. and W. Burke-White, "An International Constitutional Moment," (2002) 43 *Harvard International Law Journal* 1.

Slinckx, I., "Migrants' Rights in UN Human Rights Conventions," in R. Cholewinski, P. de Guchteneire and A. Pécoud eds., *Migration and Human Rights: The United Nations Convention on Migrant Workers' Rights* 122 (2009, Cambridge University Press).

Smolin, D.M., "Child Laundering: How the Intercountry Adoption System Legitimizes and Incentivizes the Practices of Buying, Trafficking, Kidnapping, and Stealing Children," (2006) 52 *Wayne Law Review* 113.

"Intercountry Adoption as Child Trafficking," (2004) 39 *Valparaiso University Law Review* 281.

Srikantiah, J., "Perfect Victims and Real Survivors: The Iconic Victim in Domestic Human Trafficking Law," (2007) 87 *Boston University Law Review* 157.

Stolz, B., "Educating Policymakers and Setting the Criminal Justice Policymaking Agenda: Interest Groups and the 'Victims of Trafficking and Violence Act of 2000,'" (2005) 5 *Criminal Justice* 407.

Surtees, R., "Commercial Sex Work," in R. Rosenberg ed., *Trafficking of Women and Children in Indonesia* 63 (2005, International Catholic Migration Commission and the American Center for International Labor Solidarity).

"Trafficked Men as Unwilling Victims," (2008) 4(1) *St Antony's International Review* 16.

Suzuki, E., and S. Nanwani, "Responsibility of International Organizations: The Accountability Mechanisms of Multilateral Development Banks," (2006) 27 *Michigan Journal of International Law* 177.

Toepfer, S., and B.S. Wells, "The Worldwide Market for Sex: Review of International and Regional Legal Prohibitions Regarding Trafficking in Women," (1994) 18 *Michigan Journal of Gender and Law* 4.

Townsend, G., "State Responsibility for Acts of De-Facto Agents," (1997) 14 *Arizona Journal of International and Comparative Law* 636.

Trachtman, J.P., "International Law and Domestic Political Coalitions: The Causes of Compliance with International Law," July 9, 2009, available at SSRN: http://ssrn.com/abstract=1431956 (accessed Feb. 2, 2010).

Turner, J.I., "Transnational Networks and International Criminal Justice," (2007) 105 *Michigan Law Review* 985.

Van den Wyngaert, C., and G. Stessens, "The International *Non Bis in Idem* Principle: Resolving Some of the Unanswered Questions," (1999) 48 *International and Comparative Law Quarterly* 779.

Various authors, "Symposium: Assessing the Work of the International Law Commission on State Responsibility," (2002) 13 *European Journal of International Law* 1147.

"Symposium: The ILC's State Responsibility Articles," (2002) 96 *American Journal of International Law* 773.

Verdier, P.-H., "Transnational Regulatory Networks and Their Limits," (2009) 34 *Yale Journal of International Law* 113.

Vlassis, D., "The Global Situation of Transnational Organized Crime, the Decision of the International Community to Develop an International Convention and the Negotiation Process," in UN Asia and Far East Institute for the Prevention of Crime and the Treatment of Offenders, *Annual Report and Resource Materials Series No. 59*.

"The UN Convention Against Transnational Organized Crime," in M.R. Berdal and M. Serrano eds., *Transnational Organized Crime and International Security: Business as Usual?* 83 (2002, Lynne Rienner Publishers).

Vojdik, V.K., "Sexual Abuse and Exploitation of Women and Girls by UN Peacekeeping Troops," (2007) 15 *Michigan State Journal of International Law* 157.

Vucetic, S., "Democracies and Human Rights: Why is There No Place for Migrant Workers?" (2007) 11 *International Journal of Human Rights* 403.

Warren, K.B., "The Illusiveness of Counting 'Victims' and the Concreteness of Ranking Countries: Trafficking in Persons from Colombia to Japan," in P. Andreas and K.M. Greenhill eds., *Sex, Drugs and Body Counts: The Politics of Numbers in Global Crime and Conflict* (2010, Cornell University Press, forthcoming).

Weissbrodt, D., "The Protection of Non-Citizens in International Human Rights Law," in R. Cholewinski, R. Perruchoud and E. MacDonald eds., *International Migration Law: Developing Paradigms and Key Challenges* 221 (2007, Cambridge University Press).

Weissbrodt, D., and C. Collins, "The Human Rights of Stateless Persons," (2006) 28 *Human Rights Quarterly* 245.

Weitzer, R., "The Social Construction of Sex Trafficking: Ideology and Institutionalization of a Moral Crusade," (2007) 35 *Politics & Society* 447.

Wittner, K.M., "Curbing Child Trafficking in Intercountry Adoptions: Will International Treaties and Adoption Moratoriums Accomplish the Job in Cambodia?" (2003) 12 *Pacific Rim Law and Policy Journal* 595.

Zhang, S.X., and S.L. Pineda, "Corruption as a Causal Factor in Human Trafficking," in D. Siegel and H. Nelen eds., *Organized Crime: Culture, Markets and Policies* 41 (2008, Springer).

Zilbershatz, Y., "International Law and the Palestinian Right of Return to the State of Israel," in E. Benvenisti, C. Gans and S. Hanafi eds., *Israel and the Palestinian Refugees* 191 (2007, Springer).

3. Documents and Reports of Intergovernmental Organizations

Ago, R., "Second Report on State Responsibility," UN Doc. A/8010/Rev.1, reprinted in [1970] 2 *Yearbook of the International Law*, UN Doc. A/CN.4/SER.A/1970/Add.1, 271.

Association of Southeast Asian Nations, ASEAN *Responses to Trafficking in Persons: Ending Impunity for Traffickers and Securing Justice for Victims. Update and Supplement* (Oct. 2007).

   Criminal Justice Responses to Trafficking in Persons – ASEAN Practitioner Guidelines (2007).

Beesey, A., "From Lao PDR to Thailand and Home Again: The Repatriation of Trafficking Victims and Other Exploited Women and Girl Workers – A Study of 124 Cases" (2004, International Organization for Migration).

Bhabha, J., and C. Alfirev, "The Identification and Referral of Trafficked Persons to Procedures for Determining International Protection Needs" (2009, UN High Commissioner for Refugees).

Council of Europe, *Explanatory Report on the Convention on Action against Trafficking in Human Beings*, ETS 197, 16.V.2005 (2005).

Council of Europe and United Nations, *Trafficking in Organs, Tissues And Cells and Trafficking in Human Beings for the Purpose of the Removal of Organs* (2009).

Ennew, J., K. Gopal, J. Heeran and H. Montgomery, *Children and Prostitution: How Can We Measure the Commercial Sexual Exploitation of Children? Literature Review and Annotated Bibliography* (2nd ed., 1996, UNICEF).

García-Amador, F.V., "First Report on International Responsibility," UN Doc. A/CN.4/ SER.A/1956/Add.1, reprinted in [1956] 2 *Yearbook of the International Law Commission* 173.

International Criminal Police Organization, *Trafficking in Human Beings – Best Practice Guidance Manual for Investigators* (2nd ed., 2008, General Secretariat of the International Criminal Police Organisation).

International Labour Office, *General Survey of the Reports Relating to Conventions Nos. 97 and 143 and Recommendations Nos. 86 and 151 concerning Migrant Workers* (1980).

   ILO Action against Trafficking in Human Beings (2008).

   Forced Labour: Casebook of Court Decisions (2009).

   The Cost of Coercion (2009).

International Labour Organization, International Migration Programme, *ILO Multilateral Framework on Labour Migration: Non-Binding Principles and Guidelines for a Rights-Based Approach to Labour Migration* (2006).

   The Demand Side of Human Trafficking in Asia: Empirical Findings (2006).

International Law Commission, *Draft Articles on Responsibility of States for Internationally Wrongful Acts, Report of the International Law Commission on the Work of Its Fifty-third Session*, UN GAOR, 56th Sess., Supp. No. 10, at 43, UN Doc. A/56/10 (2001).

Fragmentation of International Law: Difficulties Arising from the Diversification and Expansion of International Law, UN Doc. A/CN.4/L.682 (Apr. 13, 2006).

International Organization for Migration, *International Response to Trafficking in Migrants and the Safeguarding of Migrant Rights* (1994).

Trafficking and Prostitution: The Growing Exploitation of Migrant Women from Central and Eastern Europe (1995).

Trafficking in Women from the Dominican Republic for Sexual Exploitation (1996).

Trafficking in Women to Austria for Sexual Exploitation (1996).

Trafficking in Women to Italy for Sexual Exploitation (1996).

Trafficking of Women to the European Union: Characteristics, Trends and Policy Issues (1996).

Data and Research on Human Trafficking: A Global Survey (2005).

Identification and Protection Schemes for Victims of Trafficking in Persons in Europe: Tools and Best Practices (2005).

Inter-Parliamentary Union and United Nations Children's Fund, *Combating Child Trafficking*, Handbook for Parliamentarians No. 9 (2005).

Office of the UN High Commissioner for Human Rights, *Human Rights and Poverty Reduction: A Conceptual Framework*, UN Sales No. HR/PUB/04/1 (2004).

The Rights of Non-Citizens (2006).

A Legal Framework for the Possible Criminalization of the Demand for the Labour Outcome of Trafficking in Persons (2008).

Commentary to the United Nations Recommended Principles and Guidelines on Human Rights and Human Trafficking (forthcoming, 2010).

Organization for Security and Co-operation in Europe, *Compensation for Trafficked and Exploited Persons in the OSCE Region* (2008).

Pearson, E., *The Mekong Challenge: Human Trafficking: Redefining Demand* (2005, International Labour Organization).

Rijken, C., *The European Legal Framework to Fight Trafficking in Human Beings* (2005, International Organization for Migration).

UNESCO and the Coalition against Trafficking in Women, *The Penn State Report: Report of an International Meeting of Experts on Sexual Exploitation, Violence and Prostitution* (1999).

United Nations Children's Fund, *Birth Registration: Right from the Start*, Innocenti Digest No. 9 (Mar. 2002).

Guidelines for the Protection of Child Victims of Trafficking (Sept. 2006).

UN Economic and Social Council, Office of the United Nations High Commissioner for Human Rights, *Recommended Principles and Guidelines on Human Rights and Human Trafficking*, UN Doc. E/2002/68/Add.1 (May 20, 2002).

UN General Assembly, *Guide for Policy Makers on the Implementation of the United Nations Declaration of Basic Principles of Justice for Victims of Crime and Abuse of Power*, UN Doc. E/CN.15/1998/CRP.4 (Apr. 17, 1988).

UN High Commissioner for Refugees, *Handbook on Procedures and Criteria for Determining Refugee Status under the 1951 Convention and the 1967 Protocol Relating to the Status of Refugees, 1979*, UN Doc. HCR/IP/4/Eng/REV.1 (1979, reissued Jan. 2002).

Guidelines on International Protection: Gender-Related Persecution within the context of Article 1A(2) of the 1951 Convention and/or its 1967 Protocol relating to the Status of Refugees, UN Doc. HCR/GIP/02/01 (May 7, 2002).

Guidelines on International Protection: "Membership of a Particular Social Group" within the context of Article 1A(2) of the 1951 Convention and/or its 1967 Protocol Relating to the Status of Refugees, UN Doc. HCR/GIP/02/02 (May 7, 2002).

Sexual and Gender-Based Violence against Refugees, Returnees and Internally Displaced Persons: Guidelines for Prevention and Response (May, 2003).

Guidelines on International Protection: The application of Article 1(A)(2) of the 1951 Convention and/or 1967 Protocol relating to the Status of Refugees to victims of trafficking and persons at risk of being trafficked, UN Doc. HCR/GIP/06/07 (Apr. 7, 2006).

United Nations Inter-Agency Project on Human Trafficking, "Exploitation of Cambodian Men at Sea: Facts about the Trafficking of Cambodian Men onto Thai Fishing Boats" (2009), available at http://www.no-trafficking.org/reports_docs/siren/siren_cb3.pdf (accessed Nov. 30, 2009).

UN Office on Drugs and Crime, *Legislative Guides for the Implementation of the United Nations Convention Against Transnational Organized Crime and the Protocols Thereto*, UN Sales No. E.05.V.2 (2004).

Travaux Préparatoires of the Negotiations for the Elaboration of the United Nations Convention against Transnational Organized Crime and the Protocols Thereto (2006).

Toolkit to Combat Trafficking in Persons (2008).

Anti-Human Trafficking Manual for Criminal Justice Practitioners (2009).

Combating Trafficking in Persons: Handbook for Parliamentarians (2009).

Global Report on Trafficking in Persons (2009).

Model Law on Trafficking in Persons, UN Sales No. E.09.V.11 (2009).

World Health Organization and UNAIDS, *WHO/UNAIDS Guidance on Provider Initiated HIV Testing and Counselling in Health Facilities* (2007).

Zimmermann, C., and C. Watts, *WHO Ethical and Safety Recommendations for Interviewing Trafficked Women* (2003, World Health Organization).

4. Other Documents and Reports

Allain, J., "The Definition of 'Slavery' in General International Law and the Crime of Enslavement within the Rome Statute," speech given at the Guest Lecture Series of the Office of the Prosecutor, International Criminal Court, Apr. 26, 2007.

"A Legal Consideration of 'Slavery' in Light of the *Travaux Préparatoires* of the 1926 Convention," paper presented at the conference "Twenty-First Century Slavery: Issues and Responses" in Hull (UK), Nov. 23, 2006.

"Mobilization of International Law to Address Trafficking and Slavery," paper presented at the 11th Joint Stanford-University of California Law and Colonialism in Africa Symposium, Mar. 19–21, 2009.

American Bar Association, Rule of Law Initiative, *Human Trafficking Assessment Tool* (2005), available at http://www.abanet.org/rol/publications/human_trafficking_assessment_tool.shtml (accessed Feb. 2, 2010).

American Law Institute, *Restatement (Third) of the Foreign Relations Law of the United States* (Philadelphia: ALI, 1990).

Anderson, B., and J. O'Connell-Davidson, *Trafficking: A Demand-Led Problem? A Multi-Country Pilot Study* (2002, Save the Children).

Bindman, J., and J. Doezema, "Redefining Prostitution as Sex Work on the International Agenda" (1997, Anti-Slavery International).

Brookings Institute, *Handbook for Applying the Guiding Principles on Internal Displacement* (2000, Brookings Project on Internal Displacement and the UN Office for the Coordination of Humanitarian Affairs).

Byrnes, A., M. Herminia Graterol and R. Chartres, "State Obligation and the Convention on the Elimination of All Forms of Discrimination Against Women," UNSW Law Research Paper No. 2007–48 (July 19, 2007).

Canadian Council for Refugees, "Migrant Smuggling and Trafficking in Persons", Feb. 20, 2000, available at http://www.ccrweb.ca//traffick.htm (accessed Dec. 1, 2009).

Canadian HIV/AIDS Legal Network, "HIV Testing of UN Peacekeeping Forces: Legal and Human Rights Issues" (2001).

Cerone, J., "State Accountability for the Acts of Non-State Actors: The Trafficking of Women for the Purposes of Sex Industry Work" (unpublished paper, on file with the author).

Chuang, J., "Rescuing Trafficking from Ideological Capture: Anti-Prostitution Reform and Its Influence on U.S. Anti-Trafficking Law and Policy," forthcoming, draft paper presented at the Columbia Law School, Center for Gender and Sexuality Law, Feminist Theory Workshops, Dec. 8, 2009, http://www2.law.columbia.edu/faculty_franke/FTW2009/Chuang%20Paper.pdf (accessed Feb. 2, 2010).

Clapham, A., and M. Garcia Rubio, "The Obligations of States with Regard to Non-State Actors in the Context of the Right to Health," Health and Human Rights Working Paper Series No. 3 (2002, World Health Organization).

Cedrangolo, U., "The Optional Protocol to the Convention on the Rights of the Child on the Sale of Children, Child Prostitution and Child Pornography and the Jurisprudence of the Committee on the Rights of the Child" (UNICEF: Innocenti Research Paper, April 2009).

Centre for Reproductive and Sexual Rights, *Bringing Rights to Bear: An Analysis of the Work of UN Treaty Monitoring Bodies on Reproductive and Sexual Rights* (2001)

Connors, J., A. Byrnes and C. Beyani, *Assessing the Status of Women: A Guide to Reporting under the Convention on the Elimination of all forms of Discrimination against Women* (2nd ed., 1996, International Women's Rights Action Watch (IRWAW) USA and the Commonwealth Secretariat).

Dariam, S., "Uses of CEDAW in Addressing Trafficking in Women" (2003, International Women's Rights Action Watch).

D'Ascoli, S., and K.M. Scherr, "The Rule of Prior Exhaustion of Local Remedies in the International Law Doctrine and its Application in the Specific Context of Human Rights Protection," European University Institute Working Paper LAW No. 2007/02 (Feb. 19, 2007).

David, F., "Human Smuggling and Trafficking: An Overview of the Responses at the Federal Level" (2000, Australian Institute of Criminology Research and Public Policy).

Trafficking of Women for Sexual Purposes, Australian Institute of Criminology Research and Public Policy Series No. 95 (2008), available at http://www.aic.gov.au/documents/1/C/E/{1CE51DE9–5346–4565-A86B-778F895BF9E1}rpp95.pdf (accessed Nov. 30, 2009).

David, P., F. David and A.T. Gallagher, "International Legal Cooperation in Trafficking in Persons Cases" (2010, ASEAN, United Nations Office on Drugs and Crime, Asia Regional Cooperation to Prevent People Trafficking, forthcoming,).

Dent, J.A., *Research Paper on the Social and Economic Rights of Non-Nationals in Europe* (1998, European Council on Refugees and Exiles).

Derks, A., "From White Slaves to Trafficking Survivors: Notes on the Trafficking Debate," paper presented at the Conference on Migration and Development, May 4–5, 2000.

Dottridge, M., *Handbook on Planning Projects to Prevent Child Trafficking* (2007, Terre des Hommes).

Dungel, J., "Command Responsibility in International Criminal Tribunals," paper presented at the National Consultative Summit on Extrajudicial Killings and Enforced Disappearances: Searching for Solutions, July 16–17, 2007, available at http://sc.judiciary.gov.ph/publications/summit/Summit%20Papers/Dungel%20-%20 Command%20Responsibility%20in%20ICT.pdf (accessed Nov. 29, 2009).

Eide, A., "Promoting Economic, Social and Cultural Rights: Obligations of States and Accountability of Non-State Actors," paper presented to the Second Global Forum on Human Development: Human Rights and Human Development, Oct. 10 2000, available at http://hdr.undp.org/docs/events/global_forum/2000/eide.pdf (accessed Nov. 25, 2009).

European Women Lawyers Association (EWLA), *Resolution on Trafficking in Human Beings regarding the future European Convention on Action against Trafficking in Human Beings*, adopted by the EWLA General Assembly, Mar. 18, 2005.

Freidrich, M.G., A.N. Myer and D.G. Perlman, "The Trafficking in Persons Report: Strengthening a Diplomatic Tool," UCLA School of Public Affairs (May 8, 2006).

Gallagher, A.T., "Trafficking and the Human Rights of Women: Using the CEDAW Convention and Committee to Strengthen National and International Responses to Trafficking in Women and Girls," background paper for the UN Economic and Social Commission for Asia and the Pacific, Expert Group Meeting on the Promotion and Implementation of CEDAW, Trafficking in Women and Violence against Women, Oct. 3–5, 2005.

Global Alliance Against Trafficking in Women, *Collateral Damage: the Impact of Anti-Trafficking Measures on Human Rights Around the World* (2007).

    Human Rights and Trafficking in Persons: A Handbook (2000).

Global Alliance Against Trafficking in Women, Foundation against Trafficking in Women, International Human Rights Law Group, "Human Rights Standards for the Treatment of Trafficked Persons" (Jan. 1999).

The Global Campaign for Ratification of the Convention on Rights of Migrants, http://www.migrantsrights.org/campaign.htm (accessed Nov. 29, 2009).

Global Commission on International Migration, *Migration in an Interconnected World: New Directions for Action* (2005).

Goodwin-Gill, G.S., "Forced Migration and Human Rights," paper presented at the Expert Meeting on International Legal Norms and Migration, May 23–25, 2002.

Hoffman, R.L., "Effective Countermeasures against the Trafficking in Human Beings and Smuggling of Migrants" in UN Asia and Far East Institute for the Prevention of Crime and Treatment of Offenders, *Work Product of the 122nd International Training Course: Effective Administration of Criminal Justice to Tackle Trafficking in Human Beings and Smuggling of Migrants* 80 (2002).

Hughes, D.M., *The Demand for Victims of Sex Trafficking* (2005).

Human Rights Watch, *A Modern Form of Slavery: Trafficking of Burmese Women and Girls into Brothels in Thailand* (1993).

    Rape for Profit: Trafficking of Nepali Girls and Women to India's Brothels (1995).

    Shattered Lives: Sexual Violence During the Rwandan Genocide and Its Aftermath (1996).

    "Are You Happy to Cheat Us?" Exploitation of Migrant Construction Workers in Russia (2009).

    Workers in the Shadows: Abuse and Exploitation of Child Domestic Workers in Indonesia (2009).

International Centre for Migration Policy Development, *Anti-Trafficking Training Materials for Judges and Prosecutors* (2006).

The Relationship between Organized Crime and Trafficking in Aliens (1999).

International Council on Human Rights Policy, *Irregular Migration, Migrant Smuggling and Human Rights: Towards Coherence* (2010).

International Council on Human Rights Policy and Transparency International, *Corruption and Human Rights: Making the Connection* (2009), available at http://www.ichrp.org/files/reports/40/131_web.pdf (accessed Feb. 1, 2010).

International Movement Against All Forms of Discrimination and Racism, *Final Report: South Asian Dialogue on Trafficking in Women and Children, Towards the Adoption of a SAARC Convention*, Feb. 11–12, 1999, Colombo, Sri Lanka.

Jennings, K.M. and V. Nicolić-Ristanović, "UN Peacekeeping Economies and Local Sex Industries: Connections and Implications," MICROCON Research Working Paper 17 (2009).

Jones-Pauly, C.C., *Report on Anti-Trafficking Laws in Six Countries (Austria, Belgium, Czech Republic, Federal Republic of Germany, Italy, Poland) and Compliance with the International Conventions against Trafficking* (1999).

Knaus, K., A. Kartusch and G. Reiter, *Combat of Trafficking in Women for the Purpose of Forced Prostitution* (2000, Institute for Human Rights).

La Strada International, *Violation of Women's Rights: A Cause and Consequence of Trafficking in Women* (2008).

Lam, J., and K. Skrivankova, *Opportunities and Obstacles: Ensuring Access to Compensation for Trafficked Persons in the UK* (2009, Anti-Slavery International).

Lim, L.L., "Trafficking, Demand and the Sex Market," paper presented at the International Symposium on Gender at the Heart of Globalization, Mar. 12, 2007, available at http://www.gtm.cnrs-bellevue.fr/site-gtm/Clq%20Mond%2007/Lin%20Lean%20Lim.pdf (accessed Feb. 1, 2010).

Lutz, C., M. Gutmann and K. Brown, "Conduct and Discipline in UN Peacekeeping Operations: Culture, Political Economy and Gender," Report submitted to the Conduct and Discipline Unit, Department of Peacekeeping Operations, United Nations (Oct. 19, 2009).

Mattar, M. "The International Criminal Court (ICC) Becomes a Reality: When Will the Court Prosecute the First Trafficking in Persons Case?" (Protection Project, 2002).

Ministry of Labour and Social Welfare (Lao PDR) and UNICEF, "Broken Promises, Shattered Dreams: A Profile of Child Trafficking in the Lao PDR" (2004).

Monheim, J., "Human Trafficking and the Effectiveness of Asylum Policies," Saarland University Center for the Study of Law and Economics (CSLE) Discussion Paper No. 2008–01 (2008).

Morrison, J., and B. Crosland, "The Trafficking and Smuggling of Refugees: The End Game in European Asylum Policy?" UNHCR Evaluation and Policy Analysis Unit (EPAU) Working Paper No. 39 (Apr. 15, 2001).

O'Connell Davidson, J., and C. Farrow, "Child Migration and the Construction of Vulnerability" (2007, Save the Children).

Opeskin, B., *The Influence of International Law on the International Movement of Persons*, United Nations Development Programme, Human Development Research Paper 2009/18 (2009).

Pécoud, A., and P. de Guchteneire, "Migration, Human Rights and the United Nations: An Investigation into the Low Ratification Record of the UN Migrant Workers Convention"

(Global Comm'n on Int'l Migration, Global Migration Perspectives No. 3, 2004), available at http://www.iom.int/jahia/webdav/site/myjahiasite/shared/shared/mainsite/policy_and_research/gcim/gmp/gmp3.pdf (accessed Nov. 19, 2009).

Physicians for Human Rights, "No Status: Migration, Trafficking and Exploitation of Women in Thailand: Health and HIV/AIDS Risks for Burmese and Hill Tribe Women and Girls" (2004).

Project Victims in Europe, *Implementation of the EU Framework Decision on the standing of victims in the criminal proceedings in the Member States of the European Union* (2009, Portugese Association for Victim Support (APAV)).

Redress Trust, "Implementing Victims' Rights: A Handbook on the Basic Principles and Guidelines on the Right to a Remedy and Reparations" (2006).

Rehn, E., and E. Johnson Sirleaf, *Women, War and Peace, The Independent Experts' Assessment on the Impact of Armed Conflict on Women and Women's Role in Peace-Building* (2002, UNIFEM).

Renshaw, C., "The Globalisation Paradox and the Implementation of International Human Rights: The Function of Transnational Networks in Combating Human Trafficking in the ASEAN Region," paper presented to the Law and Society Association Australia and New Zealand (LSAANZ) Conference: W(h)ither Human Rights, Sydney, Dec. 10–12, 2008.

Richards, S., M. Steel and D. Singer, "Hope Betrayed: An Analysis of Women Victims of Trafficking and Their Claims for Asylum" (Feb. 2006, POPPY Project).

Saito, K., "International Protection for Trafficked Persons and Those Who Fear Being Trafficked," UNHCR Research Paper No. 149 (2007), available at http://www.unhcr.org/research/RESEARCH/476652742.pdf (accessed Nov. 19, 2009).

Schloenhardt, A., "Migrant Smuggling: Illegal Migration and Organised Crime in Australia and the Asia Pacific Region" (2003).

Smith, H.M., and C. Smith, "Human Trafficking: The Unintended Effects of United Nations Intervention," paper prepared for the Annual Meeting of the Midwest Political Science Association, Chicago, Illinois, April 2010.

Surtees, R., *Listening to Victims: Experiences of Identification, Return and Assistance in South-Eastern Europe* (2007, International Centre for Migration Policy and Development).

Taran, P.A., and G. Moreno-Fontes Chammartin (International Labour Organization), "Getting at the Roots: Stopping Exploitation of Migrant Workers by Organized Crime," paper presented at the International Symposium on the UN Convention Against Transnational Organized Crime: Requirements for Effective Implementation, Turin, Feb. 22–23, 2002

US Department of Justice, "Model State Anti-Trafficking Criminal Statute" (2003), available at http://www.justice.gov/crt/crim/model_state_law.pdf (accessed Nov. 29, 2009).

US Department of State, "Trafficking in Persons Report" (2009).

"Trafficking in Persons Report" (2008).

US Government Accountability Office, "Human Trafficking: Better Data, Strategy and Reporting Needed to Enhance UN Antitrafficking Efforts Abroad," July 2006, available at http://www.gao.gov/new.items/d06825.pdf (accessed Nov. 22, 2009).

Warnath, S., "Examining the Intersections between Trafficking in Persons and Domestic Violence" (2007, USAID and Creative Associates).

Wijers, M., "Keep Your Women Home: European Policies on Trafficking in Women" (unpublished manuscript, 1998).

Wolte, S., "Armed Conflict and Trafficking in Women" (Deutsche Gesellschaft für Technische Zusammenarbeit (GTZ) GmbH, 2004), available at http://www2.gtz.de/dokumente/bib/04–5304.pdf (accessed Feb. 1, 2010).

Wyler, L.S. and A. Siskin, "Trafficking in Persons: U.S. Policy and Issues for Congress," Congressional Research Service (2010), available at http://www.fpc.state.gov/documents/organization/139278.pdf (accessed June 9, 2010).

Zhang, S., and K. Chin, "Characteristics of Chinese Human Smugglers: A Cross-National Study" (Oct. 2002).

Index

Printed in Great Britain
by Amazon.co.uk, Ltd.,
Marston Gate.